SINGAPORE

A HISTORY OF ITS
TRAMS TROLLEYBUSES & BUSES

VOLUME ONE 1880's to 1960's

F. W. YORK AND A. R. PHILLIPS.

DTS
Publishing

First published 1996

ISBN   1 900515 00 8

Published by DTS Publishing Limited
PO Box 105, Croydon, Surrey

Printed by KPC Group, Ashford, Kent.

© F.W. York and A. R. Phillips 1996

British Library Cataloguing in Publication Data. A catalogue record for this book is available from the British Library.

FRONT COVER: *Main picture*; Tram 38 and AEC 603 trolleybus 32 at Tanjong Pagar with a mosquito bus about to overtake—an interesting comparison between the solidity of trams and trolleybuses and the small size and fragility of the seven-seater. The latter was in fact no more than a car chassis—albeit a large American one—given a timber passenger body. The livery of the tram reflects the 'Shanghai period' of cream body with green at appropriate locations to indicate 1st class. As the distinction between the classes was one of space and not of comfort, the rule was that 1st was always that the leading end bench was reserved for 1st class passengers; when the tram reversed, the opposite end then became 1st, hence only the 'front' nearside corners being green—the offside being labelled 3rd. It is of note that on trams, the classes were designated 1st and 3rd while on trolleybuses it was 1st and 2nd. The windows of both vehicles were unglazed, the only protection required in a tropical monsoon climate being adequately provided by slatted, or louvred, shutters that kept the torrential rain out while allowing some circulation of air. Note also the distinctive 'Shanghai period' fleet numbers, bold without garters or other embellishments and, finally, the bilingual route number blind which shows that trolleys used the route numbers right from the start. *(National Tramway Museum photographic collection, Crich Derbyshire)*

TITLE PAGE: A fine view of a 'trackless tram'. From looking at this view, it is clear to see why the public were to carry on using the term 'tram'. This picture shows 15 on a trial run, complete with a row of solemn looking officials on board. *(National Tramway Museum photographic collection, Crich Derbyshire*

BELOW: An interesting aerial view of Finlayson Green bus terminus with a collection of Dennis Falcons, Bedford OBs, a Ransoms trolleybus and what may be a prewar Albion tucked away in the middle. The roof of the timekeeper's hut can be seen behind the bus far right. The other buildings are shops of one kind or another, including a seamen's store, left and general store with newspapers next to it. *(F. W. York collection*

Singapore

A History of its Trams Trolleybuses and Buses
Volume One - 1880's to 1960's

Contents

Acknowledgements

The authors would like to express their thanks to the following persons without whose help they could not have produced this book in its present form. In Singapore, to Mrs. Lily Tan of the Singapore National Archives and Mr. Loo Ing Heng of Singapore Bus Service, the staff of the Straights Times picture library and the late Mr. G. L. Poulier of the Singapore Traction Company (1964) Ltd. In Britain, to Messrs. R. Atkinson, J. B. Horne, J. H. Price, J. Whitehead, and I. A. Yearsley, who together with Mrs. R. Thacker and her colleagues at the National Tramway Museum (Crich) resolved so many problems concerning the early tram and trolleybus history; the erstwhile public relations departments of Albion, Ford, Guy, and RSJ, and to Mrs. R. Thistlewood of the BCV Trust Archives (Chorley): and to Roger Smith for allowing us to use his cartographic skills.

The unstinting help of the foregoing allowed us to expand our manuscript, broaden our knowledge, and supported our belief in the value of telling what we both find to be the fascinating story of a hitherto little known transport system. Finally, we must extend our thanks to Mike Davis who must be described as both the matchmaker and midwife: he brought us together, and presided over the delivery of the final product.

A. R. PHILLIPS / F. W. YORK   APRIL 1996

Photographers

DEDICATION

I am deeply grateful to Ron Phillips and Mike Davis for readily agreeing that I might
dedicate the historical text of this work in memory of my late wife,
Mary Choo Lian Eng (1926 - 1979).

Often it has been remarked that any true enthusiast, in whatever direction his or her interests lie, tends to be selfish, not in the unpleasant sense but rather with a tendency to place those interests ahead of all other aspects of life. In reflection I value very highly the patience with which Mary tolerated my interest in transport without having any understanding as to how or why I should maintain such a fascination. For example, she could never understand why it would be, if we were going shopping on a Saturday afternoon, we would ignore the lines of empty Traction Company 18's standing at Tampines Terminus, and instead fight our way onto the crowded Ponggol bus for the ride up the hill to Paya Lebar, in order that we could ride into town on a number 4 trolley-bus. Nor could she appreciate the importance I placed to cycling what was to be in total a vast distance armed with note book and camera in order to observe happenings throughout the island at the time of the Great Strike, nor why I would wish to spend valuable days off tucked away amongst the files of 'The Straits Times' in Cecil Street, or the silence of the Raffles Museum. She seriously worried but once, and this was due to a misreading of the railway timetable; one day I decided to see how far into Malaya I could travel by train, and return home on the same evening. It seemed that the Day Mail to Kuala Lumpur would reach Gemas at 1.00pm, having left Singapore at 8.30am. The down mail was shown as leaving Gemas at 1.30pm, but as the train upon which I was travelling drew into the station, the down platform was deserted, and this would be very unusual as most people intending to travel arrived an hour early. After managing to raise a sleepy ticket office clerk, I was to learn that the down train would depart at 1.30, but the next morning. Slight panic, for Gemas was a high security zone, not yet declared 'white' under the terms of the prevailing emergency. A telegram was sent home, and a mixed train which would meander down the line stopping everywhere would at least

carry me away from Gemas. The crew were very friendly indeed, even to the extent of allowing a footplate ride for part of the way, but this was really too hot for comfort. Otherwise, during some of the longer bouts of shunting at wayside stations I was able to wander off and listen to Trojan buses come phut-phutting through the jungle. The crew took me as far as Segamat and gave me an evening meal, but thereafter it was a case of trying to sleep on the station platform, midst dozens of others, until the down *night* mail arrived at 5.00am. Transport in general was hardly popular in our household for some time after that, but through Mary I found a great interest, respect and love of Singapore and the people of that nation.

This work also serves as a means of expressing thanks to Mary's brother, Choo Tian Chwee, who without complaint completely reorganised his teaching schedules during my visits at the time of the first merger. Each evening would be spent pouring over maps in order to locate the more obscure terminal points, and the following day would embrace hours of driving trying to find them. In hindsight I calculate that we must have accumulated a vast mileage, and perhaps hundreds of photographs, thanks to his boundless generosity.

Other members of the family assisted by trying to obtain copies of the route guides as they were published, whilst Choo Tian Seng tried his hand, with great success, at recording the barren wastes which had been Whitley Road when the 17A was first introduced, whist it was Alice Yap who was able to provide the first photographic hints as to what the Sentosa RT's and RTL's looked like.

It is difficult to remember just when this work was started. Certainly more than forty years ago, and during that time I have received much assistance from a great many sources, both corporate and individual. Alas, because of the time scale, many of those who gave their help are no longer with us in order to see the finished work.

F. W. YORK   TITCHFIELD COMMON, HANTS, JUNE 1996

Mary Choo Lian Eng poses for her husbands's camera in the shade of Malayan Airways Dennis Teal, SR1063, one of two purchased by the airline in the 1950's.

A Brief Introduction to Singapore

In order to put the present city state of Singapore in its historical context, a brief history is appropriate, leading up to the founding of the early settlement of the island, believed once to have been known by the Chinese, c1330, as Tan-ma-xi, or Tumasik, derived from *tasek*, meaning lake or sea or even island. By 1535, however, the name Singapura, or Simhapura, appeared in the *Sejarah Melayu* (Malay Annals) which attributes the name to the son of Raja Chulan of India, and the daughter of the god of the sea, who saw a beast on the island and mistook it for a lion. (*Singha* in Sanskrit means lion and pura a town.) (SOURCE: 'OLD SINGAPORE' BY MAYA JAYAPAL—OXFORD UNIVERSITY PRESS NEW YORK 1992.)

The present day interpretation of the modern name 'Singapore' is said to mean 'Lion City'.

It was on 28th January 1819 that the *'Indiana'*, carrying Sir Thomas Stamford Raffles, dropped anchor off the island of Singapore. A party including Raffles went ashore and found a small hutted settlement of local people, the Orang Laut, near the mouth of the river under their *batin*, or chief, the Temenggong of Johore. Most other people lived in boats, making a living from the sea.

Raffles immediately decided that this was the place to establish a trading post and sought to quickly formalize the position. Unfortunately, the Temenggong felt that it was for the Sultan of Johore to give his consent but the position had been vacant for about two years, there being a dispute between his two sons, the younger having usurped the throne from his absent elder brother. Raffles had the elder, Tengku Long brought back to Singapore and with an annual payment of 5,000 Spanish dollars for Long and 3000 for the Temenggong a lease on Singapore was quickly settled on the morning of 6th February 1819. This lease gave the East India Company the right to maintain a settlement for an unspecified period.

At this point it might be of interest to summarise the activities of the (British) East India Company—there was also a Dutch East India Company, trading between what is today the Indonesian archipelago and The Netherlands. The East India Company was a commercial company, chartered by Queen Elizabeth I in 1600 and was given a monopoly of the trade between England and the Far East. The Company set up factories in numerous locations in India and by 1652 these numbered 23. Bombay came to the British Crown in 1662 and was granted to the East India Company for £10 per year. In the 18th century the Company became, in effect, the ruler of a large part of India and a form of dual control by the company and a committee of Parliament in London was introduced by Pitt's India Act of 1784. The monopoly of the China trade was ended in 1834 and after the Indian Mutiny in 1857, the Crown took complete control of territories hitherto 'ruled' by the Company; the India Act 1858 abolished the company.

Six years after its being leased to the East India Company in 1819, Singapore was placed under the Presidency of Bengal but to be governed from India was found to be intolerable to the businessmen in the now flourishing port. However, following the demise of the East India Company in 1858, as a result of the Indian Mutiny the previous year, Singapore passed to the Crown and subsequently into the hands of the British Colonial Office on 1st April 1867, after which it formed part of the Straits Settlements—1867 to 1942.

It was during this latter period that we take up the threads of Singapore's transport history with the introduction of the steam tramway in the 1880's but, before we do so, it is important that the reader is familiar with the subsequent history of Singapore so that the descriptions of the events related by the authors in the narrative can be better placed in context vis à vis contemporary circumstances.

Singapore remained a part of the Colony of the Straits Settlements—other members were Malacca, Penang, Cocos Islands, Christmas Island and Labuan—until the island was surrendered to the Japanese invaders who then occupied it and named it Syonan—Illustrious Light of the South—changing the calendar from the 'western' year of 1942 to the Japanese 2602.

Following the surrender of the Japanese in September 1945, Singapore was initially governed by an interim British Military Administration (BMA) and was created a separate and self-governing British Crown Colony in 1946.

BELOW: Illustration from a postcard showing 'Singapore, Boat Quay', probably in the 1880's

Singapore. Boat Quay.

During the remaining 1940's and the 1950's, communist inspired unrest in adjoining Malaya occasionally spilled over into Singapore, inflicting racial and political stress and the same cause encouraged the belief that the British had abandoned the local people to their fate in February 1942 and that their return was therefore unacceptable. A remarkable degree of stability was achieved, however, given the circumstances, including a multiracial community, which in some cases found peaceful coexistence difficult to accept.

The now well known Lee Kuan Yew became Prime Minister in 1959. With the withdrawal of the British from the region, Singapore joined the Federation of Malaysia in 1963 but seceded in 1965, alleging discrimination against the federation's Chinese community.

A new, independent Republic of Singapore, within the Commonwealth, was thus formed in August 1965 and this remains the situation in 1996.

Lee Kuan Yew remained Prime Minister after independence, not standing down until 1990 and, under his stewardship, Singapore developed rapidly from a somewhat backward colony into the commercial and financial entrepôt that it is today. It is also a major centre for new export industries. Today its inhabitants enjoy a standard of living unequalled in eastern Asia outside Japan and oil rich Brunei.

Geographical Location

Singapore lies at the southern end of the Malaysian Peninsula, from which it is separated by the Straits of Johore, approximately one mile (1.609km) wide at their narrowest. This places Singapore only 1° north of the equator and thus the monsoon climate varies from very warm to hot throughout the year with high relative humidity and high annual rainfall.

To the west, and south lie the islands that form the Indonesian archipelago with the major island of Sumatra only a few miles distant across the Straits of Malacca.

Geographical Composition and Area

In 1996, The Republic Singapore comprises Singapore Island and 57 small islands and islets of which only one, Sentosa, has any significance to this book. Altogether, the area of Singapore is 240 sq miles (622 sq km), just over half the size of Hong Kong to the north east. Originally covered with luxuriant rain forest, Singapore Island is now largely cleared and nature has been tamed to suit the requirements of a modern, largely urban society, and as a consequence there are few truly wild placed left. What jungle that remains is now managed along the lines of a theme park and caters for the recreational aspirations of Singaporeans.

The City of Singapore lies on the southern coast of the island and has grown in recent years into a magnificent city with modern glass office towers standing in close and harmonious relationship to such retained and restored traditional buildings as Raffles Hotel and its surrounding area. There *are* old, buildings but these are few and off the beaten track—usually traditional-style shop-houses; universal in the Colonial period.

There were a few low hills when Raffles arrived in 1819 but these have largely been levelled and Singapore Island is best described today as being mainly flat. There are a small number of small rivers, of which the Singapore River enters the city area where once it was the main landing place for cargoes unloaded by lighters from ships anchored in The Roads. There remain today some godowns of the old style along the river banks upstream of the central business district.

Political Status, Trade, Rule of the Road

The history of Singapore has been described but the political status of this city state has evolved from Colonial—governed by a Governor appointed by the British Foreign Office—first to being (briefly) part of the Federation of Malaysia, then to become the sovereign Republic of Singapore in 1965. The first Prime Minister, Lee Kuan Yew, saw the need for a strong approach to reducing interracial tension and the style of government is that of a democratically elected, liberal democracy, with a firm line being taken against dissent. The Head of State, President Ong Teng Cheong, has been in office since 1993 and Prime Minister Goh Chok Tong succeeded Lee Kuan Yew in 1990.

The geographical location of Singapore has led it to become a trading crossroads and it would be difficult, today, to name any type of trade that is not carried out, either in, or through, the Republic. It remains a major seaport and Changi International Airport has emerged to become one of the most modern in the region.

As with so many countries in the region, the Rule of the Road in Singapore is that of driving on the left. At one time this rule was almost universal from India to China and Japan—exceptions being the countries formerly a part of French administered Indo-China. Today India and Japan still adhere to the left-hand rule while China has moved to the right.

Matters Demographic

When first settled by Raffles, the entire population was of Malay racial origin but the arrival of the British, largely from India, brought in their wake a considerable population from the subcontinent. Encouraged by the prosperity of the embryo colony, the Chinese brought their skills and trades and it was from their ranks that the earlier forms of transport were introduced—largely in the form of the man-powered rickshaw.

In 1992, the racial mix was as wide as ever with Chinese accounting for 75% of the population, Malays 14% and Tamils 7%. Although Malay is the National tongue, Chinese, Tamil and English, are all official. In effect, English is the lingua franca and often the language of business.

There remain distinct areas of ethnic population, not the least being the busy China Town, together with 'Little India'. Being predominant, the Chinese have spread widely as their prosperity has improved; their residential areas now being dictated by their degree of affluence—a comment true also of the other ethnic groups but to a much less noticeable extent.

Employment is almost entirely devoted to what might be described as 'urban occupations', only a small minority being occupied in agriculture of other rural pursuits.

External Transport.

As already mentioned, Singapore is a hub of commercial sea and air traffic and this has been true—at least of the sea element—since the earliest settlements by Malays who traded between the surrounding islands. There followed traders from India and Arabia and, during the 15th century, Portuguese explorers made their early visits to the region, to be followed by other Europeans, not least the Dutch, who colonised much of what is today Indonesia. The British traders required stable conditions and a number of Settlements were established—Singapore being a later acquisition, as we have learned, in 1819. Trade by sea was one thing but, with British interests throughout the Malay peninsula, a railway was constructed as far south as Johore Barhu from where connection by ferry was made with the Singapore Railway from 1902. The latter was physically joined to the Federated Malay States Railway (FMSR) in 1923 although it had been purchased by them in 1918.

The feature that permitted the physical connection of the two railways was the construction of a causeway across the mile wide Straits of Johore, opened in 1923. This carried a single-line railway and a road, allowing free movement of vehicles between the two adjacent, then, British controlled territories, The Federated Malay States and Singapore. The causeway has, in recent years been widened to allow a dual-carriageway road to be built across the Straits.

The early days of air travel were catered for by an airfield at Seletar where the first land-plane services were catered for until the opening of Kallang International Airport in 1936/37. This could not only handle the larger aircraft then coming into service but, being adjacent to the sea, it could also service the requirements of the long-haul flying boats—Imperial Airways from London and QANTAS from Sydney. The flying boats only went as far as Singapore in those days, passengers transferring lines for their onward journey. A disadvantage at Kallang was that the main runway was crossed by a main road! This was all very well until the coming of the Comet—the world's first jet airliner—in the 1950's; the road traffic could be safely stopped upon the approach of an aircraft but, on the short runway, a Comet could not and they were consequently sent to the RAF airfield at Changi. With the coming of the second-generation jets—Boeing 707 and DC8—there was no alternative but to build what was to become what must be the world's shortest-lived international airport at Paya Lebar; opened in 1965, it was closed and replaced by the present-day Changi International in 1982—but not before being host to a regular, if short-lived, Concorde service to and from London in the late 'seventies. Today Changi International, evolved from the famous Royal Air Force station, handles the aircraft of all the major regional airlines, together with those of the majority of European, Middle-Eastern, Australasian, American and Asian carriers as well—both passenger and freight.

Internal Transport

As Singapore grew and internal transport became necessary and the horse was introduced by Europeans quite early on and a distinctive local four-wheel carriage evolved, referred to variously as either 'paludin' or 'gahrrie'. The rickshaw was an early arrival, brought by the Chinese who expanded the scope of their man-powered carriages until they were counted by the thousand. With very low fares, the rickshaws offered fierce competition to both steam and electric trams. It was not until the arrival of management ideas from Shanghai that tram—and subsequently trolleybus—fares were reduced to compete; with spectacularly good results. As already mentioned, there was a Singapore Railway but this was mainly a local connection with mainline services in Malaya proper. A double-deck motor bus was reported in the mid 1900's but there is even earlier reference to 'omnibuses' in the early 1890's when an experimental electric railway was planned between Singapore Town and Kranji for Johore Bahru. Local press reports predicted that it would be an improvement 'on the omnibus'. The electric railway on that route was not to become a reality in full until the Mass Rapid Transit reached Woodlands in the 1990's—a hundred years later.

Within the modern city, car usage is restricted in the Central Business District with the result that a frequent and efficient service is offered by two major bus operators. Taxis cater for short journeys otherwise made by private car and fares on all modes are inexpensive on an international scale.

At the twenty-first century approaches, a light rail proposal is progressing.

This book contains a large amount of information not previously published but, in order to make it acceptable to the general reader, some detail has been omitted. If you, the reader, have further information to offer, please do not hesitate to contact the authors via DTS Publishing Limited, PO Box 105, Croydon, Surrey CR9 2TL, United Kingdom.

CURRENCY: UNLESS OTHERWISE STATED, WHEREVER DOLLARS OR $ ARE REFERRED TO IN THE TEXT THIS REFERS TO STRAITS DOLLARS OR, SINCE 1946, SINGAPORE DOLLARS.

BELOW: Battery Road in the 1880's, illustrating the use of horse drawn hackney carriages, known locally as Gharries, a term believed to have originated in India.

Chapter One
Early Tramway Days

The Singapore Tramway Company

Origins and early development

The United Kingdom in particular, and Europe in general, lived through the effects of the Industrial Revolution and thousands of factories turned agricultural communities into engineering workshops, producing machinery to be sent to all parts of the world. To convey these cargoes, ever larger steam ships were constructed, and the opening of the Suez Canal in 1869 served to further emphasise the importance of Singapore as the trading crossroads of the Far East. Shipping companies were swift to recognise the expense and time consumed by the need to transship cargoes to and from vessels anchored off shore in the Roads, whilst the coaling of steamships from lighters was both laborious and filthy.

Deep water docking became essential if the projected expansion of trade was to be accommodated and a site was selected due west of the Singapore River, some two miles distant, at New Harbour, with the Albert Dock being opened during 1879. Two companies were involved: the docking facilities were provided by The Patent Slip and Dry Dock Company (later to become The New Harbour Dock Company) whilst wharves were provided by The Tanjong Pagar Dock Company; there was a merger during 1899 under the latter title.

Two major points of growth may now be seen - the town set around Singapore River, being the seat of administration, culture and residence, whilst the needs of the New Harbour witnessed the growth of a second township. Separated by perhaps two miles, in between lay beaches occupied by junks and tonkangs, their spars and rigging thrown into bold relief by a backcloth formed by Mounts Wallich, Erskine and Palmer. To travel between the town and the harbour required the crossing of these hills, but already a more convenient link was being formed: in order to provide more land whereby the town could expand, Mount Wallich was to be removed, the resulting spoil being tipped into Telok Ayer Bay, a massive task of reclamation. Where once the sea had lapped against the side of Telok Ayer Street, new ground was created, over which would be constructed Robinson Road and Cecil Street, amongst others, in the fullness of time. The need for an efficient public transport service came to be recognised and, as early as 1871, plans were prepared for a railway line which would link the harbour with the town but nothing further was done, perhaps due to the presence of the remaining hills.

The Tramways Ordinance, 1882

A decade later, Messrs. Joseph Cheney Bolton, William Ker and John Ross, each of Glasgow, Gilbert McMicking and Robert Jardine, of London, and a local gentleman, James Graham, formed the British East India Syndicate to make application to the Municipal Commissioners in order to construct and work street tramways. The powers obtained under the Tramways Ordnance, 1882, allowed for:

First: a single line commencing at Crawford Street, Rocher, proceeding along North Bridge Road, South Bridge Road and Tanjong Pagar Road to Tanjong Pagar Docks

Second: a single line commencing near the Pauper Hospital, Sirangun Road (note the early form of spelling for Serangoon Road), proceeding along Sirangun Road, Selegie Road and Middle Road, there to make a junction with the first line in North Bridge Road, thence to High Street to the West End of the Esplanade

Third: a double line commencing on Collyer Quay and proceeding along Robinson Quay, Anson Road and the new road along the line of the Docks to a terminus at the Borneo Company's Wharf

Fourth: a single line commencing in Boat Quay near Thomson's Bridge, passing along Boat Quay, then by way of Bonham Street through Commercial Square, to connect with the third line on Robinson's Quay

Fifth: a single line commencing at Boat Quay and passing along Market Street to connect with the third line at Robinson's Quay.

In addition, in the event of a bridge being constructed near the Government Offices or Court House, thus crossing the Singapore River as it meets the sea, an extension would be allowed to link the terminals of the lines at the end of the High Street (Second) and Robinson Quay (either fourth or fifth), always provided that such a bridge be of sufficient strength and width to, carry a tramway (some names have changed over the years so that Commercial Square is now Raffles Place and Robinson Quay thereafter became Collyer Quay in its full length back to the riverbank). As set out in the Ordinance, the lines would reach the whole of the town as then constructed, but blanket powers were included to allow for the extension of any of routes provided for, or the construction of completely new lines anywhere on the Island should the promoters so wish. Finally, authority was given for the construction of passing loops and sidings as might be required subsequent to a build-up in traffic.

BELOW: A view of the main entrance to the Tanjong Pagar Dock Company premises as seen from the Boustead Institute in 1892. Although indistinct, the sharp-eyed can make-out two steam trams with passenger trailers. *(National Archive of Singapore*

The infrastructure

Rails of grooved steel were to be used, to be laid on sleepers of either iron or wood and after laying down the rails, the Promoters would be liable for the making-up of the carriageway to the condition which applied before the work started.

Once the work was complete, the maintenance of the whole highway became the responsibility of the local authority and this can be seen as a most interesting departure from the situation in the United Kingdom where the tramway operator was responsible for the roadway up to a distance of eighteen inches beyond the outside rail.

Because the quality of roadways was not particularly good, protection was extended to the Promoters against other road users making use of the rails for such would be regarded as trespass with a penalty of one-hundred dollars in respect of each misuse being decreed, such fines to be paid to the promoters as a form of compensation.

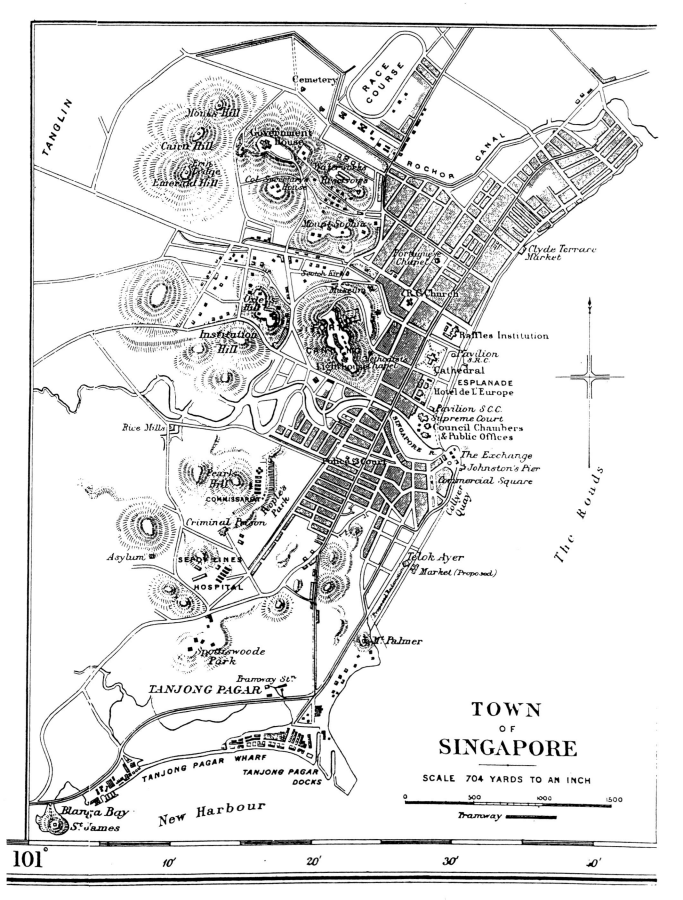

MAP: This is a reproduction of a map published in 1887 as an enlarged insert to a map of the whole of Malaya. It is, nevertheless, very helpful in showing the extent of development at that time and is doubly useful in showing the route of the steam tramway in relation to streets, the river, etc.. *(Reproduced by Courtesy of the British Library, London.)*

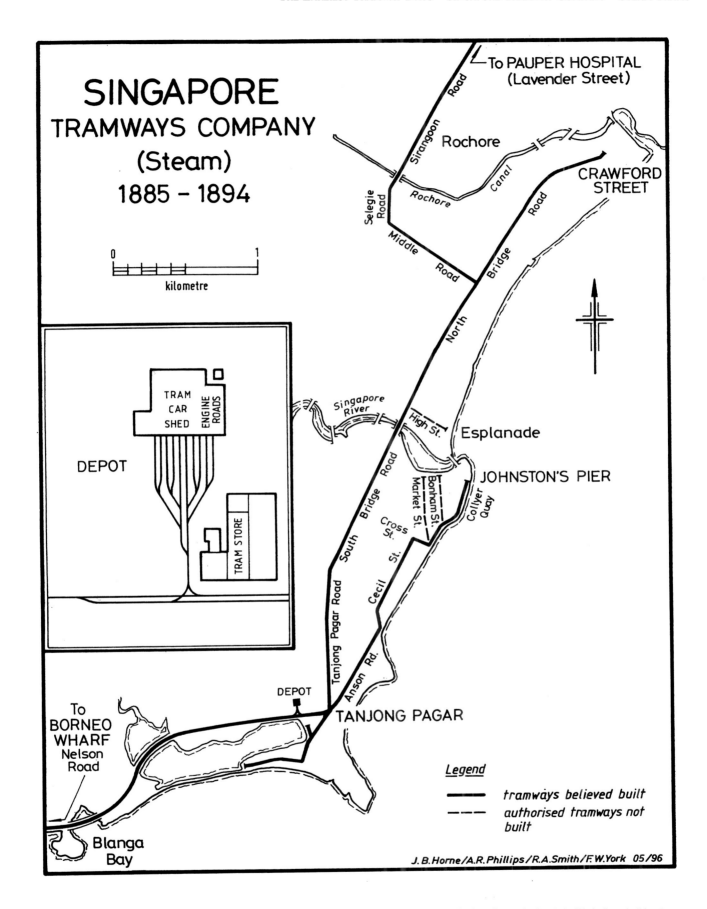

MAP : This map shows the metre gauge steam tramway network of Singapore. The section inside the Tanjong Pagar dock estate, it is believed, did not carry a passenger service. The choice of gauge was probably influenced by a desire to be compatible with other railways in South East Asia, including those of the French. This map is to a similar scale as that of the 1887 map opposite.

The track gauge was mentioned as being 4ft 8½in "or of other such gauge and construction as might be approved by the Governor in Council".   In the event, a gauge of one metre was eventually chosen.

Concerning the motive power to be used, the promotors could use animal power, steam, compressed air or electricity.   Certainly, the Promotors had steam in mind from the outset and regulations were set for the employment of locomotives, viz:

That: -
i)   they be fitted with an indicator showing the speed of the car;

ii)   they be fitted with a fender suitable for pushing aside obstructions;

iii)   they have a special bell, whistle or other apparatus whereby warnings could be sounded to other road users;

iv)   they be equipped with a seat for the driver so placed as to provide him with the clearest view of the road ahead;

v)   the locomotive should be free from noise produced by blast or the clatter of machinery and that the whole of the machinery should be concealed from view at all points above a height of four inches from rail level;

vi)   likewise the fire used on the locomotive would need to be concealed from view and all precautions be taken to prevent the escape of smoke, sparks or fire from the locomotives.

Having obtained their Powers, the Promoters launched the Prospectus of THE SINGAPORE TRAMWAYS COMPANY on 8th December 1883 and, although the required capital cannot be said to have flooded in, sufficient cash was to hand in order that groundworks were able to commence during the latter part of 1884, with the laying of the first rails on 7th April 1885, leading to the opening of the first regular service over the Tangjong Pagar to Johnston's Pier section as from 3rd May 1886.

To serve the opening of the service, fourteen steam tram engines were ordered from Messrs. Kitson and Company in 1885, to be followed by two further examples in 1887.   An unknown number of double-deck passenger trailer cars were also ordered but their pedigree is unknown.   Details of rolling stock, as far as is known, are more fully described on pages 154-6.

Extensive operating premises were secured at Tanjong Pagar with well equipped workshops which, together with the two

---

Steam Tramway: Fares and tariffs

The Company was in business to carry both passengers and freight and the Table of Charges makes for interesting study:

PASSENGER FARES:
1.   From Rocher to the Central Police Station, or the reverse thereof, or any part thereof: First Class 10 cents; Second Class 6 cents.
2.   From the Central Police Station to Tanjong Pagar, or the reverse thereof, or any part thereof: First Class 10 cents; Second Class 6 cents.
3.   From Sirangun Road to High Street, or the reverse thereof, or any part thereof: First Class 10 cents; Second Class 6 cents.
4.   From Colyer Quay or Boat Quay to Tanjong Pagar or Borneo Company Wharf, or the reverse thereof, or any part thereof :   First Class 12 cents; Second Class 6 cents.

RATES FOR GOODS:
1.   for coals, coke, charcoal, stone, lime, salt, sand, fire-clay, cinders, dung, compost, manure, bricks, slags, tiles, slates, metals;
                                                  per ton: 20 cents;
2.   for sugar, coffee, flour, corn, rice, dyewood, timber, gambier, sag, tapioca;
                                                  per ton: 20 cents;
3.   for cubic gambier, pepper, hides, fish, earthenware and light iron castings;
                                                  per ton: 30 cents;
4.   for rattans and copra;   per ton: 35 cents;
5.   for manufactured goods, cotton and other wools, matches, drugs (except opium), provisions and all other merchandise, wares or articles;
                                                  per ton: 30 cents;
6.   for opium;   per chest: 20 cents;
7.   for every parcel, not exceeding 7lbs in weight   5 cents;
        exceeding 7lbs but not exceeding 14lbs in weight   10 cents;
        exceeding 14lbs but not exceeding 28lbs in weight   15 cents;
        exceeding 28lbs but not exceeding 56lbs in weight   20 cents;
8.   for parcels exceeding 56lbs and for all other cargo not enumerated in the published lists, such rates as the Promoters consider fit (with prior approval of the Governor in Council and with a Notice published in "The Government Gazette").

---

additional locomotives, points to a degree of optimism for the Company's future, but such hopes were doomed to disappointment within a decade.

Success and Decline

At first the lines seemed to have been a success, to such an extent that plans were prepared to continue the line through the town to Geylang Village.   Another bridge presented itself as being a problem, this being Lyon's Bridge over the Kallang River.   The problem would be neatly solved by converting the existing bridge for use by the steam trams (an early example of the principle of reserved track) with another constructed in cast iron for use by all other forms of transport.

Roads of the day were very poor and carriers were quick to appreciate the fact that the smoothest ride that they could have was found along the tram lines.   Thus, bullock carts began to appear constructed to a gauge of one metre and the tramway service was considerably slowed by cars having to follow in their path with the driver quite insensible to the insults that were following him.   As a last resort, police action was called for but the problem could never really have been called solved.   This practice was not unique to Singapore: a well documented instance is that of Lisbon, where the tramways were reconstructed to a gauge of less than one metre, but even so an ingenious horse bus operator, Eduardo Jorge, built vehicles of a similar wheel track in order to compete with the trams, charging very low fares.

The steam tramway in Singapore failed because it could not meet such a challenge mounted by well entrenched local interests, namely the rickshaw pullers, porters, and carriers, who could do all that the steam tramway offered to do at substantially cheaper rates.   The tariffs demanded by the tramway were high: its fuel and machinery had to be imported, and there were impatient shareholders expecting dividends on the capital invested to set up the operation. The local management failed to lower charges to counter the local challenge (if, indeed, this were possible), and after only three years of operation the Directors made an approach to the TANJONG PAGAR DOCKS COMPANY with a view to selling the tramway as a going concern.   (By this time the Docks Company held several varied commercial interests within the Settlement, and it had been calculated when launching this approach that at least the docks to town section could be a valuable addition to those interests.)

The approach to purchase was rejected and so, following a further year of struggle, the Directors gave up and placed the system into the hands of Messrs. CRANE BROTHERS, Auctioneers, in order to obtain the best price possible.   A mere $186,000 (Straits Settlements currency ($1 equalled 2sh 2d or 11.66p Sterling)) was realised, the purchaser being THE TANJONG PAGAR DOCKS COMPANY.   No doubt appreciating the difficulties of the tramways' operations but, at the same time, viewing the possibilities which might be found, those Directors were astute in obtaining the whole operation at what must have been less than scrap value.

Under new management

Economies were made wherever possible.   For example, several of the cars had their upper decks removed to cut maintenance costs to a considerable degree, whilst making savings in the amount of coal consumed by the locomotives.

Whether any consideration had been made to cuts in the fare scales must be left to speculation but, what is certain is that the scales as first introduced were much too high - a six cents minimum fare for even the shortest ride was truly a nonsense, as the humble rickshaw could offer a door-to-door service for half the price.

As the year 1892 came to a close, so did the Tanjong Pagar to Rochor section, with the line from Borneo Wharf down Anson Road to Collyer Quay being retained for freight only working.   Serious consideration was given to the electrification of the section but such technology was still in its infancy and the end came on 1st June 1894.

The closure carries an interesting footnote: the carriageways were quickly cleared of tram rails and a large quantity were purchased by the Hongkong & Shanghai Bank who used them in the construction of a new vault.   We can only suppose that the passenger cars went for scrap, whilst some of the freight wagons would have been further employed along the wharfs.

But what of the locomotives—less than ten years old but built with a possible life of forty years?

Conclusion

Those versed in the history of tramways will know that it is highly unusual for a steam tramway to be closed down and dismantled, and for a decade to elapse before an electric tramway took its place. What is perhaps more remarkable is that the electric tramway was constructed and worked over the same routes, and with the same lack of perception, as the steam line. No lessons had apparently been learned, and the electric trams too failed to thrive. The fares were too high to meet local competition and few steps were taken to attract passengers. After a series of technical problems, mainly cable faults and the break-up of poor track foundations, the tramways company became bankrupt and the system almost derelict. It was then saved by the astute General Manager of the Shanghai Electric Construction Company, who had since 1908 operated the Shanghai tramways along a path of continuously soar-ing passenger totals, fare revenue, and profits. This was achieved by setting cheap fares, three classes of accommodation to suit the local conditions, and obtaining the best from the ethnically mixed labour force. An additional element was the Manager's own commercial skill: for example, he used the company's traction poles to good effect by painting, in Chinese, the fare to the end of the line at every stopping place. On the intervening poles, he painted a number indicating the position in which the driver should have his control handle (to ensure optimum speed/minimum power consumption at that particular point on the journey) With such attention to detail, the Shanghai tramway manager found himself in control of the most profitable tramway system in the world!

Choice of gauge

The eventual choice of a gauge of one metre for a line in a British Colony is unusual but would appear to have been in line with a general agreement for a network of railways throughout South East Asia, including French Indo-China. the subsequent railway and the electric tramway built in Singapore also used this gauge and, in the early twenties, the Singapore Railway was physically linked across a causeway with the lines in Malaya, with connections into Thailand and on into French Indo-China. The steam tramway promoters, no doubt, envisaged transhipment of goods at Singapore Docks into wagons capable of carrying said goods to distant destinations.

THIRD CLASS   THIRD CLASS

LEFT: NOT Singapore. This illustration of a Johore steam tram trailer is included in the absence of any suitable Singapore views and serves to show the arrangement of steam trailers in general and one in another, nearby, tropical location in particular. This example, unlike those in Singapore, had an enclosed lower saloon. *(J. B. Horne collection*

Early electric experiments—1891 to 1892

A trial run

16th September 1891 and weird and wonderful things were happening at New Harbour Dock. Having no apparent connection with the by now established Singapore Tramway Company, one Mr. Buckley had invited no less a person than His Highness The Sultan of Johore and several notable Singapore citizens to witness "certain preliminary trials of an exceedingly rough and ready tramcar". It was said that Mr. Buckley had been examining the feasibility of constructing an electric tramway to link the town with Kranji on the northwest coast of the Island and across the Straits from Johore Bahru. He needed to mount a full-sized demonstration and, to this end, had constructed a temporary track, extending only one hundred and eighty feet along the dock side, with an overhead wire suspended from untreated poles placed alongside. Power was provided by a New Harbour Dock Company generator but current reached the 'tramcar' motor by means of a person on board holding a makeshift trolley-pole in contact with the overhead wire. Highly dangerous, it would seem, and reports in the Straits Times for 17th September 1891 tell that:

> "The experiment was accompanied by many obstructions and much waste of power, from the fact that the engine produced too much power and would have produced too high a speed, involving much waste of power in what is called gearing down. Further, the track was of the very roughest description, as was the truck".

For all that, the objectives sought by Mr. Buckley had been gained and His Highness made several trips up and down the line for, with Royal Approval being so much in evidence, who could decry anything that Mr. Buckley might propose.

The proposed line

The Straits Times also tells us that to travel between Singapore and Johore Bahru involved the use of rickshaws and a form of horse omnibus - the earliest known recorded reference to an omnibus to gain the attention of the authors - or else the traveller might go to the expense of hiring a private carriage. At best, an average speed of five miles per hour might be hoped for and Mr. Buckley considered that the construction of a tramway would halve the journey time - although there was little he could think of which might replace the sampan crossing of the Strait. His dream was an electric line which would carry both passengers and produce, opening up residential plots for the use of Eurasians and middle-class Europeans - who by now were having great difficulty in meeting the high rents which were being charged in what was fast becoming an over populated town - besides bringing into town the fruits and vegetables grown on the farms along the line of route, so that villagers could enjoy great prosperity.

A line of route was suggested, at the town end having a terminus at Kadang Kerbau. This is a crossing with Serangoon Road and would have provided a natural connection with the existing steam car service into town. Bukit Timah Road would be used until reach-

RIGHT: A woodcut used to illustrate a number of contemporary tramway journals, showing the Kranji Electric Line in its jungle setting, close to the bungalow of His Highness The Sultan of Johore. It was also reported that the Sultan of Pahang rode on this occasion. *(Street Railway Journal, January, 1893 and the London 'Graphic'*

ing the junction with Scott's Road. Recalling the 1871 suggestion to build a railway, the Government had taken such a proposal seriously and set aside a strip of land six miles long towards Bukit Timah Village, to be used for the railway, should a line ever be constructed. Mr. Buckley would use this designated strip until such time as it was required for its intended purpose. Then, for the final six miles to Kranji, his line would be placed on a reservation alongside the main Bukit Timah Road. With such a high proportion of off-street running, the plan provided for only five stopping points, although more would be added as the expected traffic increased.

Financing

The strangest aspect of the whole idea concerned the financing of the project. Mr. Buckley intended to meet the whole of the cost - estimated at rather less than £1,000 a mile - from his own resources although, if any friends *asked* to be involved, then he would be pleased to accept their offer.

Late nineteenth century transport history is littered with somewhat eccentric schemes which flare into the public domain very briefly and then die away, never to be heard of again. Not so with Mr. Buckley, for a report in the Straits Times, dated 12th September 1892, provided an account of the opening of the first mile of the line:

"on the invitation of H. H. The Sultan of Johore, a large number of visitors from Singapore had an opportunity of seeing the line at work: and if they so desired, as a good many did desire, they also had the pleasure of being whirled along the line at a speed of from eight to nine miles per hour. A large number of ladies were present, some of whom looked upon the method of travelling as being of rather a doubtful pleasure and forbore the privilege of being able to say that they had travelled on the first electric line in Singapore and, possibly, the Far East".

An operating title had been obtained, namely THE KRANJI ELECTRIC

LINE, laid to metre gauge and with an overhead line constructed by THE SINGAPORE TELEPHONE COMPANY. Mention was made in the technical presses of the United Kingdom and of the United States of America, with the former tending to be - somewhat understandably in those days of Empire - the more appreciative.

A woodcut shows the power car to be of boxlike appearance, with little attempt towards beauty, and being capable of hauling two trailers. The background is of jungle and - as the press story tells of the line passing close to H. H.'s bungalow - and that visitors had come from Singapore - it follows that this one mile had been constructed at the Kranji end of the line.

Although a great time seems to have been had by all, the happening could only be regarded, in the longer term, as being an extended experiment and, if things did not work out, then, as the Straits Times was able to comment:

"It may also be mentioned that the gauge and the carriages which are at present at work.....are in every way suitable for work on the MUAR RAILWAY. We understand that this course of action was adopted so that in case of the thing not turning out unsuccessful, all the rolling stock along with the rails and sleepers could be transferred to the Muar Railway".

(In passing, this does open an interesting avenue for further historic research. From the reports we can assume that H. H. was keenly interest in railways, whilst a United Kingdom manufacturer does have on file a photograph of a tramway locomotive named 'Johore' and, hitherto, the assumption had been that this had worked in Singapore. If there was a tramway at Muar, a town in the State of Johore, then this might have been the locomotives' home.)

The Kranji Electric Line passed into history and left no trace of its passing. Elsewhere, difficulties were the order of the day.

The Singapore Railway—1902

"Saya pigi tanan anjing Tuan", a comment made by a disinterested passer-by in Tank Road on the morning of the 16th April 1900; roughly translated, " I go to bury my master's dog".

The Acting Governor in full regalia, despite the rain, in the presence of the town's leading citizens, was cutting the first sod to herald the birth of the Singapore and Kranji Railway, destined to follow much the same line of route as favoured by Mr. Buckley, to

provide ferry connections across the Strait, so that passengers could then continue journeys into the Malayan States and so the dream unfolded, eventually to reach Bangkok.

While it was not a tramway, and possibly inappropriate in the context of this book, its early years the Singapore Railway was a very lightweight affair and performed the role of a short shuttle service between–originally–the Tank Road terminus in Singapore Town and

Woodlands, for the ferry across the Straits of Johore to Johore Bahru

Tank Road soon proved to be an unwise choice of 'town' terminus, being some two miles distant from the main commercial centre and there was a need to extend back to the New Harbour, thus bringing to life the original proposals of 1871, local stations on this extension being provided at People's Park (in what is now called 'Chinatown'), Borneo Wharf, and Pasir Panjang. On the 'main' line other local stations were opened at Newton and Cluny Road and, out in the countryside, at Bukit Timah, Bukit Panjang,

Kranji to the terminus at Woodlands. The Hunslet Engine Company provided the first locomotives, 1-4, during 1901, whilst numbers 5 & 6 followed during 1907.

The line was transferred by sale to the Federated Malay States Railway (FMSR) in 1918. In 1923 the line lost its isolation when it was physically connected to the main Malay railway system, following completion of a causeway with road and railway, between Woodlands and Johore Bahru. Thereafter the line lost its local nature and became an extension of the FMSR main line

ABOVE: An early Singapore Railway train that ran wholly within the confines of Singapore Island, between its Tank Road southern terminus and Woodlands Station, near Kranji, opposite the mile-wide strait from the town of Johore Bahru. *(National Archive of Singapore*

RIGHT: Tank Road Station with its line of rickshaws—fierce competition for the trams and later the trolleybuses. The elaborate design of the station and its clock tower, the norm during Victorian/Edwardian eras, befitted its status as a main terminus, despite the shortness of the original line that it served. Although this was the terminus for passenger services, the Singapore Railway continued in a south-westerly direction as a goods link to the dock estate. *(F. W. York collection*

Tank Road Railway Station — Singapore.

Straker-Squire double-deck Motor Omnibus–1906

It is of interest to pause for a moment to view an interloper on the Singapore transport scene. The outward growth from the business area caused the construction of suburbs and, in turn, created the demand for public transport. Certain residents, however, were violently opposed to having tram lines laid down outside their houses, and for this reason some sections of the town were left unserved—notably along the palatial Orchard Road.

'So it happened that an enterprising gentleman brought to the island what was reported as being a Straker-Squire double-deck motor bus, and set it to ply for hire along Orchard Road in 1906. The service lasted as long as the vehicle itself, and when the supply of spare parts was exhausted, the (concept of the) motor bus was removed from the scene, not to die altogether, but to be dormant for more than two decades.' In the 1960's your Author commented, 'What did pass for ever was the regular use of double-deckers.' Time was to change that.

Chapter Two
1901-1927—The Electric Tramways

With the advent of the Twentieth Century, the United Kingdom was in a ferment of tramway construction, with electricity becoming the recognised form of motive power. The larger concerns built their own generating stations and would provide surplus current to the local authorities for street lighting and other purposes. As the home market became saturated, promoters of such schemes looked overseas in the hope of finding rich pickings, and so it was that, during 1901, SINGAPORE TRAMWAYS, LIMITED, was registered in London under the Provisions of the Companies Acts 1862 - 1900, with the objective of constructing and working a system of tramways throughout the Settlement of Singapore.

Having set up a corporate body, the next step involved protracted negotiations with the Municipal Authorities in Singapore, the result of which was the enacting of THE TRAMWAYS ORDINANCE OF 1902, powers which in one form or another were destined to set the pattern of transport services within the municipal boundaries for the next seventy years.

The document which formed the ordinance was massive, setting out rules and conditions governing construction and operation, indicating penalties for any breach in those conditions, and granting protection for other utilities having their equipment located near the proposed routes. Paragraph 3 carried the greatest significance, in that the Company was granted exclusive rights to provide services over the thoroughfares in which the tramways were laid, and no other company would be allowed to construct tramways within the Settlement unless any such projected line had first been placed on offer to the Company (and should the Company decline to accept such an offer then, by implication, the other bid would be allowed to go ahead, a period of three months being allowed for consideration).

Since the steam tramways had closed, the town had continued to grow, and the original roads pattern into the adjacent rural areas as planned by Stamford Raffles, east towards Geylang and due north-east in the direction of Serangoon proved to be natural traffic arteries, whilst the land between the town and New Harbour was becoming ever more densely populated. In planning their lines the surveyors of the Company were in fact recreating and extending the routes once worked by steam, as follows:

Tramway number 1—commencing at a point in Telok Blangah Road opposite the entrance to Keppel Harbour Dock, thence in and along Telok Blangah Road, thence in and along Keppel Road to the entrance to Tanjong Pagar Docks at the intersection of Keppel and Tanjong Pagar Roads.

Tramway number 2—commencing by a junction with Tramway number 1 at the entrance to Tanjong Pagar Docks at the intersection of Keppel and Tanjong Pagar Roads, thence in and along Tanjong Pagar Road, South Bridge Road and North Bridge Road to Jalan Sultan, thence in and along Jalan Sultan between North Bridge Road and Victoria Street, thence in and along Victoria Street between Jalan Sultan and Kalang (sic) Road, thence in and along Kalang Road and Gelang (sic) Road to the municipal boundary on Gelang Road.

Tramway number 3—commencing with a junction with Tramway number 2 at the intersection of Tanjong Pagar and Anson Roads, thence in and along Anson Road and Telok Ayer Street at the intersection of Cecil Street thence in and along Cecil Street and the northerly side of Finlayson Green, in and along Collyer Quay terminating at or near a point opposite Johnston's Pier.

Tramway number 4—commencing at the intersection of Bras Basah and Beach Roads, thence in and along Bras Basah Road to the intersection of Princep Street, thence in and along Princep Street to the intersection of Selegie Road, thence in and along Selegie Road and Serangoon Road terminating in Serangoon Road at the municipal boundary.

Tramway number 5—commencing by a junction with tramway number 4 in Serangoon Road near Rumah Miskin Police Station, thence in and along Lavender Street and forming a junction with tramway number 2 in Kalang Road.

The lines thus authorised did not represent the maximum route pattern, and two other significant sections were built and opened from the first day, namely the tracks along Mackenzie

BELOW: The interior of the twelve road car shed at Mackenzie Road, Singapore. Cars of both crossbench and combination type can be seen together with, on the extreme left, the fron part of one of the three bogie motor goods vans. *(Tramway and Railway World, December 7, 1905*

Road leading to the car sheds, and what in later documents appears as:

Tramway number 6—commencing in High Street at a point opposite the Europa Hotel, thence in and along High Street to the intersection with Hill Street, thence in and along Hill Street to the intersection with River Valley Road, thence in and along River Valley Road and Tank Road terminating at a point near Orchard Road.

In addition to laying out these tramways the Company was granted the Authority to construct a Power Station whereby to generate current for its own use, and further, for the supply of electricity to the Municipal Commissioners and the Government, but *to no other party*. Electric street lighting, albeit in limited form, was on the way.

A considerable amount of detail was concerned with the precise layout of the lines—for instance, where single line with passing loops was used, wherever such was practicable the passing loops should be within sight of each other. Also, any section of single line could be doubled at any future time: as new, tramways 1 and 3 would be double tracked throughout and located at the centre of the roads, and tramway 2 would be double as far as Kalang (*sic*) Bridge, but from thence—as far as the terminus—single line with passing loops would be sufficient. Crossing Victoria Bridge the lines would be interlaced (that is to say, the lines would be set one inside the other, forming in effect a section of single line working, but without the need for points). A major item of work involved the construction of a 'trams only' bridge in order to cross the Kallang River. True, there was a public crossing at this point, but it was quite unsuitable for trams. In the wider sense, the Powers granted under the Ordinance did allow the Company to alter the level or widen any bridge, road or street, over or along which they were allowed to operate, or indeed construct any embankments or divert any streams as required, but all at their own expense.

Tramway number 4 was indicated as being double until reaching Serangoon Road, whereafter it could be singled with an adequate number of passing loops, but without hinting at what point along the main road this change could be made. The answer seems to be Rumah Miskin Police Station, where there was a junction with tramway number 5 which was single track with passing loops, located at the northerly side of the road. Where double track was used, then traction poles (carrying the overhead equipment) would be located down the middle of the road between the running lines, the exceptions being Tanjong Pagar Road and Collyer Quay, where side poles were to be used, the same being provided along the single track sections. Whilst the Municipal Commissioners established and were responsible for their own street lighting programme (by gas), it fell to the Tramways Company to ensure that the traction poles located down the middle of roads were illuminated during the hours of darkness.

Some roads were paved, others were not, and the municipality found an ideal 'golden goose' to further its highways improvements schemes: once the tramways were laid in Tanjong Pagar Road, the Company would be required to fully make-up the whole of the carriageway, and in Geylang and Serangoon Roads, to construct and make-up fully metalled road surfaces to a

ABOVE: The construction of the tramway in Singapore was undertaken largely by muscle-power—a large labour force aided bullocks. Haulage was also provided by a steam lorry. In front of the latter can be seen the massive jaws of the 'Jim Crow' used for curving the rails. *(Charles E. Box*

BELOW: Thermit welding was in its infancy in 1905 and it is quite extraordinary to learn that it was used to make rail joints throughout the system from the outset. Here the encapsulated chemicals raise the temperature to make a secure weld. *(Charles E. Box*

distance of eleven-and-a-half feet from each side of the outer rails, and with the track gauge being set at one metre (a strange combination of Imperial and Metric measurements) a firm carriageway of some twenty-six feet became available to other road users.

Earlier mention was made of the need to protect the interests and workings of other utilities: these were the telegraph cable owned by the EASTERN EXTENSION AUSTRALASIA AND CHINA TELEGRAPH COMPANY and the telephone lines operated by the ORIENTAL TELEPHONE AND ELECTRIC COMPANY, such protection to be given both during construction, and against any possible chemical decomposition by action of electric current (meaning that cables placed under ground could rot if not properly protected) during the working of the lines.

Sea water could be piped to the Power Station for cooling purposes, provided it was returned after use! Much more serious —and reaching into the distant future, when others would take over the role of the Tramways Company—if, after the tramways had been in use for three years representations should be made to the Governor-in-Council either by the Municipal Commissioners or by twenty persons being Ratepayers, to the effect of the public not being in receipt of the full benefit of the tramways, the Governor having first satisfied himself that a prima facie case had been presented to him, could order the setting up of a Court

take precedence over the Company management, although the Company would not be allowed to suffer financial loss under such circumstances, with the correct fares and freight charges to be paid. The Company would operate a fleet of freight wagons, for besides the more conventional carriage of passengers by tram, contracts could also be made or published for the carriage of animals, parcels, merchandise and minerals. A list prepared in English, Chinese, Malay and Tamil languages, showing all fares and sundry charges, would need to be placed at a prominent position in each car, provided that if there should be any variation between the English and the other languages, then the English version would prevail. The Company should not accept any coinage other than that which was the normal legal tender within the Colony, and should there be any breach in this stipulation, they—the Company—would be liable to a fine of ten dollars. Whilst the precise timings of the various services would be at the usual business discretion of the Company, the Municipal Commissioners could request, in writing, the running of at least two cars over each route each way, morning and evening during the normal working week, not later than 7.00 a.m. and no earlier than 5.30 p.m., for the conveyance of workmen at reduced fares. Furthermore, the Company was to arrange for a "complete and continuous service for the carriage of passenger's baggage between Tank Road railway station and the Docks in

LEFT: In order for the trams to cross the Kallang River—spelt Kalang in some contemporary documents—a separate bridge was built for the tramway, alongside the original road bridge. While there was a single track at this point, there were separate overhead wires for each direction. Here a tram moves away from the camera onto its private right of way as other road traffic passes over the bridge to the left of the picture. Construction of this bridge delayed the opening of the Geylang tram service. *(Charles E. Box*

of Enquiry (Municipal Ordinance VIII of 1876). Then, if such a Court found the complaint to be justified, the Governor-in-Council could issue an Order requiring the Company to provide such a service as to meet the public need, and could include in that Order particulars as to the number of cars which would be required and the time tables to which they should work—indeed, the casting of long shadows.

If, without good cause or for reasons beyond the control of the Company, any section of the tramways remained unworked for a period of three months, then the Municipal Commissioners would have the option to purchase the undertaking, in part or as a whole. Against such emergency provisions, routine options to purchase were available first after thirty five years and, if not then exercised, at intervals of seven years thereafter, dates being calculated from the enactment of the Ordinance (viz. 25th March 1937, 1944, 1951, 1958 etc.).

Paragraph 37 of the Ordinance concerned the basic dimensions of the cars *and trailers* which might be used, only cars with flange wheels suitable for running on rails being permitted, with no car to exceed six feet six inches in width. The Governor-in-Council would be allowed to requisition all, or part, of the tramways for military purposes (the carriage of troops and the materials of war) and, at such times, Military Authority would

correspondence with the trains of the Singapore-Kranji Railway".Once more there is a reference to the Tank Road tram route, despite the fact of its omission earlier in the document!

Licensing

Concerning the licensing of rolling stock, each vehicle would be registered with the Registrar of Hackney Carriages, from whom a licence would be obtained indicating the number of passengers to be carried or the weight of goods to be carried thereon. The fee was fixed at twelve dollars per vehicle per annum, with the actual registration being conducted in such a manner so as to interfere as little as possible with the operation of normal schedules—in other words, the Registrar should not cause the whole fleet to be taken out of service at the same time in order to meet the needs of registration.

The main schedule of the Ordinance carried an instruction which would weigh heavy not only on the Company, but also on its successors over the next six decades, demonstrating the arrogant approach to business as set towards the end of the Victorian reign: "all engines, boilers, electrical generating apparatus and power station equipment, car bodies and electrical equipment including motors, shall be of British manufacture, and the Governor-in-Council may, in case the same or any of them

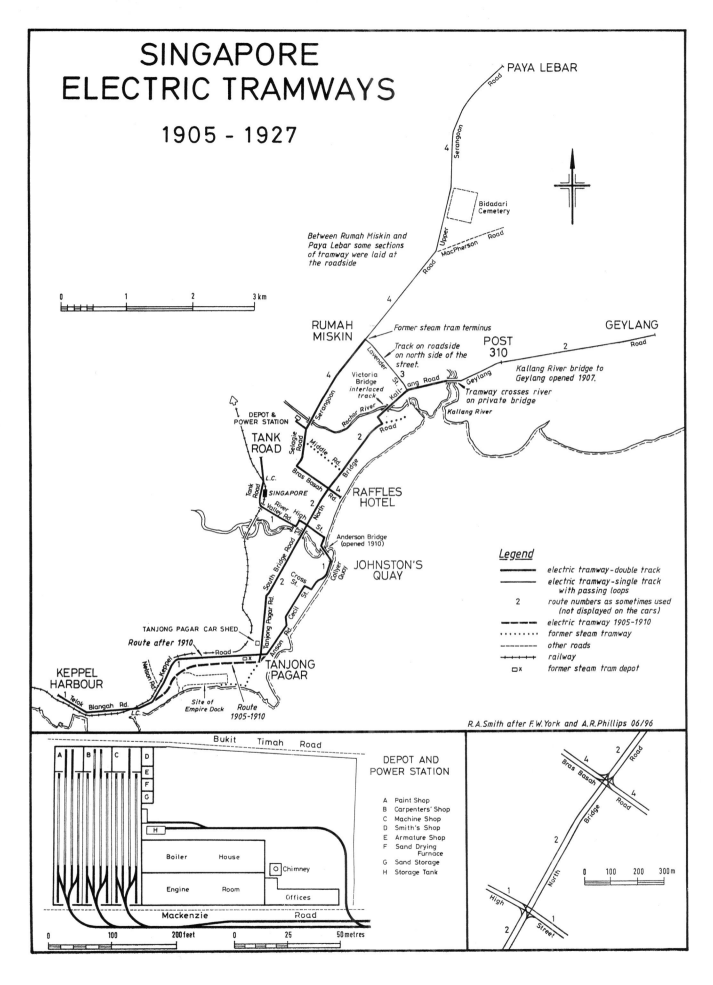

SINGAPORE ELECTRIC TRAMWAYS

1905 - 1927

PAYA LEBAR

Between Rumah Miskin and Paya Lebar some sections of tramway were laid at the roadside

Bidadari Cemetery

Upper MacPherson Road

RUMAH MISKIN

Former steam tram terminus

GEYLANG

POST 310

Track on roadside on north side of the street.

Kallang River bridge to Geylang opened 1907.

Victoria Bridge *interlaced track*

Tramway crosses river on private bridge

Kallang River

DEPOT & POWER STATION

Rochor River

TANK ROAD

Selegie Road
Middle Rd.
Bras Basah Rd.
Bridge Road

L.C.

SINGAPORE

River Valley Rd.
Tank Road
High St.
North St.

RAFFLES HOTEL

Anderson Bridge (opened 1910)

JOHNSTON'S QUAY

Collyer Quay

South Bridge Road
Cross St.
Cecil St.

TANJONG PAGAR CAR SHED

Route after 1910

Tanjong Pagar Rd.
Anson Rd.

Keppel Road
Nelson Rd.

KEPPEL HARBOUR

Telok Blangah Rd.

L.C.

Site of Empire Dock

Route 1905-1910

TANJONG PAGAR

Legend

▬▬▬	electric tramway-double track
———	electric tramway-single track with passing loops
2	route numbers as sometimes used (not displayed on the cars)
– – –	electric tramway 1905-1910
··········	former steam tramway
- - - -	other roads
+++++	railway
□x	former steam tram depot

R.A.Smith after F.W.York and A.R.Phillips 06/96

0   1   2   3 km

DEPOT AND POWER STATION

Bukit Timah Road

A Paint Shop
B Carpenters' Shop
C Machine Shop
D Smith's Shop
E Armature Shop
F Sand Drying Furnace
G Sand Storage
H Storage Tank

Boiler House

Chimney

Engine Room

Offices

Mackenzie Road

0   100   200 feet

0   25   50 metres

Bras Basah Road
North Bridge Road

High Street

0   100   200   300m

19

shall not be of British manufacture, forfeit the same and for this purpose remove the same and dispose thereof as he may see fit for the benefit of the Government".

Fares and classes of travel

In operating their cars the Company wished to provide two-class accommodation, although in preparing fare charts three were shown. Routes were not divided into stages, but rather cut into sections, thus

	First	Second	Third
Between Johnston's Pier and the entrance toTanjong Pagar Docks, for any distance	20c	15c	10c
Tanjong Pagar Docks to or from the end of Tramway number 1, for any distance	20c	15c	10c
Tanjong Pagar Docks to or from High Street, for any distance	20c	15c	10c
High Street to or from Lavender Street, for any distance	20c	15c	10c
Lavender Street to or from the end of Tramway number 2, for any distance	20c	15c	10c
Lavender Street to the end of Tramway number 4, for any distance	20c	15c	10c
For any distance on Tramway number 5	20c	15c	10c
Reduced fares under Section 46 of the Ordinance, any distance	–	12c	8c

Commenting in the kindest terms, this structure was both odd and expensive. For example, any passenger wishing to ride from Johnston's Steps through to Keppel Harbour would need to purchase two sections, at second class rate 30 cents for the through ride—but—for the short journey traveller riding, say, from the last stop in Anson Road across to the first stop in Keppel Road, on the 'any distance' rule would also need to purchase two sections, which was ridiculous. Again, if we regard the currency exchange rate as being one Singapore dollar to two shillings and four pence Sterling, then it becomes difficult to reconcile the charges with those charged on trams working in the United Kingdom, for the fifteen cents fare would roughly translate as threepence halfpenny, and it is doubtful that even the longest journey would carry such a high rate, the general average standing at a one penny fare (and many 'home' companies were able to offer half-penny workmen's tickets, with a few examples of special one-farthing early morning fares, that is to say, one fourth part of one penny). Simply to make a currency conversion does not place the situation into direct comparison, for whilst the

wages in the United Kingdom might only be a few shillings a week, per capita incomes in Singapore were lower still.

In devising a three-class division of accommodation, the thinking seems to have been that First Class would be the preserve of European expatriates, Second class for the local professional classes, whilst Third Class would cater for artisans and house servants. In the eventuality, the design of the cars as they were brought into service would not allow for three divisions, and even to have two caused a great deal of difficulty, not to be fully overcome until near the end of tramway operations.

Freight traffic charges

In addition to the passenger cars, a considerable amount of freight haulage was anticipated, and to this end tramway locomotives and freight wagons were acquired. The scale of charges for the carriage of goods makes most interesting reading, the rate quoted being for each mile travelled:

1. Horse, mule, or other beast of draught or burden, per head   15 cents;
2. Ox, cow, bull or head of cattle, per head   15 cents;
3. Calf, pig, sheep or other small animals, per head   10 cents;
4. Coals, coke, culm, charcoal, cannel, limestone, chalk, lime, salt, sand, fireclay, cinders, dung, compost and all sorts of manure and all undressed materials for the repair of public roads or highways, per ton   20 cents;
5. Tin in slabs, tin ore, iron ore, pig iron, bar iron, sheet-iron, hoop iron, plates of iron slabs, billets and rolled-iron bricks, slags and stone, stones for building, pitching and paving tiles, slats and clay (except fireclay), all wrought iron not specially designated, and for heavy iron castings including railway chairs, per ton   35 cents;
6. Sugar, grain, corn, flour, hides, buffalo horns, gambier cube, gambier illipe, nuts, copra, pine-apples in cases, rattans, coffee inbags, gums and gutta in cases and baskets, oil cake in rolls, canes, pepper, coconut oil in casks, dyewoods, eathenware, timber and metals (except iron), nails, anvils, vices and chains, and for light iron castings, per ton: 40cents;
7. Cotton and other wools, drugs except opium, manu-factured goods and all other wares, merchandise, fish, articles, matters or things, per ton: 50 cents;
8. For Opium, per chest   30 cents;
9. Small parcels not exceeding seven pounds in weight: 5 cents;
10. Parcels between seven and fourteen pounds: 10 cents;
11. Parcels between fourteen and twenty-eight pounds: 15 cents;
12. Parcels between twenty-eight and fifty six pounds: 20 cents.

RIGHT: Singapore has always enjoyed a colose relationship with the sea and this view at Jardine's Steps shows that the trams were also closely associated with the port. Here a tram makes its way past a rickshaw, and a coulpe of bullock carts as it approaches the quay, alomgside which a steam ship is tied-up. The nostalgic atmosphere is enhanced by a gas lamp and an old-fashoned telegraph post. *(Charles E. Box*

carriage of a light design imported from India, hailed in the same manner as the modern day taxi, and which charged just a few cents per mile. The 'third-class' rider was already well served by a great number of rickshaw pullers, who had numerous 'stations' located around the town.

For any parcel exceeding fifty-six pounds, the charge would be set at the discretion of the Company's agent. As far as passenger's baggage was concerned, up to sixteen pounds could be carried free of charge, after which every hundred-weight and part thereof would be charged as a second-class fare (those who framed these charges were very sharp in some directions, for there was a proviso indicating that small items sent in large aggregate amounts, such as bags of sugar, coffee, meal and the like, although made up into small parcels, should not be deemed as such, and the term 'parcel' should refer only to single packages).

From the foregoing there can be little doubt as to the intention of the Company to become established as a major freight haulier, albeit tied to their tramways, the terms of the Ordinance seeming to preclude the use of carriers' carts. Certainly, the fleet would include sufficient rolling stock whereby freight trains could be worked, but to do this there would be a need to construct sidings and wharfs away from the passenger lines, and into the premises of the larger customers in order to make bulk deliveries. This does not seem to have happened, and the most minute study of maps prepared before 1920 do not reveal any such sidings. If the wagons were used at all, then it must have been for the transport of coal and other essential materials between the docks and the generating station, to the side of which an extensive yard with a network of sidings was to be found.

Other transport

Against these rather grand proposals, what forms of transport were already established in the town, and from whence the hoped for traffic would be drawn? The 'first-class' passengers, if they were sufficiently wealthy, might already own their own carriage, besides which they would have their homes along what was to become the prestigious section of town, flanking Orchard Road, in which direction tramways were not projected. For the 'second-class' passenger there was the gharri, a horse drawn

The rickshaw

The rickshaw itself was a light structure, containing a seat for a single passenger, and with a shade to give protection from the mid-day sun or monsoon rains. Two large wheels supported the body, forward of which extended a pair of long shafts, between which the puller would position himself. When at rest the ends of the shafts were down on the ground, the whole contraption being tilted forward. Once a passenger (with her child, or chicken, or fresh vegetables bought from the market) was safely seated, the puller had first to lift the shafts, and thus place the rickshaw on an even keel, before breaking into a trot. To modern eyes, this can appear to have been an humiliating form of employment, but the little carriages stayed within families, and passed from father to son and at least provided a measure of independence. A very useful service was provided, for fares would seldom be greater than a few copper coins and many of the European 'young bloods' would use them, which in no way distressed the pullers, for they were able to turn cents into dollars (the story is told of a gambling den located at Bukit Timah, well away from the disapproving eyes of their Seniors, to which the young men would travel utilising relay teams of rickshaws. In similar fashion a relay race was organised all the way to the shores of the Johore Strait). The rickshaw pullers were tough, but were not blessed with long life expectations. Equally they were strong in their opposition to the prospect of tramways in town, and having been a major cause of the demise of the steam tramway, were soon to demonstrate their displeasure once more.

Official Regulations

With construction of the lines well in hand, it then fell to the Municipal Commissioners to make Regulations—equivalent to British 'bye-laws' drawn up by the Town Clerk—to govern the precise manner in which the cars would function, and the passengers behave. The resulting document was published on 7th July 1905, and contained some interesting requirements, not all of which were met. The rules on illumination were as to be expected, namely that every car in service between sunset and sunrise should carry two lighted lamps, one at either end, with the headlight showing white and that at the rear being red, with both lights being so constructed and located so as to be seen at a distance (although no indication as to what the distance might be was declared). The interior of each car should be given sufficient lighting, but, except in the instances of special charters, no passenger would be allowed to perform or play any sort of musical instrument. Likewise, no person afflicted with smallpox or any other contagious disease should ever be allowed to travel by tram, and should it happen that the conductor should find any such person to be aboad, he should first have the passenger removed, and make a report to the Medical Officer of Health instantly. The tram would be taken from service, and could not be used again until it had been disinfected to the complete satisfaction of the Medical Officer. Concerning the cars themselves, they would need to be constantly maintained in good order, painted and varnished both inside and outside and appointed for the safe carriage of passengers and their safety when boarding or alighting. Each car would be fitted with bells for communication between the conductor and driver. The outside would carry the fleet number in numerals not less than six inches tall, with the same number being repeated inside the car in such manner and position as to be visible at all times. Attached to each car, in the English, Chinese, Malay and Tamil languages and placed in a prominent position, would be a 'label' stating the destination of the car, using letters not less than two-and-a-half inches long. In fact, fleet numbers on the Singapore cars were quite small, and contained within a garter device, and destination signs, when used, were minimal, and certainly not multi-lingual as stipulated above.

Speed limits and Stopping Places

Regulations governing speed were also set out, thus:

The speed at which cars could pass through facing points, whether fixed or movable, should never exceed four miles per hour, with the same restriction being placed when rounding curves with a radius of sixty feet or less. Compulsory stopping places were listed, at crossing places, and with each car being bought to a complete halt thirty feet before arriving at the crossing, then to proceed over the crossing at a speed no greater than four miles per hour.

These stops were to be made

1—the crossing of South Bridge Road with Cross Street
2—the junction of South Bridge Road with Circular Road
3—the crossing of North Bridge Road with High Street
4—the crossing of North Bridge Road with Stamford Road
5—the crossing of North Bridge Road with Bras Basah Road
6—the crossing of North Bridge Road with Middle Road
7—the crossing of North Bridge Road and Rochore Road
8—all railway crossings.

From this list it will be noted that only two of the street crossings carried tramways, so it will be seen that the majority of

these were purely for the taking up and setting down of passengers rather than indicating points requiring a measure of protection for other road users. They were:

Tramway number 1—at P and O Wharf, Borneo Wharf and Tanjong Pagar Dock Entrance

Tramway number 2—at Kreta Ayer Jinrickshaw station, The Police Court, High Street, Bras Basah Road, Arab Street, the junction of North Bridge Road with Jalan Sultan, Lavender Street, 2° milestone Gelang (sic) Road and Tanjong Katong Road

Tramway number 3—at the entrance to Telok Ayer Street, at the junction of Telok Ayer Street with Cecil Street and Market Street.

Tramway number 4—at Princep Street junction with Bras Basah Road, Kadang Kerbau Police Station, Rumah Miskin Police Station, Macpherson Road and at the entrance to Bidadari (the vast cemetery located along Upper Serangoon Road slopes)

Tramway number 5—being so short, had nothing indicated.

Tramway number 6—had just one, at the River Valley Road entrance to the railway station.

Additional 'request' stops could be sited as the Company might wish (subject to consultation with the Municipal Commissioners) and each stopping place would be marked by a metal 'Tram Stop', the flag of which would be to a design duly approved by the Commissioners.

Except for the various Notices and 'labels' previously mentioned, the Company were forbidden to display any other material on the cars, so that at least for the time being, advertising was out. The form of the tram stops was unusual: they took the form of circular metal plates, bearing a large numeral, this being the number of the route.

Junction of High Street & North Bridge Road, Singapore

LEFT: The routes of two tram services cross at the junction of High Street and North Bridge Road, probably *circa* 1920. The picture is full of interest; the left hand car appears to be in a lighter livery than the car facing the camera, both have advertising boards and at least one carries a 'Shell' advertisement on the rocker panel. Below the roof advertising boards there are what appear to be route boards and there is evidence of them on the second car although they have not become apparant in other photographs. To the right is a traction post from which is hung a tram stop and fare stage indicator. Also just visible in the right background are the girders of Elgin Bridge. Rickshaws and a gas lamp add period touches. NOTE: The advertisements for Shell and Continental Tyres indicate the post-First World-war pepriod, although no motor vehicles can be seen.

compulsory stops were sited as a means of protecting other traffic, of which there would be little in the forms of easily controlled mechanical vehicles—instead, there would be heavily laden carts drawn by bullocks who might take fright and stampede if suddenly confronted by a speeding tramcar rushing out immediately ahead of them, whilst man powered vehicles should be allowed to continue on their way unimpeded.

The original Ordinance had granted powers for the construction of additional tramways anywhere within the Settlement, and we must take note of Tramway number 6 as mentioned in the Regulations, but not mentioned in the original ordinance nor the draft fare structure.

Further compulsory stopping places were listed, although

In a continued examination of the Regulations, further hints can be drawn concerning the possible movement of freight over the tramways, for paragraph 16 forebade the use of trains consisting of more than one motor car and one trailer at any one time, except between the hours of 10.00 p.m. and 5.00 a.m.

Construction

The Company had been Incorporated, the Powers to construct and operate obtained, and later in the span between 1902 and 1905, Regulations drawn up under which the service could operate. All that remained was the construction of the whole undertaking, a task requiring considerable skill and good forward planning. As a first step, a central site had to be acquired from

which all other works could proceed, and to this end a large block of land located between Mackenzie and Bukit Timah Roads was purchased and cleared: the frontage extended some 422 feet facing Mackenzie Road, whilst that side nearest to Selegie Road was 228 feet in depth, with the opposite end being slightly wider at 240 feet. Here would arise the headquarters, with the street frontage being divided into three unequal sections, each having a different style of architecture. Approached from the Selegie Road end, first came the Administration Block, in turn joined onto the Engine Room of the Power Station, with the boiler room behind. So vast was the equipment to be installed that the Engine Room rose to a three storey height. The end of the site was occupied by the extensive car sheds. Behind the office accommodation rose the chimney, unusually made of steel, and rising to such height that it remained a landmark of the town for many years to come. As the offices did not require a great deal of land, sufficient space remained for the laying out of an extensive yard, an ideal place for accumulating rails, copper wire, traction poles and all of the other equipment needed during the construction period.

Back in the United Kingdom the main industrial centres were closely linked with all of the major ports by railways, and the docks provided with all of the latest heavy lifting gear. The importance of Singapore as a port had grown to the extent of having several shipping lines able to bring the required machinery, and on frequent schedules. Hence the need for careful planning, for the engineers did not wish to receive too much in advance of the work they were actually doing, although there is some evidence that they were able to obtain a lease on the former steam tram depot at Tanjong Pagar, and this would have been a useful depository being so close to the docks. The Promoters in London were ASSOCIATION GENERAL LIMITED, engaging Messrs. ALFRED DICKINSON (of London and Birmingham) as Consulting Engineers, to them falling the task of preparing all detailed plans and specifications and, at a later date, to superintend the progress of the work. The main contractors to do the work were to be DICK, KERR AND COMPANY (with offices in London, but more noted for their world renowned factory at Preston).

The Power Station and Headquarters

To transport the rails, the wires and the poles would not have presented too many problems, but as for the boilers and engines, these would have been a very different matter, for although they would have been disassembled as far as possible, the remaining size and weight must have been elephantine. A pair of steam driven traction engines slowly hauling their loads over the none-too secure road surfaces, inching their way over the bridges across the Singapore River, and creeping around the edge of town in order to reach Mackenzie Road, these must have been sights to bring out the crowds. As far as we can tell, all went according to plan, and the walls of the power station rose up as the machinery was installed. In this respect, not everything had to be imported, for there had been established extensive brickworks during the earliest days of the Settlement, and skilled bricklayers and masons had already been able to provide the town with many fine buildings. Thus, good quality red bricks were on hand, with doors and window surrounds and copings set off with white stone. Considerable attention was given to the obtaining of maximum natural light, and the needs for ventilation, so that every roof was crowned by a full length and quite high conduit, the sides of which were provided with heavy duty slatting which encouraged the free flow of air.

A visitor, when first entering the engine-room of the power station, would be overwhelmed by sheer size, not only of the accommodation (190 feet long by 48 feet wide) but more so by the machinery, the principal items of which were two main traction sets of 500 kilowatts, one steam lighting set, one motor generator lighting set, and banks of associated switch gear, whilst inside the boiler house would be found no less than eight 'Lancashire' boilers arranged in two banks of four, and with each boiler capable of evaporating 6,000 lbs. of water each hour, and with a working pressure of 175 lbs. per square inch. The vast engine room was free of clutter, making available a considerable area of free floor space, being achieved by locating condensers and water supply pipes in the basement. The main contractors for the supply of heavy machinery were YATES AND THOM (of Blackburn) who constructed the traction sets, whilst Dick, Kerr and Company had been responsible for the generators and various switchboards.

23

Before moving further along Mackenzie Road, a few minutes might be well spent taking a closer look at the yard, entered by a single line by way of a gate at the corner of the site nearest to Selegie Road, following the boundary wall until reaching the half way point, then making a turn of ninety degrees allowing passage behind, but remaining clear of, the rear of the power station. Some sixty feet short of the car sheds was to be found a facing junction, with the 'main' line going ahead to terminate hard against a storage bunker, whilst the 'branch', going off to the right, formed a general purpose siding (in later years it was found that the yard was much too large, and a covering of mixed vegetation spread across those parts which had fallen into disuse, with a measure of control being maintained by a small number of goats!)

The third section of the buildings, the all important car sheds (a term used on a local basis rather than the more usual 'tram depot', perhaps due to the need of obtaining maximum ventilation resulting in a more open structure than would be found in the

(19 feet high) in order to enter the paint shop, this being one of three quite distinct workshops located at the rear of the shed. Roads 4 and 5 were for normal parking, whilst 6 and 7 passed through similar doors to gain access to the carpenter's shop. 8, 9, and 10 were again for parking out of service, with 11 going through into the machine shop, and 12 was for parking.

The sheer size of the headquarters overall reflected the high hopes being entertained by the Company, for Singapore was expanding and it was expected that the tramways business would likewise expand. The car shed presented a visual declaration of this spirit of optimism, for the accommodation thus described should have a comfortable capacity for about eighty trams, that estimate ignoring the short stubs for disabled cars.

The Track

The tracks were laid with grooved rail weighing 95lb. per yard, and all rail joints were welded by the Thermit process. The

LEFT: This view of tracklaying serves to show the rails laid on a longitudinal strip of concrete with tie-bars at intervals to maintain the gauge. The track was back-filled with water-bound macadam which gradually allowed water to undermine the foundations; the cause of great problems in the future. The tramway in Hong Kong was backfilled with concrete from the outset and this presented difficulties only when track renewal time came round. Another unusual feature for the day was the continuously welded rail; another feature rejected in Hong Kong. *(Charles E. Box*

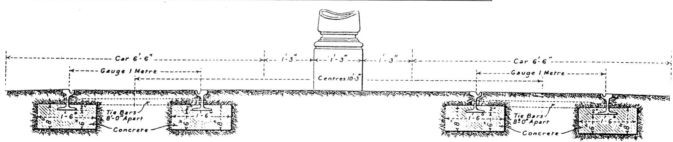

Cross Section of Street with Double Track and Centre Poles

United Kingdom). The frontage extended 138 feet, whilst in depth the maximum dimension of the site was utilised, so that the rear wall faced onto Bukit Timah Road. The access line from Selegie Road was double to a point opposite the engine room, thereafter becoming single, with three junctions in succession leading through doors and into the shed, where each track faced junctions to form four parking roads (thus giving a total of twelve interior roads): beneath each road was a full length inspection pit. From each group of three, the two outermost roads contained trailing points at the start of each road, and from each of these points there ran a short section of track coming to the wall facing Mackenzie Road, of such a length as to be able to accommodate one tram. Thus, provision was made for a maximum of six cars to be stored out of service whilst awaiting repairs or repainting, should the workshops be fully occupied. If the roads be numbered 1 to 12 from left to right, then 1 was for normal service parking, whilst 2 and 3 passed through a pair of sliding doors

base of the rails was bedded into concrete, but instead of laying a bed of concrete the full width of the track, the contractors laid a longitudinal strip of concrete, eight inches deep by eighteen inches wide, running directly under each rail. The road surface was then made up to rail level, using macadam, well rolled and consolidated. The macadam referred to is not the modern and waterproof tar macadam, but the original road surface pioneered by the Scottish engineer who invented the system of using graded crushed stones to produce a firm self draining surface. After a few years, problems arose with the Singapore tracks, as the frequent rains, draining through the stone surface, tended to undermine the concrete foundation of the rails and cause flexing of the continuous welded rails under the weight of a passing tramcar. This would not have been so had the rails been laid on a solid raft of concrete, but this in turn would have presented drainage problems if covered by the traditional macadam. With hindsight, the solid concrete raft and an impervious surface, such as stone setts, would have been much better.

LEFT: The massive brick-built tramway premises at Mackenzie Road showing, nearest to the camera, the three entrance doorwars to the car sheds—a combination car is turning into the farthest—and beyond is the huge power station building, the steel chimney for which can be seen belching smoke high above all. *(Charles E. Box*

BELOW LEFT: From the other end, the Mackenzie Road buildings looked no less impressive and the great chimney—a local landmark—can be seen to advantage. *(John Rossman collection*

Singapore Electric Tramways Power Station.

The Tramcars

Fifty passenger cars were obtained for the opening of the services, all single deck and mounted on a single four-wheeled truck.

Bodywork was of two patterns, the most numerous (thirty cars) being of the cross-bench type, open at the sides and with bench seating located in rows across the width of the body, there being ten such rows. Passengers boarded the tram by way of a footboard running the length of the car.

The other twenty cars were of the 'combination' type—also known as 'California'—having a central enclosed section and able to provide conventional saloon accommodation with seating along the sides, whilst at each end would be found open platforms with cross-bench seats.

The question remains, but ever will be without an answer "Why were two such different types of car purchased?". Had the Company been so obsessed by the theory of different classes of accommodation? Certainly the combination cars would be well suited to meet such a policy, with a saloon being set aside as first-class and the platforms as second, although it remains impossible to judge how a third class could be incorporated into the structure. The real difficulty would be in making obvious divisions on the cross bench cars (although we have suggested that certain benches might be designated as 'first-class' but then, in purely operational terms, how could they be used thus?). Perhaps the anticipated ratio between those paying first and second class fares suggested that the majority would be the latter, and so a more intensive service should be provided, using the cross-bench cars solely as second-class, although to maintain a two-to-one service of cars would produce problems with scheduling, particularly when individual cars needed to be taken out of service for prolonged periods, such as for the repair of accident damage. It is of note that in Hong Kong, almost identical trams of both types were operated as two-class cars from 1904 until replaced by double-deckers from

25

1912. (It is of note too that the Hong Kong system used very much more substantial track foundations)

In order to cater for the anticipated carriage of freight, three types of rolling stock were obtained. The mainstay was a trio of motorised vans, that is to say, capable of self propulsion in the same manner as a passenger car, and looking very much like an ordinary tram except in having no side windows, their place being occupied by two sliding doors.

The remainder of the rolling stock comprised fifteen covered goods vans, and a like number of open wagons, all of which were mounted on four-wheeled trucks and intended for haulage by the motor vans.

The contract to build the Singapore tramcar fleet was won by Dick, Kerr & Co of Preston, Lancashire, who had a vehicle building subsidiary, the United Electric Car Company—also of Preston—whose factory was just across the road from that of Dick, Kerr. In fact, the car building arm, the United Electric Car Company, had only that year—1905—been formed by merging the Electric Railway & Tramway Carriage Works Ltd with the English Electric Manufacturing Co, hence the almost identical Hong Kong cars of a year previous being referred to as having been constructed by the Electric Railway & Tramway Carriage Works. Construction of the trucks was sub-contracted to Brill.

Both types of car, cross-bench and combination, were shipped to Singapore in sections for local assembly although it is possible that one of each might have been assembled at Preston before being knocked-down again for shipping.

All cars passenger were on the same 4-wheeled Brill 21E, 6ft 6in wheelbase truck and were powered by two Dick, Kerr 25hp motors of type 25-B. Controllers, also by Dick, Kerr were of 'Form C'.

Although widely referred to as being 'identical' to the Hong Kong cars of 1904, the Singapore version was without the clerestory roof of the former.

In addition, there were a number of shorter cross-bench cars whose precise origins remain the subject of further research.

(A fuller description of the cars is given in Part Two of this volume.)

In transporting the cars from the United Kingdom, shipping charges were based upon both weight and volume, so exporters devised a system of sending the trucks and bodywork in sections, to be assembled in the local workshops (it was the custom of the manufacturers to complete at least one representative of each batch so ordered at their works, so as to check measurements and fittings, then to dismantle again for shipping). A second order for passenger cars was placed in 1907, for ten more of the cross-bench variety.

Overhead and monsoon drains

Whilst all was being prepared in the vicinity of Mackenzie Road, construction of the lines was going ahead, the streets in the town being torn open and roads of substance being constructed through groves of palm trees. Feeder cables were being located in trenches, track was being laid, and traction poles from which the overhead wire would be suspended were being planted: no great problem along these sections when they would be placed at the centre of the road, but calling for careful planning when set at the road side—severe flooding which can occur during the monsoon seasons provide a need for deep drainage ditches to be set alongside most main roads, at points reaching a depth of five feet. For most of the year they are dry, and being largely uncovered, lurk as a trap for the unwary. Come the rains and they become raging torrents. In the designs of the town shop-houses, the upper floors project over the lower, supported by substantial pillars along the edge of the roadway. The resulting 'five foot way' is available for pedestrians, although many shop keepers would allow their produce to spill out onto the paving. The monsoon drains and covered five-foot-way meant that traction poles needed to project into the roadway, and were liable to become a traffic hazard.

As for materials, the civil engineers would have little difficulty in obtaining supplies on a local basis: taking the island as a whole, the topographic features are, in the main, flat and low lying. The highest hill is to be found at Bukit Timah, rising to 177 metres, and the longest river Sungei Seletar, flowing 14.5 kilometres. There are three quite district geological zones, the central hilly district focused on Bukit Timah, but also including Bukit Gombak, Bukit Panjang and Bukit Mandai, from which could be drawn the required granite chippings as required in the track bed. To the south-west, beyond Keppel Harbour, quantities of shale and sandstone form a succession of scarps and vales, to be drawn on as required. To the east loose sand and gravel formed a belt extending from Katong through Geylang and on towards Changi. Light jungle was being cleared, and swamps were being drained so that, in due course, the works were complete. Oddly enough, the plan was to open the whole system as a going concern, rather than section by section as the appropriate work was completed, although this decision may have been influenced by the date when the generating plant was ready. One section did not open immediately: to complete the projected line to Geylang, it was necessary to build a bridge across the Kallang River. This was placed parallel to and on the seaward side of the existing bridge, and by July 1905 it was not yet complete. The route to Geylang was eventually opened in 1907.

RIGHT: Tanjong Pagar tramway junction with a crossbench car taking the left fork towards Tanjong Pagar Road which in turn leads to South Bridge Road. To the left of the carriageway can be seen the deep monsoon drain, sometimes two or three feet deep and which can become a raging torrent in the monsoon season. Lamp posts and, often, traction poles were located in the carriageway clear of the deep gully. On the tram, canvas side screen nearest the camera has been pulled-down and others are partly down. There is a bullock cart plodding away in the same direction as the tram, while a Malay police officer approaches the camera watched by an Indian officer behind him. (Charles E. Box

The Cables

The installation of underground feeder cables for the Singapore tramways was sub-contracted to Messrs. Callender's Cable and Construction Company, a firm well experienced in this type of work in Britain and abroad. Callenders installed the similar cables in Hong Kong and Shanghai, yet in the case of Singapore serious breakdowns began to occur after only a few years. This can only be attributed to water penetration, partly because of the unsealed roads and pavements, and partly due to the frequent heavy rains and high humidity.

Takeover

Meanwhile, back in London, financial dealings had seen the taking over of Singapore Tramways by the SINGAPORE ELECTRIC TRAMWAYS, LIMITED. English interests were involved, in the sense of other tramway concerns in addition to individual shareholders, and there remains an *understanding* that the HASTINGS TRAMWAYS COMPANY were in some manner associated. Memorandum and Articles of Association were registered under the Companies Acts, 1862 to 1900, on the 29th March 1905, and besides setting out the financial structures, in the main confirmed the objects and purposes of the original Company, taking over the Powers gained by the Ordinance.

The first Manager to be appointed was Mr. Lewis D. Tandy, who arrived from London on 15th February 1905. His first task was to negotiate with the Contractors, so that by stages he could take control of the tramways, by now almost completed, on behalf of his employers. A major task would be to recruit and

The Opening

The target date for the opening of the tramways was set for 15th March 1905, but such optimism was not well founded, and in the event it was not until July that one car was able to venture forth for the official inspection prior to certification as being fit for use by the public: happily, details of the Inspector's tour survive: leaving the depot, the line as far as Paya Lebar was first subjected to scrutiny, then retracing the route to the terminus in Bras Basah Road at Beach Road. A spot of shunting and using the connecting curve linking Brash Basah Road with North Bridge Road, the car was reported as moving 'at good speed' to Keppel Harbour. Retracing to Tanjong Pagar, Anson Road was followed to Johnston's Steps. The only means of leaving town would be to ride to Tanjong Pagar and back down by way of South Bridge Road, etc., but it seems that either the inspecting party had tired of the ride, or else was able to declare itself quite satisfied by what had been seen. Clearly the tracks to Tank Road, and as far as the Kallang Bridge were not ready to be inspected at this juncture.

As recorded by 'The Straits Times' for 25th July 1905: the lines were opened to the public with little formal ceremony.

"Punctually at seven o'clock this morning, the first tramway (sic) of the new electric service emerged from the power house (sic) at Mackenzie Road and hummed down the five-cent run from the Station to the Raffles Hotel. There were not many guests to see the ceremony that celebrated the inauguration. Mr. John Anderson, who came down to watch the first car load, did not risk himself as a passenger, and there was only one lady

LEFT: This photograph is dated July 1905 but the figures giving the day could be either 22nd or 29th. With the tramway opening on 24th July this was not the opening day but a few days before or after. With the then recent takeover bringing about a change of name, there had been no attempt to change the company title from the 'Singapore Tramways Limited' as shown here on the dashboard garter, to 'Singapore Electric Tramways'. The ubiquitous bullock cart once again features in this view. *(Charles E. Box*

train his staff: the more senior posts at Head Office would be filled by expatriate personnel brought from London, but there had to be found time and wages clerks, ticket room staff, stores assistants and the like, in order that the administrative side could function properly. In the workshops the needs were for electricians, carpenters and allied trades, in the generating station the call would be for boiler house attendants and stokers, outside work would need crews to maintain track and overhead wiring and lastly, but perhaps most important in the public eye, motormen and conductors. To recruit so many men would not be easy, for Singapore was very much a boom town, constantly attracting new immigrants, so that new buildings and associated works made constant demands on available labour, and with almost a promise of employment more families were attracted, with even more demand for accommodation, and so the wheel kept turning. Also to be brought from the United Kingdom was a small team of traffic inspectors, and it was to them fell the task of driving instruction.

passenger on the car, Mrs. Palliser. Mr. Tandy acted as host and conductor. He had his cash bag and his bell punch strapped about him, soldier fashion: and it is painful to state that he collected fares from everybody. Even the Press was not exempt. Neither was the lady. When it got to Raffles Hotel the car was turned back and ran away to Serangoon. This cost twenty cents extra".

Whilst the style of reporting might be regarded as being rather quaint, it does reveal an important fact: that there was little public interest in the coming of the trams, not even in the novelty sense—meaning that people might be desirous to take a ride just to see what it would be like, but without any intention of becoming regular users. Passengers would be needed on a regular basis, and from the very first day, but they did not come, instead seeming to prefer their established modes of travel—why change, and deprive the rickshaw man of the few cents he might charge for the same journey? The second revealing point was that the very high scale of fares as previously provided for had been recognised as being uneconomic, and very much revised downwards—the 'five cents' charge mentioned would be most unusual, as these would be 'first-class' passengers (itself introducing a further pointer in the direction of the theory that a class system could not be introduced).

New Speed Restrictions

After two months of operation, new rules were imposed concerning speed limits, which became:

Tramway number 1—10 miles per hour, except through Keppel Village, wherein the speed of any car should not be allowed to exceed 5 m.p.h.

Tramway number 2—between Tanjong Pagar Dock and Jalan Sultan 6 miles per hour, between Jalan Sultan and Kalang Bridge 8 miles per hour between Kalang Bridge and the municipal boundary 10 miles per hour.

Tramway number 3—8 miles per hour, except around the curves near Telok Ayer Street, Market Street and D'Almeida Street, where the speed should not exceed 4 miles an hour.

Tramway number 4—from Beach Road to Kadang Kerbau, 8 miles per hour from Kadang Kerbau to the municipal boundary 10 miles per hour.

In addition, the Company were instructed to ensure that the grooves in the rails around all curves were kept well greased. There were instructions concerning the operating of the trams. For instance, drivers of cars at a standstill should give one stroke on the foot gong before moving away, and give notice of the car approaching a stopping place by two strokes on the gong in rapid succession, as often as required. The conductor was required to remain on the rear platform of his tram whenever travelling up or down a gradient in excess of 1 in 25 in order to be on hand to apply the brake in case of emergency (although the only incline of this nature was along Upper Serangoon Road).

Rickshaw competition

To state the case in modest terms, early results and experiences were very disappointing, figures indicating that passengers carried each day remained constant at about eleven thousand, whereas accommodation was available to carry five times that number. This was but one problem, and another was congestion—although the Ordinance had specified the tracks being of the exclusive use of trams, a surprising number of carts appeared with wheels to the 'gauge' of one metre, allowing them to fit snugly into the tram tracks. Altercations passed back and forth between the various drivers, but the trams were the ones always being blocked. Then there was the menace of vandalism, with small boulders and baulks of wood being placed across the track, inviting disaster. On one occasion a car was making a fair turn of speed down the hill of Upper Serangoon Road when it struck one such obstruction. Car and track parted company, with the impetus carrying the tram across the roadway and into the compound of a neighbouring house. Little damage was caused to the tram, but recovery was very difficult. A lesson had been learned, and fearful of such violent action against the trams being allowed to continue, with possible damage to rolling stock and injury to passengers, Mr. Tandy made public an offer of one thousand dollars for information which could lead to the arrest of the instigators of what was described at the time as being "a plot to wreck the trams". The police provided several plain clothes officers to maintain observations, and their efforts were crowned with success in the arrest of just two coolies. They were brought to trial charged with placing stones and wood upon the lines (in Court the story was enlarged somewhat.) The driver of a tram had become somewhat incensed by the behaviour of a bullock cart handler who could not, or would not, get his vehicle clear of the tram tracks. An argument developed to the extent where blows were exchanged, the man with the bullock cart coming off worse. From this relatively small, and one could venture to suggest everyday, upset, there was magnified a situation which brought a sharp focus onto a general discontent against trams. Two coolies alone could not have been responsible for so many acts of placing stones, and which required police observations at many places. The rickshaw pullers stood to suffer the greatest losses, and it was they who tried to organise a boycott: a Chinese language newspaper during 1907 published a violently worded attack, using as their reason for doing so a need to continue Chinese Conservatism, partly based upon the lessons which were being provided by the newly demonstrated strengths of Western trades unions. The speed of the cars and the need for overhead wires (the latter being a direct reference to the poles located in the centre of the road or projecting from the five-foot-way) were the cause of many accidents. Trams presented a threat to 10,000 rickshaw coolies, and therefore it was a duty placed upon the various Chinese Guilds to combine in an organisation to continue to boycott the trams. Violence in the printed word, flavoured with a generous measure of exaggeration, for whilst there will be no doubt that some rickshaw pullers were put out of business, surely their total number had never been as high as was stated and they were to survive, albeit in reducing numbers, for more than thirty years. To read between the lines and with great care, the attack must be seen as a warning of the increasing expansion of 'foreign' businesses throughout the Far East, and as the Guilds were able to exercise great influence and pressures amongst the Chinese residents, the reasons for disappointing results are not hard to find).

Disappointment and sale

Such was the extent of the disappointing results that, during the first year of workings, the Company was once again to change hands, being obliged to enter into an agreement with the EAST INDIA CONSTRUCTION COMPANY, LIMITED, under which the latter were to acquire the whole of the business for a consideration of £730,000, but changed the name of the company to the SINGAPORE ELECTRIC TRAMWAYS LIMITED. Besides lower than anticipated passenger revenues, there was a smaller than planned demand for current to provide street lighting as might be requested by the Municipal Commissioners. Even worse was the discovery that feeder cables were showing signs of being defective, with no less than twenty miles needing to be replaced before the end of 1906. Under the severe tropical climatic conditions the insulating materials were breaking down, and it was hoped that, once the programme of replacement had been completed the problem would have been solved—it was not, and was destined to happen again.

Meanwhile, the natural growth of commerce as reflected by the volume of shipping handled through the Port as a whole, was destined to have some effect on the pattern of routes. A legislative Paper of 1906 indicated that a substantial rebuilding of the walls flanking the Singapore River had become a matter of urgent necessity, with the deepening of the river being incorporated at the same time. To this plan would be coupled a means of providing sheltered accommodation just outside the river mouth and a waiting area for incoming barges, being a method of reducing what had become heavy congestion at the river mouth. The Paper anticipated that the increased movement of goods would see a corresponding increase in the various banking and insurance services, and so a further need was recognised, namely a more direct road link between the business houses located along Collyer Quay and the Government departments centred on Empress Place. A new Bridge, of grand proportions, would cross the river a few yards inland from the meeting with the sea, and would incorporate tram lines in order to link the Johnston's Steps terminus with that in High Street.

In similar fashion similar increased capacity was needed by the Docks Company, and in order to meet their expansions new land would have to be created. To this end a reclamation scheme was prepared involving those areas of marshland which spread along the inland side of Keppel Road being drained, and then infilled. Once the new ground had settled Keppel Road would be subjected to a long deviation, taking it almost one-quarter-of-a-mile inland for the length between Tanjong Pagar and Nelson Road, in the vicinity of Borneo Wharf. The old road, once taken out of use, would then be sealed and in company with the new land, incorporated within the docks security limits. Wheresoever Keppel Road went, the tramway would need to follow.

Slowly, but very slowly indeed, some headway was being made to encourage passengers to travel by tram, and whilst the Company Chairman in his report for 1909, was pleased to note these increases, he was bound to admit that the most persistent difficulty remained the popularity of the rickshaw. Using the most obvious weapon in the fight to attract custom, fare scales had again been reduced but even so the financial year had closed with an ultra-modest profit of only £134. However tiny, the books were in the black, for the drastic reduction in charges to three cents per section, boosting the average daily number of riders to 32,000, still short of expectations but in the belief that the slow increase would continue, allowing a further order for ten more cars to be placed, all of which were to the 'combination' pattern, and being placed into service during the early months of 1908.

Anderson Bridge—extensions

Named after Governor Sir John Anderson, the new bridge linked the banks of the Singapore River, and new tramway services were able to be brought into use as from 12th March 1910. The layout along Collyer Quay was altered so as to provide double track throughout, with a crossing place left at Johnston's Steps. Once through the girders of Anderson Bridge the lines kept over to the side of Empress Place closest to the office blocks, then to pass round into High Street in order to make an end-on link with what had been that terminus. Two services were to be routed across the bridge: first, cars which had worked from Keppel Harbour to Johnston's Steps would now continue by way of High Street to Tank Road railway station (of great convenience for the carriage of baggage from trains to the docks). Secondly, the opportunity was taken to remove the Paya Lebar service from the rather remote terminus in Bras Basah Road into the business heart of the town, using North Bridge Road, High Street and Anderson Bridge in order to use a new terminus in the form of the crossover outside Johnston's Steps. This meant bringing into use two sets of curves hitherto used only by depot

before making a precise turn into Anson Road, whilst trams coming up Tanjong Pagar Road and seeking to turn into Keppel Road (the Lavender Street to Nelson Road service) required the locating of a new double track junction. As a result of all these works, cars from Geylang terminating at Tanjong Pagar, became isolated on a short spur (rather surprisingly, no attempt was made to retain that part of the old line as far as the docks main gate— perhaps the presence of a railway level crossing caused the decision to leave that terminus where it was). History does not reveal the effect this slightly expanded tramway network had upon the fortunes of the Government Railway: be it sufficient to say that, by 1910, the local stations beyond Tank Road had been closed, although the railway was much in demand for the movement of goods from the docks.

An Aside

To digress for a moment, it is of interest to review the progress, and otherwise, of other forms of transport for, in varying degrees, they will make marks insofar as decisions and the setting of policies be concerned. For example, the wonderments of aviation briefly touched Singapore on 17th March 1911, when together an Englishman and Frenchman managed to get a flimsy aircraft off the ground in order to demonstrate powered flight. Out on the highway, the calendar needs to be turned back to 1896 in order to witness the importing of the first automobile: for many years thereafter motor cars were to remain very much in the province of the extremely rich, and they served only to displace the larger private carriages. However, by 1907 the motor taxi was making severe inroads into the business activities of the gharries, so that by 1911 this horse drawn mode of conveyance was all but finished. The first motor bus had come—and gone, leaving little trace of it's passage through history— an anonymous gentleman of much enterprise supervised the off-

RIGHT: In many ways, Anderson Bridge has become as well known a feature of Singapore as many other landmarks and here a combination car approaches the Empress Place, having just crossed the girdered structure shortly after it was opened in 1910. *(John Rossman collection*

bound workings, from Bras Basah Road into North Bridge Road and from North Bridge Road into High Street. About a quarter of a mile of new track had been installed, but the consequent revision of services brought about an increase of two route miles. The section in Bras Basah Road between North Bridge road and Beach Road merely took on the role of infrequently used spur, for special workings if required, or the occasional short working thence to Macpherson Road.

1910 also saw the opening of the new Keppel Road, which had involved the construction of two miles of new tramway. The revised alignment had no effect on the pattern of routes, but did require considerable alterations to the layout at Tanjong Pagar. Instead of the lines from town merging where Tanjong Pagar and Anson Roads met in a simple junction, then to proceed in a gentle curve into the 'old' Keppel Road, having been moved so much further inland cars destined for Anson Road needed to first cross Tanjong Pagar Road and use a short section of connecting road

loading of a double decker omnibus, a Straker-Square. The year was 1906 and, looking around for a route upon which to work, discovered a gap in the tramway network then being constructed. Orchard Road became the obvious choice and so he applied for, and was granted, a licence to operate. Alas, the mechanical facts of life soon became known to him in the form of numerous breakdowns, and the lesson of running a bus service went beyond simply sitting behind a steering wheel or collecting fares. The novelty soon went away, as did his few passengers, who were happy to return to their more usual forms of transport.

Tramway Fares and schedules

A Schedule of Fares and Sections dated 21st August 1911 reveals the manner in which the tramways had settled down. Of great importance is the fact of two classes of fares being shown, and that there had been a further reduction in charges, which had become quite reasonable. Fares for each section on each route had been set at 5 cents First Class and 3 cents Second class. The colour of tickets, 5 cents and 3 cents White, 10 cents and 6 cents Blue, 15 cents and 9 cents Yellow and 20 cents and 12 cents Green, with the first class tickets being overprinted by two red lines. For the purpose of identification route numbers were shown, although these were not carried in service.

Route number 1—Tank Road to Keppel Harbour. Section 1: Tank Road terminus to Johnston's Pier; 1A: North Bridge Road to Market Street; 2: Johnston's Pier to Tanjong Pagar; 3: Tanjong Pagar to Paulau Brani Ferry; 4: Borneo Wharf to Keppel Harbour—with a full distance fare of 20 cents First class and 12 cents Second class.

Route number 2—Tanjong Pagar Dock to Gaylang (sic). Section 1: Tanjong Pagar to Bras Basah Road; 1A: Cross Street to Arab Street; 2: High Street to Lavender Street; 3: Arab Street to Post 310 (Gaylang Village); 4: Post 310 to Gaylang terminus at Tanjong Katong. Full distance fares as above.

Route number 3—Lavender Street, fare between Serangoon Road and Gaylang Road 2 cents only.

Route number 4—Raffles Hotel to Paya Lebar. Section 1: Raffles Hotel to Lavender Street; 2: Lavender Street to Bidadari; 3: Bidadari to Paya Lebar terminus. Full distance fares of 15 cents First class and 9 cents Second class.

The timetables section also showed service revisions, as follows:

Route number 1—Tank Road to Keppel Harbour, first car to leave Tank Road at 6.30 a.m. and Keppel Harbour at 6.30 a.m., with the last car from Tank Road at 10.50 p.m. and Keppel Harbour at 10.54 p.m. Between these times cars would run at intervals of six minutes until 6.00 p.m., after which the intervals would become 8 minutes. A late car would leave Keppel Harbour for Depot via North Bridge Road and Bras Basah Road at 11.30 p.m.

Route number 2—Through service, Tanjong Pagar to Gaylang, first car to leave Gaylang at 6.44 a.m., Tanjong Pagar at 6.48 a.m., with the last car from Gaylang at 10.45 p.m. running through to Tanjong Pagar, and from Tanjong Pagar at 10.32 p.m. running through to Gaylang. Between these times cars ran at 8 minute intervals. A late car would leave Gaylang for the Depot via Lavender Street and Serangoon Road at 11.16 p.m., and any passenger travelling on this car who might wish to travel in the direction of Tanjong Pagar may do so by alighting at Lavender Street and boarding a fresh car from the latter, the last car for Tanjong Pagar leaving Lavender Street at 11.33 p.m. However, such passengers would need to take note of tickets being valid only on the car upon which it was issued.

Route number 3—Tanjong Pagar to Lavender Street, first car to leave Tanjong Pagar at 6.30 a.m., Lavender Street at 6.00 a.m., last car to leave Tanjong Pagar at 11.56 p.m. and Lavender Street at 11.33 p.m. Between these times cars ran at intervals of 3 minutes, with a late car leaving Tanjong Pagar for Depot via North Bridge and Bras Basah Roads at 12 midnight.

Route number 4—Raffles Hotel to Paya Lebar, first car to leave Raffles Hotel at 7.00 a.m., Paya Lebar at 6.24 a.m., with cars to leave Raffles Hotel for Lavender Street only at 10.44 p.m., 11.00 p.m., 11.16 p.m., and 11.24 p.m., with the last car to Lavender Street returning only as far as the Depot. Between these times the service would operate at

8 minute intervals until 9.04 p.m., after which they would run at 15 minute intervals. On Saturdays and Sundays cars would run at 8 minute intervals until the last car, 11.04 p.m. from Paya Lebar (last car from Raffles Hotel, 10.28 p.m.).

The guide provides several interesting items, not the least being to reflect a decline in route mileage, with the Paya Lebar service coming back to the original terminus in Bras Basah Road, and with the 'route number 3' being cut back from Nelson Road (half way along Keppel Road) to Tanjong Pagar. Of greater import, the fact of a 2 cent fare only being shown for 'route 3', without a choice of class and without a ticket of this denomination being shown. We can calculate the journey times for each route as being 1, 40 minutes, 2, 44 minutes, 3, 27 minutes and 4, 36 minutes, although from these estimates must be subtracted two or three minutes lay-over time.

As already mentioned, the cars carried little route information, and certainly never showed the route numbers indicated above. One obvious reason for this was the fact that in general only one route passed along a given street, so passengers did not need to check that the car was going to take them in the direction they wanted. There were, however, some short workings, particularly at the start and end of the working day, so for a period trams carried very small plates, carrying the initials of the destination for which they were bound e.g. KH = Keppel Harbour. There is evidence that long route boards were carried at one time at cant rail level on the car sides, but such would have been cumbersome to change.

Meanwhile, the volume of traffic in forms other than trams continued to grow, and as a means of assisting to maintain smooth flow, the Company was required to station 'signalmen' at the major street crossings in order to ensure that trams were able to find a clear passage, whilst 'points boys' were employed to change the points as required by approaching tramcars (previously this was done by the driver, with consequent delay to approaching traffic from the rear).

Track Degeneration

As a result of the service revisions passengers loadings settled down to a satisfactory level, but other troubles began to surface. The feeder cables still required constant attention, but far more serious problems began to present themselves, being associated with the tracks. The original method of laying the track bed had, at the time, been both revolutionary and cheap, having the rails set onto longitudinal beams of concrete. After less than ten years of use it could be seen that such a bed had insufficient strength, leading to rails sinking out of lateral alignment, resulting in damage to the surrounding roads surfaces and undue wear on the cars themselves. By 1913 the unpleasant fact had to be faced in that the whole of the tracks would need to be reconstructed, this time using the more conventional method,

Collyer Quay, Singapore.

LEFT: A tram standing at Collyer Quay, Johnston's Steps before 1910. It displays KH—Keppel Harbour—in black on a small white plate in the windscreen. Later on, under Shanghai management, these plates were replaced by route boards which the reader can see by turning to Part B of this volume. Note also the fare stage point (1) and the timekeeper's hut on the right—some of these huts survived into the 'seventies. From the absence of a fleet number or garter on the dash, it can be deduced that this is a combination car—such cars carried these insignia on the side panels. *(John Rossman collection*

utilising a solid bed of concrete throughout. A programme of relaying was prepared, and if carried through would see the whole of the system dealt with by the end of 1915. Alas, events in Europe could not allow this to happen, for—under the terms of 'Imperial Preference'—the required materials could only be obtained from the United Kingdom where industry was concerned only with weapons of war. 1915 should have been the year when the tramways drew clear of their problems, but in fact was to mark the start of a decline which could only end in disaster.

By the end of 1914, five miles of reconstruction had been completed, and the poles located along the centre of North Bridge Road had been removed, replaced by single lines of poles located at the west side of the carriageway, with bracket arms from which the wiring to serve both directions of travel were suspended.

Generators under strain

Other maintenance work needed to be conducted on a basis of 'make-do-and-mend', as it would be several years before new materials could be received. This situation was carried over into the generating side of the business: like passenger revenues, the demand for street lighting was showing a gradual increase, and the position had been reached where the power station was working to full capacity. Without a margin to handle a spare load none of the original machinery could be closed down for prolonged periods in order to allow the carrying out of heavy maintenance, at least, not without a serious disruption of services.

The urgent need for a back-up method of providing power was recognised: steam was fast losing the prime position as the means of generating electricity and diesel engines were proving to be an attractive alternative. Initial installation of a unit was less complicated, meaning that first capital costs could be much lower, and without the need for a complex network of flues, bereft of great boilers and fireboxes and miniature mountains of coal, and with a small exhaust pipe taking on the role of great chimney, such equipment made very small demands on space. On the other hand, as these were very early days in the life of a new technology, there could be no guarantee that a diesel set would be trouble free.

To have chosen diesel sets as a means of replacing the coal fired plant in total would have been unwise in the extreme at this stage, for the original equipment should still have several useful years of working life in hand. As a back-up system, and always provided that they could be kept working, diesel sets had obvious advantages, and three sets were installed in the power station, the first of which was brought on line during 1915 but the engines which had been obtained soon began to demonstrate their temperamental behaviour, their method of working being a complete mystery to all except the chosen few who had received special training in the subject.

Little detail has survived concerning makers, save to record that there was one larger set with which to provide traction current, and two smaller in order to meet the needs of street lighting. As to their capabilities in service be it sufficient to say that, subject to the frequent breakdowns which were to be expected, the smaller units were able to give good accounts of themselves, whereas the larger unit, a constant source of trouble, met with a truly serious breakdown during 1917. Without spare parts being available, it was to remain out of use for many years.

What of the freight motors? Apart from internal works duties, little is known of their regular employment but, alas, they did have an occasional purpose, albeit in melancholy form. At the entrance to New Harbour was the small island of Blakang Mati, once the haunt of pirates and then a place to which fever victims were transported to meet their end. More recently it had been developed as the sea defence of Singapore, and was occupied by units of the British Army. Without the wonders of antibiotics and the knowledge of fevers, many were the soldiers who were unable to survive illnesses brought about by tropical conditions. The deceased soldier would be brought, in his coffin, by ferry to Jardine's Steps. Close by, at the Nelson Road terminus, one of the freight motors would be waiting, with both side doors open and the floors both clear and clean. The coffin would be placed aboard, the officer in command of the detail take a seat in the rear driving compartment with the rest of the burial party being seated on the floor at each doorway. The car would then be driven at a funereal pace through the town by way of Tanjong Pagar Road and the junction used by depot bound cars from North Bridge Road into Bras Basah Road, thereafter to follow the Paya Lebar route as far as the Christian Cemetery located in Upper Serangoon Road.

If all good things are destined to come to an end, then so too do those which are bad. The war in Europe finally ceased, but if anybody expected conditions as they were pre-1914 to return overnight, they were to be sadly disap-

LEFT: In order to reduce the strain on the original steam powered generator sets and provide a back-up for both the tramway and the street lighting commitment, in 1915, three diesel generating sets were installed—one large back-up for steam, plus these two these two 240hp units. To the left can be seen the rough edge of the concrete floor, cut back to permit installation of the diesel units. *(F.W.York collection*

pointed. Although factories in the United States could have met the need for urgent supplies whereby to complete the reconstruction of the tramways, the purchasing agents were still tied by the need to buy only British goods, and home based factories would be fully occupied in meeting demands from United Kingdom customers who also had pressing needs to catch up with long neglected maintenance programmes.

Seven-seat buses

The one major item of progress to emerge from the conflict had been concerned with the internal combustion engine, both in aviation and concerned with road transport. What had been somewhat of a novelty even during 1914 emerged as a reliable method of transport, served by an army well trained in matters of construction and maintenance, and with driving becoming a commonplace skill. In the United States of America the automobile industry had found little difficulty in switching factories to civilian production, and the assembly lines swept on with hardly a pause. Having been built, a market was needed for this vast number of cars and light trucks, and the Far East proved to be very receptive. Years before, the gharrie was giving way to what was then the traditional form of taxi cab, similar to those which would be seen on the streets of London and Paris. The newly arriving imports were at once attractive to, of all people, the rickshaw pullers, who saw in them a means of expanding their limited fortunes, an opportunity to rise above the degrading physical aspects of their trade, and an ideal weapon whereby they might join battle with the hated trams and win back the custom which was slowly being drained away from them.

Being of American manufacture, the motor car chassis tended to be much larger than anything produced by their British counterparts, for upon them could be mounted a somewhat primitive bus body giving accommodation in the most nominal terms, for seven passengers. The resulting buses were then put to work over the most renumerative routes in the town, and if the roads concerned were already being served by trams, then that was just too bad, for it would be a war with no holds barred. The terms of the Ordinance did allow the Company to operate buses of their own, but were in no position to do so, for the small profits which were being recorded up to 1917 turned into a loss when those accounts were prepared.

Decline

Having reached 1921 it was plain to see that the earlier troubles experienced with the feeder cables had not been cured, and of those

---

Singapore Municipal Omnibus Service

In his report for 1921 the Registrar of Vehicles had this to say: "The large bus is nearly extinct, as it cannot compete with the seven seater. These latter show no signs of decreasing in number in spite of the efficient tram service now running". His use of the word 'efficient' to describe the state of the tram service does seem to fly in the face of other happenings, but the point which really requires attention is the reference to 'the large bus'. Whose might these have been? It seems that the answer lies with the Municipality,

Until 1920, there were no bus services whatsoever in Singapore. The Municipality took the view that buses represented the way forward in providing cheap and efficient transport to districts outside the area served by the tramways, and took the initiative by ordering five Albion 17 seat buses. These were placed in service from 17th September 1920 on a route from Telok Ayer Market to Pasir Panjang (Cement Works), which ran every 30 minutes, between the hours 6am to 9am and 2.30 to 5.30pm The vehicles were divided into First and Third Class compartments. On 3rd November, 1920, the service was revised: the route was extended from Telok Ayer Market to Finlayson Green, at the city end, but was cut back from the Cement Works to Reformatory Road (nowadays Clementi Road) at the suburban end. The reason for the curtailment was a familiar one for the times: Pasir Panjang Road was unsuitable for bus traffic, and the buses were perceived as the cause of the deterioration of the surface.

On the 22nd November 1920, the Municipal Commissioners, having taken note that some private buses were operating on the same road, commenced a second route, using one bus, from Finlayson Green to Tanglin Barracks. When the accounts were declared at the end of the year, the bus operation was just in profit. Like Singapore Tramways, the undertaking had a very high scale of fares, so some reductions were made early in 1921, to make the service more attractive. This did little to encourage traffic on the Tanglin Barracks route, where there was competition from others' vehicles, and this service was withdrawn from 30th June 1921. The displaced bus was put to work on a new route, Finlayson Green–Thompson Road, commencing 23rd July 1921, and which seems to have enjoyed some success. A fourth service, introduced 17th September 1921, from Finlayson Green to Telok Kurau, was soon declared a failure, and the vehicle used was transferred to the Thompson Road service. The end of year accounts were disappointing, with a loss representing one sixth of expenditure. The undertaking continued into 1922, but closed down in June, a victim of the high fares and fierce competition from the owner operated mosquito buses—although that sobriquet had yet to be bestowed on the seven-seaters.

---

which had been relaid during 1906 a total of four miles again required replacing. Further financial outlay for which provision had not been made, so that competition from the small buses, of which there were less than one hundred at this time, could not be tolerated. Accordingly an appeal was made to the Municipal Commissioners for protection under the terms of the Ordinance, but the only response was a request to the individual owners that they should come together in order to form an Association, and work over allocated routes. This would have been SINGAPORE OMNIBUS SERVICE, and although Chinese thinking can draw great strength from associations, this was one to which they did not feel to be naturally drawn, and as there was nothing mandatory in the scheme, it could go no further.

To have based the appeal on the provisions of the Ordinance might be seen as tit-for-tat action on the part of the Company, for complaints had been made on such a scale as to require the Governor-in-Council to appoint a Commission "to make a diligent and full enquiry as to whether the Public are afforded the full benefit of the tramways". In addition, the Commissioners should also examine the proposal that the undertaking should be purchased by the Municipality. The Report was published on 24th June 1921, and was damning in content: for instance "the worn out track makes it impossible to keep the cars in anything like good repair and all of them need complete rebuilding. Delayed maintenance of the cars occasioned by the war, and long overdue renewal of the track have brought both to the state where they are worth little more than scrap value", and "The steam plant has not been overhauled thoroughly for many years, and the load on the station is too great to allow the sets to be laid off long enough to get proper attention". If there was to be a purchase, then the land and buildings would be assessed at market price, but little value could be placed on rolling stock and fixed equipment, "the track is valued as to three-quarters of a mile newly laid. The rest is valued only at the selling price of the rails after removal and reinstatement of the ground. The feeder cables are heavily written down because of their history. The insulation material is not of the kind recommended for this climate". The hardest blow concluded the Report, "If the Commissioners decide to purchase the undertaking it is recommended that the tramway service be suspended and the Station employed solely for the purpose of lighting: and that the reconstruction of the track and the replacement of the cars be taken into hand as soon as possible: and at the same time that a new Power Station be built, capable of supplying a full tramway service and the increasing needs of the town".

Into Receivership

The Municipality would not buy, and with annual losses by this time reaching £50,000, there remained only one course of action which could be taken, in the appointment of Sir William Plender as Receiver. His task was to 'sort out the mess', which was to embrace several years of patient negotiations with the basic objectives of saving the tramways if this was at all possible but, if not, then to ensure that the town was provided with a reliable form of transport. Wisely, Sir William sought professional help from within the industry, and with the arrival of 1922 an approach was made to the SHANGHAI ELECTRIC CONSTRUCTION COMPANY, with the hopes that not only would they be a source from which advice might be drawn in order to cope with the existing situation, but further that there might be an injection of capital from an enterprise which was proving to be a financial success. A great deal of investment would be required for the complete rehabilitation of the system which, when completed, would lead to a general reorganisation of the business. This was the advice tendered to Sir William, that in order to bring the accounts back into balance, and then project into the black for the future, there would need to be drastic rethinking and changes in policies, involving alterations in the staffing structure, a complete recasting of the fare scales in an effort to provide cheaper rates, the resumption of frequent and reliable services, and a general increase in the speed of cars.

Mr. Donald McColl, who was then the Manager of the Shanghai concern—and who, by a happy coincidence, happened to be passing through Singapore on his way back from home leave—was able to advance his own opinion, namely that all of the objectives could not be met if there was a continued use of trams, and so suggested that the Company might consider opening negotiations with the Commissioners in order to obtain a new Ordinance (valid for a period of thirty years and then for periods of seven years thereafter), with the purpose of replacing trams by trolleybuses. In retrospect such advice is hardly surprising, for although the railless car, trackless trolley, or trolleybus (call it what you will) was not at that time being regarded with any degree of seriousness within the international transport industry, Mr. McColl had demonstrated great energy in this direction, and managed a flourishing system at Shanghai. By transferring such confidence to Singapore, he could see the major problems being overcome with the minimum of expenditure.

Hesitation and Hope

If 1922 be seen as ending in a welter of suggestions and schemes, then 1923 became the year of hesitation, of rethinking, and of those responsible for making decisions not being able to fully embrace the concept of trolleybus conversion. The trams found themselves granted a reprieve, or rather were placed upon probation, with a serious programme of rehabilitation being launched in a final effort to keep the system alive. To this end the top priority was awarded to the rolling stock, and whilst work needed to be done to the 'combination' cars, it was the unpopular 'cross-bench' fleet which received the most drastic attention. By removing the benches and then panelling the sides to waist height they adopted the same pattern as the 'combinations'. These conversions took the opportunity for the class-system of accommodation to be fully realised.

Classes of travel

Both types of tram were rebuilt so as to have two classes of accommodation, labelled FIRST CLASS and THIRD CLASS, although the trolleybuses subsequently used the designations FIRST CLASS and SECOND CLASS. The car livery was altered to all-over cream, with dark green applied to the leading entrance and compartment. As trams were double-ended, this means that the seats used for First class travel on the outward journey became Third Class for the inward journey, and vice-versa. This illustrates the point that First Class did not indicate (as it does nowadays) a more luxuriously appointed and spacious compartment in which to travel but merely a less crowded space, free—in the thinking of the times—from the presence of the poorer working classes. The rationale behind this system was that, by reducing the fares considerably, a large number of new passengers would be attracted to the trams which, as a consequence, would become more crowded and hot. The greater number of passengers paying less would still bring more revenue to the Company than the lesser number paying more. However, the existing passengers who were used to uncrowded vehicles and to paying higher fares would not be driven away from the trams if they were provided with a First Class area and placing this at the front would be cooler.

For the system to work, it was necessary for passengers to know that the First Class area was situated at the front and so the trams were painted in the distinctive way as seen in the photographs. When the single-ended trolleybuses took over, the front saloon was permanently devoted to First Class travel which had the advantage of an increased flow of air entering by the open platform when the bus was in motion—it might be said that this was an early example of 'air-conditioning', especially when compared with the less well ventilated and more crowded Second Class rear saloon.

At this time, a third-class trailer was built but there is no evidence to suggest that there was more than one, nor that the one was used in service other than experimentally. In fact to do so would have required elaborate loops or other new trackwork, uneconomic at such a late stage.

LEFT: In order to identify their traction poles (those that hold aloft the overhead conductor wires) it is common tramway practice to individually number them. In this case, the number—probably 189—is used just for identity purposes. One in particular—Post 310—became as well known to passengers as to the tramways staff as it was used to identify a reversing point on the line to Geylang at a location where, in early days, there was little development. It is understood, however, that there were dwellings in nearby jungle clearings to justify short turning cars. Cross-bench car no 5 was about to be turned, probably at Keppel Harbour terminus, possibly when on test prior to entering service.

Advertising and pole numbers

One of the policies which needed changing in order to attract more revenue was concerned with external advertising, and some but not all of the cars were provided with long display boards located at the lip of their roofs, and for the length of the car. Clear destination displays were also called for (overlooked thus far, despite the Ordinance), and to meet this requirement a set of spring loaded clips was located above the dash and at the bottom of the windscreen. A white painted board with black lettering would fit into this clip, with the destination shown in the English language only (again, despite the terms of the Ordinance). By this time 'Post 310' had become a regular short working along the Geylang line. A word of explanation is necessary here: Post 310 was the number of the traction pole at the point where it was convienient to turn certain cars—being at nowhere in particular and thus, without an established local name, the post number was the best way to identify the location and later even appeared on trolleybus destination blinds. Most tram and trolleybus undertakings, of necessity, number the poles that support the overhead wires, and in Singapore this seems to have been done at one time with very

bold figures, hence the source of this unusual destination name.

On the engineering side, two of the erstwhile freight motors had become works cars, taking fleet numbers 61 and 62. There was also at least one tower wagon (used for inspection and repairs to the overhead wiring) and this (or these) had a pair of bullocks as motive power. Usually, British tramways acquired their tower wagons from the contractor who constructed the system.

New fare scales

Although the foregoing was to result in some improvement in receipts, the position was still to be regarded as being unsatisfactory, and at long last an *official* comparison was made between the fares being charged in Singapore with those currently applied in the United Kingdom. The realisation duly dawned, but not enough encouragement was being directed towards the short distance traveller who should have been providing the bulk of revenues, and a new system of stages was introduced with the passenger needing to travel less than one-and-a-half miles as the target. Once the new charges were appreciated, the reaction was both rapid and dramatic, for whilst average receipts from

BELOW: In the last days of trams, under Shanghai management, major efforts were made to rehabilitate the cars which had deteriorated badly due to lack of revenue. Here in the Mackenzie Road car sheds, a number of trams are seen undergoing repair. Note a complete pre-fabricated front body-frame in the centre of the picture, behind which is the carpenter's shop. To the left was the paint shop and to the right the heavy machine shop. With the tram fleet out on service for the day, the workshop staff have pleanty of room to work on these cars. *(F.W. York collection*

individual passengers dropped by 42% there was an overall increase in receipts of 95%. On their own these figures would be a nonsense, until it be realised that there was a staggering increase in riders, up by 235%, helped by an increase in car miles operated of 41%, with passengers carried per car mile and receipts drawn from each car mile, increased by 137% and 38% respectively, proving the need for the short distance traveller. To complete the encouraging statistical record, average occupancy of the cars rose to 45%, which was almost double the returns of earlier years (but still left room for considerable improvement, especially when compared with Shanghai which reckoned on an average occupancy of 96%). Starting with hesitation, 1923 ended with hope, for the years of mounting losses had closed with a profit of £23,000, and this after meeting the costs of the extensive rehabilitation programme to date. The new staff were settling into their posts, either having been recruited in the United Kingdom or else seconded from the Shanghai tramways. Not only had the trams been saved in the short term, but it seemed as though a prosperous future lay ahead for them. The Phoenix had risen from the ashes—but—for some reason it faltered in flight, then to come crashing to the ground once more. After all of the genuine efforts and expenses to return the undertaking to a viable situation, the whole project was dropped with amazing suddenness, and it seems that almost overnight decisions were taken to rid the streets of trams as swiftly as possible.

SET to STC

A timetable of change

3/8/22 Sir William Plender appointed Receiver of Singapore Electric Traction (SET), with powers to deal with the Shanghai Electric Construction Company (SECCo).

18/4/23 A draft agreement between Receiver, Singapore Commissioners and SECCo was ratified—for formation of a Railless System.

10/7/23 Receiver and SECCo agreed to form and register SINGAPORE TRACTION COMPANY LIMITED (STC), with a view to taking over SET and "institution of a system of railless electric traction".

This was *possibly* the first time that a tramway proposed *total* substitution by trolleybuses.

1/10/25 ORDINANCE NO 7 or SINGAPORE TRACTION ORDINANCE was passed. STC granted 30-year monopoly to run trolleybuses and buses.

The Ordinance *allowed* for a freight car—ie trailer—for animal goods, merchandise, parcels.

After this STC became a new company—still registered in London—wholly owned by SECCo, the Receiver having been paid £367,000 in SECCo shares. STC regained independence on 25th July 1935 by paying £100,000 to Shanghai Electric Construction Co.

14/8/26 **First trolleybuses** on tram conversion service Geylang—Tanjong Pagar, plus new route 'Post 310'—Outram Road Vehicles comprising chassis constructed in UK, bodies manufactured in Shanghai as 'completely knocked down' (ckd) kits of parts and finally assembled on the chassis in Singapore.

12/3/27 Second stage of tram to trolleybus conversion; Tank Road—Keppel Harbour.

Soon after: Third stage: Rumah Miskin—Lavender Street—Finlayson Green.

8/4/27 Fourth stage: Bukit Timah (Mackenzie Road)—Finlayson Green.

4/9/27 **Last tram**—trolleybuses take-over Paya Lebar—Finlayson Green

4/3/29 STC first ran motor buses.

1929 Elgin Bridge completed and trolleybus routes extended; 90 trolleys in stock serving 19 route miles.

1932 Further extensions

1935 108 trolleys running on 10 routes.

The success of the system lay in the agreement with the Town Commissioners to lay "substantial roads with smooth durable surfaces". This, no doubt, was due to persuasion by the Shanghai company, for similar roads existed there, which allowed solid-tyred trolleybuses and unsprung 6-wheel (3-axle) motor buses of the China General Omnibus Co to run with success.

All-change—to Trolleybuses

A draft Ordinance seeking to use trolleybuses was prepared by the Company and sent to the appropriate committee within the municipal administration for due consideration. Formal approval was granted at a meeting held on 13th November 1924. However, at a full meeting of the Commissioners in order to give further consideration to the proposals several major objections were registered and which would require detailed negotiations. A special sub-committee was formed in order to protect the interests of the Commissioners, for they were refusing any extension of the 'tramway' concession on the grounds of an incompatibility of interests between the parties over the state of the roads over which the trams operated. There was a flurry of cablegrams between Singapore, London and Shanghai, and the use of this medium rather than the more conventional letter post indicates the urgency of the situation. Indeed, it may well have been the state of the roads which caused the sudden change of feelings towards the trams, for if the reconstructed tracks were located in a fine, metalled surface, but the outside lanes of the highway remained in a rather battered condition, then much embarrassment would be caused to the Commissioners.

To return to the negotiations, on behalf of the Company a request was made that they should be released from the obligation of supplying current for public lighting. Immediate action could not be afforded, for an alternative source of supply would need to be found before the Company could be so released, but the promise was made that the matter would be given favourable consideration, given time. Having gained an advantage point, the Receiver looked for more, expressing the fear that any Company who might seek to take over the failing tramways might, at some future time, find itself in direct competition with the Municipality: the Commissioners committed themselves to a declaration of intent, that they would refrain from any form of competition over any roads adequately served by any successor Company, but at the same time, they let it be known their refusal to restrain other possible competition by the restriction of licences to other persons. Representatives of the Company did not take kindly to the latter part of the declaration, retorting that motor bus competition was unfair, if only because the owners were subjected to low rates of taxation. Happily, this point was accepted as being justified, and a formula would be devised with the objective of introducing a system of equity between all public service vehicles.

Tramway Finale

The final event in this unhappy saga had to be the formal winding-up of SINGAPORE ELECTRIC TRAMWAYS LIMITED, and a Bill was placed before the Legislature whereby all the rights and obligations contained within the 1902 Ordinance would be transferred and directly vested in the SHANGHAI ELECTRIC CONSTRUCTION COMPANY until such time as another Singapore company could be formed. The Bill was not passed 'on the nod' and the considerable debate once again focused attention on the state of roadways, and hardly surprisingly the Bill provided "on the road where the roadway has been reconstructed by the Municipality, such road formerly having been a tram route, the Company shall pull out the tram lines and run trolleybuses, with the Municipality making good the rest of the road, and in return for making the substitution the company would be granted the concessions which (it sought)". It became clear that, whatever form the 'new' Company might take, a close rapport would need to be established with the Municipal Highways Department, and future events were to show how an ingenious system of working together was evolved. As to the financing of the project, the Company was to meet half of the sinking fund plus interest on the loan of two-and-a-half million (Singapore) Dollars authorised by the Government for the reconstruction of roads.

Harmony amongst the negotiating parties having been reached, there was enacted the SINGAPORE TRACTION COMPANY ORDINANCE of 1925: by it the trams were finally doomed, and with the Municipal Commissioners acting as midwives, the SINGAPORE TRACTION COMPANY, LIMITED (incorporated in the United Kingdom) was born.

The change from trams to trolleybuses as seen by Sir Thomas Stamford Raffles from his lofty vantage point. **LEFT**, a rebuilt short-cross-bench car, now a saloon, pases the founder of Singapore while not many months later **(CENTRE)** one of the AEC 603 trolleybuses follows a slightly different path as witnessed by the polished road surface marking its line of route—in the mid 1920s the trolleybuses were the only vehicles running regularly enough on a semi-fixed path to create such defined paths. The tramway centre-pole traction post stands as a reminder of the former mode of transport but it is debateable whether or not the tram lines have been lifted. On both cars the frist-class accommodation can be easily distinguished by the green (darker in these views) sections—the tram has second-class leading whilst the trolleybus, being single-ended, has first leading. A second trolleybus is visible behind the head of Raffles. *(Both the above from the John Rossman collection*

BELOW: Tanjong Pagar terminus and trolleybus 13 is about to turn and return to Geylang. it cannot overtake tram 20 which is using the trolleybus overhead, its own wire having been cut short of the trolley wires and insulators inserted as it takes on the role of span-wire. It is notable that the trom is on the wire usually set aside for negative return. Of note is the narrow spacing of the trolleybus wires, so that the two trolleys on the trackless car are not running parallel. In later years, the wires were spaced-out to at least 18 inches; Singapore overhead wiring was later in part changed to the wider 24 inches as introduced on trolleybus systems built in the mid-nineteen thirties and after. *(National Tramway Museum, Crich, Derbyshire*

Chapter Three

The Largest Trolleybus System in the World - and Beyond

"An Ordinance for authorising the working and using of trolley vehicles, omnibuses and other vehicles within the Settlement of Singapore"

This, the short title of Ordinance number 7 of 1925, dated 5th. June, sealed the fate of the tramways, and in their stead would produce the very latest in traction thinking and equipment. Although the Powers contained within the Ordinance were to be granted to the SHANGHAI ELECTRIC CONSTRUCTION COMPANY, paragraph 3 directed the formation of the SINGAPORE TRACTION COMPANY, to be established within the twelve months: an interesting schedule provides details of mileages concerned, dealing first with those roads which were already served by the tramways, as shown in the accompanying table.

Road	From	To	Miles
Telok Blangah Road	Keppel Harbour Dock	Kampong Bahru Road	.63
Keppel Road	Kampong Bahru Road	Anson Road	1.50
Anson Road	Keppel Road,	Telok Ayer Street	.35
Telok Ayer Street	Anson Road	Cecil Street	.08
Cecil Street	Telok Ayer Street	Robinson Road	.49
Collyer Quay	Robinson Road	Johnston'S Pier	.24
Fullerton Road/	Johnston's Pier	Hill Street	.56
Anderson Bridge/High Street Hill Street	High Street River Valley Road		.08
River Valley Road	Hill Street	Tank Road	.42
Tank Road	River Valley Road	Orchard Road (terminus)	.42
Tanjong Pagar Road	Anson Road (terminus)	Neil Road	.61
South Bridge Road	Neil Road	Elgin Bridge	.70
North Bridge Road	Elgin Bridge	Jalan Sultan	1.31
Jalan Sultan	North Bridge Road	Victoria Street	.07
Victoria Street	Jalan Sultan	Victoria Bridge	.15
Kallang Road	Victoria Bridge	Grove Road	.76
Gaylang (sic) Road	Grove Road	Municipal Boundary (Term.)	1.76
Bras Basah Road	Beach Road (terminus)	Princep Street	.53
Princep Street	Bras Basah Road	Selegie Road	.08
Selegie Road	Princep Street	Bukit Timah Road	.38
Serangoon Road	Bukit Timah Road	Macpherson Road	1.99
Upper Serangoon Road	Macpherson Road	Municipal Boundary (Term.)	1.87
Lavender Street	Serangoon Road	Kallang Road	.64
Mackenzie Road	Selegie Road	Tramway Depot	.13

Authorisation was given for two short extensions beyond the Paya Lebar and Geylang tramway trerminals, viz.,

Road	From	To	Miles
Upper Serangoon Road	Municipal Boundary	Yio Chu Kang Road	.12
Changi Road	Municipal Boundary	Joo Chiat Road	.09

and also for the construction of two entirely new routes, as follows:

Road	From	To	Miles
Victoria Street	Jalan Sultan	Stamford Road	.98
Hill Street	Stamford Road	High Street	.26
New Bridge Road	River Valley Road	Outram Road	.93
Bukit Timah Road	Mackenzie Road	Selegie Road	.34
Rochore Canal Road	Selegie Road	Bencoolen Street	.24
Rochore Road	Bencoolen Street	North Bridge Road	.30

Thus, to the former tramway mileage of 15.75 a further 3.26 miles was obtained, with what might be termed the standard 'upon any other route within the Settlement of Singapore after the previous approval in writing, etc." clause. Furthermore, powers were incorporated into the Ordinance for the operating of motor buses, a) upon any trolley bus route in whole or part, and b) upon any other route in the Settlement once approval in writing had been obtained. As if drawing on the 1902 Ordinance, approval was also given for the operation of a freight service, working the cars "by electric power transmitted thereto through the trolley vehicle equipment", and allowing the use of a trailer, whereby there might be carried "Animals, goods, merchandise and parcels". Other paragraphs were very similar to the 1902 document, particularly in connection with the breaking up of roads and the protection to be given to other utilities, the rights maintained by the Municipal

Authority to order enquiries should the service provided by the Company be shown as not being up to the standard required by the travelling public. The option to purchase was rather different, being within six months following the expiration of thirty years, and thereafter at seven-yearly intervals, thus 1955, 1962, 1969, etc.

Paragraph 32 contained the Exclusive Privilege;

"The Company shall, until the Commissioners have purchased the Undertaking under the Powers conferred..... have the exclusive privilege of using trolley vehicles on the roads forming the trolley routes....and no further grant shall be made to any person of the right to work or use any carriages or vehicles running on fixed rails or on a specially prepared track or moved by electrical traction".

The Company did tend to place their own interpretation on the exclusive rights as being applied to motor buses in later years.

There was to be nothing complicated in the fares structure. Being set at 10 cents per mile First Class and 5 cents Second Class, with any fractions being deemed to be one mile. Higher fares could be charged only after application be made to, and approval received from, the Municipal Commissioners. As far as the carriage of animals and goods were concerned, the question of charges was to be left open for future consultation, if and when such traffic was sought.

The need to purchase only British made equipment was given an extension:

"If at any time in the future the Company ... become ... a foreign company or a company under foreign control, or if the Powers and Authorities by this Ordinance conferred become vested in any foreigner or foreign company .... the said Powers and Authorities shall forthwith cease .... and shall no longer be exercisable".

The expression "foreign company" meant any business not incorporated in, or under the laws of, and had not the principal place of business in, some part of what was then the British Empire.

Conversion to Trolleybuses

Ordinance 8 made the formal transfer of Powers from SINGAPORE ELECTRIC TRAMWAYS LIMITED to the newly created SINGAPORE TRACTION COMPANY and, thereby, the Tramways Ordinance of 1902 was repealed. For a while the Traction Company would need to operate tramcars in their own right, but despite all the hard work carried out in order to rejuvenate the undertaking, a five year programme for their replacement was considered by the new management to be adequate. Although the accounts had at long last moved into the black, there was to be no great outpourings from the cash reserves in order to effect the conversion, and instead much of the equipment to be used in the initial stages could be drawn from stock held at Shanghai. Orders placed with manufacturers in the United Kingdom were in the Shanghai Company name, but with delivery to Singapore. The Associated Equipment Co. (AEC), of Walthamstow, had designed a special

LEFT: The AEC 603 trolleybus chassis as illustrated in Commercial Motor magazine as part of a feature on the supply of a motor-and-trailer pair to the Shanghai Electric Construction Company, the Traction Company's parent company, where the model was also used by CFTE, the French operator in Shanghai. (As far as is known only the one trailer was ever built.) From this, the set back front axle can be clearly seen—a feature more of the 1990's than the 1920's although the solid tyres put it firmly in its time frame. This chassis lacks the motor—supplied by Bull—and controller unit—supplied by EMB—and mounted beneath the driver's seat.
(Commercial Motor

trolleybus chassis, the 603, for Shanghai use, but their order books would only show a few of these being as for use in Singapore, despite the fleet growing to a total of one hundred and eight vehicles. Of the bodywork, the majority of the teak fittings were fashioned in the Shanghai workshops, then being crated for shipment to Singapore, with final assembly being carried out in the tramway workshops so that, by this method, all chassis, motors, controllers, trolley equipment and body fittings were common to both operators.

The conversion of the line equipment was to be carried out by the Company's own crews, and the immediate problem was, once again, labour, or rather the lack of it. All trades involved with the building industry continued to enjoy the boom which continued to witness the remarkable growth in Singaporean population, and the only solution would be yet a further import of labour. On the mechanical side, to assist with the overhead line conversion an AEC 2° ton lorry was purchased, equipped with an Eagle Engineering three-section tower wagon. Two electric arc lights were included as standard equipment, power for which was drawn from the lorry engine, allowing for work to continue during the night whilst normal tramway traffic was halted. A capacious box, set behind the cab, contained an impressive range of tools. The full width cab provided accommodation for a three-man crew plus the driver. Of course, a single tower wagon would not in itself be sufficient to tackle all of the work involved, and either further similar units were obtained, or else the trusted bullock powered towers of the tramways days were pressed into service.

The measure of goodwill established between the parties during the negotiations leading to the 1925 Ordinance was to bear fruit in a programme for removing the rails once the tramway service had been withdrawn, a pattern of work being devised which was, and maybe remains to this day, unique of its kind. As Stage 1 the overhead line required attention, and where single side poles were supporting the wires and some traction poles remained located in the middle of the road, these needed to be replaced by new poles located along each side of the roads served, from which span wires were hung across the roadways, in turn carrying the running wires. The tram service could continue to function whilst this work was in hand. When the first stage was completed, the roadway was divided into three strips, with the tram lines occupying the centre strip (with the exception of Lavender Street, and perhaps portions of Upper Serangoon Road, where the rails were set to the side of the road). The Municipal Commissioners, through the Public Works Department, then commenced work to reconstruct the highway along the first strip, trams continued along their paths, and all other traffic was diverted onto strip number three. When the 'new' road, reconstructed to a standard capable of carrying the much heavier traffic

associated with trolleybuses, was completed, then other traffic was brought over from strip number three to use number one, and reconstruction of number three was put in hand. Upon completion, the way was open for trolleybus services to be operated over strips one and three, the trams were withdrawn, and the rails removed from strip number two. The actual change over could be made within the course of a working day, and a contemporary press report demonstrated that a clerk might travel to his office in the morning by tram, but return home by trolleybus. There seems to have ben no call for formal 'closure' or 'opening' ceremonies as had been so much a part of the municipal transport scene in the United Kingdom. Indeed, except for the fact of not needing rails to travel along, the new conveyances looked so similar to the trams which they were destined to replace, and furthermore, were destined to be known as 'trams' for many years into the future. The foregoing serves to examine the method which would be adopted whereby the new facilities would be launched, route by route.

Meanwhile, in the workshops the fleet was taking shape; sturdy machines designed for long lives (but, in the event, giving much longer lives than their designers could ever have foreseen). Mechanical equipment comprised motors built by Bull of Stowmarket, controllers from E.M.B. of West Bromwich. Mounted onto the rugged chassis was bodywork of substantial construction, devoid of any attempt of modernity—not even a windscreen!

Whilst the livery colours might be seen as commonplace, the method of application certainly was not. Two basic colours were used, dark green and cream, but applied in vertical form in order to give kerbside identification of the compartments.

Returning to 1926, and preparations are almost complete. Of the additional powers granted, advantage had been taken to construct the 'new' route along Victoria Street, Hill Street, etc., to the General Hospital in order that a driver training facility was available. The arrival of trolleybuses rather than the passing of trams was a matter of public interest, by Singapore standards to be widely reported in the Press. From *'The Straits Times'* dated 13th August, 1926:

"A start is to be made tomorrow morning with Singapore's service of trolleybuses otherwise known as railless trams.

The service to be inaugurated is that between Joo Chiat Road (beyond Geylang) and Tanjong Pagar and the rail cars will cease to operate along this route. Trolleybuses will also run along Victoria Street and New Bridge Road to the General Hospital. The old type of trams will continue to run on the other routes until the changeover has been made when Singapore's tramway service will be completely of the railless variety.

"About thirty buses are being put on the road forthwith. There will be a seven minute service from Geylang and a three minute service between Post 310 and Upper Cross Street. Buses will run every five minutes from Upper Cross Street to the General Hospital and from Upper Cross Street to Tanjong Pagar.

An Illuminated Bus. A special illuminated bus is to be run tomorrow evening starting from Bras Basah Road at 7.36 and following a circuitous route extending to Geylang in one direction and the General Hospital in the other and returning to the depot at 11 o'clock.

The inauguration of the trolleybuses is an important contribution to the solution of Singapore's traffic problem. They are attractive looking vehicles which run remarkably smoothly and silently. The drivers have been thoroughly trained during the last three months, and the Traction Company management is confident that everything will work well. All concerned have been working hard to get everything in readiness, and tomorrow's inauguration marks an interesting occasion."

The following day was a Saturday, and the 'Straits Times' was able to expand a little more on what had been published the previous day:

"At five-thirty this morning Singapore's first service of trolleybuses came into operation, and thirty of these brightly painted capacious and comfortable vehicles left the tramway depot according to their scheduled times to operate on the Geylang - Tanjong Pagar route.

Tonight the Tramway Company will run a car illuminated with 650 lights arranged in various designs, and decorated in a suitable manner. This car, which will run continuously over the tramway routes from 7.30 to 11 p.m. will be a striking advertisement for the new transport service.

The complete transformation of the present tram system will not be effected until 1928, when the Municipal programme of road reconstruction will be finished.

No alterations have been made in the schedule of fares now in operation."

The story was not yet declared as being dead by the editorial staff, for under the heading "Singapore Trams" a further item was published on 25th August, 1926, reading:

"Concurrent with the introduction of railless cars on the Geylang—Tanjong Pagar route, the taking up of the old worn-out trams lines will proceed, writes Mr. D. B. McLay, Executive Municipal Engineer, in his Annual Report. All users of Singapore Roads will be glad to see them go. They have been a source of concern and expense to this Department for many years, and of annoyance—if not danger—to the general public. The road space now occupied by the old track will of course be reconstructed with suitable foundations and surfaced with asphalted paving or reinforced concrete, to correspond with the type of construction already provided on the outer portions of the routes.

When the conversion to the new system is complete the number of railless cars on the roads will be some 60 per cent more than the number of rail cars now in use, with three minute services in the more densely populated parts of the Town and six minute elsewhere.

The need for substantial roads with smooth durable surfaces is therefore apparent, which explains the considerable activities of the public utility departments and companies, dealing with underground work, so much in evidence during the past few years, and of the Road Department who followed them up with new foundations and pavements. The public have had to put up with much inconvenience but better amenities for users of the roads are now definitely foreshadowed".

This trio of reports form a valuable collection in that they provide a indication of public anti-tram feelings, but it is rather a pity that journalistic licence should be taken in the description of the vehicles used.

More to the point, the headways quoted (7 and 3 and 5) do tend to supply an answer to the mystery of Elgin Bridge. This was a major crossing of Singapore River linking North Bridge—and South Bridge Roads. There is considerable confusion in dates as drawn from official records, for it is stated that the third bridge at this site, built of iron lasted until 1925 which, if correct, does indicate that the tramway service must have been interrupted. The new, and present, structure was completed during 1929, with the official opening being on 30th. May, and it was an often repeated frustration contained within the Traction Company Annual Reports that Elgin Bridge, or the lack thereof, was having an adverse effect on the smooth introduction of the trolleybus system. However, the contemporary reports are quite precise in their stating of a service between Geylang and Tanjong Pagar, so how was this obtained? If a temporary foot bridge had been provided for pedestrians for the duration of construction work, then it would have been a simple matter to turn trolleybuses on either side of the river, although the obvious disadvantage to this idea would have been the need for the civil engineers to have a quite substantial and secure site away from the public from which the work could be done. At first sight there might be the operational problem of trolleybuses being kept away from the rest of the network on the Tanjong Pagar side, but shown on maps as being a Tramway Depot in 1927, is a building not far from the site of the original steam tram depot, and which it is believed may well have served as a bus depot for one of the Chinese Bus companies at a later date. In the absence of any formal explanation, both of these suppositions could have been possible, but the correct solution must be

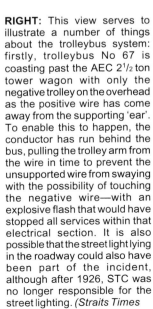

RIGHT: This view serves to illustrate a number of things about the trolleybus system: firstly, trolleybus No 67 is coasting past the AEC 2¹/₂ ton tower wagon with only the negative trolley on the overhead as the positive wire has come away from the supporting 'ear'. To enable this to happen, the conductor has run behind the bus, pulling the trolley arm from the wire in time to prevent the unsupported wire from swaying with the possibility of touching the negative wire—with an explosive flash that would have stopped all services within that electrical section. It is also possible that the street light lying in the roadway could also have been part of the incident, although after 1926, STC was no longer responsible for the street lighting. *(Straits Times*

found in that timetable: North Bridge and South Bridge Roads run parallel to Victoria and Hill Streets and New Bridge Road, and no great distance apart. The timings suggest that both services ran together as far as Upper Cross Street, which had been wired, with Tanjong Pagar bound vehicles using that thoroughfare in order to reach South Bridge Road and normal route. Even so, had this have been the arrangement, then it is difficult to understand why a shuttle service of tramcars could not have been maintained along the full length of North Bridge Road, unless, of course, the track was life expired to the point of being dangerous.

Shortly after the opening a further five trolleybuses were able to enter service over 6.25 route miles, whilst a further twenty chassis were reported as being in shipment from the United Kingdom, with ample body components being held in store awaiting their arrival. Revenue earned during the five weeks to the end of the financial year was £7,987.2s.3d. (when translated from Singapore dollars) as compared with the tramway earnings of £89,188.7s.8d. drawn from the complete system over the whole of the year, less those five weeks of trolleybus operation. Royalties to be paid to the Municipal Commissioners had been set at two cents per trolleybus mile, and during those five weeks The Municipality earned £362.10s.2d. (one hundred cents to the Straits dollar; one dollar equalling two shillings and four pence, giving 15,544 miles operated—a very healthy start). The accounts indicated that there was a small but unspecified income from the sale of recovered tramway material, no doubt as scrap, but on the debit side the training of tramcar motormen to become trolleybus drivers had been quite an expense.

Power Supply

Meanwhile protracted negotiations continued with the Commissioners, whereby instead of electricity being generated by the Company for the purposes of public street lighting, the roles

ABOVE: A 1st class passenger boards a route 6 trolleybus at Collyer Quay circa 1930. The roof-boards carry the slogan "Travel by Trolleybus and Save Your Money". *(Allen Morrison collection*

would be reversed, with traction current being purchased from the municipal power station. High tension alternating current would be converted into low tension direct current. Supplies from the Company to the town were terminated as from October 1926 and so, allowing time for the construction of the substations, there was an anticipation that the purchase of current could commence as from 1st January, 1928 which meant that the Company would no longer have the task of keeping the tired generating equipment functioning but instead could dismantle and sell off all of the gear and then put the site to another use. Experience quickly indicated that the fleet would be due to expand in dramatic fashion, and further depot accommodation would become essential.

The next tramway to be converted was that linking Tank Road with Keppel Harbour, as from a date during March 1927, and bringing in a further 4.75 route miles of trolleybus operation. However, the promises of high revenues from the new system were somewhat dented, the reason was seen in the continued closure of Elgin Bridge and, of a much more serious nature and coincidental with the latest conversion, the town was riven by civil disturbances, albeit not in the violent sense. Instead there was included a complete boycott of all of the trams and trolleybuses by the Chinese sections of the community, exploited to the full by the rickshaw pullers. A highly organised and close-knit body of men, they were finding themselves to be much harder hit in business terms by trolleybuses than ever they had by trams, although that had been bad enough in recent years. Services continued to be operated, but in the main all the vehicles were empty of passengers. Once again, and for the third time, the entrenched interests of the rickshaw pullers were attempting to bring down the transport system.

With Geylang, Tanjong Pagar and Keppel Harbour served by trolleybuses, it was a natural move to remove trams from the short Lavender Street branch. Only the Paya Lebar route remained, and conversion work was well in hand along Serangoon Road. The by now familiar programme of road reconstruction was followed within purely urban surrounds, but when reaching the countryside at the start of Upper Serangoon Road, with long stretches of track located at the side of the highways, some difficulties must have been experienced of a nature to cause delay. Therefore, a terminal loop for trolleybuses was installed at the junction with Macpherson Road, giving the most unusual situation within which both trams and trolleybuses worked in as far as Bras Basah Road, although the trolleybuses were then extended beyond the tram terminus to Finlayson Green.

By 30th September 1927, sixty-six trolleybuses were at work along six routes, with an operational route mileage of 15°. The total of nineteen routes miles contained within the Ordinance would soon be reached, the missing miles being the outer section of the Paya Lebar tram service and, by implication, the approaches to Elgin Bridge. The pattern of operations in the town centre was becoming complex, with several routes sharing common thoroughfares, and so it became time to introduce service numbers displayed on the vehicles. Such numbers, it is believed, had been in use for some time, but were not displayed on the vehicles. The pattern of tramway services was such that no two routes passed along the same street, but the trolleybus network was, from inception, much more complex. As delivered, the trolleybuses had a roof mounted destination indicator, and this was soon supplemented by a number box beneath the canopy. It was this platform, with its central headlamp, and which was equipped with tramway style lifeguards at road level, which perpetuated the use of the term 'tram' for these vehicles. In Great Britain, Ipswich and Hastings are towns where the term 'tram' also survived for similar reasons. The routes were as follows:

1. Tank Road at the junction with Orchard Road to Keppel Harbour via High Street.
2. Geylang and Tanjong Pagar.
3. Post 310 (Geylang Road) and Outram Road (at the General Hospital).
4A. Finalyson Green and Macpherson Road.
5. Rumah Miskin and Keppel Harbour via Lavender Street and South Bridge Road.
6. Bukit Timah Road at the junction with Mackenzie Road and Finlayson Green.

1927 came to an end, and its passing took the last of the trams, with the replacing trolleybuses working to their new terminus at the junction with Yio Chu Kang Road in Paya Lebar Village. The number 4 was allocated to this final tram replacement service, and the existing 4A was continued. In all, eighty vehicles were required for full service over the whole network. Changes from trams to trolleybuses no longer had any interest with the public, and the final depot bound journey went unnoticed and unrecorded. Nevertheless, there does remain the unanswered question, "what was the fate of the rehabilitated rolling stock?". It is difficult to believe that, after so much work and money had been expended on at least some of the cars, they should have gone for scrap with many years of economic life having been injected into them. A reasonable reply would be that, even if complete cars were not transferred, then a considerable amount of equipment might have been transferred to the 'parent' concern in Shanghai, for whilst there was a substantial pro-trolleybus policy there, such installations would be complimentary to a flourishing tramway network, not replacements (and one of the few foreign visitors allowed to visit that city half a century later was able to observe some trams still running). It is also a known fact that some tramway rails were transferred to Shanghai.

41

LEFT: Approaching Anderson Bridge and two trolleybuses, 22 and 38, follow the white line that helps the driver keep the bus under the overhead as they cross the emptyness of Empress Place. Across the Singapore River is the Fullerton Building, an early Singapore landmark. *(Commercial postcard*

Delays in the shipment of vital equipment created delays in the construction of the planned substations. Nevertheless, much preparatory work was in hand, including the conversion of the former power station. Part of the premises would house the Mackenzie Road substation, with the rest of the interior being restructured as office accommodation. Outside, the storage yards were cleared, half of which were roofed over in order to provide further vehicular storage, and the remainder being prepared as a hard standing. The arrangement to take current from the town supply could not start until February 1928, and only then through Mackenzie Road feeding the whole network. The second substation, located at Keong Saik Road (off New Bridge Road and close to the terminus of service 3) was brought into service during April, after which it soon became evident that costs in respect of current were more than halved as compared with Company generation.

1928 was notable in that the success of the trolleybuses was recognised, to the extent of application being made for the construction of a further six miles of new route. Close coordination was maintained with the Public Works Department in order that the planting of traction poles could be scheduled to match the rebuilding of the side roads along which the new routes would be placed. By the end of the year ninety trolleybuses were available for service, whilst a further fifteen were in varying states of construction, alongside which were also seven petrol omnibuses, almost complete.

Once again the private bus owners were making their presence felt. True, the constant outward expansion from the

LEFT: Approaching the camera in Empress Place, after crossing Anderson Bridge, is trolleybus 104—the highest numbered vehicle that the authors have found in a photograph. The quality of the print does not show the detail of this bus from the last batch of these vehicles. It is probable, however, that the modified cab area with its deep valance above the driver, with its integral destination and route number screens were incorporated from new. *(John Rossman collection*

centre of the town into the rural districts was able to provide a fair return on some of their investments, but there remained others who would not readily accept the role of pioneer, and instead sought the easier pickings by working over trolleybus routes. At the time the problem was not serious and, although the Company did not enjoy any form of extraction of revenue considered to be rightly theirs, the trolleybuses were showing very agreeable returns. That the situation might change for the worse was recognised, and so the decision was made to make a start with the operation of a small number of motor buses, so that a tool with which to meet competition would be to hand should the need arise.

The Wearn Group dealt with the bulk of commercial vehicle orders placed in Singapore, and one subsidiary, Malayan Motors Limited, was instrumental in obtaining seven G-type chassis from Dennis Brothers, of Guildford. The chassis were shipped in completely knocked down form, to be assembled in the workshops of Malayan Motors for Mackenzie Road for the fitting of bodywork. As with the trolleybuses, this was to Shanghai design, and contained components sent from there, and in overall appearance the design was a considerable advance when set against trolleybuses. Being of the bonnetted or 'normal control' pattern (that is to say, with the engine forward of the driver) a full width cab was provided, the driver being afforded the protection of a glazed, two-piece windscreen, the upper portions

the 1930's), followed by an appropriate number. In later years, as the older vehicles were scrapped, the numbers could be used again—and again.

Traffic on offer in the general area surrounding the docks called for a more extensive service, but not all the way to Keppel Harbour. In order to meet this need a turning circle was constructed at the junction of Keppel Road with Nelson Road (what had been the Borneo Wharf destination in tramway days), to become the terminus for service 5. There was a general strengthening of services, and vehicles which might at one time have been surplus to immediate requirements now came into traffic.

In all cases a further 4 minutes lay-over time at each terminal needs to be added to the double journey time. It is interesting to note how once past the built-up area ending at Macpherson Road, service 4 seems to speed up on the remainder of the journey to Paya Lebar so as to return the highest average speed. Service 6 has already become the Cinderella of the network, and was destined to remain so, but the lowest average speed must be seen in the fact of almost the entire length of the route being through congested town streets.

STC Introduces Buses

If any lesson was to be learned from the tragic conflict of 1914–1918, it was that war could embrace the whole of the world and so, from the British point of view, steps should be taken to ensure

July 1927
Routes Authorised by Traction Ordinance

No	Terminal Points	Miles	Double Journey Time (Minutes) Running	Lying	Services (Minutes)	Cars	Average M.P.H
1	Tank Road and Keppel Harbour	4.77	62	4	6	11	8.67
2	Geylang (Joo Chiat Road) and Tanjong Pagar	5.45	86	4	6	15	7.27
3	Post 310 and Outram Road	3.62	56	4	4	15	7.24
4	Paya Lebar and Finlayson Green or Beach Road	5.84	74	4	6	13	8.98
4a	Macpherson Road and Finlayson Green	3.85	56	4	6	10	7.70
5	Rumah Miskin and Nelson Road	4.79	68	4	6	12	7.98
6	Mackenzie Road and Finlayson Green	2.30	44	4	12	4	5.75
						80	

LEFT: Trolleybus running schedule copied from a 1927 Traction Company map which—interestingly, along with other official legal documents—was buried by Management before the Japanese finally took Singapore in February 1942. The casket was successfully recovered in 1945. As this was to accompany coloured lines of route, the colour key has been omitted from this table.

of which were capable of being hinged outwards and up, thus provided adequate ventilation. The cab was separated from the passenger compartment by a bulkhead, the upper portion of which was without glazing but instead was fitted with a number of vertical metal bars, once again to assist with the free flow of air. A single entrance was located at the rear, having the protection of knee-to-waist doors, while seating was provided for about twenty passengers on polished hardwood bench seating. They were painted in the overall green livery associated with 'first-class', relief being found in the polished teak woodwork, and black roof. This did not imply increased comfort but a less crowded environment.

After a period of driver training, operational use of the seven commenced as from 4th March 1929, the route chosen being already wholly served by trolleybuses in that it was a variation of service 2 from Geylang to High Street, but then running to a town terminal at Finlayson Green. The reason for not seeking out new ground over which to introduce the motor buses would be either to ensure that a frequent alternative was close to hand in case of breakdowns, or else to counter private bus competition along Geylang Road. Whatever the reason might have been, the Annual Report for that year stated, "It is intended to proceed actively with the development of this form of traffic". The introduction of the petrol buses also saw the birth of what was an almost unique system of vehicle registration, in that the Company was given the exclusive right to S.T.C. (note the full stops, to be used well into

the protection of Imperial interests on a global scale. Stamford Raffles had brought with him a military presence, which had been allowed to grow at garrison level. However, with Singapore being recognised as being at the crossroads of trade routes leading to and from, and within, the Far East, the decision was taken to construct a massive Naval Base to the north of the Island, between Sembawang Malay Village and Woodlands, overlooking the Strait of Johore. The plans formulated during the mid-1920's would take ten years to complete, and the hive of activity at the site appeared as a fruitful traffic potential to the Traction Company. The Dennis G's, numbers 1-7, having served their apprenticeship, were drafted on to a new service running for fourteen miles by way of Thomson Road, Upper Thomson Road, and Sembawang Road to a terminus which was designated as being 'Seletar', rather confusing in fact, as Seletar Village was some distance further along the shoreline. A most unexpected Traction Company venture, for the majority of the journey was well beyond the municipal limits, the country roads looping around an almost ceaseless series of sharp bends surrounded by semi-jungle, from time to time bursting out into a clearing occupied by a village, taking on a role which by rights should have been left to the private owners. Enjoying the success of early motor bus operations, orders were placed for a further ten similar machines, these to become 8 to 17. In all respects they would be similar to those already in service, apart from their weight, which would be two hundredweight the greater.

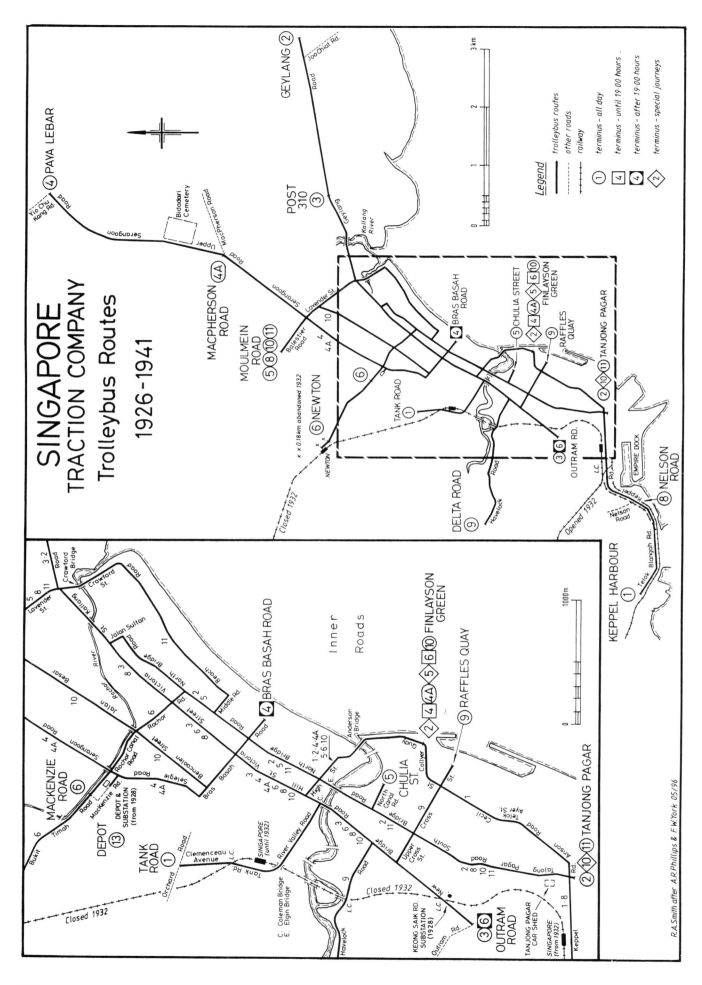

SINGAPORE
TRACTION COMPANY
Trolleybus Routes
1926-1941

R.A.Smith after A.R.Phillips & F.W.York 05/96

LEFT: Singapore is situated about one degree north of the equator and has a monsoon climate with its attendant lush flora. Before the coming of urbanisation, many of the outer limits of Singapore Town—let alone the island itself—were semi jungle with palm growth surrounding most major roads, including those served by trolleybuses, such as No 9 seen here on Geylang Road en route for the town and Tanjong Pagar on route 2. Note the tri-lingual destination, bi-lingual route number and supplimentary destination under the canopy. To the left of the picture are two seven-seat mosquito buses. *(F. W. York collection*

Trolleybus Extension

Under the additional powers obtained as a result of the application of 1927, the trolleybus system continued to grow by a further 3.31 route miles. In order to provide a 'back-door' approach to the main business area surrounding Collyer Quay, a spur was installed from Service 2 at South Bridge Road along Canal Road to a terminus at Chulia Street. Service 6 was taken a short distance further along Bukit Timah Road to a new terminus at the junction with New Cemetery Road, whilst at Rumah Miskin, the Lavender Street line was taken across Serangoon Road in order to enter Balastier Road, thence to proceed to a new terminus at Moulmein Road at The Green. The major new constructions would introduce two new routes: hitherto, trolleybuses like the trams before them had followed the generally north-east towards the south-west streets pattern as thought out by Stamford Raffles. A new route was to be directed in a westerly direction, and Raffles Quay was chosen as the town terminus, just along the road from Finlayson Green. Passing through the heavily populated section of 'Chinatown' surrounding Cross Street, and crossing into the aforementioned Upper Cross Street, service 3 was joined for a short section in New Bridge Road. Although Cross Street had not previously carried a service, it had been well served at either end, but entirely new territory was to be opened up once the new route entered Havelock Road, the full length of which was to be followed until reaching a terminus at the junction with Delta Road and Alexandra Road. The traffic potential could not have been very great, for on the right hand side when riding out of town the land was mainly mud flats laced with tributaries which, once combined, formed the Singapore River, whilst to the left, having passed the junction formed by Outram Road and Kim Seng Road, there was fairly open countryside

occupied by a scattering of small kampongs, stretching away to the somewhat isolated Lunatic Asylum, the bulk of Mount Faber, and then to Keppel Harbour. Buildings were to follow, but when they came they tended to be godowns rather than residential, and such was the anonymity of the surroundings that when fare tables came to be published stages could only be identified by the number painted on the appropriate traction pole. This new route was a little over two miles in length, and could claim some interest in having a railway crossing in the line running onwards from Tank Road to the docks.

The other major route recognised the massive residential construction which had been developing the square, three sides of which were formed by Victoria Street, Lavender Street and Serangoon Road. Perhaps half of the district, up to the Second Milestone, had been built up as far as Syed Alwi Road, but beyond Kampong Boyan the open spaces had caught the eye of speculative builders, and the quiet and rather select thoroughfare which was Jalan Besar, flanked by generously spread bungalows and compound houses set amidst considerable open ground, was rapidly being transformed by long lines of multi-storeyed shop houses, the lines broken only to accommodate a web of side streets. Once constructed the new route along Bencoolen Street and Jalan Besar linked Bras Basah Road with Lavender Street, to add a further one and one third miles to the map.

Thus far, whilst some streets in the central areas carried more than one service, each individual route had sections wholly of its own. A new link was provided between Moulmein Road and

RIGHT: Geylang village grew quickly and required a short extension to a purpose-built trolleybus station (illustrated on a later page). Here, trolleybus No 6 stands at the original Geylang terminus of route 2, prior to its extension to the bus station The timekeeper's hut can be seen to the right of the picture, under the shade of palm trees. *(John Rossman collection*

Nelson Road using the wiring of established services, viz., from the Moulmein Road terminus service 5 was used as far as Kallang Road, then the 3 to Upper Cross Street, travelling thence in order to meet the 2 in South Bridge Road, turning right towards Tanjong Pagar and joining the 1 to travel along Keppel Road and the terminus at Nelson Road. At the same time, and to prevent the over servicing of Keppel Road, the 5 service was diverted in order to serve the newly established Chulia Street terminal.

Moving into 1930, and the pattern of expansion was repeated, albeit on a much small scale. Service 6 was expanded to pass through Newton Village to a new terminus alongside Newton Railway Station, whilst a further new route was added. Coming along Lavender Street, instead of turning into Kallang Road, the new line passed straight ahead in order to enter Crawford Street, passing beneath the shadow of the great gas holders and over Crawford Bridge, in order to serve the fishing communities and markets located along the length of Beach Road, but turning inland once more by way of Middle Road and joining North Bridge Road. In the event, this route had less traffic potential than that which had been constructed along Havelock Road, and eventually would be worked on a most uneconomic half-hourly headway.

The allocation of service numbers had been extended in order to cater for these new extensions, thus:

5. Chulia Street and Moulmein Road via Lavender Street
6. Finlayson Green and Newton Railway Station
7. (this number was not used during the years of trolleybus operation)
8. Moulmein Road and Nelson Road via Lavender Street, Victoria Street and Keppel Road
9. Raffles Quay and Delta Road
10. Moulmein Road and Outram Road via Jalan Besar
11. Moulmein Road and Tanjong Pagar via Beach Road and South Bridge Road
12. (this number was not used during the years of trolleybus operation)
13. Depot only (from all points)

With all new orders for new vehicles having been met, the trolleybus fleet stood at 108, and working over what was to prove the maximum route mileage of 24.23. It was the proud boast of the Company that they, in 1930, owned and operated "the largest trolleybus system in the world". True, other cities elsewhere would soon overtake this claim, but in view of the pioneering nature of the work involved, the achievement was one in which all concerned could take pride, not the least the Town itself. The Company was to play host to many visitors who came to see "how it was done", some with tramways which might require converting, others seeking to apply the cost effectiveness of electricity to their transport undertaking. They were many, and are known to have included Rangoon, Mandalay, Hong Kong and, ironically, one or two Japanese authorities. A flavour of the times is beautifully captured in the text of a postcard, postmarked 3rd September 1930, and showing High Street: "This road contains most of the Indian and Japanese shops in Singapore for curios, silks etc. At the far end on the left is the side of the Europe (sic) Hotel. The pavements are under cover. In the foreground is a Malay policeman..... the trams, as you see, are trackless". On an international stage, trolleybus technology was set to depart from the concept of being a tram without rails, and by the mid-1930's the Singapore network would have appeared as obsolete, most particularly as there was no move to convert from solid to pneumatic tyres.

RIGHT: By the early 1930's, the mosquito bus, buzzing and darting about in search of passengers, had become a great nuisance to the Traction Company, and steps were taken to regulate their activities. Until this time the main chassis favoured by the owner-drivers—often former rickshawmen or their families— was the Ford Model T. Here such a vehicle is seen by the Mosque, under the trolleybus wires. Without exception these seven-seaters has timber-built bodies with an entrance at the back. Seating was probably, three aside on benches and one facing backwards behind the driver. *(National Archive of Singapore*

Whilst enjoying the reputation of being the world's largest, statistics for 1930 recorded passenger receipts as being 1,648,752 Singapore dollars (and increase of 179,246 compared with the previous year), vehicle miles run 4,744,053 (an increase of 792,073) passengers carried 42,869,745 (once again an increase, of 4,040,456). When converted into Sterling, the one fall recorded was in passenger receipts per mile, set at 0.66 pence. History was repeating itself, and there had been a reduction in fare scales as compared with those allowed for in the Ordinance.

Not all of the energies were being directed towards the trolleybus fleet. With an expanded number of motor buses available, the route of the experimental service was altered, removing the branch to Finlayson Green and instead having motor buses duplicating the full length of the 2 service to Tanjong Pagar. In addition, finding that motor buses would be quite acceptable along Orchard Road, a new route was opened as far as the entrance gates leading into the Botanic Gardens. Being the most exclusive residential part of town, there was a dual need, one to take middle management employees without cars to their offices around Finalyson Green, and the other to allow servants to reach market. The result was two widely separated terminals in town, one on Raffles Quay and the other outside Beach Road Market.

The Mosquito-bus

If called upon to describe a mosquito, all of the definitions would have to be unpleasant: a pest capable of bringing disease, travelling an erratic course, and living from the life blood of the victim it stung. The origins of the widely applied term 'mosquito-bus' have passed unrecorded, but such was the name by which all private buses had become known by the early 1930's. Whilst it was true that there had been a general tightening of the licensing regulations when the tramways had appealed for the protection of the Municipal Commissioners, with the passing years a general attitude of relaxation had been allowed to set in so that, in common with the mosquito, the private buses hunted as if in clouds. World trade was in deep recession, and in the normal course of events this would have hit the Company's business hard as passenger loadings fell away. The same conditions sent the sales representatives desperately seeking orders for the large motor car chassis being churned out of factories in the United States, and the former rickshaw pullers loved them. The whole situation degenerated, depending on the individual's point of view—the Company realised that if some form of restriction was not imposed and the protection granted under the terms of Ordinance, then their business would be killed off. Amongst some of the travelling public was the quite natural attitude that private

enterprise with local roots deserved their support and they gave it.

The method of operation employed by mosquito-bus owner-drivers was quite simple. First select the road over which you intend to operate, the most popular being trolleybus routes 2, 3 and 4. Be it from the terminus or some major traffic pick-up point en route, make sure you have a full load before you start, and with a seating capacity of eight this would not be difficult. Charge a fare lower than the trolleybus scale, and since it was possible to obtain a short distance second-class ride for as little as three cents, then the owner would have to have a very rapid turnover of passengers. Be prepared to set down passengers at any point along the route, but if you set one down make sure that you pick up a replacement before moving off again. The fact of the Company's motor bus routes working through lightly trafficked districts goes far to explain why they were not targets for such invasions, not only this, but also indicates why the Company could not use their own motor buses to beat off the intruders, for if they did, such action would be depriving the trolleybuses of revenue. It seemed to be a hopeless task.

As might be expected, speed was the key element of the modus operandi, in conjunction with which was the ability of the owner to work extraordinarily long hours, the individual starting out before dawn and possibly carrying on well in to the evening of the same day. Seeing that their presence was being more welcomed than opposed, the Traction Company being the only obvious voice of protest, the numbers continued to grow so that, at length, they were competing amongst themselves as well as with trolleybuses. The moods changed, and some operators commenced to work without scruple—for instance, if travelling in one direction with a full load, but spotting a crowd wishing to travel in the direction from which he had just come, an emergency stop would be made and the passengers ordered from the vehicle, without any refund of fares. Then a U-turn to pick up those who were waiting. Maintenance was scant, and this factor when combined with furious driving on the part of a man suffering the effects of extreme fatigue, led to an inevitable spate of accidents, often with tragic results. The Police Authority were obliged to take a firm stand, and became allied to the cause of the Traction Company.

Meanwhile, consideration had been given to the extended use of motor buses, to assist the trolleybuses without being in competition with them, and to open up new territory for the Company. The duplication over service 2 was ended, and instead the motor buses were used to penetrate the suburb which had grown up around Tanjong Katong, lying to the east of Geylang Road, whilst the town terminus was at Raffles Quay. In a similar fashion motor buses were superimposed over the length of service 4 but going beyond Paya Lebar for a further mile to a terminus at the junction with Tampines Road, at Somopah (seemingly a road junction in the heart of the countryside, but move away from the main road through the surrounding groves of palm trees and you would discover many fine compound houses of wood construction, served by a pattern of unmetalled roads). Both of these new facilities would have been

natural extensions to the trolleybus network, but the prevailing world situation would have made any decision to invest in traction equipment very unwise.

More STC Buses

Whilst the Dennis buses continued to give service, in order to cope with the hoped for expanded traffic once unfair competition had been dealt with, somewhat larger buses would be needed. The rather surprising choice was the Ford type-AA (and, to avoid any misunderstanding of the Imperial Preference rule, these were produced by the Ford Company of Great Britain, which was at that time completely independent of the United States concern). The orders were placed with a local factor, who in turn passed it to Ford of Malaya, from whence they were passed to the parent company. When the orders were met the chassis were despatched completely knocked-down to Ford of Malaya for assembly, who then delivered to the factor, who in turn made the ultimate delivery to Mackenzie Road. The time scale involved leads the Ford Company to believe that amongst the orders would be the last to leave the original factory located on Trafford Park Industrial Estate, near Manchester, and the first to emerge from their giant new complex being established at Dagenham, Essex.

Railway Diversion

Meanwhile, for several years previous, there had been much activity on the railway, preparing the Singapore Deviation. The little trains which had been provided by the Government Railway had been displaced by great mail versions of up to twelve bogie-coaches hauled by large 'Pacific' locomotives. Although the tracks were located on a reservation set between Bukit Timah Road and Dunearn Road, these trains had no place midst the growing traffic, and the crossings as they approached the town were a great inconvenience. The Causeway linking Singapore with Johore Bahru had been opened to freight traffic as from 17th September 1923, with passenger traffic and the official ceremony following on 28th June 1924. The problems were instantly recognised, and plans drawn up to break the original line at a point between Bukit Timah and Bukit Panjang stations. Whereas the old line had been quite straight in its approach to town, the deviation would need to wander somewhat in order to gain height to make a crossing of the main road at right angles and by a fine girder bridge. A new station was constructed at Bukit Timah, of a size anticipating a considerable growth in traffic, the new line then to pass through semi-jungle along the western periphery of the town, finally to cross the boundary and reach a fine new terminus in Keppel Road, no great distance from Tanjong Pagar (but a considerable distance from the town centre when compared

RIGHT: An unidentified Ford-AA stands outside the world-famous Raffles Hotel sometime during the late 1930's. This building, an integral part of Singapore's heritage, has been refurbished and in the 1990's stands as a reminder of less hectic days. Todays traffic rushes past Raffles three abreast in each direction but to venture inside is to rediscover tranquillity. (*Straits Times*

with Tank Road). Only the width of Keppel Road separated the new station from the docks, and it was to serve this traffic potential that the deviation was built—being the heyday of steamships, a convenient link was forged between London and Southampton and many up-country Malayan destinations. Local traffic was also considered, with stations being located at Tanglin and Telok Blanga. Because of the indirect approach involved, nine miles of new railway had been constructed, opened for traffic by the Governor as from 2nd May, 1932.

Besides the grand new station building, a locomotive shed was included within the site in company with extensive marshalling yards, connected to the docks by a crossing of Keppel Road - shunting activities within the yards was, as a rule, handled by Docks Company locomotives.

There was a debit side to these works. The removal of the old line inwards from Bukit Timah resulting in the closure of the stations at Farrer Road and Newton meant that, in the latter instance, any interchange of traffic which there might have been between local trains and service 6 had come to and end, leaving the trolleybus terminus to be somewhat remote as far as further traffic might be concerned. The result was the first abandonment of a short section of trolleybus line with the new terminus being in Newton Village.

The traffic pattern of service 1 was also altered with the closure of the former terminal station at Tank Road, for without a great deal of residential property along the length of River Valley Road and now devoid of those seeking to catch a train, traffic beyond High Street became very light. On the other hand, the other end of the route did serve the new railway station, so loadings into town from that end would have increased.

The opening of the deviation meant that freight trains destined to work to and from the docks no longer were required to work beyond Tank Road through Chinatown, and the crossing in Havelock Road was removed. Other railway happenings comprised the laying of extensive patterns of private branch lines from Tanglin into the various military camps which were in the process of being established there and out towards Pasir Panjang, although it is believed that the working of these lines was by War Department locomotives. As part of the military build up, an airfield was being laid out at Changi, in the north-east corner of the island, and a railway was also constructed here.

Independence from Shanghai

Notwithstanding the troubles being created by the mosquito-buses, more drama was hinted at with a short paragraph appearing in the Traction Company's Annual Report dated 5th February, 1934, reading:

"On 13th September last, resolutions were passed for altering the Constitution of the Company in such a way as to release it from the control of the Shanghai Electrical Construction Company Limited".

and then, in the following year:

"For some time past, negotiations with the Shanghai Electrical Construction Company Limited, have been proceeded with a view to the release of this Company from the Management Agreement, the cancellation of the Shanghai Company's participation in profits and (on a winding up) in surplus assets, and the abrogation of it's special voting rights. The negotiations have now reached the stage when an offer to buy out the Shanghai Company's rights for the sum of £100,000 in cash has been accepted, subject of the formal sanctions which will be necessary, and to legislation in the Straits Settlements".

Authority was obtained in the form of the Singapore Traction Transfer (Amendment) Ordinance, 1935, passed by the Legislative Assembly on 26th . August and assented to by the Governor on 6th September.

STC Motor Bus Services

As will be shown in the following section, the growth of the private, or 'Chinese' bus required regulation but, before embarking on a study of the territories to be taken by the Chinese companies, a look at a Guide dated 1st January, 1935 serves well to reveal the extent of Traction Company motor bus operations, and the services numbers allocated:

13. Depot only (in common with trolley buses, and used from all points when running in).

15. 15A. 15B. 15C. Tanjong Pagar OR Chulia Street OR Raffles Quay to Telok Kurau Road at Joo Chiat Place *or* Joo Chiat Place at Telok Kurau Road via Changi Road OR Katong Village at Joo Chiat Road via Tanjong Katong Road OR Joo Chiat Road OR Grove Road. (Subsequent research has been unable to unscramble the exact routings followed by each of the suffix-lettered routes, although the basic 15 operated between Raffles Quay and Katong Village via Tanjong Katong Road. In effect, the variations were able to provide a blanket coverage of the rapidly developing districts to the east of the main Geylang Road).

16. Raffles Quay to Seletar.

17. Raffles Quay to Botanic Gardens.

17. Beach Road Market to Botanic Gardens.

18. Finlayson Green to Tampines Road.

18. Finlayson Green to Norfolk Road (this was a branch from the main Serangoon Road, turning off just before reaching Rumah Miskin in order to travel by the back streets to a terminus close by the turning loop for Moulmein Road trolleybuses).

On trolleybuses, stages were charged at 2 cents second class and 3 cents first class up to thirteen stages, thereafter maximum fares were 8 cents second and 12 cents first-class, although only a through journey on service 1 was sufficient to attract the 12 cents maximum, with 2 and 4 realising first-class maximum charges of 10 cents. With motor buses being first-class only the 3 cents minimum and 12 cents maximum prevailed throughout, except in the instance of the ultra-long 16. Here a minimum of 6 cents was in operation, rising by 3 cents for each following two stages until reaching a maximum charge of 45 cents for the full journey. With sparse habitation along the route, most stages were identified by the respective milestone, with the terminus being designated '15th milestone', itself some five miles beyond Seletar Village.

The Chinese Bus Companies

Meanwhile, the Municipal Commissioners had been directing their attentions towards the swarms of private—mosquito—buses raging through the streets. Chapter 133, Paragraph 326 of the General Municipal Ordinance of 1933 went to great length in setting out the rules and conditions under which licences to run motor buses would be granted but, poor draughtsmanship drew the teeth from any proposed action, for nobody had thought to define what a motor bus actually was, and there was to be a wait until the Municipal Ordinance of 1935 was to declare, "...'Motor omnibus' means a hackney carriage which is a motor vehicle intended or used for the conveyance of passengers, and in which the passengers are charged separate and distinct fares for their respective seats".

Genuine operators would have no difficulty in obtaining licences, providing that their proposed routes were not in conflict with the Traction Company, or, if the routes which were proposed coincided in part with established Traction Company facilities, the written approval of the Company first be obtained. What was certain was that the Geylang Road and Serangoon Road routes had to be cleared of mosquito-buses at once, and the owner-drivers should get together in order to form well regulated companies. Many of the owners were in agreement with this proposal, no doubt encouraged by the thought of having a better regulated working life. Those who did not are thought to have taken their vehicles and fled to the north, where similar cut-throat competition was given to the municipal trams of George Town, on the island of Penang.

In general usage the new companies were known as 'Chinese' bus companies, in no sense in any derogatory fashion, but merely as an instant means of identifying them as against the 'English' Traction Company.

In the most general terms, the creation of the Chinese companies can be seen at extending the established Traction Company routes out into the rural districts, with passengers having to change from one to the other at a number of meeting places. At this time there were very few cross country roads suitable for carrying bus traffic, and the territories developed on and around those main roads radiating from the town. It would be quite untrue to suppose that all of the Chinese services halted at the precise line of the municipal boundary, for several were able to cross to penetrate quite deeply, but nevertheless were unable to reach the

LEFT: This illustration from an unknown newspaper shows two mosquito buses after 'regulation'. They are referred to as six seaters but most other evidence supports the seven-seat capacity. Chassis for these little buses were usually large private car models—of US origin, such as Studebaker—or such small truck chassis as the Ford A type (a smaller version of the STC Ford AA buses). *(Singapore Bus Service (1978) Limited*

town centre. Starting from the east coast, and moving in an arc in an anticlockwise direction around the island, there were:

KATONG-BEDOK BUS SERVICE: from the junction of Joo Chiat Road with East Coast Road along East Coast Road and Bedok Road to its junction with Changi Road (this was at Simpang Bedok Village, close to the 9th milestone). Livery red, mileage 4.6 and vehicles required 12.

CHANGI MOTOR BUS SERVICE: (a) from the junction of Geylang Road with Changi Road to Changi Road at 14th milestone, opposite Changi Police Station (9.5 miles), (b) from the junction of Geylang Road with Changi Road to Kampong Batak via Changi Road (2.25 miles), and (c) a special night service from 10.30p.m. to midnight and later if necessary on Fridays, Saturdays and holidays, from Union Jack Club to Changi Barracks via North Bridge Road, Jalan Sultan, Kallang Road, Geyland Road and Changi Road (14 miles). Livery red and white, total number of vehicles required 15.

From the foregoing, it will be seen that both Katong-Bedok and Changi had end-on connections with Traction services, the former with the 15 pattern, and the latter trolleybus service 2. Of (c), this was provided solely for military personnel seeking a night on the town, and would not have been available for local travel. (The Union Jack Club had been established for non-commissioned members of the services, and was located opposite St. Andrews Anglican Cathedral, the North Bridge Road side).

PAYA LEBAR BUS SERVICE: (a) from the junction of Geylang Road with Paya Lebar Road, to the Royal Air Force Base (at Seletar, but not to be confused with the Naval Base some miles distant), or Yeo (sic) Chu Kang Village, via Paya Lebar Road and Yeo Chu Kang Road - after 6p.m. service extended to Geylang Lorong 3 via Sims Avenue, and (b) from the junction of Upper Serangoon Road and Tampines Road to the junction of Tampines Road with Changi Road (7 miles). Livery yellow and green, vehicles 14.

At the Geylang end, (a) met service 2 about a mile inwards, and then travelled along the boundary line in order to meet up with service 4 at Paya Lebar Village. There were four 'Worlds' located around the town, bright amusement parks which drew considerable crowds during the evening. The Happy World was located in the junction formed by Geylang Road and Grove Road, the famed "Post 310" terminal of service 3, and it was to this point that the evening extension of (a) was directed, although not being allowed to travel by way of the main Geylang Road, but rather shunted into the parallel side road, Sims Avenue. Thus, the mileages of (a) were 7.9 when working to the Base, 7.6 with the village as the destination, to which would be added a further 1.5 during the evening.

PONGGOL BUS SERVICE: from the junction of Boundary Road (in Paya Lebar Village) with Teck Che Terrace to the end of Ponggol Road via Lim Twa Tow Road and Upper Serangoon Road (6 miles). Livery yellow, number of vehicles 6.

With just the matter of the turning loop around the Terrace to take into account, this formed an end on connection with trolleybus 4, but did result in a duplication of route with Traction Company 18 for the mile down the hill to the junction with Tampines Road, representing the only direct competition to be met.

TAY KOH YAT: from the junction of Macpherson Road with Serangoon Road to the end of Aljunied Road near Geylang Road (1.9 miles). Livery yellow and white, buses 2.

On the face of it, one of the funny little operations providing exceptions to every rule, being well within the municipal limits, at a range of three to four miles out of town. At one end there was a connection with the 4A terminal, and at the other service 2 along Geylang Road, but with very little in between, so that it becomes certain that this was a route which the Traction Company did not wish to work. As history will later reveal, this two vehicle business was very much the tiny acorn from which mighty oaks will grow.

SELETAR MOTOR BUS COMPANY: from Beach Road at Clyde Terrace Market to Seletar Village and the Naval Base via Arab Street, Rochore Canal Road, Bukit Rimah Road, Kampong Java Road and Thomson Road (14 miles). Livery red and black, number of vehicles 24.

This proved to be a most interesting development for, once reaching Bukit Timah Road, the same route was followed as used by the Traction Company 16, who, in keeping with the loose terms of the Ordinance restricting their sphere of operations to within the municipal boundaries, was then required to withdraw.

Furthermore, with a terminus in Beach Road, adjacent to the town terminal of service 17, the town centre was very nearly reached, but, as the streets to be followed in order to gain Rochore Canal Road crossed the Traction routes rather than duplicated them, then an element of direct competition could not be seen to exist.

GREEN BUS COMPANY: (a) from Queen Street to Johore Bahru, via Ophir Road, Rochore Canal Road, Bukit Timah Road, Woodlands Road and over the Causeway to Johore Bahru, (15.2 miles) (b) from Queen Street to Lim Chu Kang, via Ophir Road, Rochore Canal Road, Bukit Timah Road, Chua Chu Kang Road at the 17 1/2 milestone (17 miles), (c) special night service (Fridays, Saturdays and Sundays) from Tengah (Military bases) to Union Jack Club, via Chua Chu Kang Road, Bukit Timah Road, Selegie Road, Bras Basah Road, Queen Street, Armenian Street, Coleman Street and North Bridge Road (14 miles). Livery Green, number of buses 35.

Here again (c) was only for the use of Army and Royal Air Force personnel.

Green Bus Company services duplicated trolleybus 6 between Newton Village and Rochore Canal Road, but, as this was in the main open country (to the one side occupied by extensive cemeteries and on the other the grounds of Government House) there would be little local traffic on offer between the two points. Instead, the

LEFT: A press cutting showing a bus of the Green Bus Company together with, presumably, its driver and proprietor. These 'Chinese' buses carried the registration number in no less than seven locations; front and rear, both sides, facing forward and rear on the roof and inside. Presumably this was to assist in identifying wrong-doers. *(Singapore Bus Service (1978) Limited*

Kampong Bahru Road (1.6 miles), and (b) from 7p.m., the junction of Hill Street with River Valley Road, Merbau Road, Havelock Road and Kim Seng Road (1.6 miles). Livery blue and white, fleet strength 12 buses.

If the presence of Tay Koh Yat in original form seems to be a mystery, so the activities of Kampong Bahru bring forth a greater puzzle, for route (a) could have been natural extensions to the trolleybus network, with one terminal meeting with service 2 at Maxwell Market, passing close to the 3 terminus when passing along Neil Road, and with the Nelson Road turning point being common with trolleybus 8, and with service 1 passing. As the considerations of future trolleybus operations policy was being debated in London about this time, let it be sufficient to note that, without any motor bus services which could have been extended through Kampong Bahru, we must accept that this was a route which the Traction Company rejected as one they would wish to operate, with much the same decision being taken concerning the evening workings to the Great World , for such was (b).

KEPPEL BUS COMPANY LIMITED: from the junction of Tanjong Pagar Road with Keppel Road to West Coast Road at 7 1/2 milestone via Telok Blangah Road and Pasir Panjang Road (8 miles). Livery blue, total number of buses 35.

The only concern to be registered with limited liability and, as the Traction Company, carried the message "Incorporated in the United Kingdom" on the reverse of their tickets, so Keppel proudly stated "Incorporated in Singapore" on the back of theirs. This was a route over which major competition could have been provided, as common route was followed with trolleybus 1 between Keppel Harbour and Tanjong Pagar.

A total of twelve Chinese bus companies were in operation, with a combined fleet of 171 mosquito buses, nowhere near the

transfer points around Queen Street must have been the life blood of the 6 service.

JURONG OMNIBUS SERVICE: from the junction of Bukit Timah Road with Jurong Road to the end of Jurong Road (10.8 miles). Livery green and white, number of vehicles 4.

With the Bukit Timah Road terminal more than eight miles distant from the town centre, this was certainly the most rural of Chinese bus operations.

NGO HOCK MOTOR BUS COMPANY: from Eu Tong Street to junction of Alexandra Road with Telok Blangah Road via New Bridge Road, Outram Road, Tiong Bahru Road and Alexandra Road (4.5 miles). Livery green and red, number of buses 6.

Although there was an overlapping with trolleybus 3 between Outram Road and Eu Tong Street, the distance involved was not sufficient to create competition.

SOON LEE BUS COMPANY: from Upper Pickering Street to Ulu Pandan Road via Tiong Bahru Road, Tanglin Road, Napier Road and Holland Road, with, after 11a.m. on weekends, a diversion of route to serve Kim Seng Road and Seng Poh Road (7.7 miles) and (b) Upper Pickering Street to Great World Amusement Park via New Bridge Road, Outram Road and Kim Seng Road (1.8 miles). Livery yellow and red, total fleet 6 buses.

There was the same degree of overlapping with trolleybus 3, and with the same negative result. In hindsight, what does appear to be rather strange is the lack of interest on the part of the Traction Company to serve the Great World, for this amusement park was located well within the town.

KAMPONG BAHRU BUS SERVICE: (a) from Maxwell Road Market to junction of Telok Blangah Road and Kampong Bahru Road and/ or Nelson Road via Neil Road and

RIGHT: Chinese bus flanked on the left by a taxi and on the right by two young men wearing trousers at that time the height of fashion in England, the 'Oxford-bags' for which, it might be expected, some form of protection would be required from chain-oil. Both the taxi and the bus carry the circular plate inscribed with the letters H. C. S., together with a separate single letter 'H' on the radiator. The function of these is unclear but revolves around the classification as Hackney or Hackney Carriage—but why both? *(F. W. York collection*

clouds which hitherto had been plaguing the trolleybus services. Although many of the owner-drivers had left the Island, others were to stay, and through them there was to be born a new menace, namely the pirate-taxi. Nor should it be thought that the elimination of the mosquito buses could be obtained in one fell swoop, the interim period being spread over almost one year, during which Company inspectors would be required to make regular tours of the routes in order to collect evidence of unlicensed operators still at work, whilst police patrols were strengthened in case there might break out demonstrations of public dissatisfaction at the taking away of what many had come to regard as their personal form of transport. Whilst there could be seen a clear case for expanding trolleybus operations and a growth in the fleet, motor buses were chosen instead, and whereas their number stood at thirty-seven at the close of the 1933-4 accounting year, no less than an additional fifty-five were placed into service following the regulation of the role of the Chinese buses.

Clouds of War

Had the trolleybus fallen from favour in Singapore? Certainly not, but the Directors in London were being very careful in their considerations of vast capital expenditure. After all the termination of the Management agreement would be a financial burden for many years yet to come. It is interesting to note that, even as late as 1940, the Shanghai company continued to order their special AEC chassis, much improved to the extent of having pneumatic tyres and a more stylish bodywork. Instead, corporate eyes were observing the clouds of war generated by the Sino-Japanese conflict, and considering how far and how soon these would spread. Not so the expatriate reactions, for had not the giant Naval Base been commissioned at the end of 1935, the Royal Air Force aerodromes at Tengah and Seletar being added to at Changi, and Army camps dotted all over the Island? Should war ever come Singapore could suffer no harm, certainly not from the Japanese.

Despite the international slump of the mid-1930's commercial trade fuelled the constant expansion of Singapore, bringing forth a need for more housing which in turn required more transport. Fifty years previously it was the steamship and the needs of docking facilities which had shaped the growth of the town and dictated the pattern of the tramways, and now it was the turn of the new form of international travel, the airliner, to have a similar effect. The first civil flight (that is to say, as a means of transporting passengers and freight rather than as an adventurous exploit) had arrived during 1928, and progress was to continue over the next five years, albeit at a casual rate. The date worthy of note was 3rd. May, 1933, when Singapore became a regular staging post on K.L.M. ROYAL DUTCH AIRLINES route linking Amsterdam with Batavia (now Jakarta), using Fokker aircraft. Seven months later, IMPERIAL AIRWAYS were able to bring London

just one week away, using Armstrong Whitworth 'Atlantic' aircraft. Events were moving quickly, with 1934 seeing the birth of QUEENSLAND AND NORTHERN TERRITORIES AIR SERVICES, more usually known as QANTAS, previously a pioneer Australian domestic carrier, but now adding the magic words 'EMPIRE AIRWAYS' to it's title. Imperial Airways held a half interest in the reconstructed business, and together they were able to fly a route to link London with Brisbane, with Imperial Airways handling the 'western' leg as far as Singapore, and QANTAS the remainder to Brisbane. The only airfield capable of handling the increasing civil traffic was at Seletar, rather remote from the hotels at which passengers would need to rest during their overnight stops. Further stimulus was provided by the Empire Air Mail Scheme, under the terms of which all first class mail for Empire destinations and carried by Imperial Airways, or associated carriers, would be carried by air at normal United Kingdom postage rates. The demand outstripped all predictions, leading to an order being placed by Imperial Airways for no less than twenty eight Short type-S.23 'Empire' flying boats; fortunate indeed that Seletar was equipped as a flying boat base. With the much larger DC2 and DC3 aircraft soon to be flying, a new international airport was required, and a suitable site was located just across the Kallang River, with Geylang Road to one side and the line of the east coast to the other, so that, in addition to accommodating land planes, the Kallang Basin could be developed as a seaplane base. The former, in company with the associated hotel, opened during 1937, with sea planes being able to use their base during the following twelve months.

What did all of this mean in terms of the Traction Company? Trolleybus service 2 and 3 received a substantial boost, from construction workers during the building months, and from regular staff once the business was fully operational. Indeed, the terminal of service 3 was close by the main gates of the airport, and it is hard to understand why no change was made to the unhelpful 'Post 310' designation, given such an opportunity. Motor buses bound for Katong by way of Grove Road now had to cross the main runway—at first a traffic policeman was on hand to control traffic movements, soon to be replaced by barriers and traffic lights.

Further complications had been added to the 15 group of services with the introduction of 15D, and even perhaps 15E, so a complete recasting was called for, resulting in

15.	Raffles Quay and Tanjong Katong via Tanjong Katong Road
16.	Raffles Quay and Tanjong Katong via Joo Chiat Road
20.	Raffles Quay and Telok Kurau via Grove Road
21.	Chulia Street and Telok Kurau via Grove Road, covering all of the roads previously served, but in a much simplified fashion.
22.	Tanjong Pagar and Telok Kurau was, in fact, an exact duplication of trolleybus 2, extended beyond the Geylang terminus.
19.	Moulmein Road (at the trolleybus terminus) to Thomson Road

---

Staff and Administration

The STC was a London based Company operating a business thousands of miles distant in a multiracial city. This posed many problems, especially as a transport company required workers of varying skills and aptitudes. The managerial staff was European, with other staff of Chinese, Malayan, Indonesian and Indian origin. Each nationality would itself have sub-groupings of religion, language and customs, for example, many Indian employees expected periods of extended leave in order to revisit their homeland, whilst other had to have meal breaks tailored to their special dietary needs.

Communications were another problem. In general, an important notice would be composed in English, and the Company would request the Senior Magistrate to have his interpreters devise written versions in Chinese, Urdu, Tamil and Jawi (Indonesian). Although literate, many conductors were weak on writing, and waybills were normally filled in at termini by the starters. These men, who like the drivers, conductors and ticket inspectors, wore a khaki drill uniform had a kiosk where they were stationed to signal drivers when it was time to start. Further work on the waybills had to be done at the Mackenzie Road Ticket Office, which was bigger than was usual for a company the size of the STC. Each conductor had two ticket boxes, big and small, and these were used on alternate days. Although Bell Punch tickets, printed in Great Britain, were issued, they were cancelled by hand clippers—extra well coppered and electroplated to cope with the humid climate—and not by the usual ticket punch which recorded the exact number of passengers, and retained the ticket clippings which could, at the discretion of the company, be used as a counter check. The Singapore ticket clerks had enough to do completing waybills and filling in the cash Pay-in slips for each conductor (work that was usually done by conductors themselves in other locations).

Cash was handled by a Chinese *compradore* (a term derived from the Portuguese word for 'buyer', but which in this case means a cross between a banker and a foreign exchange merchant) who was under bond to the company. He collected and banked all the cash, and was able to advise and inform the management on many other matters to do with business otherwise denied to them by language and culture.

Police Station was a shuttle which in effect extended the Norfolk Road branch service, still numbered 18, off Serangoon Road.

A most interesting feature of motor bus operation concerned the use of a Traction Company bus over the former route 16 to Seletar. Whether it was allowed to carry passengers is open to debate, for the purpose of the one journey a day was to act as a newspaper van, carrying newspapers to the Naval Base, under the provisions of a long term contract entered into with the Straits Times Press. An ideal task for one of the ageing Dennis buses.

That a measure of extravagance might be seen in the provision of service 22 can be explained in the growth of the motor bus fleet, by now numbering over one hundred vehicles. After the initial orders placed with Dennis, loyalties remained firmly with Ford chassis. By 1937 something larger was required, and to this end a small number of Leyland Cub chassis were obtained, of the bonnetted, forward-control style. A rather surprising choice, for the manufacturers had produced this model with light country workings in mind, not the heavy town traffic through which these would be called upon to serve. In the event, they were destined to give good accounts of themselves.

In another direction, Geylang was no longer a rural outpost, the village itself having long been swallowed up, and the expansion outwards of traditional shop-houses was bringing considerable congestion at the Joo Chiat Road junction. Further along Changi Road a plot of land remained vacant, and to this the trolleybus route was extended, to turn within the confines of a purpose built trolleybus station. Concrete being the most popular of building materials then in use, this was used to provide two platforms, in the midst of which would be found the timekeepers hut, with the rest of the available space being provided with an awning in theory to provide comfortable waiting area for passengers, but which in practice became an obvious trading place for many hawkers. Of the platforms, the inner was used by service 2, whilst the outer was designed for convenient transfer to the private buses which would work beyond into the rural districts.

Mr. George Marshall, then the local manager, had great faith in the trolleybuses, and believed that there should be a considerable expansion of the network into the new residential districts, so that future orders for new vehicles should include trolleybuses. His proposals were put together as a formal report, which he was able to present to the Board of Directors during this home leave of 1938. He was given a very patient hearing, but in the end all of his proposals were turned down. That relating to extensions foundered on the previous doubts as to the international situation and the unwillingness to invest further capital. The proposal to buy new vehicles was rejected on the grounds that, as trolleybus design had advanced so far as to provide vehicles which could be described as being luxurious, then to introduce just a few within the existing fleet could create public dissatisfaction, and finance would not be available to make a complete replacement. Even the proposal made by Mr. Marshall that the existing fleet would be modernised by the conversion to pneumatic tyres and the fitting of windscreens was refused on the grounds of the cost involved with dealing with all one hundred and eight vehicles. The policy decision was that the motor bus fleet should be steadily expanded and a disappointed Mr. Marshall returned to his post with firm but polite instructions to forget his trolleybus plans.

The Leyland Cubs were working the Katong group of services with obvious success, so much so that it was decided that even larger buses would be an advantage. To this end the first orders were placed with Albion Motors Limited, for twelve of their Victor chassis, the first of which entered service during 1938, and starting an association between operator and manufacturer which would extend over almost two decades. Once the whole batch were earning their keep, the opportunity was taken to withdraw all of the Dennis buses.

Meanwhile, the numbers of Chinese buses had been growing, although there was little change in the basic design and carrying capacity. The fact of these fleet expansions provided to be fortunate, for during 1938 industrial relations between the Traction Company and the employee's trade union became very strained, to the extent of negotiations seeking to resolve whatever problems had been involved reached stalemate. As a consequence a strike was called, to be effective as from 7th July. With both sides being firmly entrenched, the Municipal Commissioners exercised their powers under the 1925 Ordinance, and ordered that cases should be heard by an independent tribunal of arbitrators, whose findings would be binding on both sides. In the meantime, the town could not be left without transport, and again using powers so granted, invitations were extended to the Chinese companies to move onto Traction Company routes, with short term licences being granted. Once again, all applications were made for the Geylang and Serangoon Roads routes, and most of the side routes had to remain unserved. Likewise, although the fleets had grown, these were not to the size whereby all of the rural commitments could be fully met, and so the outlying districts had to suffer drastic reductions. Thus, the arrival of the Chinese buses on the town routes was not wholly popular, most particularly with the Union, who regarded any service however crude it might be, as detracting from their cause. Whilst there were some variations in the pattern of routes worked, the major change was the concentration of all services to a central terminus located between Raffles Place and the rear of the General Post Office, so that a police surveillance could be maintained in case of violence. The passengers were not too pleased, for some, having recently tasted the comforts on offer from the 'big' buses, found it very difficult to adapt to the cramped conditions on offer by what many still saw as being mosquito buses.

BELOW: The trolleybus and Chinese bus interchange station, built at Geylang in the late 1930's, at the end of a short extension from the original Geylang village terminus. Trolleybus 29 is on the outside road reserved for service 2 while Changi Bus Co No S.347 awaits to depart for Changi, being in effect an out of town extension of the No 2 trolleybus. The timekeepers hut can be seen on the platform, beside the front of No 29. It will be noticed that the trolleybus has been modified with improved weather protection for the driver in the form of a deep valance—but no windscreen! *(F. W. York collection*

FAR LEFT: Although not necessarily connected with the Traction Company dispute described below, the Chinese buses continued to fulfil a function and grew in numbers although not in size or carrying capacity. Here a swarm of workers rush for the limited number of seats. *(Singapore Bus Service (1978) Ltd.*

LEFT: This photograph is dated 4.1.36 and timed at 4.55pm, giving the impression of its being from some sort of surveillance operation—possibly to crack down on illegal operations. *(Singapore Bus Service (1978) Ltd.*

The strike was to last six weeks, with a full return to work as the first trolleybus left the depot in the early morning darkness of 21st August. Whatever the cause of the dispute, the Company must have lost, for they were called upon to meet the costs of the tribunal, namely £1,121.14s. However, the financial effects of the strike on the accounts were not as bad as they might have been, for revenue which had been lost was to a degree regained when rickshaw pullers called a strike, this also lasting six weeks.

The extension from Joo Chiat Road junction to the trolleybus station at Geylang had given a minute increase in route miles of 0.6, providing a total of a little over 25 miles in all.

World War II

3rd September 1939 and the United Kingdom, in company with her colonies, was once again in a state of War, although it would be some time before any effects would be felt in Singapore. By 31st October of that year a further twenty five Albion Victors had been placed into service, bringing the motor bus fleet to one hundred and twenty eight. As a precaution, older buses due to be withdrawn were taken out of service, but placed into store rather than disposed of.

Weather conditions gave more trouble than any war being prepared for many thousands of miles distant. Exceptional rainfall during 13th November was greater than even the deep monsoon ditches were capable of dispersing. Severe flooding caused the 17 service to be suspended for most of the day, but then the troubles really started. Flood waters found their way into the feeder cables, and throughout an area bounded by Finlayson Green, South Bridge Road and Tanjong Pagar Road dozens of trolleybuses were stranded, with their unfortunate passengers having to make their way through the gathering waters as best they might. Happily, the engineering staff were soon in attendance to effect repairs, proving that the problems presented by nature could be dealt with, whereas those created by man would be far more difficult to solve.

There was an increasing volume of complaints being made against the bus operators. For one example, ribbon developments which had spread along Bukit Timah Road beyond Newton and towards Bukit Timah Village, the territory of the Green Bus Company. Timetables had been improved to the extent of offering a five minute headway throughout the day, but even so the demand for capacity far outstripped that which could be given by the small buses—on inward journeys, each bus would be filled by the time the 7th milestone had been passed, so that all the driver then had to do was to keep his foot down and work nonstop into town. Good for the business of the bus company, but very bad for the humour of intending passengers. Other rural districts from which complaints

were raised were Upper Serangoon, as served by the Ponggol Bus Company, and the territory along the east cost, of Katong Bedok. The reason for these complaints lay in one of the first effects of the war, namely petrol rationing, so that many persons (in particular middle and lower management expatriate staff) who might never have used a bus, found that they had to limit the use to which they put their cars—but the same restrictions in petrol supply meant that there would be little point in the Chinese companies seeking to make dramatic increases in their fleets.

The Traction Company recognised more problems, not the least being that they could not expect to receive any further deliveries of new vehicles for the duration of hostilities, both due to industrial production in the United Kingdom being geared to military production and a shortage of shipping space. A policy of make-do-and-mend was introduced, reworking spare parts wherever possible in the engineering shops in order to build up replacement stock, whilst older motor buses which might have been due for withdrawal were kept in service, albeit as helpers during the rush hours.

Perhaps a sign of the times, but on the occasion of Chinese New Year, February 1940, passengers along the Bukit Timah Road found that the private bus owners had introduced a self awarded surcharge of 5 cents on all fares, in addition to charging children full adult rates. Increased expenses incurred over the holiday period were given as being the reason for this unofficial step so that, by the fourth day of the festival, fares should have returned to normal. Not so, and a number of conductors were discovered still to be charging the excess, with the difference being diverted into their own pockets. Incidents of this nature were many, and not confined within the passenger transport industry. A general malaise was settling over the Island, as the terrible war news from China provoked a restlessness which in turn saw a lowering of standards.

Oddly enough, whilst giving a hearing to the ever rising volume of complaints, the Municipal Commissioners decided to appoint an enquiry into the workings of the Traction Company—we can only assume that, by so doing, there might emerge a picture of how transport in general was being able to operate under deprived circumstances, a much easier task than investigating each Chinese bus company. Even more odd, the terms of reference of the enquiry included an investigation into the possibility of Chinese bus owners being allowed to work the Traction Company routes, which in turn seems to indicate that the Commissioners were seeking a whipping-boy as a means of stemming the flood of complaints. It had been expected that the enquiry would last for just a few days, but in the event three months occupied their deliberations. The contents of the resulting Report could hardly have come as a surprise to anybody who had regarded the problems with an open mind, namely, that a good service was being provided to the absolute limit of existing resources, and if the Traction Company was experiencing a shortage of vehicles, then so too were the Chinese owners. No case had been made for the relaxation of the terms of the 1925 Ordinance.

When the findings were made known, there was an instant reaction from the motor factors in the town, who stated that there was an abundance of new vehicles to be had, and they would be most happy to accept all orders which might be directed to them. No doubt the United States of America would have been their source of supply but, with fuel shortages likely to become even more severe, they were making a desperate bid to put some life into a flagging industry. As for more general public comment, the *Straits Times* went against the more usual flow by being somewhat mildly critical of the Chinese bus companies, reminding their readers that as long ago as April 1933, with the decision being taken to get rid of mosquito buses, there was an opportunity for the formation of an Association of private bus owners, but the chance was allowed to pass. Had it been taken, the private companies would be better able to meet the prevailing crisis. Even so it would be quite wrong to maintain the impression of the concept of the mosquito bus style being carried into perpetuity, as a report in the *Straits Times* dated 9th December shows:

"A motor bus resembling a type popular in London has been introduced into Singapore for the first time by a private transport company to service the Beach Road to Seletar route. It is streamlined an provided with cushioned seats of the tubular type, including arm rests. The seating arrangements are different from those to which Singaporeans are accustomed. There is a wide entrance to the rear. Two more vehicles of this type will be placed into service by Mr. Tay Koh Yat".

How very unfortunate that this report did not carry an illustration, for what could this vehicle have been? Of greater interest insofaras the Singapore history is concerned is the suggestion that Mr. Tay Koh Yat had obtained an interest in the Seletar route, for such a magnificent machine would hardly be put to work on his shuttle service along Aljunied Road. One firm point is made, in that one Chinese operator had set out no only to emulate the degree of modernity hitherto only available from the Traction Company, but to surpass in the degree of comfort on offer.

The *Straits Times* had made matters relative to public transport into a crusade, and some months following the report a complete turn around, with travellers appreciating just how well the Traction Company in particular were performing under the prevailing conditions, and the management should not be distracted from their already difficult task by a need to constantly look over the corporate shoulder in case competition should be allowed to creep onto their better served routes. This mood of favour and understanding could not have arrived at a better time, for the effects of constant overworking were beginning to place excessive burdens onto the maintenance staff as the fleet became increasingly tired, needing to spend ever longer spells out of service due to mechanical failure. The subsequent loss of vehicles had to be reflected in a general reduction of headways: to give one example of how this policy had to be applied, trolleybus service 10 linking Moulmein Road with Outram Road had to be cut to an off-peak frequency of ten minutes, half of normal.

The war in Europe was no longer to be ignored, and various schemes were launched in order to raise money help the war effort, one of which was the War Fund. Amongst the contributors were the Green Bus Company with 500 dollars, Kampong Bahru Bus Company 200 dollars, Jurong Bus Company 100 dollars, Changi Bus Company 50 dollars, and Ngo Hock Bus Company 20 dollars. The regionally produced ingredients of war, tin and rubber, were commanding high prices, and the Traction Company considered that, as a result, the spending power of the population was increased, a fact being reflected in the substantial operating profit enjoyed by the Company as recorded in the 1940 accounts. The point was missed in that with the other major commodity of war, petrol, being in short supply, then the Company's profits were being drawn from a captive audience. Financial success to this degree could only be short lived, for costs involved in keeping the ageing fleet in service would be bound to rise and, as inflation was moving into the markets, local staff were being paid a cost of living allowance in order that they should not suffer the effects of these rising prices.

The success enjoyed by the oil engined Albions had been such that further units would be brought into service as older buses "dropped out of service" (direct quote, a singularly unfortunate choice of words under the circumstances), and an order for a further thirty had been placed during August 1940. To quote from the Annual Report:

"We are making every effort to expedite delivery but the date at which we will obtain it is at present quite uncertain. Postponement beyond the date at which the older vehicles become unserviceable would be a serious matter".

They would never be delivered.

The opening days of 1941 brought to Singapore tangible signs that the fingers of war could indeed touch the fortress with the promulgation of blackout regulations. On all buses and trolleybuses interior lighting had to be reduced to a maximum of one sixty watt bulb, shaded, whilst destination displays and headlights needed to be dimmed by the application of a thin coating of blue paint, and a somewhat bizarre happening was the conversion of a trolleybus to an ambulance—it is difficult to see how such a facility could be used in the event of air raids bringing down the wires, but at least there were some people who were taking the war news seriously.

Disquiet was once again building up amongst the residents living along Bukit Timah Road, to the extent that a petition had been presented to the Municipal Commissioners asking that improved transport facilities be provided. If the Traction Company were to assist, bearing in mind that the district in question fell beyond the normal sphere of operations, then there was naught to be done as far as an extension to service 6 was concerned. However, running parallel but a mile or so distant from Bukit Timah Road, there was service 17. From the original terminus at Botanic Gardens there had been an earlier extension to Farrer Road at the junction with Holland Road, and by the time now concerned had reached Holland Village. The petitioners sought a branch from the 17 service to run the full length of Farrer Road in order to reach Bukit Timah Road. When such proposal was put directly to the Traction Company it had to be rejected, albeit with genuine regret, as the petrol rationing situation could not allow them to contemplate the introduction of new routes. Within the ramifications of the municipal administration those responsibilities connected with all forms of public transport fell upon the Registrar of Vehicles, and it was representatives of that department who next made an approach to the Traction Company in an effort to break the impasse. Although the Registrar needed to give weight to the terms of the Ordinance, it was also he who held overall responsibility for the administration of the petrol rationing scheme with the ability to judge priorities so that, if the Company were able to provide some assistance, then it would not be at the expense of their carefully husbanded fuel supplies. Agreement having been reached, the following public announcement could be made:

"As from 7th March 1941, at the request of the Registrar of Vehicles, the Singapore Traction Company is operating, as an experiment, a service of omnibuses (during the morning and evening office peak hours), between Finalyson Green and Jurong Road, via Collyer Quay, Empress Place, High Street, Hill Street, River Valley Road, Tank Road, Clemenceau Avenue and Bukit Timah Road. Times will be as follows:

Morning   First bus leaves Jurong Road at 7.00 a.m. and at 20 minute intervals until 9.40 a.m.

Evening   First bus leaves Finalyson Green at 4.00 p.m. and at 20 minute intervals until 6.40 p.m.

Saturday   (mid-day) First bus leaves Finalyson green at 12 noon and at 20 minute intervals until 3.00 p.m.

Sunday service will operate from Kadang Kerbau to Jurong Road, returning via Bukit Timah Road and Mackenzie Road, first bus leaving Kadang Kerbau at 8.00 a.m., first bus leaving Jurong at 8.20 a.m., last bus leaving Kadang Kerbau at 6.50 p.m., last bus leaving Jurong at 7.10 p.m.

Given service number 25, in theory this should have gone far to meet the demands of the residents, particularly as an all day service was given on Sundays, even if Kadang Kerbau was a somewhat unlikely inner terminal. In practice all was not well, as the oldest of the Fords held in stock were used, which being less than reliable, meant that breakdowns were happening almost on a daily basis. A twenty minute running time on a twenty minute frequency compressed into a three hour operating span meant that one bus broken down would cause complete disruption. All in all, it was the best which could be provided, and no improvements could be directed towards the 25, for the same story was beginning to be repeated all over the system.

In order that no section of the community should be worse treated than any other a general reorganisation of services was introduced during May, with a greater emphasis being placed upon the greater reliability of the trolleybuses. The same basic routes were maintained, but with a computation of terminals. For some examples of how the pattern was organised, service 2 gained a 'branch line' passing along High Street in order to cross Anderson Bridge to reach Finalyson Green (in fact, a reintroduction of the very first motor bus route, but this time using trolleybuses). A number of journeys on the 2 were turned at Post 310. Likewise, trolleybuses 5 and 10 also had workings to Finalyson Green. On the motor bus side, some of the older members of the fleet put in an appearance from time to time as 2's to Finalyson Green, and the 17 made regular short workings to Tyersall Avenue (which was just another name for the original terminus at Botanic Gardens). Many of the Katong group of services received workings to Chulia Street.

Invasion and Destruction

8th. December 1941, and for the first time there was a breaking of the long gathering storm clouds. The street lights were shining brightly when, a little after four o'clock in the morning, the first air raid siren began to wail. One by one other sirens began their wail of doom, and the town was quickly ringed by the beams of searchlights probing the sky but finding nothing. Then the bombs began to fall, with loud explosions being heard from the Finalyson Green area and afterwards the docks. The sounds of the attacking aircraft faded, and still the street lights shone brightly. Of course, the immediate lesson to be learned from this first air raid called for a massive application of blackout regulations, but the deeper effect was the depth of disillusionment felt by the indigenous population for, as they had not been able to beat off the enemy, the British in general had suffered a serious loss of face. All aspects of life reflected this fact, and the Traction Company had to take its share of a serious decline in discipline. As one notable example, the driving of trolleybuses reached the point of being downright dangerous in some cases, with drivers working off their frustrations in high speeds. Their observations of stopping places became fictional, comprising a fast approach , then violent braking to almost bring the trolleybus to a halt but not quite, followed by fierce accelerating away again, with a scramble of passengers trying to board or leave, in danger of their lives. Once aboard, travel was acutely uncomfortable, for vehicle springs had not been designed for this sort of punishment, and standing passengers had to suffer the indignities of being thrown about during these excessive changes of speed. Indiscipline also touched some of the conducting staff, who introduced a self-devised ruling that only exact fares could be tendered to them, and anyone not handing over the correct number of cents had a very real chance of being ejected at the next stopping place, or worse, have the conductor take his higher value note or coin and then, when a request for the change was made, receive only a curt *"Nanti"* (Malay - "Wait") but with the change never forthcoming. Another feature of indiscipline was a growing degree of absenteeism, but this needed managerial understanding for, if the air raids were to continue, men felt the more pressing need was to be with their families. It fell to the military command to make soldiers available

to keep some essential service operational, but this generosity did not extend to public transport services. Quite the reverse, for the demands of the emergency caused the military to exacerbate the tribulations of the Company: on 8th. December the first Japanese landings were made on Malayan soil, at Kota Bharu, in the State of Kelantan. It soon became obvious that these landings were not being contained, and reinforcements needed to be rushed the long journey up-country. The Traction Company were instructed to make their buses available, to travel in convoy of not less than twenty—but not more than thirty. The telephone call came through in the middle of the night, to be taken by the Accountant, who was on the premises in his capacity of Group Warden, Air Raid Precautions. Not unexpectedly he hedged at the prospect of handing over a great part of the motor bus fleet, but the request swiftly changed to being an order. The Manager was called from his bed, and together with other members of staff vehicles were selected, in company with a team of volunteer drivers. A service van loaded with spare parts and drums of fuel, and accompanied by a small contingent of fitters, vital to the operation as the vehicles chosen to go were the ancient Fords. The whole exercise mounted with remarkable swiftness, and within hours of the telephone call being first received, the convoy was moving across the Causeway never to be seen again (their fate would have been destruction in the coming battles, or requisition by the occupying forces. Likewise, of the teams of drivers and fitters, news was vague).

Faltering morale and indiscipline brought about other instances of situations which could have turned very nasty: some time after the convoy had left a driver walked into Mackenzie Road garage to say that his bus had been stopped whilst in service and the passengers ordered off by two soldiers. They said that the army had requisitioned the vehicle, but the driver stood his ground and asked for some form of written authority for their actions. He produced a 'Witness Slip' carried by all the traffic staff, and asked that the men should record their name, rank and numbers, and also their units,. This they did, and then drove off in the bus. From the garage a hasty call was made to military headquarters at Fort Canning, who were able to identify the Unit as being Australian, but presently serving in North Africa. A little later the bus was discovered, a complete wreck, with even the cylinder block smashed, a mark of the orgy of destruction which had caused the end of this particular Ford.

As the military authorities had not taken to diesel engined vehicles of their own as yet, it seemed natural that, when making requisitions orders, they should look for petrol units. The Royal Navy were also unable to meet their own requirements, and so had to obtain several buses from the Traction Company, with a major difference in that these were the subject of formal hiring contracts rather than outright requisitioning. Situation—some of the latest Albions would have been involved. The Chief Engineer received a frantic message from the Base, to say that one of the buses most urgently required for naval transport, could not be made to start. The naval mechanics had checked it over and could not locate the problem. A company engineer made the long journey, and he too could not diagnose the trouble, at least, not until making an inspection of the fuel tank, and finding it filled with *ships'* fuel, of a grade burned in destroyers.

These incidents help to demonstrate the almost unbelievable background against which civilian transport services had to be

---

Concrete and Cabbages

As stated in the text, one of the remarkable things about the changeover from trams to trolleybuses in Singapore was the agreement with the local highway authorities to reconstruct the roads with suitable foundations and smooth surfaces to permit the trolleybuses to run successfully. Many early bus and trolleybus systems were forced to give up because the vehicles cut up the road surfaces and damaged underground pipes or cables.

The Singapore authorities were worried in particular about rutting, fearing that the heavy solid tyred trackless trolleybuses would cut tracks in the roads, because of their regular pattern of running. Rutting is still a problem on the inner lanes of British motorways, much used by the heaviest vehicles. However, in its 1927 report, the highway authority recognised the need for "substantial roads with smooth durable surfaces" and stressed the importance of dealing with underground services and the provision of adequate foundations.

Another hazard to be dealt with was that of the street vendors, who during, the cabbage season were wont to strip off the outer leaves of their wares and throw them into the carriageway. These leaves would become compressed by the solid tyred trolleybuses and other traffic, producing a greasy surface likely to cause skidding!

provided. In the municipal catchment area the major strain was placed upon the trolleybuses, although frequent air raids were causing increasing measures of damage to line equipment and vehicles. There was a desperate shortage of rolling stock, and at last the Imperial Preference clause had to be set aside, at least for the duration of the emergency. The motor factors had already said in public that they were not short of chassis and the Traction Company were able to obtain a total of forty seven, in the majority being American built Fords, with the remainder Canadian built Chevrolet 'Maple Leaf' chassis. Of these, twenty had been sent to the body builders, but it is difficult to even presume that any actually entered service with their purchasers.

One solution was for a Chinese bus operator to be invited back into town, and the story is told in the *Straits Times*, 22nd. December 1941:

> "After several years absence red mosquito buses made their appearance on Singapore city streets again this morning. They consist of a fleet of twelve 9 seaters of the Katong-Bedok route which are now supplementing the Singapore Traction Company's services. The route along which the mosquito buses ply is East Coast Road, Geylang Road and North Bridge Road, with a terminus in Bras Basah Road, the return journey being made by Victoria Street. Residents of the Katong and Bedok area are now served by buses from their terminus at Geylang Serai, then up along the East Coast Road to Bedok, and then on to Changi. This measure is designed to relieve the congestion in the areas north of the Geylang Road to which a large portion of the East Coast evacuation have been moved".

The implication was that the fleet of the Katong-Bedok company would be fully utilised by running into the central area, and so it fell to the Changi Bus Company, in making the diversion along Telok Kurau Road, etc., to cover the unserved Katong-Bedok territory. It is to be hoped that sufficient Changi buses were in stock in order to cover the route which made up their own territory, which otherwise would have been left unserved. Christmas morning was chosen by the Manager of the Katong-Bedok Company for the making of a public announcement. He said:

> "In order to relieve the residents in the Katong and Geylang districts of difficulties experienced at the present moment in getting buses, especially at the peak hours in the morning and evening, the Acting Registrar of Vehicles has been kind enough to arrange extra buses from this Company to run into town from Telok Kurau to Bras Basah Road via East Coast Road, Katong Road, Geylang Road, Kallang Road, Crawford Street, Beach Road and Bras Basah Road, returning via Victoria Street and the same way again. The terminus of this route in Bras Basah Road is the Rex Hotel, and buses will be collected as this point in the evening to convey passengers to Geylang and Katong. Buses will leave and run strictly to scheduled time, i.e., during the peak hours during the morning and evening buses will leave the bus stands at intervals of three minutes and the journey from one stand to the other must be completed in eighteen minutes. The rate of fares will be the same as the Traction Company's".

In theory, the service would duplicate service 15, but in practice the diversion along the 11 route along Beach Road would indicate a measure of limited stop in operation. Although every ship sailing for the United Kingdom or Australia had been evacuating families, many of whom had resided in the Katong district, on the other hand the semi-rural aspects of the east coast had proved to be attractive to those town dwellers who sought refuge from the threat of air raids. Whilst the reintroduction of a mosquito bus service might have been useful, the real winners in this awful situation were the pirate-taxis, for there were any number of large private cars just waiting to be picked up, and ideal for such a function.

By 24th January 1942 chaos and restrictions had become so severe that all bus services were curtailed to operate for a maximum of thirteen hours per day, from 6.00 am until 7.00 pm. The tempo of the drama was fast approaching a climax as January gave way to February. The wail of air raid sirens had become part of everyday living—and dying . The docks, railway station, power station and gas works, all were prime targets, but the long lines of shop houses bordering Geylang Road were devastated, whilst the kampong compounds were no match for high explosives. The streets were a tangle of broken traction poles and fallen overhead wires, whilst trolleybuses stranded out in the open were easy targets for destruction. The military had tried to blow the Causeway in an attempt to halt the advance of enemy forces, but to no avail, as beach landings at Kranji brought rapid advances along Bukit Timah Road, and later from the Naval Base by way of Thomson Road, whilst the fate of the Island was finally sealed following further landings along the east coast, bringing hostile forces through Katong and along Geylang Road. The end came on 16th February 1942 when, to British eyes, the impossible happened, and a surrender was effected, the formal ceremony being conducted in the factory of the Ford Motor Company of Malaya, Bukit Timah.

To understand the atmosphere, read the words of Arthur Swinson, writing in 'The Fall of Singapore':

> "The city by now was in a state of complete chaos, its population doubled by 500,000 refugees. Overhead hung a thick pall of smoke from the burning oil tanks. Though the streets which were choked with abandoned vehicles wandered troops without officers or orders. Sometimes a column would hang about for hours, having lost its way. In doorways deserters sprawled and others staggered around drunk, having looted liquor shops. Inevitably there were fights and drunken brawls. Looting by now was on a vast scale. Thousands of cigarette packets littered the pavements and children wobbled around on bicycles too big for them. Deserters drove cars from the showrooms and careered around wildly until they were smashed up. The food shops were looted too, and women and children could be seen hurrying along with dressed chickens, sacks full of tinned food, or flour and rice. The cinemas were crowded, mainly with troops. Every hour or so there would be another air raid and the bombs would be heard exploding on the houses. People would start running out to nowhere in particular: with no shelters yet built there was nowhere to run to. All over the city, fires were burning but few people took any notice. They were doomed and they knew that there was nothing they could do about it".

Chapter Four
1942–1945—The Era of The Rising Sun

ABOVE: Battery Road and Fullerton Square (see page 7). This was the scene soon after the surrender by British forces to the Japanese on Monday 16th February 1942. So commenced the Era of the Rising Sun. *(Straits Times)*

On the morning of Monday 16th. February, 1942, Tokyo Radio broadcast:

"The Imperial Forces of Dai Nippon have concluded the Malayan Campaign. The Rising Sun now floats over the much boasted impregnable fortress of Singapore. Within the breathtaking space of fifty-five days our invincible forces swept the British out of Malaya. This is a record unparalleled in the military history of the world. From today, the sixteenth day of the second month of the seventeenth year of Shora, 2602 years from the Glorious and Everlasting Era of Jimnu Tenno, a new chapter in the history of our great and imperishable Empire begins. From today Singapore becomes Syonan, the "illustrious Light of the South" ....Singapore is dead, now arises Syonanto the warm and radiating light of the south, the imperishable capital of the southern regions............"

(It is not the function of this work to dwell upon the Japanese action nor administration, either military or civil, except to the point wherein reflections might be found in the provision of a passenger transport network. The wider story has been presented in many variations, giving the British, Japanese, Chinese and Straits-born versions as to what life was like, and all history is written with bias. Be it sufficient to say that most of the public utilities including transport, were given little, if any, coverage in these accounts.)

The document of surrender took effect as from 5.15p.m. on Sunday 15th. February, but the advancing armies were halted at the perimeters of the main town in order that a measure of order could be established. Those who had appeared to have been photographers, office clerks and hotel waiters emerged in their true role as the first rank of some form of Japanese administration, but were insufficient in number to take complete control. For, so rapid had been the advance, the military forces were not accompanied by any number of high-ranking officials capable of taking over civil government. Under the control of a token military presence, squads of British and Australian prisoners-of-war were given the task of clearing the streets. Those members of the Traction Company Staff who had remained at their posts were brought from the internment camps to which they had been immediately sent, in order to sort out the tangles of fallen wires and to salvage as much as possible of the trolleybus fleet, with a view to restarting some form of service. The task was daunting, for in addition to the wide spread air raid damage which had not allowed a single route to be untouched, there would be a measure of 'scrap recovery' by the authorities, resulting in much copper wire being sent to feed the war factories of Japan.

To be obsolete proved to be the saving grace of those trolleybuses which were intact, for there was no move to send them for service in Japan (unlike Rangoon, whose almost new fleet of Ransomes trolleybuses were sent (possibly to Tokyo) - at this time the Japanese did not have a trolleybus industry of their own, with the few prewar orders that had been placed from within that country having been met by manufacturers in the United Kingdom).

Tokyo time

Local time was discontinued, and in the future Tokyo time would be observed. As this was three hours ahead of the sun, so to speak, the result insofar as the population was concerned was chaotic, so that if a transport service, when eventually introduced, advertised a starting time of 7 a.m., then the sleepy traveller would be at the stop for what was, in truth, 4 a.m. In practice many households kept two clocks, one to show 'official' time, and the other recording the precise point of the day as indicated by the sun.

It fell to the railway to reintroduce the first passenger transport services, although on a rudimentary basis. The first train arrived festooned with flags bearing the rising sun, but thereafter accommodation on offer could range from first class coaches right through to open freight wagons. In the absence of time tables, the intending passenger would arrive at the station, there to take his chance. He might need to wait for a few hours or else there might not be a train for several days. Too long a wait might attract the attention of the patrols of military police, so that even to contemplate making a journey could be none too comfortable, in more ways than one. No fares were charged for this haphazard facility.

On the streets of the town the rickshaw pullers were back at work, although their progress was interrupted by frequent barriers placed across the roadways, points for identity checks. In all fairness it should be pointed out that the Japanese found this mode of transport abhorrent, and it was not unknown for their soldiers, when stopping a rickshaw at a check point, to force the puller and passenger to exchange places, then to show great pleasure at the efforts of the passenger as he struggled to get the carriage moving again. Under this regime the rickshaw was finally to disappear, replaced by the tri-shaw, a bicycle with sidecar developed from the rickshaw concept. Remaining fearfully hard work, but at least the man could sit upright

Changes

Meanwhile, work was progressing at the Mackenzie Road workshops to bring surviving members of the fleet to readiness for service. The S.T.C. emblems were removed, and instead Japanese characters reading "Syonan-Si Siden", in white and on the green livery of the trolleybuses, were applied. The clearing of the main roads and replacement of damaged overhead wiring and feeder cables reached the stage at which the first trolleybus service could be started, as from 16th. March, 2602. With a form of railway service on offer, it was a natural choice to have the railway station as one terminus, hence there would have been a need to provide a terminal loop at this point. From here the route touched Tanjong Pagar before passing down to town by way of Anson Road, across Finlayson Green into High Street, thence into North Bridge Road on to Lavender Street, finally reaching the other terminus at Moulmein Road. Fare scales were based on prewar practice, and both first-and second class accommodation was available. An interesting inclusion in the official notice advertising this event read "Tickets of the former trolleybus service will not be valid. New tickets are being issued and must be paid for in the usual way". Service was due to start at 10 a.m., Tokyo time.

Whatever future trolleybus services might be provided would depend on the availability of trolley vehicles, for it was found that only fifty-three had survived to the extent where they could be used. On the motor bus side, Syonan-Si Siden had been able to collect sixty-nine complete vehicles. Public declarations by the military authorities were almost a daily happening, and one of the earliest "........hoped for an early restoration of the public transport system in Syonan". An edict published on the day following the restart of the trolleybus service demanded:

"1. All individuals and concerns that operate bus services in Syonan must bring their vehicles to the Military vehicles department in Middle Road before 23rd. of this month.

"2. Those who have surrendered their buses to the Military authorities must report so and bring along particulars of their vehicles.

"3. From now on the bus service will be operated by the City Authorities. No private individual or concern will be allowed to operate a bus service. By Order. "

The reference to Middle Road indicates the headquarters of the Registrar of Vehicles, whence all vehicle licensing was transacted in prewar times. History can be found casting its own shadows, for here we find the establishment of a *single island-wide bus operator,* although in this instance it was destined to survive only for three years. As a result of this order, any surviving so-called "mosquito-buses" were gathered together, and then taken to Mackenzie Road for overhaul and operation for service.

Nevertheless, attention continued to be directed towards the trolleybus operations, so that, a fortnight after the reintroduction of the first service, a second came into use, this time linking Post 310 with Tanjong Pagar. Given an advertised frequency of every five minutes, the first departure of the day from Post 310 was due at 7.50 am., and the last at 6.30 p.m. Having such a short working day as compared with 'normal' times, raises the question as to whether there was a shortage of crews besides vehicles? Such drivers and conductors as were able to resume their duties wore the same uniforms as previously, but stripped of all S.T.C. insignia, instead sporting an armband which declared that they were employees of the City Authority, again in Japanese script.

Whatever the case, it became possible to introduce a third trolleybus service as from 8th April, this time from a suburban terminus at Macpherson Road and working into Finalyson Green. The advertised timetable showed similar starting times as with the previous pair, but was due to work an hour longer during the evening.

Now that a network was taking shape, the opportunity was taken to reintroduce service numbers:

1. Railway Station to Moulmein Road
2. Post 310 to Tanjong Pagar
3. Macpherson Road to Finalyson Green.

Route numbering

There was no deliberate attempt to follow the former pattern of numbering, and so it must be seen as coincidence that the new service 1 followed the 'old' 1 as far as High Street, and that the new 2 had, in fact, been introduced as a short working over the 'old' during the emergency reorganisation. Improvements as they might be made were concerned with the operating day, and the 13th April showed a marked revision, for whilst starting times were put back slightly to 8 a.m., final journeys from each terminus went back a long way, to 10.15 p.m. Not only were shortages of staff and rolling stock being coped with, but the conditions of life must have been eased to the extent that people felt able to go out to seek entertainment during the evenings.

Thus far all efforts had been directed towards the re-establishment of at least some trolleybus services, and little had been done as far as motor bus operation was concerned. The trolleybus was seen as being the major efficient carrier, and motor bus operation would be in the form of extensions reaching out beyond the wires. At 7.50 a.m. on 15th April the first motor bus service was quietly brought into use, starting from Post 310 and serving Geylang Road as far as the junction with Joo Chiat Road. After only a few days it was found possible to extend the service for the length of Joo Chiat Road in order to reach Katong. Obviously, work on repairing the wiring for the length of Geylang Road had not, by this time, been concluded, but in the event the motor bus was not to remain for very long, with the full trolleybus service resuming as from the 24th April, at least, as far as the junction with Joo Chiat Road. Shortage of rolling stock would not allow for any duplication of services at this juncture, and accordingly the motor bus was cut back to work a shuttle between Geylang and Katong only.

With the release of some vehicles, a similar operation saw the introduction of another motor bus route, this time from the Macpherson Road trolleybus terminal by way of Upper Serangoon Road to Paya Lebar, on a nine minute frequency. As yet, motor bus routes were not given service numbers.

The City Administration looked for happy crowds to throng the streets on 29th April, celebrating Tentyo-Setu, 'Our Emperor's Birthday'. Buildings were decked with flags and bunting, and the citizens were to watch enthralled as military parades passed. To add to the general scene, five trolleybuses and five motor buses were dressed overall with flowers, and then sent out to tour the town for the whole of the day, although not in revenue service.

Winning the peace

As far as Syonan was concerned, the war was over and Japan had won. The victors had now to win the peace, and propaganda was one of the weapons most widely used. Great stress was laid on the vision of a great future for Ma-rai-ee (the 'new' name for Malaya) in general and Syonan in particular, as revealed by the "Syonan Times" dated 2nd May, 2602, under the headline "Good work of public transport services", but bearing all the hallmarks of being an official communique rather than the work of the editorial staff:

"The fact that there has been almost a complete resumption of the Public Transport Services within less than three months from the Fall of Singapore reflects great credit on those responsible for its reconstruction. In spite of the extensive damage to cable posts, electric cables, roads, etc., there was a resumption of part of the trolleybus service within a month of the occupation of the island. Today trolleybuses and motor buses ply on all former routes except along Tank Road and Orchard Road, affording a convenience to town workers living in the suburbs. Incidentally, the speedy resumption of the service has also been a means of providing employment for hundreds of drivers, conductors and inspectors and skilled mechanics, who would otherwise have been out of work for longer periods.

Although it will take a little time before the destroyed vehicles are replaced, the service such as it is today serves the public in a manner which calls for no complaint".

With three trolleybus services and a couple of motor bus operated connecting shuttles, nobody could possibly think that even a tiny percentage of the former island-wide network of services had been reintroduced. The rural communities had been ignored so far, and in the town a concentration of limited resources had been directed towards the major traffic arteries. The sting-in-the-tail of the item was the clear demonstration of the fact that free speech was a thing of the past, and any person who dared to complain would be in serious trouble.

The rickshaw—and tri-shaw—men were enjoying a boom period, and a further form of transport which found itself to be resurrected was the horse drawn gharrie, in decline since the days of the electric tramcar and at the point of oblivion when faced by the fleets of taxis which filled the streets prior to the war. Now a number had managed to emerge in order to take a role in solving the lack of transport.

New Services

The first motor bus service in its own right, as opposed to being a trolleybus feeder, was quite sensational. Commencing as from 6th May with the service number 19, it was to work from a town terminus at Finalyson Green, going around the Padang in order to reach Beach Road Market, then onwards by way of Rochore Road, thereafter passing the full length of Bukit Timah Road, crossing the by now repaired Causeway to end at a terminus in the Market Place at Johore Bahru. The first bus was timed to leave Finalyson Green at 8.10 a.m., returning from Johore Bahru at 10.00 a.m., with an hourly frequency being on offer. The through fare would be 89 cents. What endowed this service with historical importance is that it was to represent the only time during which a direct service was provided linking Johore Bahru with the centre of Singapore town.

On 26th May, trolleybus 3 was able to be extended beyond Macpherson Road to Paya Lebar, in turn allowing the feeder motor bus between these points to be withdrawn. Instead, having been given the service number 18, the new route was once again to extend trolleybus 3 down the hill to pass the prewar terminus at Tampines Road junction, to continue along the full length of Upper Serangoon Road until reaching a terminus at the Police Station opposite Ponggol Road, thereby providing the second excursion into a rural district.

The pace at which a restoration of services was moving became quicker, for the following day was noteworthy in that a former trolleybus route was re-established, but using motor buses. Under the service number 17, the route linked Finalyson Green with Newton, and whilst this would appear to be a duplication with the 19, as the latter worked along Bukit Timah Road, an area from which many complaints had been voiced during the months of the emerging emergency and based upon the increased residential presence, it would seem that the introduction of the 17 was a means of turning away short distance riders from the 19, a theory supported by fare tables showing a 6 cents minimum charge on the 19, twice that of the 17.

Paya Lebar—a hub

In a small way Paya Lebar was to become a hub in the network of services now emerging, for on 4th June service 20 began to operate, leaving the terminus of trolleybus 3 to travel by way of Yio Chu Kang Road to Niyako Byoin (little by little Japanese place names were introduced - this was the City Hospital, itself a misnomer, as it stood many miles from the city, and in later years became known as Woodlands Hospital - although it was also miles away from Woodlands!).

June 2602 was to prove most active as far as the rural districts were concerned, with the introduction of a further long distance service, given the number 21. Having an inner terminus at Beach Road Market, a common route was shared with the 19 as far as the town end of Bukit Timah Road, then branching away to run the length of Thomson Road in order to reach Sembawang Village (although this terminal was still shown as "Seletar", as with former operators).

From the 8th May, the trolleybus routes from Post 310 to Outram Road, and from Newton to Outram Road, were restored as services 4 and 5.

Conditions were such that consideration could be now be given to the reintroduction of cross-suburban routes, and the hitherto short shuttle

LEFT: Trolleybus No 2 decorated with the flags of Nippon soon after the commencement of the occupation in February 1942. The irony of the scene is that the trolleybus, probably driven by a Chinese driver, is *apparently* being bowed to by the Japanese soldier, whose bowed head is to be seen on the extreme right of the picture. In fact, it is the flags to which he bows so low. The STC insignia has been removed from the side of the vehicle but the white painted characters in its place are reported to say 'south facing trolleybus'. This could be a reference to Syonan—Light of the South— or that the translation can be differently interpreted; it is a Japanese phrase expressed in Chinese characters. (Straits Times

20 was to receive extensions from both ends. The full length of Paya Lebar Road was used to gain access to Geylang, whilst from Miyako Byoyin buses were continued along Yio Chu Kang Road as far as the junction with Jalan Kayu, thence to the main gate at R.A.F. Seletar. (How strange that the former presence of the Royal Air Force should be recalled in this manner).

In these extensions the pattern of feeding into the trolleybus services was continued, and an even greater strain was placed on the Geylang Road service as from 21st. June. The late 1930's had seen a web of motor bus routes designed to serve Katong and the residential districts located along the east coast. History was now to repeat itself, although without the benefit of through journeys into town. A service 15 was brought back to the area, but this time working directly back from Geylang way of Changi Road until reaching a terminus at the $8^1/_2$ milestone. After a while, the service was extended by making a turn into Bedok Road up to Bedok Corner. Service 22 had been the Joo Chiat Road shuttle, but now was able to continue from Katong Village along East Coast Road until it too reached Bedok Corner. The 23 was a variation on this theme, only to use Joo Chiat Road as far as Joo Chiat Place, so as to reach Telok Kurau Road Corner.

Return of services to the 'Chinese' bus area

Little by little, coverage was drawn back to those trunk roads which had been the territories of the Chinese bus companies, at least in part. What had once been the Keppel company's service returned with the introduction of the 25s, as before starting from Tanjong Pagar, but only reaching the $6^1/_2$ mile along Pasir Panjang Road, at Reformatory Road.

Service number 17 did not float free for very long, being used as from the 12th July on a service linking Finlayson Green with a truly rural terminal at Ulu Pandan. Even to the use of the service number and using Stamford-, Orchard-, and Holland Roads as far as Holland Village, this was the same as in Traction Company days—did any passengers notice the coincidence?

July was also to bring a further extension to the trolleybus network in that service 1 moved from the Railway Station to Nelson Road.

To complete the account of activities during that month, service 18 was to provide considerable interest. The outer end was to receive a short extension, from the Police Station up to the shoreline at Kang Kah. However, from Paya Lebar it was to follow the 3 trolleybus all the way to Bras Basah Road, with a terminus outside the Raffles Hotel. To provide such a measure of duplication did seem to indicate that the period of resuscitation was almost complete inasmuch as the town area was concerned, although the rural areas still seemed to be poorly served. There was a further press statement dealing with public transport published on 19th July, 2602, reading:

> "Plans for the reconstruction and extensions of the existing transport system in Syonan are receiving the careful attention of the authorities concerned, although their main problem is the restoration of transport facilities to normal. In spite of wartime conditions Syonan-si- Siden has restored and is now operating fourteen transport routes in and around the city, whilst it is at the moment considering the opening of seven additional routes on which mosquito buses will operate.
>
> The first of these will be a service starting from Raffles Quay, along Cross Street, New Bridge Road, River Valley Road and up to Alexandra Road junction.
>
> The second will start at the Harbour Board end of Kampong Bahru Road and will follow Outram Road, Kim Seng Road and end at Napier Road.
>
> The third will run from Finalyson Green to Balastier Road. The fourth will run from the junction of Geylang Road and Joo Chiat Road up to Kampong Meylayu. The fifth starts at the same place as the fourth and will run along Changi Road to Changi Village. The sixth will connect Tampines Village with Changi Road while the seventh will run from Paya Lebar to Ponggol.
>
> At the moment the transport system in Syonan is provided by diesel engined omnibuses, the electrically operated trolleybuses, large numbers of which were destroyed during the recent hostilities in the island.
>
> To make up the deficiency in large transport vehicles, the authorities are repairing and refitting scores of former mosquito buses at the Syonan-si Siden headquarters at Mackenzie Road. Better cars were being sought, either in Syonan, or to be sent from Nippon".

In making an analysis of this report, perhaps the most interesting item is that hitherto the motor bus services were maintained by the faithful Albions, although there is also photographic evidence that suggests that some, if not all, of the Leyland Cubs were also to remain. That 'scores' of mosquito buses were in the process of passing through workshops serves as an indication of almost the total fleets of the former Chinese bus operators being taken into stock. As for the prospect of a supply of 'better' cars being brought in from Japan, there has got to be strong element of doubt as to this happening in any great number, if at all (although here again there is photographic evidence which purports to show a Japanese bus at work in Singapore - however, this was a time of war, and Japanese industry, in common with all of the protagonists, was geared to military production).

Charcoal burning gas buses

Local industry was encouraged to assist with the solution to the transport problem, not only concerned with the shortage of vehicles but, equally important, restrictions in the supply of fuel. If diesel and petrol were short, on the other hand charcoal was plentiful. The Flying Eagle Company, with workshops at Kallang, devised a system whereby power could be generated using a charcoal burning boiler, producing gas. Syonan-si Siden made a number of petrol engined buses available to the Company for conversion, and these had a vast array of equipment mounted directly onto the bodywork, at the rear. The device comprised four major components, namely the charcoal burning boiler, a gas generator and convertor, a gas accumulator and a discharging unit. The boiler contained a separate water tank to act as a heat regulator. Once generated at the boiler, the gas passed through a pipe into the convertor which filtered out all sediment. Once purified the gas passed along a further pipe to a storage tank located under the driver's seat, from whence it was drawn into the carburettor. Great claims were made for the buses so equipped - with a load of thirty-five passengers they would be capable of a maximum speed of thirty miles per hour, whilst in economic terms it was reckoned that a pick full of charcoal would be sufficient to keep the bus running for a whole day and night. It has not been possible to obtain a precise definition of how much by weight comprised "one pick full", but the running costs were claimed to be no more than one cent per mile. If these contraptions had been a success, then the whole of the automotive industry would have been revolutionised, but in truth operations were beset by a catalogue of breakdowns and minor explosions, and the end result may never be known.

The local network centre on Geylang became a further strengthened as from 20th August with the introduction of motor bus 16, having a split route - working out by way of Geylang Road, one section branched off in order to serve the Malay Settlement at Kampong Melayu, whilst alternate buses continued along Changi Road, turning right into Telok Kurau Road to terminate at the junction with Joo Chiat Place, completing a pattern in conjunction with the 23 service.

Also as from 20th August, trolleybus 1 became the subject of extensive rerouting in that, instead of using Jalan Sultan and North Bridge Road, it was to continue along Victoria Street and New Bridge Road as far as Upper Cross Street, turning along that thoroughfare in order to regain the original line to serve Tanjong Pagar Road. This move coincided with what was to prove to be the final reinstatement of a section of trolleybus route: given the number 6, it was an exact replacement of the Traction Company's 'old' 1, once again linking Tank Road with Keppel Harbour.

Shortages and route identification

In an atmosphere of shortages, linen for destination blinds was a luxury beyond contemplation. Traction Company stock would be used wherever possible, but as the Albions were working to destinations never before reached by them, those fitted would more often than not be inappropriate. Therefore, a new system of route identification was required, and to this end square coloured boards were introduced, these to be carried at the front of all buses. With a limit to the number of single colours, combinations were painted in diagonal form. The question of route identification needed to be given serious consideration, for with the network of services now being provided being so different in terms of route followed and destinations served when compared with pre-occupation times, prospective passengers could be easily confused. It is not possible to say as to whether the overhaul of the former Chinese company buses included full repainting into a common livery for this might have been an unnecessary luxury. Nevertheless , having been taken into a pool, it is doubtful if the Chinese buses were able to return to their former territories, where travellers would have recognised their bus from its livery.

The new services which had been promised in the report quoted as from 19th July came into operation as from 19th October and with a much greater number than the seven which had been enumerated . Details of the colour identification were also made public, and in addition there was also a major revision of the frequencies. The complete listing of routes is set out in the table below, for it does represent the maximum pattern of routes which was worked by Syonan-si Siden. From this point onwards there would set in a decline:

Trolleybuses the mainstay

This new network clearly shows the trolleybus as being the main support for public transport, with most, but not all, of the motor buses being a supplement thereto. Also clearly shown is the manner in which the town area has received most attention, although based on the frequencies quoted and the short distances covered by most of the services, the majority of routes could be served by a single vehicle. Even so, some of the main thoroughfares were able to enjoy two or three different services, particularly Serangoon Road, and in allowing such measures of duplication, there must be seen an improvement in the fleet of operational buses.

One or two of the services are worthy of particular note, if studied in tandem with the promise contained within the previous statement of intent. Service 28 might be seen as keeping half a promise, for although what had been stated was "the sixth will connect Tampines Village with Changi Road", in fact it was to start from Paya Lebar Village but then only reach Pasir Ris Village, three miles short of Changi Road. Again, that which emerged as service 30, linking Geylang with Changi Village, was only able to reach the 11th milestone along Changi Road, some three miles short of the village. The reason would seem to be obvious, in that the work which had been started by the Royal Air Force in constructing a base had been taken over and much expanded by the Imperial Forces, so that the area beyond the 11th milestone would have become a high security zone. The most unusual of the new services was the 31, forming as it did a direct link between Geylang and Ponggol, a facility not provided before, nor indeed after, Syonan-si Siden.

Syonan was being integrated into the Imperial Empire, and little by little civil administrators were beginning to arrive in order to take over appropriate departments from the military. This inflow of new population required accommodation, and of course they sought the best. The band of desired properties formed an arc around the northwest periphery of the town, and therein lay the need to provide services 51-53. Although it has not been possible to locate exact route details, they would have passed through the high quality inner suburbs.

Service 29 deserves a particular place in history, albeit in a debit sense, being the first of the former trolleybus routes to be replaced by motor buses on a permanent basis. Other sections of trolleybus routes were not given coverage at all by Syonan-si Siden, these being the old 10 along Bencoolen Street and Jalan Besar, and the old 11 in Beach Road.

In addition to the public services, there were four routes provided for the Japanese military on a free-of-charge basis. The central terminal was in Orchard Road, from which the routes radiated to various camps and military installations.

2602 had still to produce small variations, in that as from 19th November trolleybus 3 and motor bus 27 had a post 7.00 p.m terminal at Tanjong Pagar in lieu of Finlayson Green.

End of the class system

An important change which had been anticipated with the resumption of trolleybus services actually took thirteen months to realise. In a proclamation dated as operational from 10th March 2603 there was stated:

"1. The existing system of 1st. and 2nd class is abolished

2. New fares are set accordingly to that of the former second class, i.e., one section 2 cents.

3. For military and Gunzoko the fares will not be charged for the time being"

Editorial comment was soon to follow, and because of the fascinating information contained therein, is recorded in full:

"With the introduction of the new type of one-class trolleybus on Syonan thoroughfares, passengers will be charged according to the present second-class rates.

The new fare will come as a boon to all travellers by street-car, particularly city workers residing in the suburbs, for a definite saving will be in their travel expenses.

For instance, while passengers paid 10 cents for a first-class ticket from Paya Lebar to Finlayson Green, they will in future be required to pay only 8 cents, the present second class fare.

The new street car, which has no separate compartments (for 1st. and 2nd. class passengers) has already made its appearance on the streets, with more to follow".

'New' trolleybus

Another source records "a locally manufactured trolleybus" as being placed on the Tanjong Pagar route.

SYONAN-SI SIDEN
Route Colours and Service Frequencies
17th October 2602

TROLLEYBUSES

Service Number	Route	Colour	Interval
1	Moulmein Road—Nelson Road	White	10 minutes
2	Geylang—Tanjong Pagar	Red	3 minutes
3	Paya Lebar—Finlayson Green	Blue	6 minutes
4	Post 310—Outram Road	Yellow	14 minutes
5	Newton—Outram Road	Black	11 minutes
6	Tank Road—Keppel Harbour	Pink	20 minutes

OMNIBUSES

Service Number	Route	Colour	Interval
15	Geyland—Bedok	Green-Yellow	44 minutes
16	Geyland—Kampong Melayu	Red-Green	16 minutes
17	Holland Road—Finlayson Green	Red-White	22 minutes
18	Finlayson Green—Upper Serangoon	Yellow-White	13 minutes
18	Bras Basah Road—UpperSerangoon	Yellow-White	10 minutes(*)
19	Finlayson Green—Johore Market	Yellow-Black	22 minutes
20	Geylang Police Station—R.A.F. Seletar	Yellow-Red	20 minutes
21	Seletar—Beach Road	White- Black	17 minutes
22	Geylang—Bedok	White-Pink	44 minutes
23	Geylang—Bedok	Black-Blue	44 minutes
24	Beach Road—Bukit Panjang	Pink-Blue	40 minutes
25	Tanjong Pagar—Reformatory Road	Blue-Yellow	13 minutes
25	Tanjong Pagar—Gillman Barracks	Blue-Yellow	25 minutes
26	Telok Blangah—Napier Road	Blue-White	irregular
27	Thomson Road—Finlayson Green	Red-Black	14 minutes
28	Paya Lebar—Pasir Ris Village	Green-Black	15 minutes
29	Raffles Quay—Delta Road	Blue-Red	60 minutes
30	Geylang—Changi Village	Pink-Black	15 minutes
31	Geylang Police Station—Ponggol	Green-White	25 minutes
50	Mackenzie Road—Railway Station	Orange-Green	30 minutes
51	Mackenzie Road—Railway Station	Brown-White	15 minutes
52	Mackenzie Road—Dalvey Road	Violet-White	20 minutes
53	Mackenzie Road—Sea View Hotel	Pink-Yellow	25 minutes

(*) Service after 7.00p.m.

"Painted green and silver throughout, this trolleybus was built lower to the ground, and with two doorways, one near the driver and one at the rear".

Photographic evidence of a very sad number 18 has survived, showing it to be very close the description given. The conclusions which must be drawn are that, from amongst the severely damaged vehicles which were recovered, parts were taken in order to make a trolleybus capable of service. The original body was retained, but inside the bulkhead dividing the compartments had been taken out, causing obvious weakening to the main structure. The near side rear entrance bows down to the roadway, a feature which when new, might have given the impression of a lower chassis line. Whether other trolleybuses were produced or so treated, it becomes impossible to comment, except that, had it been so, then the overall life span of the fleet would have been much lowered.

Discipline and speed limits

Discipline was inflicted on the population in a variety of ways. Intention of one such exercise was promulgated by Tokubetu-Si (the City Council) Notice number 206, entitled "Re-third practice safety first week (Traffic Control): "It is hereby notified that in order to raise the spirit of observing traffic rules and to acquire safety as well as pleasantness in traffic, we have decided to have a Safety First Week for the third time. Therefore, we request the full cooperation of the public to acquire our aims as follows-

1. Period of operation from 20th. April to 26th. April, Syowa 18, inclusive, between the hours of 9 and 19 o'clock.
2. Area where Safety First Week will be observed - within Syonan-to.
3. Main purpose of the training-

Kind	Speed within City	Speed outside City
Motor Cycles	25 m.p.h.	45 m.p.h
Cars	25 m.p.h.	45.m.p.h
Lorries	25 m.p.h.	35 m.p.h

   ii)   strict observance of traffic signals and signs
   iii) strict observance of stop line
   iv) training cars to turn right and left at junctions
   v)   training of pedestrians at junctions
   vi) training of morality within trolleybuses
4. Model of regulated speed of cars: during this period a model of regulated speed of cars with special signs will be in use, and those who overtake these cars shall be treated as violators of the traffic rules"

Of the foregoing, it is 3(vi) which catches the eye, with wonderment as to the degree and form of immorality which might have been flagrant aboard trolleybuses. In fact, comment made by "Syonan Shimbun" (which we know better as being "The Straits Times", indicated "One eye sore is the manner in which people cling to trolley-cars and omnibuses, much in the same manner as bees to a hive". Even so, the travelling public, not the authorities, were to be castigated: "Talk of putting more buses on the road in circumstances at present prevailing savours of thoughtlessness, for surely even if materials were available, there should be some far-sighed scheme designed for the people themselves". They were instructed to be "..more methodical and public-spirited, and to make adjustments to their departure times". The theme was continued after the conclusion of the Safety First Week, noting that passengers had been asked not to block doorways, nor to smoke nor spit whilst aboard. An editorial declared passengers to be "... better behaved than ever in the past", but as for crews, "... the drivers and conductors of our public transport system have been known to be entirely oblivious of the fact that they are there to serve the public", being accused of "...maltreating the commuters and moving off before boarding or alighting". A conclusion had to be drawn, namely that neither measures nor warnings would improve the overburdened transport situation, but rather the provision of more vehicles, and in truth the opposite seemed to be happening.

Services renumbered

During March 2603 notice had been given of the intention to renumber many of the by now existing services, and whilst this came into effect as from the 10th July, what in practice the scheme was to achieve was a drastic reduction in services. So

much of the trolleybus network, so painstakingly restored, was again abandoned, due to the fact of the ancient AECs becoming beyond repair in increasing numbers. As they failed they were taken from the road and dumped in the yard to the side of the garage in Mackenzie Road, and from these hulks parts would be removed as required in order to keep the others going. Cut by half, the new network retained the busy Geylang to Tanjong Pagar route, but renumbered as service 1. Second in importance was the line to Paya Lebar, renumbered as service 2 during the daytime and when working to Finlayson Green, to become 2A after 18.38 hours when the alternative terminus at Tanjong Pagar was used. (Note that by now the twenty-four hour clock had been adopted). Service 3 linked Moulmein Road with Outram Road, and thus completed the reduced trolleybus system.

The pattern of motorbus services had also to suffer major shrinkage, with many through facilities into town being withdrawn, and the remaining stumps returning to the role of being trolleybus feeders. Of the motor bus fleet capable of working, their use was concentrated on the eastern coastal strip, so that Geylang and Katong were able, in theory, to retain fragments of their local route pattern.

To summarise the most important changes, 15 became a circular route, starting at Geylang and working by way of Joo Chiat-, East Coast-, Telok Karau- and Changi Roads back to Geylang: 17 was cut short at Holland Road, no doubt at the Village: 18 ceased to work into town but instead started at Geylang Police Station, once again becoming a feeder of new trolleybus 1, and also to trolleybus 2 when passing through Paya Lebar in order to reach the terminus in Upper Serangoon Road: the 'original' 23 disappeared, and a new 23 started from Finlayson Green and then working by way of Cecil Street and Anson Road in order to reach Keppel Harbour, a direct replacement of the recent trolleybus operation between these two points: a new 24 replaced the original 29 over the Delta Road route, but going beyond the original terminus in order to reach Alexandra Road: the branch to Gillman Barracks was cut from the 25: the 26 was cut back at both ends, left only to work between Tanjong Pagar and Orchard Road: the old 30 took the number 27, to be cut back from the 11th. milestone to the 10 milestone along Changi Road, with a short working numbered 27A going only as far as the 6 milestone. To cater for some degree of evening entertainment, a short route numbered 28 ran between Eu Tong Seng Street (in the heart of Chinatown) to the Great World Amusement Park, between 18.08 and 23.35 hours. Noteworthy, the terminus of service 20 became 'Seletar Aerodrome'. Of all other services, nothing was to be heard, leaving the greater part of the rural districts without bus services.

Fares

The question of fares also entered into the reorganisation, not so much directed at the local passengers but rather to meet the need of some of the Japanese riders to make some contribution to revenue. Officers and enlisted men wearing uniform, or if in civilian clothes but able to produce a special badge, would still be able to travel without charge, otherwise a special, simple, fare structure would be applied, viz., I) by trolleybus 5 cents per person between any termini, or for any shorter distance, ii) omnibuses, as by trolleybuses, except, iii) the Seletar service, from Beach Road terminus to Chiyoda-Yama (this would have been some distance along Thomson Road), 10 cents per person, or else the full distance for 20 cents, and iv) the Johore Service, from Finlayson Green to Chyu-Reito (and this would be the 5th. milestone along Bukit Timah Road) at 10 cents per person, and again 20 cents for the full distance. The provision of these special rates serves to indicate the arrival of more Japanese civilian residents, and the very light scale of charges imposed upon them would have done nothing to make their presence any the more welcome.

"In fact, during the Japanese time, I have yet to take a bus. Either I walked or go along with my bicycle". Post-occupation comment by a resident, and showing that the most prized possessions of the time were indeed bicycles.

The City Council route guide for the 1st July reorganisation, as follows:

SYONAN TOKUBETU-SI
Route Guide 1st July 2603
TROLLEYBUS
1 Tanjong Pagar—Geylang
2 Paya Lebar—Finlayson Green (daytime)
2A Paya Lebar—Tanjong Pagar (evenings)
3 Moulmein Road—Outram Road

OMNIBUS
15 Geylang—Geylang (via Joo Chiat road)
16 Geylang—Kampoing Melayu
17 Finlayson Green—Holland Road
18 Geylang police Stn—Upper Serangoon Road
19 Beach Road—Johore
20 Geylang Police Stn—Seletar Aerodrome
21 Beach Road—Seletar
22 Geylang—Bedok at Changi (Road)
23 Finlayson Green—Keppel Harbour
24 Finlayson Green—Alexandra Road (daytime)
25 Tanjong Pagar—Reformatory Road
26 Tanjong Pagar—Orchard Road (daytime)
27 Geylang—Changi Road (10¾ mile)
27A Geylang—Changi Road (6¾ mile)
28 Eu Tong Seng Street—Great World (evenings)

There were happenings during 2603 which remain shrouded in mystery. Although "Syonan Shimbun" encouraged the suggestions, when talking with residents some thirty years later the responses were negative to the point of insinuating that this was not a topic for discussion, and so we turn to the writings of Mamoru Shinozaki ("Syonan - my Story", Asia Pacific Press, 1975). By August the total population of Syonan was calculated at 1,000,000 persons, and with lines of supply becoming very stretched the military administration decreed that the Island must become self supporting. As the families who lived in the rural areas would not be able to produce enough food on their small plots of land, the decree ordered that at least 300,000 persons should be evacuated, all to be Overseas Chinese. A site upon which a new town might be located was found in northern Johore State, by the name of Endau, also known in common parlance as New Syonan. It fell to Syonan Tokubetu-si to arrange the transport, and during September ten 'lorries' set out on the 136 mile journey, filled with 'happy' settlers.

A second evacuation embraced the Eurasian and Roman Catholic populations, their settlement being at Bahau, far away in the State of Negri Sembilan, so that their movement needed to be by rail.

Somewhat sketchy mention of these evacuations is made only to indicate that the whole transport administration was being put under tremendous pressures other than those generated by the normal to and fro between home and work. The serious problems were to persist, and the Tokubetusi (and the indications are that the City Council had taken direct responsibility from Syonan-si Siden by this time) issued further instructions for the regulating of the use of trolleybuses and buses, viz., if the 'Full Load' sign was displayed then there was to be no boarding, nor was there to be any standing in front of or around the driver. If these instructions were not complied with, then the conductor or inspector had the right to order the passenger off the vehicle. Such public proclamations continued to come thick and fast, although only a few directly concerned public transport. Number 309, dated 15th. December 2603, did. Reading "Use of trolleybuses and omnibuses", the directions were

i) Board of trolleybuses and omnibuses which display the sign 'Full Load' is strictly prohibited, unless special directions are given by the conductor or inspector,
ii) passengers are strictly forbidden to stand in front of or around the driver,
iii) the accommodation of these facilities will not be made available to those who do not comply with the directions given by the conductor or inspector of said buses.

The original Straits Settlements currency had been hidden away since the start of the occupation, and instead colourful notes known as "Banana Money" were in circulation, becoming ever more plentiful as inflation bit harder. A new scale of fares was brought into operation as from 1st January 2604: trolleybuses remained the cheaper form of travel, being up to two sections for 5 cents and 10 cents for three sections and beyond . Motor buses retained a graduated scale, on the Johore and Seletar services a flat rate of 5 cents per section, and over all other routes 5 cents for very two sections or part thereof.

Marking the start of the third year of Syonan-si the by now all to familiar pronouncement: by way of an introduction the public were advised that the cause of the failing public transport system had to be seen as the inability to obtain spare parts for the fleet of predominantly British built vehicles. Inspectors, drivers and conductors were lashed for not giving sufficient attention to the carrying out of their duties in an efficient manner, and then to the

LEFT: Two AEC trolleybuses sometime during the occupation, probably posed to reassure everyone that all was well and normal in what were, without doubt, difficult times. Again there are characters painted in the position formerly taken by the STC initials.
(F. W. York collection

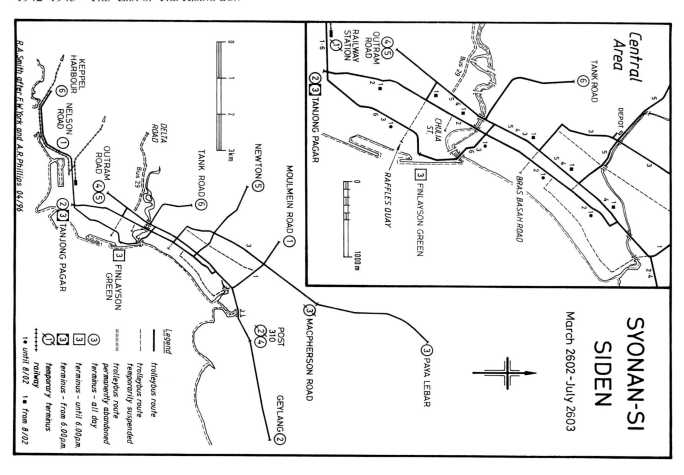

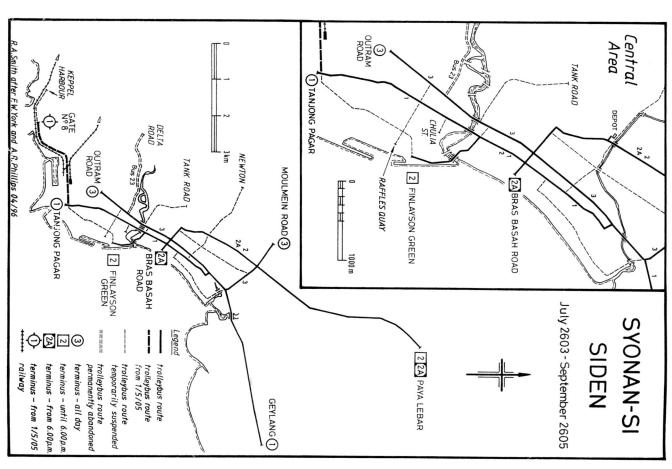

public, "walk short distances instead of burdening the buses with your additional weight". As one resident later remarked, "The main means of transport was your own two legs. You simply walked. You never dreamt of trying to get public or private transport" or again "I don't think there were any buses. I can't remember this, but I doubt that there were any buses. Either you use your bicycle mostly, or else you walk. It was common for people to walk many miles those days". Yet again "Bicycle at that time was a vital asset to everyone. Bicycle can be built for two or three at that time, so it was very vital means of transport during the occupation period".

More shortages and service 'revisions'

The military machine was learning the lessons of over-stretched supply lines, and as they had become bogged down in Burma and in their drive towards India, so increasingly there was a need to divert all of their available resources towards the war effort. In common with all civilian aspects of life, the provision of a viable transport service was pushed ever further back in the order of priorities.

The result was yet a further heavy 'revision' to take effect from 24th July. In making a study of the detail, as far as trolleybuses were concerned, the only saving which could be made was by cutting back the evening operation of 2A from Tanjong Pagar to Bras Basah Road, away went the 15 and 16, whilst the 19 was curtailed at a point described as "Johore Causeway Front", meaning that the service was no longer to leave the Island. Also lost was the 27A and the only gain which might be discovered concerns a short extension of the 28 from Eu Tong Seng Street a little further along New Bridge Road, but with the hours of operation cut by two hours daily (starting an hour later, finishing an hour earlier than hitherto). Yet again the point was made, that the ancient trolleybuses were struggling on still, but in reduced numbers. The garage yard was becoming increasingly the graveyard of their fellows, and this can be hardly surprising when the suggestion is considered that one of the lubricants used was coconut oil. Very much an example of using whatever might be able to be produced locally.

The full guide for the period is as follows:

SYONAN TOKUBETU-SI		
Service Revisions 25th July 2604		
TROLLEYBUS		
1	Tanjong Pagar - Geylang	White
2	Paya Lebar - Finlayson Green (daytime)	Red
2A	Paya Lebar - Bras Basah Road (evenings)	Red
3	Moulmein Road - Outram Road	Blue
OMNIBUS		
17	Finlayson Green - Holland Road	Red-white
18	Geylang - Upper Serangoon	Yellow-white
19	Beach Road - Johore Causeway Front	Yellow-black
20	Geylang - Seletar Aerodrome	Yellow-red
21	Beach Road - Seletar	White-black
22	Geylang - Changi Road	White-pink
24	Alexandra Road - Finlayson Green	Blue-pink
25	Finlayson Green - Reformatory Road	Blue-yellow
27	Geylang - Changi Road	Blue-red
28	New Bridge Road - Great World	Black-green (evenings only)

There was faint hope in being able to maintain even these few services, and as the months passed by, even the stock of serviceable trolleybuses declined to the point where routes were served by a single vehicle. History is famed for repeating itself, and Telok Blangah Road, which was able to witness the first operational trolleybus of Syonan-si Siden, was to be involved in the last desperate attempt at revision of services on the part of Syonan Tokbetu-Si. Whereas the original route had used an improvised terminus outside the railway station, the reintroduction of some sort of service along Keppel Road was only able to reach Gate number 8 of the Docks, that is to say beyond the prewar terminal at Nelson Road but not as far as Keppel Harbour.

The reopened section was linked with service 1 at Tanjong Pagar and worked as an extension thereto. At the same time motor bus 25 was cut back from Finlayson Green to Gate number 8, to become a feeder. These revisions came into effect as from 1st May 2605, coincidental with a drastic cutting out of stopping places in an effort to reduce further wear and tear. The end could not be far away.

The end in sight

Into August, and it was obvious that the days of Syonan-si were numbered. In the town offices emptied of Japanese staff, and there became a great demand for transport in order to move families to a evacuation centre in Jurong, from whence shipping back to Japan would be arranged. Elsewhere it was a time for the settling of old scores, and there were instances of trolleybuses being stopped and the crews dragged away to be beaten, those armbands perhaps unfairly placing them in the ranks of collaborators. Came the 5th September, and the first British warships were sighted. A small number of soldiers were landed, they being prepared for any eventuality. The civilian population were enthusiastic in their welcome, but a cold formality existed between the forces so recently at war. After all, Japanese soldiers would be needed to maintain law and order for a while longer. The formal surrender was made on 12th September, and Singapore, the Lion City, had returned.

Throughout the events spanning 1942 through to 1945, the Singapore Traction Company remained in exile in far away London. Without any firm knowledge as to what had happened to those members of staff who had remained, nor the condition of property or vehicles, Annual General Meetings were sombre affairs with little firm business with which to deal. Such business as was to hand related to drawn out negotiations with the Inland Revenue and the War Department, and the placing of claims with those Government Departments in connection with the obtaining of reparations for war damage.

By 1944, the news broadcasts were able to show that the tide was turning, and realising that there would be a great rush to place orders for new rolling stock once British industry could revert to peacetime production, the STC Board considered fleet renewal.

There was a wish to continue with trolleybus operation, but the happenings of 1941 and 1942 had proved how vulnerable the fixed equipment was to air attack. Therefore, the worst was assumed, in that Singapore might only be retaken after bombardments from air and sea, so that all of the trolleybus infrastructure could well be destroyed. Accordingly it was decided to order less than half of the prewar fleet, a total of fifty chassis, if indeed there could be found a manufacturer to accept the order. In the event it was taken by Ransomes, Simms, and Jeffries, of Ipswich, who had built trolleybus chassis during the late 1920's and through the 1930's. They had chosen to withdraw from the trolleybus market, instead concentrating on their other lines of production concerned with agricultural machinery, but agreed to supply the Singapore Traction Company—and several other overseas orders—in view of the difficult supply circumstances of the immediate postwar period.

There was little chance of being able to reactivate the last prewar order for Albion chassis, but as good fortune would have it, Vauxhall Motors were able to accept an order for seventy Bedford chassis, with a promise of early delivery subject to prevailing conditions. These buses would mark a return to the use of petrol engined vehicles contrary to previous policy. Shortly thereafter Dennis Brothers were able to accept an order for one hundred Falcon Mark II chassis. As neither manufacturer was a major supplier to the British home market, it was hoped that deliveries could be expedited.

The greatest difficulty to be overcome was dealing with the taxation authorities and agreeing as to whether the Company had been a 'continued' or 'discontinued' business. That matter took years to resolve, but for the present, the Traction Company was set fair to return to the task of serving the city of Singapore.

Chapter Five
1945-46—Slow Return to 'Normality'

7th September 1945 and the Japanese occupation came to an end: there was to follow a decade during which the Traction Company, being a British-owned concern, became the target of political uncertainty through riots and labour disputes, whilst the Chinese buses were able to develop away from the mosquito-bus pattern and progress towards the most modern vehicles which were then available.

Singapore Traction Company

In the most immediate terms, control of all civil matters was taken by the British Military Administration (BMA), which recognised the importance of reintroducing a system of public transport. To this end, they were able to hand back the Traction Company to the management as from 11th September, by which time those European staff members who had been interned in Changi Gaol, had been released and who, with typical devotion to duty, did at least attempt to resume their pre-1942 roles. Alas, the rigours of their imprisonment had taken a severe toll of their strength and most were obliged to either retire or take a prolonged period of sick leave, leaving only three in post. Mr. A. A. Ewing was appointed as General Manager, an interesting historical coincidence for, at one time, Mr. Ewing had been the General Manager of the Shanghai Electric Construction Company and, as an officer of that concern, had also been the first Manager of the Singapore Traction Company, having responsibility for the tramways replacement programme.

Concerning the physical condition of the Company's property, buildings were found to be in a reasonable condition. Where damage had been caused during the 1942 air-raids, repairs had been carried out by the Japanese, although the quality of the materials was very poor—perhaps masonry salvaged from the rubble elsewhere: rebuilding would need to be done when good quality materials became available, at an estimated cost of £14,000.

Office equipment and furnishings were quite good and capable of use until pressing needs had been met. In the workshops, an inventory of small tools showed most to be missing whilst heavy machinery was in the most urgent need of repair and a general programme of renewal needed a high priority.

Out on the road, six route miles of trolleybus overhead equipment and two hundred and twenty-five traction poles had been removed, preventing the reinstatement of trolleybus operations along the lengths of Havelock Road—service 9—and Beach Road—service 11. Oddly enough, an inspection of the fixed equipment revealed that the original thirty-six miles of mains and feeder cables had been increased by two miles, the work having been supervised by the Company's own line Engineer under the supervision of the Japanese.

To view such rolling-stock as remained could only have inspired feelings of utter despair but, at the same time, a sense of wonderment that anything was left at all, bearing in mind that, even by the standards of 1942, the AEC's, with their solid tyres, could at best be termed as obsolete. Little by little, the hulks of the trolleybuses were recovered from the dump, brought into the main workshops so that the engineering staff, using what limited resources they could find, coupled with a vast wealth of experience, could get at least some of them running again—although the Board had expressed their doubts concerning possible trolleybus operation, the local management team knew that they must use whatever they could find—so it was that, by 16th September 1945, twenty were declared to be fit for service, to be used on the two major routes; 2, Geylang to Tanjong Pager, with fifteen vehicles on a five minute headway, and 4, Finlayson Green to Paya Lebar, utilising the other five at a ten minute headway—schedules which must have been calculated with much crossing of fingers or else in the expectations of further trolleybuses becoming available. A strict limit of forty-five passengers maximum had to be applied but, in the event, the public seemed quite content to comply and there was no mad rushing and pushing whenever a trolleybus came into sight; instead, orderly queues formed, this perhaps unnatural behaviour being a relic of stern days of Japanese rule. Twenty-five years later, the Company tried to impose queue barriers at main stops in the central area but, in the 'battles to board', the metal frames were deemed to be dangerous and had to be removed.

Of the motor bus fleet, not all the survivors had been dumped in the depot yards and the staff were obliged to make a thorough search of the town and the rural districts to see if any could be found. Their efforts were spread over a long time but, as a result, forty-nine buses were collected together, of which twenty-two could be repaired reasonably quickly, eleven could be made ready for service only if spare parts could be found or improvised, whilst the remain sixteen were fit

BELOW: Following the surrender of the Japanese forces, the Traction Company found itself with but few serviceable buses with which to resume services. Those few vehicles that had survived the occupation were in a sorry state, like the very tired Albion, STC 29, seen here. Fleet numbers appear to have been carried—A16 in this case—and the registration series was re started at STC 1; both the appropriate plates are in strikingly better condition than the rest of the bus. The STC initials have yet to be reapplied.

only for scrap. The search even went as far as advertising in the 'Straits Times', the issue of 8th November 1946 carrying the appeal:

> "The following omnibus chassis, with or without bodies, belonging to the Singapore Traction Company, have been removed from the Company's premises during the Japanese occupation;
>
> Ford Type 118WF—Quantity nine;
>
> Ford Type 116—quantity two;
>
> Chevrolet—quantity eight;
>
> These chassis were bought in 1941. A suitable reward will be paid to any person furnishing information which will lead to the recovery of all or any of these chassis".

The British Military Administration continued to assist with the recovery and was able to pass a selection of military vehicles to all of the bus operators, these being in the main, of Austin, Chevrolet, Bedford, Dodge and Ford manufacture and the Traction Company was to receive chassis from the last three makes, besides receiving additional aid in the form of army engineers to assist in the workshops for a short while.

In order to meet the most immediate needs, lorry-buses were pressed into service, the only concessions to their new role being small 'windows' cut into the canvas sheeting which formed the 'coachwork' and a set of crude steps anchored at the tailboard. With others, cab and chassis were sent to hard pressed builders who were able to construct a compartment without integration of the cab. Finally, the pressure eased to the extent that chassis alone could be sent for the mounting of conventional bus-style bodywork. An average capacity of thirty seated passengers could be obtained with these bus bodied former military chassis, many of which were able to give ten years of hard service.

The Chinese bus operators

Once the British Military Administration felt justified in issuing them licences, in what form had the Chinese operators survived? Not all had done so:

JURONG OMNIBUS SERVICE became part of GREEN BUS COMPANY;

SELETAR MOTOR BUS COMPANY surrendered its workings to TAY KOH YAT—Mr. Tay Koh Yat thus gaining access to the town area but nonetheless maintained two operations some distance apart, wearing two liveries—his original blue and yellow for the Aljunied Road service and taking the Seletar red and black for what became his principal routes.

The various vehicle maker's local agents were deluged with orders for new chassis, all of which were directed towards manufacturers in the United Kingdom. The competition was tremendous with those manufacturers being swamped by the requirements of the

RIGHT: Utility bodywork, Singapore style. With the return to peacetime conditions, under the British Military Administration, the Chinese bus operators were able to cast off the constraints of their traditional seven-seater and acquired a variety of ex-military truck chassis upon which they constructed 'proper' bus bodies, albeit on the small size, probably about 16-seaters. This view, circa 1946, shows two buses belonging to the Paya Lebar Bus Service; S.2466 is a Ford while S.1151 is a Chevrolet—compare the latter with the STC emergency lorry-bus at the top of page 68. *(D. W. K. Jones*

UPPER LEFT: In order to return public transport quickly to normal, the BMA provided STC with a number of ex-military lorries for use as emergency buses. They had timber steps at the back and canvas tops to keep off sun and rain. For ventilation, large rectangular holes were cut in the canvas and some had roll-down 'blinds' to keep-out driving rain. This Chevrolet lorry-bus carried CL15 on the bonnet, indicating that it was from a stock of vehicles distributed amongst the operators until surviving buses could be made roadworthy. It was seen here working as a bus in 1945. *(D. W. K. Jones)*

LEFT: Trolleybuses were slowly brought back into service as such overhauls as could be managed could be completed. One legacy of the occupation was the loss, forever, of two-class accommodation and a new livery arrangement was introduced—probably in an effort to help make the vehicles look less run-down. The bodysides and rear, above the waist, were given a lick of white paint while the green continued the full length of the car; as they became available, STC transfers were applied to the sides, above the front wheel. Here trolleybus 15, not looking too battered, appears in its fresh paint but, behind, No 32 is still in a very dirty version of the prewar two-class livery. The rear-doorway No 18 is the third trolley in the line. *(D. W. K. Jones*

domestic market, exacerbated by the need of factories to convert from wartime production, together with a constant shortage of basic raw materials. The newly elected Labour Government used the dictum 'Export or Die', so that, when new chassis did start to arrive, in the majority, they were of a variety of designs—Vulcan, Morris, Bedford—and of types rarely seen in Britain.. It is, nevertheless, gratifying to note that British goods were favoured one-hundred percent.

BELOW: Another Chevrolet lorrt-bus, after the addition of heat protection in the form of a sheet-metal sun screen over the roof of the cab. As STC 13 (or is it 134?), CL11 moves away from Finlaysom Green, an AEC 603 trolleybus loads for Paya Lebar.

The return to a limited trolleybus service

There was a slight variation in the scale of fares, increasing the minimum to four cents, up to a maximum of ten cents, with no attempt being made to reintroduce the two-class system. The timetable provided for a start at 7.00am—of course a prompt return was made to the use of local time—working through to 9.00pm. The overstrained vehicles could not cope and efforts were redoubled in the workshop in an effort to provide twelve motor buses to cover the same route. Success in this direction could not be certain and so a form of taxi service was introduced, over Service 2, with a charge of twenty cents per person between Maxwell Market—a mile or so short of Tanjong Pager—and Geylang, and over Service 4 between Paya Lebar and Bras Basah Road with a fare of thirty-five cents. Truly, this was a return of the mosquito bus, albeit with official sanction, but their presence proved to be so popular with the public, despite the high fares, that a strain was placed on the finances of the Traction Company at a time when there was a desperate need to gather in every possible cent. Relief would only come with the receipt of new rolling-stock but the indecision of the Directors concerning the possibility

ABOVE: Although photographed in the early 1950's, after it had become a school bus, S 3926 displays typical bodywork as fitted to the ex-military lorry-buses as resources permitted during 1946. The body shows distinctive STC design features.

trolleybuses did not return. Service 6, however, did return with full trolleybus operation from 22nd December 1945 with a very gentle twenty-two minute frequency, indicating that a further three AEC's had become available for service.

Slowly back to normal

Viewing the transport industry as a whole, with such a dearth of road transport being available, in hindsight, it seems a most odd decision taken by Malayan Railways when choosing to close most of the suburban stations on the Island—at Tanglin Halt, Bukit Panjang and Kranji, although Tanglin did continue in use for military specials. The closures took effect from April 1946 and it was not until 8th May that the Traction Company was able to reintroduce a further fragment of a previous service—a one vehicle shuttle working a fifteen minute shuttle linking the Service 10 terminus at Moulmein Road with Thompson Police Station. Little by little, a measure of normality was returning, not only concerning vehicles and services but also such items as the reintroduction of concessionary fares for school children—one suggestion which was not accepted was the reintroduction of the coloured route boards as used pre-1942.

Coincidental with the renaming of Grove Road to Mountbatten Road, the first Bedford OB's were becoming available for service and it became possible to re-establish the Katong network of routes. At the same time, land in Aljunied Road which had been purchased before the war, was developed as an open air garage, destined to become the home of the Bedfords for the next ten years.

On the reverse of the Traction Company's tickets were printed the words 'Incorporated in the United Kingdom'. This fact of being a 'foreign' business brought difficulties which were not experienced by the owners of the Chinese bus companies.

In the Chairman's Report for 1945, we find the words:

"...there are other difficulties to be faced. Owing in the main to the shortage of food and tobacco, the high cost of living, the unrest inevitable after a war and the low standard of morality inculcated by the Japanese, the indigenous staff require a firm, tactful and sympathetic handling in order to bring them to a state of efficiency".

Sombre words indeed, for it must be true to observe the whole of the population as being in a state of perplexity for, whilst there had been great rejoicing at the ending of the Occupation, there was a section of society who had no wish to see the return of a British administration for, in their surrender, the British had 'lost face'. As yet there were no true Singaporeans but a mixture of many racial groups owing their first loyalties to the countries of their grandparents' birth.

of renewed trolleybus operation resulted in only fifty new trolleybuses being ordered (half the number required if the full pre-1942 service was to be reintroduced—if, in fact, a United Kingdom manufacturer could be found).

RANSOMES, SIMS AND JEFFERIES, of Ipswich, had been pioneers in the evolution of the trackless tram into the trolleybus but, they were also producers of high quality agricultural machinery. It was in this direction that they wished to trade but, recognising the difficulties current in Singapore, they did accept the order for fifty trolleybus chassis with, delivery to commence during 1947.

The Public Notices column of the Straits Times dated 13th December 1945 contained a most significant announcement:

'An omnibus service will operate between Balistier Road and Outram Road at the General Hospital, via Balistier Road at Moulmein Road, Lavender Street, Jalan Besar, Bencoolen Street, Bras Basah Road, Hill Street and New Bridge Road. The service frequency will be every ten minutes, subject to breakdowns which unfortunately are fairly frequent these days due to lack of maintenance during the Japanese Occupation. Every possible effort will be made to maintain the scheduled frequency but the indulgence of the public is asked in the event of a breakdown. Stopping places will be clearly marked on poles and fare tables will be exhibited in vehicles. This route is normally operated by trolleybuses and will revert to this form of traction as soon as trolleybuses are available.'

Thus the return of Service 10 and, although the overhead wiring was fully restored and maintained for a further fifteen years,

Indonesia and Indo-China were experiencing the pains of anti-colonial violence, whilst the civil war raging in China caused the overseas Chinese to take sides, either by inclination or under pressure. Secret Societies flourished and violence became commonplace. Against this background of conflict, many of the Company's staff found themselves held in a dilemma of conflicting loyalties; on the one hand to offer their support to a good employer—as those with long service were swift to admit—but on the other, recognised a growing nationalistic awareness prompted by outside influences.

Whilst in the business world the Company would not be alone in needing to face such problems, it was too easily seen as a target—as the next few years would painfully show.

The first postwar strike was called on 26th October, with demands that those men who had been serving up to December 1941 should be awarded a large bonus, equivalent to three months wages, plus a permanent increase of forty per cent on current wage rates. So excessive were these demands that no room was available for negotiation and an

BELOW: By the end of 1946, the first of the Bedford OB type buses had entered service to release some of the lorry-buses, either to return to being lorry-buses or to be fitted with coachbuilt bus bodies. Here Bedford OB, STC 182 (with short-lived fleet number—B33—on the bonnet side. Lurking in the left background is a lorry-bus with a 'coachbuilt' body but retaining the separate lorry cab. (*Straits Times*

appeal was made to the British Military Administration for help. Servicemen were made available to work on the buses. As a result, the strike collapsed and there was a return to work as from noon on 1st November.

Other difficulties were to follow, each of a different nature—there was the 'rice strike' of 28th August 1946, based on a demand for the provision of canteen facilities. Then came an attempt to organise a measure of self protection: hooligans and pickpockets were many and, following a number of assaults on and thefts from conductors, the staff decided to take matters into their own hands. 5th October was chosen as the day upon which concerted action would be taken and the 'battle plan' was for groups of off-duty crews to gather at selected busy traffic points. Should the conductor of a passing bus or trolleybus suspect that a pickpocket was on board, he would give a prearranged signal and the vehicle would halt alongside the waiting group who, in turn, would apprehend and question the suspect—not too gently, one would suspect: if duly discovered, the pickpocket would be marched away to the nearest police station under heavy escort. Needless to say, not everyone subjected to such a challenge accepted the situation kindly and fights are known to have broken out. The crews declared, however, that their action had been a success and they had 'cleaned-up Singapore's buses'.

As previously remarked, the Chinese operators were not disrupted to the same extent as Traction Company but they did have their tribulations which came in rapid succession and coincidentally with those of the Traction Company, the latter seeming to indicate that outside forces were possibly engaged in spreading dissent. The Keppel Bus Company, the Green Bus and later Tay Koh Yat made an agreement not to employ further staff until new buses were delivered. Green Bus withdrew the dismissal notices which had been served on seventeen ticket inspectors and timekeepers, whilst at Tay Koh Yat the seven demands made by striking crews were deemed to be too severe, the strikers were dismissed and new staff engaged.

Long distance coach travel

1946 was not without historical highlights, one of which was the formation of Singapore to Malacca Coaches, Limited, with an office and terminus at 35, Beach Road and later known as Sing Lian Express Limited, incorporated in the Federation of Malaya. The Japanese had removed the railway line between Gemas and Malacca and the railway administration were too hard pressed with their main line refurbishment programme to replace the track—and it never has been! Long distance coach travel was unknown up to this time and great enterprise was shown in obtaining Bedford chassis and the fitting of bodywork which provided passengers with a greater degree of comfort than had been experienced hitherto. The first departure was made on 20th December 1946; the original timetable being 7.30am and 2.30pm, with a very reasonable single fare of ten dollars.

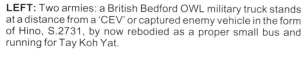

LEFT: Two armies: a British Bedford OWL military truck stands at a distance from a 'CEV' or captured enemy vehicle in the form of Hino, S.2731, by now rebodied as a proper small bus and running for Tay Koh Yat.

BELOW LEFT: By the end of 1946, the Chinese bus companies had fitted bus bodies to their military lorry chassis and typical of the type was this Ford, S 1377, of Katong Bedok Bus Service. It was common for this form of bus to have an open rear platform, more often associated with the traditional double-decker.

BELOW: At the same time as the unbodied chassis of the STC Bedford OB's were arriving in Singapore, a number of fully bodied Bedford OWB's with British austerity bodywork appeared. These may have been ex-military—for whom they were standard issue—or they may have been supplied new, through the Crown Agents. Here S 6254 is seen in the service of a private bus company, school or similar.

Chapter Six
1947—Squeeze Corruption and New Developments

Once the British Military Administration thought it fit and proper to re-issue licences, the Chinese owners went quietly about their business, rebuilding their fleets in order to cut the headways on their established routes. Being confined to the rural areas, the owners were content with buses which had started their lives as army lorries, for these were well suited to the winding roads which connected the *kampongs* located in semi-jungle terrain, besides being capable of accepting substantial overloading. Not so with the Traction Company, with an urban network to reintroduce, and a perhaps more sophisticated passenger to cater for, calling for heavier duty custom-designed passenger chassis, only to be obtained from the United Kingdom. 1947 dawned, and was filled with new hope, for this was the year which should see the first of the new trolleybuses arriving, and Dennis Falcons available for traffic. For a start, 6th January saw the Thompson Road Police Station to Moulmein Road shuttle being extended towards town by way of Rangoon Road and Serangoon Road, designated service 19.

There was the continued problem of a backlog of maintenance on all buses (other than the new Bedfords) which had been pressed into service in very poor condition, and STC still needed to cope with serious overcrowding. The situation came to a tragic head with the death of an elderly lady who, being pressed against an emergency exit by ever greater numbers of persons trying to force themselves aboard the bus in question, fell into the roadway when the door burst open, and she was killed. In an effort to prevent such a tragedy being repeated, bars of wood were nailed across all emergency doors of old buses and the trolleybuses, whilst conductors were issued with instructions to ensure that no passenger was to travel in such a position that his or her weight was fully against the door (although in hindsight it is difficult to see how such an instruction could be enforced). In a public statement the Manager said that, in the event of an emergency, the bars could be easily ripped away.

The first post-occupation Royal Visit was made on 17th January 1947 by H.R.H. The Duke of Gloucester, an event which provided several interesting traffic diversions and service revisions. For example, service 1 between Keppel Harbour and Tank Road, using motor buses pending the delivery of new trolley buses, was able to cope with two variations away from the normal route without difficulty, viz., to avoid the focal point of the ceremonials on The Padang by working via Battery Road, Chulia Street, Canal Road and North Bridge Road, and again, using New Bridge Road and Cross Street in order to gain access to Cecil Street, so vacating the whole of the business district for the duration of the visit. Such could not have been arranged had trolleybuses been in use, and it is pure speculation as to whether this flexibility of operation had been noted by the management, for this service was destined never to return to trolleybus operation, despite the overhead wiring being kept in place. Of the "true" trolleybus routes, both the 4 and the 6 services were precluded from reaching their normal terminus at Finlayson Green, instead being transferred to Chulia Street, a town terminal which

was to see little use after 1945. Of the "regular" motor bus operations, services 16 to 20 were still able to reach Collyer Quay, but needed to make their approaches around the back of town in similar fashion to the service 1. Of particular interest, once normal routings were resumed, service 1 was extended from Tank Road by way of Clemenceau Avenue to reach the terminus of trolleybus 6 at Newton.

The problem of Squeeze

January ended as a simmering volcano of industrial unrest. The Oxford Dictionary defines the word "Squeeze" as "......... forced extraction by .... official, illicit commission, percentage on goods purchased, extorted by native servant". Insofar as the coffers of the Traction Company were concerned, this simple word represented a tremendous burden, for it could be practised by many conductors (although let it not be thought for a single moment that all of the staff were involved), either for their own benefit or else to pass on as instructed by criminal or subversive political elements. The methods used were varied, the most common being the issue of a ticket of a lower face value than of the actual fare being paid, with the difference being pocketed by the conductor. Then there was the collecting of used tickets from passengers as they alighted in anticipation of resale, time and time again, although this method did require the cooperation of the passengers. A third method was for the collec-

ABOVE: " ...confined to the rural areas, the owners were content with buses which had started their lives as army lorries, for these were well suited to the winding roads which connected the *kampongs* located in semi-jungle terrain..." In such surroundings and negotiating an incomplete culvert on a newly made-up road near Pasir Ris, is Paya Lebar Bus Service ex-military Ford, S 8097, with open rear platform.

tion of fares as the passengers alighted, without the issue of any ticket, and only if there was a hint of an Inspector working the route would the dishonest conductor make the effort to move around his vehicle. This was a highly organised system of theft, and those conductors involved would need the cooperation of other employees in order that their misappropriation of fares could pass without detection, and shares for drivers, ticket clerks, time keepers and the like had to allowed for. However, so lucrative were the fields to be harvested that it was said at the time that any man seeking to be employed as a conductor would be willing to pay something like fifty dollars "coffee money" to the right person in order to obtain a job. To fight back, the Anti-corruption Branch was formed, manned by European Inspectors drawn from the ranks of servicemen who were being demobilised, and for a while activities on both sides came to resemble Chicago during the worst days of prohibition. These Inspectors would travel in groups using Jeeps, and they would stop a bus manned by a suspect crew at a time and place where such action would be least expected: once the bus had been stopped, one Inspector would stand guard over the crew, whilst a second took charge of the conductor's supply of tickets, whilst others made a painstaking examination of the passenger's tickets. However, it might be one thing to catch a guilty man, but it was another matter entirely to bring him before the Court and obtain a conviction. Very few passengers would be willing to stand as witness, either because of racial loyalty or mindful of the fact of becoming a possible target for revenge. In a four year period, only twenty cases of "squeeze" were proven before the Courts, and even so the conductors prosecuted had to be allowed to return to their duties. The dice of corruption were certainly loaded against the Company—it was said that the total loss was several hundred pounds every day, although at the time nobody could be absolutely certain of the true sum. What was sure was that in order to survive, the haemorrhaging would have to be stopped: to this end the management drew up secret plans, and on a given day every bus on a chosen route carried an Inspector, from first bus out in the morning until last bus in at night, so that the amount of money extracted by "squeeze" along that route could be determined. As a representative body, the Union was very angry indeed and, on the morning following this exercise, the General Manager had to face a deputation, whose demands were that these "insulting and provocative measures" should not be repeated, on penalty of strike action. What else could the General Manager do, save to appeal to the Union to lend its strength to assist in the stamping out of this curse?

Whilst it was conductors who played the key role, drivers devised a scheme in order to pass warnings back through a variety of signals. Should it be that the bus had just been checked or a Jeep had been spotted lurking in a side street, then it was simple to pass a message across to an oncoming vehicle, either by a code flashed on the headlamps or played on the horn—without stopping that information was relayed to the saloon, either by the backfiring of an engine, or a heavy crashing of the gearbox, a sudden bout of oversteering, flicking of interior lights, or the playing of a tattoo upon the horn, all of these were means to warn. Of a far more serious nature in view of the safety of passengers, if a sudden check of all buses on a particular route was put into operation, there might be a sudden climb in the accident rate in which buses were involved, whilst minor mechanical defects might develop and spread like a rash across the chosen route.

The Strike of 1947

Although strikes had not been unknown during the post occupation period, the first major confrontation came early in 1947. At a trial wherein three conductors stood charge with assaulting an Inspector, and were found guilty and duly convicted, the General Manager took the opportunity to speak of the evil of "squeeze" whilst in open court, and to make remarks concerning a measure of unruliness amongst some of the employees. Having due regard of the delicate balance of industrial relations in general, and within the Company in particular, in hindsight it might be thought that the time and place had been ill chosen, although it is easy to understand how there was a desire to let the public have a greater understanding of the traumatic conditions under which a resumption of normal services was being undertaken. Subversive elements within the Union saw a golden opportunity to create trouble and, after a meeting lasting two and a half hours, laid their plans.

A diary of events reads thus:

29th January: the Union Meeting

30th January: forty-eight hours notice of strike is given, if demands are not met, fifteen in all.

31st January: the Union makes an approach to the Municipal Commissioners seeking an investigation into the workings of the Traction Company, based on the opinion that "in most modern cities throughout the world public transport is provided by public bodies, why not in Singapore?"

1st February: the fifteen demands not having been met, the Union calls for a strike to commence at 8.00 am., the demands being:

a) an apology for the statements made in Court,

b) a fifty per cent increase in pay

c) the provision of living quarters, or allowance in lieu

d) full uniforms for each man

e) a lawyer to be provided to defend any criminal charge

f) buses to be kept in good order

g) two months back pay

h) a new scales of wages to be adopted

i) double pay after midnight

j) conductors to be paid interest on their deposit of thirty five dollars

k) a bonus of half a months pay to the given to each man on completion of six months service

l) raincoats for line workers

m) evidence to be collected from passengers when a conductor is charged with corruption

n) Inspectors not to issue unnecessary warnings.

(Such was the atmosphere surrounding the start of this dispute that there seemed little doubt that any form of settlement would be a

LEFT: During the previous year, 1946, the first express service had commenced—operated by Singapore and Malacca Coaches Ltd. between the places of those names. Branded 'Singapore–Malacca Express', both the fleetname and company title were changed to become Sing Lian Express Limited, registered, in the Federation of Malaya. Their original Bedford OB's were later replaced by Vulcans as seen here where we see a typical river crossing in early postwar days.

long time in coming, and thus the Municipal Commissioners, through the Registrar of vehicles, gave consent for the Chinese bus owners to commence operating over Traction Company routes.)

3rd February: Two further resolutions are passed by the Union, "That the Singapore Traction Company be sent a letter demanding the reinstatement of two dismissed workers" and "That the general body of the Union is thankful to the City Fathers for asking the Chinese Bus Companies to run their buses over STC routes for the convenience of the travelling public, and that the Union earnestly hopes that the City Fathers will allow the owners to run their buses on the Traction routes after the settlement of the strike because of the inefficiency of Singapore Traction Company buses and their inadequacy to meet public demands".

4th February: When called upon for comment, the General Manager said that the second resolution was most unusual, as the employees sought to destroy their own livelihoods.

6th February: leaflets are discovered to be in circulation addressed from the Union to taxi owners, seeking cash for the upkeep of a strike fund. Fifteen dollars a day for each taxi was being asked, whilst similar approaches were reported by the private bus owners.

7th February: At last, the principals decided to meet with a view to reaching an end to the strike. When asked how the men manage without any wages the Union Secretary told of many having found other jobs, of drivers being sent to work at the Naval Base, others returning to transport by pedalling tri-shaws, and mechanics finding a good supply of odd jobs.

12th February: The Union announce their agreement to the dispute being submitted to arbitration.

24th February: Intimidation hits hard at the private bus services: so great the determination of the Chinese owners that they were able to place a total of one hundred and forty buses into service between 7.00 am and late evening. However, on this day, by 9.00 am only nine buses were still operating, and there were reports of private crews having been beaten. Two buses were then provided with the protection of four Inspectors and four policemen, so that arrests made during the morning discouraged further intimidation and by 10.30 am buses in service had reached sixty eight.

5th March: Whether or not the Union ordered a return to work, the whole matter of the strike would be the subject of a Court of Enquiry, a decision reached by the Government following the fruitless outcome of numerous meetings between the parties. As to the question of arbitration, whilst the Manager was still in favour, there was rejection by the Union.

8th March: A change of mind on the part of the Union, who now accepted the role of an independent arbiter.

11th March: A further change of mind, and the Union declined to accept a return to work or the setting up of a Conciliation Board unless their fifteen demands were met in full.

12th March: Drastic Government action might be needed to be taken under the provisions of the Essential Regulations (Requisition of Vehicles) Order, 1947, which had passed into law some ten days previously and following the complete breakdown in negotiations between the parties. Under the Order the Government takes the powers to requisition, through the Registrar of Vehicles, any vehicle registered within Singapore, and there was a widespread public opinion that such action would be the only means of breaking the deadlock in order to get this essential service running again. Whilst it is true that the private buses were providing a service of a kind, this could only be at the expense of the rural communities from whence the vehicles were withdrawn besides which the buses themselves were of a low capacity, so that all were functioning in a seriously overcrowded condition.

17th March: The Management takes a strong line, and issues an ultimatum to the strikers, in that any employee who fails to report for duty three days hence would be liable for dismissal. The following was published as an advertisement in the local press: "The Company earnestly appeals to all employees now on strike to resume work on Wednesday, 19th March, 1947, on the understanding that the Government will take steps to investigate the demands submitted before the strike. Police protection will be offered to all employees resuming duty. The staff bus will run between Tanjong Pagar and Geylang, and also on Rangoon road, on 19th March, 1947, between 6.30 am and 8.00 am, to pick up employees. Employees failing to report for duty by 19th March are liable to be dismissed."

18th March: A small number of staff reported for work, but not enough to have buses back in service. They were the more senior members of the office and workshops departments, and although there was a certain degree of intimidation directed towards them, matters were settled without recourse to police action.

19th March: No matter how many or how few crews reported for duty, the Company was determined to have as many buses back into service as possible. The staff buses would be running as promised, and each would be given the protection of police Jeeps, whilst further police protection would be mounted for all seeking

LEFT: With no sign of the Ransomes trolleybuses promised for delivery in 1947, the ageing AEC's, the worse for their wartime neglect, were required to soldier-on, their ranks reduced to about forty-eight from an original 108 units. Here No 52 shares Collyer Quay with a military vehicle in February 1948 (a couple of months after the currency of this chapter). *(Major E. A. S. Cotton—H. Luff collection*

73

to return to work.

20th March: The efforts of the previous day sank as if a lead balloon. Clerks and technical workers were prevented from entering the Head Office by extreme provocation, although this was later denied by the Union, with the Secretary maintaining that it was the continued presence of the police which was the real intimidation.

That day saw the opening session of the Court of Enquiry, who had for the first item on the agenda for consideration the original fifteen demands. The public gallery was crowded with strikers.

22nd March : The Singapore Ratepayers Association makes its views known, urging Government action to requisition buses, military lorries and taxis in order to provide at least a skeleton service over all routes, not only under the prevailing circumstances but at any time when the Traction Company be brought to a halt by strike action. These expressed thoughts provide an interesting insight into the manner in which the public regarded the situation within which the Company was obliged to function, in that despite the high standards which might be sought in the long term, the threat of industrial actions could well remain a constant feature for the future.

26th March: The finances of the Company came before the Court of Enquiry, and in concert with other burdens to be detailed the following day, the effects of the strike meant that fares would have to be increased when workings resumed.

27th March: Hopeful signs from both sides, with the Union deciding to drop all claims in respect of back pay, whilst the Company agreed to restore the prewar practice whereby the men were allowed a twenty minute break at midday.

On behalf of the Company, the Court of Enquiry heard of fifty three buses being used by the Malayan Auxiliary Medical Service as naval ambulances and troop carriers and, not only had the buses not been recovered, but not a single cent had been paid for their hire; a claim against the military authorities was pending. Later it was also stated that, through the good offices of the British Government, the Company had made a claim against the Japanese Government for the sum of 2,750,000 Singapore dollars in respect of material damage sustained during the occupation.

1st April: The Union start the presentation of their case to be completed by 3rd April.

6th April: The President of the Court requests the strikers to return to work forthwith, confirming that the Court's findings, whatever they might be, would be retrospective from the date upon which work was resumed.

7th April: A Union meeting spurned the appeal, and further, issued a statement of denial that the strike was being financed through "Red" funds.

16th April: The only action which seems possible is to tell the public what is happening, and hope to win their support. The General Manager published a statement in which he alleged that there was continued intimidation of those staff members seeking to return to work.. But for this adverse action it would have been possible to have several buses in service. On the subject of wages, these could only be linked to the resources of the Company, and already the employees were receiving basic rates eighty one per cent higher than applied during 1941.

3rd May: Intimidation looks in another direction, with some strikers travelling in gangs on the private buses, forcing those conductors to give them free rides, and a number of cases of assault were being reported. At least one Chinese bus company was known to be employing strikers as "extra" conductors.

6th May: In the findings of the Court of Enquiry, all round pay increases are urged, such proposals being accepted by the management.

7th May: The Union vote to call off their strike "in the interests of the public and children".

8th May: 1,200 Traction Company employees were due to return to work after this strike lasting nearly fifteen weeks. At first only a skeleton service would be on offer, but within a week there were hopes that one hundred motor buses and fifty trolleybuses would be available: several new buses had arrived and would be placed into immediate commission, whilst the old fleet would require cleaning and a backlog of defects put to rights. The Union considered that they had won this particular battle, and as a form of victory parade, 1,000 men drove through the streets in a fleet of ten lorries, arriving at Mackenzie Road at 11.45 am. With the Traction Company back in business the Chinese buses were required to be withdrawn from the city area, and would make their

LEFT: 1947 saw the entry into service of the first of the Dennis Falcons for STC and here one can be seen alongside a line of small buses on 1946 Ford 'School Bus' chassis which were to remain in service into the mid 1950's. STC 62 was bodied by Lee Kiat Seng.

	final journeys into town at 4.00 am.
16th May:	Increased fares come into operation, the new scale being ten cents for three sections, fifteen cents for five sections and twenty cents for more than five sections. Thus the five cents fare was abolished and the maximum charge remained unchanged at twenty cents.
24th May:	Weighing three and a half pounds, the full report of the Court of Enquiry is published , involving six hundred and twenty four closely typed pages.
2nd June:	"There are signs that in the near future there may be an attempt at concentrated action with the object of bringing about a complete stoppage of public transport in omnibus services". This warning was contained in the Annual Report of the Registrar of Vehicles and, in making further reference to strikes, continued "Viewed generally it may be said that the organisation behind the strikes and other attempted strikes has shown considerable subtlety in creating disaffection in one company at a time". Would there be worse to come? Indeed there would. The Report throws further light on prevailing conditions, for the staff working in that Department it was said that they were dispirited and confused, having been put completely "out of gear" working to the (British) military system. Over a period of many years the Department had been constructed around a very efficient card index system of records and whilst the Japanese had, with modifications, attempted to keep the system in being, it was a matter of considerable regret that the British Military Administration had allowed it to fall into complete misuse.

1947 was not a good year for the Traction Company, and the scars left by the dispute would take a long time to heal, if ever they would, for so long as the Company remained British owned. The determination to return to an efficient service remained firm, and deliveries of new buses would be a salvation, but in the United Kingdom, fuel shortages, and hard winter conditions, caused delivery dates to slip away from targets. The political undercurrents in Singapore made life very difficult for the law abiding citizens, but for all of the difficulties, there were brighter signs to see, most particularly as the private owners thrived and expanded. Nevertheless, the "Letters to the Editor" columns were filled with demands that services be improved, that buses should be less dangerous, and that new routes be established in all parts of the town. Singapore to Malacca Coaches

were doing very well, and were able to increase their timetables to three departures daily, at 7.30 am, 11.30 am and 3.00 am, as from 2nd August, besides providing an intermediate fare to Muar at eight dollars.

Rolling-stock

Long past the promised delivery date, the first twenty-five Dennis Falcon buses had entered service, whilst other chassis were either with the body builders, aboard several ships spanning half the world, or still awaiting construction at Guildford. Of the Ransomes products there remained no sign, and the AEC's had to soldier on: by June their number had risen to fifty-one. This total was to fall again when, during the evening of 17th June, the entire front portions of two shop-houses were wrecked by a trolleybus which ran off the road near the junction of Victoria Street with Jalan Sultan. Great damage was caused by the vehicle ramming the main brick support pillars of the houses, bringing tons of timber, debris and even furniture onto the front portion. This was another loss which could be ill afforded, and by the end of the year the number available for service was down to forty-six.

Changi comes into town

An event of greater long term import occurred on 15th August when the Changi Bus Company commenced the operation of an extension of their main route, from Geylang Serau inwards over the route of the 2 trolleybus, to a terminus at Union Jack Club in North Bridge Road, opposite the Anglican Cathedral. The Traction Company Ordinance was only dented, not breached at this stage, for passengers could not be taken up nor set down on the express section from Geylang, and the headway provided over the extended section was only every half an hour (between 8.00 am and 12 midnight). Through journeys took the service number 1, Geylang to Changi Village became 2, and the short branch from Geylang to Kampong Melayu Malay Settlement service 3: the branch line brought in additional revenue to the Changi concern, for hitherto those residents seeking to reach town used the red bus in order to reach Geylang, and then needed to travel onwards by trolleybus. Instead a transfer ticket was introduced whereby they could arrive at the interchange point on a 3 and finish their ride on a 1. In fact, the extension, and the town terminus, could be seen as a convenience especially provided for Royal Air Force personnel based at Changi, and soldiers from Selarang Barracks, and for them special return fares were introduced,

RIGHT: Although small buses, the Bedford OB's were at least new and reliable and, together with the Dennis Falcons did much to raise moral—both in the Traction Company and with its passengers. STC 244 was working the 18, a route long associated with the Bedfords.

being one dollar for the complete trip, or eighty cents from Changi to Geylang. Otherwise the fare scale from the Union Jack Club to Geylang and beyond was calculated at five cents per mile, with a discount on a single through journey at sixty cents (a saving of ten cents).

First Express Services

At about this time, advertisements were placed in the newspapers seeking a new type of employee, namely bus conductresses, who, once appointed and clad in smart uniform, would work for a new company about to be launched, the SINGAPORE–JOHORE EXPRESS. The success of the Malacca Express had demonstrated the need for a similar facility linking Singapore with its neighbour across The Causeway, Jahore Bahru. True, there was a reasonable train service provided by Malayan Railways, but as ever the siting of the Singapore station proved to be an inconvenience for the short distance traveller. The Green Bus Company provided the normal stage service, but as yet the buses used were lacking in comfort, and with so many stops the journey was tedious over the full distance. This new express service had to cope with a serious geographical disadvantage, in that the Singapore terminal was located at Rochor, some two

miles distant from the main commercial centre, and passengers seeking to reach town needed to change to trolleybus 6 in order to complete their journey. Nevertheless, with a single fare of eighty cents and running non-stop between the terminals, the venture was an instant success (whether the location of the terminus had been as a measure of protection under the Traction Company Ordinance is pure speculation, although no harm would have come to the Company even if the Malacca Express terminal in Beach Road had been selected). By 1955, the express continued to prosper, with headways based at every few minutes throughout the day, and the fare still less than two dollars. Building on the success of the their main line, Singapore–Johore Express were able to provide a second service, although this could not be available to the general public, serving the security area of the Naval Base, and working thence to Jahore Bahru.

A further significant event was the reintroduction of service 3 from the 28th September, starting from Outram Road, but running beyond the prewar terminus at Post 310 to Geylang, perhaps in a bid to counter the new competition from Changi Bus: speculation which is given credibility in that scarce motor buses were used pending the availability of more trolleybuses.

LEFT: A line-up of Bedford OB's at the official launch of the Singapore–Johore Express Service, with S 630 nearest the camera. This service crossed the causeway from the northern part of Singapore island to Johore Bahru, the southernmost major town in Johore State, Federated Malay States, running parallel to the Green Bus service but, unlike the latter stopping local route, the Express ran without scheduled stop from centre to centre. Both services continue in the 1990's, the former Green Bus service now being Singapore Bus Service Route 180. More comfortable vehicles have always been used by the Express and the early Bedfords were no exception when compared with contemporary buses on the same model chassis.

LOWER LEFT: By 1955, when this photo was taken, the same OB's remained in use, supplemented by Vulcans. By virtue of its later SC-series registration, SC2811 was probably from a later batch of OBs, following the original vehicles which were S-series. All Bedfords and Vulcans had 2 + 1 seating and the Bedfords sat 21 passengers. SC 2811 is seen here, followed by Vulcan SH 106—a number re-used and still current in the mid-1990's.

Chapter Seven

1948–1955—Planting the Seeds of Change

ABOVE: 1948 dawns and the AECs still gallantly soldier on. Despite tremendous efforts by the engineering staff, the number available for service by April had fallen to forty-one. Fortunately, on 22nd April the first two Ransomes trolleybuses entered service on the Paya Lebar route amidst the slower AECs. Here AEC No 51 passes the Mosque whilst running on Route 2 during what must have been its last days in service. Alos of interest is the Ford taxi, S 1391, in the centre foreground. *(F. W. York collection*

The events of the previous year were brought to the attention of the Traction Company shareholders during the summer of 1948 with the distribution of the Annual Report and Accounts for 1947, parts of which read (it should be remembered that STC was a British company and the Report was made to the shareholders in London):

"....coming to the accounts, the loss for the year amounts to £37,830. The main causes for this loss are the Strike which lasted from 1st February to 8th May, 1947, which involved a complete paralysis of the undertaking, and the cost of keeping old vehicles on the road.

The Strike was an unnecessary proceeding and could have been avoided, without detriment to the employees, had they accepted the proposal put forward at the outset that the matters in dispute be referred to arbitration. Ultimately, the Government directed an enquiry into the whole affair to be made by a High Court Judge, who made a report recommending certain concessions. Effect to these recommendations was given by the Company and as a result the fares charged to the public were amended, the amended fares coming into force in May 1947: in the absence of any further upheaval they should permit the undertaking to run at a profit.

As will be seen from the profit and loss account, the amount allowed for depreciation has increased from £15,856 to £40,230. This increase is to be accounted for by the heavy provisions which must be made in respect of second-hand vehicles acquired since 1945 and in respect of new vehicles which have been put into service. The cost of the new vehicles is in effect double the prewar cost. Owing to more new vehicles being put into service, this item will increase during the current year and probably during the following year.

Good progress has been made in the rehabilitation programme. Of the one hundred Dennis Falcon chassis ordered in this country in 1945, eighty-eight have been shipped, of which

seventy-three have arrived in Singapore. Of those that have arrived in Singapore sixty-nine have been fitted with bodies and sixty-seven of these are on the roads, whilst four are at the body-builders.

Of the fifty new trolleybuses ordered by the Company, twenty-eight have been shipped, of which nineteen have arrived in Singapore ... It is anticipated that before the end of the Company's financial year (and remember, this Report was being delivered during mid-1948) all chassis of both classes will have arrived in Singapore and that nearly all will have been fitted with bodies and be in operation".

Reading between the lines it is possible to see an expression of hope that 1948 would prove to be a better year than that which had gone before, for to be otherwise could only mean disaster. In fact, during the early weeks of the New Year the workshops of Lee Kiat Seng started with the construction of the first new trolleybus bodies, although the speed at which this work could be carried out tended to be restricted by the volume of work in hand and in connection with the equally pressing demand for new motor buses, added to which there was still a considerable shortage of vital components. Nevertheless, a target date was set for the entry into service of the first of the new trolleybuses during the first week of March.

There was a further complete stoppage of services on 22nd February: during the previous week an on-duty conductor received serious stab wounds from which he died. As a mark of respect to him, and in order to bring public attention to the sometimes violent conditions under which traffic staff were obliged to work, the whole of the staff set aside that day as a period of mourning, with Management joining the funeral march.

The Ransomes trolleybuses arrive

A further one-day stoppage was in reply to a call made by the Singapore Federation of Trade Unions, this on 23rd April, and seen as a purely political disruption, but very much a great pity,

the motor bus fleet. The window frames appear to have remained unglazed, having the slatted screens for use during the monsoons, but some Ransomes appear to have been fitted with droplight windows of either perspex or glass. The greatest advance in comfort for the passenger, however, was the fitting of pneumatic tyres, so farewell to the loud rumbles and vibrations so closely associated with trolleybus travel. However, somebody spotted a legal problem with their introduction, in that section 18 of the original Ordinance of 1925 stated that no car should be used by the Company which, when fully loaded, exceeded eight tons in weight, and that cars could be so designed as to provide first and second class accommodation (although the operative word was 'could' and not 'should'). Somewhat belatedly there was enacted the Singapore Traction (Amendment) Ordinance, 1949, of which section 2 in part provided that "no car shall be used by the Company if the weight transmitted to the road surface by any of its two wheels, in line transversely, exceeds eight tons, or the sum of the weights so transmitted by all it's wheels exceeds, in the case of a car with more than four wheels, fourteen tons ... *provided*, that in the case of a trolleybus such maximum weights may be exceeded by ten hundredweights and no more, in each case respectively ... The weight transmitted ... shall be taken to be the weight when the car is complete and fully equipped for service with a full supply of

for it was on the previous day that the first five of the new trolleybuses was actually brought into service. The Paya Lebar route was chosen to receive them, the scheduled round trip time forced by the continued presence of the venerable AEC's having to be maintained until the complete working could be taken over by the new vehicles, at which point a general speeding up could be introduced. Meanwhile, actual operation became somewhat embarrassing, as even with the most careful driving skills, the new easily caught up with the old, and bunching was the order of the day. By this time the AEC fleet had reduced to forty-one, and the miracles which had kept them going could not be repeated for very much longer.

The 'new' represented a revolution when compared with the 'old', constructed to the dimensions then applying (in the United Kingdom) and having a maximum passenger capacity of fifty-seven persons, of whom thirty-five would be seated on cushioned perimeter benches. There was no intermediate bulkhead, a sure sign that the 'class' system was ended for ever. If seen in the United Kingdom context, then the bodywork could be placed to the mid-1930's form of design, but when viewed in comparison with all other public service vehicles at work in Singapore, they were able to represent the very last word, a view given emphasis by the choice of livery which included streamlining in cream, a touch of modernity which worked better with these trolleybuses than with

Turning circles for the Ransomes trolleybuses

One consequence of the introduction of the new trolleybuses was that adjustments were requires to the overhead wire at terminal points. The AEC 603's had 11ft 8 in wheelbases, which meant that they could turn fairly easily in a confined space but the new Ransomes had a wheelbase five feet longer, therefore the overhead line department was faced with making adjustments to the wiring at turning points. At Paya Lebar, an extension of the route some 200 yards was needed to reach a point where the roadway had sufficient width for the new, longer trolleybuses to make a 'U' turn. At other terminals, kerbs were set back and wiring was repositioned but, even so, Outram Road terminus was so confined that dewirements were commonplace and at Brash Basah Road, drivers frequently found it necessary to reverse a little in order to complete a turn.

RIGHT: Paya Lebar trolleybus turning circle, showing the widened road opposite the Bhuddist Temple (and Ponggol Bus Garage) to allow the newer and longer wheelbase Ransomes to turn. The 1949 extension had extended the wires by approximately 200 yards. Trolleybus 26, on Route 4, makes it turn after a few years in service; hence the modified livery, minus the cream band below its window level.

RIGHT: Trolleybus 10 never returned to electric traction and the arrival of the last Dennis Falcons found the route in their hands. Here Falcon STC 27, an early example, is seen under the wires turning from Lavender Street into Jalan Besar.

water, oil and fuel or electrical appurtenances, and in the case of passenger vehicles loaded with the weights of one hundred and thirty three and one third pounds person placed in the correct relative positions for each passenger for whom a seat is provided, plus similar weights for each standing passenger (if any) permitted, and for the driver and conductor (if carried ... Passenger vehicles may be divided into First Class and Second Class compartments).

Under "Objects and Reasons" (that is to say, explaining the purpose of the Ordinance but without being a part thereof) was provided the following explanation. "It is desired to increase the authorised weight of the passenger vehicles employed by the Singapore Traction Company in order to increase the range of the new models to which the Company has access when in the market for new vehicles. Because of the present restrictions in (the) weight of cars the Company is compelled to ignore many of the standard models produced by manufacturers of passenger carrying vehicles. The proposed weights are the same as those permitted in the United Kingdom, where additions to the Company's fleet are usually purchased".

Such powers would have been granted as the result of application made by the Traction Company, but as the title indicates, the result was limited to the applicant. Where did this leave the independent operators? The answer must be that, for the next few years, they would be dependent in the main on lorry derived chassis, although there would be examples of medium weight buses increasingly being taken into stock by the turn of the decade. Certainly the situation concerning the larger Ransomes trolleybuses was placed onto a firm footing, and we can only speculate as to whether there was still a firm intention to seek a full restoration of the network as it had been immediately before the occupation. (*Two marginal notes, made in pencil, on the Author's copy of the 1949 Ordinance provoke interesting thought—concerning weights carried on vehicles is noted "cars 25 and 26", which would seem to indicate that when new they had been used in weight distribution experiments, whilst in the margin, against the two class accommodation, appears "Cars 37 and 38", seeming to indicate that some form of structural trials were conducted, albeit of a temporary nature and not in service*).

12th May 1948, a day which might well be seen as the first nail in the coffin of continued

ABOVE LEFT: Trolleybus 45 comes adrift at Outram Road terminus—a not uncommon happening at this point. By the time that this photograph had been taken, the new livery of cream with green roof and 'streamline' areas had been applied.

LEFT: The difficulty of turning a Ransomes trolleybus at Bras Basah spur is amply demonstrated by No 48 whose driver is attempting to reverse into a main traffic stream. In this picture—and others—the small toplight windows above the front cabside windows can be seen. The Morris Commercial van is also of interest.

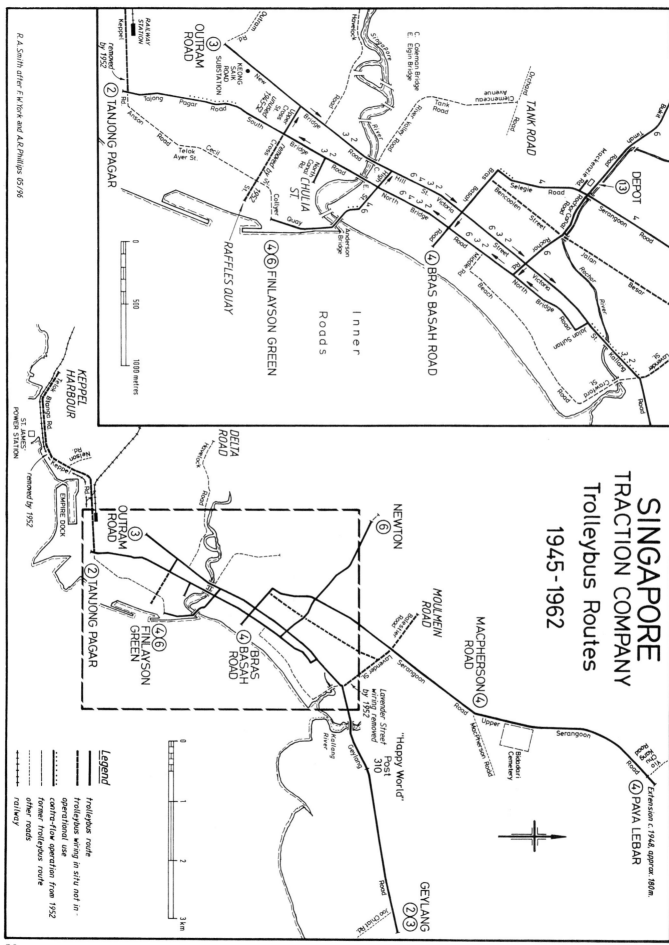

SINGAPORE
TRACTION COMPANY
Trolleybus Routes
1945-1962

R.A.Smith after F.W.York and A.R.Phillips 05/96

Legend

+————+ trolleybus route
———— trolleybus wiring in situ not in-
operational use
·········· contra-flow operation from 1952
———— former trolleybus route
———— other roads
++++++ railway

trolleybus operation, for there was brought into operation a one-way traffic scheme focused on the crossing of Kallang Road by Lavender - and Crawford Streets. In common with all other traffic, except trolleybuses, buses inward from Geylang henceforth would need to turn left into Crawford Street, cross Crawford Bridge using either the left or right hand span, then to join North Bridge Road at its extremity. Thereafter, those routes needing to reach Victoria Street would make a right hand turn from North Bridge Road into Sumbawa Road, and then left in order to retain normal routing. The cost of relocating traction poles and overhead line around this extensive diversion would have been very high, and thus dispensation was granted allowing in-bound trolleybuses to retain their route in Kallang Road against the flow of traffic. Special traffic signs were designed and positioned at the end of Sumbawa Road reading 'Beware of Trolleybuses', shaped in the style of the erstwhile 'Halt at Major Road Ahead' plate except that, as this was a non-designated traffic sign, it could not carry the statutory red triangle. For the time being, this was a relatively short section of contra working, but not inclined

Connaught Drive, Beach Road, Lavender Street, Serangoon Road and Upper Serangoon Road. The first service stop will be Rumah Miskin and the minimum fare fifteen cents. Limited Stop buses will be clearly marked as such". The object of the exercise was to provide transport for those white collar workers concentrated around the Government offices and business houses located around the central business area, and who lived in the more distant suburban districts, without the constant possibility of being forced off buses by short distance riders. Note that the non-stop section of route was by off-normal route working, avoiding the possible congestion spots of High Street, Bras Basah Road and Kadang Kerbau. The experiment proved to be an immediate success, so much so that a similar facility was introduced for inward runs on the 18 between 7.30 am and 8.45 am, with the last picking-up point being Paya Lebar, and carrying a minimum fare of twenty cents, with additional services from Katong at Joo Chiat Road along the route of service 20 at ten minute intervals between 7.00 am and 8.45 am, observing all stops in Katong as far as Arthur Road, thence non-stop to Collyer Quay by way of Mountbatten Road, Crawford Street and Beach Road, minimum fare again twenty cents. An exact reverse facility was provided during the evening between 4.45 pm and 5.45 pm, but it will be noted that the evening 18 was out of balance with the morning facility, insofar as first

LEFT: Kampong Bahru Bus Co Tilling-Stevens L6PA8, SH252, turns out of an unidentified one-way street into another upon which trolleybuses worked contra-flow, hence the warning signs 'Look out for Trolleybuses'

to endear other road users to this form of transport, as a letter to the *Straits Times* indicated: "The Singapore Traction Company is replenishing its fleet of vehicles with more than fifty trolleybuses, a type of vehicle which is surely the least suitable for this city, with its narrow streets and increasingly congested traffic. The necessary roadside poles and overhead wires are nothing but a nuisance, apart from which the system is cumbersome and unwieldy, lacking the fluidity of the self propelled bus. It is believed that this system of transport is being abandoned in some cities".

For the time being every effort was being made in order to get more Ransomes into traffic, and the hope that the AEC's could be replaced on a one-for-one basis was fast fading, the number of the old faithfuls having fallen to thirty-five shortly after those first five new entries became operational. On the motor bus side things were looking very much brighter, even to the extent where further expansion could take place over routes which seem to have become satisfactorily re-established, and taking the form of rush hour limited stop services. Service 18 was an obvious choice, for duplicating trolleybus 4 for the whole of the latter's length before going on to Tampines Road, since being reintroduced as from 7th July 1946 it had worked from town as far as Rumah Miskin on a non-stop basis, and charging a minimum fare, so that regular passengers had become well versed in special conditions. The Traffic Notice reads "Limited Stop Omnibus Service—Finlayson Green to Tampines Road. Commencing on 20th May 1948, a limited stop omnibus service will be run as an experiment during the evening peak hour from 4.45 pm to 5.45 pm, from Finlayson Green to Tampines Road via Fullerton Road,

point for setting down and minimum fare be concerned. That to Katong was, in reality, a natural development of arrangements introduced as long before as July 1946, with the introduction of evening rush hour buses starting from the junction of North Bridge Road with Bras Basah Road out to Geylang and Katong, in an effort to negate the wave of complaints concerning buses arriving filled to capacity in town.

Further revisions were made as from 3rd August, in the main extending hours of operation, although the Katong service was split, with alternative buses routed via the length of Joo Chiat Road and Geylang Road.

Improvements were to be found in all directions, and the most substantial weapon in the armoury to return to normal working was the flow of new vehicles being received by both the Traction Company and the Chinese bus owners. Nevertheless, serious overcrowding was still a very great problem, so much so that the police expressed alarm at the number of reported accidents involving passengers falling from overcrowded buses, often with fatal consequences. Those former lorries fitted with bus bodies of which considerable numbers were in service with the Chinese bus owners had an open platform at the nearside rear, whilst the Bedfords, Dennis and trolleybuses of the Traction Company favoured central entrances/exits with three steps leading up into the saloon, the short stairwell becoming seriously congested as ever more people tried to force their way onto the bus, often being left hanging on more outside than in. The police authority went as far as to suggest that sliding doors be fitted to all buses, these to be under the direct control of either the driver or conductor,

RIGHT: The Singapore Turf Club provided the Traction Company with a useful source of additional income on race days. The STC contribution was a fleet of new Bedford OBs and Fords which ran an express service from outside Raffles Hotel, while the Singapore-Johore Express introduced a similar service from the Racecourse and Johore Bahru on racedays only.

and geared in such a manner that prevented the bus from moving whilst the door was open. However worthy the suggestion might have been, prevailing conditions made it impossible to pursue (indeed, something like forty years would need to pass before such a practice became widespread). Alas, all too often it fell to conductors to face the hostile reactions of disgruntled passengers, and as the police were beginning to win their battle against general lawlessness, it was to them that the Unions turned seeking protection for their members who tried to enforce loading restrictions.

As respect for the rule of law was gradually re-established, so the extent of 'squeeze' was much reduced, although there would be a long way to travel before this evil was fully eliminated.

All operators were enjoying the effects of taking more new buses into stock, allowing for the increasing of headways on those services which had been reintroduced, and for the introduction of new services. The Singapore Turf Club was a very popular venue on race days, and the Traction Company were able to use many of the new Bedfords on an express service between Bras Basah Road outside the world famous Raffles Hotel and the race course in Bukit Timah Road, although, being well outside the municipal limits, passengers were restricted to genuine racegoers and there was no stopping on route. The Singapore to Johore Express was able to share in this popularity, and introduced a similar facility between the race course and Johore Bahru; race days only.

By December 1948, all the Ransomes trolleybuses had been delivered, meaning that the last of the AECs could make its way

to the breaker's yard. The Company Chairman in his annual address, described these vehicles as having been a magnificent tribute to the skills and quality of British manufacturing, and indeed they had been. At the same time all but ten of the prewar survivors were withdrawn, in company with most of those buses which had been based on former military trucks. Prewar practice was again resumed, with Albion being chosen to meet the future needs of the Traction Company and constant flow of repeat orders each year brought the total number in service at any given time to be reckoned in hundreds .

The Victor model also found favour with some of the Chinese bus owners, attracted by the robust construction of the chassis combined with the ability to have fitted an attractive body with a higher seating capacity than hitherto they had been able to aspire to. Always in the forefront when it came to seeking modernity, Mr. Tay Koh Yat was swift to place examples in service, closely followed by Keppel and Hock Lee Amalgamated, for each could see the growth in population and the associated development of new estates in the rural areas as a forthcoming growth in traffic, although all of the owners would be glad to get rid of the small capacity buses from their fleets as soon as possible.

As far as the Traction Company was concerned, the certain knowledge that the fleet would increase in substantial numbers year by year brought forward a pressing problem, namely where the fleet could be accommodated, for the original car sheds at Mackenzie Road had expanded as far as the site would allow, and the premises at Aljunied Road were little more than a bus park, with limited facilities available.

24,850 square yards of undeveloped land was acquired in Upper Aljunied

LEFT: The need to expand bus storage space led the Traction Company to acquire 24,850 square yards of undeveloped land adjacent to Macpherson Road. The capacity of these premises can be judged from this photograph which shows buses parked at the commencement of the 1955 'Great Strike' (qv). (Straits Times

Road at the junction with Macpherson Road (and from the latter it was to take it's name in order to prevent confusion with the other land owned in Aljunied Road). Land clearance was the first task to be tackled, and this work extended from 1949 into 1950, by which time a huge open air hard standing had been provided capable of accommodating the greater part of the motor bus fleet, for the ultimate intention was that, when the administration block had been built and engineering and staff facilities completed, then the smaller premises in Aljunied Road could be closed and the land sold, for prices were booming.

1950 and Civil Unrest

If 1949 could be seen as a good year, then 1950 was to become an unhappy spell of civil unrest, and whilst all sections of business were to suffer the effects, the British owned Traction Company was to present an all too easy target. The hazards were such that either insurance could not be obtained anywhere, or else at such premiums as to be wholly uneconomic, so that there was an obligation to create a reserve fund of a purely general nature in order to set off the results of damage caused to vehicles or property through riots or precise acts of sabotage directed against the Company.

The Annual Report of the Company for 1950 contains the following remarks made by the Chairman: "I regret to say that considerable lawlessness prevails in Singapore. Since May of last year determined attempts have been made by small gangs of young ruffians to put our vehicles, whilst in service, out of action. The attempts increased in frequency up to 11th January 1951. There was a lull for a month, after which they commenced again. Altogether twenty attempts have been made, of which eleven have resulted in considerable damage. Broadly speaking, they have followed a single pattern. Several Chinese youths, usually three, board a bus; compel the conductor at revolver point to bring it to a stop; empty it of passengers; sprinkle it with petrol; set fire to it and make off. The conductor, driver and passengers are overawed; arrests are occasionally made, but so far have let to no result. That the passengers have been supine there can be no doubt, though it may well be that they have to some extent been influenced to inaction by the failure of the police to deal with previous outrages, some of which have taken place in crowded thoroughfares".

"Though our employees have so far escaped injury, the carrying of firearms is clearly not for the purpose of intimidation only, as shown in the number of murders which have been committed".

"Over and above the losses due to gangsters we suffered losses, including three buses, during the disturbances in December. That the losses were not greater was due to the skill, courage and determination of all our employees concerned in extricating the vehicles from streets given over to rioting ... with two exceptions the staff escaped physical injury ...".

Distressing in the extreme, for once the company was truly returning to normal operating conditions, political agitation should cause dreadful problems far beyond anything normally associated with the provision of an efficient transport service. All of the transport operators had suffered, for the objectives of those sowing dissent were to close off all patterns of normal life, and instead impose the rule of chaos. A formal Commission of Enquiry was set up by the Government, whilst a further Government body was prepared to entertain claims for loss and damage caused by the riots.

To meet the additional financial burdens brought about by strife, and at a time when all other expenses were on an upward spiral, mainly materials and wages, bus operators needed to be protected from another drain on their incomes, namely pirate taxi owners, a rather heavy irony, seeing that it was from the mosquito buses of old that the Chinese bus companies were formed.

Whilst it is true that, during the immediate post occupation period when all forms of passenger transport were at a premium, a service of taxis was allowed to function over part of the Geylang to Tanjong Pagar route, but it is also true to say that with the easing of the situation, the taxi proprietors, both licensed and unlicensed, were loath to set aside this lucrative trade and instead expanded their spheres of operation to cover any major bus route which would provide a plentiful supply of customers. The modus operandi was much as before, in that a taxi driver spotting a queue would stop alongside, cram into his cab as many persons as it would take, and then speed away, either charging the appropriate bus fare from the distance travelled by his passengers, or else negotiating the rate before starting. Licensed taxi drivers would certainly keep the meter switched off. Teams drawn from the Police, the office of the Registrar of Vehicles, and traffic inspectors of the Traction Company made copious observations but no solution would be found until sufficient buses were available to accommodate all the passengers who needed to use them.

After a post-war lull the population totals began to grow again, in the natural way, by further immigration, and by a build up of British military forces and, although there was a constant flow of new vehicles coming into service, the demand was always ahead of capacity. Many employers in diverse businesses found that their own efforts towards full recovery were being at risk due to the difficulties in getting staff to work on time, and so decided to invest in their own personnel transport. Any old lorry could still find a ready purchaser, as could the military-based buses being disposed of, and these were quickly snapped up and used until such time as regular bus services became reliable. From such beginnings, long term con-

BELOW: Dennis Falcon, STC 34, following an arson attack at Delta Road on 1st May 1951. Unfortunately such attacks were all too common and resulted in great loss of money and equipment for the Company. *(Straits Times*

ABOVE: During the protracted period during which bus services attempted to keep up with demand, many schools and employers acquired their own transport for their employees' use. Many ex-military buses sold-off by the regular bus operators were snapped-up, this Dodge, S 3461 becoming the property of St Andrews School.

BELOW: S 3579, with Nan Wah Girls' School, is another example of a 1950's school bus, probably from a Chinese bus company

flights of Malayan Airways, international routes were operated by British Overseas Airways Corporation (BOAC) and the Australian airline QANTAS and as the 1950's drew to a close, all realised that their fleets of Dakotas, Argonauts and Constellations aircraft, with their low passenger capacities, would soon be rendered obsolete by the new generation of turbo-prop airliners and later by the big jets which were on the way and operating their own coach fleets became an essential—large automobiles having proved to be sufficient to date.

BOAC and QANTAS bought several of the handsome Commer-Park Royal combinations known as a 'deck and a half', whilst Bedfords were chosen for crew transport and back ups. QANTAS owned a most weird machine; a full sized Bedford chassis mounted with a body in height being on a par with the large type of private car, with a boot which appeared to have been grafted on from a Humber Super Snipe, no doubt to ensure safe passage beneath aircraft wings.

To digress into matters of civil aviation has been to demonstrate how a quite substantial European population came to be grafted throughout the Island, few of whom would expect to

BELOW: Perhaps the strangest Bedford OB that readers have cast eyes upon! This airside coach was operated by QANTAS Empire Airways and appeared to be based on the lines of a Humber Super Snipe private car. No doubt its function was to go under aircraft wings—a sort of early 'stretch-limo'.

ABOVE: Two Malayan Airways Vulcans attend the disembarkation of troops from a British military charter flight. This pair, SB 231 & SB 232 had rear luggage compartments

tractors became established, their objective being the supply of transport to schools. Although a particular contractor might build up a fleet of buses, common livery was the exception rather than the rule and instead, painting and lettering would be for a particular school.

In the widest transport sense, the increased British military presence presents an interesting study for, with the Emergency raging in Malaya, Singapore took on the roles of expanded military fortress, massive transit camp, and a rest and recreation centre. For those servicemen who would be based here, much sympathy was extended towards the married man, and increasing numbers of families were allowed to accompany their menfolk. The days of the large troopships ploughing their way half way around the globe were almost at an end, and instead we find air trooping giving a boost to civil aviation and with certain nostalgia we can recall the names of Lancashire Airways, Airwork, Eagle Aviation and Aquila Airways, flying a mixture of Handley Page Hermes, Avro York, Avro Tudor, and those lovely civilianised Sunderland flying boats. The route flown involved overnight stops on Indian territory, whose authorities would not allow the landing of troops in uniform, thus civilian clothes had to be worn, and the whole operation was regarded as a massive civil charter. To this end the collection and delivery of passengers to and from the Royal Air Force base at Changi or in the case of Aquila flights the flying boat base at Seletar was contracted out to Malayan Airways, who were able to invest in a number of handsome coaches over and above the usual Bedfords which had been sufficient when dealing with their own Dakota flights in and out of Kallang civil airport and also for crew transport.

Tilling-Stevens in their most modern form were the first choice, to be followed by Dennis Teals. Besides the regional

purchase cars, and who would thus be in need of a reliable transport service. Already enterprising landlords were snapping up the estates of neat bungalows springing up where recently there had been farmlands or semi-jungle, and the Chinese bus companies prepared themselves for the boom. Just beyond Paya Lebar one such project was taking form, destined to become Serangoon Garden Estate. The established operator in the area was Paya Lebar Bus Service, whose main route passed along Yio Chu Kang Road, which happened to be the perimeter of the developing site. Although the estate was growing up within the municipal limits, it was to the Paya Lebar Bus Service that a licence to provide a service was granted, the terminus being at Serangoon Garden Way, at the time little more than a traffic island set amongst a forest of hoardings carrying messages such as 'Site for Market', 'Site for Super Cinema', 'Site for Modern Shopping Centre' and the like. The snag was that service 3, for such it became, needed to work to the established terminus at Geylang, and most of the residents wished to reach town. Short of meeting the expense of a long taxi journey, they would need to use service 3 as far as Paya Lebar Police Station at a five cents fare, and could there transfer to a number 4 trolleybus, a perfect example of traffic feeding (there was also motor bus 18, of course, but in the mile beyond the trolleybus terminus they tended to be filled). Paya Lebar Bus Service did seek a licence for an evening express service to a town terminus near the Cathay Cinema, but this application did not meet with success, and shortly thereafter the Traction Company managed to establish its own route from Finlayson Green under the number 18A.

Changi Bus Services was also enjoying expansion. For some

ABOVE: In order to cater for traffic as it grew on the Serangoon Garden Estate, STC introduced its service 18A. In this view the houses, shops, market and cinema have yet to come as STC 228, an Albion Victor FT39ALX 44-seater, new in 1954, sets off around around the Estate. The deep monsoon drains were a trap for the unwary.

BELOW: Another operator to benefit from an increasing number of military families during the 1950's was the Changi Bus Company which introduced its service 3 to serve a series of residential roads associated with the RAF Changi air base and known as Lloyd Lees—a name straight from leafy Surrey! The usual allocation was a stylish Chevrolet Maple-leaf, Canadian-built, and with stylish Singaporean bodywork. Here SC1911 sets off to—if the destination is to be believed—Lloyd Lees on 18th January 1955.

time there had been a loop operation, starting from the main terminal in Changi Village, and then describing a circuit around the main barracks area of the Royal Air Force Station. In addition, there commenced a service with families in mind, using Upper Changi Road until leaving the military zone, then to turn

off into a series of side roads known as Lloyd Leas, within the shadow of the notorious Changi Gaol. A Chevrolet Maple Leaf was the usual type of bus used, and this became their service 3. Service 4 was a further Changi local, although required only at certain times of the day, as it's destination was Telok Paku School, a mile or so along Changi Beach. A feature of the military establishments was the vast number of civilian staff employed, and Changi Bus Service operated a considerable number of contracted services, designated by letters rather than numbers, to far parts of the island.

The outer end of Tay Koh Yat's 'main line' skirted the giant Naval Base, and a large fleet of buses was maintained on similar contract work, although the long lines of parked up vehicles resting at Sembawang Village during the daytime indicated that the oldest buses in the fleet were set aside for these duties. In stage carriage terms a short shuttle route was introduced from Nee Soon Village into the Army's Nee Soon Transit Camp, providing connections on the 'main line' for those seeking an evening in town.

Mention of the Naval Base brings to mind recollections of a very mysterious operator, H.M.NAVAL BASE BUS SERVICE and, whilst the casual passer-by could not enter the closely guarded gates to have a look, neither did the bus fleet come out onto the public roads—not, at least, until such time as their working lives were at an end when bodies might be found in scrapyards around the town. What can be said is that the fleet was generally similar to those adopted by the Chinese bus owners, followed a pattern of routes through the base according to timetables and used tickets of similar pattern to those used outside. From what could be seen, the buses, in a livery of Silver/grey and blue, were very well maintained. Details of operations and size of fleet were not included in returns published by the Registrar of Vehicles nor published in the various Government publications in which statistics relative to passenger transport might be found.

At the other extreme, one could take the ferry boat from Jardine's Steps (off Keppel Road) and enjoy free access to Blakang Mati, a small island which had become the base for the Royal Artillery (here were located the huge guns which, in theory, confirmed the 'fortress' design), and which was served by a one-vehicle operator named THE ISLAND BUS. With a terminus at The Jetty, the immaculate green-and-white Ford meandered around the rather complex road pattern; no conductor was employed and no tickets were issued. This was quite possibly the first example of one-man operation to be found in Singapore. In fact, there was no set scale of fares, and all that the passenger was required to do was, upon alighting, to drop a few coins into an old circular cigarette tin fastened to the bulkhead behind the driver.

ABOVE LEFT: The H.M.Naval Base Bus Service conducted its operations behind closed doors—or rather the closed gates of the Naval Base. Only upon retirement could the little buses be identified as this Ford, S 1237, seen awaiting disposal in 1955. It has two blind displays partially visible.

ABOVE RIGHT: Another little seen operator was Island Bus, hidden away on the small island then known as Blakang Mati. This one-bus operator had this smartly turned-out Ford , S7552, with open rear platform—probably second-hand from one of the Chinese bus companies.

A mix of demand for letting and private purchasing saw the establishment of the Frankel and Opera Estates, spreading over the virgin lands between the East Coast Road and Upper Changi Road, and just across the municipal boundary. This represented an opportunity to expand for the Katong-Bedok Bus Service who (as with Paya Lebar and Serangoon Garden Estate) introduced their own service 3 as new roads were being laid.

The needs of the indigenous population seeking to rent their homes was not being ignored, and it fell to the Singapore Improvement Trust to locate sites upon which blocks of flats would be constructed. A few isolated properties were owned within the town but major expansions were to be located further afield, to the benefit of Hock Lee Amalgamated. Within the municipal limits—and just beyond the terminus of trolleybus 3—but seemingly of no interest to the Traction Company, was Tiong Bahru Estate, built with high population density around a grid of narrow streets with very sharp corners, so that the bus company always had a need for some special short wheelbase vehicles with which to work the loop service through the estate. Further west, estates were built or expanded at Henderson Road and Alexandra Road and new services and consequently the fleet, boomed.

Thus far, the Traction Company had been content to stay within its geographic limits. The new Bedfords did have provision on their destination blinds for the reintroduction of the short lived service 25 to Bukit Timah, but this did not happen. Military considerations must have weighed heavy with the introduction of service 24: the town terminus was designated 'Shackle Club' (which itself was later renamed 'Britannia Club'), a recreation centre for off-duty servicemen, although the precise terminal was in Bras Basah Road adjacent to the Raffles hotel from where buses crossed Anderson Bridge and thereafter ghosted service 1 as far as Keppel Harbour, at which point the boundary was crossed. Pasir Panjang Road was used until reaching Alexandra Road (between the 4th and 5th milestones), using that road in order to reach the vast British Military Hospital. Here the 24s left the public highway in order to make a long circuit of the hospital grounds, a facility not granted to the other bus operators in the district. Once back on the main road the scenery was dominated by endless lines of barrack huts, the surrounding wire fences broken only by a

series of main gates and guard rooms, and coloured by a variety of Unit badges. Turning into side roads, and negotiating several open crossings of the railway, the route ended in a pleasant little cul-de-sac

BELOW: Estates of flats were providedfor the non European populations during the early 1950's and at Tiong Bahru Estate it was for Hock Lee Amalgamated to provide the bus service. The usual harshness of blocks of flats were softened by the liberal provision of roadside trees; in this case it is Seng Poh Road with Hock Lee's Morris Commercial, SC 8437 running on Route 7.

BOTTOM: For its routes through Tiong Bahru Estate, restricted by narrow streets and tight corners, Hock Lee used, amongst other types, special shortwheelbase Seddons such as SH 171, seen here in the company of a Ford and other Seddons at South Canal Road

LEFT: Albion STC 395 waits on the turning point outside Sandes Soldiers Hole on Route 24 before heading off for town—to the Shackle Club for servicemen to be precise (this latter was subsequently renamed Britannia Club). This view shows the palatial quarters allocated to British Army officers at the time. The cream livery dates the view *circa* 1955.

BELOW LEFT: The Keppel Bus Co terminus at Tanjong Pagar is host to a line of Albions, headed by SH 454 on service 3 between there and Sandes Soldiers Home. These were Victor FT39ALX models—substantial vehicles which gave years of valuable service. *(Albion Motors Ltd*

Roman Catholic), extending boundaries, a qualifying size of population, a centre of commerce providing excellent links worldwide, and above all a seat of Government. Until September 1951 those bestowing the title of city had been in technical error, but during that month there was presented to the Municipality a Royal Charter conferring upon Singapore the title of 'City' and "all such rank, liberties, privileges and immunities" as are incident to a City and further declaring, "the Municipal Commissioners of Singapore shall henceforth be one body corporate by the name and style of City Council of Singapore".

opposite Sandes Soldiers Home, a well appointed hotel at which servicemen could stay for a week or two whilst on leave. Completing the terminal double-run, the route followed a right hand turn to work around further camps until eventually arriving back at the hospital grounds.

Protection from STC Route 24 was given to the Chinese bus operators, for sections of routes already served by Keppel, Hock Lee Amalgamated, and Easy were covered. This was done by conditions attached to the STC licence, preventing passengers being taken up or set down west of Keppel Harbour, except within the hospital grounds, at Sandes Home, and at a number of points around the camps circuit. With a flat fare of twenty-five cents being charged, and with service 1 and others providing an adequate coverage between Keppel Harbour and town, the 24 seemed to carry little interest for local travellers. In due course, both Keppel and Easy recognised the need for local fares around the camps and were able to introduce diversions from their established routings.

City Status

Whilst all of this activity was taking place in the transport world, Constitutional confirmation had taken effect. For many years previously Singapore town had been looked upon as being a city, for there existed all of the attributes which went to make up a modern city, viz., no less than two cathedrals (Anglican and

---

> #### A small amalgamation
>
> DURING 1951, NGO HOK MOTOR BUS COMPANY merged with SOON LEE BUS COMPANY in order to create the Hock Lee Amalgamated Bus Company, a feature of which was the adopting of a combination of the two former liveries, green and red with yellow and red, producing a most attractive rainbow presentation. In theory, it fell to the Chinese operators to rework routes which had been served prior to the occupation. In practice, however, there was a degree of poaching onto the Traction Company's preserves but, for the time being at any rate, anything which would help to ease the situation would be tolerated.

Trolleys Face a One-way Future

What of the trolleybus network? The Ransomes fleet had settled down nicely, and seemed to be well liked by the travelling public, and full loads were the order of the day. If the Kallang traffic experiment were seen as a single nail, then what would follow during the early months of 1953 might equally represent the beginning of the end of trolleybus operation, although there would still be much to happen between the two events. Traffic congestion was becoming a serious problem, and in order to speed the flow, a vast one-way street pattern would be introduced affecting most of the central area. Between Crawford Street and Cross Street, North Bridge and South Bridge Roads would become one-way, east to west, with traffic in the opposite direction using New Bridge Road, Hill Street and Victoria Street. The immediate effect was to almost completely amalgamate service 2 and 3, and the only independent section of the 3 remaining was the very short section from Upper Cross Street to the terminus at Outram Road, just a few hundred yards.

The wisdom of maintaining the unused overhead wiring became an advantage, as there was sufficient equipment in situ along Upper Cross Street, left over from the days when services 8 and 9 were trolleybus operated. On the other hand, as service 6 inbound could no longer make a right hand turn into Victoria Street, a single set of new wires was required in Rochor Road up to the junction with North Bridge Road, from

where the 'loop' could be joined. The provision of one set of wires along the wholly new section of route tended to lay emphasis on the rather strange fact that other overhead wiring and equipment no longer to be used was kept in place and fully maintained in subsequent years, including the wiring for service 10 which, as we have seen, never did take trolleybuses after the occupation had ended.

There was a certain amount of revision of layouts at main junctions, even to the extent of ensuring that the Chulia Street spur could be made operational by providing a left hand exit. The opportunity was taken to remove a considerable amount of unused overhead from elsewhere, such as the remnants of service 1 beyond Tanjong Pagar to the Keppel Harbour terminus, anything that remained in Anson Road along the same route and that of service 9 in Cross Street leading down to Raffles Quay.

In addition to the major pattern embracing the town, there were several secondary schemes which had a detrimental effect on the trolleybus system in a conflict of passage with other road users: at Maxwell Market, outbound traffic was re-

quired to divert by way of the market and Murray Street, leaving trolleybuses to work against the inbound traffic flow. A further circus based on existing streets was formed outside the Cathay Cinema, utilising the end of Bras Basah Road, Dhoby Ghaut and Prinsep Street, again for outbound traffic, leaving service 4 trolleybuses to battle against the speeding flow of traffic, their situation made all the more perilous by the fact of the turn off Bras Basah Road being a blind corner. This was not the only hazard facing drivers on the 4, nor was it the worst for, in company with service 6, they had to cross three lanes of opposing traffic near the Legislative Assembly House. Once across, a certain amount of shelter could be drawn from a traffic island located opposite the Singapore Cricket Club whilst waiting for the opportunity to cross the three lanes rushing out of Connaught Drive. In the suburbs some form of traffic control was needed at busy junctions, one such location being

where the main Serangoon-, Upper Serangoon- and Macpherson Roads met, with additional side road traffic feeding in from Moonstone- and Kolam Ayer Lanes. Various street corners were cut back, leaving ample space for the construction of a large traffic island, this being given the name 'Woodsville Circus'. Trolleybus writing required a realignment, and whilst this was being done the turning loop which had allowed short workings over service 4 was removed, although 'Macpherson Road' still appeared on new destination blinds.

Road Improvement Schemes

Once across the city boundaries, all of the main roads had a tendency to follow a series of severe bends, some almost to horseshoe dimensions and, whilst it was possible to enjoy a swift but somewhat violent ride in the small buses, the arrival of Vulcan and Austin units into the various fleets did seem to make the

ABOVE: The restrictions placed upon public transport by the rural and winding nature of the roads caused the authorities to embark upon a series of improvements to eliminate situations as this on the 'main' Changi Road-scene of the death by heatstroke of a senior STC official when force marched to internment in Changi Gaol in February 1942. In happier circumstances two Changi Bus Co. Vulcans pass on a narrow bend in 1955. This is now a six lane super-highway.

task of drivers somewhat more difficult and the driver would need to spend most of the rural journey 'going through the box'. A vast investment in long term road improvements was implemented with early benefits being felt by Tay Koh Yat (Thomson - and Upper Thomson Roads), Changi (Upper Changi Road) and Paya Lebar (Tampines Road). An interesting footnote concerned with the latter when bus passengers were asked not to be alarmed if they should pass a car in flames, for all was to do with the filming of scenes from 'A Town like Alice'.

Meanwhile, back in the City, the major one-way system was given three months to settle down, during which constant observations were made by the various bodies involved. Where trolleybuses went against the flow of traffic some visual protection was needed and to this end reservations were established, being marked by lines of oil drums set in long lines and painted with horizontal stripes of black and white. Hardly attractive but easily

removable should the scheme be abandoned, which might also have been the reason for letting more unused than used wiring to remain in place.

The City Council did come to recognise the loss of several long established and useful links and transfer points and, in an effort to restore the balance, approached the Traction Company with the request that a form of City Circular service should be established, connecting the main shopping centres, places of entertainment, Government and commercial complexes, and the major transfer points. Special 'luxury' buses should be used and so, having accepted the challenge, the Company approached Albion Motors who were then working through an accumulation of repeat orders totalling seventy chassis, with a view to inserting an additional five chassis to a special short-wheel base specification, essential as the completed buses would need to work through some narrow streets and encounter some tight corners. Lee Kiat Seng rose to the occasion, and produced bodywork of a style instantly capable of being recognised as being something different from ordinary buses, whilst the interior boasted the, then, luxury of transverse seating. To assist with easy recognition, a reverse livery was applied, that is to say, mainly cream and with green streamline flashes. Normal destination blind equipment was contained within the front dome, but in addition route boards were contained on each side above the windows, carrying the legend 'City Circular Service', and at last service number 7 was allocated, having been passed over during the early numbering sequence as the trolleybus network was being established: perhaps it had been an unlucky number, for such things mattered greatly to the Chinese staff. Considerable advance publicity was given prior to the official launch of the route, not the least point being made that, for the first time, prestigious Raffles Place would be receiving a bus service. 7 proved itself to be unlucky for, after only a few weeks of operation, the service was withdrawn. The reason for this failure must be found in the flat fare of twenty-five cents when it is recalled that the service was intended only as a series of links, and all passengers would only be making short journeys, for the era of the tourist had yet to arrive.

BELOW: With one of the two cathedrals as a picturesque backdrop, the short wheelbase Albion Victor poses quietly for the camera, complete with side roof route boards proclaiming 'City Circular Service'. Lee Kiat Seng provided the 'luxury' bodywork to attract passengers to this service designed to make travel betweeen places of business, shopping and entertainment simple after the introduction of the one-way street system.

The first whispers of Mass Transit

If it had been a short term fear of the city centre becoming strangled by traffic which prompted the introduction of the one-way system, then long term thinking reached the conclusion that congestion could spread throughout the Island during the coming years. All concerned agreed that it was vital for all citizens to be able to enjoy maximum mobility but the private car would not be the answer.

The Public Passenger Transport Committee of the City Council had pondered long over this projection, and presented a report to the Meeting of the Council held on 8th July 1953. In content, the report implied a return to the tramcar in its modernised form. The new-style trams would not be incorporated into the existing roads pattern, but would be provided with exclusive rights-of-way. As a first move and as a means of gaining experience, it was suggested that the existing line of Malayan Railways could be converted to Light Rail, with the route to Johore Bahru being converted to double track, and the provision of a large number of 'stations' en route, close to centres of population. Should immediate electrification prove too costly, then diesel railcars could be used as an interim measure. Success was assumed, and proposals were included for the construction of new lines, the first being the obvious extension to the city centre for without such a projection any light rail operation would be as doomed as the Malayan Railways local services had been. To continue through the central zone, such a line could eventually reach Changi, with a second main line reaching out to Upper Serangoon. From a hub close to Finlayson Green, a fourth line would reach back from the converted railway in order to serve Pasir Panjang so that, in effect, all of these plans recognised the main traffic arteries which had been opened up by the original electric trams.

The purpose of the light railways would be to provide a cheap and fast service, with no outer terminus being more than a twenty minute ride from the city (alas, such wild speculation did little to make the proposals realistic, for to reach Finlayson Green from

Johore Bahru in twenty minutes inclusive of the many proposed stops would, it was claimed, involve the cars moving at speeds of eighty miles an hour). The intention being that there would be no deliberate competition with existing road transport, the plan was accepted by the City Council, who passed it on to the Government, in time reaching the desk of the Governor, who was able to express his complete support, a reaction which seemed to be shared by the public at large. Indeed, only one formal objection was entered, this from the Green Bus Company, fearing competition on their main route to Johore Bahru.

As so often happens with such a far sighted report, it was destined to follow the road taken by so many of its kind, before and since, in that, after receiving the approbation of all concerned, it was placed on some forgotten shelf in an office of Government, there to slowly gather dust. (The germs of the suggestions were not lost, however, and there were to follow 'The Rail Transit Plan for Singapore' of May 1968, and the 'Mass Rapid Transit Study' of June 1969, although both documents remain on the 'Restricted' list. Finally, whilst on a visit to Hong Kong during 1977, the Prime Minister Mr. Lee Kuan Yew was able to see the various aspects of the construction of the Mass Transit Railway then well in hand).

During 1953 the City Council presented a further task to their Public Passenger Transport Committee, to examine and report upon the prospects of coordinating all forms of public passenger transport throughout the Island, to make firm recommendations based upon their findings but, in particular, to give advice to the Council as to the practicability of their taking over the Traction Company as a going concern on 5th June 1955, the first date dictated by Section 29 of the 1925 Ordinance for such a purchase. So serious an investment of public funds would require at least that time-span and need detail examinations and reports.

At the full Council meeting of 16th October the Committee presented the result of their deliberations, which were (i) not to recommend the purchase of the Traction Company, and (ii) to draft proposals to submit to Government with a view to the preparation of Legislation providing for the creation of a single independent transport authority, to be set up no later than 5th June 1955, to (i) acquire the Traction Company, (ii) to rationalise the services of the private bus companies in preparation for (iii) the control of these companies being vested within the SINGAPORE TRANSPORT AUTHORITY as soon after the take over of the Traction Company as could be arranged. A very odd situation which seemed to present a contradiction in terms, viz "We do not want the Traction Company but we recommend the take over of the Traction Company". As it happened, the City Council did accept the Report, and during their meeting of 29th January 1954 sent a Resolution to the Government along the lines suggested, but nothing further happened. (Section 29 was quite specific in that only the City Council could take over the Company, and for such a Transport Authority to have been elected for the task might well have been the legal rock upon which the scheme foundered—the Legislative Assembly could promote a Bill in order to amend or repeal Section 29 , but this could only be done if the Company could be shown as not to be meeting their obligations under the Ordinance, whereas corporate affairs were in a state of sound good health which had not been enjoyed for many years previous).

LEFT: The unsung heroes of the trolleybus network—and the trams before them—were the service vehicles, in particular the tower wagons that allowed the line crews easy access to the overhead fittings. On earlier pages we have seen other example of tower wagons; the AEC 2½ tonner and the Morris Commercial. Here we see the vehicle used immediately post-war in the form of SA 8484, a Bedford ML, similar in frontal appearance to the OB bus but lighter and with a shorter wheelbase. Note the coiled length of overhead wire always carried in case of emergency

A double-decker bus

The afternoon of 11th October 1953 was to cast a further shadow. The setting: the bus park to the side of Mackenzie Road garage, a small group of white-uniformed European Inspectors supported by a host of khaki clad traffic staff, watched by a long line of passers-by rooted on the public side of the boundary fence but with all eyes turned in one direction. The reason, of course, for their attention was a bus, but what a bus! Never before seen by most of those watching, it was a double-decker. On loan from the General Transport Company (Federated Malay States) Limited, their number 52 (registration BA6421 in the Selangor State series) was an A.E.C. Regent Mark III, with bodywork by Park Royal, a combination which was very familiar in many fleets throughout the United Kingdom. A livery of dark green, but with mudguards and upper deck and roof in light green was not unlike that current for the Traction Company, made for any additional recognition which might be required, and the message 'A.E.C. Builders of London's buses' occupied the sides between decks. Upon arrival, a Kuala Lumpur destination blind was still in place which was, of course, replaced by a Traction Company display and the bus was ready for service.

A crew of four provided, two European Inspectors (one to drive and the other to maintain platform control) and two conductors, one to each deck. Service 18 was chosen for the first part of the demonstration and throughout the week considerable crowds gathered at each terminal hoping for a ride on the upper deck, with the lower saloon being the next best choice for the few fortunate souls who might have been able to board along the route.

To see this handsome vehicle, thundering through the spans of Anderson Bridge, was indeed a sight to behold and treasure, and the novelty value remained intense into the second week, when operation was switched to the trolleybus-worked-by-motor-bus service 10. Here, the only adverse comments, from some of the young ladies employed along Jalan Besar, who feared that as the shutters to their first floor rooms needed to be kept open, passengers might be able to look in.

Whether being novel would have been sufficient to cultivate more and new riders was an area open to doubt, for if such a fleet needed a crew of four to each vehicle, then the extra traffic to be generated would have to be greater than the capacity of the buses. The visit of number 52 thus became quite simply a good publicity exercise.

At the end of the fortnight the bus was inspected by the managements of Tay Koh Yat and Hock Lee Amalgamated, but not worked in service, whilst a press report stated that Singapore-Johore Express would have welcomed the opportunity to view.

Another afternoon, and a further shadow, but one which would have more immediate consequences: of all the vehicles likely to be encountered, the most unwieldy contraption had to be the hawker's mobile stall, a heavy metal frame incorporating a man-powered tricycle, a nightmare to get into motion but, once movement was obtained, to be kept going at all costs, no matter what other traffic might be doing. 7th September, 1953, and one such machine was making slow progress along Tanjong Pagar Road, slightly uphill so the rider was straining to keep the pedals turning, bent almost double with the effort. Behind, trolleybus 19 was fast catching up. All of a sudden, and without any prior warning, the rider seems to lose his sense of direction, and starts to veer away to the right, but 19 was already overtaking. The driver accelerated hard, hoping that he would avoid hitting the hawker and the line of traffic coming in the opposite direction, but his efforts failed and the trolleybus struck the tricycle broadside on, causing it to overturn and also for the driver of number 19 to lose control. In the acceleration mode, it managed to leap the deep monsoon drain at the side of the road, then to bury itself in a three storey high coffee shop on the corner of Cheng Tuan Street. The demolition was almost complete, almost the whole of the building collapsing onto the forward end of the trolleybus. The emergency services were quickly on the scene and within moments a vast, silent, crowd filled the side street. Outward signs of the tragedy took several poignant forms, such as a mattress standing vertical where the cab would lie buried, and a child's cot seeming to hover in the blank space where,

BELOW: As with the first experiment with double-deck operation in 1906, the 1955 trial with an AEC Regent III from Kuala Lumpa was not to herald the general introduction of the type to service with either STC or the Chinese bus companies, despite extensive in-service trials with the former and an inspection by two of the latter. No 52 in the General Transport Company fleet, BA 6421 was tried on Route 18 and later on the former trolleybus Route 10.

LEFT: In times more relaxed, Katong Bedok Vulcan SH 293, drives along the East Coast Road, at Bedok, with only a private car and the still waters of the sea for company, although one can almost feel the intense tropical heat reflected from the road surface

moments before, a family had lived. Almost beyond belief, out of the mountain of rubble an undamaged trolley pole reached out, as if seeking a wire with which to make contact. The site was cleared, and the remains of 19 were taken back to Mackenzie Road depot, in the immediate term to await a decision, but in the long term to bring a dramatic series of improvements to the fleet.

The one-way system had settled down, and the trolleybuses seemed to have been accepted into their non-flexible situation by most other road users so that, whilst no further orders had been placed in order to expand the system by reintroducing a service along the fully wired service 10, there as no reason to think that trolleybuses had no future. Therefore, 19 was sent away to the workshops of Lee Kiat Seng in order to be reborn, and the opportunity was taken to make substantial alterations to the body

drawings so that, when she came back into service, the overall impression was of the 1950's rather than twenty years earlier. (It may be that replacement parts for the rebuilding were obtained from the manufacturer, as 19 was the only one in the fleet to carry any form of 'R.S.J.' identification, and this was on the foot pedals). As time had been the major consideration during the construction of the fleet, some of the poorer quality materials which had been used required replacement and a major reconstruction programme would be put in hand following the success experienced with 19, although if forward planning in this direction was a means of reflecting optimism, such hopes were to be dashed as the clouds of the storm which had been gathering for some time burst in a fury of unrest and violence, with no area of society or industry being untouched.

BELOW: Battery Road circa 1948 and in the foreground an open lorry conveying workers to their place of employment. This somewhat overcrowded vehicle would at the very least raise the eyebrows by today's road safety standards. The variety of other vehicles gives rise to additional interest. *(Times Books International*

ChapterEight
1955 - 1956—The 'Great' Strike

'Merdeka', an honourable word, quite simply indicating the aspirations of a people to determine their own future, and insofar as the citizens of Singapore be concerned, when they first heard the word they saw no provocative connections, for the battles then raging in some of the Malayan states caused little disturbance to their secure lives. Alas, there were subversive elements at work, and they seized upon 'Merdeka' to use as their slogan for violent riots and industrial mayhem and, having infiltrated the trades union movement, could manipulate the pressing of extreme demands which would be impossible to meet, so that waves of strikes could be called.

As far as the Traction Company was concerned, 14th July 1955 simply saw the presentation of demands for increased wages, despite an agreement which had been reached during February of the previous year, which provided that once a scale of remunerations had been agreed, no further demands would be made for two years. The Management was not prepared to break the agreement, for to do

their education the first consideration within families. To take away the means of reaching school provoked the greatest public reaction to the strikes, and the Government was pressurised to act on behalf of pupils, the result being the creation of a pattern of lorry-bus services.

Several haulage contractors were able to supply vehicles which had been adapted to transport building workers between various sites, so that a 'standard' pattern of 'bodywork' had evolved: the chassis had been obtained from former military vehicles, the most popular being the Bedford QL (although quite drastic surgery would be required in order to reduce height). In most cases the original cab would be retained, with doors removed. A platform with low sides became the body so that, when not acting as a labourer ferry, the lorry could be fully employed hauling goods. Access for passengers was obtained by first stepping onto the nearside running board, then by way of a short ladder, or steps, onto the platform.

Additional facilities needed to be provided for the safety and relative comfort of the children, and these took the form of large metal hoops spanning the platform over which were draped canvases in order to provide some protection from sun and rain, and sets of bench seats along each side and back to back down the centre. For so long as the lorry was acting as a school bus an additional flight of steps was located on the tailboard (which was kept locked in place, of course).

Drivers were usually provided by the contractor, with a second man to act as a conductor whose task was to ensure safety whilst the children were boarding and alighting, and a police constable might also travel in order to assist with these precautions, and also to make sure that no person save children en route to and from school

so would not only induce a loss of £500,000 per annum (based on existing fares), but more important, would bring a 'loss of face', in effect placing the future of the business into the hands of extremists.

A firm stand was taken, and the demand rejected, so that the Union gave formal notice of their intention to strike, as from 27th September. However, the agitators were not only seeking to halt the Traction Company, but had as their target the complete closing down of all bus services throughout the island, and to this end had been building up an atmosphere of unrest amongst all of the Chinese bus companies' employees, with demands for increased pay and a catalogue of fringe benefits.

The owners were united in rejecting these demands, and as a result all buses came off the roads in concert with the Traction Company. Garage entrances were blocked by lines of pickets, and along boundary fence wires lurid banners were hung depicting the wicked actions of the greedy owners. Taxi proprietors found more business than they could cope with, and pirates swamped the main city routes, leaving the rural dwellers to cope as best they might.

Great value is placed upon children, and

ABOVE: The first priority of the community during the early days of the 'Great Strike' was to organise a means of carrying children between home and school. As the Chinese bus companies were also at first effected, the lorry-buses belonging to factories for the carriage of workers was mobilized. The condition and type of these varied widely and included this example, at work on schools service 11, covering Holland Road. The vehicle's make is uncertain but *may* be a WWII 'captured enemy vehicle' of Japanese origin. *(F. W. York* **BELOW:** Another ex-military truck in use as a lorry-bus for school services, probably a Ford (Canada), judging from the oval badge but similar cabs were used by Chevrolet (Canada). This 'bus' was serving the emergency route 1A to Geylang. *(F. W. York*

LEFT: In this October 1955 view, a protective policeman stands at the side of this lorry bus of indeterminate make, obscuring the entrance-way beside the cab to the platform. The 'schools' sign and chalked route '5A Tangong Pager' are clearly evident attached to the front bumper. Such is the esteem in which children are held by the local population—including strikers—that the police attendance was scarcely necessary. *(F. W. York*

ABOVE RIGHT: SA3592 was working the emergency school service 7 to Moulmein Green and shows clearly the children entering the vehicle by way of the nearside running-board and steps to gain access through an opening in the front-board of the lorry body and protective taupaulin. The chassis make is unclear but could possibly be a 'captured enemy vehicle' as ex-Japanese vehicles were classified. *(F. W. York*

was able to board. As a form of protection the policemen were not required, as the strikers had great respect for the children. No fares were charged, and normal stopping places were observed. On the radiator of each lorry were displayed two boards, one carrying the word 'School' in both English and Chinese, the other bearing the 'service' number and destination, viz.:

  1A Geylang Road and Geylang,
  2A Paya Lebar and Upper Serangoon Road,
  3A Katong,
  4A Newton,
  5A Tanjong Pagar,
  7A Moulmein Green,
  11 Holland Road.

Whilst all of these routes favoured the Traction Company's sphere of influence, the decision not to match the service numbers can be seen as an attempt to show a neutral stance in the dispute. Indeed, no cross town facilities were on offer, and all of the services came together at a central terminus in Waterloo Street, situated between Stamford Road and Bras Basah Road, an area within which a considerable number of schools might be found. It will be noted that

no provision could be made for children living in the rural areas, but the whole scheme depended wholly on the number of contractors who felt able, in these troubled times, to make their lorries available, and it was thought prudent by those who planned the operation to meet the greatest needs with what limited resources were available.

To the children it was a great adventure, uncomfortable as it certainly was, although towards the end of this logistic exercise some children were able to ride on two buses which joined the motley fleet, the first being a private owner's Ford ('Private' in the sense of being owned by an individual, not one of the Chinese bus companies) recently retired from the fleet of the Green Bus Company, whilst the other provided accommodation bordering on luxury, being a recently delivered Mulliner-bodied Austin, the property of the MALAYAN AUXILLARY AIR FORCE (Angry letters appeared in the press demanding to know why the extensive fleets of coaches owned by the British military were not pressed into service, and although no official response was given, it is easy to see how much a move would have been regarded as provocative, causing even more violence on the streets).

RIGHT: Recently the property of the Malayan Auxiliary Air Force, this Mulliner-bodied Austin, was one of two private-owner buses to supplement the lorry-buses, providing a little extra comfort for those children whose school might fortunately be served by it on its 1A Geylang Road to Geylang route.

LEFT: Changi Bus Co was the first to put a toe in the water and introduced a service 2, being an extension of their service from, over trolleybus 2, from Geylang to Union jack Club. An outward extension was very quickly introduced to cove the STC service 23A from Siglap Road. Changi Bus Co. Ford, S 4320, stands at the Siglap Road terminus, its emergency door open to keep the stationary bus cool in the humid heat in this very tropical, palm-lined, setting. *(F. W. York*

Supplementary Railway Service

Came November, and no settlements were in sight so that, with public exasperation reaching danger levels, the Government looked for any straw which might be clutched in order to bring at least some measure of relief. To this end an approach was made to Malayan Railways with the request that a form of local service be reintroduced. An agreement was reached, that such a service would be provided for the duration of the strike : Bukit Timah still had a regular train service, and at Tanglin use by the military had kept the station intact, but the sites at Telok Blanga and Kranji had become little more than crossing keeper's huts.

The lorry-bus concept was adopted in order to feed passengers to these stopping places, and the 'rail-bus' impression was further extended by the style of tickets used, being of thin paper to bus ticket dimensions, with destinations printed down each side (except for journeys between Singapore and Bukit Timah and Johore Bahru, when the normal Edmonson card tickets were issued). Third class accommodation only was provided, and the fares from Singapore were Telok Blangah 15 cents, Tanglin 20 cents, (Bukit Timah the standard 35 cents), Bukit Panjang 40 cents, Kranji 60 cents (and Johore Bahru 80 cents).

Considerable traffic was anticipated, so much so that the tickets were given five digit serial numbers. Alas, the crowds did not appear (three days into the service, the Author caused a slight sensation at the booking office when seeking to purchase a set of tickets: the serial numbers respective to the reopened stations listed above were 00000, 00000, 00005 and 00001).

A good idea had failed badly, and although no official reason was given, several can be contemplated. First, the trains themselves were far too grand for this type of work, comprising no less than twelve bogie coaches hauled by one of the main line Pacific locomotives, when the ideal would have been one of the Sentinel railcars working with great success on local services around Kuala Lumpur or, if they could not be spared, a sprightly tank engine with perhaps three coaches. Secondly, the public had lost the habit of travel by train, and those who needed to travel from Tanglin were within the range of pirate taxis. Thirdly, the very location of the railway station at Singapore meant that taxis would still need to be sought in order to reach the central districts. Fourthly, and perhaps the most difficult problem to be faced, was that the railway was single track, with passing loops of course, and this layout was not suitable for high density travelling, for priority had to be given to the regular services up-country, and the frequent passing of freight trains. The experiment at reintroducing train travel lasted for perhaps two weeks, and then was quietly withdrawn.

Chinese Bus Cos. settle

Meanwhile, the Chinese bus owners had maintained close negotiations with the Union, agreement was reached, and they were able to resume their services during December. Not so with the Traction Company, whose Chairman had flown out from London during the previous month hoping to mediate, but his was a wasted journey. For a while residents in the rural districts had the advantage of bus services once more, but did not take kindly to being dropped at the

LEFT: Easy Bus Co Austin SH 456, together with Keppel Vulcan SC 7068, at Raffles Quay terminus. These little Austins were specially narrow for use on the narrow lanes traversed by Easy services in the normal course of things. The resulting 2+1 seating made them less than ideal for high density operation in the central area. *(F. W. York*

ABOVE: Predictably, the trunk routes of the STC were those most attractive to the Chinese bus operators; particularly those along the Geylang and Serengoon Roads. Here Tilling-Stevens L4MA8 (badged as Vulcan), SH 122, of Keppel Bus Co, is in Geylang Road on the 16.

city boundary, and public opinion moved towards the Chinese bus companies being allowed to take over the Traction Company services. Such a move could be made only after applications to the Registrar of Vehicles for short term licences and the New Year brought hope, not for the Traction Company, but for the travelling public.

How could the Chinese operators take on such a task? The delivery of new vehicles, and the retention of some of the former military based buses which might otherwise have been disposed of, meant that most of the operators held fleets greater than their normal functions would require. Most terminals would show lines of buses laying over, but with only a single route to be served. By using every vehicle it would be possible to maintain regular services and also take advantage of the opportunities on offer within the city boundary. Changi was the first to make a move, and whereas their service 2 was a short working of the main line, operating between Geylang and Changi, it was pivoted so as to work between Geylang and the Union Jack Club, so providing cover for half of trolleybus 2. Enjoying instant success, an extension beyond Geylang was quickly introduced to Siglap Road, embracing the Traction Company's 23A service.

During the afternoon of 3rd January a small yellow bus sporting a black flash was to be seen darting along Collyer Quay, this being one of the specially narrow Austins of Easy Bus Company, perhaps the most unexpected entry into the city, for this was one operator who did not appear to have a great surplus of buses. Furthermore, the nature of the route served, being very narrow and winding lanes, called for small buses, and with a one-and-two transverse seating plan, their carrying capacity was very limited. ('One-and-two' means that, instead of having the usual double seats on either side of the gangway, on one side would be a double but on the other would be only a single seat. The first actually to reach the business centre, the little bus made a brave sight as it went past the General Post Office, admired by those who thought that they might never see a bus in service again. What Easy Bus had done was to extend their route from the Pasir Panjang end inward over service 24 of the Traction Company, although perhaps fearing that their limited resources would become overstrained, no attempt was made to reach the normal 24 terminus in Bras Basah Road. Instead, once over Anderson Bridge, a U-turn was accomplished by using the trolleybus-only lane around the Empress Place traffic island, although special dispensation would have been required to make this move. The result was a through service between Collyer Quay and Bukit Timah, albeit a very long way round, but, somewhat oddly under the circumstances, Easy Bus was

required to observe the same restrictions as applied to Traction Company 24, in that passengers could not be taken up or set down beyond Keppel Harbour, at least, not until their own routing was obtained. Perhaps an advantage in that they were able to charge the Traction Company's twenty-five cents fare, and were even able to offer a through fare of sixty cents to Bukit Timah - as ticket stocks in this denomination were not held, the rate was met by the 'marriage' of 25- and 35 cents tickets.

As might be expected those routes serving Geylang and Serangoon Roads proved to be the main attractions as far as the Chinese bus companies were concerned, so that eventually buses of many colours would be seen at work, a situation which troubled the Registrar of Vehicles: for example, Serangoon Road would be served by Tay Koh Yat, Paya Lebar, Easy and Ponggol before the dispute was finally settled, but the Registrar was worried to note that other, less fruitful, portions of the Traction Company network were being left unserved. Representations were made to the operators, asking that they should spread their operations to take on some of the less lucrative routes, as a result of which all routes bar one were able to receive some kind of service, although not always in the form as provided by the Traction Company. As with the initial moves by Changi and Easy, operators would endeavour to cover the city operations by natural extensions of their regular territory, a practice which would prove to be very much to their advantage in the not too distant future. The sole route that nobody wanted was the number 11 along Beach Road.

Towards the conclusion of the strike all of the Chinese bus companies were working in the city with one notable exception, for the

ABOVE: Paya Lebar Bus Co operating on Service 18A which, with the 18, was operated from Serengoon Garden Estate to Finlayson Green as per the STC service. Here Fargo 'Kew', SH 269, in Serengoon Garden Estate, en route Finlayson Green.

BELOW: Pretending to be a trolleybus, Fargo 'Kew' (SH 464) of Changi Bus Co stands with a sister vehicle and a third from another operator—possibly the Paya Lebar Bus Co—at the Geylang bus and trolleybus station. This bus was on the 16A—suffix letters being freely employed by operators to denote their own variations—Katong to Tanjong Pagar, an extension to STC 16, serving North and South Bridge Roads in lieu of Finlayson Green, giving almost complete cover to trolleybus 2.

ABOVE: Ponggol also had stake in the 18, along with Paya Lebar and here their Tilling-Stevens (Vulcan) SH 248 displays a hand-written '18' in the destination screen as it passes through Finlayson Green. **BELOW:** On the 9th January 1955, Hock Lee Amalgamated commenced its Service 10— Neil Road to Moulmein Road— following the exact route of STC 10. Here Hock Lee's Vulcan SH 205 passes the General Hospital

lem was faced by the Kampong Bahru Bus Company, whose own regular service was so short as to require only 5- and 10 cents tickets. Not knowing how long the strike would last it would have been imprudent to purchase stocks of higher value in their own name, and so 15-, 20- and 25 cents tickets were used bearing the name of the Katong-Bedok company.

When first starting to work into the city, the Chinese companies used the established Traction Company service numbers but, as the number of routes being served increased and their own variations were introduced, the system of numbers became less accurate, with the suffix 'A' being added at the whim of the operator. Again with one exception all destination material was bi-lingual, in English and Chinese, the exception being the Tay Koh Yat Service 1 where destination boards were wholly Chinese. Following the tentative moves by Changi and Easy Bus, 4th January became the day upon which wholesale introduction of services took place, and it becomes opportune to now present a Diary of Events:

4TH JANUARY:

Ponggol–Service 18	Tampines Road to Finlayson Green (as STC).
Paya Lebar –18 & 18A	Tampines Road and Serangoon Garden Estate to Finlayson Green (as STC).
Hock Lee–Service 19	Raffles Quay to Kim Keat Avenue (not covering STC Service 19 between Raffles Quay and Tanjong Pagar and then diverting off Moulmein Road via Kin Keat Road to Kin Keat Avenue - NOT an STC route at all.
Hock Lee–Service 19	Tanjong Pagar to Kim Keat Avenue (covering trolleybus 2 from Tanjong Pagar in lieu of Anson Road and Shenton Way, plus the extension to Kim Keat Avenue as above).
Keppel–Service 1	Raffles Quay to Keppel Harbour (being in effect an extension of their own normal service inbound from Tanjong Pagar by terminating at Raffles Quay - only one third of STC 1 was covered).
Keppel–Service 17	Raffles Quay to Botanic Gardens (short working of STC 12 as Hock Lee had a 'normal' service beyond Botanic Gardens to Holland Village
Kampong Bahru–16	Katong to Tanjong Pagar (being a variation and extension to STC 16, serving North and South Bridge Roads in lieu of Finlayson Green, giving almost complete cover to trolleybus 2).
Katong-Bedok–15A	Finlayson Green to Simpang Bedok (being an extension of 'normal' route over STC 15)
Easy Bus–Service 24	Ceased to work to Empress Place

7TH JANUARY:

Easy Bus– Service 24	New central terminus at Raffles Quay.

8TH JANUARY:

Changi–Service 2	Union Jack Club terminus discontinued, extending to Tanjong Pagar (STC 2)

Green Bus Company remained aloof, although their fleet had grown to a size wherein there would have been spares available. Indeed, this would have been the golden opportunity to extend away from the restricted terminal in Queen Street and reach the true central area but, as they covered a portion of trolleybus 6 in reaching Queen Street, perhaps this was enough. At the other end of the scale, a quite sensational move was the arrival of the coaches of Singapore-Johore Express to work service 9, serving high density of population through 'Chinatown' before passing along long lines of warehouses flanking the banks of Singapore River. Not having any of their own, tickets had to be borrowed from other operators, and the same prob-

BELOW LEFT : Raffles Quay. Amongst the services commenced on 4th January 1955 were the 17, seen here operated by Keppel Bus Co Albion Victor, SH 259, and the 15, represented by Katong Bedok Dennis 'Teal', SH 432. One wonders if the fare stage 9 plate on the post had any significance to the Chinese operators during the strike. **BELOW RIGHT:** Tay Koh Yat commenced running Service 1 on 14th January 1955 and here Commer 'Avenger' SH 343 is seen on lay-over beside the time-keeper's hut at Moulmein Road.

9TH JANUARY:

Hock Lee–Service 10	Neil Road to Moulmein Road (exact STC 10)
Tay Koh Yat–Service 2	Tanjong Pagar to Aljunied Road (this was almost a complete coverage of STC 2, finishing about one mile short of Geylang by a terminal loop formed y Geylang Road, Lorang 25, Sims Avenue and Aljunied Road).
Tay Koh Yat–Service 12	An alternative service number to above— proved *very* confusing.
Changi–Service 2	Extended from Union Jack Club to Tanjong Pagar (to complete the coverage of STC 2).
Changi–Service 22	Tanjong Pagar to Siglap Road (replaced STC 23A)

10TH JANUARY:

Hock Lee–Service 19	Route from Raffles Quay discontinued.

14TH JANUARY:

Tay Koh Yat–Service 1	Tanjong Pagar to Thomson Road. (Worked as a short of STC 1 by terminating at Tanjong Pagar rather than Keppel Harbour, requiring a revised terminating loop embracing Anson, Tanjong Pagar and Keppel Roads in order to regain Anson Road for the return journey. From Moulmein Road terminus extended to Thomson Road via Balastier Road–STC 19).
Tay Koh Yat–Service 12	Number discontinued for Aljunied Road Road working.

17TH JANUARY:

Easy Bus–Service 24	Service discontinued.

18th JANUARY:

Easy Bus–Service 18	Finlayson Green to Frankel Estate (a branch from the already established 15A but departing from the STC 15 by leaving Geylang Road to travel via Guillemand Road to reach Mountbatten Road, thence back to Geylang Road at Happy World, thus providing a short cover for STC 20)

2ND FEBRUARY:

Changi–Service 16A	Siglap Road to Finlayson Green (little in common with STC 16—in the central district, on inward journeys, used Coleman Street, previously without buses —and made acircuit of the Pedang in order to reach Connaught Drive–with High Street being used outwards).

4TH FEBRUARY:

Tay Koh Yat–Service 18	Finlayson Green to Tampines Road (as STC 18)

ABOVE: Tay Koh Yat Albion Victor SH 522 at Katong on Service 16

BELOW: Paya Lebar Tilling-Stevens (Vulcan) SH 307 at Tampines terminus

RIGHT: At the end of the strike, an STC Albion (STC 232) returns but the Tampines Road terminus is occupied by an Easy Bus Austin (SH 456) and an unidentified Paya Lebar Vulcan—probably all on the 18!

ABOVE: Rear view of Kampong Bahru Bus Fargo 'Kew', SH 448, at Katong terminus. The light blue and white livery adding more colour to the surrounding shop signs.

routings must have been very confusing to passengers but they would not need to worry for very much longer, as a settlement would soon be at hand. An interesting feature of the dispute was the neat manner in which the Traction Company fleet had been parked up in strict numerical order. Alas, with the motor buses being parked in the open, and through the monsoon season, sun and rain had taken their toll, for as the weeks extended into months so the usually bright paintwork became dulled, whilst on the more recent deliveries fitted with windows, the panes were covered in a film of grime. An air of neglect hung heavily, and there would be much work to be done before the fleet could venture back into service. At each gateway small tent-like structures were placed, housing the Union pickets, who always seemed to be quite cheerful. Not so happy the lurid banners hanging on perimeter fences, in grotesque fashion depicting the gross European shareholders whipping cowed employees harnessed to buses. For it's part the Government had appointed a Court of Enquiry, following the pattern

9TH FEBRUARY:

Changi–Service 22   Renumbering of journeys extended beyond Geyland to Siglap Road.

Changi–Service 23   An alternative number for the above.

11TH FEBRUARY:

Tay Koh Yat–Service 12   Tanjong Pagar to Aljunied Road discontinued.

Tay Koh Yat–Service 10A   Chulia Street to Whitley Road via Jalan Besar and Lavender Street (no direct comparison with any STC service, being 10 cut short at Chulia Street, 19 from the 10 terminus at Moulmein Road to Thomson Road and then into previously unserved areas to a terminal at Whitley Road, not far from Bukit Timah Road).

12TH FEBRUARY:

Tay Koh Yat–Service 16   Katong to Tanjong Pagar (as STC 16)

Changi–Service 16   Tanjong Pagar to Siglap Road (replacing to use of 22 and 23).

The use of the number 16 to cover widely separate

ABOVE: Seen working on Service 16, this Fargo 'Kew' belonging to Kampong Bahru turns left into Boon Seng Road, Katong, one of many tight turns throughout this mainly residential district

LEFT: If its in the way, cut it down! The building contractor's answer to trolley-bus overhead adjacent to the site was, in the absence of striking STC crews, to merely cut the wires and get on with their job. Standing-in for trolleys, Vulcan, SC 8691, of Paya Lebar Bus Service passes the severed wiring in Serangoon Road.

established in 1947, and both sides to the dispute had agreed to be bound by the findings and recommendations.

Return of Traction buses

The Report was published on 11th February: the company were required to give substantial increases in pay to the operational staff, whilst the Union were called upon to give a solemn undertaking to provide maximum support in the final stamping out of 'squeeze'. The afternoon of 16th February saw a few Traction Company buses back on the streets, but a period of chaos was to follow, based on the fact of the Chinese bus owners not giving advance notice of when they were to introduce, or make variations to, an emergency service, so also did they not inform passengers of their withdrawal. There were a few isolated instances of Traction Company and Chinese buses interworking on the same route but, by and large, the Chinese owners made a rapid exit from the scene.

What of trolleybuses? The fleet had been fortunate in having been stored under cover within the car sheds, but lack of maintenance had left the overhead wiring in a sorry state, mainly due to broken spacer bars causing the wires to 'come apart'. During the

LEFT: SH 425, a Fargo 'Kew' of Katong-Bedok in Guilleward Road, a 'temporary' emergency extension, destined to become permanent once the strike was over.
BOTTOM LEFT: This side view is of a Commer Commando is S 2182 of Tay Ko Yat taken at Paya Lebar International Airport, a classic example of older buses being pulled-in for further use.

TOP LEFT: Katong-Bedock Vulcan SH 294 at Frankel Estate Terminus, surrounded by signs of new construction.

CENTRE LEFT: Keppel Harbour Post Office is the setting for Vulcan SC 7168 of Keppel Bus Co. and the treminus of the route. Unlike STC buses, which made a 'U' turn, Keppel drivers were inclined to reverse their charges.

months of the dispute major bridge reconstruction work was put in hand where Serangoon Road crossed Kallang River, involving the use of cranes, the jibs of which would foul the wires. With no overhead crews available to make a realignment, the contractors simply cut away those section of the overhead wiring which formed an obstruction, the effect being to delay the reopening of service 4 until such time as the wiring could be restored. Ample accommodation could be found on buses on service 18, even if overcrowded, but not so with the 6 to Newton, onto which a couple of Dennis 'Falcons' were drafted in order to maintain the route on an interim basis. 2 and 3 trolleybuses were back in service three days after the end of the strike.

The after effects of the long strike were swift in coming, for the Chinese bus owners had tasted the rich fruit of city workings, and

RIGHT: Siglap terminus of Service 16A operated by Changi Bus Co during the strike. Here Vulcan SH 266 and (behind) a Ford rest in the heat under palm trees. Settings such as these are—sadly—a thing of the past in modern Singapore.

101

RIGHT: Private Bus S2452, an ex-military Chevrolet chassis with a bus body was one of the smaller buses working emergency schools services, in this instance to Paya Labar. This vehicle was probably purchased from one of the Chinese operators for further service on lighter duties.

RIGHT: Open rear platforms were common practice for many years but the arrangement was unusual on small, normal-control (bonnetted) single-deck buses such as this Chevrolet of Hock Lee Amalgamated, S 9326, seen here at Outram Road terminus.

BELOW: The Dennis 'Teal' was a rare bird, so sa to speak, but was present in the fleet of Katong Bedok Bus Service. Here SH430 was seen in December 1955 at the Collyer Quay terminus.

they wanted more. Indeed, someone, somewhere, had made a very fine study of the 1925 Ordinance and come to the conclusion that the monopoly granted to the Traction Company was in respect only of the *trolleybus* services, and no rights were indicated insofar as motor buses were concerned.

Such a decision did not affect the first move, which was made by Changi, who were granted the right to take up and set down passengers from Geylang into town, and such a move certainly brought severe competition to trolleybuses 2 and 3, for whilst their minimum fare was 10 cents, Changi was able to offer short stages at 5 cents, the minimum common to all of the private operators.

As from 13th October a further brand of competition was brought against trolley 3, when Hock Lee Amalgamated extended their own service 3 to a terminus at Jalan Kubor, just short of Kallang Road. Whilst it is true that, within the city the line of route followed Clemenceau Avenue and Orchard Road, those sections along New

ABOVE: Before the days of one-man-operation, front entrances were unusual in Singapore. Here a Commer (SH 370) belonging to Tay Ko Yat, works 'strike' route 10 as it turns into North Canal Road.

LEFT: Tay Ko Yat SH 373 was a Fargo 'Kew', seen here at Whitley Road terminus, an extension having little obvious passenger potential.

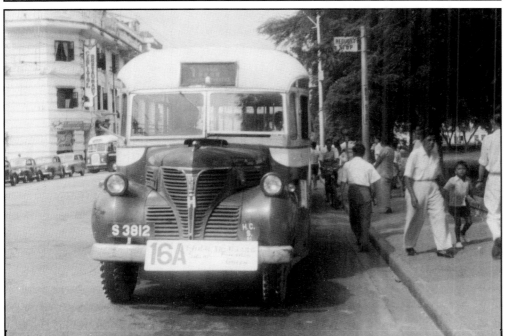

LOWER LEFT: North Bridge Road and a bonnetted Fargo—built in the USA—S 3812, of Changi Bus Company, waits by a request stop but appears to be broken-down. Of particular note, the rather heavy destination board and the positioning thereof.

RIGHT: Strike Service 15A, with Chinese, Malay and British passengers boarding at Fargo' Kew', SH 427 of Katang-Bedok at Bedok.

BELOW RIGHT: Tilling-Stevens (Vulcan) SH 256, belonging to the Keppel Bus Co Ltd, on strike Service 17 in Stamford Road, hurrying towards the city with a full load.

Bridge Road and Victoria Street brought the 5 cents fares to those travellers who hitherto had used the trolleybus.

Paya Lebar looked towards the city, and used the length of Sims Avenue in order to move away from the long established Geylang terminal, coming to a new terminus opposite The Happy World. In similar fashion, Katong-Bedok had built up quite a high degree of passenger loyalty whilst operating along Guillemand Road, and applied to make this arrangement permanent, which licence was duly granted.

Tay Koh Yat recognised the potential traffic to be found along the side roads of 'Little India', and were able to introduce loop services well within the city boundary, whilst in common with Paya Lebar (and later, Changi) the fact of the new International Airport at Paya Lebar being open created new destinations on a permanent basis. Although not reaching the central business area, the Chinese bus companies were moving deep within the city boundary, but without any form of co-ordination.

Whilst the strike was in progress, yet a further study of Singaporean public transport was being made.

RIGHT: Albion 'Victor', SH 519, of Tay Ko Yat on Service 15 at Tanjong Pagar, one of the busiest terminals. Note the Hock Lee Amalgamated bus waiting to turn.

LEFT: Changi Bus Company Seddon Mk 11 with underfloor engine—itself unusual in Singapore—SH 301 was just over a year old when the strike began and looks in fine fettle with deeply domed roof when seen here operating Strike Service 2 in the company of a Ford 'Prefect' and a turbaned gentleman on his bicycle as it passes South Bridge Road, under the trolley wires.

BELOW: Making tight turns on city bus services had not been a regular part of the daily routine for either the coaches or the crews of Singapore-Johore Express. The coach firm's appearance on Service 9 late in the strike came as a surprise—they even had to borrow tickets from other operators. Here Singapore-Johore Express Vulcan SH 111 turns from South Bridge Road into Cross Street with its service '9' route number pasted to the upper windscreen as the conductor signals the turn.

LEFT: Keppel Bus Company provided this little Chevrolet 'Maple Leaf', SC4334, with Perkins diesel engine seen standing beside Singapore-Johore Express Tilling-Stevens (Vulcan) SH 106 at Raffles Quay terminus. It is noteworthy that the most luxurious buses should be used over the least trafficed route.

ABOVE: The background to the Hawkins Report was one of strike and strife which continued for much of the time as the Commission of Enquiry was sitting. Although the Chinese bus companies were also effected by the strike of 1955-56, it was the Traction Company which was generally and continuously effected. Here is seen Macpherson Road depot with row upon row of buses that remained motionless for months on end while the population made frenzied efforts to struggle to and fro school or workplace. *(Straits Times*

Under the provisions of the Inquiry Commissions Ordinance, 1941, the Governor "deemed it expedient and in the interests of public welfare that a diligent and full examination and enquiry should forthwith be made into the following matters, namely, the public passenger transport system of Singapore and its future development", such Order being dated 3rd October 1955. So many reports and investigations had been made since the ending of the occupation that, on the face of it, there seemed to be little opportunity for a Commission to discover anything new to lay before the Governor but, in the event, the Commissioners were able to bring together the more workable aspects of previous reports and then use them as a foundation upon which to construct recommendations reaching far into the future. Five Commissioners were appointed, the Chairman being Mr. L.C. Hawkins, seconded from the London Transport Executive and thus demonstrating the sheer professionalism of the team, and from whom the report, when published, was to take a "short title". The task ahead of them would not be easy, working as they would be in an atmosphere of industrial unrest. When published on 12th January 1956, the Report was presented in twenty-seven Chapters and three Appendices, a total of 102 pages in all.

Due note was made of the rapid expansion of population and, taking the period between the financial years ending 30th September 1951 to 1954, remarked that passengers carried by the Traction Company had increased by 49 per cent, a spectacular growth by any standards, whilst vehicle mileage worked was in almost an exact proportion, up by 43 per cent, with a fleet expansion of 36 per cent offering a seating capacity growth of 43 per cent due to the introduction of larger buses. A similar rate of growth was recorded by the Chinese bus companies, with a total of 249 buses being brought into service during the four years following the end of the occupation, rising to 318 by 1951. Then, the Registrar of Vehicles had reported "At one time during the year it was thought that an amalgamation of all Chinese public omnibus services was imminent but, for one reason or another, negotiations (again) fell through. The early unification of services is of paramount importance to the public, but it is

felt that this desirable result will not be brought about by negotiation". Whilst the number of passengers carried had not shown as rapid an increase as had been experienced by the Traction Company, at 39 per cent, the seating capacity increased by an astronomical 81 per cent, with the total number of buses up by 49 per cent, an indication of the extent to which small capacity buses based on former military chassis were being ousted by larger vehicles, besides indicating that the rapid population growth tended to be concentrated within the city limits.

Although their remit was not concerned with the waves of strikes, a warning was included in the Report, viz., "...despite the remarkable record of growth, bus operators could not expect to have everything their own way, and must expect competition from private means of transport, motor cars, motor cycles (then very much in vogue) and even bicycles. When services are stopped passengers are forced to find other means of transport, which many will continue to use once normal services are resumed, to the detriment of the interests of not only of those who own the undertakings but also of the staff who are employed and find their livelihood in them". Such a warning would be difficult to ignore. The importance of the humble bicycle was further emphasised as being a competitor for both traffic and road space, for when these machines first required registration plates during 1936 their numbers stood at 60,000 but by 1955 the total was 200,000.....

The Report provided an interesting insight to working conditions and practices, surprisingly revealing that the Chinese bus companies' rates of pay were higher than those paid by the Traction Company, but that the hours of work for a normal days pay were longer with any overtime being paid at plain time rates (as compared with time and a half on the Traction Company). Again, the Chinese companies' crews would work 8, 8° or 9 hours for that normal days pay, whilst the average for Traction Company crews would be 7 hours 6 minutes for one group (believed to be trolleybus shifts), 7 hours 28 minutes in a second group (these would be motor bus crews, taking into account the need to travel from Macpherson Road garage on shift change), and as little as 4 hours 54 minutes in a third group

ABOVE: This interior view of Ransomes trolleybus No 49 shows what the report referred to as a box interior when calculating standing as a proportion of the seated capacity—in this case it was an notional frfty percent.

made up of senior men who had been retained in order to work the Limited Stop services, whereon duties were seen to be light.

Witnesses gave conflicting views concerning overcrowding. Evidence given on behalf of the Traction Company took the view that, with frequencies so improved recently, no passenger should need to wait longer than five minutes before boarding a bus upon which reasonable accommodation was available. The Registrar of Vehicles and the Singapore Improvements Trust, backed by the City Council's Public Passenger Transport Committee, presented opposing statements, the latter going as far as to state "Complaints by the public of the unsatisfactory services provided by the Traction Company have been continuous and numerous and it cannot be denied that there is ample room for improvement". The President of the Council was asked to produce some of the complaints, but his reply was that they were not kept on Council files, but dealt with by individual Councillors : a request that they should assist brought no response. The Union also gave evidence of the overcrowding which their members were unable to control, and further stated that police assistance had proved to be more effective with the Chinese companies than with the Traction Company.

The situation would be much worse, most particularly during peak periods, were it not for the private arrangements made by employers and the use of freight lorries for the carriage of staff, most particularly civilians employed at the numerous Army, Naval and Air Force establishments located throughout the Island. An estimated 10,100 persons were daily carried by freight lorries hired by the War Department. A similar situation involved the carriage of school children, a considerable number of whom were carried in privately owned or specially chartered buses, in respect of which 290 licences had been issued during 1954. It was further noted that (shortly before the strike started) the Traction Company had introduced experimental "School Children Only" buses over the busier routes but, denied the opportunity of viewing such workings for themselves, the Commissioners were unable to comment on the value of such special provision. Instead, the Report stressed that all of the foregoing staff and children should, under ideal conditions, be able to travel by regular public transport but, as they required movement during very narrow time bands, the need to produce vast increases in bus fleets, most of which would remain idle for the greater part of the day, meant that the existing arrangements provided the only practical solution for the time being. (A note of explanation: as previously noted, education was exceedingly valuable, but there were more pupils than school places. Schools devised a form of shift system, "Morning" and "Afternoon", with a great deal of studying being done at home. Pupils attending "Morning" school would be on their way between 6.00 a.m. and 7.00 a.m., whilst there would be a double-peak

at mid-day as the "Morning" pupils went home and the "Afternoon" children made their way to school, thus giving a final exodus of the day between 5.00 p.m. and 6.00 p.m., which unfortunately clashed with office workers also making their way home. Furthermore, the population was recovering from the devastation of the occupation, and the post war boom meant that the proportion of children to adults was out of balance, the average age making Singapore a very young society).

Complaints relating to overcrowding and undue waiting times were less numerous as regards the Chinese bus companies, the reason to be found in the rural and thus less populated areas served. Nevertheless, there was competition to be faced from taxis, both licensed and pirates. What was the legal situation concerning standing passengers? Two differences were current between that which was allowed to the Traction Company and to others, in that attached to the Omnibus Service Licences issued to the Chinese companies a restriction was placed on the number of standees, with a penalty for non-compliance and, whilst similar restrictions were placed on the Traction Company they faced no penalty should an excess number of passengers be carried. With such a wide range of vehicle types in service a formula needed to be operational rather than a fixed figure : for the Chinese operators one-third of the seating capacity was the figure allowed for standing passengers, with the same allowed for the Traction Company *except* for those described as having a 'box-type' body, for which the formula provided fifty per cent. (What was this 'box'? Any vehicle fitted with perimeter seating, that is to say, long benches around the sides. At the time of the preparation of the Report such a definition would have embraced the greater part of the fleet, for all of the Bedford, Dennis and earlier post war deliveries of Albion's were to this pattern, as were all of the trolleybuses). Perimeter seating did encourage overcrowding by nature of the available floor space and, whatever the evils the system might have had, did much to assist recovery post-occupation.

Now that the pressures had eased somewhat, the Registrar of Vehicles had issued instructions that henceforth all new buses should be fitted with transverse seating (two-by-two, with a central aisle) for the greater comfort and safety of passengers, and furthermore, expressed the hope that buses with perimeter seating would either be withdrawn or converted to transverse pattern as soon as possible (that last was wishful thinking, and the earliest deliveries of Vulcan and Albions made to the Chinese operators stayed as they were). A final note concerning standing passengers - the Singapore-Johore Express were allowed none!

Speeds

In judging a transport service the passenger is concerned not only with the waiting time at bus stops and the measure of comfort provided once aboard but also with the journey time. Speed of operation was seen to have a direct bearing on the quality of service. The average speed of Traction Company buses, terminal to terminal, was indicated as being 10.8 miles per hour, but that of trolleybuses only 8.9 miles per hour. It was felt that the reason for the difference was that, for the major part of their journeys, trolleybuses had to work through congested city streets, whilst most motor bus routes worked into less congested suburbs : the averages had been drawn from the whole working day (which would start at 5.00 a.m. and continue through to midnight) during which it was considered there would be long periods when traffic could flow freely, meaning that the Commissioners thought that the average speeds were too low, especially for trolleybuses. Once again the Commissioners were at great disadvantage in not being able to see for themselves and it is impossible not to think that the Chairman might have based his thinking on experience in the United Kingdom wherein, particularly during the evenings, traffic did tend to decline, even during the pre-television era. No so for Singapore, which remained vibrant throughout the operational day. The Report advocated higher speeds.

Licencing

Turning next to the system of licensing, due note was made of the differences existing between the Traction Company, functioning under the provisions of the 1925 Ordinance, and all other operators, who needed to obtain a licence from either the City Council or Rural Board when wishing to establish a new route, with which ever Authority concerned not only approving such new route but also determining the schedules thereof. The Municipal (Hackney Carriage) By-Laws, 1950, applied to the Chinese companies but not the Traction Company, in laying out penalties for non-compliance of any conditions set to the licence, in theory being valid for a period of up to one year but in practice needing renewal every six months. In as much as the Traction Company was concerned, the Commission made a minute study of the "Exclusive Privilege" granted by the 1925 Ordinance, and upheld the view that any rights concerned *trolleybuses* only, and that Section 30 of the Ordinance did not in itself protect the Company's motor bus services from competition. Therefore, over the years there had grown up an understanding that, wherever the Traction Company could be shown as providing an adequate service over a particular route (within the city boundary), then further licences for that route should not be granted. In his evidence the Manager stated "It has been the policy (of the City Council?) that we should provide the service within the city area and the other bus companies the services outside the area, and on that basis the network of routes has been built up".

The City Council maintained a Vehicles and Traffic Committee comprising six councillors, and it was they who heard the licence applications in private sessions unless any person or body had made representations concerned with the subject of the application, in which case they would be allowed to attend in order to make know the nature of their support or objections. The Committee made known its' recommendations to the Registrar of Vehicles and in some instances asked for his advice, then laid the application before the City Council in open session for confirmation. The general process was the same for all parties, except that the Chinese companies had first to advertise their applications in the Government "Gazette" and in a newspaper, and were also required to give notice to the Traction Company concerning the nature of their application. (The Traction Company did advertise extensively whenever a new route was about to commence, but this was after an application had been approved). Theory again, in that all applications should be considered within one month from the date of the publication of the advertisement in the "Gazette", but the Commission discovered a considerable backlog awaiting attention from all quarters. This situation perhaps arose from too many investigations into public transport, for the City Council had seen fit to defer the issue of any further licences until the findings of the Commission could be debated, most particularly with regard to any purchase of the Traction Company and/or the setting up of a unified transport authority. In hindsight, it is very difficult to understand such lassitude, for any such proposals would need years to accomplish and, with the public getting thoroughly fed-up with the strike, surely they would hope for an improved pattern of routes to emerge, regardless of whom the operators might be.

The Registrar of Vehicles made several illuminating remarks concerning the licensing system, regarding the existing system as being unsatisfactory because, although there was keen competition for licences as new housing projects spread across

the traditional boundaries of the Chinese bus owners territories, "there is no means of providing services where a need can be seen to exist, unless there is an application for a licence". What he meant was that everybody wanted to work those routes which appeared to be fruitful, but he did not have the powers to insist that operators should introduce services along less rewarding routes. Witnesses on behalf of the Traction Company also declared the system to be unsatisfactory (i) because Members of the City Council and Rural Board were laymen without knowledge associated with the provision of efficient public transport services, (ii) there were considerable delays in processing applications, proved to be against the public interest, and (iii) the proceedings themselves were often bogged down by unnecessary evidence and argument hardly relevant to the establishment of a new bus service. The Rural Board wished for a single licensing authority with common practice throughout, with a similar attitude being shown by the Chinese bus owners, the latter adding that having licences valid for only six months did not give security to the large sums of money involved with the purchase of new vehicles to service the new routes, which would take several years to recoup. The Commissioners accepted this argument, and recommended that three years validity for a licence would be reasonable (as then was the case in the United Kingdom, although there too moves were afoot to extend licences to five years).

The pattern of services then existing had been largely determined by quite separate developments, in-town services going under the direction of the Traction Company, whilst beyond the municipal boundaries had been pioneered by the Chinese bus owners and, to a limited extent, the mosquito buses, without the slightest hint of co-ordination between any of the participants. The development of Singapore in order to accommodate and employ a growing population (from 418,000 during 1921 to 1,210,000 at 1954, projected to 2,000,000 by 1972), coupled with the extensive improvements in families economics, produced new transport demands to be best met by a system of routes planned on an Island-wide basis, further fuelled by that increasing population being the subject of further decentralisation plans and an opening up of rural districts. Chinese operators had always been jealous of their "traditional territory" meaning that new route applications were inclined to be based on preventing an overlapping into a neighbour's territory rather than to serve the best public interest, and whilst in theory this practice might have avoided wasteful duplication and/or competition, it could be at the expense of passenger's convenience. Whether tongue in cheek or wishful thinking, the Commissioners expressed the hope that, in the interests of efficient workings, individual financial interests should be ignored, with existing route being replanned according to the natural flow of traffic, viz., (i) linking certain of the Trac-

BELOW: Two operators running over a common section of route at different fares and with the crews on different rates of pay. In the east, a Tilling-Stevens, SH 307, of the Paya Lebar Bus Service and Albion FT39, STC 399 run through picturesque surroundings approaching Paya Lebar village.

ABOVE: Thje Singapore-Kuala Lumpur Express had only recently been introduced when Hawkins' committee sat and comparisons were made between it and the SingaporeJohore Express. Although the latter was registered and operated from within Singapore, its claim that, like the K.L. Express it was an Inter-State service, was accepted and the Johore Express remained outside any proposals made by the Commission. Here a new Albion coach for the K.L.-Singapore Express is posed for the camera, registered in Singapore as SH 229; half of the fleet being registered in Malaya and half in Singapore. *(Standard Photo*

special liveries and charging a scale of fares comparable with associated stopping services but with a fairly high minimum charge in order to discourage short journey riders. With a high level of comfort being provided such services would do much to induce regular travellers to lave their cars at home.

The Commissioners made an extensive survey of the situation relative to the Singapore-Johore Express in order to give weight to their suggestions regarding limited stop services. Depending on the time of day, there were six or eight departures each hour from the Singapore and Johore Bahru terminals, with no stops to be made en route. On the Naval Base service passengers could be taken up or set down at stops within the security zone, but not once the public highway was reached. Although almost all the mileage thus operated was within Singapore, traffic was regarded as being Inter-State with the Federation of Malaya, although the company was incorporated in Singapore, vehicles were registered in Singapore and licence duty and diesel fuel tax was paid in Singapore. Representations were made by the company, arguing that because of their Inter-State status it should be treated in the same manner as the recently introduced Singapore–Kuala Lumpur Express, and the Sian Lian Express to Malacca, and be excluded from any recommendations made by the Commissioners. The answer to this valid point was that any decision reached whether or not to include the company in any unification scheme would have to depend on general traffic considerations and the long term interests of both Singapore and Johore Bahru. On the first point the company accounts had recorded a fall in the number of passengers carried in the period between 1951 and 1954 despite an increase in vehicle miles operated, from 1,157,000 down to 1,225,000. (In retrospect, the fall might well be attributed to the continued State of Emergency and the consequences for Johore State as a whole, for thereafter the company did thrive, and retain independence).

To continue the theme and provide support for the predictions made earlier, the Report made note of the high frequency stopping service provided by Green Bus, covering exactly the same route but providing between 10 and 12 buses an hour between the terminals, so that co-ordination with the Express would be appropriate. To achieve this the Express route should be extended to the city centre at Shenton Way, with stops for both taking up and setting down passengers at Bukit Timah and Bukit Panjang in the rural districts, whilst Rochore Road would remain as an additional stopping place in the city. The rather surprising conclusion to this recommendation was that, should this degree of co-ordination be achieved then not only would the Express be withheld from any unification project, but also the Green Bus Company!

This was the only precise route recommendation that was made, for the Commissioners did not regard a detailed replanning of existing services to be contained within their terms of reference : if this were so, then they would need a great deal of additional time in order to make physical inspections of the routes concerned, which again could only be carried out when the whole pattern was functioning normally, and no end to the strike was then in view.

At the time of evidence being taken the Singapore Improvement Trust was putting the finishing touches to their own Master Plan, and although the contents had not been made public, a measure of advance detail was made available. Provision was made for a considerable amount of rehousing away from the older parts of the city, and for additional accommodation to cater for the population expected to reach 2,000,00 by 1972, representing an increase of 60 per cent in seventeen years. The Plan sought to limit the amount of

tion Company route with some of those operated by the Chinese companies so as to provide through routes, (ii) extending some of the Traction Company's routes into the outer areas beyond the city limits, again with the objective of providing through routes without a change of vehicle, (iii) projecting some of the Chinese bus routes into the city centre, with the same objective in mind, and (iv) where some Chinese bus companies have routes which came close to the city centre, allowing them to continue in order to reach their true objectives (e.g., Keppel in from Tanjong Pagar, Tay Koh Yat from Beach Road, Hock Lee Amalgamated from "Chinatown" and Green Bus, in Company with Singapore-Johore Express from Queen Street), Heavy irony once again, for recommendations (iii) and (iv) were already in hand, with some reservations, even whilst the Commission was sitting, due to conditions of the "Great Strike", but as these happenings were for the duration only, then they could not be used to provide examples of the findings within the Report. All four of the recommendations were eventually adopted, but not until 1971.

Question : what had Birmingham and Singapore transport in common? Answer : bus terminals dotted around the perimeter of the central areas. In fact the Commissioners found the number of terminals to be quite undesirable, and had received evidence from several sources concerning passengers who might be required to make two changes in order to complete a reasonably straight forward journey. At North Canal Road, Hock Lee Amalgamated turned 67 buses an hour during peak periods, at Queen Street Green Bus turned 30, Hoi How Road (off Beach Road) with Tay Koh Yat turning 25, whilst the Keppel company turned 24. If every bus arrived at each terminal with a capacity load, this meant that vast numbers of passengers were being set down at points far removed from their true destinations and whilst this might have been of great benefit to the finances of the Traction Company, it meant great inconvenience to those travellers besides creating a waste of valuable road space and increased traffic congestion.

This was not to suggest that the aforementioned turning points should be eliminated altogether, as short workings were often a valuable aid for the short distance rider, but insofar as the main body of services be concerned consideration should be given to the construction of a central bus station in the vicinity of Collyer Quay. Nor was it suggested that all routes then existing should be reorganised in order to reach the city centre, for the rural districts could be best served by a pattern of feeder routes leading onto the trunk roads. Such an arrangement would encourage the introduction of longer distance limited stop services to be served by buses presented in

travel embracing the city centre by expanding existing estates and constructing self-contained new towns throughout the rural areas. Such a wide expansion reflected the need for some form of unification, and the Chinese bus owners did support this thesis to the extent of limited amalgamations whereby to reduce their numbers, but were against the formation of a single company. Their strongest point of argument was that a better and more efficient service would be provided, in the long run, by private concerns whose owners were actively engaged in the bus industry, rather than a single organisation or even state-owned. The replies to the Association were (i) common maintenance facilities for the larger fleets would lower costs, (ii) standardisation of vehicles types, with resulting reduced stocks of spare parts and the benefits of bulk buying would also reduce costs, (iii) common labour policies and staff amenities, with comparable rates of pay, could only be advantageous, (iv) only one inspecting staff would be required for each trunk route, (v) the averaging of costs over a much wider area would encourage the establishment of otherwise unrenummerative services, and (vi) would eliminate the financial risks which would otherwise accrue from a drastic recasting of existing services. The Association suggested that most of the benefits so described could be obtained by suitable arrangements between the companies, such as a Managing Committee, but the Commissioners could not agree with this point of view, for whilst they were readily able to appreciate the incentive and responsibility arising from a personal financial commitment, such might tend to become blurred if managed by a committee, with a large portion of the autonomy of the individual companies in matters of administration needing to be surrendered, whilst items (v) and (vi) could in any event be met by a merging of financial interests and therefore of ownership. To quote, "The right policy, in our view, is the unification of the whole of the Island's passenger transport services, with a common ownership and a common management". Three options were proposed, (i) directly by Government, (ii) by a self supporting department of the Municipality, or (ii) by a Public Authority. Their own choice was option (iii), quoting experiences drawn from the history of the London Passenger Transport Board, and subsequent changes thereto. Enter the word 'Nationalisation' for the first time during the deliberations of the Commission, half way through their Report, and revealing that this was indeed the declared objective of the Government. The co-ordination of services through a revised system of licensing could provide an adequate pattern of bus services, but absolute unification could be the only practical answer to outright nationalisation, based on a Statutory Limited Liability Company incorporated under a special Ordinance in much the same way as other public utilities. Such a company would be given compulsory purchase powers to acquire existing bus operators, and thereafter would have a general duty to provide adequate services and to set up machinery appropriate for dealing with staff matters.

The magnitude of such an enterprise was swiftly recognised, and the transition from individual ownerships into a unified undertaking would require careful and detailed advance planning. Step one would be to acquire the Traction Company, for having a well established organisation supported by extensive and well organised workshops, would form a base upon which the new administration could rest (not in purely architectural terms of course). Then it would be possible to absorb the Chinese companies one by one, as the new management was ready to incorporate them into the new structure, with those whose existing routes were most easily adapted into the unified pattern being the first to be purchased.

Whatever the ideal functional solution might prove to be, prevailing conditions demonstrated the need for great tact and diplomacy when setting up a machinery for dealing with staff negotiations, and once more the Commissioners needed to make clear that there was no part of their function to make observations regarding the dispute(s) then creating chaos in the city although, in order to make proposals for the future, there was a need to make

a study of the history of industrial disputes without appearing to take either side. Two Trades Unions were involved, the Singapore Traction Company's Employees Union (2,000 workers) and the Singapore Bus Workers Union (about 1,600 workers), both quite small in terms of membership. The background to the Traction Company's dispute has been presented in an earlier Chapter. In their evidence the Chinese bus owners revealed that, apart from the major dispute which was crippling their businesses at the very time they were called upon to make their statement (during November 1955 they had received from the Union a series of demands, most of which they found impossible to meet, with the result that all their buses were removed from service as from 14th November, with the exception of the Singapore-Johore Express, that concern not being a member of the owner's association. The Union refused to withdraw or amend their demands, and so the owners felt compelled to institute a formal lock-out, for the recently enacted Labour Ordinance would be far more drastic than had been anticipated in financial terms, and could be met only by either cutting staff numbers or increasing fares. Seeing a threat to their livelihood, the strike was called off, and Chinese owned buses returned to service on 29th December), their services had been affected by fourteen stoppages of work during 1955 alone : taking into account the number of operators involved this was the equivalent to fifty-seven strikes. The duration of the stoppages ranged from ten minutes to twenty-two days, often without any prior notice, and with reasons based on protests of various kinds, such as a demonstration against the Public Security Bill, and a localised disagreement when the Hock Lee Amalgamated management refused two new buses to enter service without licence plates. Lists provided by the owners indicated that buses were stopped when there was no industrial dispute involved, and that the facilities of the Unions were being used as a tool in forms of political agitation. Except for the Statutory Provisions enabling the Government to set up Industrial Courts or Courts of Enquiry, their purposes to investigate matters and events which had taken place rather than to prevent disruptive happenings, no machinery then existed between the managements and employees whereby disputes could be settled by "round the table" negotiations before reaching the point of calling strikes : furthermore, the organisation built up by the Unions should not be used for, nor strikes called for, the furtherance of purposes which did not arise out of matters directly associated with the bus industry, and a greater sense of responsibility towards the public should be henceforth shown by both sides.

The Superintendent of Traffic Police provided an interesting insight concerning bus driving, for whilst pupil drivers were given a set course in order to learn their skills by the Traction Company before being licenced for bus driving, all that candidates for such employment with the Chinese companies were required to produce was a current licence valid for the driving of large cars, then to be

BELOW: Double-deck buses were looked-at by Hawkins but it was to be more than twenty years before they were to appear agin in city service in Singapore. Also suggested were 'large maximum capacity' single-deckers but the buses that came nearest to this description, two Tay Koh Yat Sentenels (SH 190-191) and seven Commers (SH 320-2/5/43/68/70), which had front entrances and set-back front axles, were unsuccessful, both types being rebuilt to centre doorway. Here a Sentinel becomes overcrowded under 1956 strike conditions whilst working city service 12A, in Bras Basah Road.

ABOVE: Another criticism by Hawkins was that of unnecessary duplication which was wasteful of buth manpower and vehicles. Larger buses could probably have reduced this line-up of Katong-Bedok buses by a third. The tea stall does good business at the Geylang terminus of Katong Bedok, away from the STC/Changi trolleybus station / interchange.

was to educate passengers in the importance of receiving a valid ticket for the correct fare paid each time they made a journey.

A number of witnesses, the most prominent being the Registrar of Vehicles, Traffic Police, and the Singapore Improvement Trust, advocated the in-city services being worked by double deck buses. From the Traction Company came the view that although the experiment using the A.E.C. on loan from Kuala Lumpur had attracted a great deal of interest, this had been purely as a novelty, and because of the crowds which had been attracted it had been found impossible to work to a schedule. The high crew costs had made the experiment uneconomic, and it was felt that any extended use would always call for a two-conductor crew in order to prevent the carriage of standing passengers on the upper deck, and in order to exercise control on the stair well, where boarding and alighting passengers might be loath to give way to each other. The Company would be quite willing to conduct a further experiment of longer duration if such would negate the novelty factor. The Manager of the Gen-

tested by a representative of the Registry of Vehicles before being passed for bus driving.

"Squeeze" was to feature large, and the two Trade Unions in a jointly prepared memorandum laid stress on what they described as "the extent of the petty corruption prevalent within the Traction Company" adding "to date 187 conductors have been convicted and imprisoned for petty corruption" further adding that similar corruption amongst the Chinese companies was "very conspicuous by its' absence". The Unions could not condone any form of corruption, but maintained that the roots were firmly implanted in the low rates of pay of the Traction Company. In a counter statement the Manager was unable to say to what extent conductors were subject to pressures from outside sources, leading on to the Chinese owners stating that they could not accept the latter part of the Union's memorandum. Whilst "squeeze" had been unknown, corruption was first suspected during the early part of 1955, becoming swiftly prevalent to the extent of, by the time the current strike commenced, they were together experiencing a sharp and otherwise unexplained drop in traffic receipts. The methods of working the "squeeze" were exactly as encountered within the Traction Company, so that the Commissioners recommended the early introduction of ticket machines as being one method of halting the diversion of receipts. The real need

eral Transport Company made the journey from Kuala Lumpur in order to state that, even with a two-conductor crew, the use of his fleet of double deckers had proved to be financially justified. The pros and cons between double deck and large capacity single deckers were examined in detail, the latter form being based on the European low-seating, high standing capacity layout coupled with one-man operation, which might have been the ideal design for use in Singapore, perhaps because during the post occupation years of shortages crush loading had acclimatised travellers to accept standing as the norm. With further debate such an idea faded, and instead the recommendation was for the new style of double decker then being developed in the United Kingdom, which would provide seats for 70 passengers.

In the Report the Commissioners confirmed that they had learned the details of the light railways suggestions, but observed that the Master Plan had been based on the assumption of all traffic expansions being road based for at least the following twenty years. However, the General Manager of Malayan Railways was introduced as a witness, and was able to express his professional interest in the introduction of local services over the existing line as far as Johore Bahru, using either diesel power multiple unit railcars or else going for full scale electrification. He also produced plans showing there possible extensions from the existing Singapore railway station in order to reach a new terminus in the vicinity of Collyer Quay (i) a single line at ground level with road overbridges, and suitable for conversion to double track when traffic required this, (ii) a single line at ground level except for a section from a point north of Keppel Road to a point east of Prince Edward Road which would be elevated, also being suitable for conversion to double track, and (iii) to go underground at the existing station and to continue thus until reaching Prince Edward Road (and, although the point was not made, we must assume that this construction would be double track as from start). A further proposal was that a junction should be installed at Bukit Timah, then to reactivate the former railway as far as Newton at Farrer Park, there to either terminate or else to go underground in order to reach Collyer Quay. It had to be admitted that costings for these proposals had not been attempted, and the greatest problem would be the availability of land, or lack of it.

BELOW: A major benefit from recommendations to amalgamate operations would have been to provide modern central workshops instead of each operator having its own premises, each to a differing standard of efficency. Here Morris Commercial OP/R, SC9332, of Green Bus stands at the gate to the Company's office and workshop installation. Not all were as neat as this.

111

ABOVE: Hawkins urged that rural routes should be maintained by increasing the number of more remunerative base routes—itself to be achieved by the same amalgamations that would have provided better workshops. Here a Green Bus Chevrolet Maple Leaf, SC 1599, runs along the very rural Maudai Road on that Company's Route 4.

be the construction of two-thirds of one mile of new line circumnavigating that holy-of-holies, the Padang : the Padang is a great heart of green, fronting city Hall and the High Court, whereon the pomp of national ceremonies can be watched by crowds numbering thousands, whilst rather fewer might be on hand to watch the almost traditional cricket matches which grace the hallowed turves. St. Andrews Road sheltering the Anglican Cathedral to one side, and Connaught Drive with the sea beyond to the other, all might be defaced if overhead equipment came to be erected, particularly as much cutting back of mature trees would be required. Once again an opposite opinion came from a quite unexpected quarter, for the City Engineer in supporting the removal of trolleybuses from the vicinity of Empress Place was not advocating their wholesale removal, instead offering an alternative which would require the reactivation of the Chulia Street spur, with new line going beyond that "terminus" by way of Battery Road as far as Fullerton Square, although it was not made clear whether the Square would be the new terminus or if the revised route would venture onto Collyer Quay, the existing terminal being only a few hundred yards further. The merits and demerits of the principals of trolleybus operations were discussed in detail (fumes free and silent in operation, route bound and lacking in flexibility, etc.,) and it was asked if the Traction Company had prepared any plans for the replacing of trolleybuses. A negative reply was given, for as the fleet was then barely seven-and-a-half years old there remained several years of effective life ahead of them, and only when eventually they became life expired would consideration be given to the mode of fleet replacement. With considerable tact the Commissioners decided that it would be premature for themselves to express a view in the matter.

With all forms of road traffic bound to increase, the Commissioners suggested that a serious study be made into the possibility of introducing a ferry-boat "bus services", starting at Collyer Quay and following the east coast as far as Katong. As a minus, trishaws were seen as being a form of transport very much out of place in a modern city, being slow and difficult to handle however skilful the driver might be. One trishaw is able to slow a complete lane of traffic, and restrictions should be placed not their use ("is" indeed, for in 1996 a small fleet of trishaws remain active, although they tend to venture out only during evenings, a great delight to the tourist trade).

Trishaws were not the only vehicles to be deemed as being out of place - a detailed examination was made of the one-way traffic pattern, in particular of those places at which trolleybuses were required to work against the traffic flow. The scheme was admitted as being in the form of a long term experiment able to be removed if needs be. The Superintendent of Traffic Police was asked, if the scheme was confirmed and made permanent, would his Department be prepared to accept the continuation of wrong-way working? The reply was that the Police would rather see trolleybuses removed altogether but, if this could not be done, then the section at the Kallang end of Victoria Street could be accepted whilst the complex working involved at Empress Place would be tolerated as the alternative would

The reminder of the Report dealt with wide ranging general comments concerning street furnishings, for instance advocating wide uses of central refuges for pedestrians along main roads and the provision of queue barriers at major bus stops. All in all the document proved to be a most detailed examination, and as such was given international recognition so that, unlike many that had gone before, almost all of the recommendations were destined to be put into practise, albeit over a span of some thirty years. (Despite the Summary once again seeing a future for the water-bus to Katong this did not happen, but, a similar service was introduced during February 1994, linking Collyer Quay with Clark's Quay up stream along the Singapore River).

The most immediate result was the enactment on 16th April 1956 of the Omnibus Services Licensing Authority, to do exactly what the title of the Act described.

LEFT: Hawkins felt that it was essential to improve the road system island wide and here extensive works are under way to the northern end of Bukit Timah Road at Mandai. A Green Bus Tilling Stevens on the Johore Barhu to Singapore Queen Street Inter-State service passes two generations of road rolling equipment; to the left the traditional steam-roller, SA 6605, son of the traction engine, while opposite is a, then, modern Aveling-Barford diesel-engined road roller, SG 4381. It is of note that, despite Hawkins reccommendations, the two Johore services, now SBS 180 amd the Singapore Johore Express, as well as the KL and Sian Lian Expresses, still terminate at Queen Street, outside the main central district.

Chapter Ten

1956 to 1964—The Traction Company

Towards a New Company

Whatever the findings of the Court of Enquiry might prove to be, the Board of Directors were certain that the cost of the Great Strike would be enormous, and in order to generate sufficient new revenue to allow the business to survive, the local management prepared a radical application for the revision of fares, not the least being the removal of the twenty-five cents maximum charge. So great was the confidence of the new structure being approved that considerable stocks of tickets in the higher denominations were purchased and placed in store pending the end of the strike. Great was the dismay when the suggestion to go beyond twenty-five cents was rejected, and those new tickets had to be destroyed. There was something to be gained, however, in that the adult five-cents minimum was abolished, and the ten cents stages were made shorter. Needless to say, there were Chinese bus operators who very much welcomed this move, most particularly Ponggol, who found that their five cents fare from Tampines Road junction up to Paya Lebar village drew much patronage to themselves in lieu of the Traction Company's service 18, and in similar fashion to riders on Changi buses taking short rides along Geylang Road. The five cents, and the ten cents maximum, charges had to remain for school children.

As ever, tickets were supplied by the BELL PUNCH COMPANY, of Uxbridge, and the new supplies needed to be somewhat longer than hitherto in order to accommodate the increased number of stages.

Whilst the protection of revenue was the prime consideration, two other matters required urgent attention, the future development of the motor bus fleet and the continued operation of trolleybuses. Of those sections of overhead wiring which had been maintained in anticipation of trolleybuses usage returning at some time, that along Cross Street was removed during February 1953, and the remnants of service 1 to Keppel Harbour during November of the same year. The crossing outside Kellang gasworks had been left in place for some time, but hardly penetrated Crawford Street (and so may have been left in situ for feeder purposes): this crossing, and the line along Lavender Street up to the junction of Jalan Besar would have been removed about the same time.

Of the fleet, the chassis were in very good order, and capable of giving many years further service. Alas, as the bodywork had been constructed rather hastily, premature signs of wear were beginning to show, and a programme of general rehabilitation was put into hand. As it was, several modifications had already been made, as technology brought forth new items of equipment. For example, direction indicators. As delivered, the intention to make a right hand turn was signalled by the driver pulling on a metal ball, this causing a large white painted board to swing out from the side of the bodywork. Whilst this might have been very effective, the method was downright dangerous for any cyclist who might have been coming alongside at that precise moment. As electrically operated flashing trafficators became available, so they were fitted (similar direction boards fitted to the Bedford and Dennis fleets were also being replaced over a period of time). In the original form, when wishing to make a left hand turn it fell to the conductor to lean out from the steps with his arm outstretched.

Once the post-occupation replacements were on the road, the fleet comprised forty-nine identical vehicles, and one oddment. Visually the design used for the late 1940's was not unpleasant to behold, although perhaps more in keeping with designs a decade earlier. As for number 2, this had been the basis of an experiment to mount certain of the electrical equipment on the roof rather than the chassis, the idea being to provide protection in the event of monsoon flooding. To provide accommodation the front dome was extended upwards and back to the point where the trolley booms had their seating. Again in visual terms, the result was somewhat ugly, and the experiment was not extended elsewhere.

Instead, there was the attempted suicide of number 19, back in traffic and looking very smart, so that most, if not all, of the fleet would go through workshops in order to receive body rebuilds to a varying degree. The result was that many of the trolleybuses re-entered service looking quite different, the most extreme example being number 45, whose revised bodywork was akin to the 'utility' designs produced for operators within the United Kingdom during the war. With others there were

LEFT: Following their mid-life rebuilding, the once standard appearance of the trolleybus fleet changed almost to the situation where every vehicle differed visually from any one of the rest. One unusual modification that predated the main rebuilding, however, was the relocation on No 2, of the electrical resistances and other equipment to the forward part of the roof where all was concealed by a deeply domed roof which extended back as far as the centre entrance and also shrouded the sides of the trolley bases which were located further back than was normal on Singapore's Ransomes. The purpose was to prevent damage caused by driving through deep monsson flood waters. Although successful, no further trolleybuses were altered in this way.

ABOVE: The Traction Company was obliged to utilize the services of small firms for the rebuilding of its trolleybus fleet and here No 26, in the company of Albion STC 307, is receiving attention in surroundings less well appointed as Mackenzie Road.

BELOW: At least some work was undertaken 'in house', particularly the relocation of the headlights to a more outboard location and the provision of air-intakes between them. In this view, trolleybuses are in the process of having their headlights relocated further apart and being fitted with new ventilators between the headlights to assist with chassis equipment cooling. It is interesting to compare this view with that on page 34—the period in the early 1920's when the trams were undergoing similar refurbishment.

detail differences which provided a means of identifying individual vehicles at some distance. To improve ventilation throughout the chassis, grills were placed within the dash panel, but at several locations. Some of these grills were single piece, others double. Number 27 was perhaps the greatest surprise, coming back into service with transverse seating. The conversion having worked well, and being recommended by the Hawkins Report, similar work was done to eliminate the bench style of seating, although over a much longer period of time than allowed for within the current programme.

Why, then, should there be so many variations within which was a reasonable small fleet? So important was the programme that there were insufficient facilities to carry it through swiftly within the Mackenzie Road workshops. Work was contracted out, and there were many small engineering firms happy to take a single trolleybus to work on, so that they would be found hiding away in parts of the town where they would be least expected. The major body builders, including Lee Kiat Seng, were not able to take on any of the contracts, as they were fully extended in meeting orders for new buses, in numbers difficult to accommodate.

The opportunity was also taken to introduce a new styling of livery. Several variations had been tried, including number 11 in all-over green, with very drab results. When new the pattern had been green with aluminium streamlining, but the latter was changed to cream upon first repaint. Now it was found that the style as used on the ill-fated City Circular service 7 would brighten up the whole fleet, and cream with green streamlining was adopted as the refurbished trolleybuses came back into service. The Dennis fleet was also progressively repainted thus, as were some of the better conditioned Bedfords, although a start was being made with their withdrawal. Of particular interest was a major refurbishing of Bedford 157, in addition to a complete body overhaul during which it also received a new front dome incorporating a one-piece destination box, matching the style of buses entering service.

Some work was, however, done at Mackenzie Road and a walk past the car sheds at this time enabled one to view a double line of trolleybuses in various skeletal forms, such was the extent of the work being undertaken. More to the point, there was an opportunity to examine the contents of the destination blinds, to find that, indeed, full provisions were made

LEFT: Trolleybuses 14 and 41 approach the Geylang trolleybus / bus interchange, passing an Ovaltine advertisement, typical of the 1950's, as they do so. More important are the contrasting liveries with 14 in original green and silver and 41 in newer cream with green roof and flashes. Other differences include the original closely spaced headlamps on 14 while 41 has its in the new, wider-spaced, location. The black patches between the headlights of the latter vehicle are the new ventilators.

RIGHT: In order to release trolleybuses for rebuilding, a number of Route 4 duties were reallocated to Dennis Falcon diesel buses and, in initially, these ran without blinds, merely carrying a 'Service 4' plate on the front dash panel. Here Falcon STC 74, on the 4, passes a trolleybus also on the 4. Some duties were also allocated to Albions and Falcons appeared on the 6 from time to time.

BELOW RIGHT: As the refurbishing work progressed, the Falcons began to appear fitted with trolleybus blinds, as was Dennis Falcon STC 24 seen here on the 4 in High Street. It too was sporting the cream and green STC livery.

for both services 5 and 10, although, taking due regard of the dismantling of the overhead line in part of Lavender Street, the text for service 5 read 'via Jalan Besar—not only was there still hope for a return to more extensive trolleybus operation, but even a 'ghost' route revision.

With only fifty vehicles, there was no spare capacity within the fleet with which to cover these prolonged spells out of service, and as a consequence service 4 became partly replaced by motor buses. At first a blank destination screen and metal plate carried beneath the cab and displaying 'Service 4' was considered to be sufficient, but as the replacements became ever longer, so trolleybus blinds were fitted to those Dennis Falcon's more usually assigned to this duty. From time to time they would be assisted by one of the later delivery Albions, whilst the released Falcon could then spare time as a substitute on service 6.

As far as the motor bus side of the business was concerned, the point had been reached where consideration had to be given as to what would comprise the next generation. There was no doubt that the Albions had proved to be a very sound and capable machine, but with the ever increasing demands placed on the buses, both in terms of passenger loadings and other traffic to be contended with, then a heavier duty vehicle was desired. To this end contracts were placed with GUY MOTORS LIMITED, Wolverhampton, and from these initial orders there was to be found such confidence as to place the Traction Company towards the top of international lists of users of the Guy Arab Mark IV. The first chassis was shipped from the United Kingdom during September 1955, five more during each month remaining of that year, until the 132nd chassis was despatched during May of 1958—repeat orders would follow, or so it would seem! In fact, the Guy Fleet was destined to comprise 133 vehicles.

Walking past the Macpherson Road yard during mid-1956 one could catch sight of the first two chassis, painted in their dark brown transit 'livery', complete with the Birmingham-style of bonnet, for the very first time provoking a slight twinge of nostalgia. Lei Kiat Seng would be constructing bodies of handsome proportions, and very soon the first was ready to enter service. There was a small difficulty to be first overcome, for a new numbering series was to be started for the

BELOW: The STC had standardised its postwar motor bus fleet on the Albion Victor chassis and these had given stalwart service but, despite their reliability, they were becoming increasingly under rated for the traffic which they were carrying. Here STC 228 of 1954 stands alongside the chassis of a brand new 'heavyweight' Guy Arab Mk IV awaiting bodying at Macpherson Road garage. The Birmingham-style of radiator grille can be seen clearly—later examples had a flatter 'Singapore' style fromt.

RIGHT: The only refurbished Bedford OB, STC 157, was re-registered STC 201 in order to allow the Guy Arab series to commence at 157. The original Bedford with number STC201 was sent for scrap and its registration number donated to the refurbished STC 157. The rebuilt Bedford was given a large one-piece destination box and metal panelled roor, minus the troublesome canvas. In this August 1954 view, STC 201 waits at the racecourse terminus for the homegoing crowds.

Guys, as from 157, but the revamped Bedford already carried that designation and was considered fit for further service. The use of the special STC series had allowed for the re-registration of occupation survivors into a series starting again at 1, for these numbers had remained vacant since the withdrawal of the original Dennis fleet. This case would be different, in that the required number was still in service. The solution, bring in Bedford 201—swap the registration plates with 157, send the original 201 for scrap, and let the erstwhile 157 continue in the new guise until such time as the entry into service of the Guys required the use of 201. Not all of the Guy's carried the 'Birmingham' style of bonnet. By the time deliveries were completed, the majority had received a revised styling unique to Singapore, having a completely flat front, incorporating the nearside mudguard as an integrated unit. A matter of opinion, but a great deal of the visual attractiveness was lost in the altered design, which may have been required in connection with engine ventilation. Full details of these buses can be found in Part B.

Bus bodies were to spring up all over the place, divorced from their chassis, the latter resuming their original resolves once fitted with rudimentary lorry bodies. Storage sheds seemed to be the most widely observed destiny, the body of one of the Albion survivors enjoying a particularly beautiful evening of life, having been sited in an orchid farm off Bukit Timah Road, gradually to disappear from sight under a blanket of exotic blooms. Of the Bedfords which had been purchased new, quite a number were sold off for further service, to be found in the school bus fleets on the Island, whilst two were observed in service in Johore State, so that there is a reasonable chance that others were to find their way into upcountry Malaya. Others, not fit for further service, had their bodies lined up to serve as beach huts, with the growth in popularity of Changi Beach.

1955 saw small extensions to the network: following the introduction of a service to Kim Keat Avenue by the Chinese concerns during the 'Great Strike, certain buses working service 10 continued to that destination, but without an individual service number. The situation was placed onto a regulated footing by the introduction of service 14 as from 4th August, to share common route with the 10 between the latters' Moulmein Road terminus and Bras Basah Road, but then going further into the business sector and ending at Raffles Quay.

As previously indicated,the opening of the new international Airport at Paya Lebar proved to be a great attraction to all the operators in the immediate area. The Traction Company reached that destination on 14th August, but needed to compete with Paya Lebar Bus Company and Tay Koh Yat—Changi had also made an application to reach the Airport, but their application was rejected.

During the evening of 26th October, 1956 severe rioting broke out in the city, started by students and lasting for several days. Many buses were stranded along the roads affected but, in all cases, drivers and conductors stood by their buses, often in the face of extreme provocation. Under the direction of the Deputy Traffic Superintendent all buses were brought in to their respective garages, and such was the success of the recovery operation that, over all, the cost of the damage sustained amounted to no more than £50 Sterling, being the cost of replacing broken windows (it should be noted that, following on from the Dennis Falcons, windows had been glazed rather than be fitted with the slatted frames). Of a more damaging consequence of the riots, all buses were then kept off the road as part of the Government imposed curfew, and the troubles were not concluded until 30th October.

BELOW: Paya Lebar International Airport, with buses of the STC—Albion, left—and Tay Koh Yat—Ford, centre, in juxtaposition with a Douglas DC3 Dakota of Malayan Airways, while the terminal building shows signs that air freight is established with the presence of Skyways Cargo and KLM Air Freight proclaimed on signs attached to the eaves.

Merdeka Bridge

20th January, 1957, and a triumph of civil engineering was realised with the opening of Merdeka Bridge and the newly constructed express highway designed to take traffic from the city centre to the site of the old airport at Kallang, thus avoiding the congestion of North Bridge Road, Victoria Street and Kallang Road, and named Nicholl Highway. The Company at once took advantage of the opportunity to introduce a pattern of express services, these being the 25 (replacing the 16), 26 (in place of the 22) and 27 (replacing the 20), out to Katong, Telok Kuran and Siglap.

Industrial unrest would keep cropping up from time to time, but the dispute which boiled into disruption on 16th February took a very different form, in that the Union asked the management to make available one hundred buses, to be worked by the two hundred Union members who had been ordered, by the Union, to work them over service 1, 3, 8, 9, 10, 12, 14, 15, 16, 17, 18, 18A, 19, 20, 22, and 23 between the hours of 11am and 3pm, but without taking any fares (and the list of routes over which it was proposed that the buses would work is of particular interest, in that no trolleybuses would be allowed to run, and mention is made of '16 ...20... 22 , although these services were shown as having been replaced with the opening of Merdeka Bridge). The objective of the exercise is clear, that for some reason the Union sought to hurt the Company, but did not wish to lose such support as there might be for their case expressed by the general public. As far as the management was concerned, they would show themselves to be somewhat bemused over the suggestion, and could only stress their own point of view, namely that all vehicles should be out on the road and passengers pay their fares.

BELOW: The gates open and the lights go green for Albion STC 375 as it prepares to cross the main runway of Kallang Airport by Mountbatten Road. As air traffic grew, this arrangement became unacceptable and a new, larger sight was obtained for a replacement international airport near Paya Lebar.

There were still areas within the city limits that Traction Company services did not reach, although such expansion as there might be to the network would be in the form of branches leading off the established trunk routes: it would seem that, although the limited stop facilities using Nicholl Highway were very much in demand, there did remain a need for the previous routing from those who did not wish to travel all the way into town, and so the 16, 20, and 22 were reinstated. To the pattern serving Katong was added the 20B, a split route which started up as from 1st June. The 'outer terminus was at Tanjong Rhu, a somewhat isolated spit of land facing the Kallang River Estuary and a centre for boat building, but without a direct link with the city. To meet this need the 20B operated from Rhu Cross to Raffles Quay at 20 minute intervals, but in so doing the shape of the route was akin to a ladies hairgrip, with the edge of Katong being represented by the turn. Therefore, it is easy to see why the alternative 20B continued in company with the 20 through Tanjong Katong and on to a common terminus at Siglap Road (in hindsight, would it have been the intention to designate one of these splits as 20A?).

During the latter part of July 1958 application was made for a further new route, which was, in effect, a very short branch away from the main Serangoon Road at what had once been the 4A trolleybus terminus, to pass along Kolam Ayer Lane to reach the new estate then in construction. The application was duly granted, and the new service took the number 7.

Self-governing state

In the wider field of events greater happenings were shaping the course of history. On 3rd June, 1959, a new Constitution confirming Singapore as a self-governing state was brought into force by proclamation, although it would fall to the United Kingdom still to control defence and foreign affairs. The new Government decided to defer any decision regarding the possible takeover of all passenger transport undertakings, and so the Company felt able to seek further profitable routes. As a result of the 1959 General Election, the People's Action Party had been returned with a sweeping majority: in reply to a question tabled in the Legislative Assembly during February, 1960, the Deputy Prime Minister stated, "On principle, it is the policy of the P.A.P. Government to nationalise public road transport. When and how the nationalisation of the bus companies will be brought about must depend on the ability of the Government to meet the financial problem of compensating the bus companies. In this respect I would like to remind the House that there are other and more important claims to the financial resources of the State.

"We are not committed within the next five years to bring about this nationalisation, as this has not been declared as part of our Five Year Plan. Nevertheless, it will be our intention to organise and train an administrative and managerial staff to form the nucleus for a future Road Transport Authority, which will effectively take over the control of public transport. This is a prerequisite, as the complicated machinery of running public transport is not within the capability of any Government department at the moment, or for that matter, of any statutory body that can be created in the immediate future".

Of the "more important claims", housing was to be near the top of the list. The population continued to expand, and all available land within the city confines had been, or was about to be, developed. A first class job had been done by the Singapore Improvement Trust, providing low cost estates of varying sizes. The planners' ideal was seen as a maisonette dwelling, and these had been produced in considerable numbers at Macpherson, St. Michael's, and Tiong Bahru Estates. Wherever private developers were involved, they had favoured bungalows for letting to the transient military residents, but both the S.I.T. and private schemes were, in themselves, wasteful of that most valuable asset, land. The Government set up the Housing and Development Board under the purview of the Ministry of National Development; this during February 1960. The Board was to bring radical new thinking into the provision of quality housing at a reasonable cost to the purchaser or tenant, building upwards. True, the S.I.T. had created the flats in Upper Pickering Street, but sadly an unhappy reputation had grown up behind them, as they became the final destination for those unfortunate people seeking to end their lives by jumping from the top. Under the new plans, not only would the blocks rise much higher than had been seen anywhere else on the Island, but they would be grouped together in completely new towns, set well away from the traditional city. The two sites first chosen were at Toa Payoh (across the road from Serangoon Garden Estate) and Queenstown (beyond Holland Village). Both were sitting on the fringe of the city boundary but, in the fullness of time, satellite towns would be located throughout the island. More to the point, with the growth of Toa Payoh and Queenstown, a new pattern was being set which would force drastic changes in the bus services.

For the time being the Company continued as before, merely adding short extensions or branches to the established network. At some point after the conclusion of the Great Strike, certain of the 19 services had been extended across Thomson Road through a landscape made up of cleared semi-jungle to a terminus at Whitley Road—on the face of it, without any hope of attracting any traffic, for there was nobody around. Schools tend to congregate, and several had become established within the block formed by Thomson–Bukit Timah–and Whitley Roads, and it was serve these that an extension from the 17 took effect as from March 1960, as service 17A. Although students were seen as being the major source of revenue, a full, all-day operation was provided, even to the extent of being cut back from the daytime terminus at Raffles Quay to Bras Basah Road after 7.00pm, in common with the 17's. In Whitley Road the new service met head-on with the extended 19's, but no attempt was made to create a loop working. Upon arrival, vehicles from each service turned, and returned the way from which they had come. Was this because Falcons were used on the 19, whereas the salubrious residential thoroughfares leading to and including Orchard Road were deemed worthy of receiving the newly delivered Arab?

With a concentration of terminals within the general area of Finalyson Green, coupled with a drastic increase in other traffic, a review and reorganisation of stopping places was called for. Trolleybuses had been required to make what had become a very dangerous U-turn on Collyer Quay involving six lanes of fast moving vehicles, but short of constructing an extensive loop around the Green (an expense not even worth considering) they would have to remain as they were. In preoccupation days, motor buses had followed the same pattern, but during the late 1940's they had been moved to a large plot of vacant land on the seaward side of the Quay. The site had been taken by an extension of supporting services connected with the docks, and the buses had moved back to the streets. Services involved included 18, 18A, 20, 26 and 27. In the widest terms, whilst the Limited Stop variations of the 18 and 18A would join the regular daytime buses and turn by circumnavigating Finlayson Green, the others involved would use a projected terminal loop which would include the lower end of Cross Street, even to the extent of having a stop located therein designated 'Post 310'—what nostalgia, that so long after the last trolleybus had operated over service 9, one of the traction poles should remain and be used as a geographic point! Otherwise the scheme removed some of the stopping places fronting the world famous Change Alley, resulting in a speedier flow of traffic along the length of Collyer Quay. Perhaps in a spirit of over-optimism, queue barriers were located at some of the boarding points, but the citizens were more accustomed to the head-down-elbows-out-and-push style of boarding their bus home, and within a very short time the barriers had to be removed as being serious obstructions.

The foregoing adjustments had been brought into effect as from 4th January, 1961, and it could be said only as a result of a major happening less than three months earlier. Frequently the

ABOVE: The cleared semi-jungle of Whitley Road. Guy Arab STC 195 waits for the passengers hurrying out of the undergrowth at a 'Request Stop'. It is hard in these days of ultra modern Singapore, with its extensive urbanisation and high-rise, high-tec environment, to remember that scenes such as this represented development and improvement in their day.

RIGHT: Empress Place with Anderson Bridge and the Fullerton Building as a backdrop to the predecessor of the present day cone—oil-drums. Here they form part of a new traffic management that was to see the demise of Route 4 and 6 trolleybuses from the area between here and High Street. With one set of wires already removed—see the out-of-use hangers top right. The trolley on the 4 is heading for High Street and Paya Lebar

observation has been made that history has a habit of repeating itself, and the point was proved yet again. As the trams were cast aside in the midst of a period of regeneration, so it was to be with the trolleybuses. Despite the drastic programme of modification and rebuilding, the lobby who sought the removal of trolleybuses did gain a partial victory. In the previous paragraph it was noted how that dangerous U-turn had to be made, but the need to leave High Street and cross Empress Place on inbound journeys was equally fraught with danger. Therefore, the decision was taken, to remove trolleybus operations from High Street to Finalyson Green. This took effect as from 15th October, 1960, with service 6 becoming directly replaced by motor buses (Newton to Finlayson Green, but after 7.00pm on weekdays, 5pm on Saturdays and all day on Sundays and Public Holidays working Newton to Neil Road). Service 4 continued to be trolleybus operated, but between Paya Lebar and Outram Road.

At this point, the conversion of service 6 must be regarded as being a means to an end, the obtaining of an improved traffic flow along Collyer Quay, and could not be regarded as being a policy towards complete abandonment. As far as might be ascertained, there was no reduction in the size of the fleet, at last allowing for a small reserve to be maintained. Instead, there was a more serious worry with which to contend, namely the presence in vastly increasing numbers of 'pirate' taxis. It was estimated that there were 3,000 of these driven in shifts by some 11,000 drivers. Over 2,000 diesel engined taxis were estimated as working over the bus routes, which could be done over the full working day and beyond. Once again appeals were made for Government protection, but more direct action would need to be taken with the provision of faster, better sprung and therefore more comfortable buses. In order to meet this objective two ultra modern buses were ordered for evaluation, promised for delivery during May 1962 (but in fact they did not arrive until July, to enter service during August, 1962)

There was a much more serious matter to be considered by the shareholders, as best illustrated by the Chairman's Report: "It has for some time been the view of your Board that this (the Company) can operate successfully in the future only if a large measure of the control and ownership is transferred to local hands. We have taken preliminary steps towards the formation of a local subsidiary company with the intention of transferring to it our assets in Singapore. No such transfer of assets would of course be of any use without the consent of the Government (United Kingdom or Singapore?) to a transfer of the operating licence, and we understand that this will not be politically possible unless local participation is provided for at the outset. We are examining the possibility of finding suitable partners and should any change of ownership become likely we will see that you are informed".

Shortly after the above statement, during September 1961 a referendum was held to decide on a proposed merger of Singapore into Malaysia, and although the result was a popular vote in favour of the motion, the unsettled, political atmosphere meant that little progress could be made in the search for such suitable partners.

1961 saw little in the way of routes changing, but what there were carried much of interest. As from 23rd. July the 20B was varied to operated between Neil Road and Rhu Cross, but on the way doing a double run along Old Airport Road, which at one time had been the main runway of the original international airport but was now evolving as the Spine Road across the new Kallang Park Estate. The alternative 20B to Siglap Road was dispensed with. Instead , the 23A, with a town terminus in Chulia Street, was extended from Siglap Road into Opera Estate, with the rather complex proviso that, on inward journeys alternate buses would proceed i) to Changi Road via Fidelio Street and Siglap Road, or ii) to Frankel Estate via Fidelio Road, Siglap Road, Siglap Drive, and Frankel Avenue to reach Changi Road. By so doing, the Traction Company had moved very firmly into the territory of the Katong Bedok Bus Service. The following day being a Monday, the third service alteration concerned with the general district was introduced, in that the limited stop service 27, by this time linking Opera Estate with Raffles Quay by way of Merdeka Bridge, was reduced to rush-hours only (Monday to Fridays 6.45am and 9.33 am, 4.30pm and 7.19pm, Saturday 6.45am and 9.33am, 12.11pm and 2.40pm, with Sunday service withdrawn).

July 1962, and into service came STC 1 and 2, like no other buses which had ever been used by the Company. For a start they were imported in fully made up condition, and secondly had been supplied by Isuzu, a Japanese manufacturer. By their arrival the pair of Isuzu's swept away the final vestiges of the Imperial Preference clauses of the 1925 Ordinance.

BELOW: STC 2 when new shows typical aspects of Japanese transit bus design. Only STC 1 and 2 had the traditional Singapore centre entrance/exit. Of note is the non-matching window which fills the space normally occupied by the front door. These two buses were also the only ones to have airconditioning for some years to come. *(Straits Times*

As to the specification, they were more than thirty feet in length and ten feet high, with a rear mounted 6,373 cc six-cylinder engine producing 170 brake horse power. A claim was made that "rattles, bumps and grinds", would be a thing of the past, thanks to the provision of telescopic shock absorbers on both front and rear axles, combined with round bellows type suspension, again claimed to give "floating on air" travel.

For the times, the most remarkable feature of the new buses was the provision of airconditioning, although it was at once appreciated that not every passenger would welcome this ultramodern feature so that, if further orders for the model were to be placed then, a decision would have to be taken as to whether the additional plant was a necessity. In the event further orders were placed, but without the air-conditioning. As a result, after a term of touring most of the major routes, STC 1 and 2 tended to be employed on special charter duties.

Several other features which are accepted as being commonplace thirty years later were considered to be revolutionary. Push button control of the door by the driver, which could not be opened whilst the bus was in motion, and a device to set off an alarm should anybody attempt to open the emergency exit. Fluorescent lighting was also deemed to be a luxury and, as electronic wonderments were still largely unknown, the device fitted above the rear mudguard was able to 'feel' the approach of oncoming traffic at night, then to automatically dip the headlights.

The beginning of the end for trolleybuses

The die was cast: the Isuzu would be in, and the trolleybus fleet would be out. There were voices raised against the continued use of the trolleybuses, but it was the need for comprehensive development of Geylang which was the hammer below which would finally shatter the system, as the Notice dated 9th October, 1962, and issued by the Ominbus Services Licensing Authority will show:

Due to the proposed development of Geylang Serai, the Ominbus Services Licensing Authority , with the concurrence of the relevant Authorities in the State, has agree, in principle, to the conversion of the existing STC trolleybus services 2 and 3 to diesel omnibus services and to the resiting of the existing trolleybus terminus at Geylang Serai to the 6th milestone, Changi Road.

It is hereby notified that application has now been made by the undermentioned company to the Ominbus Services Licensing Authority for the existing trolleybus services, when converted to diesel omnibus services, and extended to the 6th milestone, Changi Road, to operate as follows:

Service No. 2—from Tanjong Pagar to Talok Kurau via Tanjong Pagar Road, South Bridge Road, Upper Cross Street, New Bridge Road, Hill Street, Victoria Street, Jalan Sultan, Rochore Canal Road, Kallang Road, Geylang Road, Joo Chiat Road, left into Joo Chiat Place, right into Still Road, left into Lorong 'M', left into Telok Kurau Road to turn left into Joo Chiat Place for Telok Kurau terminal lie-over: returning to town via Joo Chiat Place, Crane Road, Onan Road, Geylang Road, Kallang Road, Crawford Street, North Bridge Road, South Bridge Road and Tanjong Pagar Road.

Service No. 3—Neil Road to Talok Kurau, via New Bridge Road, Hill Street, Victoria Street, Jalan Sultan, Rochmore Canal Road, Kallang Road, Geylang Road, Changi Road, right into Still Road, left into Joo Chiat Place, and left into Karau Road for

Telok Kurau lay-over: returning to town via Telok Kurau Road, Changi Road, Geylang Road, Kallang Road, Crawford Road, North Bridge Road, South Bridge Road, Upper Cross Street and New Bridge Road.

This application will be taken into consideration after the expiration of one month from the date of publication of this Notice'.

Therein sits the reason, for the smart little trolleybus station was in the way, and had to go, the site to be occupied by a towering block of shops and flats. Strange that the Notice should define the 6th milestone as being the new terminal, when in fact the route application shows Telok Kurau Road. No great distance apart, of course, and it can be seen that services 2 and 3 continued to operate in close proximity with each other.

It was the progress being made with the vast new housing projects which prompted a major extension of the 17 service, as 17B, into Queenstown at Rumah Bomba Circus. St. Michael's Estate was also to be provided with a branch from Balastier Road as the 14A, working by way of Jalan Kebun Limau to daytime terminal at Raffles Quay, whilst after 7.00pm Upper Cross Street became the inner terminus. To complete the pattern of route expansion, there was the introduction of the rather odd 18B, working out of Serangoon Garden Estate in company with the 18A until reaching the junction of Upper Serangoon Road with Upper Aljunied Road. The 18B then used the latter thoroughfare right along to Geylang Road, turning right to approach Kallang Road and thereafter the terminus at Finlayson Green. It is difficult to understand the purpose of this routing, for there could be little advantage accruing to residents beyond Paya Lebar who might have been looking for a speedier journey into the city, for whilst they might miss the congestion building up once reaching Rumah Miskin, equal amounts would be met when passing along Kallang Road.

During what was to prove to be a short life following the rehabilitation programme, trolleybuses were to undergo two further changes of livery. In the first the cream areas were replaced by aluminium, but retaining the green streamlining, whilst at the end overall aluminium was used, with a relief band of green with a thin red stripe placed beneath the window line.

On 19th October the steamship *Fuji Maru* docked, part of her cargo comprising twenty-five Isuzu buses painted in a similar style of livery (indeed, even fitted with destination blinds, slightly unusual in that these carried black lettering on a white ground). A further ten Isuzu's were on their way. Broadly similar to numbers 1 and 2 except, as previously forecast, they

LEFT: This photograph serves two very different purposes; firstly it shows a service 4 trolleybus after that route had been diverted away from High Street, Empress Place and Finlayson Green, to a new terminus shared with trolleybus 3 at Outram Road. Secondly, the livery had been changed to largely silver with a minimum of green relief. By the time all the trolleybuses had been rebuilt, as previously discussed, numerous visual variations could be seen. No 48 was, perhaps, one of the more drastically altered and had a very angular cab with an inverted V window line; in fact very similar to many Albion Victors. The trolley base area has also been faired-in. (C. J. F. Buckland

LEFT: Following the trial of two Isuzu buses, the STC placed an order for 135 similar vehicles which, unlike the two prototypes, were not airconditioned and had front entrances as well as centre exits. Here, two of the batch are swung ashore from the Fuji Maru on 19th October 1962, complete with destination blinds—which are thought provoking in themselves—Japanese-built buses being swung ashore from a Japanese boat onto the soil of an island at the foot of the Malay Peninsula, carrying the destination 'Sussex Place'. *(Straits Times*

were no air-conditioned but, of greater note, where as 1 and 2 had only a central doorway, the new deliveries had both front and centre doors, in the hope that passengers might adapt to a 'front-entrance-centre-exit' pattern of movement on and off the buses.

The night of the 10th November, 1962, and trolleybuses ran into Mackenzie Road depot off services 2 and 3 for the last time. The next morning Isuzu's took over their routes, although such a typle allocation was possibly a touch of Company publicity, for it was not long before many of the rosters were taken by Albion's, as the Isuzu's needed to be spread around the network a little more. Of the trolleybuses, there was no need to retain such a large fleet with just a single route remaining, and so they were driven from the depot as far as the former 4A turning point, then, down poles and tow to the large yard forming Macpherson Road garage, there to await buyers from the scrap metal trade.

Midnight of Saturday, 15th December, 1962, and the role of the trolleybus was finally ended. There were no great ceremonies to mark the passing of the last service 4 car, nor great crowds around the depot to mark the entry of the final journey. It just happened, and the average citizen hardly noticed. On the following day, the *Sunday Times* (of Singapore, of course) had this to report:

"Off for good—Singapore trolleybuses. The Traction Company's trolleybus service, first introduced on the Island in 1946 (*sic*), came to an end at midnight tonight. The last trolleybuses today operated service 4, from Paya Lebar to Outram Road.

The Company will also remove the overhead wires used by the trolleybuses which have long been considered an obstacle to improving the Island's transport system.

A new era in bus travel in Singapore has opened with the introduction of the Isuzues (sic) Japanese built buses which are bringing jetliner comfort to Singapore routes

Now that the wires used by the trolleybuses are to be removed, it is even possible for the Company to introduce the 'double-decker' buses now currently in use in Kuala Lumpur.

This will bring Singapore in line with other big cities like London and Paris which use the 'double-deckers'.

The STC today announced that the new No 4 omnibus service will be operating from Tampines to Neil Road along the following routes: Upper Serangoon Road, Serangoon Road, Selegie Road, Princep Street, Bras Basah Road, North Bridge Road, South Bridge Road, Upper Cross Street, New Bridge Road to the STC terminal at Neil Road near the General Hospital. The return journey will be via New Bridge Road, Hill Street, Victoria Street, Bras Basah Road, Dhoby Ghaut, Selegie Road, Serangoon Road and Upper Serangoon Road".

Dare one suggest, about par for the course insofar as newspaper reporting goes, to forget the highly efficient service which had been introduced twenty years previous to that as reported,

whilst it is difficult to understand why the reporter considered the removal of the overhead wires as being a sound reason for the introduction of double-deckers, obviously not looking back through the files to recall the operation of the Kuala Lumpur Regent III less than a decade earlier. There was a similar story in a daily paper, telling of the passing of the 'Trams'.

In order to dispose of the electric fleet, tenders were invited by lots, as a Public Notice contained in the *Straits Times* dated 5th February, 1963, again of considerable interest:

"The Singapore Traction Company Limited—Tender Notice. Tenders are invited for Lot E: seven trolleybuses Chassis and Bodies. nos. 1, 8, 10, 23, 29, 30 and 47 with four wheels and tyres per vehicle and including traction motors.

No guarantee of condition is given or implied for any of the above equipment.

The equipment may be inspected at our Macpherson Road depot by arrangement with the Engineer-in-Charge (telephone No. 89-756 extension 7).

Tenders for the above lot should be marked 'Tender For Scrap Trolley Buses ' and addressed to The General Manager, The Singapore Traction Co. Ltd., P.O. Box 841, Singapore 9, and must be delivered by midday Friday 15th February, 1963.

It will be a condition of acceptance that the above lot will be removed from our depot immediately the sale if complete."

That was that: what, many years before could claim to have been the world's largest trolleybus system had very quietly come to an end. There was a brief note in the Accounts relative to the following year which read 'Within the balance sheet itself you will notice that there is an increase in General Reserve of £46,000, which is accounted for by a profit from the disposal of fixed assets during the year, principally the trolleybus system. It is not therefore an operational profit, and obviously not recurrent."

All overhead wiring and feeder cables were quickly removed, being the most valuable items of scrap, but many of the traction poles remained in situ for street lighting purposes until they, were felled as road widening schemes overtook the former routes. Very soon nothing tangible was to remain, save the destination blind from one of the final trolleybuses, safely held in exile in far away Hampshire.

There were some route extensions brought into effect during September of 1963, but unfortunately, the 'Confrontation ' with Indonesia broke out at about the same time, and the resulting political nervousness had been an adverse effect on passengers carried, most particularly during the evenings, resulting in a drop in revenues. Over the months there was a serious deterioration in the overall political situation, made decided worse by spells of severe rioting during July and August 1964, to be combated by the imposition by the Government of tight curfews. During those periods when the curfews were lifted efforts were made to get the maximum number of buses out into service, and although these were only able to attract light loadings, the policy was maintained by way of the Company's effort to help boosted public morale.

Again this uncertain background there had been a considerable increase in the number of pirate taxis roaming the major bus routers, skimming away the cream from revenue which the Company could ill afford to lose. Perhaps belatedly, the Government came to the realise that it was also losing out in financial terms, with falling royalties being drawn from the Company and also income from taxation. At this late stage it was discovered that there was little action which could be taken by the traffic police under the Law as it was it was constituted.

The Board of Directors met at the Registered Offices in London on 22nd January, 1964. During the meeting the London appointees tendered their formal resignations, and new Directors, resident in Malaysia, were appointed. The fact of the Company still being incorporated within the United Kingdom and having registered offices in London was due entirely to certain legal requirements, and negotiations were already in hand with the several interested parties, the end result to be the complete transfer of the business to Singapore.

At Mackenzie Road the drawing office staff were busily preparing designs for a new livery, encouraged to use every colour in the spectrum. The results were as extreme as paint charts would allow, ranging from the current favourite of aluminium with single relief band beneath the windows, to an all-over royal blue with pink lines. A new logo was called for, and here again the results were varied, but most incorporating the initial letters of the company title, whatever that might prove to be. One such design was based on the shape of the whole Island, which might have been a case of wishful thinking, whilst another had an Isuzu bursting through the letters, which would have been rather inappropriate if the new Company hoped for a substantial future.

As to the title, as the old company had become such a part of the city's infrastructure, there was no great desire to be completely divorced from what had been, thus Sharikat Berhad Trekshen Singapura (giving the initials S.B.T.S. for a logo) was proposed as being the direct translation into the Malay language, or else a combination The Singapore Traction Company Berkhidmat Untok Ra'ayat.

The new company was incorporated in Singapore on 19th September 1964, entering into an agreement with the old Company to acquire the whole of the undertaking, property and assets. The operational birth date of the new Company was 1st October, 1964, with a first obligation to discharge all outstanding obligations of the old Company as on 30th September.

The Singapore Traction Company (1964) Limited was in business. Passengers who might idly be studying their tickets would notice that the legend 'Incorporated in Singapore' had replaced 'Incorporated in the United Kingdom' but little else could be seen as changed. The same logo was carried on the sides of the buses, and the same STC registration plates identified the individual buses. The arrival of the Isuzu fleet had seen the end of the streamlined painting in the livery, and the colours chosen by the new Company marked a return to the almost pre-occupation practice, of dark green with a thin red line below the windows, with either aluminium or cream upper-works and roofs. The bulk of the older units in the fleet were destined not to receive the new colours.

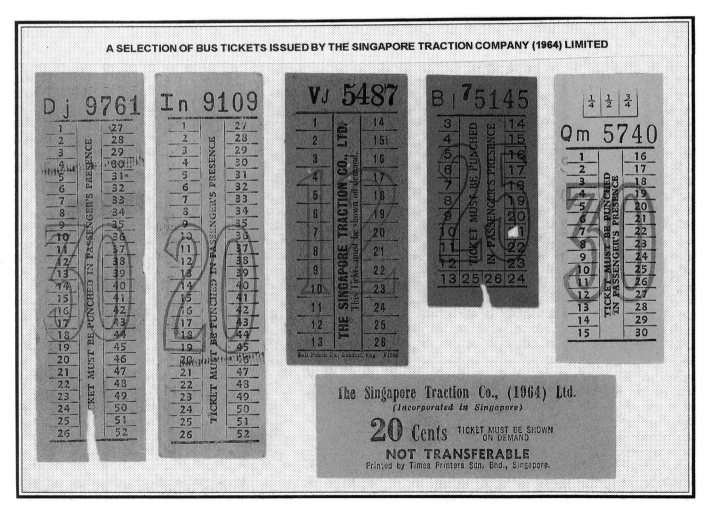

A SELECTION OF BUS TICKETS ISSUED BY THE SINGAPORE TRACTION COMPANY (1964) LIMITED

Chapter Eleven
1956—1971 Roads Leading to Amalgamation

The 'Great Strike' having been settled, the Chinese bus owners were able to look forward to a much enhanced future. First hand experience had been gained in the working of natural extensions to what had traditionally been Traction Company routes, highlighting areas well within the city boundary where they could expect to have licence applications met with success, thoughts further enhanced by the recent example of having been able to provide high density city services, even without the benefits of co-ordination, between the individual operators. Of greater value was the wealth of support which had been drawn from the public, and which might be well used in connection with the planning.of new routes.

Viewing the prospects of expansion, there was no great hurry to dispose of those military-based buses obtained immediately after the end of the occupation. Whilst these buses had, by 1956, obtained a decidedly antique appearance, closely matched by riding qualities, to keep them operational did mean that substantial reserves could be accumulated. Furthermore, they did prove to be a valuable tool when owners were called upon to provide an increasing number of charter services to carry civilian staff to military establishments. As a result

buses could be seen working well beyond their natural territorial limits, for instance: Green Bus reached Upper Serangoon., and from the opposite direction Changi Bus came into Serangoon Garden Estate. During the day Sembawang Village looked like a vintage bus rally site, with lines of bonnets packed close, waiting for out-muster time from the Naval Base, following which these ancient buses of Tay Koh Yat set off for all parts of the Island.

In order to keep these old buses reasonably economic, in most cases the original petrol engines were removed, to be replaced by the very popular Perkins diesel unit. Even so, the inflow of new buses continued apace, with the Fargo Kew by now being the most popular choice. Cycles of popularity did not seem to be very long lasting: perhaps it was a coincidence, or perhaps a campaign mounted by the agents, but with the Traction Company breaking with their own traditional chassis supplier, so several of the Chinese owners turned to Albion for their need to obtain larger and more comfortable buses (indeed, Albion was a name to loom large for a further decade, the Victor being replaced by the Viking in large numbers in the Chinese owners fleets).

ABIOVE LEFT: Tay Koh Yat's S1331 was a 20-seat Ford 'School Bus' (the model name applied by Ford to the 194 inch wheelbase bonnetted bus chassis built from circa 1941). Here the bus stands at McPherson Road terminus in October 1955. Tay Koh Yat operated some 50 normal control buses of various makes, both ex-military and purpose-built bus chassis such as this one.

LEFT: SH 383 of Tay Koh Yat at Barley Road terminus of that company's Route 9. This bus is a 'Fargo Kew', as can be seen in small chromium letters above the H on the front grille. Such chassis carried Dodge, Fargo Kew or, in later times, Commer badges and, in Spain even showed Barreios. The 'badge-engineering' was to fit the market in which the vehicle was sold.

Mixed fleets comprising less common makes had been the order of the day until now. The Tay Koh Yat fleet proved this point, having a solitary Leyland OPS, a brace of Sentinals, and a few Commer Avengers. Whether this was an attempt to better the Traction Company (and the OPS would certainly be able to do this), to evaluate the full range as available from United Kingdom manufacturers before placing more substantial orders, or simply a means of snapping up some bargains from stock held by the agents, who can say? What is certain is that having taken on the role of pioneer amongst the Chinese bus companies, the strength and modernity of the stage carriage fleet (the charters would not count in this context) would do much to support the applications for new routes within the city boundary when they came to be made.

A Further policy of Tay Koh Yat was, "if it does not work, then change it". As delivered, the Sentinel and Commer Avenger buses had front entrances, forward of the axle, a location which did tend to confuse intending passengers. On all, engine covers protruded onto the top step, and as many riders were going to or from market and would be heavily loaded, then nasty falls would always be a possibility. Most particularly with the Sentinels, to ride on them was an unusual experience, for the fore and aft pitching motion whilst at speed could provoke a sensation not unlike seasickness. The owners found the cure for all of these inconveniences by rebuilding all such buses with the traditional centre entranc/exit, and by the fitting of bulkheads between the saloon and the driver.

Green Bus developed a liking for Seddon products, even going to so far as to introduce the underfloor engined concept to Singapore. Changi Bus also obtained a couple but, in view of the regular flooding of Upper Changi Road during the monsoon season, they had to be constructed in such a manner as to leave the engine clear of possible flood waters. As a result, passengers were required to climb five steps into the saloon so that these buses, although ultra modern in concept, soon became unpopular with passengers carrying home live chickens from market—then still a common practice.

The Falcon fleet of the Traction Company had caused the Dennis name to be well seen around the city, and soon a new type, the Teal—not to be found in the United Kingdom—was to find favour with Hock Lee Amalgamated and Katong-Bedok, besides forming the basis for some coaches of Malayan Airways. These handsome but solidly constructed buses were destined to give many years of service, beyond the life of their original owners.

Although co-ordination between the owners was unknown there were several operational features which were common to all. For instance, at each terminal point, no matter how remote, would be found a small wooden shed within which would sit a timekeeper. Usually of the rank of Inspector within the operating company, each would take a spell of timekeeping on a rota basis. In additional to ensuring that departures were according to schedule, his duties involved the maintenance of the conductors' waybills. Another feature was the painting of a mark on the forward bulkhead indicating a height of three feet from the floor, a complete mystery to the casual visitor. When discovered, the reason for the mark is quite simple, and is concerned with young children. It is not sufficient to have a rule which allows a child under

ABOVE: The sole example in the whole of Singapore of a heavyweight bus chassis and of a Leyland in the service of a Chinese bus company was SH 145, a Leyland Tiger OPS. Its power and performance were indeed notable! 'where did it come from?' Unfortunately, the full history of this vehicle is unavailable to the Authors and any reader able to answer this question is requested to pass on hgis information to the Authors via the publisher.

BELOW: The appearance of the two Sentenels—SH 190 and SH 191— in the Tay Koh Yat fleet became more impressive after removal of the front doorway and its relocation amidships. (See picture on page 110.) The provision of a destination screen above the doorway in its new location is also of note.

RIGHT: Another underfloor engined design of the 1950's with only a central doorway was this Seddon Mk II of Green Bus, seen here at Newton.

CENTRE: SH 401 is a Dennis Teal, operated by the Hok Lee Amalgamated Bus Company, seen here in August 1955 at Alexandra Road, terminus of Route 3.

LOWER RIGHT: Clearly to be seen on the left of the front bulkhead is the '3ft' mark inside this metal bodied bus of the mid-fifties. The photo was taken to show the 'new-style' transverse seating as recommended by the Hawkins Report.

the age, say, of five years to travel free of charge, for in this cosmopolitan society there are several ways of calculating age, most particularly in the traditional Chinese fashion. Thus, in case of any doubt, a child can be measured against the mark, and if under three feet tall, is allowed to travel without a fare being paid.

Ticket machines were quite commonplace elsewhere in the world by the mid- to late-1950's, but they had no attraction to operators in Singapore. The pre-printed ticket was ever popular, and the Bell Punch Company of Uxbridge did obtain several substantial orders for a while. These were very similar to designs produced for use within the United Kingdom, adapted for local conditions. The majority of ticket production was handled by the Government Printing Office., with a more or less standard design, being slips of a very thin paper of approximate dimensions 5 inches long by inch wide. Made up in packs of one hundred, the tickets were carried on a plastic rack, held in place by thick bands of elastic. Hock Lee Amalgamated had an extremely long range of tickets, which must have been based upon routes, although it did prove to be very difficult to establish any firm pattern. Over the basic colour would be printed the value in an opposing shade, but of the two colours there was an almost limitless combination to be discovered. Long-term contracts were not favoured, and changes in the suppliers of tickets were frequent—several small printers took on the task, and to continue with a local content Bus and Theatre Tickets became familiar, as did the Straits Times Press. The most unusual newcomer was Bell Punch Somerville, Hong Kong, to the extact pattern of those produced in London.

Stopping places were marked by a silver painted pole carrying a 'flag', dual-coloured in the livery of the

LEFT: Buddhist temples are not generally regarded as being the place to find a bus garage but for the Ponggol Bus Service Co. this was certainly the case. Here SC 8045, a Vulcan 6PF, stands outside the temple walls while two other Ponggol buses stand within the compound. (In Hong Kong, the Ngong Ping Bus Company was owned and operated by a the monks of a Buddhist Monastery until 1973.)

CENTRE: Green Bus SH 238 on the Johore Bahru–Singapore service passes the rear of the rear of STC's Mackenzie Road depot on Bukit Timah Road. The Tilling Stevens chassis is clearly badged as a Vulcan. This service survives today as Singapore Bus Service Route 180 and has always been a local bus service observing all bus stops en route.

BOTTOM LEFT: A similar vehicle with Singapore–Johore Express, seen here in Duneau Road. As well as having a similar Tilling Stevens-badged-as-a-Vulcan chassis, the bodywork is also from the same stable as that of Green Bus SH 238 but inside their 'de luxe buses', Singapore–Johore Express fitted more luxurious, semi-high-backed seats, reflecting the 'express' nature of the service which ran without scheduled stops between Queen Street bus station, Singapore, and Johore Bahru. This service still runs in 1996 but must stop at the, now international, frontier between Singapore and Malaysia, at the Johore end of the causeway before proceeding to the bus station in Johore Bahru.

operator (red over white, yellow over green, etc). On those sections of the road served by two operators, then two 'flags' would be carried on the pole. This was in order to assist intending passengers, who would be drawn more by the livery of the bus rather than the wording on the destination indication, whereas service numbers could be without any meaning at all. Consider within the length of North Bridge Road, which carried three quite different service 1's, two 2's, two 3's, two 6's and two 8's. The practice continues today: bus stops serving different operators carry a separate flat for each one in fleet colours.

Except with the Traction Company, rollerblind destination indicators had not found much favour (here again, Tay Koh Yat was the leader in fitting the newest buses thus. Metal plates were preferred, such being placed within the usual front dome aperture. After 1954, new deliveries had clips provided beneath the windscreen into which additional destination plates could be slipped.

Whilst the owner-driver of the original mosquito buses would have kept his vehicle close to home, and carried out routine maintenance in the street, with heavier work being done at a garage, the formation of companies required a better standard of accommodation. Even so, a back yard in the midst of close packed residential premises would do, although the Ponggol company must have been unique in having premises contained within the enclosed surrounds of a Buddist temple. The late 1950's indicated that such arrangements could not continue, if only because the size of individual buses called for purpose built premises and engineering work-

shops. Against a background of ever rising land prices, new garages were constructed by most of the operators, the basic design provided for an office block with covered maintenance facilities, and a large area of open hard standing for the buses. The whole would be contained within a security fence, and unauthorised visitors would be discouraged from entering by the large red sign carrying the usual warning, tri-lingual, and emphasised by the silhouetted figure of a guard firing his rifle at an intruder.

When first introduced, vehicle registrations carried the letter S, shared by all private cars, lorries and buses. With the growth of the motor vehicle park following the end of the occupation, the system was expanded to include a second letter to designate class of vehicle, and buses were given SC, later to be followed by SH in order to accommodate all taxis and public service buses, excluding those of the Traction Company. As a general rule, there did not appear to be any means of booking blocks of numbers, the Registrar of Vehicles allocating them as each vehicle was inspected and passed as being ready to enter service. To all golden rules there must be an exception, and it is noteworthy that SH106 through to SH120 were taken by the Singapore–Johore Express, to be used on their Vulcan fleet, and is doubtful that all could have been licensed on the same day. However, after some six years of use, the Registrar came to recognise that there would be administrative advantages in allocating blocks of numbers to a particular company, particularly as orders progressed beyond the single vehicle stage, and might more usually involve half a dozen buses. In addition to the registration plate, licence discs also needed to be carried. Unlike the STC series, which could be, and was, reissued to subsequent vehicles, and even changed whilst a bus was still in service in order to provide a clear numerical run for a new series entering service, it was the intention that an SH-mark should relate only to the vehicle to which it was first issued The long passge of time showed that reuse would be needed, albeit on a limited scale. SH 101-999 and many in the SH8001-9xxx were extensively re-issued, and the series is still in limited use today.

Great changes were about to be launched which, evolving over several decades, would result in the ultra-modern city-state. Inasmuch as bus services were concerned, personal experience serves well to demonstrate the initial stages, by recalling what had been a daily bus ride, that of the Paya Lebar Bus Service along Tampines Road, a distanceh of seven miles.

That there was no hint of co-ordination between operators would become instantly apparent for, as the Changi bus came hurtling through the raw cutting which marked a recent realignment of Upper Changi Road, so the little yellow and green bus could be seen pulling away from the raised compound which fronted the shops at

Yan Kit Village. A twenty minute wait was more or less certain, but it was time well spent in chatting with the timekeeper. This end of Tampines Road was little more than a country lane, a sharp bend and steep decline leading to the junction with the main road. Thus, the sound of an engine hard at work could be heard well ahead of the bus rushing into view, to come to a screeching stop on the wront side of the traffice bollard marking the junction. Almost before coming to a halt, reverse gear was engaged, and with much shuddering and engine protests, the bus was guided back to the timekeepers' hut.

The very first ride was enjoyed during the New Year of 1953, and Chevrolet's were much in use, with the occasional Ford taking a turn. Being very much a country route, they were ideal for the task, for there were very few stretches of the route that were straight for longer than a couple of hundred yards. Shortly after leaving the terminus, three journeys each day were obliged to divert into Kuala Loydang Road, passing through surrounding palm plantations in order to serve Kuala Loyang. This had become a small Royal Navy radio station and, on reaching the main gate all passengers were required to leave the bus whilst it went on a circuit of the camp area. The interesting point here was that the through fare, terminus to terminus, was thirty-five cents, but for anybody boarding at Kuala Loyang the fare was forty-five cents. Unhappily, despite frequent requests and much searching, such a ticket was never to be found, the implications being that nobody from the camp used the bus.

ABOVE RIGHT: Paya Lebar Bus Service SC 4384 in the rural outpost of Yan Kit Village, on service 2 to Tampines Toad, in January 1956. Thevehicle is an ex-military Chevrolet, now fitted with a coachbuilt bus body with perimeter seating for 21. The operation of this route at Yan Kit Village is described in the adjacent text.

RIGHT: Whilst on Paya Lebar service 2, between Yan Kit Village and Tampines Road, the bus passed a popular picnic site near the Pasir Ris Hotel, so titled after the village of that name. A little further on one came upon the outer end of the light railway which served the Upper Serangoon Sewage Works, the tracks of which ran parallel to the road before disappearing into the jungle towards its goal. simple passenger carriages were used, probably as staff transport, and these were hauled by small single-ended petrol engines, such as this, which required the services of the turntable, seen here to the left of the picture.

Once back on board, the bus completed the double run back to Tampines Road, perhaps a quarter of an hour having been added to the journey. Then to continue through a constant succession of sweeping bends, on either side of the road, agricultural smallholdings and fish farms, eventually emerging from the simi-jungle to enter Pasir Ris Village, the largest centre of habitation along the route, close by the extensive Pasir Ris Hotel, and a popular destination for Sunday picnic parties. Shortly after leaving the village most interesting company is joined in the form of a light railway to our right. Worked by petrol engined locomotives drawing simple passengers coaches, this serves the nearby Upper Serangoon Sewage Works, and stays with us until crossing the road to Teck Hock Village, after which the line disappears into the trees to final destination unknown. Bus drivers need to take care on approaching the crossing, as entry to the village is on a downward gradient and on a bend.

With just under two miles to go to the terminus, from Teck Hock Village the road is perfectly straight, and raised on a form of causeway, with marshland either side. It forms the ideal platform for a very fast running, and with little need to observe any stops the end of the road is swiftly reached. Everybody off, and the bus runs around the traffic island which also forms the turning circle for Traction Company service 18 buses, to come to a stand alongside the timekeeper's hut, to keep company with the next bus shortly to depart.

The last ride was taken more than three years later. The new international airport at Paya Lebar was open, the threshold for which cut across the old road between the villages, and a fine new highway made a gentle curve of almost two miles to take traffic away from approaching aircraft. Being projected towards Changi, the new highway attempted to follow as straight a course as possible, and by so doing missed out Pasir Ris Village altogether. Gone, too, were the Chevrolet's, and in their place had come some of the earlier deliveries of the company's Vulcan fleet, from time to time helped out by the ubiquitous Fargo "Kews". (A small demonstration of what was to come for, when making the same journey twenty years later, it was to travel into the unknown, so vast had been subsequent developments).

Once recognition had been given to the advantages of block booking registration numbers, some interesting features were to emerge: for instance, whilst Hock Lee Amalgamated took SH 384 through to 404, the buses involved comprised Albion, Seddon, and Dennis Teal, a mixture which was destined to be repeated with increased frequency as even more new vehicles were delivered. Chinese mythology places great store on the value of numbers, some bringing good fortune whilst others can only cause disaster: for a large fleet of Fargos, Changi Bus took the registration 460 through to 479, but would not accept 465 nor 475, and would not take any of the marks which came in the 500 series, which seems to indicate that the numeral '5' was deemed to be the possible source of bad luck as far as that company was concerned. (It should also be noted that the Traction Company was loath to take registrations in their 500 series too).

As the years progressed, so the Fords and Chevrolets, in company with normal control Austins and Bedfords, were finally put to rest (although forward control Austins and Bedford SBs were still to grace several of the fleets for years to come), and their withdrawal in conjunction with the greater capacities of new arrivals and the ominous growth of private motoring, did allow for a certain economy in the size of individual fleets. One quite remarkable happening, however, was the purchase by Hock Lee Amalgamated of a small number of Traction Company Dennis Falcons, for hitherto it had not been the policy of the latter to sell off buses for further service with possible competitors. In the rainbow livery, the Falcons looked very smart indeed, although they could not have been well loved by the drivers, by this time well used to having full width cabs.

Applications for new services were made as residential development continued apace: some were granted and some were lost, some services were started, but then not renewed, and year by year the Island-wide pattern became increasingly interwoven. Bearing in mind the importance of 1964 in the annals of the Traction Company, it becomes appropriate to study the accompanying tables to understand the situation as applied to the Chinese Bus Companies at that time.

CHANGI BUS COMPANY LIMITED

1. Changi Point to Capitol Theatre (the inner terminus no longer entitled 'Union Jack Club', but the same place).

1A. every fifth bus on service 1 to divert from Changi Road along Tanah Merah Road, Nicoll Drive and Telok Paku Road before rejoining Upper Changi Road. (Number of buses required, services 1 & 1A—48 plus 5 spare)

2. Guillemard Road–Lim Ah Woo Road triangle green to Changi Point (Number of buses required—32 plus 4 spares).

3. Guillemard Road–Lim Ah Woo triangle green to Kampong Batak.

3A. Guillemard Road–Lim Ah Woo triangle green to Kaki Bukit Settlement (Number of buses required—services 3 and 3A–8 plus 1 spare).

4. Changi Village–Telok Paku English School. (Number of buses required–2 plus 1 spare).

5. Changi Village–Lloyd Leas Estate. (Number of buses required - 2 plus 1 spare).

Total number of buses required—104, but number held on the Registrar of Vehicles register—116.

Not included in the above, the loop service which ran from Changi Village to circumnavigate the large Royal Air Force Station. This would be done by extending the journey of an occasional bus from the city.

The use of the green at Guillemard Road was brought about by the plan to redevelop Geylang Serai, and the consequent loss of the trolleybus station. The terminal was shared with Katong-Bedok and Paya Lebar companies, and resulted in a short distance of common route with the former along Geyland Road.

EASY BUS COMPANY

1. From the junction of Alexandra Road with Pasir Road to Jurong Road near the Junction with Bukit Timah Road, via Portsdown Road, North Buona Vista, etc. (Number of buses required—5 plus 1 spare)

2. As service 1, but directly along Ayer Rajah Road and Clementi Road. (Number of buses required—4 plus 1 spare)

(Number of buses required—11, but number held on the Registrar of Vehicles register—12)

Whilst smaller than usual buses were still required for some of the remaining country sections of the services, this was one of the operators who was able to benefit from major highway improvement schemes. In addition, the various military camps around Tanglin had proved to be very lucrative, so that service 1 came to be of greater importance than the original working, which had become the 2.

The trunk route of the Keppel company was met at the Pasir Panjang end of the route, and a common terminal here was shared with Hock Lee Amalgamated, with whom both services were in competition up to the British Military Hospital. That part of service 1 passing through the camps area had to be shared with Tay Koh Yat and Keppel, again in direct competition, whilst at the other end of the routes, Bukit Timah Road was shared with Green Bus between the railway station and the village.

GREEN BUS COMPANY LIMITED

1.   Queen Street to Johore Bahru (number of buses required - 32 plus 4 spares)
2.   Queen Street to Lim Chu Kang Road extending to the end of Chua Chu Kang Road between 7am and 9am, 12 noon and 1.30pm and 5pm and 6pm (number of buses required - 9 plus one spare)
3.   Queen Street to Jurong, 18th milestone (number of buses required—9 plus one spare)
4.   Ban San Street to Mandai (number of buses required—8 plus one spare)
5.   Queen Street to Princess Elizabeth Estate (number of buses required—7 plus one spare)
6.   Queen Street to junction of Holland Road with Bukit Timah Road (number ofbuses required—3 plus one spare)
7.   Queen Street to junction of Dunearn Road with Swiss Club Road (number of buses required—3 plus one spare)
8.   Royal Air Force Station,Tengah to Union Jack Club, operating only on Fridays, Saturdays and Sundays, ex-Tengah between 6pm and 8pm, returning between 12 midnight and 12.20am (number of buses required—7 plus one spare)
9.   Tanjong Kling to junction of Jurong to Boon Lay Road (number of buses required—2 plus one spare)
SPECIAL—Marsiling Road to Marsiling School (one bus required, but to be of a type specified by the Registrar of Vehicles: it had to be small)
SPECIAL—Bukit Timah Garage to Ulu Pandan Sewage Disposal Works (one bus required)
Total number of buses required for services—94; number held on the Registrar of Vehicles register—110. Green Bus felt no need to carry a large stock of spare buses.

Green Bus was perhaps the most isolated of all the Chinese bus companies, serving as it did the largely country districts to the north of the city. True, there was a considerable extent of common route shared with Tay Koh Yat from Rochore Road until the junction of Bukit Timah Road with Kampong Java Road, and the short section with Easy as noted above. An end on junction with the Tay Koh Yat trunk service at Mandai was the only other point of contact.

In practice, services 6 and 7 were short workings of the services that otherwise went beyond Bukit Timah, and in a sense tended to demonstrate that there remained a need to cater for residents of that part of Bukit Timah Road closer to the central area. Buses would work outward along Bukit Timah Road, reach the appropriate junction, make a right hand turn to cross what had become to all intents and purposes a central reservation, and come straight back by using Dunearn Road.

HOCK LEE AMALGAMATED BUS COMPANY, LIMITED

1.   South Canal Road to Ulu Pandan
2.   South Canal Road to Holland Road, 5th milestone
2A`   South Canal Road to Holland Village (number of buses required for services 1, 2 & 2A—13 plus 4 spares)
3.   Alexandra Road at the junction with Telok Blangah Road to Jalan Kubor (number of buses required—25 plus 3 spares)
3A   South Canal Road to the junction of Alexandra Road with Telok Blangah Road to operate only during the hours 6am to 7pm, thereafter to be replaced by service 5. (number of buses required—5 plus one spare)
4.   South Canal Road to the Circus formed by Queensway, Holland Road and Farrer Road (number of buses required—8 plus one spare)
5.   South Canal Road to Great World Amusement Park, deemed to be a 'Night' service, operational between 7pm and 12.30am.   (number of buses required—4 plus one spare)
6. Circular service, from South Bridge Road at South Canal Road terminus, via Upper Cross Street, New Bridge Road, Outram Road, Tiong Bahru Road, Tiong Poh Road, Guan Chan Street, Chay Yan Street, Yong Siak Street, Moh Guan Terrace, Seng Po Road, Outram Road and back to South Canal Road. Condition of licence: "Omnibuses servicing this route to have 28 seats". (number of buses required—8 plus one spare)
7. South Canal Road to Henderson Road (number of buses required—3 plus one spare)
8. South Canal Road to Redhill Road. (number of buses required—7 plus one spare)
9. Park Road to Margaret Drive, Queenstown. (number of buses required—9 plus one spare)
10. Holland Road Village to Park Road. (number of buses required—10 plus one spare)
11. South Canal Road to Alexandra Hill Estate. (number of buses required—5 plus one spare)
Total number of buses required for service—113; number held on the Registrar of Vehicles register 118.

As with Green Bus, the number of spare buses is very low, and indeed there is only a surplus of five over the number required for service, a low point which demonstrates how well Hock Lee's modernisation programme had advanced.

Of the route pattern, it is apparent that the company was swift to appreciate the benefits to be drawn from the construction of the first 'new town', with services 4 and 9 reaching Queenstown. The original Singapore Improvement Trust estates were well served by the 6, 7 and 8, but the most notable area of expansion was that surroundng Holland Road, for so long the province of the Traction Company's 17, and which was to face intense competition.

So far as meeting up with other operators was concened, mention has been made of Keppel and Easy, and there was also a common route with Changi along the section from the Bras Basah Road

KATONG BEDOK BUS SERVICE COMPANY, LIMITED

1.   From the junction of Bedok Road and Changi Road to Talma Road at Lorong 8
2.   East Coast Road at Bedok Corner to Talma Road at Lorong 8. (numberof buses required for service 1 & 2—21 plus three spare)
3.   Loop services starting from the junction of Aida Street with Fidelio Street, by way of Fidelio Street, Siglap Road, East Coast Road, Mountbatten Road, Tanjong Katong Road, Geylang Road, Guillemard Road, Guillemard Circus, Mountbatten Road, Old Airport Road up to the junction with Jalan Satu, returning via Old Airport Road into Kallang Park up to its end out into Mountbatten Road, Guillemard Circus and outward route reversed: provided that, on journeys outward, alternate buses to procede along Siglap Road, Siglap Drive, Frankel Avenue, East Coast Road, thence forward. Peak hour extras into Frankel Estate between 6.30am and 8.30am, 12 noon and 2pm and 4.30pm and 6.30pm (number of buses required——11 plus two spare)
Total number of buses required for services—37: number on the Registrar of Vehicles register—46.

To have moved away from the previously long established terminal at the green triangle at Lim Ah Woo Road served to demonstrate how the company had held on to mileage for services 1 and 2, gained during the Great Strike. As for the complicated 3, this was wholly within the districts previously considered to be the sole preserve of the Traction Company. Other than these, Katong Bedok shared a short section of common route with Changi along Geylang Road, and met with Paya Lebar at Lim Ah Woo Road.

KAMPONG BAHRU BUS SERVICE, LIMITED

1.   Maxwell Road Market to Kampong Bahru Road junction with Telok Blangah Road (number of buses required—5 plus one spare)
2.   "Night Service" River Valley Road junction with Hill Street to Great World Amusement Park, 7pm to 12.30am (number of buses required—4 plus one spare)

The smallest of the Chinese bus companies, and located well within Traction Company territory, the only other operator to be reached was Keppel, the outer terminus of service 1 overlooking that trunk route.

KEPPEL BUS COMPANY, LIMITED

1.   Keppel Road stand (at Tanjong Pagar) to 9 ° milestone, West Coast Road. (number of buses required—32 plus 4 spares)
2.   from the junction of West Coast Road with Kay Hai Road to the junction of Day Road with Jurong Road at 10th. milestone. (number of buses required—2 plus 1 spare)
3.   from the junction of Pasir Panjan Road with Clementi Road to the junction of ClementiRoad with Ayer Rajah Road. (number of buses required—1 plus 1 spare)
4.   from the junction of Pasir Panjang Road with South Buona Vista Road to the junction of South Buona Vista Road with Ayer Road, the outer end being a wide loop around the Wessex Estate formed by Portsdown Road, North Buona Vista Road and back to Ayer Rajah Road. (number of buses required—1 plus 1 spare)
Total number of buses required for service—43; total on Registrar of Vehicles register—38

The latter is one of those surprises for which there is no obvious explanation, a fleet standing below expectations—it must be hoped that the spares were not often called upon.

The relationship between service 1 and the Traction Company 24 has been previously mentioned, as has the competition with Tay Koh Yat and Easy around Portsdown Road and the military bases. Other than these, Keppel was rather like Green Bus, and once past the world famed Haw Paw Villa, the traffic on offer was very much of a rural nature. Indeed, for services 2, 3 and 4, the casual traveller really did need to know the timetable, so far between were the headways. Service 2 was, in effect, an onward extension of the 1, West Coast Road at this point having become little more than a track carried on a causeway, with the sea to one side and marshland to the other. From the original terminus at 10th. milestone, a new road struck inland over reclaimed land, in time coming up to Jurong Road, so that there was an end-on connection with Green Bus. Service 4 could provide one of the most spectacular rides on the island, as South Buona Vista Road twisted and turned up the incline which was known locally as The Gap, from the peak of which the whole of the harbour lay spread out below. The keen photographer wishing to record service 4 against this setting had to be prepared for a very long wait.

PAYA LEBAR BUS SERVICE LIMITED:

1. Geylang Road at the junction of Paya Lebar Road and Royal Air Force Station, Seletar,and also, Geylang Road at Paya Lebar Road junction to Yio Chu Kang. (buses required for service to Seletar—17 plus 2 spares, and for service to Yio Chu Kang—19 plus 2 spare)
2. Tampines Road at the junction with Upper Serangoon Road to Tampines Road junction with Changi Road, with the deviations to serve Kuala Loyang at 7.00a.m., 12 noon, 1.30 p.m. and 6.30 p.m. (ex-Changi Road). (buses required for service—9 plus 1 spare)
3. Serangoon Garden Estate to Happy World. (buses required for service—9 plus 1 spare)
4. Geylang Road at juntion with Paya Lebar Road to International Airport. (buses required for service—4 plus 1 spare)
Total number of buses required for services—65. Number of buses of Registrar of Vehicles register—70.

As previously noted, Changi and Katong -Bedok buses were met up with at Geylang Road, and Changi buses again at the Tampines Road terminal. Other than these, the road through Paya Lebar village was shared with Ponggol, although there would be no competition on this short stretch. In the fullness of time the Yio Chu Kang service would reach out to touch Thomson Road, and thus provide an end on junction with Tay Koh Yat. As for the run up to Paya Lebar Airport, Changi had faded from the scene, leaving Paya Lebar to be in competition with both the Traction Company and Tay Koh Yat between Paya Lebar Road and the terminal buildings.

PONGGOL BUS SERVICE COMPANY

From Ponggol Road end to Bartley Road at Mount Vernon, with two or three buses to turn at St. Joseph's Church, 7 1/2 milestone Upper Serangoon (buses required for service—13 plus 2 spare)
Total number of buses required for service—15. Number of buses on Registrar of Vehicles register—15.

The move away from the traditional terminus at Boundary Road, Paya Lebar , for the new terminal loop by way of Paya Lebar Road, Bartley Road and Upper Serangoon Road provided the opportunity for some stiff competition, not only with the Traction Company along the main road, but also with Paya Lebar for the five cents stage along Paya Lebar Road, and in similar fashion with Tay Koh Yat along the length of Bartley Road.

TAY KOH YAT BUS COMPANY LIMITED

1. A shuttle service for school children only between the Mata Gate, Sembawang Road 15th. milestone, terminus and Nee Soon Village, to operate between the hours of 7.00 a.m. and 8.00 a.m. and 12.30 p.m. and 1.30 p.m. (buses required for service—2 without spare)
2. Hoi How Road to Rotherham Gate, H.M. Naval Dockyard. (buses required for service—4 plus 1 spare)
3. Hoi How Road to Sembawang Road, 15th. milestone, with six buses daily to turn short at Thomson Road 7 1/2 milstone. (buses required for service—29 plus 3 spares)
5. Hoi How Road to Royal Naval Air Station, Sembawang, serving H.M.S. Simbang and the N.A.A.F.I. Club, the service being required by the Royal Navy authorities. (buses required for service—2 plus 1 spare)
6. Nee Soon Village to Neen Soon Transit Camp: service required by the War Department. (buses required for service—2 plus 1 spare)
8. Sembawang Hill Estate to Havelock Road (direct)
8A. Sembawang Hill Estate to Havelock Road via Balmoral Road. (buses required for services 8 and 8A—10 without spares)
9. Paya Lebar International Airport to Havelock Road.
(buses required for service—15 plus 2 spares)
10. Bartley Road at the junction with Paya Lebar Road to Ayer Rajah Road junction with South Buona Vista Road: two buses to work short to the junction of Dunearn Road with Adam Road.
10A. Bartley Road at the junction with Paya Lebar Road to Ayer Rajah Road junction with South Buona Vista Road via Queenstown. (buses required for service 10 and 10A—9 plus 1 spare)
12A. McPherson Road junction with Serangoon Road to International Airport. (buses required for service—3 plus 1 spare)
11. Aljunied Road outside house number 17 to Upper Aljunied Road at the junction with Upper Serangoon Road. (buses required for service—2 plus 1 spare)
14A. Hoi How Road to Norfolk-Owen Singapore Improvement Trust Housing Estate, a circular service via Beach Road, Arab Street, Rochore Canal Road, Bukit Timah Road, Kampong Java Road, Hampshire Road, Race Course Road, Owen Road, Norfolk Road, Thomson Road, Kampong Java Road and back to Hoi How Road. (buses required for service—3 plus 1 spare)
Total number of buses required for services—98: on the Registrar of Vehicles register—113.

Whilst not the largest in numerical terms, the spread of the Tay Koh Yat operating territory placed it second only to the Traction Company. In a wide swathe stretching from Geylang Road in the east, closely following all the residential developments along the line of the city boundary, the red-and-black livery came within a couple of miles of the west coast (at Ayer Rajah Road), and in so doing either touched upon, or else had common sections of route, with all of the other Chinese bus conmpanies except Katong-Bedok (and that was just beyond the houses on the other side of Geylang Road). In a route planning context the Traction Company had failed to keep abreast of the times, because a pattern based on routes radiating from the city centre was their firmly held policy. By so doing, the new suburbs would be difficult to serve except by way of radial routes, and it was this need which was seized with such success by Tay Koh Yat. The result was the creation of some long journeys, such as services 9 and 10, well able to compare with the traditional trunk workings out to Sembawang. The expansion also meant that the original Tay Koh Yat workings, established back in post-mosquito bus times, and now taking on the mantle of services 11 and 12, were no longer isolated from the rest of the network.

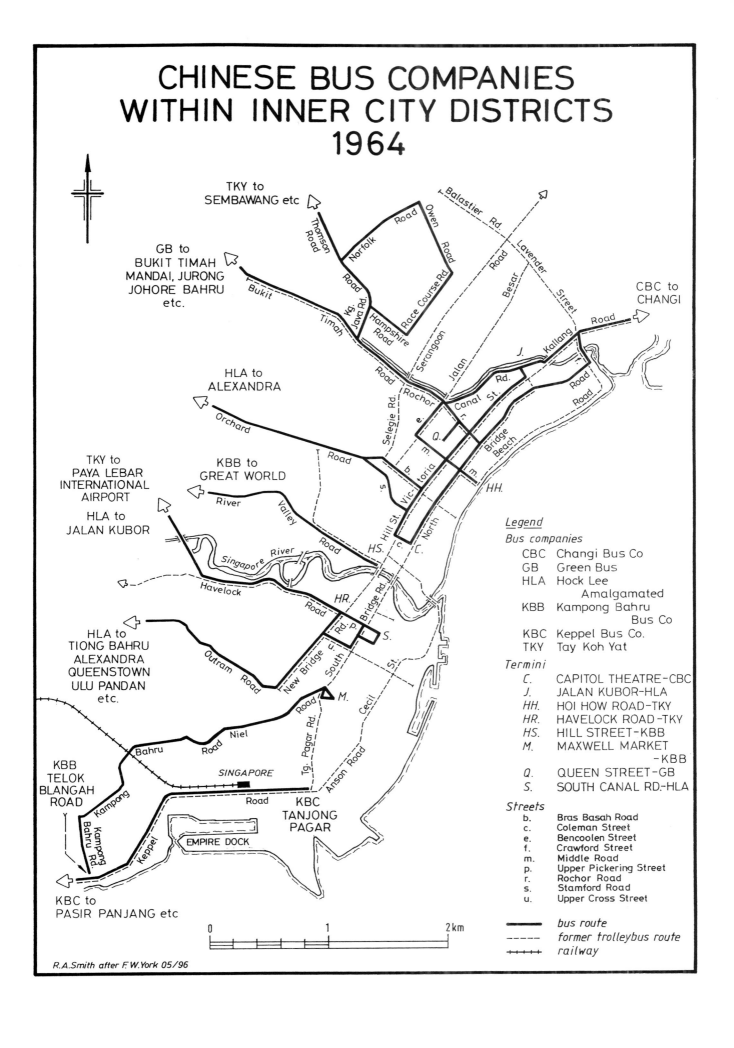

CHINESE BUS COMPANIES WITHIN INNER CITY DISTRICTS 1964

TKY to SEMBAWANG etc

GB to BUKIT TIMAH MANDAI, JURONG JOHORE BAHRU etc.

CBC to CHANGI

HLA to ALEXANDRA

TKY to PAYA LEBAR INTERNATIONAL AIRPORT

HLA to JALAN KUBOR

KBB to GREAT WORLD

HLA to TIONG BAHRU ALEXANDRA QUEENSTOWN ULU PANDAN etc.

KBB TELOK BLANGAH ROAD

KBC TANJONG PAGAR

EMPIRE DOCK

SINGAPORE

KBC to PASIR PANJANG etc

Thomson Road, Norfolk Road, Owen Road, Balastier Rd., Lavender Street, Race Course Rd., Serangoon Road, Besar Road, Kallang Road, Bukit Timah, Kg. Java Rd., Hampshire Road, Jalan, Rochor, Canal St., Selegie Rd., Orchard Road, Victoria, Bridge, Beach, River Valley Road, Hill St., North, Singapore River, Havelock Road, Bridge Rd., New Bridge Road, South, Cecil St., Outram Road, Tg. Pagar Rd., Anson Road, Niel Road, Kampong Bahru, Keppel Road, Kampong Bahru Rd.

Legend

Bus companies

CBC	Changi Bus Co
GB	Green Bus
HLA	Hock Lee Amalgamated
KBB	Kampong Bahru Bus Co
KBC	Keppel Bus Co.
TKY	Tay Koh Yat

Termini

C.	CAPITOL THEATRE–CBC
J.	JALAN KUBOR–HLA
HH.	HOI HOW ROAD–TKY
HR.	HAVELOCK ROAD–TKY
HS.	HILL STREET–KBB
M.	MAXWELL MARKET–KBB
Q.	QUEEN STREET–GB
S.	SOUTH CANAL RD.–HLA

Streets

b.	Bras Basah Road
c.	Coleman Street
e.	Bencoolen Street
f.	Crawford Street
m.	Middle Road
p.	Upper Pickering Street
r.	Rochor Road
s.	Stamford Road
u.	Upper Cross Street

——— bus route
– – – former trolleybus route
+++++ railway

0   1   2km

R.A.Smith after F.W.York 05/96

The difference between the number of buses required for service and those recorded as being currrent with the Registrar of Vehicles does not appear to leave a very wide margin by which the contract services could be managed. Perhaps the spares total would also be involved in this work, unless special registration arrangements had been made whereby to accommodate the large non-public fleet.

Although not to be seen as being part of the Chinese bus companies service network, similar recordings of other express workings into Singapore are of interest:

THE KUALA LUMPUR–SINGAPORE EXPRESS LIMITED:
From the Rochore Road terminal point to the Causeway, and from thence to Kuala Lumpur (buses required for service—2, of which 1 to be registered in the Federation of Malaya)

SING LIAN EXPRESS LIMITED
From the Beach Road terminal to the Causeway, and from thence to Malacca (buses required for service—10, of which 5 to be registered in the Federation of Malaya)

THE SINGAPORE–JOHORE EXPRESS LIMTIED
1.   Rochore Road to Johore Bahru (buses required for service—20 plus 2 spares)
2.   Singapore Turf Club to Johore Bahru (no passenger to be taken up or set down in Singapore except at the Terminal Point located within the grounds of the Singapore Turf Club) (buses required for service—2 without spare)
3.   H.M. Dockyard to Johore Bahru (no passengers to be taken up or set down in Sinapore except within the confines of the Naval Base.) (buses required for service—1 plus 1 spare)
Total number of buses required for service—26, but the total recorded on the Registrar of Vehicles register only 21, explained in part by the fact of the Company having made an application to reduce the number of vehicles to work service 1 to 16.

---

were 12,000 cabs at work throughout the Island, of which 7,000 were concentrated on the city routes, a situation which was regarded as getting worse every day. Perhaps somewhat belatedly, the unpleasant fact came to be recognised, that no normal bus service could be as attractive as an illegal pirate taxi, for he, the owner driver, was able to present a personalised function, not on a door to door basis it is true, but instead, once all his seats were taken, then speedily working the route without the need to make frequent stops. His charges would be the same as bus fare scales in the main, with other financial benefits being drawn from the non-payment of taxes, his reduced insurance premiums as for what seemed on paper to be a private car for personal use, only a small feeling of obligation towards maintenance and inspection of his vehicle, and no incentive to go to work along lightly loaded routes, nor control the number of hours that he should work. All of the bus operators were tightly controlled in all of these matters so that, in seeking free competition to obtain passengers, well regulated bus companies would always be the losers, unless they could be provided with the legal protection to which they were entitled by virtue of their public accountability.

In hindsight it would seem to be somewhat unfair that the 'new' Traction Company should be shouldered with much of the blame for the situation as now it stood. Be that as it may, as a result of a close and continuous examination of admittedly unfair competition, the 'obvious' conclusion to be drawn was that the major factor contributing to the increase and indeed the influence and success of the pirate taxis was in the inadequacy of the existing pattern of bus routes. The manner in which the Chinese companies, most especially Tay Koh Yat, had expanded beyond their recognised territorial boundaries can only mean that the criticism was directed against the Traction Company. Whoever the examiners of the problem might have been, for this was an anonymous enquiry, they were to insist that there had been little change in the overall pattern of bus services 'within Singapore' during the previous twenty-five years. Whilst good for public comment, of course, such condemnation had little historical grounding, for there were no bus services at all prior to 1920 whilst, following the demise of the electric tramways, route developments within the municipal limits had certainly kept pace with the needs of an ever expanding population.

No person of good sense would expect there to be overnight solutions, but the new Board of Directors were very much aware of the considerable changes in the locations of centres of population, and the consequent changes in the directions of travel. The STC would conduct a far reaching review of all of the existing services and, as a consquence, present to the Omnibus Services Licencing Authority, new proposals designed to take advange of the new roads leading into the satellite towns which were starting to take shape. At the same time, it was stated that such a review would not seek to infringe upon the traffic being generated by the Chinese companies. The result was the presentation of the "Twenty-nine applications" on 13th April 1965, and after due consideration the Licensing Authority were able to approve the majority in principle. However, it was then discovered that the adminstrative tasks involved in bringing the overall proposals to fruition would prove to be greater than at first thought, and a series of delays would need to follow. Computers were obtained with which to assist with the complex work, and the Company made the claim that it had been one of the few bus companies in the world able to produce schedules by this means.

Reaching the end of 1965 the fleet in service with the Traction Company numbered 450, and concern was being expressed at the

ABOVE: A Singapore registered Vulcan 6PF of the Sing Lian Express Limited. Half of the fleet was registered in Singapore, the other half in Malaya. Some coaches in the fleet were provided with toilets at the offside rear corner, complete with white glass windows, while the luxury atmosphere was enhanced by the provision of curtains at the windows to shield passengers from the tropical sun.

Two camps and pirate taxis

To the outside observer, the restructuring of the Traction Company as a wholly local company totally separated from its London ties should have resulted in a drawing together of the interests of all of the transport operators. Alas, it was not to be, and the term "the Chinese bus owners and the Traction Company" was destined to remain current for several more years. Even at employee level there was no attempt to create a single bus worker's Union, and the various problems which had beset the "old" company were set to continue during the lifetime of the new one. Not the least was the battle with pirate taxi operators, and it was now estimated that there

ABOVE: The Chinese bus companies set about replacing their mixed fleets of ex-military vehicles and by the early 1950's, some fine examples of local body production graced the streets of Singapore. Here Changi Bus Company's Austin CXD, SH 331, shows off well the Company device of intertwined initials 'CBCL' with the equivalent in Chinese forming a half-circle below.

from 9th August. Admission to the United Nations was to follow on 21st September, and Membership of the Commonwealth of Nations as from 16th October, with Malaysia as sponsor, a most pleasing gesture. Finally, on 22nd December, Singapore was declared a Republic. Here again, change would not come about overnight, but the seeds would soon be planted which, over the following thirty years, would produce one of the most co-ordinated systems of transport, both public and private, to be found anywhere in the world.

Into 1966, and history was repeating itself, and very real danger was to be found in the constant presence of the pirate taxis. Certainly the situation was as dangerous as had been the case with the mosquito buses thirty years previously, but with one major difference. Whereas then the Chinese bus companies had been able to evolve from the mosquito, now they too were victims, and if any attempt were to be made to

high age of many of that number, with the Albions soldiering on despite being well beyond their expected life. A pair of Mitsubishi buses were purchased for evaluation purposes, like the Isuzu fleet before them delivered complete, but as they had been designed for Japanese climatic conditions they did suffer a high defect rate. The major problem seemed to be their inability to cope with heavy traffic within the high ambient temperatures of Singapore, and a series of technical investigations were required before satisfactory solutions could be worked out, bringing the pair to a high state of reliability. Perhaps the extent of the remedial work was too involved, for whilst future orders still involved a Japanese manufacturer, Nissan was the chosen supplier.

On the national scene, 1965 was a year of great importance, for, in view of the differences between the Governments of Singapore and Malaysia with regard to a "Malaysian Malaysia", in one of the classic political speeches of modern times, Prime Minister Lee Kuan Yew announced the separation of Singapore from the Federation as

organise the owner-drivers, there was no place into which they could fit, so that the only action which could be taken against them would be complete elimination. As far as legal taxis were concerned, all licences had been issued, and they behaved with perfect correctness. If to be wiped out should be the only answer to this constant problem, then there is little doubt that public support for them would be generously given, and that could lead to trouble in the streets. Even at this time there were extreme political elements who would not hesitate to exploit any cause, no matter how unworthy, in order to forment trouble. The Chinese companies would solider on as best they could, but for the Traction Company only two lines of action appeared to be open. The first would be to make application for a substantial and immeidate increase in fares, but even if approval could be obtained, then there could well be a negative effect, for both existing and potential passengers might be scared away. The second, and terrible to contemplate, would be to place the whole business into voluntary liquidation. The real problem facing those seeking to exercise some form of control was the secret background to the organisation of the pirates. That some form had crystalised became clear when, on the 7th and 8th March 1966 the pirates came out on strike, and it became clear that individuals could not take industrial action against themselves. These two days served to demonstrate the extent of the damage that was being done to the revenues of the STC for, on the first day an additional 43,700 tickets were sold, whilst on the second day that figure rose to 55,800, which represented an increase in receipts of six thousand seven hundred dollars daily, by average. The government had at last taken an active interest in the on-going misuse of motor cars, having recently amended the law so that various authorities could take effective action against pirate operations. Therein might be found the root cause of the strike, an effort to win public support, but as there had not been sufficient time for the full effects of the revised legislation

BELOW: A U.S. built Ford, probably ex-military, of the Green Bus Company, on the Johore Bahru service in June 1956, makes its way past the rear of Mackenzie Road depot. A Falcon of the STC is about to depart from its home premises.

of modern bus would have to be removed from consideration. It fell to the government to decide which Agents could be recognised as an approved vehicle assembler, their decisions being announced on the 10th January 1967. The fifty-vehicle order was taken out from the state of limbo, meetings arranged with parties who might be contenders for the supply of the buses, all in the hope that they would be in service by the end of the year. Nissan had been the chosen manufacturer, and in order to meet the needs of local assembly, a tripartite business was created, formed by Lee Kiat Seng, Nissan and the Traction Company, with the latter holding a minority share at this stage. To construct the required factory, train engineers and get the production line working would take a considerable time, and so the fifty buses were, in this instance, allowed to arrive fully assembled.

to filter down, the pessimistic stances adopted by the company are not difficult to understand. One of the measures taken as a means to acheiving some reduction in costs was to withdraw 2.2% of off-peak workings, almost a panic induced step in the face of the crisis, and very dangerous, for having to wait longer at the bus stop would be the natural means of sending the prospective passenger into a pirate taxi.

The fleet as at 30th September 1966 comprised all 178 Albions, the 133 Guys, 137 Isuzus and two Mitsubishi Fusos. The Albions by now had been fully depreciated, and with the oldest of their numbers being eighteen years old, there was an urgent need for their replacement. To this end advertisements were placed worldwide, seeking tenders for the supply of fifty completely built up buses.

Local assembly

The arrival of the completely built up (bodied) Isuzus four years previously was not a compliment to Singapore industry, for the bodywork provided by the local builders was to a very high standard. It was the policy of the government now to give strong support to local industry, and in some circles there was concern at the prospect of such a large fleet of fully built buses being imported. As a counter measure, a new rate of import duty was placed on fully built buses, so high as to make the whole project uneconomic, so great as to demand the rethinking of the placing of the order. From the point of view not only of the resulting initial price but also in the future interests of fleet standardisation and thus the economic maintenance factors, the policy of the company would have to be to purchase only from a manufacturer who had an assembly plant located in Singapore, either directly or through an agent. In the making of such a decision and the setting of such a firm policy, several types

The closure for rebuilding of the bridge carrying Mountbatten Road over the Geylang River caused a major pattern of diversions to affect those services working within the Katong 'box' bringing once again a marked fall in revenue as passengers flocked to the pirate taxis. Cars were allowed to cross the temporary structure, forbidden to buses. There was also a great deal of concern being felt as to what effects of any planned extension to the one way traffic pattern might have on revenue. Increased mileages would not attract new patronage. For example, inbound services leaving Upper Serengoon Road would deviate at Woodsville Circus in order to join the newly constructed Bendemeer Road, located in a line parallel to Serengoon Road for the whole length. Beyond the Lavender Street crossing, having been joined by the extensive pattern of routes leading out beyond Moulmein Green, the need to revise the long established map would become very complicated, hence the reason for this concern. However although the advance notice of the scheme had been made public as early as 1966, with implementation due during 1968, various constructional problems caused a delay to extend into 1969. Other, if somewhat less involved, one-way traffic schemes were introduced during 1967, directly being responsible for the recasting of a large number of bus routes involving a number of companies. In the central area one such scheme embraced Orchard Road, Stamford Road and Bras Basah Road, and across the city South Bridge Road, Neil Road and New Bridge Road provoked a need to revise several terminal loops. Within the inner suburbs the former Singapore Improvement Trusts' St

LEFT: With support and protection for local industry in mind, following the mass purchases of Isuzu and Nissan buses completely built up from Japan, a company was formed to assemble ckd bodies on Nissan chassis but very few were completed, including STC 752, seen here running on Route 124. Locally assembled bodies could be identified by their almost rectangular last side window.

Balastier Road, being renumbered 38, part of the 10 linking Neil Road with Kim Keat Estate became service 30, whilst the 17A was extended on from the rapidly developing area surrounding Whitley Road as service 37, all went into Tao Payoh and proved to be an instant success, so much so that more buses would be needed in order to maintain the momentum, in effect a further stay of execution for those Albions. Other operators were swift to recognise the pot of gold awaiting them: working along Braddell Road, skirting the northern aspects of the new town, Tay Koh Yat introduced service 16, linking Havelock Road with Tao Payoh, and service 17 between Aljunied Road and Havelock Road, on the way making a very extensive loop and double run into and off Tao Payoh. The Paya Lebar service 2A was a long extension of the Changi Road to Tampines Road route, working up the road to Paya Lebar Village thence to Tao Payoh, at last forging a link between the isolated section of their business and the main operations. Similar expansions would penetrate other satellite towns, resulting in an ever more complicated interweaving of many bus services.

The directors of the STC had declared themselves to be fully in support of the government policy in the promotion of local assembly and construction of buses, and the 1968 order was placed with Singapore Nissan Motors (Pte) Limited, in which plant the company had increased its stake to 30%. In the event, it would seem that only a small number of buses were supplied from this source for, when the government lifted the taxation based restrictions on the importing of fully built up commercial vehicles, the next order for complete buses was to have been placed with Nissans, from Japan. Thus, this experiment in taking an active role in manufacturing was very short lived, but this was not the case elsewhere.

The Cycle and Carriage Company, based along the showroom lined affluence of Orchard Road, held the agencies for a variety of European Manufacturers, including Albion and Leyland. Also included was Mercedes-Benz—and the home management of Daimler Benz AG at Mannheim—were quick to realise the opportunities which would be presented if an assembly base could be provided within Singapore, not only for commercial vehicles but also to be a boost throughout the Far East for the Mercedes car. A wise move, which was shortly to result in complete control of the bus market being snatched away from the traditional British suppliers, to be replaced by a selection of Mercedes types. Although high-frame, lorry-derived models, seemed to be the popular choices in the initial stages of the enterprise, such was the constant level of demand for the full Mercedes range that the opportunity was taken to construct a new factory on land being developed between Princess Elizabeth Estate and Jurong Road, facing onto Hill View Avenue. In order that the factory was able to supply complete buses, kits were obtained from Superior Star, and a highly standardised product resulted. There might be some small variations as to indicator apertures, some operators being quite happy to continue with the single design wherein a board would be placed, whilst others wished to have double boxes to show terminals at each end of the route, and yet again Tay Koh Yat, with experience of rollerblinds, sought a large box to carry the destination flanked by one smaller in order to show the service number. As a means of reaching an even greater

Michael's Estate had to become one-way along the loop service road throughout the estate in view of the amount of unauthorised car parking which was starting to make a serious impact on the ability to maintain schedules. To follow this latter point, all the bus companies were having to face a combination of circumstances which were proving to be detrimental to the continued expansion of their businesses. As increasing numbers of flats within the new estates were occupied, so there was a constant changing in the established travel patterns of the public, for what might be gained by one operator would have been lost to another. As noted the spread of one-way traffic flows did much to exacerbate the problem but, in addition, the needs to travel were being very much reduced with the introduction of television and, as might have been expected, an ever increasing level of private car ownership, the result of which was to increase congestion at a number of key junctions throughout the island. The highways department carried out a considerable range of improvements at such sites, involving the provision of traffic islands, roundabouts or automatic signals but, for the longer term, the government had to consider the place of the motor car in the structure of society, for already it was being felt that strong control measures would soon be required. Armed with this knowledge, all of the bus companies continued to look to the future with confidence, despite the current problems.

As far as the Traction Company was concerned, although the first fifty Nissans had been bought into service during July and August of 1967, their arrival could not allow for the withdrawal of the oldest Albions. At last, firm government action was being taken against the pirate taxis, and the quite staggering increase in the numbers of passengers as a direct result meant that the company quite unexpectedly found itself short of stock with which to cope which fact went far to demonstrate the extent to which revenues had been creamed off over the years. Even so the overall financial situation could hardly be strong, being fixed into the policy of providing cheap fares over the longer distances, and the basic ten cents children's tickets. It was calculated that, if this benefit could be replaced by the more usual half-of-the-adult fare, then the annual revenues could benefit by as much as two-and-a-half million Singapore dollars. If the subsidy should remain, then the cost should be met either by the government or some other appropriate authority.

It is a most interesting fact in that, by 1967, the average mileage of each Traction Company bus had reached 39,134, which figure was considered to be greater than could be shown for many of the municipal operators of similar patterns within the United Kingdom.

Tao Payoh was growing rapidly, a new town rather than an estate, and like a magnet drew new bus services into the web of its roads pattern. The Traction Company made three extensions: service 8A which had linked Keppel Harbour to Thomson Road via

RIGHT: Tay Koh Yat SH 971, A Mercedes-Benz LP1113, represents both the new order and the simplified livery style—silver with a thin colour band—used in the late 1960's, just before amalgamation. LP1113's were widely used by most of the Chinese operators, despite their lorry-based chassis with high frame requiring steep steps into the saloon. Local bodywork was used, showing some similarity to the Isuzu and Nissan designs, with half-drop side windows and fixed upper panes.

degree of standard production there came a major change in the manner of livery presentation, in that an all over aluminium finish was adopted by several companies, with the individual fleet colour being carried in narrow bands carried beneath the windows.

1969 became noted for an extensive reshaping of portions of the Traction Company's route map. Amongst the schemes to improve road junctions previously mentioned, the most drastic saw the complete removal of Moulmein 'green', that charming little oasis of peace which sat comfortably in the junction of Balastier and Moulmein Roads, and which formed a natural bus turning circle. Being reborn as a simple "Y" junction joining a pair of dual carriage ways, and without any facility for "U" tuning, all of the services which formerly terminated here had to be moved elsewhere, and the obvious destination was to be found within the complexities of Tao Payoh. The date bringing in these alterations was 22nd June 1969, coincidental with the similar and long awaited scheme embracing Serengoon Road, Bendemeer Road and Jalan Besar. With so many established services now moved to serve Tao Payoh, additional strength needed to be provided along Balastier Road, and this was met by the introduction of service 19A from Tanjong Pagar to Thomson Road Police Station. All in all, a day which must have placed great strains both upon the crews and the patience of regular passengers.

Increased congestion was developing into a state of complete chaos, and part of the solution would be found in the removal of bus terminals from Collyer Quay and Finlayson Green, with services 15, 16, 18, 18 Limited Stop, 18A, 18A Limited Stop, 18B, 20, 25, 26, and 27, all to a new site located along Shenton Way. Fifteen years previously Shenton Way had been a fine highway constructed over a wide expanse of reclaimed land, running from the business centre out towards Tanjong Pagar, and parallel with Anson Road. On either side, nothing save a few street lamps. During the intervening period the land had been developed to a limited extent, and certainly was not able to produce very much in the way of traffic potential. What was created was the nearest approach to a central bus station as envisaged by the Hawkins Report, although on-street loading was used. Further extensions were being made to the one-way traffic patterns within the central districts, taking effect as from 17th October 1969, and it was on the same day that

the Shenton Way terminal was brought into operation.

The British Government had made known their policy to run down, and eventually close altogether, many of the overseas military bases, and Singapore was included in the list. The economy of the Republic depended to a considerable extent on the employment provided by these many establishments, ranging in size from the huge Naval Base, a complete town within itself, down to isolated little radio posts such Kuala Loyang. Singaporean energies are such that there would be no question of sitting back to bemoan the prospect of a cloud of unemployment on a vast scale building up for the near future, but instead active planning was in hand to provide counter measures. Tourism would be one possibility, but that would need to be something for the distant future. The other alternative was for the Republic to invest heavily in industry, and to this end a vast programme of reclamation had been converting the marshlands along the West Coast into Jurong Town.

The Jurong Town Corporation had been established under the Act of that title as from 1st June 1968, to develop and manage industrial estates throughout Singapore. The town was provided with a 3000 feet deep water wharf, and a further 1,260 feet of wharfage suitable for coastal and lighter traffic. Reclaiming an off-shore island would provide for the expansion of the port, besides making more valuable land available. Further inland, the area was served

RIGHT: Jurong Development Cpn. The swamps from which Jurong New Town rose, seen at the West Coast Road before the developers had completed much more than a survey. Keppel Bus Co Bedford OB, S 3012, makes its way beneath interesting cloud effects and with dense palm growth behind it.

by a total of twelve miles of internal railway, connecting with the main line of Malayan Railways, whilst there were forty-four miles of first class roads. The Jurong Road was declared a Free Trade Zone as from 1st September 1969.

For the bus operators a traffic potential almost without limit, and a perfect demonstration of the changing pattern of population movement. For those years whilst Jurong was no more than a tiny rural village, and territory had belonged to Green Bus, with Keppel arriving from the coastal strip recently. Service 3 remained the principal access to Jurong, but to this was added service 10, starting from a point along Bukit Timah Road opposite Singapore University, and then threading a route along many of the new side roads until reaching a terminus at Taman Jurong near Jalan Peng Kang: service 11 from the Staff Quarters in Jalan Peng Kang to Jurong Shipyard, and service 12 between the same terminal points but using a circuitous route.

As for Keppel, their service 6 started from the traditional terminus in Keppel Road close by Tanjong Pagar, then to work along the full length along the west coast before turning into Jalan Bahru Selatan, proceeding through the town to a terminus at Jurong Shipyard.

Nor was Hock Lee Amalgamated to be denied access, introducing their service 14 from New Market Road close to Upper Cross Street, passing through Queenstown in order to reach Jurong Town and a terminus at Jalan Boon Lay. What of our pioneer, would Tay Koh Yat be able to participate in this traffic bonanza? After all, Jurong was a very long way beyond the traditional territorial boundary. The answer was 'Yes', for Tay Koh Yat brought in a service 5 from Gagak Selari Barat to pass through what had been the exclusive Hock Lee Amalgamated territory, including Queenstown, eventually leaeving that popular terminus at Jurong Shipyard. Retaining a further belief in the importance of providing cross country connections, there was also service 7, which at the Jurong end had a terminus at Jalan Bukit Marah, passed through Queenstown, and then went on to reach Tao Payoh. Although in fact the one terminus just touched the fringe of Jurong, nevertheless, this service made contact with the three sections of the island which were witnessing the most rapid change. Even the tiny Easy Bus Company was able to make a contribution to what would develop into a highly complicated map, but not, as might have been expected, from the Pasit Panjang end of their route, but rather from a junction with the long established service 1 at Clementi Road near Bukit Timah Circus, to pass along Upper Ayre Rajah Road in order to gain access to Jalan Ahmad Ibrahim, the trunk road through Jurong Town, to a terminus in International Road.

Not to be left out, the Traction Company introduced a new service 17A as from 7th December 1969, from a city terminus at Shenton Way (and by implication, this fact must also have seen the 17 and 17B removed from the previous terminal at Raffles Quay). In common with most of the Chinese routes, Jalan Ahmad Ibrahim was included along the line of route, afterwards taking side roads in order to reach a terminus outside the Mobil Oil Refinery.

Whilst it has been possible to establish the starting date for the 17A, we can only assume that the arrival of so many other bus companies was a process of evolution, spread over a period, although the time factor would be quite narrow. There are two obvious conclusions to be drawn, the first being that the traditional territorial concept had been lost forever, whilst the Traction Company was now prepared, and authorised, to work far beyond the confines as suggested by the terms of the original Ordinance, with a considerable proportion of this service lying beyond the city boundary. Would the company attempt further long route expansions elsewhere? It would be a very doubtful proposition, for whereas the throughfares on the other buses might stand at sixty or seventy cents, the Traction Company were still tied to the ruling which fixed their maximum charge at twenty-five cents. To remain viable, heavy patronage would be needed, particularly from short distance riders, but the problem of fare scales again went against the Traction Company, their minimum fare of ten cents being undercut by the continued presence of a five cents charge by competitors along common sections of route.

The previously mentioned 'Twenty-nine applications' had seen the reintroduction of a service 5 to the Traction Company, having been unused since the pre-occupation years at which time it was a trolley bus working. The number had been given to as long cross-city venture linking Siglap with Holland Village. Also, the peculiar service 24 had been extended beyond the loops-around-the-camps also to reach Holland Village. As from February 1970 the Holland Village terminal was closed, and the 5 and 24 together were transferred to a new terminal at Commonwealth Avenue, in the heart of Queenstown.

For the Traction Company the statistical picture looked quite healthy. The fifty completely built up Nissans were brought into service during October 1969, and shortly thereafter forty-three locally assembled by Singapore Nissan Motors were able to join the fleet together allowing for additional traffic needs to be met in company with the withdrawal of forty-six of the oldest Albions (and it is worth noting that not all of these 'old-timers' went for scrap, several being refurbished, indeed even rebuilt, by contractors for use as school buses). The expanded fleet allowed for increased mileages to be worked, rising from 18,659,890 during 1969 to 21,133,681 for the following year. This factor, when combined with the increased success in combating the few remaining pirate taxis, witnessed an increase in adult passengers carried over the same periods from 91,838,227 up to 103,555,162, although there was a decline in the number of school children carried, down by 1,276,962, being due to the increased number of special school vehicles being operated throughout the Republic.

BELOW: A decline in the number of school children carried by public buses was, in part, accounted for by the increase in the numbers of privately owned school buses operated either by schools or on their behalf by contractors. Some, like the Dennis Stork (**left**) SR 1241, were purpose built school buses—the Stork was a favourite with the London County Council at the time. The Vulcan, SCB 1135 (**right**) is believed by the photographer to have been new to Singapore–Johore Express but in this view was sponsored by the Singapore Football Association for San Shan School. Note the additional window bars.

ABOVE: Some school buses were former Traction Company vehicles such as this Albion FT 39 seen here in the ownership of the Paya Lebar Methodist Girls School and re-registered in the School Bus series as SCB965

In the wider sense, the 'Hawkins Report' had presented a range of possibilities, although the suggestion that trolleybuses be scrapped had been subsequently adopted. It fell to the Wilson Report (otherwise the White Paper on the re-organisation of the Motor Transport Service of Singapore), to put the majority of those suggestions into practice.

The Steering Committee of the Singapore Bus Study Group looked to Australia in order to appoint their consultant, and on 17th June 1970 appointed Mr R P Wilson, who was then the Traffic Manager of The Municipal Tramways Trust, Adelaide. His report was completed by 26th November and received the formal acceptance of the Steering Committee on 2nd December.

Pointing out that eleven companies were operating a total of one hundred and seventeen services, there had developed a considerable amount of wasteful duplication and overlapping of routes, the ideal solution to which would be the merging of all services into a single operation. A single organisation with single ownership and single management would not be appropriate at the time, but the amalgamation of the Chinese companies into three operational groups would be a move in the right direction. By so doing, the ability to plan for future expansion might be made more productive for passengers, but even with four companies remaining the creation of future new towns could eventually lead to further duplications. Emphasis was laid on the ideal being a single transport authority, in time.

As to the pattern of the new route network, it was agreed that a pattern of radial services should be maintained, using the main arterial highways and connecting the major areas of urban development with specified areas of the city, viz., (a) the commercial areas south of the Singapore River in the vicinity of Collyer Quay, Shenton Way and Robinson Road, (b) the Chinatown district around South Bridge Road, Neil Road and New Bridge Road, (c) the administrative complex near North Bridge Road and High Street, and (d) Orchard Road. However, in order to avoid overlapping and duplication of individual services within the central area and also to make the best use of rare road space required at terminal points, it was suggested that the radial routes be linked so as to pass through the city, east and north-east across to west and north-west. Besides easing traffic congestion, there would be benefits to many passengers who would be able to make through journeys without having to change buses.

In preparing the report, due regard had to be taken of all roads carrying a bus service, and it was recommended that no existing service should be withdrawn, but, on the under standing that a complete recasting be called for, it would not be certain that the same destinations would be reached as hitherto.

One point made in the Hawkins Report which did not find support concerned the provision of express or limited stop services. The fact that the Traction Company had been using such facilities to Upper Serengoon, Serengoon Garden Estate and Katong with a degree of success had passed without comment. Instead it was argued that such should only be provided when there were large numbers of passengers who required to travel between two specific points, and where such services were able to show significant reductions in travelling time compared with stopping services. It was considered that the areas with the highest density of population (Toa Payoh, Queenstown, St Michael's Estate and Macpherson Estate) were reasonably close to the city centre, and this factor, when seen in conjunction with the high traffic densities of other road users seeking to reach the city, would not be conducive to the time saving required.

Questions concerning the frequencies to be provided were found to be difficult to answer with any degree of certainty. Two major difficulties contributed to an undercurrent of doubt, both in a sense, being based on the lack of exact statistics. Perhaps the most important lack was an even reasonable estimate as to the numbers of extra passengers to be accommodated once pirate taxis were finally eliminated. Secondly, a major disadvantage was to be found in the wide range of vehicle types then in service with the resulting variations on capacity. For the purpose of the scheduling exercise, the weighted average of the authorised carrying capacity of the buses then in service was set at 53 passengers: in hindsight, this figure does appear to be somewhat high, although it should be stressed that this was not the seating capacity. Therefore, the recommendations were made on the basis of peak-hour loadings being a 50 passenger load per vehicle, but was at once discounted as being too high to enable a satisfactory standard of service to be maintained, it being dictated by the total number of buses being available for service. It is highly unusual for a report such as this to argue with its own findings, but maybe there was a case for presenting all the possible options, as the writer of the words would not be putting the suggestions into operation. To continue with the theme, it was reasoned that if the schedules were to be constructed to such a formula as a general rule, with experience elsewhere showing the method to be inadequate, then the results could only be serious overcrowding coupled with over-long waits at bus stops to be endured by prospective passengers. The target figure would need to be brought down to a rush hour capacity of 43 passengers per bus, but by so doing it was reported that there would be insufficient buses available, bringing the conclusion that problems would persist in matters relating to scheduling until more buses, built to a standard specification, could be brought into service.

Of what size should the fleets be? Based on the weighted average, 1418 buses would be required to work the revised route pattern. To this total should be added a 10% margin of emergency spare vehicles with which to cover mechanical breakdowns and accidents on the road and absence from service during terms of heavy workshop maintenance, slightly rounded up to produce an overall total of 1560 buses. Alas, as of the 31st December 1970, the Registrar of Vehicles only carried 1542 buses on the register. If, as seemed to be sensible, the lower figure be adopted, then the number required for service rises to 1560, and adding on the 10% reserve, arrives at a grand total of 1815, showing a deficiency of 273 buses. Therein was the need to present alternatives, for other scheduling was based on the higher capacity figure, which would almost certainly mean severe over crowding during the peak periods, or else the lower figure was adopted in the knowledge that a substantial number of journeys could not be run. Later experience would show that the emergency reserves needed to be kept exactly for that purpose, for the new companies, having taken in such mixed constituents, were to experience severe problems regarding the obtaining of spare parts, and breakdowns tended to become the rule rather than the exception. Furthermore, the Report laid stress on the fact of the calculations not having taken into account the number of time expired buses which were due for replacement, nor was any attempt made to forecast the extra patronage which might result from the natural growth in the population. Consideration was given to the world wide trend towards a greater increase in the use of private motor vehicles and a consequent decrease in the use of public transport patronage and that there existed no sound reason to assume that, in the evidence of growing economic development, that such a pattern would not be followed in Singapore. However, any loss of traffic in this matter would be made up by the continued population growth so that, in looking to the future, it was anticipated that the total fleet strength should stand at 2000 by June 1973.

In view of the considerable financial outlay which would be involved with the expansion of the fleet, it was suggested that further detailed studies should be made with a view to obtaining an ideal standard Singapore bus. There was also a proposal that mini-buses would be used primarily for the transport of school children, also to be used as worker's contract buses during the peak periods. As such a scheme had seemingly been approved elsewhere, the Report indicates that there would be a need to ensure that the mini-buses were indeed used only for the purposes as mentioned. The Report felt compelled to give even starker warnings, saying that in no circumstances should the mini-buses be permitted to ply for hire for the carriage of passengers at individual fares, in competition with the regular bus services, most particularly during off peak periods when the levels of patronage on the regular bus services had a vital effect on the profitability of the operating companies. Furthermore, the mini-buses would be restricted in number in order to ensure that the over servicing on their routes could not adversely affect their own profitability, and also for ease and control of regulation. No additional licences should be granted until such time as a proper investigation was able to show that there was a genuine need for the proposed service, and that it would not detract from any existing mini-bus or regular service. If the operators of the minibus services were to become dissatisfied with their profitability, then there would be the temptation to operate illegally in much the same manner as had been adopted by the pirate taxis. There would be little point in the various government authorities following their own decision to remove illegal taxi operations if a new form of pirate was allowed to spring up in their place. Earlier the question was posed, "Where would the pirate taxi owners go?", and the answer was being anticipated, "Into mini-bus operation", and if they did, then they would become an even greater problem.

Whether as a result of the publicity given to these warnings or not, it is difficult to say. What is certain is that there were very few mini-buses to be seen throughout Singapore during the early 1970's. It is certainly true that the concept of the mini-bus was far in advance of thinking on the subject in the United Kingdom, wherein such vehicles as there were happened to be van conversions. As long ago as the mid 1950's the Trojan chassis was a popular choice to have mounted thereon a 'proper' bus body. Bodywork was built in Singapore for the STC, but in this case the Sarawak Transport Company. Trojan buses also featured on rural services in Malaya. Such minis as were to be found in Singapore at the time the Report was being prepared were generally Mercedes, although the Leyland name could be seen now and then.

As to the type of bus best suited to the needs of Singapore, standardisation should be the key in order to meet mechanical eco-

UPPER RIGHT: An STC minibus—built in Singapore but not for use there. In this case the initials represent Sarawak Transport Company but had the authorities decided that Singapore's needs would be best served by minis, then the means to build them was in place. Trojans were popular in the Borneo territories and in Malaya itself but aggressive marketing meant that others were to supply the lion's share of the Singapore market for small buses.

MIDDLE RIGHT: The popular appeal of Mercedes-Benz was to lead to that make being prevalent in the small school and factory bus market and here we see a Mercedes mini lettered for the Sembawang Hills English School as it passes through Sembawang Village.

RIGHT: Leyland were able to offer the unusual looking 'Leyland 90', a light 2-ton payload truck chassis and these were bodied in Malaya, although the pug-like front incorporated panels supplied by Leyland and more generally associated with the 'LAD' cab built for Leyland Albion and Dodge. The Leyland 90 owed its heritage to the Standard Motor Company.

nomics. Perhaps due to their limited use throughout Australia, double deckers did not receive a mention. Instead, it was pointed out that articulated buses were proving to be quite popular in some European countries, and whist they would certainly provide the essential capacity, the length and weight involved might prove damaging to Singapore highways. This observation was not supported by the facts, for roads were built to the highest standards, and only in the older central areas where sharp corners would be encountered, or along some of the truly rural lanes to the North of the island, would it be likely that any real difficulty might be encountered. The ultimate suggestion was that a larger single deck bus of rigid chassis specification, able to accommodate an average peak hour loading ranging between 60 and 72 passengers depending on the seating arrangements, would be ideal, and Mercedes were happy to oblige. Based on conditions then prevailing, with the larger and standardised buses, the number required for service would be 1182 and adding on the 10% spares margin, the ideal fleet strength should be 1300: experiences in the near future would prove these statistics to be very wide of the real needs. Nevertheless, it was estimated that before June 1973, no less than 300 life expired buses would need replacing, and the suggestion that withdrawals should be based on carrying capacities rather than age, for the capacities which they provided could be replaced by only 215 new buses of the larger size.

Notwithstanding the policies of the Traction Company which, under normal operating circumstances, had always purchased chassis designed wholly for bus work, the Report made comments concerning most buses then in service as being constructed on truck rather than bus chassis, as a result tending to have high steps and floors which could slow down loading and unloading. In addition, elderly or handicapped persons could find the steps difficult to negotiate. On the worldwide transport scene a demand was becoming apparent of the need for buses to be designed with the lowest possible floor and step height, so that most of the major manufacturers were providing a positive response to such demands. A strong recommendation was made that the operators in Singapore should look to these designs, and the government could assist by making concessions on tax or import duties. If such was not financially feasible then the opposite approach could be taken, with the bus companies being deterred from purchasing new buses with high floor lines by means of a super tax placed on the import duties charged on such vehicles.

Although not mentioned by name, the Nissan fleet of the Traction Company were commended in that they were provided with pneumatically operated doors, opened and closed by remote control by the driver. All other buses on the island either had no doors at all or else doors to be manually operate and which were thus left open almost on a permanent basis. Such conditions presented a serious safety hazard, as passengers could be thrown from the vehicle when

a corner be turned at speed, and also the continued presence of an open access did largely contribute to the overcrowding of buses during the peak times, with the conductor unable to control whatever was taking place on the steps. Concerning this particular problem, it was suggested that regulations be introduced making it mandatory for all future bus deliveries to be fitted with pneumatic doors, to be under the control of the driver.

Except for many of the ex-military chassis, mainstay of the post-occupation fleets, and since the demise of the mosquito buses, a central doorway had been the standard feature of Singapore buses, used by all operators. The Report saw this as being a major cause of bus stop delays, as passengers seeking to leave the bus clashed with those who were trying to push their way on, with neither side being willing to stand aside for a few moments. It was considered that buses to the new size could be fitted with two doors, with one to be used for boarding and the other as an exit. Such a radical change in design would be needed in order to work the cross-city routes with greatest efficiency, as there would be as many passengers wishing to board as there would be leaving the bus, whereas under the existing regime, during the morning peak everybody would be getting off, and in the evening would be getting on. A two door design would also allow passengers to 'move along the bus', for all too often with the central entrance passengers would tend to congregate around the doorway making it impossible for other passengers to board, Whilst ample empty space might be available towards the front and rear of the bus.

It was noted that the driving compartment was completely closed off from the rest of the bus, required by Regulation. This was considered to be a most unusual feature, which served no useful purpose, representing instead a waste of space which might otherwise be used to some advantage. One of the proposed doorways could be fitted ahead of the front axle without any reduction of passenger accommodation, and the recommendation was made that regulations should be drafted with a view to permitting the use of buses so constructed. Mr Wilson was not to know that Tay Koh Yat had already tried this design with their Sentinel and Commer buses, and look what happened to them! The Traction Company, however, found the arrangement on their Isuzu and Nissan buses quite satisfactory.

Of course, thoughts associated with the forward doorway were leading in the obvious direction, to introduce a note pointing out the trend towards the one-person operation of buses, with the driver collecting fares or inspecting pre-purchased tickets. Whilst there was no immediate sign of Singapore turning towards such a method of operation, as the estimated life of new buses was placed at seventeen years, then serious thought should be given to producing a design for new buses which would be suitable for one-person operation. As it happened, the government was more concerned with the maintenance of full employment throughout the Republic, and

LEFT: Apart from nine buses in the Tay Koh Yat fleet, only the Isuzu and Nissan buses of the Traction Company had been purpose built with front entrances beside the driver and separate centre exits, making them suitable for one man operation and, as far as can be seen, the arrangement worked quite well. Here, still in Traction Company livery and carrying its original number, Isuzu STC 54, now owned by Associated Bus Service, takes a break in quiet rural surroundings at the end of 'post-amalgamation' Route 94. The lack of outward change meant that many less well informed passengers hardly noticed the final demise of the Singapore Traction Company (1964) limited

would not have looked kindly to a great army of conductors being put out of a job. As to the proposed age of buses, here again the government was not in line with the findings expressed in the Report, and policy was set out under which the life span should be eleven years.

To devise a unified fare structure must have caused a headache or two, although it was realised that a common structure must be adopted throughout the systems. Although as much duplication as possible would be eliminated, nevertheless there would remain areas within which all four operating companies would be providing services, certainly within the central areas, and to a certain extent around the outer residential districts. Differing fare scales as between individual companies would result in grave anomalies which would certainly lead to adverse effects on the operating ability of one or more companies.

In general terms, by 1970 two fare scales were operational, that of the Traction Company being higher than the Chinese bus companies over shorter distances. Despite having higher charges, the Traction Company had sustained losses during the years leading up to 1970, whilst the Chinese companies had, on the whole, enjoyed good profits. Whilst any increase in fares always proves undesirable, the only method of achieving uniformity without having to increase some fares would be to adopt the Chinese companies scale in respect of the short to medium journeys, but then fix the maximum adult fare at 25 cents, as was the need with Traction Company. By so doing, many of the travellers over existing Traction Company services could look for a five cents reduction in their fare, but, based on the returns for years previous, the Traction Company would not be able to sustain such a drop in revenue of this magnitude. Likewise, under such a scheme, the Chinese bus companies would stand to lose quite heavily if the 25 cents maximum was to be imposed, as their longest routes carried the scale beyond 60 cents, and as a result the longer routes might not be operated.

Obviously a compromise had to be found, and the accepted answer was a new scale graduated in 10 cents steps, viz., 10, 20, 30, 40 up to a maximum of 50 cents, the opinion being that from the passengers point of view more would gain from lower personal charges than would have to pay more, the Traction Company would benefit by having their maximum charge doubled, whilst any reduction in revenue accruing to the Chinese companies would be the minimum possible, as there were estimated to be few passengers who were inclined to travel through routes: for such value as high figures might have, the estimate was that the Traction Company's revenue might be down by 700,000 Singapore dollars as against 1969, whilst the total income for the combined Chinese companies could rise by a staggering 3,900,000 Singapore dollars. Already the Traction Company could be seen as being very much the poor relation under the planned merger.

Considerable merit was seen in the 10 cents children's fare as used by the Traction Company, and the proposal was made, and subsequently came into operation, that this facility should be extended island wide. As new schools had a tendency to be grouped quite close together, it was at the bus stops serving them that crowds could be encountered. It was suggested that fares collection at such busy points would be made more complete by the introduction of mobile conductors selling tickets before the arrival of the bus. As a result fewer fares would go uncollected, and such a scheme might go far in covering its own costs. It would also be an ideal means of examining the possibility of introducing ticket machines, but neither suggestion was followed through.

With a linking of routes across the city central area much thought would need to be given to the siting of stopping places and the extent to which additional road space might be required. As it was the existing terminals in New Market Street (Hock Lee Amalgamated), Hoi How Road (the main terminal for Tay Koh Yat) and Murray Street would no longer be required, whilst there would be a reduction in the number of buses using those at Neil Road (Traction Company), South Canal Road (Hock Lee Amalgamated), Chulia Street (Traction Company) and Queen Street (Green Bus). On the other hand, Shenton Way would certainly become overcrowded, and an alternative sight should be sought. Swiftly to become accomplished, a large space was located 'just across the road', and Prince Edward Road Became a very busy city terminal, almost up to the standards of being a bus station, but lacked facilities for waiting passengers.

Bearing in mind that the Report was adopted during December 1970, the question as to when the merger should take place became a very serious matter to be considered, with several outside departments being involved with projects which would have a bearing on the functioning of bus services, and it was felt to be unwise to introduce what would be a complete recasting of existing bus services whilst there was evidence of the possibility of further changes being called for no sooner had passengers become used to their new routings. Additionally, the 'new' bus companies would need to be given a reasonable time span within which to prepare for the changeover, for they would be unable to commence the complex and time consuming task of preparing their new schedules until the plan had been made public. Whilst the end of 1970 was first chosen, upon a further consideration of the outside factors, mid-April 1971 was chosen.

Traffic management as a whole was the prime reason for the short delay; (a) in order to provide adequate road space to accommodate the proposed bus flow, investigations were being made with a view to reversing the traffic flow along Cecil Street in order that it might be used as a bus route, thereby taking some pressure off Robinson Road, but which would involve considerable roadworks;

LEFT: Untouched by the machinations in the Singapore bus industry, the express companies, Singapore–Johore Express, K.L.–Singapore Express and the Sing Lian Express to Malacca worked on, consolidating their own businesses. Here a Malacca registered Dennis Teal of Sing Lian Express negotiates Singapore traffic as it threads its way to the Bukit Timah Road and the border between Singapore and Johore State on the Johore side of the Causeway. This vehicle has no toilet facility.

(b) there was a proposal to establish a mini-bus-station in Fullerton Square, but the design of the loading platforms and shelters could not be speedily completed: this would not be a terminal, but an enlarged stopping place for through services travelling West to East along Collyer Quay; (c) the work involved with the reconstruction of Canal Road between Pulau Saigon Road and New Bridge Road would not be completed, and this fact when viewed in conjunction with the proposed reversal of traffic flow in Upper Hokkien and Upper Pickering Streets would need careful consideration when determining the pattern of routes through the particular area; and (d) most sensible of all considerations of the date of implementation, advanced the point of April being the main period of school vacations, during which there would be a considerable easing off of pressures on the bus companies. An ideal time to introduce the sweeping changes, with an opportunity to concentrate on dealing with initial teething troubles.

Even so, four months would not be over-long, for not only would preparations for the merger need to be put in hand, but the existing operations would need to continue unhindered until vesting-day. The public would need to be given the widest information possible, and to this end Guide Books were produced in both the English and Chinese languages, both official and 'private' versions. Thousands of metal plates needed to be prepared in order to carry the new service numbers, and destination plates to carry on the fronts and sides of buses. The Traction Company would need to surrender their destination blinds in exchange for these plates although, oddly enough, those buses of Tay Koh Yat which did carry rollerblinds managed to have new ones supplied. Before moving on to the precise constituents which would emerge during April, the report took some time to look to the distant future. If the suggestions contained within the report could be adopted in full, then there should be an adequate bus service for the immediate years, but the bus might not be able to cope with the demands which would arise in the decades yet to come. Therefore, it would appear that the only alternative means of providing an adequate public transport system would be to proceed with the construction of an underground or overhead fixed rail mass rapid transit system (and such proposals were already under consideration elsewhere within the Government)

The end of the Chinese Bus Companies was nigh: in their place would be established the Western, Northern, and Eastern Groups - Western would be the smallest, embracing Keppel, Hock Lee Amalgamated and Kampong Bahru as Associated Bus Services (PTE) Limited, Northern would be the largest, combing Easy, Tay Koh Yat and Green Bus as United Bus Company (PTE) Limited, whilst the Eastern Group would take in the most mixed fleets, combining Paya Lebar, Ponggol, Changi and Katong-Bedok as Associated Bus Services (PTE) Limited. Fleet colours were light blue for Amalgamated, Yellow for United and red for Associated, which coincidence would prove to make life a little easier for users of the former Changi and Katong-Bedok services. The Traction Company would continue to use its own livery.

Meanwhile, in Parliament, steps were being taken to repeal the Singapore Traction Ordinance, 1935. The outsider might consider that this was not before time, as so many of the provisions had been set aside in normal operational processes. Perhaps this was a move to keep the Statute Books in a tidy state, or else a means of removing the rights of the City Council to purchase the company. Elsewhere the Registrar of Vehicles had taken note of the increasing use of school buses, and taxis specific for the carriage of school children, and had introduced two new registration marks for these purposes, viz., SCH for taxis and SCB for school buses.

There can be no doubt that the Traction Company in particular was steeling itself to meet the forthcoming chances. Earlier in the year the appointment was made of a consultant, drawn from the International Executive Service Corps, being Mr. R. J. O'Connor, who was able to bring with him some forty years of experience within the transport industry, twenty four years of which were spent with a bus company owned by the Union Pacific Railroad and whose routes ran parallel to the railway. By 1955 he had risen to the posts of Vice President and General Manager, until such time as the company was purchased by the internationally famous Greyhound Corporation, rising within that organisation to become President of Central Greyhound. His initial appointment was for three months, which suggests that he would be on hand to witness the immediate effects of the merger. In the event Mr O'Connor remained with the company for only four months, and had left before publication of the Wilson report.

On the vehicle side, the total fleet strength as at 30th September 1970 stood at 553 buses, which somewhat contradicts the figure carried in the report which had reported a strength of 464, albeit as on 31st December. The difference seems to tally with the continued withdrawal of the Albion stock, and it is understood that none remained in service at the time of the merger. Instead, once the demand for school buses had been met, an export market was discovered for the later models which retained a modern appearance and, having been well maintained, were forecast to have more years of service remaining. A number were shipped to Sarawak, and as the Sarawak Transport Company used a similar livery and logo, little save a tidying up needed to be done to them.

In another direction, the company pre-empted the Wilson Report by completely rebuilding two of the Guys, 170 and 172, to what was termed the 'transit layout'. Full fronted bodywork was fitted, with the radiator grille being skilfully blended into the design, the principal feature being the provision of a rear entrance and front exit. The American derived thinking was given further emphasis by the provision of a line of small standee windows located above the main window frames. Any further conversions to this style were halted by the prospect of a merger.

RIGHT: Despite the attempt by STC to modernise two Guy Arabs, STC 170 and STC 172, they remained unsuitable for ome man operation and no further conversions were undertaken by either the Traction Company or their subsequent owners who introduced numerous examples of Mercedes Benz LP1113 s with front entrances by the driver. One of the modernised pair stands beside STC 178, a largely original Guy Arab Mk IV, inside Mackenzie Road depot.

Government was concerned at the increase in air pollution being generated by traffic and, rightly or wrongly, regarded buses as being major contributors. As a counter measure, legislation was introduced which required the replacement of bus engines after five years of use. The Traction Company were not slow to comply, and a programme was put into hand whereby no less than 135 buses had been, or were being, re-engined by the end of 1970. (As a matter of absolute fact, it is not clear as to whether brand new engines needed to be obtained, or whether existing engines could be removed, then be most thoroughly overhauled. What is certain is that the requirement was to lead to somewhat bizarre problems for the company in later years.)

The Government was also involved with a serious undercurrent of political disturbances, and between 1968 and 1974 there was a number of arson and bomb outrages which were seen as being the responsibility of communist or pro-communist trouble makers. The STC did not escape a share of these incidents, despite no longer being a British owned business, and during 1970 was to suffer one bus burned at Lim Ah Poon Road (14th June), two buses burned at New Bridge Road terminus and one bus burned at Lorong 1 Toa Payoh terminus (1st August)

Following the upsurges in population connected with Queenstown, Jurong and Toa Payoh, such expansions as remained with the Chinese companies were somewhat limited in scope: Green Bus had a service A from Queen Street to the campus of Nanyang University, operational between 7am and 9am, 12 noon and 1.30pm and 5pm and 6pm: Changi no longer ran their service 2, but had introduced a long needed direct link between Kaki Bukit Malay Settlement and North Bridge Road as service 6, while service 7 was a short working of the main line, starting at 8° milestone, Changi Road to North Bridge Road: Paya Lebar had got around to sort out the designation of their trunk route from Geylang Road, that to RAF Seletar, leaving Yio Chu Kang took 1B. They had also added to their presence around Tao Payoh loop with the introduction of service 5 from RAF Seletar, leaving Yio Chu Kang Road to make a very extensive double run through Serengoon Garden Estate and Tao Payoh before coming back in order to proceed to Lorong 5 near the Happy World. Katong-Bedok had dropped the use of service 1 as a short working, leaving the 2 to be their trunk service, which was a reversal of the original pattern during which the 2 was an occasional extension from the 1. With the particular needs of the school children in mind, service 4 had been introduced as a circular between Kallang Airport Estate and Tanjong Katong, working between 6.30am and 8.15am, 11.30am and 2pm, and finally between 5.30pm and 7.30pm, from which can be drawn the extent of school hours. Finally, Easy Bus had managed a short extension to pass across Pasir Panjang Road in order to reach Labrador Villa Road and the un-named lane which led to the British Petroleum Refinery, on the way crossing over a short section of railway track left in the roadway since abandonment half-a-century previously.

The script had been prepared, and the players were being rehearsed. The properties had been allocated, and the lines were being learned. No doubt with considerable apprehension, all awaited the raising of the curtain on would prove the most momentous reorganisation of passenger transport perhaps anywhere in the world, and the date for the opening performance, Sunday 11th April 1971.

The Chinese Bus Companies
Statistics of Amalgamation 1967-1972

	1967	1968	1970	1971	1972
Eastern Group of Companies					
Paya Lebar Bus Service	71	72	101	128	—
Changi Bus Company	98	98	119	187	—
Katong-Bedok Bus Service	47	49	56	76	—
Ponggol Bus Service	15	16	19	19	—
Associated Bus Services (Pte) Ltd				69	*924
Sub Total	231	235	295	479	924
Northern Group of Companies					
Tay Koh Yat Bus Company	137	137	182	227	
Green Bus Company	107	107	125	157	
Easy Bus Company	11	11	18	18	
United Bus Company (Pte) Ltd				46	*711
Sub total	255	255	325	448	711
Western Group of Companies					
Hock Lee Amalgamated B.Co	127	127	158	183	
Keppel Bus Company	42	42	48	57	
Kampong Bahru Bus Service	14	14	15	23	
Amalgamated Bus Company Limited				33	*377
Sub Total	183	183	221	296	377
Singapore Traction Company					
	500	500	577	510	See note *
Grand Total	1169	1173	1418	1733	2012

Note*: The vehicles of the Singapore Traction Company were distributed amongst the three amalgamated companies after the STC was placed into receivership later in 1971. They were split as follows:
To Associated Bus Services   218   (SH 8919-9136)
To United Bus Company   155   (SH 9137-9291)
To Amalgamated Bus Company   34   (SH 8885-8918)
In addition, 29 more STC Guy Arab buses were reregistered SH 9292-9,9305-25 after the initial allocation and were allocated to Associated Bus Services. These are not incorporated in the above figures, which are taken from a published report.

Epilogue
The demise of the Traction Company

The story of the 1971 amalgamations and reorganisations belongs in Volume II of this work, but the present volume has told the almost complete history of the Singapore Traction Company, which together with its direct predecessor, Singapore Electric Tramways, served the city from 1905 until 1971, and it is felt best to bring down the curtain on the STC here and now. The Company will figure as a 'minor character' in Volume II, but it is indeed the 'tragic hero' of this first volume. Within months of the April 1971 amalgamations of the Chinese Bus Companies and the restructuring of services, the STC was swallowed up by the newly created three headed dragon consisting of the Amalgamated, Associated, and United bus companies. The very titles suggest a close knit group plotting the downfall of the 'old enemy', but that was not so. Nor was it the STC cast in the role of King Lear, dragged down by greedy offspring.

The Singapore Traction Company collapsed into insolvency and passed into receivership because the reorganisation of services left it with no important role to play. The three other companies were given a sector of the island and city to serve, to the north, east and west, and the STC was left in its traditional central sector, but without the protection of the now repealed Ordinance of 1935. Much of the STC's revenue had been derived from passengers boarding at the city (and STC) boundary from outer-suburban services which were not allowed to penetrate far over the STC routes. Thus the first

pearance of the STC, and the failure of the three regional companies to do what was asked of them.

The long history of the SET/STC is beset by weakness of management. Only during the period between 1922-1935, when the Singapore undertaking was under the control of the dynamic and financially very succcesful Shanghai Electric Construction Company, was there a firm and inspired hand guiding company affairs. Otherwise the undertaking lurched from one crisis to another: the tramways suffered from collapsing track and unserviceable cars, the trolleybuses from obsolescence, the whole undertaking from sequestration in 1942, the post-war company from shortages, staff unrest, prolonged strikes, civil disturbances, pirate taxis and increasing urban traffic congestion. There were some good things: the bus engineering staff built up an efficient and standardised bus fleet, and some of the principles established by the STC engineers live on today in the modern fleet of buses serving Singapore. The weakness of the STC was of management of the commercial side of the business.

Disposal

Of course, when the end came in the autumn of 1971, the STC did not simply fade away. The assets passed to an Official Receiver, and the large fleet of buses was disposed of to the three large bus companies, a different quantity to each, in accordance with territory and route allocation. As a general rule, STC buses were allocated on a semi-permanent basis to the same route each day, and remainned so allocated until a visit to the repair shops would take a bus off the road for a period, or a route allocation would be changed in accordance with a change in passenger traffic. This system persists too in the present day, and at the time it was easy for a route and all its buses to be passed over to a new operating company, although the route might well be subsequently changed. Vehicles that were under repair or awaiting repair were also transferred to the new owners, and it is interesting to note that some surviving papers of the period, listing the buses for disposal, are marked "engine seized", "no gearbox" etc. alongside the buses that were transferred as non-runners. Of course, the Receiver sold off the buses at a notional price (book value), and the oldest Guy Arabs, which were probably valued at scrap price rather than as working vehicles (in other words, in the language of accountants, they were "written off") were excluded from sale in the first instance, although they were transferred a little later on to the Associated Bus Service.

ABOVE: Halcyon days. STC 115, the last of the Dennis Falcons, stands at the town terminus of Route 9. note the lack of other road traffic, also the timekeeper's kiosk and 'Fare Stage 9' sign to the right. This picture is the epitome of STC operations during the nineteen fifties.

and maybe the most important reason for its downfall was the loss of monopoly rights, even though they had been eroded here and there by 1971.

A second cause was the company's aquiescence in the new arrangements. With a fleet of buses numbering almost 500 (and as must follow, a substantial labour force) it should have fought hard to obtain a proper slice of the routes in the reorganised scheme. But if we cast the STC as a 'tragic hero' (that is to say, a personality whose downfall is caused by faults inside himself, and not primarily because of the actions of others), it was a fault of management not to have obtained a good network of routes. There were, perhaps, those who felt that the STC with its long tradition of service should have been chosen as the nucleus of a new island wide transport company, which would subsume all the Chinese Bus Companies, but this would never have worked, for reasons that will be told elsewhere. The creation of such an entity had to wait for the disap-

price rather than as working vehicles (in other words, in the language of accountants, they were "written off") were excluded from sale in the first instance, although they were transferred a little later on to the Associated Bus Service.

The Guy Arabs in particular, but also many other buses from the STC fleet, did not last long in the service of their new owners. The Guy Arabs fell victim to their age (their average age was some fifteen years) and their inability for use as one man operated vehicles. Others were unfamiliar to the drivers and engineers of the three companies, and they preferred either familiar models or the brand new Mercedes-Benz and Albions that were then flooding in from the locally established assembly plants. Very many STC buses found themselves out of service and parked neglected in the corner of the open compounds then in use as depots, often missing essential parts, and especially the registration plates, which were transferred to new vehicles. Only some of the Nissans, many of which were almost new, served a full term with the regional companies and were later transferred to the fleet of the Singapore Bus Service.

When the STC foundered and its buses were transferred to new owners, the Registrar of Vehicles was faced with a dilemma: the STC registration numbers belonged to a now defunct body. Consequently, all the buses transferred were allocated new numbers in the standard SH seriers used for buses and taxis. The numbers SH 8885-9325, with a few gaps, were issued in the early part of 1972 to all the ex STC vehicles then still extant. For the first few months with their new owners, the STC buses continued to carry their old numbers, and as they also carried STC colours, many passengers probably did not realise that the Traction Company was no longer in business. As an indication of ownership, the three regional companies applied a thin coloured band to the erstwhile STC livery (red for Associated, blue for Amalgamated and yellow for United).

The two large premises owned by the STC did not pass to the new companies, which already had various sites (mainly open) for parking buses. The large open site at Macpherson Road lay weed grown for a while, but was eventually sold off for housing purposes. The original tramway premises in Mackenzie Road were at first used to lock up the redundant buses, but were later demolished and the site redeveloped.The buildings had, of course, been modified since the abandonment of tramcar operation. The brick built tram shed backed on to Bukit Timah Road, and so when trolleybuses were introduced, a series of openings in what had been the back

wall were cut in the brickwork to allow the trolleybuses and later buses to run through. Both the trams and subsequent rubber tyred vehicles up to 1955 were quite narrow single deckers, and could fit the rows designed to accommodate the metre gauge tramcars of 1905, but it is doubtful if the former tram shed was suitable for the longer and wider (and later double deck) vehicles of the seventies.

This epilogue does not aim to give the fullest details of the final days of the STC, which properly belongs in the opening chapter of the next volume, but to acquaint the reader of the sudden death of a company whose history has been the main theme of this book. A verdict would state 'suicide' and not 'murder', for the Traction company chose liquidation when it found its revenue seriously reduced by the reorganisation of services of April 1971. In a way, some of the spirit of the STC lingers on in the present SBS, although this is no direct descendant, but any former STC employee returning to central Singapore today would recognise certain features from the past. Such would be the dignified livery, the well-established company emblem applied to vehicles and other fixed items, controlled advertising on vehicles, the vehicle standardisation and allocation systems, and a general sense of order. This latter never quite came to rule the registration and fleet numbering systems, which in both the case of the STC and the SBS, have just been allowed to grow "like Topsy". Although both authors would have appreciated a more logical numbering system, it must be said that the idiosincracies of the two schemes have led to many hours of challenging study.

As has already been stated, the story of road transport in the city and state of Singapore will be continued in a second volume, which will show how in a period of thirty years Singapore was given one of the finest public transport systems in the world, and one of the few that has seriously taken on the problem of controlling the private car in an urban centre.

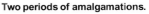

Two periods of amalgamations.

 ABOVE: as a result of the demise of the STC, its bus fleet was disposed of between the three recently formed 'regional' operators. Seen here after its transfer to Associated Bus Service, the former STC 617 crosses Anderson Bridge having been re-registered SH 9048 by ABS. It is being followed across the bridge by a Ford R226, SH 615, of the United Bus Company, a bus that was absorbed in 1973 into Singapore Bus Service where it became SBS 6191T. The apparently hign route number, 3030A, carried by the Nissan, is in fact two numbers, separated by an unhelpfully thin stroke—ie 30/30A.

BELOW: The second amalgamation occurred in 1973—but that is another story, to be told in Volume Two. Suffice it to say that this Nissan, seen here as SBS 4115C, had made three transitions, having been new in 1967 to the Singapore Traction Company as STC 648. In 1971, it was absorbed into the Amalgamated Bus Company as SH 9048 (later SH 9048L), finally passing to the Singapore Bus Service in November 1973.

Dispersal of STC Bus Fleet, 1971

407 buses were earmarked for disposal to the three regional companies. These were divided into three groups, nominated A,B, and C, according to age and type. Group A consisted of the Nissans, some of which were almost brand new, Group B consisted of the Isuzus, and Group C consisted of the newest of the Guy Arabs.

The vehicles were dispersed amongst the three companies as shown on the listing below by their initials:

ABC = Amalgamated Bus Company
ABS = Associated Bus Service
UBC = United Bus Company

A few vehicles, consisting of one Isuzu and 29 Guy Arabs were sold at a later date to Associated Bus Services, these including the oldest of the Guy Arabs, and these are marked # in the listing below.

Some vehicles in the groups shown were not passed on, and these are shown as "scrapped". It is probable that some of the reregistered vehicles saw little if any service with their new owners, as at the time of sale they were off the road for repair, and such buses were more likely to have been cannibalised for spare parts. The fact that new registrations were issued does not mean that the vehicles were licensed for use on the public roads: many of the registration plates were quickly surrendered and applied to new buses, of which a large number was put on the road during 1971-2.

STC	SH	Co.	STC	SH	Co.	STC	SH	Co.	STC	SH	Co.
STC 1	SH 8919	ABS	STC82	SH 8970	ABS	STC180	SH 9298	ABS#	STC453	SH 9025	ABS
STC 2	SH 8920	ABS	STC83	SH 8971	ABS	STC181	SH 9293	ABS#	STC454	SH 9026	ABS
STC 3	SH 9137	UBC	STC84	SH 8972	ABS	STC182	SH 9314	ABS#	STC455	SH 9027	ABS
STC 4	SH 9138	UBC	STC85	SH 8973	ABS	STC183	scrapped		STC456	SH 9028	ABS
STC 5	SH 9139	UBC	STC86	SH 8974	ABS	STC184	SH 9299	ABS#	STC457	SH 9029	ABS
STC 6	SH 8921	ABS	STC87	SH 8975	ABS	STC185	scrapped		STC458	SH 9030	ABS
STC 7	SH 8922	ABS	STC88	SH 9166	UBC	STC186	SH 9315	ABS#	STC459	SH 9215	UBC
STC 8	SH 8923	ABS	STC89	SH 9167	UBC	STC187	SH 9316	ABS#	STC460	SH 9216	UBC
STC 9	SH 8924	ABS	STC90	SH 9168	UBC	STC188	SH 9317	ABS#	STC461	SH 9031	ABS
STC10	premature withdrawal		STC91	SH 8976	ABS	STC189	SH 9294	ABS#	STC462	SH 9032	ABS
STC11	SH 8925	ABS	STC92	SH 8977	ABS	STC190	SH 9295	ABS#	STC463	SH 9033	ABS
STC12	SH 8926	ABS	STC93	SH 8978	ABS	STC191	SH 9323	ABS#	STC464	SH 9034	ABS
STC13	SH 8927	ABS	STC94	SH 9169	UBC	STC192	SH 9324	ABS#	STC465	SH 9035	ABS
STC14	SH 8928	ABS	STC95	SH 9291	UBC#	STC193	SH 9325	ABS#	STC466	SH 9036	ABS
STC15	SH 8929	ABS	STC96	SH 9170	UBC	STC194	SH 9318	ABS#	STC467	SH 9037	ABS
STC16	SH 8930	ABS	STC97	SH 9171	UBC	STC195	SH 9189	UBC	STC468	SH 9038	ABS
STC17	SH 8931	ABS	STC98	SH 9172	UBC	STC196	SH 9190	UBC	STC469	SH 9217	UBC
STC18	SH 8932	ABS	STC99	SH 9173	UBC	STC197	SH 9191	UBC	STC470	SH 9218	UBC
STC19	SH 8933	ABS	STC100	SH 8979	ABS	STC198	SH 9192	UBC	STC471	SH 9219	UBC
STC20	SH 8934	ABS	STC101	SH 8980	ABS	STC199	SH 9193	UBC	STC472	SH 9220	UBC
STC21	SH 8935	ABS	STC102	SH 8885	ABC	STC200	SH 9194	UBC	STC473	SH 9221	UBC
STC22	SH 9140	UBC	STC103	SH 9174	UBC	STC201	SH 8896	ABC	STC474	SH 9222	UBC
STC23	SH 9141	UBC	STC104	SH 9175	UBC	STC202	SH 9195	UBC	STC475	SH 9039	ABS
STC24	SH 9142	UBC	STC105	SH 9176	UBC	STC203	SH 9196	UBC	STC476	SH 9040	ABS
STC25	SH 9143	UBC	STC106	SH 9177	UBC	STC204	SH 9197	UBC	STC477	SH 9041	ABS
STC26	SH 9144	UBC	STC107	SH 9178	UBC	STC205	SH 9198	UBC	STC478	SH 9042	ABS
STC27	SH 9145	UBC	STC108	SH 8981	ABS	STC206	SH 9199	UBC	STC479	SH 9043	ABS
STC28	SH 9146	UBC	STC109	SH 8886	ABC	STC207	SH 8993	ABS	STC480	SH 9223	UBC
STC29	SH 9147	UBC	STC110	SH 9179	UBC	STC208	SH 8994	ABS	STC481	SH 9224	UBC
STC30	SH 9148	UBC	STC111	SH 9180	UBC	STC209	SH 8995	ABS	STC601	SH 9225	UBC
STC31	SH 9149	UBC	STC112	SH 8982	ABS	STC210	SH 8996	ABS	STC602	SH 9044	ABS
STC32	SH 9150	UBC	STC113	SH 8983	ABS	STC211	SH 8997	ABS	STC603	SH 9045	ABS
STC33	SH 9151	UBC	STC114	SH 8984	ABS	STC212	SH 8998	ABS	STC604	SH 9046	ABS
STC34	SH 9152	UBC	STC115	SH 8985	ABS	STC213	SH 8999	ABS	STC605	SH 9226	UBC
STC35	SH 9153	UBC	STC116	SH 8986	ABS	STC214	SH 9000	ABS	STC606	SH 9227	UBC
STC36	SH 9154	UBC	STC117	SH 8987	ABS	STC215	SH 9001	ABS	STC607	SH 9228	UBC
STC37	SH 9155	UBC	STC118	SH 8988	ABS	STC216	SH 9002	ABS	STC608	SH 9229	UBC
STC38	SH 9156	UBC	STC119	SH 8887	ABC	STC217	SH 9003	ABS	STC609	SH 9230	UBC
STC39	SH 9157	UBC	STC120	SH 8888	ABC	STC218	SH 9004	ABS	STC610	SH 9231	UBC
STC40	SH 9158	UBC	STC121	SH 8889	ABC	STC219	SH 9005	ABS	STC611	SH 9232	UBC
STC41	SH 9159	UBC	STC122	SH 8989	ABS	STC220	SH 9006	ABS	STC612	SH 9233	UBC
STC42	SH 8936	ABS	STC123	SH 9181	UBC	STC221	SH 9007	ABS	STC613	SH 9234	UBC
STC43	SH 8937	ABS	STC124	SH 9182	UBC	STC414	SH 9200	UBC	STC614	SH 9235	UBC
STC44	SH 8938	ABS	STC125	SH 9183	UBC	STC415	SH 9201	UBC	STC615	SH 9236	UBC
STC45	SH 8939	ABS	STC126	SH 9184	UBC	STC416	SH 9202	UBC	STC616	SH 9047	ABS
STC46	SH 8940	ABS	STC127	SH 9185	UBC	STC417	SH 9203	UBC	STC617	SH 9048	ABS
STC47	SH 8941	ABS	STC128	SH 9186	UBC	STC418	SH 8897	ABC	STC618	SH 9237	UBC
STC48	SH 8942	ABS	STC129	SH 8890	ABC	STC419	SH 8898	ABC	STC619	SH 9238	UBC
STC49	SH 8943	ABS	STC130	SH 8891	ABC	STC420	SH 8899	ABC	STC620	SH 9239	UBC
STC50	SH 8944	ABS	STC131	SH 8892	ABC	STC421	SH 8900	ABC	STC621	SH 9240	UBC
STC51	SH 8945	ABS	STC132	SH 8893	ABC	STC422	SH 8901	ABC	STC622	SH 9241	UBC
STC52	SH 8946	ABS	STC133	SH 8894	ABC	STC423	SH 8902	ABC	STC623	SH 9242	UBC
STC53	SH 8947	ABS	STC134	SH 9187	UBC	STC424	SH 8903	ABC	STC624	SH 9243	UBC
STC54	SH 8948	ABS	STC135	SH 8990	ABS	STC425	SH 9204	UBC	STC625	SH 9244	UBC
STC55	SH 9160	UBC	STC136	SH 8991	UBC	STC426	SH 9205	UBC	STC626	SH 9245	UBC
STC56	SH 8949	ABS	STC137	SH 9188	UBC	STC427	SH 9008	ABS	STC627	SH 9246	UBC
STC57	SH 8950	ABS	STC138	SH 8991	ABS	STC428	SH 9009	ABS	STC628	SH 9247	UBC
STC58	SH 8951	ABS	STC139	SH 8992	ABS	STC429	SH 9010	ABS	STC629	SH 9248	UBC
STC59	SH 8952	ABS	STC157	scrapped		STC430	SH 9011	ABS	STC630	SH 9049	ABS
STC60	SH 8953	ABS	STC158	SH 9305	ABS#	STC431	SH 9206	UBC	STC631	SH 9050	ABS
STC61	SH 8954	ABS	STC159	SH 9306	ABS#	STC432	SH 9207	UBC	STC632	SH 9051	ABS
STC62	SH 8955	ABS	STC160	scrapped		STC433	SH 9208	UBC	STC633	SH 9052	ABS
STC63	SH 9161	UBC	STC161	SH 9307	ABS#	STC434	SH 9209	UBC	STC634	SH 9053	ABS
STC64	SH 9162	UBC	STC162	SH 9319	ABS#	STC435	SH 9210	UBC	STC635	SH 9054	ABS
STC65	SH 9163	UBC	STC163	scrapped		STC436	SH 9211	UBC	STC636	SH 9055	ABS
STC66	SH 9164	UBC	STC164	SH 9296	ABS#	STC437	SH 9012	ABS	STC637	SH 9056	ABS
STC67	SH 9165	UBC	STC165	scrapped		STC438	SH 9013	ABS	STC638	SH 9057	ABS
STC68	SH 8956	ABS	STC166	SH 9308	ABS#	STC439	SH 9014	ABS	STC639	SH 9058	ABS
STC69	SH 8957	ABS	STC167	scrapped		STC440	SH 9015	ABS	STC640	SH 9059	ABS
STC70	SH 8958	ABS	STC168	SH 9320	ABS#	STC441	SH 9016	ABS	STC641	SH 9249	UBC
STC71	SH 8959	ABS	STC169	SH 9309	ABS#	STC442	SH 9017	ABS	STC642	SH 9250	UBC
STC72	SH 8960	ABS	STC170	SH 9292	ABS#	STC443	SH 9212	UBC	STC643	SH 9251	UBC
STC73	SH 8961	ABS	STC171	scrapped		STC444	SH 9213	UBC	STC644	SH 8904	ABC
STC74	SH 8962	ABS	STC172	SH 9310	ABS#	STC445	SH 9214	UBC	STC645	SH 8905	ABC
STC75	SH 8963	ABS	STC173	SH 9297	ABS#	STC446	SH 9018	ABS	STC646	SH 8906	ABC
STC76	SH 8964	ABS	STC174	SH 9311	ABS#	STC447	SH 9019	ABS	STC647	SH 8907	ABC
STC77	SH 8965	ABS	STC175	scrapped		STC448	SH 9020	ABS	STC648	SH 8908	ABC
STC78	SH 8966	ABS	STC176	SH 9312	ABS#	STC449	SH 9021	ABS	STC649	SH 9252	UBC
STC79	SH 8967	ABS	STC177	SH 9321	ABS#	STC450	SH 9022	ABS	STC650	SH 8909	ABS
STC80	SH 8968	ABS	STC178	SH 9313	ABS#	STC451	SH 9023	ABS	STC651	SH 9060	ABS
STC81	SH 8969	ABS	STC179	SH 9322	ABS#	STC452	SH 9024	ABS	STC652	SH 9061	ABS

STC	SH		STC	SH		STC	SH		STC	SH	
STC653	SH 9062	ABS	STC684	SH 9086	ABS	STC715	SH 9265	UBC	STC746	SH 9122	ABS
STC654	SH 9063	ABS	STC685	SH 9087	ABS	STC716	SH 9266	UBC	STC747	SH 9281	UBC
STC655	SH 9064	ABS	STC686	SH 9088	ABS	STC717	SH 9267	UBC	STC748	SH 9282	UBC
STC656	SH 9065	ABS	STC687	SH 9089	ABS	STC718	SH 9268	UBC	STC749	SH 9123	ABS
STC657	SH 9066	ABS	STC688	SH 9090	ABS	STC719	SH 9107	ABS	STC750	SH 8915	ABC
STC658	SH 9067	ABS	STC689	SH 9257	UBC	STC720	SH 9108	ABS	STC751	SH 8916	ABC
STC659	SH 9068	ABS	STC690	SH 9258	UBC	STC721	SH 9269	UBC	STC752	SH 8917	ABC
STC660	SH 9069	ABS	STC691	SH 9259	UBC	STC722	SH 9270	UBC	STC753	SH 8918	ABC
STC661	SH 9070	ABS	STC692	SH 9260	UBC	STC723	SH 9271	UBC	STC754	SH 9283	UBC
STC662	SH 8910	ABC	STC693	SH 9091	ABS	STC724	SH 9272	UBC	STC755	SH 9124	ABS
STC663	SH 8911	ABC	STC694	SH 9092	ABS	STC725	SH 9273	UBC	STC756	SH 9125	ABS
STC664	SH 9071	ABS	STC695	SH 9093	ABS	STC726	SH 9274	UBC	STC757	SH 9126	ABS
STC665	SH 9072	ABS	STC696	SH 9094	ABS	STC727	SH 9109	ABS	STC758	SH 9284	UBC
STC666	SH 9073	ABS	STC697	SH 9095	ABS	STC728	SH 9110	ABS	STC759	SH 9285	UBC
STC667	SH 9074	ABS	STC698	SH 9096	ABS	STC729	SH 9111	ABS	STC760	SH 9127	ABS
STC668	SH 9075	ABS	STC699	SH 9097	ABS	STC730	SH 9275	UBC	STC761	SH 9128	ABS
STC669	SH 9076	ABS	STC700	SH 8913	ABC	STC731	SH 9276	UBC	STC762	SH 9129	ABS
STC670	SH 9077	ABS	STC701	SH 8914	ABC	STC732	SH 9112	ABS	STC763	SH 9130	ABS
STC671	SH 9078	ABS	STC702	SH 9098	ABS	STC733	SH 9113	ABS	STC764	SH 9131	ABS
STC672	SH 9079	ABS	STC703	SH 9099	ABS	STC734	SH 9114	ABS	STC765	SH 9132	ABS
STC673	SH 9080	ABS	STC704	SH 9100	ABS	STC735	SH 9115	ABS	STC766	SH 9133	ABS
STC674	SH 9081	ABS	STC705	SH 9101	ABS	STC736	SH 9116	ABS	STC767	SH 9134	ABS
STC675	SH 9082	ABS	STC706	SH 9102	ABS	STC737	SH 9117	ABS	STC768	SH 9135	ABS
STC676	SH 9083	ABS	STC707	SH 9261	UBC	STC738	SH 9118	ABS	STC769	SH 9136	ABS
STC677	SH 9084	ABS	STC708	SH 9103	ABS	STC739	SH 9119	ABS	STC770	SH 9286	UBC
STC678	SH 9085	ABS	STC709	SH 9104	ABS	STC740	SH 9120	ABS	STC771	SH 9287	UBC
STC679	SH 8912	ABC	STC710	SH 9105	ABS	STC741	SH 9121	ABS	STC772	SH 9288	UBC
STC680	SH 9253	UBC	STC711	SH 9106	ABS	STC742	SH 9277	UBC	STC773	SH 9289	UBC
STC681	SH 9254	UBC	STC712	SH 9262	UBC	STC743	SH 9278	UBC	STC774	SH 9290	UBC
STC682	SH 9255	UBC	STC713	SH 9263	UBC	STC744	SH 9279	UBC			
STC683	SH 9256	UBC	STC714	SH 9264	UBC	STC745	SH 9280	UBC			

Singapore Municipal Council—Atkinson-Walker light locomotives

To accompany an article about the locomotive manufacturer, in their July 14, 1928 edition, *The Locomotive* reported that Messrs. Atkinson-Walker Wagons Ltd. had supplied examples of their metre gauge light locomotives to the Singapore Municipal Council, stating: "The light locomotive illustrated by Fig. 4 is one of several recently shipped to Singapore. The engines fitted to these locomotives have two cylinders, 7in bore by 10in stroke....". The general arrangement was similar to that of Sentinels in having a vertical boiler and small high-speed steam engine driving via two single-roller chains with the two axles being connected by chains rather than rods.

The purpose of these engines is unclear but the SMC *possibly* provided locomotives for use inside the dock estate, on rails which were the successors to the original steam tram lines built to serve the Tanjong Pagar quaysides. Alternatively, they *may* have had something to do with the closure, in 1927, of the electric tramway which was connected to the railway system of the Tanjong Pagar Docks Co. As the rails extended outside the docks, it was possibly felt by the Docks Co. that the Municipal Council should provide motive power for use outside the authority of their dockyard railway system. The original freight line connecting the docks with Tank Road and the original Singapore Railway was not superseded by the rerouted FMSR line until May 1932.

The Authors would welcome additional information on this subject.

ABOVE LEFT: Reproduction (including original caption) of an illustration in a contemporary journal of light locomotive No 2 as acquired by Singapore Municipal Council *circa* 1928. Just where these locomotives ran is unclear—perhaps on the rump of the docks tramway system after the arrival of trolleybuses. (Atkinson-Walker went out of business shortly after the locomotive shown was built, and was reformed in 1933 as Atkinson Lorries (1933) Limited, builder of diesel engined trucks.
(The Locomotive, July 14, 1928—courtesy J.B.Horne

LEFT: Disconnected sections of metre gauge rail remained as late as 1956 and this piece of isolated street track remained in the street as a reminder of days gone by. The presence of a check rail rather than grooved rail indicates that this was not part of the street tramway system—at least not in its latter days.

Appendix A — The First Guide Book

Hitherto, the local press had been the ideal means of advertising the facilities on offer to the Company, although the size of such advertisement in order to cover the complete system must have been rather expensive. Conditions had improved as regards income and the re-establishment of routes, so that by August 1955 issue number 1 of the "*Trolleybus and Omnibus Guide*" was published. A pocket sized volume of fifty-six pages plus covers, and with a page size of four and a half inches by six and a quarter inches, full particulars concerning routes, fares, times and a map were provided, at a selling price of 20 cents. The cover colours of green and buttermilk came very close to matching the newly introduced vehicle livery, and the front carried a photograph of a newly delivered Albion in company with recently rebuilt trolleybus 45 standing in Mackenzie Road (whilst on the rear cover was a birds eye view of Macpherson Road garage, featuring perhaps one hundred buses in neat ranks, the most obvious of which were many Dennis Falcon models).

The quality of the paper used was not high, once past the card covers, the pages had the yellowish tinge so often associated with wartime emergency publications seen in the United Kingdom. Nonetheless, the contents were most comprehensive, starting with a short historical resume, and then General Information and Hints to Passengers, which really served to reproduce the Bye-Laws, but in readable fashion. There came an index of services next, and as the network was much the same as listed in previous sections of this appendix, it is not proposed to make a full account once again at this point. However when moving onto the individual service pages, we are able to draw a quite reasonable timetable of services in their latter days, as shown in the accompanying table.

A study of these timetables reveals the trolleybus as a mode of transport at its best, giving a frequent headway over some eighteen hours a day. There is no need to look for the reason why the Geylang to Tanjong Pagar line had become the premier route, and, with the combination of service 3 over most of the route, a total of some four vehicles every ten minutes, clearly there was always a trolleybus in sight. You have just missed one, well not to worry, for the next is only a couple of stops away. (As far as frequency is concerned, there is some doubt as to whether service 2 would have remained supreme had the full system been brought back into use, as will be seen a little later in these notes).

The definition of the term "Night Service" would seem to be the headways worked as from the conclusion of the evening peak hour - thus, there is no night service shown for service 4. The term might seem rather strange to English understanding, but it will be recalled that night falls every day of the year between a time range only of 6.00pm until 6.30pm, without any evening as known in the United Kingdom. The transition from afternoon to night is very short.

As pointed out in the main work, service 6 was least frequent of the trolleybus services, although it is a matter of further interest to see how he frequency was increased during Sunday night, usually the poorest time of the week in terms of revenue (but again, as seen by English eyes).

To look at those former trolleybus services, the pattern was much the same as shown above, with frequencies during the off peak period of 7 minutes on service 1, 4 minutes over service 8 as far as Tanjong Pagar but with alternate buses going the full route to Keppel Harbour, service 9 having on offer a five minute headway, and poor service 11, always the poorest of poor relations, unable to do better than a bus every 28 minutes. So ever it was! If service 2 were to discover a rival, it would be service 10, which showed a most remarkable off peak headway of a bus every 2 minutes, even on Sunday, reducing to 3 minutes for a Night Service. Such was the amount of traffic generated from along Jalan Besar that a "School Specials" timetable needed to be superimposed over the main public schedule, with such specials operating at seven minute intervals during school hours (which extended through most of the day), Monday to Saturday. If such an intense service tends to amaze, then wait, for there was even better!

The second of the trunk routes was that along Serangoon Road, but we find that service 4 could offer no more than daytime 8 minute headway. What happened during the years leading up to 1955 was that motor bus 18 had been developed rather than trolleybus 4, so that the former could now show a headway during the peak periods of a bus every 1 minute, with a 2 to 3 headway during daytime off peaks, staying at 3 minutes after the evening peak was over until 10pm, and then further reducing to 6 minutes until close of service with the last bus of the day leaving Tampines Road terminus at 1.01am. These times also applied to a Sunday. Close headways were also provided on the 18A service, which divided from the 18 in Paya Lebar village, that is to say, more or less at the trolleybus terminus, giving a peak hour frequency of 4 minutes, off peak of 10, and a night service of between 10 and

EXAMPLE OF LATTER DAY TROLLEYBUS TIMETABLE FROM GUIDE BOOKS

Service	From	Weekdays		Saturday		Sunday	
		First bus	Last bus	First bus	Last bus	First bus	Last bus
2	Geylang	6.00am	12.19am	6.00am	12.19am	6.00am	12.19am
	Tanjong Pagar	6.00am	12.23am	6.00am	12.23am	6.00am	12.23am
3	Outram Road	6.04am	12.33am	6.04am	12.33am	6.00am	12.33am
	Geylang	6.00am	12.14am	6.00am	12.14am	6.00am	12.14am
4	Paya Lebar	6.30am	6.46pm	6.30am	6.46pm	6.30am	6.46pm
	Finlayson Green	7.06am	6.10pm	7.06am	6.10pm	7.06am	6.10pm
6	Newton	6.03am	11.10pm	6.03am	11.16pm	6.03am	11.09pm
	Finlayson Green	6.25am	7.12pm	6.25am	7.18pm	———	———
	Outram Road	7.20am	11.35pm	7.26am	11.41pm	6.16am	11.34pm
2	Peak Service	3 minutes		3 minutes		3 minutes	
	Off Peak Service	3 minutes		3 minutes		3 minutes	
	Night Service	7 minutes		7 minutes		7 minutes	
3	Peak Service	8 minutes		8 minutes		8 minutes	
	Off Peak Service	8 minutes		8 minutes		8 minutes	
	Night Service	8 minutes		8 minutes		8 minutes	
4	Peak Service	8 minutes		8 minutes		8 minutes	
	Off Peak Service	8 minutes		8 minutes		8 minutes	
6	Peak Service	11 minutes		11 minutes		13 minutes	
	Off Peak Service	15 minutes		15 minutes		13 minutes	
	Night Service	14 minutes		14 minutes		13 minutes	

11 minutes. Small wonder that the trolleybus did not seem to be needed very much. (If we compare the relationship of the 2 and 3 services along Geylang Road, we find that the major rivals, namely the 15 and 16 motor buses, off peak headways Monday to Saturday stood at 6 minutes, reducing to 10 minutes on Sunday). All other motor bus schedules were much the same, with one exception being the 24, which could only boast a bus every hour for most of the time, the only difference being during the peak hours of Wednesday to Sunday, down to half hourly, the night service Wednesday to Saturday also half hourly, and the Sunday night service further reduced to 20 minutes. (One wonders why traffic was ultra light on Monday and Tuesday?) Thus, the 24 was left with the honour of having the least frequent regular service within the whole of Singapore.

The guide was also able to introduce the special racecourse service, to operate on Race Meetings Days only. Buses would operate from a terminus in Bras Basah Road to and from an outer terminal actually within the compound of the Race Course, via Selegie Road, Bukit Timah Road and Dunearn Road, observing stops as required as far as Newton trolleybus terminus, but then to be non-stop to the Race Course. As required, the first bus would leave Bras Basah Road at 11.30am and continue at frequent intervals until 7.00pm. (A list of race meetings was appended to the timetable)

The section dealing with fare charts was able to devote a page to each individual service (except 18 and 18A which were capable of being combined without confusion to the reader). The subject of fares is dealt with in a separate Appendix to the guide.

Being of limited size, no attempt was made to provide a comprehensive street index, but a listing of the more popular places sought by visitors and residents alike was essential: Churches, Cinemas, Markets, Hotels, Parks, etc., listed with the services which passed by. Therefore, all such points could easily be found within the STC network: the text has listed the few points served by all of the post war trolleybus network, but we could calculate the hub of the whole system as being located outside the Capitol Cinema, served by all STC services except 1 and 9 (the City Hall was listed as being served by all services except 9, but this was not strictly true, as North Bridge Road, along which the trolleybuses ran, was distant by a complete city block, quite a few minutes walk from the nearest stopping place, and out of sight).

At the time of publication, the exchange rate between the Singapore dollar and Sterling remained at the long established eight dollars and fifty-seven cents to the pound. Therefore, those who care to indulge in mental arithmetic will realise that an equivalent and approximate cost of sixpence, the booklet was a trifle expensive. The cover price must have been determined by the fact that no advertising material was included. Sales were quite good, for the citizen of Singapore is much more likely to keep such a booklet in his home than in his English counterpart. Future editions were anticipated for publication, but the question is to at what interval does not seem to have been considered, service cuts and fares increases being unknown.

So much for the Guide Book. Years were to pass before a further attempt was to be made with a view to publicising the services, and a different presentation selected. The folding map, given away without charge, with costs met by a wide range of products advertising, appeared with a publishing date of April 1962. When folded, the page area was five inches by seven and a half inches, rather large for convenient pocket carrying. Fully open, the page measured twenty inches by fifteen, the actual map being ten inches by seven. The whole network was contained thereon, and very fine and therefore clearly read print was used. Two colours were employed, with red indicating the Company's routes, and black 'other main roads'. It is interesting to note that none of the publicity used by the Company had ever made reference to the Chinese bus operators, and the map used in the Guide Book gave the impression that wide areas of the outer districts within the city boundary had no bus routes at all. It just so happened that the 'other main roads' in this case indicated the routes served by the Chinese operators, but without any direct reference to the competition. Also on the map appeared a host of large black dots, their purpose to indicate

the sites of new housing estate developments, and in a way shadows were being cast ahead.

Services were listed by numbers and roads served in the broad margin either side of the map and, by this time, the number of trolleybus routes operated was down to three, with the 6 to Newton having been converted to motor bus operation. By and large the route pattern was much the same as well described previously—added was a short service 7 branching from Serangoon Road to serve Kolam Ayer, the opening of the new international airport at Paya Lebar (miles away from Paya Lebar as served by trolleybus 4) had resulted in the introduction of service 12, to be a means of helping service 10 a new route had been introduced to Kim Keat Avenue, somewhat beyond Moulmein terminus, and given the number 14, service 17 had also received a branch, leading off Orchard Road along Stevens Road to a terminus at Whitley Road and called 17A, with the opening of the new international airport the site of the displaced airport became the basis of Calling Park housing estate, to be served by a wandering new service called 20B, working to a terminus at Rhea Cross, but involving a considerable amount of double running to and from the extremities of the erstwhile main runways (of which more in another section of this Appendix). The main work has made mention of various limited stop services introduced during the mid-1950s, but of the traditional routes only the 18 and 18A were shown as still having this facility. On the other hand, a brand new group had been introduced, in part to replace those which had been superimposed over stopping services serving Chatting, numbered 25, 26 and 27, their object, to quote the map, "designed to give city workers, etc., a faster non-stop run via Nicoll Highway (and) operate every morning and evening from Mondays to Fridays, and at morning and mid-day on Saturdays. No service at night, on Sundays or public holidays". The Race Course service was shown as working every day that there was a race meeting at Singapore or the Federation of Malaya: the reason for the latter was quite simple, once you know the Singapore law concerning the placing of bets. Such transactions could only be lawfully carried out within the premises of the Turf Club, and thus, although there might not be a meeting at the Singapore Course, if you wanted to play a wager on a horse running in Malaya, then you had to go to the Race Course to spend your money.

Five display advertisements were carried at the head and foot of the map, ranging from such mixed subjects such as a tyre retreading service to the Singapore Steam Laundry. Turn over the page, and two colour printing is once again found, this time in blue and black, which is just as well: the page is divided into sections, ten in all and of differing sizes, the largest of which is devoted to the Company, who present a diagram showing how their services radiate from Collyer Quay to places of importance, such as the Airport, the Railway Station, Sultan Mosque, Botanic Gardens, etc., etc. Collyer Quay is shown as half of the sun, rising from above the horizon, whilst the routes are shown as rays. What then is the point being made? Well, should red ink have been used on this side as well, then there would have been provided a very good likeness of the Japanese "Rising Sun", and memories are not that short. Some of the advertisements, such as that for a vitamin tablet which was claimed as "good for men of middle age and advancing years", placed by Yee Loong the Tailor, and by Ngo Hock Auto Spares, were bilingual in English and Chinese, whilst the automotive industry was represented by the local agents for Dagenite batteries, and by Far East Motors extolling the virtues of Lucas genuine spare parts. Of eye catching proportions was the display by Malayan Motors, calling attention to the most recent engineering marvel, the Morris Mini-Minor. Of company interest, the largest individual advertisement, again in Chinese and English, was placed by Messrs. Lee Kiat Seng, from their delightful address in Kallang Pudding Lane, telling that they were bus, coach and motor body builders, and featuring in an illustration Guy Arab STC 465. The passing traveller could be forgiven for thinking that the whole fleet comprised Guys, for once refolded for carrying, the cover of the map featured Guy STC 474 on service 19.

149

There was not quite so long to wait for the next publication, this being during 1964 and thus the last to bear the words "Incorporated in the United Kingdom" after the company title. Indeed there was a very English flavour to the particular work, and one can only assume that a member of the staff had been on holiday in London, seen the new style of map used by London Transport, designed for easy reference without complete unfolding, and decided to do the same. The result was very useful, and provided a mixture of the best features contained in the book of 1955 and the map of 1962. Gone were the advertisements, although as before the map was issued free of charge. The map occupied the whole of one side of the sheet, and was printed in several colours, viz., red for Traction Company services, black for 'other main roads', all on a green background, but with the two garages shown as red blocks, and with the sea and reservoirs shown in blue. A grid system was superimposed for reference. Places of interest were also indicated.

On the other side of the sheet a whole wealth of information was given, including that blue rising sun. The by-laws were reproduced in full, lists of services and routes followed, a complete fare charge for each service, and lists of first and last timing over each route. There was also a panel to act as the cover. When it is realised that the size of the sheet, when open, was twenty four by eighteen inches, it will be appreciated that the type used in the printing of so much detail was so small as to be almost beyond reading, especially the first and last times. Nonetheless, it was very neatly done.

With the demise of the trolleybuses, the title became the 'Bus Guide'. The manner in which the trolleybus routes were absorbed into the motor bus system is told within the main text.

A quick glance through the list of services shows that the peripheral housing developments were attracting a certain amount of expansion of Company services, although once again, rather in the form of branches from the traditional routes rather than completely new projections—the quite recent 14 gave birth to the 14A into St Michael's Estate, and the 17 was strengthened by the 17B to Jalan Bukit Merah at Queenstown, besides itself being extended to Sussex Estate. The limited stop 18 and 18A's worked down to Geylang Road into Nicoll Highway, and there was a new 18B service which provided a stopping service over the above, certainly as far as Geylang Road: Nicoll Highway was banned to stopping buses, except that on the limited stop 18 and 18A services, buses would stop if required at the People's Association Building for the short remaining operation of the day after 6.00pm. Service 20B became even more of a happy wanderer by having a school hours extension to Siglap, over the established 20 route - the fare tables indicated that the extension was not solely for the use of school children. The other new 'Service' was the tourist special, between the docks and Raffles Place.

BELOW: Cover of the First Guide Book to be issued by the Singapore Traction Company in August 1955

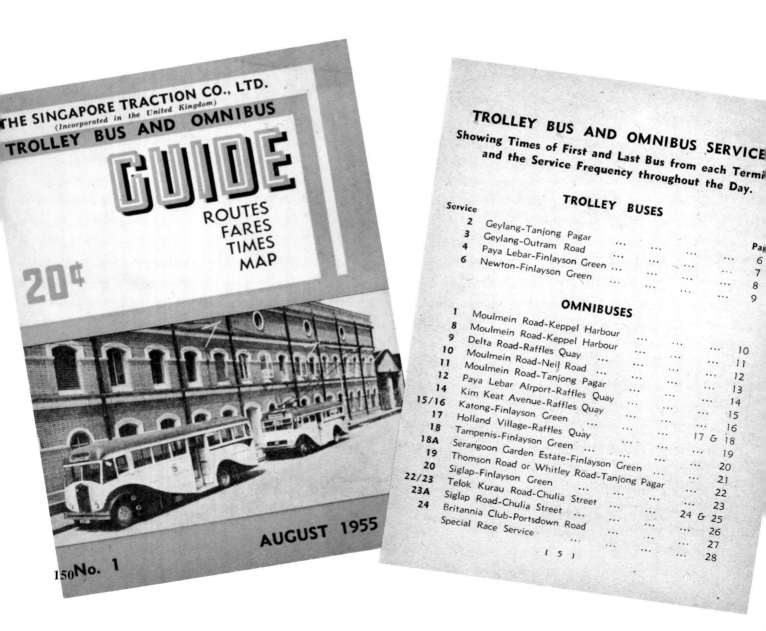

TROLLEY BUS AND OMNIBUS SERVICES
Showing Times of First and Last Bus from each Terminus and the Service Frequency throughout the Day.

TROLLEY BUSES

(5)

RACE COURSE SERVICE

1. On Race Meeting Days only.

2. Buses operate from Bras Basah Road to and from the Race Course via Selegie Road, Bukit Timah Road and Dunearn Road. (Non-stop from Newton to Race Course/Race Course to Newton).

3. The Service commences from Bras Basah Road at 11.30 a.m. and continues at frequent intervals until 7.00 p.m.

Singapore Racing Fixtures 1955.

August	- - - -	13th, 17th, 20th.
September	- - - -	24th, 28th.
October	- - - -	1st.
November	- - - -	19th, 23rd, 26th.

TO PASSENGERS—It will be greatly appreciated if passengers will report any unusual service on the part of Drivers and Conductors which merits commendation.

(28)

FARE TABLES

TO FIND THE FARE FOR ANY JOURNEY:

Note the two sections between which you wish to travel. Look along the cross column opposite the lower section point, and in the square joining that column with the upright column headed by the other section point, the fare for the journey will be found.

Example:

Service No. 2 — If you board at Lorong 12 and wish to travel to Cross Street, the fare would be 20 cents.

Remember you may travel two Sections for 10 cents, four Sections for 15 cents, six Sections for 20 cents and all the way for 25 cents.

SCHOOL CHILDREN
(UNDER 16 YEARS OF AGE)
SPECIAL FARES

6 A.M. TO 7 P.M.

ADULT FARES	SCHOOL CHILDREN
CENTS	CENTS
10	5
15	
20	10
25	

(29)

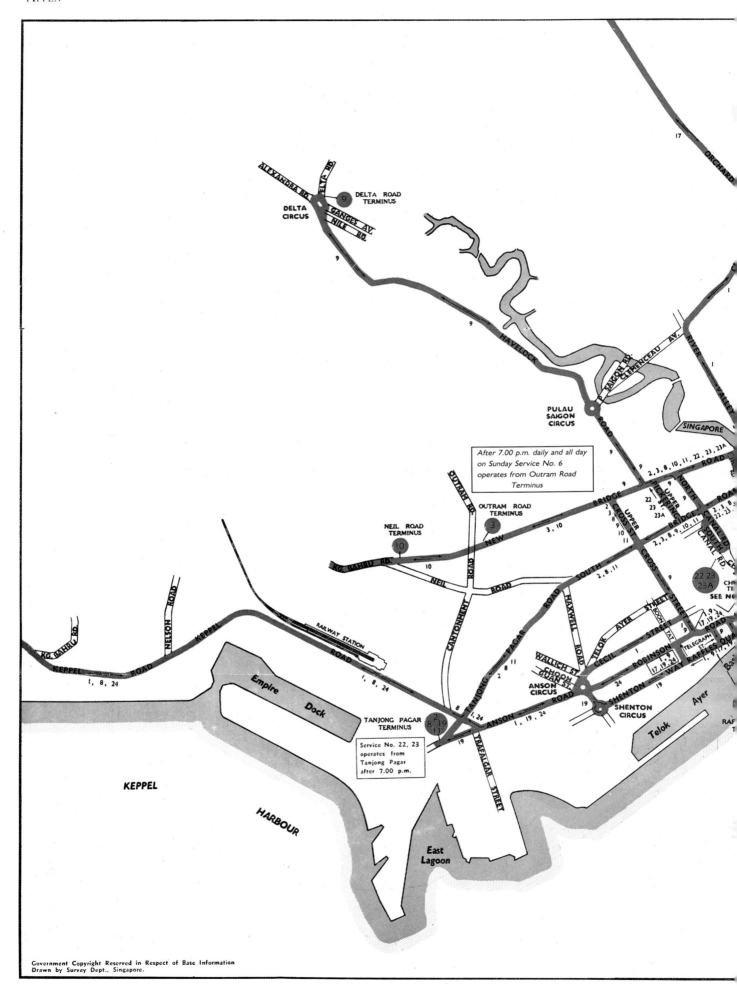

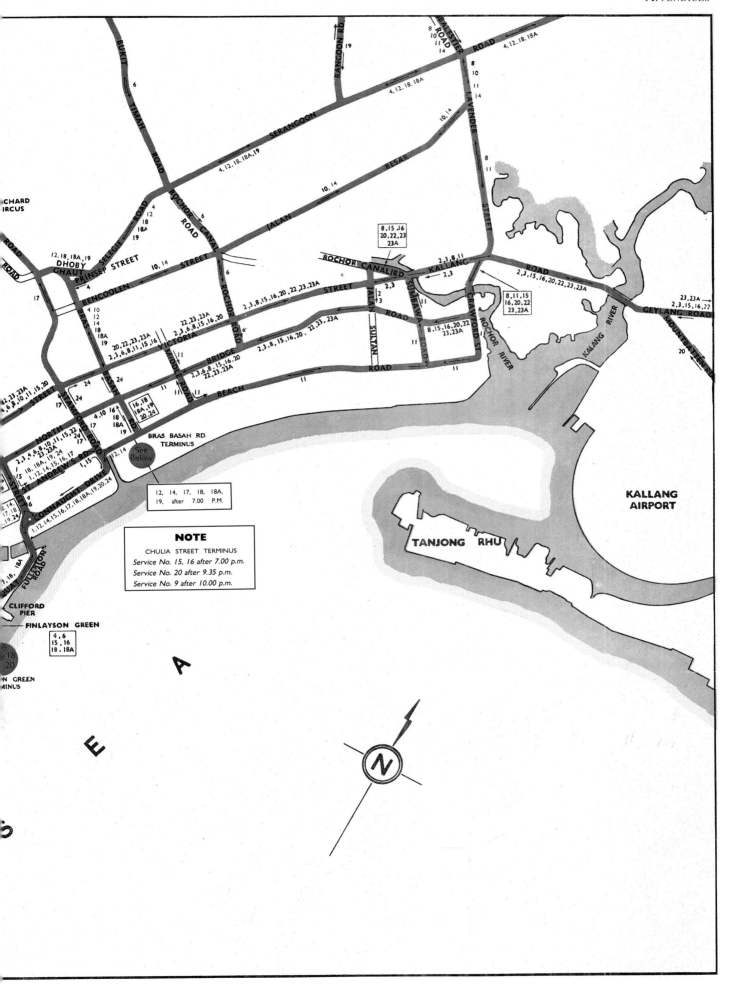

BUKIT TIMAH ROAD

SERANGOON ROAD

KANGOON RD.
19

BALESTIER ROAD
8
10
14

ROAD
4,12,18,18A

6

4,12,18,18A

JALAN BESAR

LAVENDER STREET
8
10
11
14

4,12,18,18A,19

10,14

10,14

8
11

CHARD IRCUS

ROAD

ROAD

12,18,18A,19
DHOBY
GHAUT

PRINSEP SELEGIE STREET
4
12
18A
19

ROCHOR CANAL ROAD
6

10,14

STREET
6

8,15,16
20,22,23
23A

ROCHOR CANAL RD.

KALLANG

2,3,8,11

ROAD
2,3,15,16,20,22,23,23A

23A
2,3,15,16,22

GEYLANG ROAD

17

BENCOOLEN

2,3,8,15,16,20,22,23,23A STREET

2,3
2,3

SUMBAWA ROAD

8,11,15
16,20,22
23,23A

KALLANG RIVER

MOUNTBATTEN RD

4 10
12
14
18
18A

22,23,23A
2,3,6,8,15,16,20

JALAN SULTAN ROAD
2
3
11

CRAWFORD ST.

ROCHOR RIVER

20

20,22,23,23A
2,3,6,8,11,15,16

VICTORIA
11

BRIDGE ROAD
6

2,3,8,15,16,20,22,23,23A

8,15,16,20,22
23,23A
11

11

22,23A
6,8,10,11,15,20

24
24

24

2,3,6,8,15,16,20
22,23,23A
11

11

BEACH
11

16,18
18A,19
20,24

17

4,10
18
18A
19

16
18
18A
19

BRAS BASAH RD.
TERMINUS

KALLANG
AIRPORT

NORTH
2,3,4,6,8,10,11,15,22
23,23A

24

ANDREWS ROAD
1,15

12,14

See
Below

18,18A,19,24

1,12,14,15,16,17,18

CONNAUGHT DRIVE

12, 14, 17, 18, 18A,
19, after 7.00 P.M.

TANJONG RHU

7,18,18A

1,12,14,15,16,17,18,18A,19,20,24

FULLERTON ROAD

CLIFFORD
PIER

FINLAYSON GREEN

4,6
15,16
18,18A

18
20

N GREEN
MINUS

NOTE

CHULIA STREET TERMINUS
Service No. 15, 16 after 7.00 p.m.
Service No. 20 after 9.35 p.m.
Service No. 9 after 10.00 p.m.

A

E

N

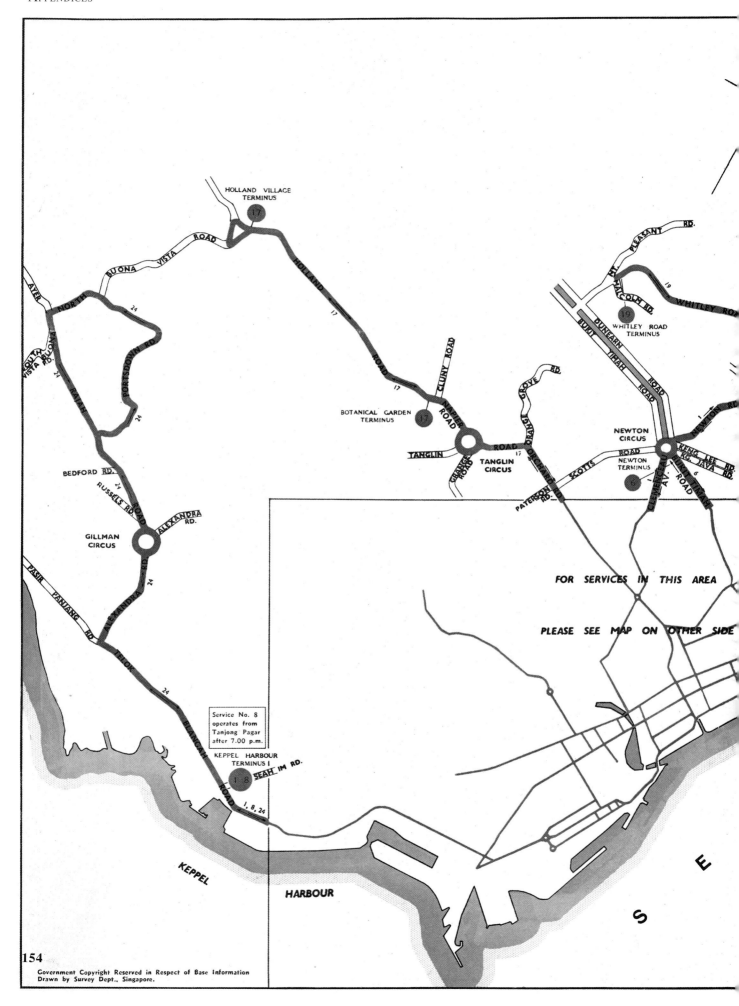

HOLLAND VILLAGE
TERMINUS

17

BUONA VISTA ROAD

AYER

NORTH

SOUTH VISTA RD.

RAJAH

PORTSDOWN RD.

24

24

24

HOLLAND ROAD

17

17

17

CLUNY ROAD

NAPIER ROAD

BOTANICAL GARDEN
TERMINUS

17

TANGLIN

ORANGE GROVE RD.

TANGLIN CIRCUS

CHANGE ROAD

ORCHARD RD.

17

PATERSON RD.

SCOTTS ROAD

NEWTON
CIRCUS

NEWTON
TERMINUS

6

CLEMENCEAU AV.

BUKIT TIMAH ROAD

KING ALBERT RD.

KG. JAVA RD.

NEWTON RD.

MT. PLEASANT RD.

MALCOLM RD.

DUNEARN ROAD

BUKIT TIMAH ROAD

19

19

WHITLEY RD.

WHITLEY ROAD
TERMINUS

BEDFORD RD.

RUSSELS ROAD

24

GILLMAN
CIRCUS

ALEXANDRA RD.

24

PASIR PANJANG RD.

ALEXANDRA RD.

TELOK

BLANGAH

24

Service No. 8
operates from
Tanjong Pagar
after 7.00 p.m.

KEPPEL HARBOUR
TERMINUS

1 8

SEAH IM RD.

ROAD

1, 8, 24

FOR SERVICES IN THIS AREA

PLEASE SEE MAP ON OTHER SIDE

E

S

KEPPEL

HARBOUR

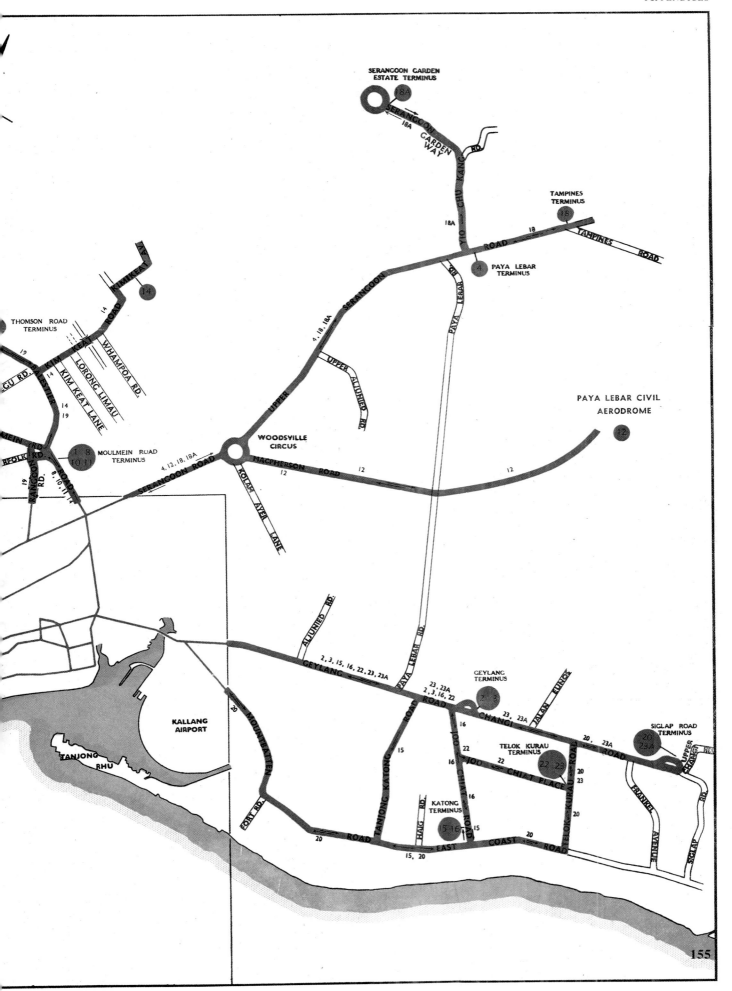

FARE TABLE

Omnibus
SERVICE No. 1
MOULMEIN ROAD and KEPPEL HARBOUR
(via CLEMENCEAU AVENUE)

Fare Stage No.

16														MOULMEIN ROAD
15	10													THOMSON ROAD
14	10	10												NEWTON
13	15	10	10											EMERALD HILL ROAD
12	15	15	10	10										ORCHARD ROAD
11	20	15	15	10	10									DAMAR ROAD
10	20	20	15	15	10	10								HIGH STREET (North Bridge Road)
9	25	20	20	15	15	10	10							FINLAYSON GREEN
8	25	25	20	20	15	15	10	10						McCALLUM STREET
7	25	25	25	20	20	15	15	10	10					TANJONG PAGAR
6	25	25	25	25	20	20	15	15	10	10				RAEBURN PARK
5	25	25	25	25	25	20	20	15	15	10	10			NELSON ROAD
4	25	25	25	25	25	25	20	20	15	15	10	10		GATE No. 8 S.H.B.
3	25	25	25	25	25	25	25	20	20	15	15	10	10	KEPPEL HARBOUR

(34)

FARE TABLE

Omnibus
SERVICE No. 8
MOULMEIN ROAD and KEPPEL HARBOUR or
TANJONG PAGAR

Fare Stage No.

15													MOULMEIN ROAD
14	10												JALAN BESAR
13	10	10											LAVENDER STREET
12	15	10	10										ARAB STREET
11	15	15	10	10									BAIN STREET
10	20	15	15	10	10								HIGH STREET
9	20	20	15	15	10	10							UPPER CROSS STREET (New Bridge Road)
8	25	20	20	15	15	10	10						WALLICH STREET
7	25	25	20	20	15	15	10	10					TANJONG PAGAR
6	25	25	25	20	20	15	15	10	10				RAEBURN PARK
5	25	25	25	25	20	20	15	15	10	10			NELSON ROAD
4	25	25	25	25	25	20	20	15	15	10	10		GATE No. 8 S.H.B.
3	25	25	25	25	25	25	20	20	15	15	10	10	KEPPEL HARBOUR

(35)

FARE TABLE

Omnibus
SERVICE No. 22/23 & 23A
CHULIA STREET and TELOK KURAU or SIGLAP ROAD

Fare Stage No.

7													TANJONG PAGAR
8	10												WALLICH STREET
9	10	10											CROSS STREET or CHULIA STREET
10	15	10	10										HIGH STREET
11	15	15	10	10									SEAH STREET
12	20	15	15	10	10								ARAB STREET
13	20	20	15	15	10	10							LAVENDER STREET
14	25	20	20	15	15	10	10						FIRESTONE FACTORY
15	25	25	20	20	15	15	10	10					LORONG 12
16	25	25	25	20	20	15	15	10	10				LORONG 28
17	25	25	25	25	20	20	15	15	10	10			GEYLANG POLICE STN.
18	25	25	25	25	25	20	20	15	15	10	10		JALAN EUNOS or EVERITT ROAD
19	25	25	25	25	25	25	20	20	15	15	10	10	LORONG MARZUKI or TELOK KURAU
20	25	25	25	25	25	25	25	20	20	15	15	10	10 SIGLAP ROAD

PLEASE RETAIN YOUR TICKET UNTIL YOU LEAVE THE BUS. IF YOU LOSE IT YOU MAY BE REQUIRED TO PAY YOUR FARE AGAIN.

(46)

FARE TABLE

Omnibus
SERVICE No. 24
BRITANNIA CLUB and ALEXANDRA DISTRICT
(via PORTSDOWN ROAD)
(Return via BUONA VISTA ROAD and AYER RAJAH RD.)

Fare Stage No.

20											RUSSELS ROAD
26	15										PORTSDOWN ROAD
23	20	10									SANDES HOME
20	25	15	10								RUSSELS ROAD
3	25	20	15								KEPPEL HARBOUR
4	25	25	20	10							GATE No. 8
5	25	25	20	10	10						NELSON ROAD
6	25	25	20	15	10	10					RAEBURN PARK
7	25	25	25	15	15	10	10				TANJONG PAGAR
8	25	25	25	20	15	15	10	10			C.I.D. HEADQUARTERS
9	25	25	25	20	20	15	15	10	10		FINLAYSON GREEN
10	25	25	25	25	20	20	15	15	10	10	CONNAUGHT DRIVE or EMPRESS PLACE
11	25	25	25	25	25	20	20	15	15	10	10 BRITANNIA CLUB

(47)

156

Appendix B — Reminiscences

Reminiscences One: Through Chinese Eyes—Images taken from family conversations

It is the 25th April 1936, the tenth birthday of Mary Choo. At the time she was living with her family in the Staff Quarters located in the grounds of Middleton Hospital, at which establishment her father was employed as a Senior Laboratory Technician. Although very gentle, and kindly by nature, Father was very strict, and despite having the busy Moulmein Road trolleybus terminus within sight of the hospital main gates, the children were not allowed to use public transport to and from school. To do so might be an invitation to dawdle instead of hurrying directly home, or perhaps to divert altogether in order to spend an hour or two in the home of a friend, instead of getting on with the all important homework. Worst of all, there would be the danger of precious school books being left behind on the seat of a trolleybus, never to be seen again. Therefore a long standing contract had been agreed with a rickshaw man, who was to come punctually every morning in order to take Mary to school, giving a literal door to door service: if on arrival her mind contained some small kind of mischief, such as slipping away to look in at the market, she would only need to glance over her shoulder to see the eyes of the rickshaw man still upon her, to remain there until she had passed through the entrance and into the charge of her teachers. Such were his instructions, and he carried out his contract to the letter, for such work was to be highly valued. True, there was still work to be had for rickshaws, but it was more difficult to find, for the days when one passenger could be put down and another immediately appear were over, and increasingly long proportions of the day could be spent waiting for a fare. Such tourists as there were would still like to sample the novelty of such a ride, but otherwise motor cars, taxicabs and trolleybuses were taking all the trade.

Even so, the youthful mind turned towards rebellion to the adult observer of a very mild nature, but to one who is only ten years old, then very daring indeed. Besides, whilst the rickshaw ride was very convenient, it could be rather uncomfortable, especially during the rain seasons, with protection from the elements being provided by a large drape of oilskin hung across the otherwise open front of the small carriage, with just a small slit for ventilation and vision. Otherwise, to travel thus was a very claustrophobic experience. More important, her friends seemed to find very exciting things to do on their way home from school, and gradually Mary found ways of avoiding the watchful eye of the rickshaw man as he waited at the gate. Instead, she would go with her friends, perhaps to explore the market or the endless rows of shops along each road, or visit their homes, or just ride, talking all the way. After some periods of scolding, Father bowed to the inevitable, and she was allowed to make her own way: the rickshaw man lost his contract, which, in a way, was rather sad—similar situations were unfolding all over Singapore, to be placed under the general heading of 'Progress'.

At this time, Mary went to Saint Anthony's Convent school, located in Victoria Street. This meant that, from the nearby terminus, her direct trolleybus would be the service 8, which would be able to give almost as good as the door-to-door transport previously the province of the rickshaw man. For this reason she shunned the 8 whenever she could, for such are the contrary ways of young women. She might find herself on board a service 5 car, and this did not please her very much, as the nearest stop at which she could alight, in North Bridge Road, involved her in a walk through the narrow streets in between that thoroughfare and Victoria Street, and this she did not like very much. Service 10 was much more agreeable, for this promised a walk through the confusion of traders stalls at the point where Rochor Road met Bencoolen Street, and the eye was blessed with a riot of colour provided by the mounds of fresh fruits and vegetables, and the nostrils assailed by the delightful scents of

small skewers of meat being roasted over a charcoal fire, or deep pans of frying fish or noodles: it is a fact that all times of day or night there is a demand for cooked food. Mary had her breakfast at home, so she could only look. The fourth alternative, which could not be taken very often because of infrequency, was the 11 service, an ideal way to end a hard day spent amidst the strict discipline of school: to travel thus meant being able to go to Arab Street, to gaze at the rich cloths, the precious metals and semiprecious stones laid out in the shops of those traders for which the district had already earned a long-standing fame. Then the ride skirted the vast Beach Road fish market, quiet in the late afternoon but still able to leave its mark in the air, and most exciting of all, went by the fishermen's villages on the one hand, and the cramped, mean little streets filling up the space leading back towards North Bridge Road on the other—the oldest and most crowded part of the town, already showing marks of decay, just a little frightening to look at, and certainly not to be seen except from the safety of a swiftly moving trolleybus.

To any child of this age, to go for a trolleybus ride only in the company of similarly aged friends or classmates, and without stern authority of an adult, just had to be an adventure. First, the trolleybus comes rumbling along the road towards the stopping place, and the giggling knot of schoolgirls lightly jostle each other to see who can be nearest to the actual spot at which the vehicle comes to a halt, thus being the first to scurry up the steps leading into the second-class compartment. With beatific looks upon their faces they pay their two-cent fare to the conductor (no matter which route they travel by, they always seemed to pay just two cents, no doubt because this was all the fare that their parents gave them). Then, whilst that hard working man made his way through the thick press of passengers towards the rear of the compartment, some of the more daring of our heroins would steel up from their seats and then, as quick as a flash of lightning, push their way through the dividing swing doors and into the first-class compartment. How snug and genteel it seemed, for more often than not they could expect to have all of the half dozen seats to themselves: if not, then it was fun to crowd around that door leading onto the drivers platform, watching him at his work and experiencing a thrill of mild wickedness at the sound of his harsh words as he cursed the ancestors of some pedestrian wandering almost without purpose across the roadway—happily, the young ladies seldom, if ever, understood the meaning of the shouted words, but they did sound terrible. There can be little doubt that most conductors were aware of the game of compartment swapping, but few were prepared to do anything about it. What would they gain by demanding an extra cent here and there, and was there not more than enough to be done coping with the crowds in the second-class compartment? An adult doing that would be a different matter, for there would be presented the chance of a first class argument, an exchange of views which could become quite heated and which would add some spice to what might have been a hectic but boring day—but these were only children—so it was that, upon reaching their stop, the girls were able to alight from the front platform, carrying the impression of being young ladies of quality until the illusion were broken by yet another attack of the giggles.

There was another quite frequent journey to be made, but this time with all the adult members of the family, and therefore a different approach was to be taken, namely to be seen but not to say a word, to sit wherever indicated and not to move therefrom unless instructed. The family was setting out to visit a favourite aunt who lived in the heart of jungle country, somewhere beyond the 8° milestone, Changi Road. Her house was surrounded by many fascinating natural things which, by this time, had become largely lost to the wholly town dweller: there were trees to be climbed, fishes to be harried, fruits to be gathered and then consumed, all dominated by the small jungle creatures to be avoided. All combined to make the journey into an exciting expedition, and the good behaviour could not long be held in check, any more than can a volcano. To start the day there had to be the short walk to the trolleybus terminus, and there was never any need to wait, for service 5, 8 or 11 would suit the purpose of the family by taking them to the end of Lavender Street. There alighting, they would stand for a short while on the corner opposite the mighty gas holders, and within a few minutes along would come a trolleybus on service 2 which would be taken for the ride to Geylang terminus. Here, the town ended and the countryside began, and to go further meant using a mosquito bus—of recent memory, and still so-called, although in fact operated by the properly constituted Changi Bus Service Company—to go as far as the 8° milestone. Being a large family and a small bus the whole vehicle would be filled, with some of the older brothers being obliged to ride on the next bus. The headway was quite frequent, and so the separation would not be for long. The buses were bright yellow by livery, which might have been selected from a popular hue employed by most mosquito bus owners, or else it might have been an interim measure prior to the later, and most familiar, red and white (or sometimes aluminium instead of the latter) so closely associated with Changi buses. After a bumpy and rather furious ride, the bus reaches the 8° milestone, and at once empties, with the crowd of erstwhile passengers making their way along one of the several red dirt tracks leading away from the main road, until they are quickly hidden behind a vast green curtain of trees, bushes and high grasses, with only the sound of their diminishing laughter to mark their progress—the civilisations of the town seemed to be a world distant.

Reminiscences Two: **Through European Eyes**

Dealing as we are with personal recollections, and having taken a look at the Chinese bus, it becomes opportune, before rejoining the main text, to regard that mode of transport through European eyes—forty years later, Mrs P. Ewells recalled "I lived in Changi, which is roughly fifteen miles from Singapore. My late husband was in the Army, and we were there from 1933 to 1936. Trams ran in town, but at Changi, it was rather isolated then, the only means of getting into town was by taxi. However, they did run a small five-a-side 'Piggi Bus' which was definitely for natives: no windows or protection of any sort from the tropical storms, and they used to travel at terrific speeds, through jungle roads, rounding all corners on two wheels.

"One day the Army laid on a coach for the Army wives to go into town to a Jumble Sale. The Roman Catholic Padre in fact arranged it, which of course we had to pay for. We went to the Jumble Sale, and the coach brought us back to the NAAFI Club for a meal, and we were told that we could look round the shops and be back at a certain time, ready for the journey home. My friend and I went off to the shops, but when we got back (in plenty of time) the coach had gone, leaving us behind. Service pay in those days wasn't very much, so we couldn't afford a taxi, and in any case we had always promised ourselves a ride in a Piggi-Bus before we left Malaya. Everyone thought we were mad at the time, but this seemed the opportunity to try it. So we boarded the bus, much to the astonishment of the natives, and we experienced the most hair-raising ride of our lives. My friend just hung her head over the sides and was seasick all the way.

"They dropped us outside the Royal Artillery Guardroom, and when we got to our married quarters the Padre was there, as well as our husbands, not knowing what to do. We never did live down our ride on the Piggi-Bus, but we never wanted to repeat the experience"

Elsewhere in this account the fact is recorded that Commissioned Officers serving with His (later Her) Majesty's Forces were not allowed to travel on the trolleybuses nor motor buses of the Traction Company, and it would seem that a similar rule applied to enlisted men so far as the Chinese buses were concerned, as the account given by Mrs Ewells does indicate that a problem could exist concerning Insurance, in case of an accident. It is well to remember that these were closely akin to the mosquito buses which had so hurt the trolleybus operations, and it is not hard to visualise those kind of driving conditions in the busy streets of the town. A final point worthy of note is the terminology applied by Europeans to the Chinese buses—in no sense is the term intended to be derogatory, for the spelling provides the true meaning of the nickname, 'piggi' being the Malay verb 'to go', thus giving the 'go-bus' in the sense of 'get-up-and-go', or in other words, a very fast and ruthless sort of bus.

BELOW: Possibly the 'Piggi-Bus'? Changi's US-built Fargo, S 3810, on Route 1 to Changi Camp Theatre.

PART B

TYPE BY TYPE DESCRIPTIONS OF THE TRAMS, TROLLEYBUSES AND BUSES OPERATED IN SINGAPORE FROM THE 1880'S TO THE 1960'S

ABOVE: Possibly the least attractive livery adopted by the Singapore Traction Company was a plain all-over silver, relieved only by a green band. Here Albion FT39L, number STC 308 is checked by the regulator as it passes the request stop and fare stage—both indicated by metal 'flags' on the lamppost—only recently relieved of its primary function as a traction pole for the trolleybuses. Buses of this type are described on page 202.

BELOW: The Chinese bus companies operated a wide variety of buses with numerous makes of chassis. Here a Canadian built Chevrolet Maple Leaf picks up passengers for owner Tay Koh Yat. Few details of these early post-occupation buses have become available and this type should be grouped with others of similar style on page 222.

The Singapore Tramway Company—Steam Trams
Rolling stock

0-4-0 steam tram engines

Singapore Tramway Company placed an order with Messrs. Kitson and Company in October 1884 for fourteen of their non-condensing 0-4-0 tram engines with which they would inaugurate the service the following year. These engines—works numbers T169 to T182—were delivered in 1885–6 and were followed by a further two, T225 & T226, ordered in January 1887 and delivered later that year. The addition of the two extra locos indicates that the early fortunes of Singapore Tramways Company had appeared promising.

Having regard to the regulations referred to earlier and to the fact that there were many horses also using the streets, the locomotives were of the totally enclosed type, with valances covering all the motion and wheels to within four inches of the rail level. This not only kept mechanical noise to a minimum but also prevented the hapless from becoming caught and injured by connecting rods and valve gear—these latter requirements being

SPECIFICATION: Tram engines	
Builder:	Kitson & Co Ltd
Makers numbers:	T169-182; T225 & T226
Maker's class:	Singapore class: Iron Cab—non-condensing
Wheel arrangement:	0-4-0- tram engine
Cylinders:	8in x 12in
Driving wheels:	2ft 4¼ in
Wheelbase:	5ft 0in
Date built:	1885 (T169-82) —14 1887 (T225/6) —2
Total:	16

general for street-running steam locomotives and were not specific to Singapore.

Rather than the windows which surrounded British tram locos, these engines had open sides beneath their canopy roofs.

BELOW: This maker's photograph is the only definitive view so far discovered by the authors to illustrate the Kitson steam tram locomotives supplied to Singapore Tramways Company in 1885, this example being No 6. (*Science Museum photographic collection, London*

The passenger trailer cars

Of the passenger cars, little detail has survived. In the main, contemporary United Kingdom practices were followed in that the cars were double-deck with a four-wheel bogie at each end and of considerable length. The most noticeable departure form general UK practice being the provision of the entrance/exit doorway at the centre of the body, rather than have platforms at each end.

The lower saloon was provided for first-class passengers and, with the stairway to the upper deck being placed opposite the entrance, it was possible to divide the first-class accommodation into smoking and nonsmoking compartments.

Second-class fares had to climb to the upper-deck and, although there were glazed screens at each end and a roof to offer protection from any smoke or sparks which might escape, the accommodation provided was quite spartan, with back-to back knifeboard seating on simple wooden benches, divided longitudinally down the middle by a central backrest so that passengers sat looking outwards over the side of the car.

The roof was supported by a series of stanchions, themselves given a measure of added strength by the inclusion of an horizontal handrail running the length of the car sides. Set into the end bulkheads at roof level could be found large oil burning lamps serving dual purposes, forward to give some warning to other road users during the hours of darkness, whilst the back light could have been of some limited benefit to passengers. To provide added protection during the monsoon seasons, large tarpaulin screens were carried in a rolled-up condition, located in sections under the edge of the roof, to be used at the discretion of the conductor.

The cars were reportedly licensed to carry sixty passengers and would work with a crew of three, viz: the locomotive driver plus a conductor for each deck. Communication was by a strong cord which passed the length of the lower saloon, across the gap between car and locomotive, there to be anchored to a striker, allowing signals to be sent by the 'lower' conductor to be sounded on a gong in the driver's compartment. The upper deck conductor would need to rely on blasts given on his hand whistle.

Of the number of cars in stock, no actual total can be given but it seems reasonable that there could have been as many as the re were engines.

Materials for their construction would have been sent from the United Kingdom and assembled at the depot. The Company had been very fortunate in being able to obtain an extensive site at Tanjong Pagar, on the corner of Lim Teck Kim Road and facing onto the main line. Besides the car sheds, full workshop facilities were provided.

ABOVE: Not many photographs have been found to illustrate the Singapore steam tram engines and their passenger trailers. In this greatly enlarged view, the general features can be made out but the car is largely obscured by steam from the engine. *(National Archive of Singapore*

BELOW: Line drawing interpretation of the possible arrangement of a Singapore steam tram double-deck passenger trailer car, based on the above photograph and using the proportions of the car illustrated on page 13 of Part A. The location of the stairway ascertained from available evidence.

GENERAL ARRANGEMENT ONLY—NOT TO SCALE

Dimensions taken from a broadside photograph of a similar car

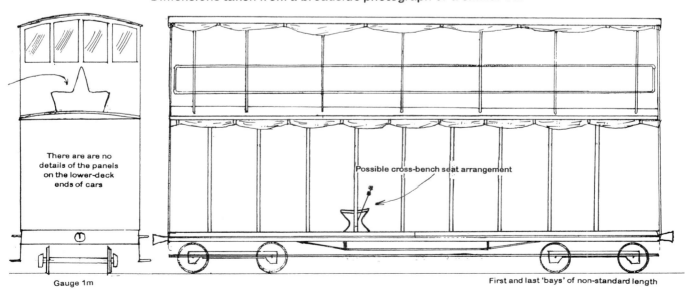

There are are no details of the panels on the lower-deck ends of cars

Possible cross-bench seat arrangement

Gauge 1m

First and last 'bays' of non-standard length

No details of lower-deck seating available except that these were cross-bench cars
The location of the staircase is uncertain

Cross-bench cars—10-bench type

ABOVE: Maker's illustration of it Singapore-design for an open-sided 'cross-bench' car—very similar to those it supplied to the Hong Kong Tramway Electric Company the previous year (1904) for use there on a 3ft 6in gauge system. The Singapore cars differed in not having a clerestory roof, reducing their height by eleven inches over the trolley plank.

The most numerous (thirty) of the original 1905 cars were of the cross-bench type, open at the sides and with bench seating located in ten rows across the width of the body. Passengers boarded the tram by way of a footboard running the length of the car.

The roof was supported by a series of varnished wood stanchions, located in such a manner as to coincide with the positions of the seats, thus providing support for the roof and acting as an additional anchor for the seats. The lower ends were bolted to heavy cast iron mouldings set adjacent to the foot board.

Protection for the driver was provided by three glazed droplight windscreen panels reaching from the dash to the underside of the roof; more usually, however, the cars were worked with them in the down, or open, position. Only when subjected to monsoon rains did drivers require protection as Singapore, just north of the equator, has no cool season.

Whilst the crossbench design might have been almost ideal for tropical weather conditions, they could not have been popular in use, for the conductor could only pass along the footboard in order to collect fares—and do so with the tram was in motion. This was a common tramway practice in days when speeds were relatively low and other traffic light. From the passenger's point of view, it could be very difficult to reach or leave the middle seats, particularly if those on the outside proved unwilling to move.

Protection from the extremes of climate—in Singapore this includes blistering sunshine, high humidity and torrential rain—was provided by spring-loaded, pull-down, roller-blinds which fitted between each pair of vertical pillars, the latter having grooved edges to accommodate the striped canvas. It was possible to pull down the blinds either fully or partially, as required by prevailing conditions.

The crossbench cars could carry 40 passengers—ten rows of four, less two places immediately behind the driver—and passengers were carried on reversible bench seats of the type where the

SPECIFICATION: 1905 cross-bench cars—10-bench type

Fleet numbers :	Initially 1–30 (unconfirmed)
Trucks:	Brill 21E
Wheelbase:	6ft 6in (*1981 mm*)
Motors:	2 x Dick, Kerr 25B, each of 25hp (*18.6kW*)
Controllers:	DB (form C)
Body make:	United Car Company—assembled by Singapore Tramways.
Seats :	40—ie 4 per bench
Length over platforms:	28ft 0in (*8535mm*)
Total length overall:	29ft 0in (*8839mm*)
Width over body:	6ft 1in (*1854mm*) over the body
Width over roof:	6ft 4in (*1930mm*) at the roof
Height:	10ft 0in (*3048mm*) from rail to the upper surface of the trolley plank
Height inside at centre:	6ft 10in (*2083mm*)
Track gauge:	1 metre (*1000mm*)
Date built:	1905 (30 cars); 1908 (10 cars)—the latter *may* have been the short, seven-bench cars whose length would be less than above.

Note: Dimensions based on manufacturer's brochure

conductor was required to swing the back-rest at each terminus to change the direction faced by passengers.

To prevent passengers from falling from the 'offside' of the vehicles, protective bars were provided that could be pulled down from a stowed position below the roof valance, to lock in place at elbow level to a seated passenger. These appear to have fallen out of use by the early 1920's and photographs reveal that they were missing completely.

Destination equipment was minimal and appears, at one time, to have taken the form of the initial letters of the destination in black on a small white rectangle in the centre windscreen. For instance, a car heading for Keppel Harbour would show 'KH' while another going to Rochore would have 'R' showing. Later, plates were carried in the centre windscreen showing the name in full.

Trip-gate and tray lifeguards were provided from the outset and the way ahead was illuminated at night by large, roof-mounted, headlights.

In addition to these 10-bench cars, there are photographs of shorter, 7-bench, cross-bench cars and a description of these follows.

ABOVE: Crossbench car No 21 seems to be the subject of much scrutiny in this view—possibly the initial inspection by the Railway Inspector in view of the attire of the gents involved. Members of the Indian community also seem fascinated by the spectacle, giving support to the 'new' suggestion. The three-piece front windows can be seen to advantage, as can the glazed windscreens which have been fully lowered. The edge of the canvas side screens can also be seen here, behind the arched cantrail. *(F. W. York collection*

BELOW: In their latter years, Singapore Tramways was placed under the management of the Shanghai tramways in, and a new livery was adopted, possibly light grey. Here Car 52 shows its early 'Shanghai' livery, also identifiable by the plain fleet number without surrounding garter. These cars were later to have one end bench designates as 'First class' and many were subsequently rebuilt as saloon cars by panelling the sides between the pillars and having perimeter seats in place of benches. The elbow-level side guard rails can be seen lowered nearest the camera and raised on the far side. *(F. W. York collection*

The Combination Vestibuled Cars

ABOVE: An illustration from the United Electric Car Company's brochure illustrating the combination-car for Singapore which, like the crossbench cars, differed from the similar cars for Hong Kong in not having a clerestory on the roof, having un-glazed drop louvres in place of windows, and being of metre gauge. The trolley-base and spring arrangement illustrated here was not, however, of the type shipped and used in Singapore

The other twenty cars were of the 'combination' type—also known as 'Californian'—having a three-bay central section enclosed and able to provide conventional saloon accommodation with inward-facing bench seating along the sides and a central gangway, whilst at each end were to be found open platforms with fixed crossbench seats arranged with two benches placed back-to-back. . These were intended to seat four passengers abreast. Allowing for two spaces lost behind the motorman, the total seated capacity was probably 32 passengers.

The open sections were protected from the weather by roller-screens of a pattern similar to those of the crossbench cars, but wider as the stanchions on the open platform were of the same spacing as the window pillars of the enclosed section.

The enclosed saloon had three arched windows on each side, each with glazed drop-lights. For protection from the sun when the windows were in the dropped—open—position, spring-loaded, pull-down roller-blinds were provided but were of a dark colour, ie, not striped canvas as fitted by the open crossbench sections.

SPECIFICATION: 1905 Combination stock	
Fleet numbers :	Initially 31–50 (unconfirmed
Trucks:	Brill 21E
Wheelbase:	6ft 6in
Motors:	2 x Dick, Kerr 25B, each of 25hp
Controllers:	DB (form C)
Body make:	United Car Company–assembled by Singapore Tramways.
Seats :	32—16 inside; 16 outside.
Length over platforms:	28ft 0in (8535mm)
Total length overall:	29ft 0in (8839mm)
Width over body:	6ft 3in (1905mm) over the body
Width over roof:	6ft 6in (1981mm) at the roof
Height:	10ft 0in (3048mm) from rail to the upper surface of the trolley plank
Height inside at centre:	6ft 10in (2083mm)
Track gauge:	1 metre (1000mm)
Date built:	1905

Note: Dimensions based on manufacturer's brochure

The conductor was able to travel inside the saloon and be able to stand on the platform when collecting fares from outside passengers. These cars were licensed to carry 32 passengers (if eight were carried on each platform, then this would leave a total of sixteen in the saloon, eight on each side, which seems to be accurate).

TRAMCAR NUMBERING

It is difficult to be precise on this subject, as in the early days car numbers were not prominently displayed, and in latter days the cars were rebuilt and renumbered randomly.

Initially, the passenger cars are *believed* to have been allocated numbers in the following manner:

1–30   cross-bench, 1905
31–50   California cars, 1905
51–60   cross-bench, 1908

Goods wagons were certainly allocated:

1–15   open wagons
16–30   vans
31–33   motorised vans

After the Shanghai takeover, cars were rebuilt and renumbered in no apparent order of types. Motorised vans 31–33 became 61–63 (33/63 unconfirmed), maybe before the Shanghai period. It is not known if the unmotorised goods wagons survived the full life of the system and no photographs have revealed a van. Detail of the car numbering is likely to remain obscure in the absence of archival material on the car fleet.

RIGHT: An unidentified California car in rural surroundings, with its roof-mounted headlight silhouetted against the sky, also showing the unusual trolley-spring arrangement to advantage. The practice of carrying the fleet number only on the side of combination cars makes identification difficult.

BELOW: Another picture where some sort of inspection appears to have been under way. Also involved, appear to be two Chinese gentlemen in front of car No 50 which, like all combination cars, carries its fleet number on the side of the central saloon. Here too, the canvas blind-type weather screens can be seen in the raised position, while one pane of the three-piece windscreen has been raised. Singapore trams retained the headlight in a roof mounted position until their final days in the mid-1920's. *(F. W. York collection*

For comparison... Two posed views of the original Singapore Tramways cars—**ABOVE:** A 'Combination Vestibuled' car, showing to effect the central saloon with cross-benches on the outer platforms. **BELOW:** A 1905 cross-bench car with ten rows of benches with swing-over backrests, each bench nominally seating four persons. *(Author's collection from a contemporary journal*

Short 7-bench cars

Although it is known that the original crossbench cars were of ten-bench layout, there was also a number of shorter cars with only seven cross-benches which may have been the ten additional cars purchased in 1908. These had longer platforms than the ten bench cars and offered, latterly at least, first-class accommodation on at least one end-bench, the narrow arched valance above the entrance to the platform being inscribed FIRST CLASS. From photographs, one such car was numbered 12.

The short crossbench cars had seats to carry about twenty-eight passengers, if calculated at

SPECIFICATION: Short cross-bench cars—7-bench type	
Fleet numbers :	Believed to have been 51–60 initially
Trucks:	Brill 21E
Wheelbase:	6ft 6in (1981 mm)
Motors:	2 x Dick, Kerr 25B, each of 25hp (18.6kW)
Controllers:	DB (form C)
Body make:	Probably Union Electric Car Co. Ltd.
Seats :	35 approx
Length over platforms:	Approx 24ft (7315mm)
Total length overall:	Approx 25ft (7620mm)
Width over body:	6ft 1in (1854mm) over the body
Width over roof:	6ft 4in (1930mm) at the roof
Height:	10ft (3048mm) from rail to the upper surface of the trolley plank
Track gauge:	1 metre (1000mm)
Date introduced:	Possibly 1908

about four or five persons per bench—benches on at least one platform were designated 'first class' with a capacity for four passengers. While it is believed that there were first-class seats at *one* end, the platforms at *both* ends were longer than on the ten-bench cars.

The overall length and number of bench seats aside, the shorter cars were generally as per the description of the 10-bench type previously described.

Like their full-length counterparts, the 7-bench short cars were rebuilt as saloons shortly after the Shanghai Electric Construction Company had assumed control in 1923, the main difference being that there was only one entrance each end, each side.

LEFT: An unidentified short, seven-bench, crossbench car apparently off the rails, presents a good broadside view of its arrangements. Clearly seen here is the longer 'bay' that forms the platform, with the inscription '1ST CLASS' above. The lighter, post-1923 livery had been applied. *(J. H. Price collection*

BELOW: In this photograph, so full of interest, short crossbench car, No 12, overtakes a bullock cart on Serangoon Road circa 1910. Note the destination initials in the windscreen—'R' to Rochore. *(Allen Morrison collection*

Upper Serangoon Road, Singapore

ABOVE: One of the reconstructed cars built new as a crossbench car. All the bench seats except those at each end, facing the platform, have been replaced by longitudinal, inward-facing seating for about thirty passengers while of the remaining bench-seats, that at one end only was designated as a four-seat, first-class 'compartment'. The central saloon was accessed by way of two entrances on each side. The original running gear was retained. *(Commercial Motor— January 15, 1925*

1923/24 Rebuilt Crossbench Cars

At the time of the decision to replace the tramways, only about 10% of the cars were available for traffic due to a backlog of maintenance brought about by the lack of revenue, itself a direct result of an excessively high fare structure. Restructured management repaired the cars to improve car miles run and reduced the fares, providing a massive increase of 95% in receipts, allowing further improvements to be paid for.

These improvements included rebuilding much of the tram fleet and the trams found themselves granted a short reprieve with a serious programme of rehabilitation being launched in a final effort to keep the system alive. Whilst some work was needed on the 'combination' cars, it was the unpopular 'crossbench' fleet which received the most drastic attention.

Mechanically, the running gear and electrical equipment was brought up to standard; the majority of the work being to the bodies.

The crossbench seats were removed and replaced by inward-facing, longitudinal seats but it is believed that one bench was retained at each end with one of these forming a four-seat, first-class compartment—at the leading end only end only.

By removing the benches and then panelling the sides to waist height, they adopted a similar pattern to that of the 'combinations', the result being hardly pleasing to the eye, for the panels had been inserted in between the stanchions supporting the roof, giving a crude appearance, akin to starved cattle—although a photograph shows that at least one car had neatly panelled sides. No attempt was made to fit weather shutters into the resulting window frames, instead, the rolled canvases, fitted when new, were left in place (although the conductor was no longer required to roll up, or down, these blinds on the offside of each car when arriving at a terminus as had been his duty when these were true "crossbench" cars). Inside the resulting saloon, the usual longitudinal seating was located, with two short bench seats remaining on each platform. However "hit-and-miss" the system might have previously been, these conversions took the opportunity for the class-system of accommodation to be fully realised.

SPECIFICATION OF CARS: 1923-24 reconstructed stock	
Fleet numbers :	Unidentified
Trucks:	Brill 21E
Wheelbase:	6ft 6in
Motors:	2 x Dick, Kerr 25-B
Controllers:	DK form C
Body make:	United Car Company–reconstructed by Singapore Tramways.
Seats :	First-class: 4 / Second-class: 30 (approximately)
Bodies reconstructed:	1923/24
Length over platforms:	28ft
Total length overall:	29ft
Width over body:	6ft 1in
Width over roof:	6ft 4in
Height:	10ft 0in—rail to top of trolley plank
Track gauge:	1 metre

ABOVE: Rebuilt cross-bench car No 41 in 'Shanghai' livery, showing the 1st class signwriting above the entrance at one end only. This method of denoting the first-class entrance was superseding by using diagonally opposite corners. The style of panelling between the pillars led to comments of looking like the ribs of starved cattle—see the lower photo on page 151! This car shows the destination 'Post 310' which for years was the only applicable name for the short working on the Geylang Road, beyond the Kallang River, to the east of the city. 41 was freshly repainted by comparison with other cars of the time. When Shanghai management took control, the system was very run down and only a few cars were in full working order and looked very dilapidated. *(F. W. York collection*

Short-cars

The shorter 7-bench cars were similarly modernised, the four centre bays having flush panelling while the outer bays had inset panels.

LEFT OPPOSITE: A detail from an earlier photograph (page 36, top) showing the extent of rebuilding afforded the shorter, 7-bench, cars. In this case, panels have been fitted over some pillars to give a less ribbed look. The dark green area around the corner of the car denoted the 1-st class entrance whenever that end was leading; the diagonally opposite corner was similarly painted green.

RIGHT: Another detail from an earlier picture to show car 5, a rebuilt short cross-bench car.

1905 Non-passenger stock—Freight motors 31 to 33

In order to cater for the anticipated carriage of freight, three types of rolling stock were obtained. The mainstay was a trio of motorised vans, that is to say, capable of self propulsion in the same manner as a passenger car, and looking very much like an ordinary tram except in having no side windows, their place being occupied in the main by two sliding doors. The major difference with the passenger cars was that each of these cars was mounted on a pair of Brill 21G equal-wheel bogies with Dick, Kerr 25-b quadruple type motors and D.K. form 'C' controllers.

These cars entered the fleet with a dual role in mind, the first to act independently for the carriage of parcels or small crates capable of being accommodated within their own bodywork, whilst the second put them in the form of locomotives, hauling trains of non-motorised wagons. A railway-like feature of the motor-cars was the fitting of a large buffer at each end, mounted at a central point towards the bottom of the dash.

By the 1920's, two of the erstwhile freight motors had become works cars, taking fleet numbers 61 and 62. If viewed head-on then their appearance would be hardly changed, but in elevation the double doors had gone, to be replaced in the case of 61 by wagon-like drop sides, leaving the upper halves of the

SPECIFICATION OF CARS: 1905 motor freight trams.	
Fleet numbers :	31-33; later renumbered 61, 62 (? & 63?)
Trucks:	2 x Brill 21G-equal-wheel
Wheelbase:	?
Motors:	Dick, Kerr 25b
Controllers:	D. K. DB1 form 'C'
Body make:	United Electric Car Co.
Seats :	Nil
Length over body corners:	18ft 0in
Length over vestibules:	24ft 0in
Width over body:	6ft 1¼in
Width over roof:	6ft 6in
Clear height inside:	6ft 9in—at centre
Payload:	8 tons

bodywork open while 62 has water tanks and open sides.

One of the freight motors was sometimes to be seen traversing the streets of Singapore at a solemn funereal pace as it conveyed the coffin of an unfortunate soldier who had succumbed to one of a number of tropical diseases in the days prior to the introduction of modern drugs. While, in theory, any one of the three could have undertaken the task, it is highly likely that one car was earmarked for this duty as it had to be immaculately turned-out, to military standards. It is quite likely that the car used for this duty was the third freight motor, left unaltered with its side doors.

BELOW: The freight motors as built were fairly plain box cars with a driving position at either end. The van portion was provided with double sliding doors each side, while the driving compartments were open either side and. Like the trams, the ends were fitted with three-piece windows. Tramway-style fenders were provided just below the line of the underframe which itself had a central buffer/coupler of the type common on narrow gauge railways and, possibly, of a type compatible with the Singapore Railway and the railway in the docks. The normal use for the couplers was to attach the freight motors to short trains of goods trucks owned and operated by SET themselves. *(F. W. York collection*

LEFT: Freight motor No 31 shunts goods trucks into the depot yard at Mackenzie Road with a whited suited gentleman in a pith helmet at the controls while another looks on. The trucks were carrying timber but were also used for the carriage of coal for the boilers in the power station, the iron plated chimney of which can partly be seen in the bottom photograph.

CENTRE: Seen here lurking behind a pile of coal, one of the freight motors, by now re-numbered 62 and redesignated as a water carrier. The keen eyed can see the twin tanks inside the open sides of the car.

BOTTOM: Freight motor No 61 had been converted to a drop-side truck but retained its roof, albeit braced by turnbuckles to add strength amidships. *(All F. W. York collection.*

Open Wagons and Vans

The remainder of the rolling stock comprised fifteen four-wheeled open wagons, with provision for tarpaulin covers, and a like number of covered goods vans, all of which were fitted with railway-style running gear with horn-guides and not tramway-style trucks. (No photographs have been located showing a van.) The purpose of the vans would have been similar to that of the motor-cars, namely the carriage of parcels and the like, particularly where protection from the weather was required. The open wagons would be concerned with general bulk cargo; coal being an obvious example. All of the stock was designed for a maximum payload of six tons.

Tower Wagons

There was also at least one tower wagon—used for inspection and repairs to the overhead wiring—and this (or these) had a pair of bullocks as motive power. Unfortunately, no photograph has been turned up.

BELOW: From this manufacturer's illustration, it would seem that there had been envisaged a role for tarpaulin covered wagons but later photographs show them with the support frames removed. The centre buffer/couplers can be seen in this view together with the more tramway-like fender, below underframe level.

RIGHT: A line of open wagons being unloaded in the Mackenzie Road yard, the track layout of which can be seen from the map on page 19.

SPECIFICATION : 1905 Open trailer freight wagons	
Fleet numbers :	1–15 (open wagons); 16–30 (vans).
Trucks:	Railway-style horn-guides
Motors:	None
Body make:	United Electric Car Co.
Length over headstocks:	12ft 6in
Length over collision fenders:	14ft 6in
Width over sides:	6ft 1in
Width overall:	6ft 6in
Height from floor to tarpaulin cover:	7ft 0in
Payload:	6 tons
Tare weight:	3 tons 7 cwts 1 qtr

Some other cars— and a trailer

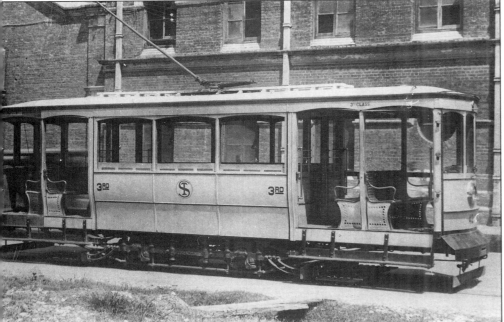

UPPER LEFT: As can be seen from this illustration of No 42, the partially enclosed combination cars had their accommodation redesignated to 1st and 3rd class as fares were reduced by the Shanghai management after takeover. This arrangement allowed the better off more space on the car. Obviously seen here in the 'Shanghai' period 42 carries cream livery with green at one end to denote the first-class area. As already mentioned, the area devoted to first-class was changed so as to always include the leading row of seats, whichever direction the car was facing..

CENTRE LEFT: In this photograph (taken from the cover picture) the combination car, No 38, has had more drastic changes made to its accommodation. The saloon has been extended by one bay either end and the first-class area is now identified by the green corner as the car approaches the intending passenger. The diagonally opposite corner was also painted green for when the car was running in the opposite direction. A more significant modification has, however, been carried out. Provision has been made for towing a trailer. The trip-gate has been modified and there is a flat rail, to restrain the coupling bar, fitted between trip-gate and fender.

LOWER LEFT: In Shanghai, the SECCo operated a successful fleet of trams which hauled trailers and it seems that trials were carried out in Singapore, although no reference to such trailer operation has been discovered by the Authors. What did appear was a trailer car, pictured here outside Mackenzie Road depot, which may or may not have operated in service. The need for run-around loops at termini makes it unlikely that this was more than an experimental one-off car. The trailer closely resembles those used in Shanghai. It could have been lent by Shanghai; it could have been built there for Singapore or it couls have been built in Singapore to Shanghai design. Whatever it was, it was branded 3rd class and in this photograph shows a 'Route 3' board.

In order to provide Singapore with trolleybuses to re-place the trams, the management in Shanghai ordered 80— later to total 108— AEC Model 603 two-axle chassis to the same specification as those used by its Shanghai Electric Construction Company and, later, by Compagnie Française de Tramways et d'Eclairage, the operator of trol-leybuses in the French Concession of Shanghai.

The 603 was unusual for its time in having a set-back front axle, thus permitting a true front entrance.

Bodies were designed in Shanghai where they were constructed, following which, it is believed, they were sent 'completely-knocked-down' (ckd) to Singapore for local assembly.

Mechanical equipment included a 50hp type motor built by Bull of Stowmarket, Suffolk; a type-T controller from E.M.B. of West Bromwich; suspension was provided by nine-leaf front springs with eleven-leaf springs at the rear, car-ried on heavy-spoked, solid-tyred wheels, with tyres provided by Dunlop. Further statistical data: wheelbase 11ft 8¾in; all up weight unladen 5 tons 13 cwt; an overall length of 26ft 6in; height from the roadway to the roof 9ft 10in with a roof camber of 8in; height of front fender from the road 1ft 4in; height of life guard from the roadway 4in; front dash panel to front of fender 4¼in; and distance from the trip guard to the front of the life guard 3ft.

SPECIFICATION OF CARS: 1925 AEC trolleybus stock.	
Fleet numbers :	1-108
Chassis:	AEC 603
Motors:	Bull 50hp, type RV 612
Controllers:	EMB type-T
Body make:	SEC (Shanghai) ckd kits assembled in Singapore
Seats:	First-class: 8–FEX / Second-class: 30–CEX
Length of frames:	22ft 8¾in
Length over body:	26ft 6in
Width over body:	? ; Front track: 5ft 1¾in; Rear track: 5ft 7⅝in
Height:	9ft 10in—over roof
Wheelbase:	11ft 8¾in
Unladen weight:	5tons 13cwt

On the rather narrow platform, the driver was provided with a seat in the normal driving position, with foot controls and a warning gong pedal of tramway pattern, protected by the substantial dash panel. A normal steering wheel was provided, most of which was visible above the dash, but the driver was not given the protection of a windscreen.

Mounted onto the rugged chassis was bodywork also of substantial hardwood constructionand much like contemporary tramcars. A bulk-

BELOW: A posed official view of one of the AEC 603 trolleybuses when new, showing clearly the two-class passenger accommodation with white painted first-class steps at the front where the body was a deep green. The rear part of the body was a cream colour and carried second-class passengers who entered through the centre doorway which had double, spring doors which opened only inwards. The photographer probably thought the crowd of small boys was better controlled by including them in the picture rather than trying to make them go away from this obviously very exciting spectacle. Again, almost by right, a bullock team has managed to get into the picture! The destination screen was mounted above the canopy while the route number was hung below. Not long after entering service, an intermediate point was displayed in the top of the nearside front (first-class) window. *(National Tramway Museum, Crich, Derbyshire*

LEFT: A broadside, offside, view of an AEC 603 early in Singapore trolleybus days as it waits between duties at the Geylang terminus of Route 2. *(John Rossman collection*

head, into which was set a doorway, separated the driver from the first-class accommodation, so that intending passengers would use two steep steps ahead of the front wheel, leading from the road onto the driving platform, and then pass through the doorway. To assist with the climb, a short hand rail was located on the main bodywork to their right, whilst to the left a long stanchion was in place between the bottom step and the underside of the roof, thus adding strength to that particular corner.

Viewed from the offside, the body would be seen as of nine-bay construction, each very short, but not of equal size, the two bays forming the first-class section being somewhat larger than the rest. With the front axle located midway under the forward compartment, the space left between the roadway and the underside of the body was protected by a tramway-style tray and lifeguard, with five-bar metal side-guard.

At waist height the panelling ended with a sill which supported the window frames when in the closed position. The windows were not glazed, but comprised fine slats, or louvres, set into a teak frame, to be raised only to provide protection from the rains. Above the windows was a further set of louvres, perhaps six inches deep which, if glazed, could be described as 'top-lights'. On the nearside, the second 'top-light' from the front, over the first-class section, was glazed to form a side destination indicator

The second-class compartment accounted for almost three-quarters of the body, with the first two nearside bays being occupied by the entrance-exit with recessed double-doors. The inward-opening doors had hardwood frames with inset louvres, similar to the window shutters, and their top rails were in line with the waist rail. They were only about two feet deep and sprung into the closed position. One main stanchion was anchored in the bottom step, rising into the underside of the roof and was cranked outward an inch so at knee-to-waist height in order to accommodate the doors when these were in the closed position.

As the space between the roadway and the bottom step leading to the doors was not great, only two guard rails were required (and practice was to prove the essential need for these, as passengers attempting to reach this quite narrow and steep passage way whilst the vehicle was moving would be quite likely to fall. The guard rails did not continue beyond the rear wheels.

Bulkheads divided the first and second class sections, into which similar short, louvred, doors were located.

Three rear window frames were provided, and, unlike the sides, it seems to have been the usual practice to work trolleybuses with the outer two louvred frames in the closed position, possibly to help prevent swirling dust from entering the saloons. Two red-eye marker lights were fitted at the rear upper corners of the bodywork and alongside that to the left was located a glass plate upon which was painted the fleet number, white numerals on a black ground. A length of rope ran the width of the body, anchored at top corners of the roof with just a little slack. Onto this rope were clipped the trailing ends of the trolley retrieval ropes, one to each boom, with the eye of the

The AEC 603 trolleybus

The AEC model 603 trolleybus was the first mass produced trolley vehicle to have been built by an established motor bus manufacturer, using a chassis, wheels and axles of proven design. It was also the only 'primitive' trolley bus to have been built in large numbers (over 200 were constructed over a five year period) and which continued in manufacture beyond its time. It also represents the first major adoption of foot pedal control and a set back front axle. The latter allowed not only for a front entrance position under the supervision of the driver, but a short wheelbase which gave the vehicle the ability to turn in narrow streets. Model 603 was supplied to just three overseas customers as tabulated below:

Year	To Shanghai (S.E.C.Co.)	To Singapore (S.T.C.)	To Shanghai (C.F.T.E.)
1925	10		
1926	52	40	
1927	8*	50	
1928		15*	
1929	3*	3*	2*
1930	10*		

The chassis numbers are known for the groups marked*
603163-70 to Shanghai Electric Construction Co.
603A189-203 to Singapore Traction Co. (91-105)
603A204/6/7 to Shanghai Electric Construction Co.
603A205/8 to Shanghai (Compagnie Française de Tramways et d'Eclairage—French Settlement)
603A209-11 to Singapore Traction Co. (106-8)
603212-221 to Shanghai Electric Construction Co.
Other chassis, apart from the two marked, may have been supplied to Shanghai's French Settlement—Compagnie Française de Tramways et d'Eclairage—which is also known to have operated tramcars of similar design to those of SECCo, and with which company there was an element of joint working. Vehicles in the French Settlement drove on the left, which was the rule of the road in China in general until 1946.

RIGHT: Accidents are never to be taken lightly and photographs of them must always serve a purpose and never be merely to enthuse over, as they are frequently the cause of personal grief. In this case, the good reason is that no other photograph so far discovered shows the destination indicator without the valance later fitted right around the front of the canopy. An offside rear view mirror has also been fitted. Possibly, planting traction and other poles in the roadway was more hazardous than at first thought—rickshaws were also particularly at risk. *(Straits Times*

clip being of sufficient size to allow for a complete sliding movement along the ropes. There would be no tension on the retrieval ropes, which looped down to a point just below the window sill, then up again to the clip. In case of dewirement, the booms could be manhandled with ease with the conductor reaching out of the back window. Rising from each side of the roof at a point directly over the rear wheels was a metal frame, its two vertical arms each ending in a trolley pole retaining hook—a crossbar giving added stability.

Other equipment included a single headlamp set at the centre of the dash—on the first vehicles into service no glazing was provided, leaving the simple bulb unprotected. Therefore, a glass was provided, to be supplied with a bright metal surround. These early deliveries entered service with large destination boxes mounted on top of the roof, over the head of the driver, with script in the English, Chinese and Malay languages. Service numbers were shown in a small supplementary box set under the canopy above the drivers head, with the numerals shown in English and Chinese. Although the original destination boxes were large, the need to show destinations in three languages left no room for the listing of intermediate points, and so, for a very short while and only during the earliest period of trolley-bus operation, additional route information was shown in a further box carried inside the canopy and close to the entrance to the first-class saloon. The first departure from this layout came when the destination box was relocated—suspended—beneath the canopy, to the offside of the route number box.

For whatever reason, the pattern was not considered to be ideal, and later batches had a different arrangement, with previous deliveries being converted to match: in fact, the change in design was quite radical in visual terms, a deep valance being attached to the front and sides of the driver's canopy, into which were set two apertures, the larger to carry the destination and the smaller a route number. The deep valance was also added to the similar Shanghai cars and helped to give a greater measure of weather protection to the driver.

Whilst the livery colours might be seen as commonplace, the method of application certainly was not. Two basic colours were used, dark green and cream, but applied in vertical form in order to give kerbside identification of the compartments. The dash and platform area was green, as was the first class accommodation as far back as the centre doorway, thereafter cream was used for the second-class area.

The woodwork of doors and windows was not painted, but instead treated with several coats of varnish. In general black was chosen for the roof, although for a while white had been used on a few vehicles, no doubt in order to keep interiors cool but, as this colour was liable to staining by wire-lubricating materials, droplets of which would fall from the overhead from time to time, white was not practical. Side guards have been described as having been red-oxide or brown, and the wheels were black.

Class denominations were shown by '1st' and '2nd' in English and Chinese, placed to the right of the respective doors, oddly enough, repeated on the offside. Within the space of the first-class panels would be found the Company motif, a large 'S' embracing a somewhat smaller 'T', and with a small 'c' being held in the upright of the 'T', the three letters being contained within a circle (this logo

LEFT: A detail study of the front end of trolleybus 38 showing the deep valance into which was incorporated the destination and route number blind boxes. It will be noted that the destination 'Post 310' is in three languages while the route number is in two, Chinese and English. Also to be seen is the STC badge of encircled initials, together with the 'flap' style of direction indicator—seen in line with the '1st' sign on the bodyside. *(Straits Times*

LEFT: A good rear view of an AEC as it crosses Anderson Bridge towards Empress Square—with Raffles statue just to the left of the bus, in the background. The arrangement of ropes attached to a bar across the back of the roof can be seen, as can the usual arrangement of only having the centre shutters open. No 15 was advertising Great Eastern Assurance, a company within the same group as the STC. *(Straits Times*

was based upon the Shanghai version, identical except that the 'c' was not used, and despite the fact of 'Tramways' not being included in the Shanghai company title). The letters were either black or white, according to the contrast of the colour upon which they were applied. A large fleet number, in white, was located beneath the headlamp.

Inside, the first-class compartment must have been quite claustrophobic, having accommodation for only eight passengers, four to each side on longitudinal seats set between the bulkheads. The payment of the higher rate of fare would be reflected in a measure of comfort provided on the seating, but whatever material had been used would need to be strong, easily cleaned, besides being unattractive to those indigenous insects which would devour anything. Therefore, upholstery would be useless, and the most likely covering would have been cane (rattan) in hardwood frames (as used until the 1980's on Hong Kong's trams). Having passed through the swinging connecting doors, the second-class accommodation would give one the impression of considerable space, the bench seat around the

sides in nominal terms carrying thirty passengers, with a clear floor space within which almost unlimited numbers of standing passengers would ride and for whom leather handgrips suspended from bars running the length of the compartment were provided. Communication between the conductor and driver was by means of a bell cord running the length of the vehicle.

By and large the complete trolleybus fleet, when delivered and in service, would have been sufficiently standard as for any one vehicle to be identical to any other. Mention has been made of the rebuilding of the destination displays but, in time, certain little detail differences were to be noted, no doubt as a result of accident damage and the like. In common with early tramway days, the Municipal Commissioners were not very happy at the prospect of advertising material being carried, but when they relaxed such attitude the displays were not mounted directly onto the bodywork. Instead, brackets were mounted along the roof sides in order to carry boards showing the commercial message, and in a similar fashion a wooden framework was positioned beneath the rear windows onto which a

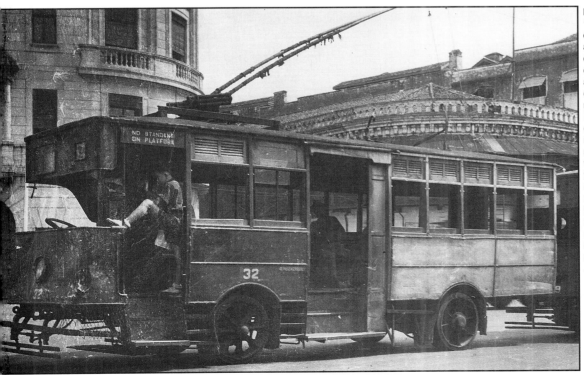

LEFT: Trolleybus No 32 in 1945, very shortly after the end of the occupation stands at Collyer Quay in a very run down and dirty condition. The class system had been done away with but the distinctive colours of the two compartments can still just be seen. It was to take many months of hard work with precious few resources to get fifty of the survivors back to a roadworthy state. This car is in the all-green livery adopted during the occupation after removal of the two-class system. White side window surrounds were added after liberation to brighten the appearance of the trolleybus fleet, as shown on page 68. *(D. K. W Jones*

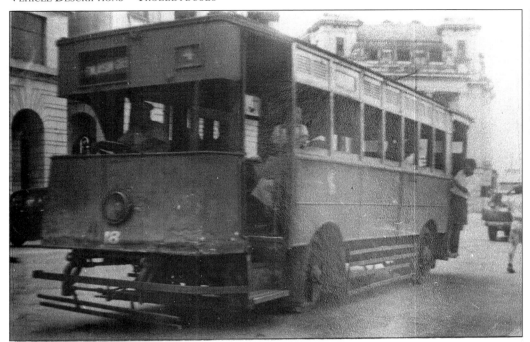

panel carrying the required advertisement could be screwed. However, there does not seem to have been any great desire to encourage this form of revenue, and not all of the trolleybuses were thus equipped.

Rebuilt Car 18

As recorded in Part A (pages 61/2), trolleybus No 18 was modified during the Japanese occupation and converted to one-class, front entrance, rear exit. The internal bulkheads were removed which must have compromised the structural integrity of the body. As the vehicle aged—prematurely—the rear end sagged where the new rear exit had been cut into the bodyside but, as it was capable of being coaxed to run in service, it lasted long enough to be photographed in 1945 by D. K. W Jones.

Although the two-classes were never to return, no further cars were rebuilt in the manner of No 18.

BELOW: The AECs have almost reached the end of their particular road as No 3, possibly in High Street, picks-up a lady passenger. One of the photographer's next photographs will be that seen opposite, of a Ransomes Sims & Jefferies with gleaming new paint and bright fittings. *(C. A. Poskitt*

Ransomes, Sims and Jefferies—1948   *Nos 1–50*

It was described earlier (page 65), how, as the war in Asia showed signs of coming to an end, the Board of the Singapore Traction Company, exiled in London, saw the necessity of placing orders for new rolling stock in good time as, with the war in Europe coming to an end, manufacturers would be inundated with orders both for home operators and for export. In the event it proved difficult to place the order for trolleybuses but, fortunately, in a temporary change of policy and at the behest of the British Government, Ransomes Sims and Jefferies, of Ipswich, Suffolk, agreed to accept the STC order. From afar, it was uncertain just how badly damaged the infrastructure of the trolleybus system might be when returned to its owners, particularly as the means to liberation might include bombardment, so it was decided to place an initial order for just fifty trolleybus chassis suitable for single-deck bodywork—less than half the prewar fleet of 108 AEC's.

Ransomes, Sims & Jefferies chassis

Ransomes, Sims & Jefferies began as manufacturers of agricultural machinery at Ipswich, Suffolk, and it is claimed that in 1842 they produced the world's first self-propelled steam traction engine. Various firms in the area were involved in the production of such machinery; one such manufacturer, Garrett, began building trolleybuses, and was joined by Ransomes, and a third firm, Bull Motors Ltd. began to produce traction motors. The municipal transport undertaking in Ipswich became one of the first to substitute trams with trolleybuses, and indeed operated no motor buses until the fifties.

SPECIFICATION OF CARS: 1948 RSJ trolleybus stock.	
Fleet numbers :	1-50
Chassis:	Ransomes, Sims and Jeffries
Motors:	?
Controllers:	?
Body make:	Lee Kiat Seng
Seats:	B35+17C
Length:	27ft 0in
Width:	7ft 6in
Height:	?
Wheelbase:	Approx 16ft 3in
Unladen weight:	?

When the Shanghai Electric Construction Co placed its first order for the AEC type 603 trolleybus, the electrical equipment comprised Bull motors, and EMB resistances, a combination which proved to be an excellent choice. In effect, the SECCo chose three well made parts to make a whole, and Singapore, which received 108 AEC 603s, was well served by them.

In 1925, AEC conducted a trial of a 603 trolleybus, from the SECCo order, pulling a trailer, and this took place on the Ipswich system. It would be another twenty years before Ipswich again played its part in the Singapore story, although in the meantime Georgetown, Penang, built up a substantial fleet of Ransomes trolleybuses. The early Ransomes machines for Ipswich were similar in style to the

BELOW: This early view of a Ransomes Sims and Jefferies trolleybus was taken while the AEC's were still in service but, unfortunately no views that include both old and new types have been discovered. The newness is evident, especially in the normally grimy area of the trolley bases and springs which, in this case, gleam in the sunlight. The early condition of the Ransomes trolleybuses with closely spaced headlights, three, chrome-plated bumper bars and dark green livery with cream streamlining. This vehicle, like the majority, but not all, had top-lights above the drivers' cab front side windows. In this instance the windows have full-drop side windows but others has louvred shutters to the end of the 1950's. *(C. A. Poskitt*

AEC 603s, with set back front axles to allow for an entrance doorway alongside the driver, and some of those in the Ipswich fleet which were built with solid tyres lasted for as long as the AECs in Singapore. It was not long, however, before Ransomes introduced pneumatic tyres, and began to build their own electrical equipment. The aim was to produce a compact and lightweight motor, and in this field they were successful. At first, the quest for lighter weight was to assist the introduction of pneumatic tyres, but later, because Ransomes began to export trolleybuses, it was to construct lighter vehicles to operate in places where axle loadings were restricted. An example is Rangoon: in the late thirties this town began to build up an extensive system using lightweight trolleybuses. Curiously, in pursuit of an order from Rangoon, Leyland Motors considered obtaining lightweight electrical gear from Ransomes, a competitor, but the only company at that time with expertise in this field. Many of the vehicles built for use in Britain and South Africa were double deckers, but Ransomes specialised in the production of "small light-type" vehicles for use overseas.

Such was Ransomes success in the late twenties and thirties that it not only built trolleybus chassis, but also bus and trolleybus bodies. The Second World War put an end to this activity, and the Company chose to build other types of equipment after 1945. The demand for motor bus chassis was so great in the postwar period, that the British government suggested that Ransomes build a small number of trolleybuses to fulfil the needs of overseas customers. In fact, the Company produced three orders, for Port of Spain in Trinidad, for Drammen in Norway, and for Singapore. In each case, the chassis were essentially to prewar dimensions and specification, and of "small light-type" (Ransomes did not have a more precise nomenclature for its trolleybuses!) It should be born in mind that the Ordinance under which the STC operated restricted the size and weight of trolley vehicles, and the Ransomes chassis were as close as possible to meeting the restrictions (other British makes would have been heavier). This does not mean to say that the vehicles were obsolete in design, but that vehicles in many countries at the time

ABOVE: Rear view study of a trolleybus. The positions of the rear route number and fleet/registration number can be clearly seen as can the three bright metal rear bumper bars. Of note ate the trolley wires spaced at 24 inches—compare this with earlier photographs where a narrow spacing of 18 inches, or less, was used.

BELOW: Trolleybus No 6 after rebuilding in a style almost unchanged from the original, suggesting that the work was carried out at Mackenzie Road. The headlights have been moved further apart and the ventilators are where the old headlights had been. Wooden slatted shutters are in evidence in this example which has been repainted into the mid-1950's cream and green.

were being constructed longer and wider. Singapore certainly did not require longer trolleybuses, as even with the Ransomes there was a problem caused by the length of wheelbase, and therefore greater turning circle, than that of the existing short wheelbase AECs. Overhead wiring had to be modified at certain terminal points to allow the new vehicles to turn. As already stated, Georgetown Municipal Transport in Penang also used similar chassis. chassis.....

Bodywork was built in Singapore by Lee Kiat Seng whose design followed closely that of the Dennis Falcon motor buses ordered simultaneously with the trolleybuses. The frontal arrangement, of course, differed from those of the Falcons in having the, by then, conventional full width cab associated with trolleybuses since the early 1930's. In fact, although the postwar style appeared to eyes accustomed to the AEC 'trackless trams', it too was actually dated, being more akin to a mid-1930's design than mid-1940's, by British standards.

Experience of post-occupation operation with both the motor buses and AEC trolleybuses, all of which were one-class with centre entrance/exit, led the Company to specify such a layout for the Ransomes. Although new thinking had resulted in relocation of the entrance position, the prewar standard perimeter seating was retained with sparingly upholstered seats covered in leathercloth of a variety considered to be indigestible to the host of hungry tropical insects, so intent upon devouring everything that they might come upon (see photo page 107). The official capacity (painted on the side of every bus in Singapore) was for 35 seated and seventeen standing passengers.

Initially, full-drop, slatted shutters were provided to protect passengers from the elements as the windows were unglazed but, quite soon, some Ransomes trolleybuses appeared with glazing, also of the full-drop type, but it is uncertain as to whether both shutters and glazing were—or could be—provided within the same window frame.

The driver's cab was provided with both offside and nearside

LEFT: No 28 is still relatively original, except for its cream livery. The headlights are in the original position but it has received flashing arrow direction indicators. Behind and to the left, No 19 has a rebuilt cab and destination screen rubber gasket mounted and flush with the front dome, probably following the accident described in Chapter 10 of Part A where other illustrations of trolleybuses in various rebuilt condition appear.

BELOW: No 13 retained much of its original dash panel but received deeper cab side windows in order to help driver visibility of the kerb.

ABOVE: The pristine No 16 posed for the camera probably when brand new. It had the small top-lights above the front cab side windows and glazed droplights in the main passenger saloon windows. *(F. W. York collection*

LEFT: Another view of No 16 some years later after having a rebuilt cab—but possibly not as a part of the refurbishment programme as the headlights remained at the original close spacing. The inverted V windscreens and cab side windows are similar to those on earlier postwar Albions. It had, however, acquired the later cream livery.

boors, of which the latter could only be opened from inside as a precaution against unauthorised entry.

Deep, three-bar, chromium-plated bumper bars (fenders) were fitted front and back but destination indicators were only provided for at the front, in a wide, one-piece, raised box which incorporated, in English only, both end of route place names and a route number only. At the rear, a square plate showing the service number only was placed in the lower half of the nearside back window. The latter comprised a three-piece arrangement with two smaller windows either side of a wider central pane. Above the right hand rear window was the plate carrying the combined, unprefixed registration/fleet number.

Delays in production due to postwar shortages of materials caused production to fall behind into the era of the coal strike and very cold winter of early 1947, resulting in the first chassis not arriving at Singapore until the closing days of 1947. Bodying was commenced by Lee Kiat Seng early in 1948 and it was, finally, on 22nd April that year, that the first five Ransomes entered service on Route 4, the Paya Lebar service.

Mid-life rebuilding

When the Ransomes' bodies were constructed, there was tremendous pressure on the body makers to produce new vehicles as quickly as possible and also, those materials such as well seasoned timber, which would normally be used were in short supply. All this

combined to ensure that, after nearly a decade of service under harsh conditions, body weaknesses were becoming an ongoing problem. To rectify the situation, the entire fleet of fifty trolleybuses was sent for a comprehensive body rebuild, with chassis also receiving thorough attention. With so many vehicles requiring attention within a relatively short period, the Company deemed it prudent to either undertake the work themselves at Mackenzie Road workshops or, when that reached capacity, involve the services of small bodyworks, often one-man businesses. Although the body framing was largely retained, the resulting vehicles were hardly the standardised fleet of the past. While the output from Mackenzie Road was fairly consistent in appearance, bodies rebuilt by outside contractors were very nearly all different, with some looking like wartime utility buses once found in the UK. Many received cabs which followed the lines of the Albion fleet, some of which were themselves rebuilt under similar circumstances.

At this juncture, the opportunity was taken to improve the ventilation of electrical equipment slung under the saloon floor and, to achieve this, additional ventilators were incorporated at the front dash, usually located in the space left when the headlights were relocated nearer to the corners of the body. The grilles of these vents were painted black, or dark green, with the fleet number placed between. A few had a single vent and in this case the number was above. In both cases, with the new cream livery, the number had a dark background, giving the illusion of a single, continuous ventilator unit.

BELOW LEFT: The final silver livery which was to see the trolleybuses out. Here No 5 displays a curious devise beneath the trolley bases—possibly an experiment to prevent interference with the newly introduced television.

Decorated Vehicles

Many public transport companies, in Britain and in countries of the erstwhile British Empire, celebrated royal events with decorated vehicles. Two of the examples depicted on these two pages are quite remarkable, indeed, they are unparalleled.

BELOW: The first STC decorated vehicle illustrated, a trolleybus chassis disguised in the form of a crown for the coronation of H. M. King George VI in May 1937, is the only known example of a decorated trolleybus built upon a **bare chassis**. Not only that, the chassis was a **Thornycroft** (trolleybuses of this make are numbered in single figures) and came from Shanghai, where it had been rendered surplus by the delivery of new AEC 603Ts (a pneumatic tyred version of the AEC 603s used in Singapore). It will be noted that this vehicle retains its lifeguard at the leading end. The supply of this chassis in 1937 is but one example of a continued link between Singapore and the Shanghai Company after the severance of the financial link in 1935. *(Singapore Traction Company*

BELOW and RIGHT OPPOSITE: The second vehicle is a Bedford OB coach—a Bedford OB Coronation Coach! Based on the redundant chassis of STC 190, it was constructed to commemorate the coronation of H.M.Queen Elizabeth II in June 1953, and is seen outside Mackenzie Road Depot, with a retinue of uniformed coachmen. Note the Bedford radiator, the front wheels disguised by false spokes, and the large ornamental rear wheels situated aft of the true rear axle, here masked by the 'postillions'. The second view, taken at night alongside the former power station generating house, itself adorned with flags and fairy lights, shows off this unusual vehicle to full effect. *(Both Singapore Traction Company*

Colourful decorations were also provided in various places in the town by different community interests, such as the Coronation Arch erected by the Indian Merchants in High Street.

The first excursion into motor bus operation by STC saw an initial purchase of seven Dennis G-type chassis, probably ordered very early in 1928. The chassis were completed and then completely knocked down (ckd) and crated for reassembly in Singapore by Malayan Motors, having left the Dennis factory at Guildford all together on 23rd July 1928. The order by STC had been handled by the Wearn Group, Singapore agents, through Tozer, Kemsley, a well known motor dealer of the day and had chassis numbers 70350 to 70356. The assembled chassis weighed approximately 1ton 17cwt.

Following the pattern set by the trolleybuses, ckd bodies were prepared by Shanghai Electric Construction Company for local assembly in Singapore at the Mackenzie Road premises of the Traction Company. The only similarity between the bodies of the trolleybuses and the Dennis was the method of construction and assembly. The Dennis bodies were more advanced in appearance, although still behind European styling.

Despite their being of the bonnetted type—driver behind the engine—they were provided with a full-width cab, the windscreen to which was glazed and the upper half hinged upwards to provide a flow of air when it was not raining. The bulkhead between the driver and passenger compartment was unglazed but physical protection for the driver was provided by vertical metal bars.

Passenger access was by a single doorway behind the nearside rear wheel and was fitted with two inward-opening swing-doors extending from knee to waist level and similar to those fitted on the trolleybuses. Perimeter seating was provided on hardwood benches for *approximately* 20-passengers, plus ten standing. Although first-class fares were charged throughout, this was to promote a less crowded atmosphere and did not imply any degree of comfort.

Side windows were unglazed, being protected by drop-louvres to provide protection from monsoon rains while permitting an

VEHICLE SPECIFICATION:	
Registration numbers:	STC 1-17
Chassis:	Dennis G-type
Engine:	Dennis 4-cyl rated at 17.9 hp petrol
Transmission:	4-speed, sliding-pinion manual gearbox
Body make:	SECCo (Shanghai) ckd kits assembled in Singapore
Body layout:	B20+10REX—inward swinging doors (capacity approximate)
Date introduced:	1929 (1-7) & 1930 (8-17)
Withdrawn:	1938
Total:	17
Length:	?
Wheelbase:	11ft 10in
Unladen weight:	STC 1–7: 2tons 15cwt 3qtr; STC 8–17: 2tons 17cwt 1qtr

airflow through the saloon. Above each side-window was a louvred ventilator or the same proportions as a standee top-light window, had the latter been fitted.

The weight of the body was about 18cwt, giving a total kerb weight (including driver and conductor) of 2tons 15cwt 3qtrs and these seven—S.T.C. 1 to 7— entered service on 4th March 1929.

STC 8–17

A second order was placed for a further ten Dennis G-type—chassis numbers 70598–70607—and, following similar purchase, construction and assembly procedures, these left the Dennis factory at Guildford, England, on 7th January 1930. They entered service later that year—allowing about six months for shipping and assembly of chassis and body.

The only known difference was that the total kerb weight was nearly two hundredweight greater than S.T.C. 1–7 at 2tons 17cwt 1qtr, of which the chassis was 1ton 18cwt and the body 19cwt 1qtr.

Livery, for all seventeen, was green edged with black, as on the first-class portions of trolleybuses.

BELOW: The only picture of a Singapore Traction Company Dennis G-type that has become available to illustrate the type. The drop-louvre shutters in each side window can be seen as can the louvres in the 'top-light' position. This example is STC 16 of the second—1930—batch which had a single destination box without separate provision for a route number blind.

Ford type AA

STC 18-102

When the STC required further motor buses, it was not to Dennis that they turned but to Ford. Ford products manufactured in Britain were included under the Imperial Preference, low duty, scheme operated within the then British Empire.

The Type AA was a light bus chassis and, as was the case with the Dennis G's, a ckd body was prepared in Shanghai by SEC and sent to Singapore for assembly on the chassis. It is not clear if the chassis was also locally assembled from ckd parts.

The design of the largely timber body was based on that for the Dennis and was visually similar—only the radiator grille, bonnet and wheels being markedly different.

In all probability, the bodies had perimeter seating and a combined total seating + standing capacity of about 30 persons and again first-class fares applied—hence the green livery with black trim.

Two large headlights were provided, mounted on a large radius bar attached each end to the inner face of the front 'wings' for which they also acted as a stay. Small sidelights were mounted in neat streamlined nacelle atop each front mudguard. Unlike the Dennis G's, the Fords had a chrome plated bumper, or fender, at the front.

The drop-louvre windows, toplights, passenger doors and entrance were all as per the Dennis. (*qv*). Destination equipment did, however, differ, the Fords having separate roller-blinds for route number and destination, both appearing in English and Chinese

The Ford AA series was delivered in three main batches; S.T.C. 18–27 appearing in 1933; S.T.C. 28–37 in 1934 and 38–102 in 1935. Interestingly, the first of the Fords was withdrawn as early as 1938 when 21 examples were disposed of. The remainder are believed to have met their doom in the jungles of Malaya during the Japanese advance down the peninsula when a large number were commandeered to transport Commonwealth troops to forward areas up country, from which, it is believed, neither the buses nor crews returned.

VEHICLE SPECIFICATION:	
Registration numbers:	STC 18-27, 28-37 & 38-102
Chassis:	Ford Type AA
Engine:	Ford 4-cyl
Transmission:	Four-speed, crash gearbox
Body make:	SECCo (Shanghai) ckd kits assembled in Singapore
Body layout:	B20+10REX—inward swinging doors (capacity approximate)
Date introduced:	1933 (18-27); 1934 (28-37); 1935(38-102)
Withdrawn:	1939 (18-3<u>8</u>); 1942-1945 (remainder)
Total:	75

BELOW : A depot view of Ford AA buses showing the detail differences between them and the preceding Dennises. A prewar Albion PK series Victor can also be seen on the far left.. *(Straits Times*

LEFT: S.T.C.62 seems to be having a spot of trouble as it receives attention from a pith-helmeted gentleman whilst a peak capped employee looks on—probably the driver. An AEC trolleybus advertising 'Tiger Beer' is about to overtake in the middle of the road. The bilingual route number and English only destination are clear in this view. *(From the collection of Singapore Bus Service (1978) Limited.*

BELOW: A line-up of almost military precision, as the light reflects off the opened windscreens of all but one Ford. This photograph was probably taken after the majority had been withdrawn and before they had been requisitioned by the military and sent off to way in upcountry Malaya in January 1942. Neither the buses nor their drivers were ever heard of again. *(Straits Times*

Leyland Cub

STC 103-112

Leyland Motors of Lancashire established a separate factory at Kingston upon Thames, Surrey, to build a range of lightweight trucks and buses in the 1930's. these were known as the Cub range and were designated KG (Kingston Goods) or KP (Kingston Passenger). Most had the driver seated behind the engine but bus companies, anxious to carry as many passengers as possible, required a side cab—forward control—version. Petrol and diesel engined versions were built and, apart from Britain, the Cub model found favour with overseas customers, particularly in India.

For introduction in 1937, the STC ordered (in August 1936) "a side drive Kingston Passenger oil engine Mark II" version of the Leyland Cub, representing a new configuration for a Singapore bus but one which would endure for some time. Leyland, however dissuaded the STC from taking the diesel engine following complaints from a number of overseas customers about this power unit and so the Singapore Cubs were to be petrol engined.

Bodywork was based on designs produced earlier by Shanghai for the Dennis and Ford buses but was most probably produced in Singapore, following STC's separation from SEC in 1935. Leyland supplied the bonnet and front wings, headlights and the large wing-mounted sidelights.

VEHICLE SPECIFICATION: Leyland 'Cub'	
Registration numbers:	STC 103-112
Chassis:	Leyland Cub Model SKPZ2—forward control
Engine:	Leyland—petrol 4.7litre, 6-cylinder
Transmission:	4-speed, constant-mesh gearbox
Body make:	STC
Body layout:	B33FD, perimeter seating
Date introduced:	1937
Withdrawn:	(1942-45?)
Total:	10
Length:	24ft—nominal
Width:	7ft 6in
Height:	?
Wheelbase:	15ft 6in
Unladen weight:	Approximately 3ton 18cwt 0qtr (Similar vehicles in Rangoon)

The biggest change, apart from being forward control, was that the entrance was moved to the front of the saloon and had a single, hinged, two-piece, full-length, folding door. An emergency door was located behind the offside rear wheel. Seating remained of the inward-facing—perimeter—variety with slatted hardwood benches. Drop-type slatted louvres protected the unglazed windows in wet conditions while louvred 'top-lights' were fitted above each window and the doorway, as well as over the canopy above the engine. In the front of the canopy there was a destination and route-number screen , beside the latter was a

BELOW: The Leyland Cubs delivered in 1937 were bodied by STC themselves, without recourse to the Shanghai-based SEC from whom STC had split. Here STC 108 demonstrates well the body style with unglazed side windows. Louvred drop-panels could be pulled-up in monsoon rain to protect the passengers without completely cutting off ventilation in high temperatures with the 99% humidity prevalent at such times. It is believed that all these 'Cubs' were destroyed during the occupation or during the fighting that preceded it. Note the large Leyland fitted headlights and swept back mudguards.*(F. W. York collection*

further small louvred vent. The roof met the bodyside just above the 'top-light' vents and the front 'dome' was angular—the only styling 'curves' were the Leyland provided front wings and the valance between the canopy and front door pillar.

A feature apparently introduced on the Cubs was the unusual offside direction indicator which took the form of an arm about 18 inches long, hinged from outside the cab door, which the driver flipped out to 90 degrees when indicating a manoeuvre to the right. The manner of operation could not have been simpler for the driver merely leaned out of the cab window and with his hand deftly swung the arm outward—at just the right height to catch a hapless cyclist or rickshaw puller in the face. When new, the Cubs were painted green with black trim and with a matt black roof—probably covered with stretched canvas. Latterly, roofs and mudguards were painted white.

Precise details of the fate of the ten Cubs is uncertain but it is believed that none survived the occupation to be reinstated in September 1945.

It is noteworthy that by taking the petrol engined version of the Leyland Cub, the Traction Company operated buses identical to a type being supplied to London Transport who took eight petrol engined Leyland Cubs in 1936, numbered C106-113

ABOVE: This offside view of Leyland SKPZ2 'Cub', S.T.C. 105 in near original condition, shows off well the emergency exit behind the rear wheelarch. Like the Fords before them, the Cubs had front bumper bars, only in this case they were double. An electric horn can just be seen above the bumper bar in line with the nearer radiator side piece. Later pictures show a bulb-horn so, presumably, electric horns could not cope with the wet conditions found in a tropical monsoon climate. *(Straits Times*

(CLX 543–550), of type SKPZ2, for use on a service between the central London railway stations. These were based on the same chassis as those supplied to STC although they were fitted with distinctive 'deck and a half' bodywork by Park Royal, similar to the bodies illustrated on Commer chassis on page 230.

BELOW: This broadside aspect of a well loaded Cub shows passengers on the side bench seats and a large crows standing. The 'flap' used to signal a right turn is attached to the driver's cab door, below the bulb-horn. This 'flap' type of indicator lasted into the postwar era on new STC buses. Also evident is the later prewar livery style with white or cream mudguards and roof. *(F.W. York collection*

Albion Victor PK115

STC 113-149

After the Leyland Cubs, the STC turned to Albion Motors for twelve more oil engined chassis of similar dimensions. These comprised four that had been ordered by the China General Omnibus Co. (CGOC) of Shanghai, built in 1937 and eight built early in 1938. All but one were powered by the Gardner 4LK diesel engine, the other having a Perkins Panther engine. The wheelbase was five inches longer than that of the Leyland Cubs but in general, the Victor PK115, introduced in 1935, was a medium weight passenger chassis very similar to the side cab Cub and used by similar customers. It was, like the Cub, also available as a normal control chassis. There is no known connection between the China General Omnibus Co. and the STC and the purchase of four chassis originally intended for the CGOC is just chance. It seems that the Shanghai based bus company substituted its order for four oil engined Victors with one for four 3-axle (6-wheel) Valkyries, a heavier duty chassis powered by a Gardner 5LW engine and fitted locally with centre entrance bodywork. The four 2-axle Victors already built were constructed to a special overseas standard, as shown by their designation SpPK115 (the preceding 'Sp' indicating their difference from the standard model) and so they would have been transferred by Albion Motors to the Traction Company order. Albion had many customers in India and Africa and their bus chassis, robust and simple in construction, soon found favour in Singapore. The first twelve, STC 113-124 introduced in 1938, gave such satisfaction that an order for twenty-five was placed for delivery in 1939. These became STC 125-149 and would have been followed by a further batch carrying the numbers STC 150-179 but for the war in Europe.

The body style of the first Albion, STC 113, and probably the first four, was almost identical to that of the Cubs of 1937.

VEHICLE SPECIFICATION: Albion PK115	
Registration numbers:	STC 113-149 – (plus 150-179 never delivered)
Chassis:	Albion SpPK115
Engine:	Gardner 4LK (one vehicle – Perkins Panther)
Transmission:	4-speed Albion manual gearbox
Body make:	STC
Body layout:	as built B40FEXD — perimeter benches Post-1945 rebuilds B40CEX (capacity approximate)
Date introduced:	1938-39
Withdrawn:	Some survived to 1945/6 (others 1942-45?)
Total:	37
Length:	approx 26ft
Width:	7ft 4in
Wheelbase:	16ft 4in
Unladen weight:	?

The chassis numbers of those Albion SpPK115's delivered were as follows:

1938 delivery
25014F	built 1/37
25017I/J/K	built 6/37
25020L	built with Perkins engine
25021K/L	built 3/38
25022A/C/D/E/F	built 2/38

1939 delivery
25025G/H/I/J/K/L, 25026A/B	built 3/39
252026E/F/G/H/J/K	built 4/39
25027B/C/D/E/F/G/H/I/J/K/L	built 5/39

BELOW: The first Albion for STC was bodied following a style first seen on the Dennis G-type in 1929 and designed by the Shanghai Electric Construction Co for its then Singapore associated company. Comparison with the body of the Leyland Cub illustrated on the previous two pages shows the evolution—the Albion being half a bay longer behind the rear wheels. The same hardwood bench seats can be seen, complete with a neatly lathe-turned 'leg', just inside the entrance, next to the metal stanchion. *(F.W.York collection*

Differences included the replacement of the louvres in the top-lights by glass, an additional half-length side window bay at the rear overhang and 'spats', or trims, over the rear wheels, a styling feature very much in vogue in the 'thirties . The valance between the canopy and front body corner pillar was extended downward and forward in a continuous curve to meet the rear of the front mudguard. Sidelights were mounted at the extreme front of the mudguards, with large headlights either side of the businesslike Albion radiator. Bulb-horns were fitted from new.

From STC118 onwards, the body style differed and showed distinct signs of drawing away from the influence of Shanghai, albeit in minor ways.

The most noticeable change was to the shape of the front dome which lost the severe lines of the Shanghai style and became rounded, curving down to join the upper edge of the windscreen. Other feature differences included the curve of the swept-back front mudguards and a more even pillar spacing giving six similar sized side windows. The livery was changed, with the addition of white window surrounds and 'streamline' painted embellishments around the front and rear wheel-arches.

Survivors

The exact number of Albions to survive the occupation remains uncertain but the group, STC 1-15 (1945 series), were 'long term' survivors—and all were Albions. STC 16 upwards were 'short term' survivors and *not* necessarily Albions

At least two Albions, STC 5 & 8, were refurbished—possibly also rebodied—largely to the original design, but altered to have a centre entrance. With the prewar vehicle registration number system lost, the surviving buses were re-registered commencing at STC 1. Photographic evidence reveals three Albions, STC 5, STC 8 and STC 29, as survivors, STC 5 and 8 having the centre doorway. After some time back in service, STC 8 was rebodied and renumbered as STC 288 in order to release STC 8 for a later Albion, by which time it had become a staff bus.

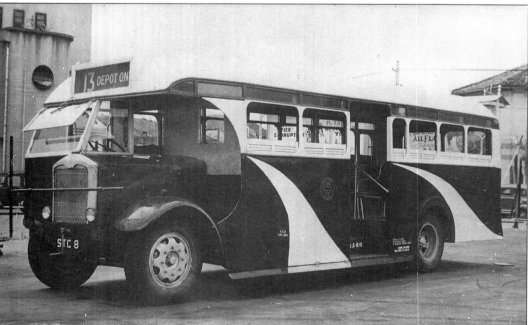

ABOVE: STC 120 probably when new in 1941 showing the improved styling when compared with the previous batch. Note the revised livery and evenly spaced body pillars. *(Straits Times*

LEFT: STC 8 in 1946 after being either extensively rebuilt—with a centre doorway—or completely rebodied. Unfortunately, no records survived to show which pre-1942 registration had been carried by this bus. The Louvred shutters in the windows can be seen clearly in this view. *(F.W. York collection*

ABOVE LEFT: The very end for pre-1942 Albion PK115, STC 5 as it lies derelict 'somewhere in Singapore'.

ABOVE RIGHT: The one time STC 8 in the 1950's after becoming a staff bus. Its 1945 registration had been transferred to a new Albion and the old PK115 had become STC 288.

Ford   114/116/ 118WF   STC 180-191

Very little can be told about these Fords except that, with the war in Europe having effectively cut Singapore off from its suppliers, the 'Imperial Preference' rules were waived to allow STC to acquire additional new bus chassis fro the United States of America. It was from that country that in late 1941 the Traction Company received 12 Ford chassis of semi-forward control layout, giving a short 'snub-nosed' bonnet. The only photograph known to the authors is a 1945 view showing a very dirty, neglected bus, with its body showing the same basic design as used for the later pre-1942 Albions except that it had an open rear platform.

VEHICLE SPECIFICATION:

Registration numbers:	S.T.C. 180-191
Chassis:	Ford { 118WF - 180-188. 116 189. 114 190-191.
Engine:	Ford
Transmission:	Manual crash gearbox
Body make:	STC contractor
Body layout:	B ??R
Date introduced:	1941
Wheelbase:	?
Unladen weight:	?

Photograph
The only known photograph of this type appears on page 67

Chevrolet

It is of note that eight Chevrolet chassis were also ordered in 1941 but were not delivered due to the occupation.

Ex-military chassis

With the occupation ended by mid September 1945, the task of moving people quickly outstripped the tattered resources of the Traction Company, whose vehicle park had been depleted to little short of junk. While the workshops slowly got to grips with the task of making buses roadworthy—for at least a minimum safety standard was expected—the interim British Military Administration made available a variety of military vehicles for temporary use as lorry buses. These varied widely in make and a few in original, unconverted condition, are illustrated on page 68.

As the situation gradually improved, probably with the arrival in 1946 of the first Bedford OBs, bus bodies of various conceptions were constructed on the ex-military chassis. Some took the form of a square 'coachbuilt' box-shaped saloon mounted on the chassis behind the original lorry cab, while others were given complete bus-style. Very details of specification can be traced but, no doubt, students of military vehicles may have some answers.

Additionally, there were those vehicles which were captured from the enemy—at least one complete Japanese bus was reported as having been in Singapore during the occupation. Initially classified 'CV' these Captured Vehicles were but reports suggest that they were later re-designated 'CEV'—Captured Enemy Vehicle. There can be little doubt that these were the least sought after types, both on grounds of distaste but also the more practical reason, lack of spare parts.

Many Ford, Chevrolet and Dodge military chassis were bodied as conventional small, bonnetted, buses and many served the Traction Company well. With supplies of new buses and trolleybuses being delayed by the privations and shortages of postwar Britain, these military buses stayed on longer than anticipated and gave STC trojan service.

RIGHT: After sale for further use as a Private Bus and re-registered S 9822, this ex-military Bedford OXD truck chassis had been fitted with a passenger compartment of boxlike proportions but with a refined coachbuilt appearance. Engine was Bedford WD-type, 6-cyl, petrol, 27.34hp, with an 85.72mm x 101.6mm bore and stroke. The wheelbase was 111inches

BELOW: Unfortunately, not so much detail is known about the chassis of this Chevrolet, except to say that it was right-hand drive and, as such, may have been from the Canadian factory. Again, no photograph of such a vehicle has been discovered of this type whilst still with STC and this substitute view shows what had become S 3484 whilst working for Tuan Wong School in the early 1950's.

Bedford OB

Although not generally thought of as a prewar chassis type, the Bedford OB had been introduced before hostilities commenced in September 1939 and continued and continued to be made into 1940 when all bus production was stopped by the government, by which time only 73 had been built.

The chassis ordered by STC were probably all that could be obtained at the time and would have represented a backward step in vehicle size. However, they were new and they were very reliable, allowing workshop staff time to attend to rehabilitating the prewar and ex-military fleet.

The chassis was the standard Bedford product with a 14ft 6in wheelbase and 84bhp, 6-cylinder petrol engine. The driving position, while set back was more semi-forward than normal-control. Unlike the OL truck in the same series, the OB handbrake was located on the offside, not near the centre, due to the majority of bus bodies on this chassis type having access to the driving position from inside the vehicle and in this respect the STC examples were no exception.

Upon arrival in Singapore, Hock Hin Thye provided the bodywork which broke with prewar tradition and introduced the centre entrance/exit

The roof was covered with stretched canvas which was bituminised to make it weather proof. Side windows were unglazed but featured standard tropical monsoon shutters with louvred slats which could be pulled up in torrential rain while maintaining a small degree of air circulation. Above the side windows was a shallow top-light or standee-window and all these were glazed.

Destination equipment at the front was in two parts; a narrow destination screen above the driver's side windscreen and a larger square route number above the nearside windscreen—both were fitted with roller blinds.

VEHICLE SPECIFICATION: Bedford OB

Registration numbers:	STC 157 to STC250—some later renumbered
Chassis:	Bedford Model OB
Engine:	Bedford 84bhp, 6-cylinder petrol.
Transmission:	Bedford 4-speed manual gearbox
Body make:	Hock Hin Thye
Body layout:	B ? C
Date introduced:	1946
Total:	94
Length:	Approx 24ft 6in
Width:	7ft 1in approx
Wheelbase:	14ft 6in
Gross vehicle weight:	7tons 3cwt

As was the case with some Albions which survived the occupation, a small fleet number was carried on the bonnet side of the Bedfords, the number in this case being prefixed by 'B'. However, little is known as to the extent of the use of fleet numbers, neither for how long they were used, nor which classes of vehicle carried them.

Following a pilot overhaul to assess the feasability of refurbishing the fleet of Bedford OBs, STC 157 emerged with a single destination screen displaying both route and route number on a single blind, just as on the Albions, Falcons and Ransomes. No further examples were so treated and quite soon the refurbished STC 157, was re-registered STC 201 in order to allow the Guy Arab series to commence at 157. The original Bedford with number STC201 was sent for scrap and its registration number donated to STC 157. The rebuilt Bedford was also given a metal panelled roof, minus the troublesome canvas. See photo page 116

BELOW: Bedford OB, STC 186 (with small numerals on the bonnet side), demonstrates a degree of over crowding in this Straits Times press photograph but clearly shows a passenger seated alongside the driver who was enclosed inside a small 'cab' area, surrounded by a metal grille behind and a glass screen to his left. A separate offside cab door was provided, an unusual feature on an OB. An illustration of a Bedford OB, STC 182, when brand new, appears on page 69 of this volume. *(Straits Times*

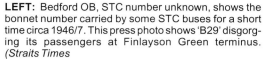

LEFT: Bedford OB, STC number unknown, shows the bonnet number carried by some STC buses for a short time circa 1946/7. This press photo shows 'B29' disgorging its passengers at Finlayson Green terminus. *(Straits Times*

BELOW: STC 208 stands alongside a civilian registered, Phase 1 Standard Vanguard at the time when these were so familiar as staff cars for the Armed Forces in British overseas bases, including Singapore.

LEFT: By the mid 1950's, STC had changed its fleet livery to mainly cream with green roof and trim, including the bonnets of the OBs. Those which retained the bituminised canvas roof covering retained black roofs, such as STC 164 in 'new' livery. Of interest is the retention into this era of the offside direction indicator 'flap' to be seen here in extended position below the window of the driver's cab door.

BOTTOM LEFT: A very down at heel Bedford receives attention at the roadside and at the same time displays how the tropical heat and wet have caused the canvas roof covering to deteriorate.

Ford (USA)
194" wheelbase 'School Bus' chassis

Following shortly after the Bedford OB's, STC received twelve Ford (USA) chassis of similar type to those acquired by China Motor Bus in Hong Kong at about the same time and, probably, for the same reason, ie, that STC was desperate for additional buses and the local Ford agents could supply quickly. In Hong Kong the Imperial Preference rule was not waived and the taxation authorities added 15% to the price;. Given similar Colonial Governments, there is nothing to suppose that things were any different in Singapore.

In general appearance, the 'School Buses' bore a family resemblance to many of the ex-military chassis upon whose chassis bus-style bodies had been fitted. The main differences being the much shorter wheelbase, the corresponding overall length, and much higher chassis frame.

The 'School Bus' chassis were low-framed, specifically designed for passenger work, and of the bonnetted type, with driver behind the engine. The driver was further sat further back than on British-built types, such as the Bedford OB or Austin CX, leaving less room for passenger accommodation. From photographic evidence, the STC buses differed from those with CMB,

VEHICLE SPECIFICATION: Ford (USA) 'School Bus	
Registration numbers:	STC 251–262
Chassis:	Ford (USA) Model 1946 'School Bus'
Engine:	Ford G8T, 8-cyl, petrol, 90.7bhp
Transmission:	Ford 4-speed manual gearbox
Body make:	Hock Hin Thye
Body layout:	B ? C—Peripheral seating for about 30
Date introduced:	1946
Total:	12
Length:	approx 24ft 6in
Wheelbase:	194 inches (16ft 2in or 4.92 metres)
Unladen weight:	? —Similar vehicles in Hong Kong were 3tons 7cwt

Hong Kong, in that the front axle was of the narrow track variety with the result that the front wheels appeared to be set under the front wing or mudguard.

Headlights were incorporated as a part of the wings and the whole appearance has a distinct North American flavour.

The body was constructed in Singapore by Hock Hin Thye and conformed to the 'standard' STC appearance, with narrow toplight windows above each side window. Only the toplights were glazed.

BELOW: The Ford 'School Buses' did not survive as long into the 1950's, when most of the photographs in this volume were taken, as did the Bedfords and other early post-occupation buses. As a result, of the immense collection of photographs available for selection, only this one has come to light of a Ford, STC 256, although others do feature in a line-up shown on page 74.

Dennis Falcon Mark II

STC 16-115

The Directors of the STC, isolated in London, and in the confidence that eventually their company would be returned to them after the cessation of the war against the Japanese, had placed advance orders for new postwar buses in the same way as they had done for trolleybuses. From 1942, it was possible to place orders for buses with British manufacturers, but doing so was merely to be allocated a place in the queue for vehicles that would not be built until the war was over. The last new prewar buses had been the Leyland Cubs, and Leyland did not intend to resume production of lightweight buses at the Kingston-on-Thames factory, so the Directors of the STC looked at equivalent chassis from other manufacturers. Both Guy and Dennis built small numbers of lightweight bus chassis featuring a half-cab arrangement: Guy had the Vixen model, and Dennis the Falcon. These both found customers outside Britain, notably in India and China, although the war had interrupted production and neither type had been built in large numbers. Perhaps because Guy were concentrating on the production of the Arab, under an arrangement whereby Guy and Daimler could build double deck buses, and Bedford single deck buses, for the British Government, who in turn allocated these scarce vehicles to British operators in urgent need of new stock, the STC placed an advance order for 100 Dennis Falcon chassis.

As things turned out, not only was this to be the largest order for this type of bus chassis, it was also to be the only order completed by Dennis in the postwar period for this type. British operators received a number of Dennis Falcons of the normal control variety, which were suitable for operation by one man. The postwar versions were nominated Falcon Mark II, the half cab forward control variety as used in Singapore being the P2, whilst the normal control version was the P3 or P4., with a final updated version called P5. The STC buses carried the chassis numbers 101P2 -200P2....note that Dennis, at this time, showed the vehicle type after the serial number, and also began each different series with the number 101, so 101P2 was the first of the type.

The Falcon was a purpose built passenger chassis, powered by a Gardner 4LK diesel engine, driving through a four speed

VEHICLE SPECIFICATION: Dennis Falcon

Registration numbers:	STC 16-115
Chassis:	Dennis Falcon Mark II
Engine:	Gardner 4LK
Transmission:	4 speed manual gearbox
Body make:	Lee Kiat Seng
Body layout:	B35 + 17C
Date introduced:	1947-8
Withdrawn:	between 1957-1964
Total :	100
Length:	approx 27 feet
Wheelbase:	17 feet 6 inches

manual gearbox. The braking system was hydraulic. The exposed radiator was characterised by the unusual narrow shape, tapering towards the base. In its half cab form, the STC Falcons looked like a scaled down counterpart of the standard heavyweight single-decker widely used on British roads, and—until the advent of the STC Guy Arabs in 1956—represented in Singapore by one sole bus, a Leyland Tiger, in the fleet of Tay Koh Yat. Apart from this bus, only the STC operated vehicles with British style half cabs. Other aspects of the scaled down nature of the Dennis Falcons were the wheelbase, one foot shorter than the usual wheelbase of contemporary full-size single deckers, and the lower floor level, particularly when compared with the Albion Victors. A seating capacity of 35 was still achieved within the limited dimensions of these buses. Other operators, such as Green Bus, no doubt took note of the advantage of placing the driving position at the side of the engine, and converted normal control vehicles to forward control in order to increase the seating capacity.

Several of these buses were destroyed in arson attacks (see page 83) and one was rebodied *circa* 1956 to become STC 260. Few STC buses were ever rebodied but this particular vehicle was additionally unusual as it became the only full-fronted Dennis Falcon—illustrated on the following page.

BELOW: The 100th and final Dennis Falcon, STC 115 stands in hot sunshine as it is posed for the photographer in almost original condition. The apparent absence of either shutters or glazing in the side windows is evident. The bodywork bore great resemblance to that of the contemporary Ransomes trolleybuses

LEFT: STC 20 in post-1955 livery, showing the modified destination screen with rubber mounted glass. In this view, the louvred shutters in the side windows are partially raised and the driver sips tea at a roadside cooked food stall convieniently located near the bus stand.

CENTRE: The rear view of a Dennis Falcon, showing the registration number repeated—on the roof, above the central window pillar and in the lower rear panelling behind rubber mounted glass.

Rebodied Dennis Falcon STC 260

A number of STC buses were destroyed by arson during strikes and other civil disturbances. One Dennis Falcon so damaged was considered to be fit for further use, and so a new body was constructed to the design then current for Albion Victors. This Falcon, therefore, became unique as the only example of its type with a full front, and resembled at first glance buses of the series STC300-330, although slightly shorter. It took a then vacant number STC 260: this later passed to STC 10 when it was renumbered to make way for Isuzus.

LEFT: STC 260, referred to in the text as the only Falcon to be rebodied with a full-width cab, with the result looking not unlike an Albion.

199

Albion Victor FT39N

STC 116-156 and 263-287

The postwar fleet still contained examples of the Albion marque that had survived the wartime period, and it is not surprising that a repeat order should be placed with Albion Motors Limited to follow on after the Dennisses. With an exposed radiator but a full front, the Albion series FT Victors were intended for passenger use, but were derived from a truck design, and indeed many were used as lorries or vans in Great Britain. Their chief merit was robust construction and good ground clearance, and Victors were exported to many parts of the world. In Singapore, they appeared in both the STC and some of the fleets of the Chinese companies.

Production of the Albion Victor FT39N commenced in 1947. The chassis was shorter than the Dennis Falcon, with a wheelbase of 15ft 11⁵/₈ins. The power unit was a 4-cylinder diesel engine of Albion manufacture, which drove via a four speed constant mesh gearbox. The brakes were of the vacuum-servo assisted type. The driving position was alongside the engine, but no examples are known of fitted with a half width cab. In Singapore, the full width cab was the normal arrangement on most buses of the 1945-1955 period, and the layout persisted locally much longer than elsewhere, many bus chassis intended to have forward entrances, and therefore fitted with set back front axles, still being equipped with bodywork in which the driver was provided with a full width cab as late as the mid-sixties.

In all, 66 Albion Victor FT39N chassis were built for STC, and these were fitted with 32 seater bodies with central entrance/exit by the body contractor to the Company, Lee Kiat Seng. The registration numbers allocated were in two sequences, STC 116-

VEHICLE SPECIFICATION: Albion FT39N	
Registration numbers:	STC 116-156, 263-287
Chassis:	Albion Victor FT39N
Engine:	Albion 4-cylinder diesel
Transmission:	4 speed con-mesh manual gearbox
Body make:	Lim Kiat Seng
Body layout:	B32+16C
Date introduced:	1949-51
Withdrawn:	??
Total:	66
Length:	approx 27 feet
Length	26 feet
Wheelbase	15ft 11⁵/₈ins

156, which took the numbers up to the point where Bedford OBs intervened, and STC 263-287. Then, in order to separate the subsequent buses which had a slightly longer wheelbase, and therefore an increased seating capacity, a few numbers were left unused, and Albion Victors continued upwards from STC 300.

STC116-135 were based on chassis built in 1949, and had a style of body obviously derived from that fitted to the Dennis Falcons, but without the half cab. The front panel and radiator were the same as supplied to the Albion FT series trucks, and so neither came as low as was usual on passenger chassis, giving the front a rather old-fashioned appearance. Like the Falcons, the Victors had a fender bar across the radiator. During their lives these buses sported several variations of the STC colours, and one arrangement of the livery attempted to make the frontal

BELOW: When new the early postwar Albions FT39N Victors had windscreens which sloped downwards away from the centre and had a corresponding cab side-window which also sloped downwards. This bus, STC 139 was from the second (1950) delivery but differed little from the original first (STC 116 to 135 batch. Here STC 139 shows off the styling of its Lee Kiat Seng body to advantage and a number of features can be seen. There is a 'bus full' sign in the toplight of the window immediately in front of the doorway; the doorway does have doors fitted but, in practice, these were seldom used in service, being manually operated by the conductor. *(Albion Motors photo, courtesy F. W. York*

LEFT: First series (STC 116–135) Albion Victor FT39N, STC 132, shows how the windscreens were rebuilt with a horizontal lower edge, together with correspondingly rebuilt cabside windows which have acquired neater, radius corners. This photograph also illustrates the type in the '1952' livery first tried on STC 1–5 (qv). (*F. W. York collection*

CENTRE LEFT: STC 127 in original livery whilst on Learner driver duties, the modification to the windscreen is highlighted by the style of the paintwork.

LOWER LEFT: STC 271 of the 1951 batch shows the slope of the cab windows is extended to include the window in the cab door. The other major difference was the destination indicator which was behind a screen, the glass of which was set flush into the front of the roof dome and mounted in rubber.

appearance less severe by suggesting a sloping rather than a straight bottom to the windscreen. One, maybe more, members of this group of buses received a rebuilt front of the style described below for STC 136 onwards.

STC 136-159, STC 263-270 were the order for 29 chassis built in 1950, and were similar to the previous batch except at the front. The windscreen bottom sloped down, as did the side windows of the driving cab to give a double benefit: the driver had better visibility, and the external visual effect was less harsh. There was also less taper on the cab sides, adding a couple of extra inches to the width of the front face of the bus. Both this and the previous group were built new with a row of small glazed lights at cant rail level, a relic of the prewar buses fitted with slatted shutters in lieu of glazing, but most Victors lost this feature upon rebuilding.

STC 271-287 comprised an order for 17 chassis built in 1951, and on which the bodies showed a further stage in the evolution of the STC concept of the Singapore bus body. The small glazed lights were omitted and a rain guard was now situated above the glazed side windows, which continued to drop downwards into the body sides. At the front, the destination indicator was housed directly into the roof dome, rather than be mounted in a separate box. Further bodies of this aspect were built in 1951 on long wheelbase Victors, which instead of carrying the numbering onwards from STC 288, began a new series at STC 300.

Albion Victor FT39L and FT39AL   STC 300-413

The Victor FT39L had a wheelbase one foot longer than the FT39N model, thus allowing an extra four seats to be installed in a slightly longer body. Otherwise the model was identical to its predecessor, and together with its variant, classified FT39AL, it became the most numerous form of Albion Victor in the STC fleet. In all there were 31 of type FT39L, dating from 1951-2, and registered STC 300-330, and 83 of type FT39AL, dating from 1952-4, and registered STC 331-413

The first fifty received bodies seating 36 passengers, exactly four more than hitherto, but the next thirty-seven had 37 seats, and the remainder 40 seats. This change of capacity was the result of a changeover to forward facing seats. It must be admitted that the dimensions allowed for seat spacing were not over generous, but there were strict rules on carrying capacity, and these persist to this day in Singapore. Two facts must not be forgotten. The first is that the stature of some Asian peoples tends to be smaller than that of Europeans, and the second is a practical point and well known amongst bus designers. It is dangerous to build buses in such a way that they can be easily overloaded. By putting the maximum number of seats into a bus, a limit is placed on the spaces available for standing passengers, and the seats and stanchions attached to them provide support for those who are obliged to stand. It is not unknown in some of the less well regulated places in the world for buses to be denuded of seats in order to increase capacity: the result can be an unstable and overstressed vehicle. The STC policy (shared by all Singapore bus companies) was to place passengers evenly distributed and sitting down inside the vehicle. Passengers forced to stand, and those moving out of seats when boarding or alighting, would have plenty of handgrips to hold. Of course, STC until this time had operated trolleybuses and motor buses with longitudinal seats (or lateral bench seats), but they belonged to an earlier era when traffic speeds were low. The move to transverse seating was as much for safety and better comfort, as it was to be yet another improvement in the STC designed bus.

STC 300-310 were constructed on chassis built in 1951, and form a continuum of the style adopted for STC 271-287, and were

VEHICLE SPECIFICATION: Albion Victor FT39L / AL

Registration numbers:	STC 300-330—(type FT39L)
	STC 331-413—(type FT39AL)
Chassis:	Albion Victor
Engine:	Albion 4-cylinder diesel
Transmission:	4 speed constant-mesh manual gearbox
Body:	Lee Kiat Seng
Body layout:	36+18 standing—(STC 300-349)
	37+17 standing—(STC 350-376)
	40+13 standing—(STC 377-413)
Date:	1951-4
Withdrawn:	between 1968-70
Total:	114
Length:	approx 27ft
Width:	7ft 4 ins
Wheelbase:	16 ft 11½ in

Chassis number check:

FT39AL	1952	19 (STC 331-349)—A
	1953	27 (STC350-376)—B
	1954	37 (STC377-413)—C

A—Albion records give 20 chassis (3/52 & 6/52)
B—Albion records give 28 chassis (7/52 & 12/52)
C—Albion records give 38 chassis (3/52 & 6/52)
The reason for one each chassis of each type is unclear.

followed by STC 311-330, on chassis built in 1952. During this year, Albion Motors made a small modification to the chassis design, and further vehicles were classified FT39AL. In motor engineering, it is quite common to use the letters A, B, C, etc. to indicate variations to a basic product, but Albion was unique in also using the first twelve letters of the alphabet to form part of the chassis number. After the Second World War, the letters G and I were omitted from the sequence, so that from 1945 until Albion production ceased in the 1970s, the ten letters A,B,C,D,E,F,H,J,K,L were the equivalent of a final digit on Albion Motors' chassis numbers.

BELOW: In this offside view of STC 304, the longer of the wheelbase of the FT39L—and AL—is apparant when compared to the earlier FT39N on the previous two pages. The body styling follows the trend set by the last FT39N's, STC 271–287, but the cab side windows sloped lower than previously.

ABOVE: STC 320, an FT39L, in original condition, stands posed in front of some imposing Colonial architecture. The distinctive ribs along the lower body sides were a feature of Lee Kiat Seng bodywork for some years. Even for this formal posed photo, the folding passenger doors remained open and functionless, possibly due to their being manually operated under difficult operating conditions.

BELOW: STC 391 of the later, 1954, batch, was an FT39AL seen here passing the Railway Station in June 1956, when just two years old. The body has a more refined windscreen arrangement where the lower margins are radiused and the entire screen each side opens from hinges at the top, rather than the earlier arrangement where just the upper part could be opened for additional ventilation.

Albion Victor FT39AL & ALX   STC6-10 & STC222-41

(STC 6-10 later re-numbered STC 242–246)

The final development of the Albion Victor in the STC fleet was to take place in 1954-5, when twenty of the extended wheelbase FT39ALX model were placed in service, fitted with bodywork seating 44. STC 222-31 of 1954, and STC 232-41 of 1955 took numbers now vacated by scrapped vehicles, but five additional buses of similar type were also delivered in 1954 and took the numbers STC 6-10. As Albion records do not show five further vehicles sold direct to the Traction Company, it is assumed these came from stock held in Singapore by Progress Motors, then the Albion agents.

The bodywork fitted was not dissimilar to previous designs, but the following differences can be pointed out. The bodies were longer, and had an extra row of seats: the windows were of half-drop type, that is to say, the upper part of the glazing let down over the lower half: previous designs had windows which let down into the body sides, and the bodies had flat sides, without any ribs or ridges. The next new vehicles for STC, the Guy Arabs, were to develop this body style further. These vehicles also adopted the cream livery, with green roof and side flashes.

The all-metal bodies (STC 232–41) were further distinguished by the use of longer window bays.

VEHICLE SPECIFICATION: Albion FT39ALX

Chassis:	Albion Victor FT39ALX (STC 222–41) or, FT 39AL (STC 6–10)
Engine:	Albion 4 cyl. diesel
Transmission:	4 speed con-mesh gearbox
Body:	Lee Kiat Seng
Seating capacity:	B40 + 13C (STC 6-10) B44 + 14C (STC 222-241)
Withdrwn:	by 1971
Total:	25
Length:	30 ft 0 ins—STC 6-10: approx 27ft
Width:	7ft 6 in
Height:	?
Wheelbase:	16ft 11½ (STC 6-10) or 18 ft 0 in (STC 222-4)

The Albion Victor continued in production after 1955 for another three years, but STC 241 was the last for STC. The Chinese bus companies continued to use the long FT39ALX, which was unique to the Singapore market, for a while, but it was eventually replaced by the VT series, and then the very succesful Viking.

LEFT: STC 240, A Victor FT39ALX and the penultimate Albion Victor of the STC fleet, is seen in August 1955 standing at a Request Stop. The side windows and smooth flat sides of the body are features shared by the subsequent Guy Arabs. The longer wheelbase is evidenced by the additional, but slightly smaller, side window ahead of the centre doorway, when compared with bodies on the FT39AL chassis, below.

LOWER LEFT: STC 7 was photographed on route 18A one month before, in July 1955. Note that the window arrangement is different, as too is the cab door and front roof design. To allow access to the cab, two stirrup like steps are attached to the right hand side of the front mudguard (a feature also seen on STC 240).

Albion Victor FT39AN

STC1-5 *(later STC251-5)*

STC placed an order for five of the shorter wheelbase Victor chassis in 1953, in order to build five special 'luxury' buses, with transverse seating, for use on a City Circular Service. This required buses of the shorter length in order to negotiate certain tight corners and congested streets. As this was an additional order, placed after the main order, Albion Motors supplied five chassis (chassis numbers 73712C/D/E/F/K) that had originally been built for sale in Australia. To make them readily distinguishable from other STC Albions, these were painted in a 'reversed' livery, with cream replacing green, and vice-versa. This was a common practice at this time amongst British bus companies, to distinguish coaches used on interurban services, and therefore fitted with luxury seating, from urban buses which otherwise might be similar to look at.

Inside, however, there was a marked difference—these five buses were the first to have transverse (forward facing) seats arranged in pairs along each side; evidence of their 'special' nature.

These Albions with their well appointed bodies were soon to find themsleves on ordinary duties, as the City Circular Service, allocated route number 7, was a failure. The attractive livery, however, was not deemed a failure and was subsequently adopted

VEHICLE SPECIFICATION: Albion FT39AN

Registration numbers:	STC1-5 (later STC251-5):
Chassis:	Albion Victor FT39AN
Engine:	Albion 4-cylinder
Transmission:	Manual constant-mesh gearbox
Body make:	Lee Kiat Seng
Body layout:	B30+15C
Date introduced:	1952
Total:	5
Length:	approximately 25ft
Width:	7ft 4 ins
Wheelbase:	16ft

in a slightly modified form for the entire bus and trolleybus fleet.

When new, these vehicles took the numbers STC 1 to 5, now brought back into use for the third time. In July 1962, with the arrival of the first Isuzu rear engined Japanese buses, the lowest STC numbers were reallocated yet again. STC 1 and 2 were renumbered STC 251 & 252 with the introduction of the two air-conditioned prototype Isuzus, to be followed later in the year by STC 3 to 5 when the first main batch of Isuzus was disembarked.

BELOW: For its ill fated 1952 City Circular Service, the STC ordered five short wheelbase Albion Victor FT39AN which were given high specification bodied by Lee Kiat Seng. The most striking difference from buses in the fleet hitherto was the reversal of the two main colours, green and cream, making up the then current livery. With cream body and green roof and embellishments, STC 1 stands outside the body manufacturer's premises. The change of livery was a success—the City Circular Service was not. After a few weeks, the five little Albions were relegated to regular bus duties. An offside view of one of these short Albions appears on page 89 of this volume.

AEC Regent III—double deck demonstrator

Following the debut et debacle of the Straker-Squire in 1904, there was a gap of almost fifty years before a double-deck bus was to carry passengers in Singapore. Although the AEC type 603 trolleybuses had been an undoubted success, STC had never purchased any motor buses by that firm, and AEC perhaps felt it was time to reintroduce their products to Singapore.

In October 1953, a double-decker AEC Regent III from the fleet of the General Transport Company, Kuala Lumpur (KL), was sent to Singapore on demonstration. It was newly repainted in the dark green, with light green roof and wings, of the GTC, but had a specially applied slogan between decks, which proclaimed 'AEC Makers of London's buses' This vehicle was an AEC Regent III with preselective gearbox and 9.6 litre engine, and bore a Park Royal body of the usual British 'provincial' pattern, except for the provision of tropical ventilation.

The bus, GTC No.52 (registered BA 6421 in KL), was used for two weeks in STC service and, for the first week it ran on service 18, Finlayson Green–Tampines, and for the second week it was operated on STC's most frequent motor-bus service 10, Moulmein Road–Neil Road. Subsequently the vehicle was inspected by the Tay Koh Yat and Hock Lee Amalgamated companies and it is believed that the Singapore-Johore Express also showed interest.

Whilst with STC, the double-decker caused a 'mild sensation', with crowds of passengers wishing to ride on the top deck. It was 'five-man-operated', with a driver, two conductors and two inspectors. The use of two conductors on double deckers is not uncommon outside the British Isles, but the need for the inspectors was special to this case: they were there to control the crowds, and to ensure there was no standing on the upper deck.

No orders for double-deckers were to ensue at this point in time. The probable reason was that a bus seating 56 and with room for 5 standing, and which required a three man crew, which weighed over 8 tons and was driven by a 9.6 litre engine offered no advantages over a 44 seat single decker, with room for 18 standing passengers, which weighed less than 6 tons and was driven by a 7 litre cngine. The next order for single deckers did, however, show that some features of the AEC had been appreciated: STC ordered a batch of 5LW powered Guy Arab IVs, with preselective gearboxes. These re-introduced the half cab layout in the STC fleet, and were the first motor buses on heavy-weight chassis.

Almost twenty years were to pass before a double-decker reappeared on the streets of Singapore, and this time, as described on the following page, it really was a London bus! But that is a story for Volume Two.

VEHICLE SPECIFICATION: AEC Regent III	
Registration numbers:	BA 6421 (Kuala Lumper)
Chassis:	AEC Regent III
Engine:	AEC 9.6 litre
Transmission:	Fluid flywheel and pre-selective gearbox
Body make:	Park Royal Vehicles
Body layout:	H30/26+5Rop
Date on demonstration:	1953
New:	1950
Total:	1
Length:	26ft
Width:	7ft 6in
Height:	14ft 3in
Wheelbase:	16ft 3in
Unladen weight:	8tons 2quarters 1pound

LEFT: Despite its long drive from Kuala Lumpur to Singapore, the Park Royal bodywork of AEC Regent III, BA 6421, of the General Transport Company of Kuala Lumpur looks in pristine condition as it stands posed for the press at the Macpherson Road premises of the Singapore traction Company in October 1953. The advantages of double-deck operation were apparently not appreciated by the STC Board and the only feature of the model to receive acclaim—and orders—was the Wilson-type pre-selective gearbox fitted in Guy Arab Mk IV single-deckers. *(Standard Photo)*

ABOVE: The impressive sight as the first modern double decker to run in service in Singapore crosses the Singapore River beneath the equally impressive girders of Anderson Bridge whilst operating on Route 18.

BELOW: The view in this photograph could *almost* have been of a sunny day in England. The AEC Regent double decker looks quite at home behind a line of STC single-deck buses. Operating conditions were quite similar to those in Kuala Lumpur, to the north, the home ground of the AEC, but, despite this, the management of the Traction Company felt ill at ease with having to control crowds of passengers unused to double-deckers. Regionally, Kowloon was also successfully operating double-deckers, using two conductors.

Guy Arab Mk IV

The purchase of Guy Arabs represented a break with tradition in several ways. For the first time, STC placed an order for heavyweight chassis, of a type designed for the rigours of city traffic. Similar chassis, although built with a shorter wheelbase, were also in use in Asia with the China Motor Bus Company in Hong Kong, whose fleet of such vehicles, some single and some double deck, was—with the inclusion of Arab Mk V's—eventually to total over five hundred. Although the terrain over which the Guys had to operate differed between Hong Kong and Singapore, the Arab IV's in both locations were powered by the Gardner 5LW engine, renowned for its economy, which drove through a spring-activated, Wilson preselective gearbox, operated by a floor mounted lever. This arrangement differs from the system found, for example, on many of London's buses, in which the gearbox was operated by means of a lever fitted to the steering column. On some makes and/or models, this remote lever changes the gears by of compressed air. The Singapore Guy Arabs did not have a compressed air system, therefore the brakes were actuated by vacuum and the gears changed directly by means of the floor mounted lever.

Other new features of these buses was the overall width of eight feet (all previous Singapore buses had been at least six inches narrower), and the fitting of the then fashionable and oddly named 'tin fronts'. This term, slightly derogatory and beloved by traditionalists who preferred buses to have exposed radiators, can be regarded in this case as semi-official, as Guy records refer to the front panels supplied as 'tinwork'. The first

VEHICLE SPECIFICATION: Guy Arab Mk IV:	
Registration numbers:	STC 157-221, STC 414-481
Chassis:	Guy Arab Mk IV–single-deck
Engine:	Gardner 5LW 'economy' version
Transmission:	4-speed Wilson preselective, epicyclic, gearbox
Body make:	Lee Kiat Seng, all-metal
Body layout:	B42+14CEX
Date introduced:	1956-1959
Withdrawn:	1971—dispersed to amalgamated bus companies
Total:	133
Length:	30ft (nominal)
Width:	8ft
Height:	9ft 9in (approx)
Wheelbase:	18ft 6in
Unladen weight:	6 tons 11 cwt 3 qtrs — or 6tons 4cwt 3 qtrs (S'pore front)

Singapore order for 30 Guy Arabs had bonnet assemblies and fronts of the type generally known as 'Birmingham fronts', named after the city which first specified that particular design. Some Guy Arabs later carried 'Johannesburg' fronts, whilst contemporary Daimler buses sported 'Manchester' fronts, although in Hong Kong, 90 Daimlers for Kowloon Motor Bus had the Birmingham style.

The STC also appears to have felt the desire to have a frontal design all of its own, for when the next order for Guy Arabs was placed, the specification called for no front structure to be supplied, except that a radiator grille and a Guy badge was to be packed with each chassis upon dispatch. These parts were subsequently incorporated into a front end design built locally....there were several variations of what we might call the 'Singapore front', but it cannot be exactly compared with the designs actually made by Guy and fitted to the chassis before sale

BELOW: The first thirty Guy Arab Mk IV's ordered by STC had the so-called 'Birmingham' or 'tin' front with a very rounded cowl incorporating a grille typical for the type. The grille had a Guy badge and, above this, was the 'Red Indian' inscribed 'Feathers in our Caps'—the then current Guy trade mark. The cab of these first Arabs were distinctive in having the offside cab window angled towards the front giving a narrower windscreen than on Hong Kong variants—and indeed than on later STC buses. Here STC 157—the first of its type—poses for the press. Of note are the small rectangular windows in the front bulkhead and the chrome plated front bumper. *(Straits Times*

to the purchaser. The 'Singapore front' caused another modification to be made by the manufacturer. Guy Arabs supplied with factory made front end assemblies had, in common with most other buses of this style (i.e. front engined, with the driving position alongside the engine) the electrical control box mounted on a cross bulkhead behind the driver's seat. This box controls the lighting and various electric circuits, and usually contained the starting button. As most of the Singapore chassis were being supplied without the front end structures, Guy supplied extra lengths of cabling to allow this box to be fixed ahead of the driving position, to the right of the driver.

The Guy Arab chassis were delivered to Singapore in *completely knocked down* (ckd) form. The STC called for an unusual variation of ckd. The general procedure when bus chassis are supplied in ckd form is for the manufacturer to pack all the necessary parts into wooden crates, generally in multiples of 2 or 4, and the assemblers can then put the vehicles together piecemeal over a period, and possibly they might intermingle parts. The STC order called for the chassis to be assembled and road tested in Great Britain, and then to be dismantled and packed for shipping and reassembly at destination. It follows that, because of this method, the chassis were more likely to fit together without any problems, but they were more expensive to purchase because of the labour costs in Great Britain for assembly, testing and disassembly. Of course, chassis prepared in this way would arrive at destination with some pieces already attached that it was not necessary to remove in order to fit the pieces in crates. The method described above is distinct from the modern practice of building vehicle chassis, and removing the wheels and a few oddly shaped parts, so that the ready assembled chassis may then be placed in a sea-going container.

The Singapore Guy Arabs had a very distinctive appearance, not only because of the locally produced front end design, but because of the extra width, the long wheelbase (18' 6") and the

ABOVE: This view of STC 160 at Serangoon Garden Estate was taken soon after introduction of the Guy Arabs and while the estate was still under construction. The curious design of the cab offside can bee appreciated with its narrow windscreen and wider front panel. The school children's uniforms would not have looked out of place in Britain on a hot summer's day

apparent low overall height. The chassis were of the Arab Mark IV type, not the later Mark V which did have a lower set chassis, so the squat appearance of the Singapore Guy Arabs was partly an illusion created by the width, and by the rather shallow roof profile of the locally produced all-metal bodywork. This was clearly evolved from the standard STC bodies as fitted to Dennis Falcons and Albion Victors: the most distinctive and obvious feature being the central entrance/exit. However, the older STC

BELOW: The premier member of the Guy Arab type in Singapore, STC 157, shows-off its offside and allows us to see that it weighed 131 hundredweight 84 pounds or 6 tons 11 cwt 3 qtrs as more usually quoted in the UK in those pre-metric days. Although bodied by Lim Kiat Seng in Singapore, the front dome bears a distinct resemblance to Metal Sections pressings as used on Guy Arab single-deck buses of the China Motor Bus Co in Hong Kong. (Straits Times

buses were based on narrow chassis with fairly high chassis frames, whereas the Arabs were based on a wide chassis with a cranked frame to allow for the fitting of either double or single deck bodywork. Aft of the rear axle, the chassis frames swept down to allow for a rear platform, should the vehicle be fitted with a double deck body, so the overall height of the passenger saloon on this class of vehicle could be kept down. The low-set bodies of the Guy Arabs were ideal for the smooth level roads of the STC operating area, but when they were dispersed to the amalgamated companies after 1971, they found less favour with operators whose buses had to pass over less smooth roads outside the city limits. From the passengers' viewpoint, the main features of these buses were the spacious interiors and smooth gearchanges effected by the 4 speed Wilson pre-selective gearboxes, which no doubt the drivers appreciated too once they had mastered the slightly different driving technique required.

The STC seemed well satisfied with the Guy Arabs, and placed regular repeat orders between 1955-1958 until there was an eventual fleet of 133, numbered STC157-221, STC 414-481. All of these were built to an identical specification (with the exception of the type of front supplied with the initial order), and when the final batch of ten chassis was ordered, it was decided to up-date the specification of the final vehicle, which would be fitted with air operated brakes and a fully automatic gearbox,

BELOW: The General Post Office has, for generations, been a focal point in Singapore standing at Collyer Quay where the steamships from Europe once docked before the days of nonstop jetliner travel. Here on 19th February 1961, Guy Arab, STC 419 runs under the trolleybus wires on 19th February 1961 with, apparently, only the crew aboard whilst working the 18. The 'Singapore-grille' is quite clear in this view.

together with power operated steering. At the eleventh hour, a cable was sent from the Guy representative in Singapore to the Guy factory in Wolverhampton, quoting a memo he had received from the STC management. It stated "we have decided to have the standard type of epicyclic gearbox fitted to this chassis, and leave the matter of the automatic gearbox in abeyance until such time as we are considering the purchase of additional chassis." So the last chassis was quite standard and maintained the tradition of mechanical standardisation upheld by the STC since its inception. It was also the very last British made bus to be obtained by the Company!

Orders and chassis

The first order was placed with Guy in 1955, for 40 chassis, with an option to increase the order by 18 provided that if this option were exercised within a reasonable period, deliveries of the additional chassis would be made as if they were part of the original order. In fact, the number of chassis in the second order was increased to 43 as the first Guy Arabs proved to be so satisfactory in service. The Company Manager wrote of them:

"The performance of those now on the road leads us to believe that our expectations of economical running maintenance will be justifed. The drivers find them easy to manage in traffic, and they have no difficulty in accustoming themselves to the new method of gearchanging"

The second order (43) gave equal satisfaction, and was followed by a subsequent one for 25 more, which was itself followed by a final order for 25, making up the grand total of 133. The Guy Arabs were intended to replace 49 Bedford OBs, and the 98 remaining Dennis Falcons (two of the 100 had been destroyed maliciously). As revealed above, the ordering and commissioning of these vehicles took the form of a 'rolling programme', spread over the years 1955–8, and with slight changes being made to the design of the bodies. After the first batch had been built by Guy, the new 'Singapore front' was fitted locally to all subsequent chassis. This was designed around right angles rather than curves: the dash panel was a flat sheet which was both cab front and the front of the engine compartment. The front wings were flat-topped, the bonnet was quite broad, and left the engineers plenty of room to service the Gardner 5LW engine. As new, the front incorporated a grille, supplied by Guy and embellished by a Guy badge, which gave the buses their identity. (It should be pointed out, however, that the design of grille was also fitted to Crossley, Daimler and AEC buses in Great Britain, and was by no means exclusive to Guy Motors.) As time went by, many of the STC Arabs lost the original front grille, and their original looks were changed by the substitution of 'home-made' grilles of

ABOVE: This picture of STC 192 when new illustrates several of the features of the Singapore specification for the Guy Arab Mk IV. Looking under the canopy, the three high and small windows set in the front bulkhead may be distinguished. Inside the drivers cab, no control box can be seen mounted on the bulkhead, and on the original photograph the handbrake (to the driver's right) and gear selector (to the driver's left) may just be picked out. Note also the flat-topped wings, containing the lamp assemblies, and the flat sheet of metal forming the cab and bonnet front, upon which the standard 'Birmingham' grille is attached. The single roller blind indicator is supplemented by the brackets, seen under the canopy on the bulkhead, into which a metal plate with route information could be slotted. Many Guy Arabs later received an array of three roller blind indicators. *(F.W.York collection*

BELOW: This splendid view of STC 161 was taken at Serangoon Garden Way with wide expanses of open land on either side, soon to support many high quality bungalows. Behind is an FT39 Albion. The 'Birmingham' front anf Guy 'Indian Head' motif and Gardner engine scroll can be seen on the filler cap and top of the grille respectively. The fleet number appears on the offside cab door for the first time.

various 'anonymous' designs.

The first order for 40 was placed in 1955, and 30 of these, with the numbers STC 157-86, entered service in 1956. The chassis numbers of these 30 vehicles, plus the 10 which entered service in the following year, STC 187-96, comprised:

FD72895/7/9,72900/l/2
FD72916/68/9/73/4
FD784/6/7/8/92,
FD73002/3/6/10/2
FD73020/1/2/3/32
FD73052/3/4/5/60
FD73169/72/3/4/5/6
FD73197/8,FD73203

The second order for 43 was placed with Guy Motors in March 1956, and at the time it was recorded that "it has not yet been decided whether the front canopies (sic) are required, but only Guy emblems and radiator grilles". This reference should more correctly have referred to bonnet assemblies rather than 'canopies', and it tells us that the frontal design of the first batch, by then with the body builders in Singapore, was being evolved. It is probable that the change from 'Birmingham' front to 'Singapore' front commenced with STC 187, but this has not been verified. The chassis which made up the order for 43 were built in batches of five or six, as shown in the list below, and took the numbers STC 197-221, STC 414-31.

All bar the last one entered service during 1957.

FD73358/9/64/5/7/68
FD73456/69/71/8/3
FD73538/9/41/2/4
FD73610/l/5/6/27
FD73645/51/8/60/2
FD73663/5/7/72/5/6
FD73685/92/3/6/7
FD73716/46/7/8/52/6

The third order was placed with Guy Motors in January 1957, and again these were built so as to be supplied to the shippers in groups, the last being dispatched in September.

FD73766/7/8/9/75/6
FD73812/3/6/7/24/32
FD73851/2/6/8/9/61
FD73913/4/5/7/9/20/67

These all entered service during 1958, taking the numbers STC 432-456 They were followed by the final group, which in fact was made up of an order for 15 plus an order for 10, placed with Guy Motors in January 1958 and March 1958 respectively and delivered during April-June of the same year. A slight modification was made to the leaf springs on this group and, as already explained, the last chassis, originally intended to have air pressure brakes and a fully-automatic gearbox, was delayed whilst the STC pondered the matter, and it was eventually delivered in standard form. The numbers allocated to these final Guy Arabs were STC 457-481 which entered service in 1958 (STC 457-474) and 1959. The chassis numbers are not all known.

FD739084/6/7/8/9/90/4
FD74005 plus 17 more.

LEFT: This depot view shows three types of Guy styling. Nearest the camera is one of the two Arabs converted to full-fronted 'transit buses'; second is a bus with a 'Singapore' front; next are three similar vehicles with 'Birmingham' fronts. Of the latter, two display the modified canopy with three-piece destination blinds, while the other (fourth from left) retains its original 'domed' canopy with single-destination screen.

LOWER LEFT: By the time that this photograph was taken, 'transit-bus' Guy Arab STC 170 had been re registered SH 9294 by its new owners ABS—Associated Bus Service. The extent of the conversion went beyond the full-front and dual doors; the windows were replaced by rubber-mounted, sliding units, each with a pair of small top-lights above. After the amalgamations, the three-piece destination arrangements were reduced to just a route number.

All metal bodywork

The bodies for this class of bus were built entirely from aluminium to a design by STC. Construction was by Lee Kiat Seng who received the chassis after final assembly and road testing by STC. The bodies had a flat floor and, compared with existing STC vehicles, had a more spacious layout than ever before seen in Singapore. The extra six-inches of width improved the circulation of both passengers and conductor throughout the interior and the seating was laid out to maximum effect. The front and rear of the saloon had full width bench seats, each for six passengers. Except for the pair of inward facing seats for two over the rear wheel arches, all other seats faced forward and all seats were upholstered and covered in leathercloth type material.

Ventilation was by means of square framed half-drop glazed windows and through the entrance which, although equipped with doors, was usually left open to assist the flow of air. The rear of the bus, which was angular and without curves—which would have reduced both width and height—had two opening windows. This part of a single-deck bus often houses an emergency door, but this was situated at the front offside, adjacent to the front bench seat.

As the Guy Arab bodies were constructed of aluminium, the STC was clearly tempted by the idea of leaving the gleaming silver coloured vehicles unpainted, or at least mainly so. In the mid-1950's, several British bus operators, such as Liverpool Corporation and South Wales Transport, experimented with unpainted buses and a special sheet metal (Birmabrite) was produced for the purpose. It was found, however, that in time, the unpainted metal became tarnished and was difficult to clean. STC produced several full colour drawings to illustrate the effect of using new colours and areas of 'silver' on the Guy Arabs, before settling on a modified colour scheme which still retained the traditional green on the lower panels. A decade later, the use of unpainted and silver painted panels was revived by the three regional formed by the amalgamation of the Chinese companies and the practice carried over into the early days of the Singapore Bus Service in 1973.

These buses were the last to have bodywork designed by the STC: all future purchases were of ready made vehicles designed by Japanese manufacturers.

BELOW: In rural surroundings, Guy Arab, STC 204, lays over between trips on Route 1A before heading back into town and Raffle's Quay. This bus is in the short-lived STC livery of silver relieved only by a green band and the various lettering and STC badge of encircled initials. The flat, 'Singapore' front can be easily recognised in this view. *(Choo Tian Chwee*

Isuzu single-deck buses

STC 1-137

STC 1 & STC 2

The first two Isuzus, STC 1 and 2, entered service in July 1962 and were like no other buses which had ever been used by the Company. Firstly, they were imported in completely-built-up (CBU) condition; secondly, they had been supplied by the Japanese manufacturer and, thirdly, they swept away the final vestiges of the Imperial Preference clauses of the 1925 Ordinance.

STC 1 & 2 were just under 31 feet in length and ten feet high, with a rear mounted 6,373cc, six-cylinder engine, producing 170 brake horse power. A Company claim that "rattles, bumps and grinds", would be a thing of the past, was made to emphasise the provision of air-bellows suspension on both front and back axles.

For the times, the most remarkable feature of the new buses was the provision of air conditioning, although it was at once appreciated that not every passenger would welcome this ultramodern feature and subsequently STC 1 and STC 2 tended to be employed on special charter duties—after a term of touring most of the major routes.

Several other features which are accepted as being common-place thirty years later were considered to be revolutionary. The door was under the control of the driver from push-buttons in the cab and could not be opened whilst the bus was in motion; a device was provided to set off an alarm should anybody attempt to open the emergency exit. Fluorescent lighting was also deemed to be a luxury. Electronic wonderments were still largely unknown but there was a device fitted above the rear mudguard that was able to 'feel' the approach of oncoming traffic at night, then to automatically dip the headlights.

The bodywork styling was typical of contemporary Japanese practice—itself evolved from American designs of the 1940's and not unlike some PCC trams.

Surprisingly, STC 1 & 2 were delivered with the traditional Singapore centre entrance although both the chassis and body designs were suitable—indeed intended—for a front entrance,

ahead of the front wheel and beside the driver. In place of the front door, a square window, similar to the driver's signalling window, was provided. Behind this were two bays, each with a rectangular passenger window over the front wheel. The centre doorway was about fifteen inches behind the wheel-arch followed by a further five bays with rectangular windows. The last side window was of partially radiused outline to conform to the lines of the rear dome. Above the main rectangular side windows there was a glazed top-light or 'standee' window, rubber mounted with radius corners—the first top-light behind the doorway being utilized as a side destination indicator. Each side window was capable of opening but instead, as had hitherto been the norm, of the glazing either sliding laterally or dropping into the bodyside, on the Isuzus it was raised, sliding up behind the top-lights. Exceptions were the opening windows beside the driver and another behind the doorway, all of which slid laterally.

A feature of this American-Japanese design was the way the panelling of the roof was extended down below normal cantrail level to accommodate the top-lights of the side windows.

The driver's windscreen was of four parts—a central section of two almost square flat panes, flanked by two curved corner

VEHICLE SPECIFICATION: Isuzu BR351, 20P, 20PA or 20PA2

Registration numbers:	STC 1-137
Chassis:	Isuzu model ⎧ BR351P—1962 —STC 1/2, 3–37 ⎨ 20P—1963 —STC 38–87 ⎩ 20PA2—1964 —STC 88–137
Engine:	Isuzu 6,373cc; 6-cyl; 170 bhp
Transmission:	6-speed manual gearbox as new-later reported as Allison fully automatic.
Body make:	Isuzu—monocoque
Body layout:	⎧ STC 1-2: B42+14CEXD,a/c ⎨ STC 3-137: B38+19FED,CXD
Date introduced:	1962–64
Total:	137
Length:	30ft (approx)
Width:	8ft
Height:	10ft (approx)
Wheelbase:	?
Unladen weight:	?

NOTE: These buses were transferred to Associated, United and Amalgamated Bus Companies in 1971.

BELOW: The air-conditioned STC1 is nearest to the camera with non-air-conditioned SCT 15 a short distance behind, skirting the Padang, in this late 1962 view, probably posed. The single centre entrance of the nearer bus contrasts with the dual doorway arrangement of STC 15, a 'production' vehicle. While STC 1 has its windows down (closed) to retain the cool, air-conditioned ambiance within, STC 15 has its side windows open wide to reduce the heat in its naturally ventilated saloon. *(F. W. York collection*

glasses. None of these had an opening facility and to provide an alternative airflow for the driver, a small metal-flap-type ventilator was located at his ankle level in the dash panel. A similar vent was provided on the nearside. Above the windscreen was a metal sun-shield.

Across the front dome were arranged five 'torpedo' shaped marker lights which were more ornate than of any particular use and did not meet any legislation that required their fitting.

The motor for the air-conditioning plant was located under the floor—see the grille behind the door in the accompanying photograph—and cool air was ducted across the roof from front to back to be vented into the saloon through outlets in the ceiling.

The American image was completed by the provision of a deep chrome-plated bumper—fender—across the front.

These buses introduced a new silver—aluminium paint—livery, relieved by a green and red band below the windows. Also new were the black-on-white Japanese-style destinations indicators with place names only in Roman lettering—Malay and Chinese being dropped at this time. A separate route number screen was placed immediately to the offside of the destination and a combined route number/destination screen was fitted in the top-light of the side window immediately behind the centre entrance.

STC3-137

Also in 1962, but following some months later on 19th October, as recalled in Part One of this Volume, 25 Isuzus were unloaded from the *SS Fuji Maru* in Singapore—a further ten arriving a few days later. These were the frontrunners of ongoing for buses from Japan

The 1962 delivery were all on the Isuzu BR315P chassis but, although generally similar, the 1963 and 1964 series were of the 20PA and 20PA2 model respectively.

There were two major differences between these 'production' buses and STC1 & STC 2. In the first instance, the case for air-conditioning had not been proved and thus they were not so fitted—no grilles in the side panels or ducts on the roof. In the second case, these buses were provided with front entrance doors

ABOVE: Although of questionable quality, this photograph of Isuzu STC 44, taken at Collyer Quay in November 1965, serves two purposes: firstly to show the array of roof mounted ventilators associated with the non-air-conditioned forced-air ventilation system. The second reason is more personal. During his three-week 1965 visit, Mike Davis, the publisher, lover of British buses abroad, took three rolls of 120 film, of which, ironically, only this shot 'came-out'! *(Mike Davis*

and a centre exit—two bays further back than the single door on the first two. The side destination screen was moved forward to the first bay behind the front doorway.

In most other cases, the foregoing detailed description of STC 1 & 2 relates also to the later buses. At some point, the layout of the destination screens was altered to three-piece and later buses were delivered so fitted. A minor difference was the provision of a slightly larger ventilator for the driver.

All the Isuzus were painted silver with the green and red band below the windows as on the first two. Later on, the fleet, including the Isuzus, was returned to a more traditional green livery with silver roof and window surrounds.

LEFT: Overhead wires remain in place but trolleybuses have passed along Geylang Road for the last time. Here STC 16 lets off an elderly lady from the centre exit doorway while the front entrance doors also remain open. The Japanese-style destination indicators were later to include names in Chinese but the Malay script was seldom seen thereafter. *(F. W. York collection*

A detail difference between STC3–87 and subsequent Isuzus, was the back window which had been of three distinct sections, each separated by a body pillar, the centre window having an opening sliding ventilator. From STC 88 upwards, this arrangement was replaced by a large single 'wraparound' aperture, with three separate glass sections—a main centre segment flanked by two more curvaceous pieces—each pane being separated from its neighbour by a thin strip of 'H'-section metal channel. No provision was made for ventilation in any of the three pieces.

Re-engining

As revealed in Part A, Ch 11, the Government introduced a requirement that bus engines should be replaced after five years use. This may explain the appearance of the Nissan 'UD' trademark on numerous Isuzus at the time of their transfer to the three 'Chinese' companies in 1971.

There were press reports that some engines had been replaced by General Motors (USA) units in an effort to reduce smoke emmissions—Isuzu being a part of the GM empire. It is also believed that Allison—also part of GM—fully automatic gearboxes were fitted at the same time as they were re-engined.

UPPER LEFT: STC 109, newly transferred to the Amalgamated Bus Company, who had neatly painted and masked the single destination screen to take a central route number, thus giving the appearance of a three-part display.

LEFT: This rear view of STC 65 was taken after the vehicle had passed to United Bus Company (Pte) Ltd. The new owner had changed the colour of the line below the side windows from Traction Company's red to yellow—just discernable in a monochrome illustration. The three-piece rear windows of STC1–87 are also illustrated.

BELOW LEFT: The later Isuzus, from SCT 88 upwards, had revised back windows, there being a single aperture with three glass sections, each separated by a narrow strip. It will be noted that this particular bus has a 'UD' sticker, probably indicating that it had been re-engined using a Nissan Diesel 5.67 litre unit—UD being the Nissan logo.

Mitsubishi—*single deck buses*   *STC 138-139*

A pair of Mitsubishi buses were purchased for evaluation purposes, like the Isuzu fleet before them delivered complete, but as they had been designed for Japanese climatic conditions they did suffer a high defect rate. The major problem seemed to be their inability to cope with heavy traffic within the high ambient temperatures of Singapore, and a series of technical investigations were required before satisfactory solutions could be worked out, bringing the pair to a high state of reliability. Perhaps the extent of the remedial work was too involved, for whilst future orders still involved a Japanese manufacturer, Nissan was the chosen supplier.

STC Fleet—New vehicle summary 1962 to 1971

Year	Numbers	Model	Builder	Layout
1962	1-2	Isuzu BR351P	Isuzu	B42+14a/c
1962	3-37	Isuzu BR351P	Isuzu	B38+19
1963	38-87	Isuzu 20 PA	Isuzu	B38+19
1964	88-137	Isuzu 20 PA2	Isuzu	B38+19
1964	138-139	Mitsubishi-Fuso	Mitsubishi	B39+19
1967	601-650	Nissan RX102K3	Fuji Heavy Industries	B37+18
1969	651-699	Nissan RX102K3	Fuji Heavy Industries	B35+17
1969	700-749	Nissan 4R94	Fuji Heavy Industries	
1970	750-774	Nissan 4R94	Singapore Nissan Motors	B38+19

Nissan—*single deck models RX102K3 and 4R94—STC 601–774*

For reasons already described in Part A (Ch 11, 'local assembly'), No new buses were introduced between the last Isuzu in 1964 and 1967 when further cbu Japanese-built buses arrived in the form of fifty Nissan model RX102K3 with bodied built by Fuji Heavy Industries (these became STC 601–650). Like the Isuzus, the Nissans were of the, then current, standard Japanese transit-bus pattern. A further delivery of RX102K3's was made in 1969—49 in total (STC 651–699) which suggests that one vehicle may have lost due, possibly, to transit damage.

Following the 1969 delivery the chassis specification changed to Nissans 4R94 which appears to have generally similar, probably being an updated RX102K3.

Mechanically, all the Nissans had a 5.67litre diesel engine, mounted at the rear, which drove via a fully-automatic gearbox. No provision was made for air-conditioning on any of these buses.

VEHICLE SPECIFICATION: Nissan RX102K3 and 4R94

Registration numbers:	STC 601–699 RX102K3
	STC 700–774 4R94
Chassis:	Nissan models as above
Engine:	Nissan 5.67 litre rear mounted—some reportedly replaced by GM units
Transmission:	Initially 6-speed manual, subsequently Allison fully-automatic gearbox
Body make:	Fuji Heavy Industries cbu except STC750–774 assembled by Singapore Nissan Motors from Fuji parts
Body layout:	STC601–650: B37+18FED,CXD
	STC 651–666 (?): B35+12FED,CXD+o/sCD
	STC668–699: B37+18FED,CXD
	STC 700–749: B38+19FED,CXD
	STC 750–774: B38+12FED,CXD
Date introduced:	See below.
Total:	174
Length:	31ft 7ins (STC 700–74 may have been two inches longer—unconfirmed)
Width:	8ft
Height:	10ft 6in (approx.)
Wheelbase:	?
Unladen weight:	STC 601-699: 7tons 13cwt 3qtr 19lb
	STC700-774: 7tons 10cwt 3qtr 20lb – individual buses differed

BELOW: This view of a Fuji bodied Nissan RX102K3 whilst still quite new and with STC, shows the shaped jack-knife-style front door—both doors hung from their respective forward pillars—and the very narrow last side window. The three-piece destination and route number screens were fully used in STC days. STC 612 was at Collyer Quay in 1967, en route for Tanjong Pager—former trolleybus route 1. *(Late C. J. F. Buckland*

ABOVE: STC 602 in very suburban —almost British—surroundings shows most of the distinguishing features of its type: peaked 'dome', upward opening side windows without top-lights (the upper half *did* open downwards but was an unpopular option), a roof cluttered with marker-lights and ventilator intakes and dual doorways, each immediately in front of its adjacent wheel-arch. By the time that this photo was taken the bus had passed to Associated Bus Company (Pte) Ltd..

LEFT: The offside of the Fuji body featured a centre emergency exit of the conventional floor-level type. The small window seen on the nearside view also appeared on this side. Working on the 191A, STC 699 was the last of the RX102K3 chassis and had also passed to Associated.

These buses were 31ft 7in long and had bodywork that followed similar principles to the Isuzus, with the front entrance ahead of the front wheels and the centre exit immediately ahead of the rear wheel-arch. Side windows were horizontally divided; the lower half sliding upwards and the lower half dropping down, although in practice the lower half was more usually open, giving a face-level flow of air. No top-light standee windows were provided; instead the upper half of the main side-windows extended upwards to meet the roofline, the panels of which were extended downwards over the doorways, forming a shallow awning. Behind the last rectangular opening window each side was a very narrow, rubber-mounted fixed window, possibly only three inches across and, because of the curve of the rear dome, its upper margin was lower than the top off the adjacent main windows.

Windscreens were of the four-piece type, with two flat main screens and two curved corner panels. Being non-opening, large ankle-height vents were located in the dash panel to allow the driver a flow of fresh air. A single-piece rear window was fitted at the back which was its self flatter—less curvaceous—than on the Isuzus.

The power-operated front and centre passenger doors were of the two-piece, jackknife, type, hinged from the forward door pillar and were under push-button control by the driver.

The usual roof-clutter associated with this type of bus or coach was largely ventilation scoops but also included five 'torpedo-shaped' front roof marker lights.

From new, the front canopy, or 'dome', was of the 'peaked' type, with three flush mounted destination/route number screens; the offside screen for the route number was smaller than the other two which showed outer and inner termini in Roman script only.

At the rear, large grilles of expanded-metal mesh protected the engine cooling fans, belts and pulleys—not unlike the arrangement adopted on the Leyland National.

The body capacity and layout for STC601-650 was B38+19FED,CXD.

Offside doors

All buses—with the exceptions mentioned below—in the series STC 601-699, had a centre offside emergency exit door at floor level but an unusual feature of a small number of Nissans

ABOVE: STC 655, another ex-Traction Company bus now working for Associated, serves to show the offside doors fitted to a small number of buses in its immediate number range. Clearly seen here are the rear roof marker lights, the rear window with three panes in a single opening and the exposed fans, belts, etc., hidden only behind a mesh grille.

in the second series—STC 651–69— was the provision of power-operated offside centre doors in the manner frequently found on airside buses. The purpose of these doors is open to debate as no convincing reason has so far been offered—any reader having this knowledge might like to pass it on to the publisher. Buses identified from photographs include, STC 651 (confirmed as the first), 652, 655, 662 and 666. STC669 definitely did not have the offside doors which leaves the finishing number open. The seating capacity of these buses was reduced accordingly, being B35+12FED,CXD+o/sCD. STC 666 was later rebuilt to have 38-seats—probably after removal of the offside doorway.

Chassis Model 4R94
STC 700–749

Referred to here as the 700-series (chassis numbers were 1891–1940, in order), these fifty buses had Japan-assembled FHI bodies but differed in a number of minor ways from the preceding RX102K3's although the engine remained the 5.67litre unit as before with fully-automatic transmission. They were, however, approximately three hundredweight heavier—exact weights seemed to vary from bus to bus but typical seems to have been 7tons 13cwt 3qtrs 19lbs.

Although official records supplied some years later give the overall length as 31ft 7in, the same as the 601-series, it is possible that they were very slightly longer at the rear overhang, allowing for the emergency exit door to be placed behind the rear wheel-arch and for the provision of a larger non-opening last side window with a pronounced curve to the rear margin. In most other respects the bodies of these were similar to 601 etc.

STC 750–774

These buses (chassis numbers 2168–2192) had their bodies assembled in Singapore in accordance with Government wishes

LEFT: STC 715 was a Nissan 4R94 with a Japan-built body by Fuji Heavy Industries. The location of the offside emergency door behind the rear wheel and the larger last side window do suggest that there was an extra two inches on the rear overhang when compared to the 601-series. In this case the bus had passed to United Bus Company (Pte) Ltd. who had painted the band below the windows yellow.

ABOVE: Commencing with STC 750, the bodies on Nissan chassis were assembled by 'Singapore Nissan Motors' and although generally similar to STC 700-740, there were differences. Most noticable was the rectangular last side window in place of the radiused type of the Fuji-assembled buses. A further difference was that there were only three roof-mounted 'torpedo-style' marker lights at the front; the other two being lowered to a position either side of the destination screens. Here STC 767 works the 42 to Jurong in the service of Associated Bus Services (Pte) Ltd.

LEFT: By the time this photograph was taken, Singapore Nissan bodied STC 752 had been in the fleet of Amalgamated Bus Company Ltd. long enough to have been re-registered as SH 8917—it was subsequently taken into SBS stock in November 1973 becoming SBS 4600K.

but after the last had been delivered, circumstances changed and only these twenty-five were completed. Body parts were supplied by Fuji heavy Industries for 'Singapore Nissan Motors' to assemble in the tripartite—Nissan, STC (30%) and Lee Kiat Seng—owned factory at Jurong Industrial Estate.

These Singapore Nissan bodies differed in a few details to those assembled by Fuji in Japan but may have been about 96lbs lighter. Seating, etc. was B38+12FED,CXD—seven less standees.

Principal external differences included the rectangular last side window each side (which, on STC 700–749, was a radiused, rubber-mounted pane) and three, instaed of five, roof-mounted 'torpedo' marker lights. The remaining two makers were located in the front panel, above the windscreen, either side of the destination/route number screens.

Re-engined buses

As referred to under the Isuzu heading, there was a Government requirement to replace bus engines after five years service and there was press comment to the effect that the Nissans were unpopular with residents near bus interchanges due to their high-revving engines. As well as the Isuzus, there was also reference to their being given General Motors replacement encines. Eye witness reports suggest that there were Nissans fitted with fully automatic gearboxes, despite there being close-up photographs of gear levers amongst the drivers controls.

The Vehicles of the Chinese Bus Companies

The various types of bus operated by the Chinese Bus Companies in Singapore are described in the following pages, in alphabetical order of make, and with brief technical details. With very few exceptions, all the vehicles listed were supplied to Singapore as chassis, and local coachbuilders constructed the bodies. The style of the coachwork is distinctive to Singapore and Malaya.

Fleet lists form the final section of this volume. These give details of the registration numbers, make and type, and type of body fitted, with extra notes where applicable. The type of body is shown in the form of a code system, the elements of which are as follows:

B   single deck bus (or C coach, luxury seating)
 followed by a figure; the seating capacity (+ standing capacity)
F   front entrance door
C   central entrance door
RP   rear entrance door with open platform
 (EXAMPLE B23+5RP indicates a 23 seat bus with open rear platform which is authorised for five standing.)
Other abbreviations used from time to time to best describe vehicles are as follows:
 n/c normal control (driving position behind front engine)

f/c   forward control (driving position at the side of engine)

The descriptions begin with pictures of the utility type vehicles drafted in to build up the fleets in 1945-46, many of which used ex-military chassis.

This section has been compiled with the Singapore reader in mind, but British readers too will find it of use, as many of the types of bus supplied to Singapore from the British Isles were export models, and not found in any numbers, if at all, in Great Britain.

Two types of bus which were very unusual in Singapore are illustrated below.

SH 145 was a Leyland Tiger, thousands of which were to be found in all continents but only one of which came to Singapore. The oil drum was acting the part of a traffic bollard, once a familiar feature prior to the days of the ubiquitous 'cone'.

SH 191, one of a pair of underfloor engined Sentinels of which four were imported by George Lee (Chassis numbers 4/40/74, 4/40/75, 4/40/76 and 4/40/78) of which only the Tay Koh Yat pair have been traced.

Utility type vehicles 1945-46

Illustrated on this page are three types of normal-control chassis of American origin. Although widely used for buses in many countries, these vehicles, with their long bonnets, were not really ideal for passenger work as so much of the length was taken up by engine and driving position. The narrow front track and wide rear track also gives them an unbalanced appearance. The roomy bonnet, however, gave the opportunity to fit diesel engines if so desired. Certain British bus chassis built for normal-control, such as the Austin CXB, Bedford OB, and the Fargo (Kew Dodge) show a much more compact front end, maximising the space for the passenger compartment.

TOP RIGHT: A Chevrolet of Tay Koh Yat, with a Ford in the back ground.

ABOVE: S7517 an American Dodge of Tay Koh Yat illustrates how only just over half of the length of the vehicle is used for passengers. Also of note are the unglazed side windows and, untypical for this type of vehicle, the front doorway, and.

RIGHT: S905 - Keppel Ford S905 clearly shows the open platform of the locally constructed body. The style of body is very similar to the normal-control Ford on the next page.

LOWER RIGHT SG4646 The Keppel tow car on Ford chassis clearly shows the characteristic narrow front and wide rear track. This vehicle was probably converted from a bus, as it has a home made cab. As new it would have had a factory built windscreen or complete cab.

BELOW: This view of Island Bus Ford S 7552 shows clearly the rear platform arrangement and perimeter seating, both standard features on buses built on ex-military chassis.

TOP RIGHT: STC Trolleybus 2 stands at the terminus at Paya Lebar (note tight turning circle). Although not a large vehicle, the Ransomes trolleybus appears to dwarf the Ford 14-seater of Tay Koh Yat and makes the point that many of the utility single-deckers were no more than 'grown-up mosquito buses'

RIGHT: A snub-nosed Ford, S 3223, of Tay Koh Yat leads TSM SH270 and a normal-control Ford with central doorway. These buses were working a contract service along Upper Serangoon Road in September 1955.

ABOVE RIGHT: Green Bus S3894 is an ex-military Ford car, thought to be a Dodge (USA) used for general duties. In the background are the body of S2451, divorced from its chassis, and what appears to be the body from a "lorry bus".

RIGHT: This Tay Koh Yat Private Bus is based on a large motor car chassis, and with its rear door, is clearly derived from the mosquito bus design.

Albion Victor series

Victor FT39

The Albion FT39 series has been fully described in the section devoted to the vehicles of the STC, and no further technical details will be given on this page. Suffice it to say that the Chinese Bus Companies, particularly Tay Koh Yat and Hock Lee Amalgamated, saw the Albions of the STC giving sterling service, and chose themselves to place substantial orders for this type and its successors. The FT39 laid the foundations for 30 years of business between Albion and various bus operators in Singapore.

In parallel with the STC, the Chinese companies moved from the shorter FT39N chassis to the longer FT39ALX, thus taking the seating capacity from about 30 to about 45. Central doorways were the norm on all these vehicles.

Victor VT17

The FT series was replaced from 1959 by the Victor VT series of chassis. The chief models of note, all of which shared the same mechanical components, but which differed in dimensions and purpose, were VT19, essentially intended as pantechnicons, and VT15, VT17,

VEHICLE SPECIFICATIONS: Albion Victor	
Chassis:	Albion Victor VT17AL/VT17BL
Engine:	Leyland 0350, or 0370 (VT17BL later models)
Transmisson:	5 speed constant mesh gearbox
Length:	27ft 6ins
Width:	7 ft 6 ins or 8 ft
Wheelbase:	17ft 3 ins

VT21, and VT23, which were passenger models. The VT21 was a model intended for the British market and to be a close rival to the Bedford SB range, whilst the VT23 was a special model, of which 100 were built for the Kowloon Motor bus Company of Hong Kong The VT15 was an Albion engined version of the Victor, which found favour especially in the South African market.

The general export model of the Victor was the VT17, made in normal and heavy duty form, and differing from the previous FT series in a number of ways. The front axle was set back slightly, and the chassis was able to carry wider and longer bodywork. At first the well known Albion radiator was supplied, but then some chassis were fitted with a front end as used on the Leyland Comet passenger chassis. Leyland Motors had taken over Albion in 1951, and the new VT series was part of a programme to move away from traditional Albion designs, and re-launch Albion as builder of medium weight trucks and passenger chassis in the Leyland range, leaving the parent company with heavyweight vehicles. Consequently, the new Victors used many components sourced from Leyland Motors, including the 0350 engine, as used in the Leyland Comet. The model chosen by the Chinese Bus Companies was the Victor VT17AL , very much of the same configuration as the Dennis Teal and Seddon Mark 17.

As stated above, the front axle of the VT19 was set back slightly, and Albion took this process a step further in 1963 when the Viking VK41L model was introduced to replace the Victor. This chassis had a front axle located in such a way as to allow an entrance alongside the driving position, which both aided safety and permitted operation by one person.

ABOVE LEFT: TKY SC5335 is one of the earliest FT39Ns of the postwar period. These, like STC 116 - 134 of the Traction Company, were built smaller all round dimensions then the later Victors.

LEFT: Hock Lee Amalgamated SH482 is a typical example of an Albion Victor FT39ALX. It is seen here in late 1955. Those not familiar with Singapore should note the deep storm drain on the right. (Standard Photo

Albion Viking VK41L

As already stated, the Viking VK41L was a redesigned version of the Victor, suitable for a front doorway. Singapore buses, however, were almost universally fitted with centre doorways, and a few buses delivered in the mid-fifties with front doorways had had these taken out, and the driver became isolated in a full width cabin, as hitherto on most of the forward-control buses.

Albion Motors and Leyland must have been very surprised to find that Vikings were being fitted with full width cabs, but then "the customer is always right," and in fact a large number of Vikings in the Tay Koh Yat and Hock Lee Amalgamated fleets were constructed with centre door bodies.

VEHICLE SPECIFICATIONS: Albion Victor	
Chassis :	Albion Viking VK41L
Engine:	Leyland 0370
Transmission:	5 speed constant mesh
Length:	30-31 feet
Width:	7 ft 6 ins or 8ft
Wheelbase:	16ft 1 in

Mechanically the Vikings carried on the traditions of the earlier Albions: a straightforward and robust chassis using the uprated 0370 engine, mounted at the front, but with sufficient room to allow passengers to board ahead of the front axle under the supervision of the driver. Only in Singapore was this feature not utilised, and the driver given the benefit of a roomy cab, and leaving the conductor in charge of the passenger saloon.

LEFT: Katong Bedok SH225 has a neat 31 seat body which appears to be of all metal construction. It could have been assembled from a kit of parts imported from Great Britain—many Albion FT39Ns were supplied so to India and Africa.

CENTRE: Changi SH772 is a Victor VT19 and illustrates the 8-feet wide bodywork fitted on the narrow track of this Albion. The width is emphasised by the traditional radiator. (Choo Tian Chwee

LOWER: SH 908, a Viking VK41L ex-Tay Koh Yat, seen here running for United Bus Company, has a full width drivers cab. Compare this photo with Mercedes Benz SH955 on page 235

Austin CXB and CXD

The Austin Motor Co. of Birmingham built a large number of light military vehicles during the Second World War, and its post war production developed the range for civilian use. A normal-control bus chassis, evolved from a truck, and looking like a cousin of the famous Bedford OB, formed the basis of a passenger range which was publicised as the 'Austin Coach'. This chassis was available in normal-control or forward-control configuration, and could be converted by the operator if so desired (usually from normal-control to forward-control, rarely the other way round.) The normal-control version ex-factory was the CXB, the forward-control version the CXD.

Austins of the above types were found in the fleet of Changi Bus and Easy Bus. Changi Bus SH 193/4/6-9 appear to have been CXBs converted to forward-control in Singapore, as they carry unusual and anonymous front grilles, whereas the later SH 326-31 have Austin front panels. Similar fronts appear on the Austins used by

VEHICLE SPECIFICATIONS: Austin CX	
Chassis:	Austin CXB/CXD
Engine:	Perkins P6
Transmission:	4 speed manual gearbox
Length:	27ft 0 ins
Width:	up to 7 ft 6 ins
Wheelbase:	15 ft 0 ins

Easy Bus, whose buses needed to be especially narrow. The Tay Koh Yat fleet contained a number of vehicles of great interest, included amongst which were a number of Austin CXBs.

After merging with Morris to form the British Motor Corporation, Austin continued building its single deck bus range, mainly for export, and the marque was to reappear in the bus fleets of Singapore in the early 1970s.

ABOVE: S 2766 of Changi Bus is an Austin K4 lorry chassis adapted for passenger use, and equipped with a rear entrance (open platform) body of typical early post war Singapore style. The sharp-eyed will note that the passengers are all moving towards the rear to alight. The K4 chassis was later developed into the passenger chassis known as the CXB. The K4 had a shorter wheelbase, at 13ft 1˙ins.

LEFT: SC 4636 of Tay Koh Yat is a bonneted CXB, and shows much in common with the Bedford OB. This bus dates from about 1948-9, and although it looks quite like contemporary British touring coaches on the OB or CXB chassis, this vehicle had a full width cab and longitudinal wooden seating.

226

ABOVE: Changi SH 196, seen here at Geylang trolleybus interchange carries a plain grille that suggests that this class of bus was converted from normal control, although we are listing these buses as type CXD.

BELOW: Changi SH 326 carries an Austin made front grille, and is a longer wheelbase forward-control chassis. It is seen here turning from Coleman Street into Hill Street.

Bedford

A make well represented on the roads of Singapore, where many examples of Bedford trucks were to be seen in the four decades following the end of the war. The Bedford OB bus chassis was supplied to the Traction Company to help it re-establish city services after the heavy losses incurred during the 1942-5 period, and a description of this type of bus can be found under the entry for STC 157-250.

The Bedford range from 1931-1940 included parallel bus and truck models, hence the catalogue at the outbreak of war contained the OL (model 'O' lorry) and the OB (model 'O' bus). As the factory turned to wartime production, the O series was redesigned slightly, and both lorries and buses continued in production, for military and limited civilian use. The Bedford petrol engined OWB bus was supplied for military transport and as the only available single deck bus for British transport companies. When the war ended, Bedford was able to resume building OBs, whilst many surplus ex-military OWBs came onto the market.

Singapore had not been in an active theatre of war, so few OWBs reached its shores. The STC took the bulk of the OBs that could be spared, so very few of a make which was very numerous in other parts of the world, and which was ideally suited to Singapore bus

operators' needs, actually ran there. By the time operators were free to choose, the OB had less appeal, being fitted with a petrol engine, and without a base of OBs, the SB model, which could be diesel powered, failed to follow in any numbers.

VEHICLE SPECIFICATION: Bedford OB and ML	
Chassis:	Bedford Model OB
Engine:	Bedford 84bhp, 6-cylinder petrol.
Transmission:	Bedford 4-speed manual gearbox
Date introduced:	1946
Length:	Approx 24ft 6in
Width:	7ft 1in approx
Wheelbase:	14ft 6in
Chassis:	Bedford Model ML
Engine:	Bedford 76bhp, 6-cylinder petrol.
Transmission:	Bedford 4-speed manual gearbox
Wheelbase:	11ft 11in

LEFT: Changi S 3238 is probably an OWB chassis, fitted with an early post war rear entrance body, and seen here at Kampong Melayu in a jungle setting

LOWER LEFT: The Keppel Bus Company was the only Chinese Bus Company to build up a small fleet of Bedfords. Here Bedford OB S 7618 is seen along the West Coast.

ABOVE: Private Bus SF 8290 is an OWB model ex British Armed Forces. It has been modified slightly from its original condition, the British built bodywork now having more opening windows for the Singapore climate.

CENTRE LEFT: S1942 is a small Private Bus based on the 11ft 11in wheelbase Bedford ML type lorry chassis.

LOWER LEFT: Tay Koh Yat SH 135 is an example of an ex-British Military—believed in this case to have been RAF— wartime specification Bedford OWB with wartime 'utility' body. It is being followed by another normal-control bus built on the chassis of an ex-military truch of US origin.

Commer

Several distinct models from the Commer passenger range appeared in Singapore, and are described under separate subheadings.

Avenger III (T85A)

This chassis was powered by a Rootes TS3 diesel engine mounted in an inclined position at the front, with a slightly set back axle. The three cylinder two-stroke engine had been developed by Tilling Stevens, who were taken over by Commer's parent organisation, and was a lively if noisy performer in both Commer buses and trucks. The set back axle of the Avenger Mark III (model T85A) allowed a front doorway of restricted width to be fitted, and the Avengers in the Tay Koh Yat fleet were unique in their time with this feature. The passengers did not, however, find this convenient when the bus was crowded.

Commando 17A

The Commer equivalent of the Bedford OB was model 17A, which was also known as the Commando. In production between 1946-9, over 1700 were built, and of these several hundred were bodied as airport coaches. The order was first placed on behalf of the RAF, which was in charge of civil aviation soon after the end of the Second World War, but many of these vehicles were eventually de-

VEHICLE SPECIFICATION: Commer T85A

Chassis:	Commer T85A
Engine:	Rootes TS3
Transmission:	4 speed manual
Length:	30ft 0ins
Width:	8ft 0ins
Wheelbase:	17ft 6ins

ABOVE: A line up of Tay Koh Yat SH313 (Albion FT39N) and Commer Avengers SH343, SH320, SH368 and SH321, all for working route 9, Havelock Road-Bartley Road. The very narrow front door is apparent, the boarding passenger having to negotiate the narrow space between wheelarch and engine.

VEHICLE SPECIFICATION: Commer 17A

Chassis:	Commer 17A
Engine:	Commer 4.086 litre petrol
Transmission:	4 speed manual gearbox
Length:	
Width:	7 ft 6 ins
Wheelbase:	15 ft 9 ins
Bodywork:	Park Royal Vehicles , London

BELOW: QANTAS Empire Airways deck-and-a-half Commer, S 6153, had been with the Royal Air Force in Singapore before its transfer to the Australian airline.

livered to British Eurpoean Airways and British Overseas Airways. A number of these coaches were stationed at foreign airports into which planes of the British fleets operated.

These special airport coaches had a raised rear section to allow passengers' luggage to be stowed beneath the floor. Very comfortable seats for 20 passengers were fitted, and the petrol engines added to the atmosphere of refinement of these distinctive vehicles. Those allocated by the RAF to Singapore Airport included vehicles registered 08 AC 24, 08 AC 56 and 08 AC 71 in the British military series. At least one of these was reregisterd for use by QANTAS, the Australian airline, as S 6153.

SH240

Tay Koh Yat SH240 and SH282 are Commer's of an unknown type. They could be war time vehicles rebuilt, post-war Commandos reconstructed as forward-control, even perhaps rebuilds of the ex RAF airport coaches. SH240 is seen here at Hoi How Road.

Dennis Teal

The Dennis Teal was yet another example of a passenger model based on a truck design, in this case the Dennis Pax. The front end shared the sloping dash and set-back front axle of the Pax truck, and the extended wheelbase of this passenger chassis produced especially for the Singapore and Malayan market allowed a seating capacity of up to 46 to be accommodated within an overall length of less than thirty feet. Not a great many of these robust chassis were built, but they were very rugged, and were some of the few earlier vehicles that allowed the Chinese bus companies to last well into the era of the three regional bus companies. In some ways they were similar to the Albion Victor VT series, both with regard to layout and construction, and shared with this model the quality of being a 'good work horse', a straightforward chassis that used well proven truck components and, in the case of the Teal, the well regarded Perkins P6 engine.

Teals were operated by Katong Bedok Bus Service and Hock Lee Amalgamated, and a pair registered SR 1062-3 entered service

VEHICLE SPECIFICATION: *Dennis Teal*
Chassis: Dennis Teal
Engine: Perkins P6
Transmission: 4 speed manual gearbox
Length: 27 ft 6 ins
Width: 7 ft 6 ins
Wheelbase : 17 ft 6 ins

in September 1955 with Malayan Airways in Singapore, as the earlier airport buses, two fairly new Tilling-Stevens, had too small a capacity for the larger passenger planes then coming into service. A few Teals were produced for service in Great Britain as removal vans, and this too is a feature in common with the Albion Victor VT models

The Dennis marque was also represented in Singapore by the 100 Falcon buses supplied to the STC. A small number of these were sold for further use after withdrawal by the Traction Company: one became a full-fronted School Bus, whilst another, SH 757, joined the Hock Lee Amalgamated fleet, and was one of the few vehicles outside the STC fleet with a half-width cab.

LEFT: Katong Bedok SH430, as seen from the rear, with the overhang hang even more evident. Note the rear indicator panel over half of which is used to repeat the registration number.

BELOW: The same bus seen here at Frankel Village, was new in December 1955, and shows the greater length and width permitted by this chassis, as compared with earlier vehicles. With a seating capacity of 46, it could carry twice as many as the older normal-control types, and the wide bodywork in some ways copied the interior layout of the STC Guy Arabs.

Fargo (British Dodge)

Modern times have seen a spread of so-called 'badge engineering' - the practice of attaching badges to vehicles that are not strictly the name of the company that built them. The example dealt with on this page has a long history.

As long ago as 1928, the Fargo Motor Corporation was established in Detroit, USA, by the Chrysler Motor Corporation, in order to market commercial vehicles. From 1931 certain Dodge trucks from America were badged as Fargo in order to increase the market penetration of Dodge products, selling them through the Fargo agency. From 1935, British built Dodge trucks also benefited from this arrangement, and were accordingly badged as Fargo or Kew-Fargo (Kew, in Surrey, was the location of the Dodge factory).

The British operation had begun in 1927, assembling U.S. built trucks, but from 1935 it had its own range of trucks and a small bus chassis, all made in Britain but for the engine and gearbox. These vehicles were variously marketed as Dodge, Kew-Dodge or Kew-Fargo. The range was extended gradually, and in the postwar period an export-only passenger chassis was introduced, which like the Albion Victor and Dennis Teal, was closely linked with a 6/7 ton pantechnicon chassis. At first, the passenger model was built in both forward and normal-control versions, but the latter was later dropped. The bonnet and cab structure for this model was a bought in unit which was also used by other manufacturers (Ford and Leyland *inter alia*), and during the post war era, the Dodge commercial vehicle range never really established a style of its own. In appearance, the normal-control bus chassis resembled a similar product by Ford,

and like similar Ford and Austin products, was capable of conversion to forward-control by the operator. Hence Green Bus, which took a series of British Dodges (badged as Fargo) of the 86AL/P6 type, converted them all by moving the driving position forward and thereby increasing the passenger capacity.

As Dodge had no specific badge or radiator panel, the frontal design of forward-control Dodges was at the discretion of the coachbuilders. In Singapore, a variety of designs emerged, perhaps the most confusing being the one which used a Seddon derived front panel, which included a Fargo badge similar to that of Seddon as well! The passenger model was upgraded in the 1960s, and became known as the KS60, being then parallel with the Bedford SB and the Austin FF110: all three of these models figured in the fleets of the merged Chinese Companies. The British Dodge factory was closed in 1967, and the product range was taken over and merged with that of the Rootes Group, later to market some Commer models under the Dodge or Fargo names.

The photographs below will illustrate the various faces of the Fargo in and around Singapore, the ones on this page showing the transformation of one bus in particular.

THE SAME BUS:

The picture **RIGHT** shows Green Bus SH 136 in July 1955 in Dairy Farm Road as a normal-control vehicle, fitted with factory made front end, of a design also shared with Ford Thames ET6 and ET7 models. The cab sides of the bus body taper in to match up with the front end.

The **LOWER** picture shows SH 136 again, seen in Bukit Timah Road one year later, and now a full-fronted normal-control vehicle. The driver now sits in a wide cab, but there are two distinct clues to the former design. The first is the narrow track of the front wheels, now sunk deep inside the wheelarches and fitted with a ribbed ring to act as a foothold for those wishing to climb into the cab, and the second is the position of the steering wheel, closer to the engine than would be on a vehicle built for a full width cab. (Compare with the position of the steering wheel on SH 965 on the following page.)

UPPER LEFT: Tay Koh Yat SH520 shows one type of anonymous grille used on Fargos

LEFT: Katong Bedok SH427 illustrates a body by a different coachbuilder and a different front grille.

LEFT: Another (later) style is seen on SH950 (seen here running for Associated Bus Service) with another variant sported by SH598, ex Ponggol, also now with Associated.

LOWER LEFT: SH965 is a smart vehicle with Ponggol. The anonymous grille carries the word 'Fargo' in chrome lettering. BELOW: The driver of Green Bus Fargo SH 287 fills his water can from a standpipe while the radiator filler-cap has been removed in anticipation of being refilled.

Mercedes-Benz — 300 series

Until Singapore became independent, the importation of motor vehicles from outside the British Commonwealth was not possible. Mercedes-Benz, therefore, was a late comer to the Singapore bus scene, although in the seventies it became an important force as will be seen in Volume II of this work.

Like many British vehicle manufacturers, Mercedes-Benz built a range of vehicles for home use in Germany and other European countries, and another for exportation to countries where the operating conditions favoured lighter vehicles with high ground clearance. This range tended to be based on the mechanical units used in lorries, with forward mounted vertical engines, manual gearboxes, and a chassis upon which local coachbuilders could construct bodywork of their chosen type. The German and European market for buses at the time in question was moving towards integral, low floor, rear engined buses, in which the bodywork was required to be loadbearing and manufactured to very strict dimensions, for both structural and safety reasons.

VEHICLE SPECIFICATION: Mercedes-Benz	
Chassis:	Mercedes-Benz
Engine:	Mercedes-Benz OM321, 110 bhp diesel
Transmission:	5 speed manual gearbox
Length:	approx 30 ft
Width:	approx 8 ft
Wheelbase:	??

Katong-Bedok Bus Service was to be the first user of the Mercedes-Benz in Singapore, with a number of 40 seat centre entrance buses of the traditional Singaporean style, powered by the OM321 engine. This power unit gave satisfaction, and was installed in at least one of Katong-Bedok's TSMs. The fleet was generally well looked after, and many of the older Katong-Bedok buses passed into the Associated Bus Service fleet, and were eventually replaced by new generation Mercedes-Benz buses assembled in Singapore.

ABOVE: Katong-Bedok SH 782 on service 2 shows the lines of its locally built body incorporating an elliptical grille, featuring the Mercedes-Benz three pointed star, which copies the German firm's contemporary styling. *(Choo Tian Chwee*

LEFT: Another view of the service 2 terminus at Bedok Road in June 1969 shows a Mercedes-Benz, and two TSMs. SH 224, the vehicle in the centre, repowered by Mercedes-Benz, has lost the Vulcan badge in favour of the Mercedes-Benz emblem. *(Choo Tian Chwee*

ABOVE: Tay Koh Yat SH 953 shows the revised livery introduced with all-metal buses. The colours are now just flashes over the wheelarches and much of the vehicle is either unpainted or silver. This bus shows well the early Singapore-built, all-metal, bodywork which was quite attractive and displayed some familiar design features, particularly in the front dome and roofline, previously incorporated in traditional timber built buses.

BELOW: SH 958 is one of the very first of hundreds of truck chassis based buses which were introduced in order to speed up modernisation of the Singapore bus fleets. This bus is based on the LP1113 chassis, and the front and windscreen were factory built. It is seen here in the service of Associated Bus Services. Compare the high floor level of this vehicle with the other Mercedes-Benz illustrated on this page.

Morris OP/R

The Morris OP/R (these letters signify Oil-engined, Passenger chassis, Right-hand drive) was introduced in 1948. In many ways it represented a forward-control version of the popular Bedford OB, a model which was not built with a forward driving position, but which was often rebuilt as such by owners, particularly in Scotland and Australia. The Morris chassis was made available with petrol or oil engine, and over 650 were built, most being placed in service in Britain, Singapore and Malaya, India and Ceylon, and the Middle East.

The overall dimensions were compact, and this model bridged the gap between the small 20 seat rear entrance buses based on military type chassis, and the medium sized Albions and Commers. It was closest in style and layout to the Vulcan 6PF, but the latter was lorry derived, whereas the OP/R was designed as a passenger carrying chassis, and it was the final such chassis designed and produced by Morris before the merger with Austin to create what became known as the British Motor Corporation. It therefore has nothing in common with certain later bus chassis badged Morris, but which were really identical to Austin models.

VEHICLE SPECIFICATION: *Morris OP/R*	
Chassis:	Morris OP/R
Engine:	Saurer designed diesel engine 4.25 litre
Transmission:	Manual 4-speed gearbox
Length:	
Width:	7ft 4 ins
Wheelbase:	14ft 11 ins

BELOW: Tay Koh Yat SC7700 seen on display when new. Of interest in the indicator display shown when box was empty of usual route screen, and the front, rather than centre, entrance. Quite a few TKY buses had the door in what was an unusual position in Singapore at the time. *(Straits Times*

Seddon—Mark 4 and Mark 6

Seddon Diesel Vehicles Limited specialised in the construction of medium weight and lightweight trucks and buses. Up to ten different types of bus chassis were produced, the majority of which were exported from Great Britain mainly to Africa, Asia and South America, during the period covered by this volume. The models imported for use in Singapore were quite distinct, and are dealt with under separate headings.

Seddon Mark 4

This model was similar in concept to the Albion FT series Victor and Vulcan 6PF in being a lorry derived passenger chassis, designed to carry 29-31 passengers. The factory built frontal panel was common to both Seddon buses and lorries and featured a plain rectangular exposed radiator. The power unit generally fitted was the Perkins P6 diesel engine, of 4.73 litres capacity, driving through a constant-mesh gearbox. Used by several of the Chinese Bus Companies, it was not as numerous in Singapore as it was in Malaya.

A feature of Seddons was the emblem carried in the centre of the radiator, formed by the words '**Seddon DIESEL**' inside a circle. On certain other Seddon models (as described below) the emblem was placed on the frontal grille, or plain front panel, and was distinctive enough to proclaim the make of the vehicle

VEHICLE SPECIFICATION: Seddon Mark 4/Mark 6	
Chassis:	Seddon Mark 4/Mark 6
Engine:	Perkins P6
Transmission:	4 speed manual gearbox
Length:	Mark 4 - 27ft 0 in
	Mark 6 - 30ft 0in
Width:	7ft 6 ins
Wheelbase:	Mark 4 - 14ft 11ins
	Mark 6 - 16ft 4 ins

from a distance, in the same manner as the Mercedes-Benz three-pointed star, or the Vulcan vee-shaped badge. However, there were on the roads of Singapore a number of Fargos that, in the absence of a factory fitted front of distinctive appearance, were equipped locally with frontal panels that looked very like those of Seddon vehicles, and which in addition carried a circular emblem inscribed 'Fargo'. (For further details see under Fargo)

Seddon Mark 6

The Mark 6 was a longer wheelbase version of the Mark 4 described above, and was the equivalent of the Albion FT39AL, being suitable for bodywork of up to 30 ft in length.

BELOW: Seddon Mark 6 SH346 of Changi Bus Company passes Yau Kit village on route 1, destined for the Capitol Theatre.

The Mark 10 midibus is exemplified by SH395, one of the several owned by Hock Lee Amalgamated Company for use on a route passing over narrow roads. An almost identical vehicle, registered SB3775, was a 'Private Bus' in the Paya Lebar Bus Company fleet.

Seddon Mark 10

Seddon were one of the earliest British manufacturers to build vehicles that are nowadays referred to as 'midi-buses', that is to say small capacity vehicles designed from the outset for passenger use, and not modifications of vans. Midibuses usually seat between 20-30 passengers, and whereas they began as vehicles for use on routes with narrow roads or light loadings, nowadays they tend to be deployed on urban services with high frequencies. In their day, they were often referred to 'personnel carriers', and were used as staff transport.

The Mark 10 employed a 4 cylinder diesel engine, and was only two thirds as long as a normal bus of the day. In Singapore, the Paya

VEHICLE SPECIFICATION: Seddon Mark 10	
Chassis:	Seddon Mark 10
Engine:	Perkins P4 (4 cylinder diesel)
Transmission:	manual gearbox
Length:	21 ft 6 ins
Width:	
Wheelbase:	11ft 8 ins

Lebar bus Company used one for private hire or staff transport, whilst Hock Lee Amalgamated required some very short vehicles for a route along narrow roads with tight curves.

Seddon Mark 11

The Seddon Mark 11 is quite a rare model in the Seddon range, and was designed as a cheaper option to the underfloor engined bus and coach chassis which major manufacturers introduced from 1950 onwards. Most of these featured a 'flat' engine, otherwise known as 'horizontal', in which the engine block was modified, and auxiliary equipment relocated in order to give an engine of low height which could be fitted beneath the floor. Such engines were regarded by some fleet engineers as difficult to access, and were more prone to overheating and damage from dusty roads. Seddon produced a chassis which featured a vertical engine mounted beneath the floor, and which was essentially a version of their standard passenger chassis with repositioned axles and mechanical units. One disadvantage of using a taller engine was that the floor height was raised. This did not matter very much if the vehicle was used on express service or as a touring coach, but the Mark 11s in Singapore, such as SH301-2 of the Changi fleet, and SH446-7 of Green Bus, were used on busy crowded services, and the three high steps which had to be surmounted by boarding passengers, who were often burdened with bags and bundles, were far from ideal. Another disadvantage of the under-

VEHICLE SPECIFICATION: Seddon Mark 11	
Chassis:	Seddon Mark 11
Engine:	Perkins R6
Transmission:	
Length:	30ft 0 in
Width:	7 ft 6 ins or 8 ft 0 ins
Wheelbase:	16 ft 6 ins

floor engine was the danger from flash floods, so common in Singapore's tropical climate. The Mark 11 did not find success in Singapore, and all subsequent Seddons used by the Chinese Bus Companies were of the normal forward engined type. Seddon replaced the Mark 11 by the Mark 19, a chassis with a slightly lower floor level, and which used a 'flat' engine produced by AEC. Green Bus later demoted their Mark 11s to School Buses, where the high carrying capacity was an advantage, and the passengers were nimble enough not to mind climbing the steps.

Seddon Mark 17

The Mark 17 was an up-graded version of the Mark 6, with the choice of an extra long wheelbase to allow for bodywork of up to 33ft 0 in length. The front axle was slightly set back, and the central radiator was replaced by a futuristic grille, which could be incorporated by the body builders into the front of the bus. The engine fitted was a more powerful version of the famous Perkins P6, designated R6. Thus the Mark 17 was of the same concept as the Dennis Teal and Albion Victor VT17, and was supplied to numerous customers around the world. Its chief merit over some of the other similar makes of bus in its era was the saloon floor level, which was quite low and reached by two steps.

VEHICLE SPECIFICATION: Seddon Mark 1	
Chassis:	Seddon Mark 17
Engine:	Perkins P6 or R6
Transmission:	4 speed manual gearbox
Length:	30 ft to 33 ft
Width:	7 ft 6 ins or 8 ft 0 ins
Wheelbase	17 ft 10 ins

THIS PAGE ABOVE: SH796U, seen in later days with United, shows the greater length and 'fish mouth' front of the Mark 17.

OPPOSITE PAGE LEFT: SH301 is an underfloor engined Seddon Mark 11 of Changi Bus Company seen here in Changi Village. Comparison with the vehicle behind shows the high floor level.

TSM (Tilling-Stevens)

At the 1948 Commercial Motor show, TSM introduced a new 'lightweight' model. The Company's heavyweight K series vehicles had been selling to coach operators rather than to service bus operators, and there was a need to introduce a cheaper chassis in order to retain custom. The new L series chassis was designated L6PA7, which indicated a Perkins P6 oil engine, and a 17 ft 3 ins wheelbase, and it was supplied without a front radiator, to allow coachbuilders to fit front panels to suit body styling.

TSM also built Vulcan trucks and buses, and the Vulcan passenger chassis was now dropped in favour of the new lightweight TSM. In Singapore and Malaya, where Vulcan was building up a customer base, the new TSM was badged as a Vulcan. This was nothing new, as prewar TSMs supplied to Hong Kong also carried Vulcan badges, although in the postwar period a large number of TSM K series sold to Hong Kong were regis-

VEHICLE SPECIFICATION: TSM L6PA7	
Chassis:	TSM L6PA7
Engine:	Perkins P6
Gearbox:	4 speed manual
Length:	27 ft 0 ins
Width:	7 ft 6 ins
Wheelbase:	17 ft 3 ins

tered under the TSM name. The Singapore coachbuilders fitted the TSMs with false radiator shells to resemble the erstwhile Vulcan front end styling in many cases, and probably slightly more TSMs badged as Vulcans were sold in Singapore than true Vulcans. In 1953 the TSM business was acquired by the Rootes Group (proprietors of Commer, *inter alia*), and so the supply of this type of bus ceased.

LEFT: A mock Vulcan radiator is incorporated into the front of SH 380 of the Tay Koh Yat Bus Service. It is seen here when one month old, on route to the airport on service 9, in October 1955.

LOWER LEFT: SH 377 of Kampong-Bahru shows a different frontal styling, but is otherwise virtually identical to SH 380.

Vulcan 6PF

The Vulcan Motor & Engineering Company of Southport, a maker of trucks and buses, found itself in financial trouble in the 1930s and was eventually was taken over by Tilling-Stevens of Maidstone. Under new ownership, the Company became known as Vulcan Motors Limited In order to retain favour in certain markets, Tilling-Stevens supplied vehicles built to its own design equipped with Vulcan badges. Perhaps because it was best known as a builder of buses, the parent company began to produce a truck from 1945 under the Vulcan name, and from this a simple bus chassis was derived. Both truck and bus were known as the 6PF model, even though as a truck there were differences in wheelbase and springing. Tilling-Stevens also continued to produce bus chassis and electrically driven goods vehicles under its own name.

The 6PF was quite popular in Singapore, where many buses with the distinctive sloping front scuttle and central mesh grille were bought by the Chinese Bus Companies. Katong Bedok, Changi, Ponggol, Keppel, Kampong Bahru, Paya Lebar, Hock Lee Amalgamated, Sing Lian Express and the Singapore-Johore Express all took

VEHICLE SPECIFICATION: Vulcan 6PF	
Chassis:	Vulcan 6PF
Engine:	Perkins P6
Transmission:	4 speed manual
Length:	
Width:	7ft 4 ins
Wheelbase:	

this model. Further buses of this type were also to be found in Malaya. The chassis had much in common with the 6/7 ton truck, and was powered either by a Vulcan petrol engine or the Perkins P6 diesel. It was dropped when the manufacturer was taken over in 1950 by the Rootes Group, a vehicle manufacturer amongst whose marques were Commer and Karrier, but for a while it was substituted in the Singapore market by Tilling-Stevens' own medium weight bus chassis, although this was a slightly larger vehicle than the 6PF. As had happened before, the Tilling-Stevens vehicles were badged as Vulcans in order to retain customer loyalty.

RIGHT: Ponggol SH182, seen here in Paya Lebar Village in November 1954, is a typical example of the Vulcan 6PF, fitted with Singapore built 31 seat bodywork.

LOWER RIGHT: Singapore - Johore Express SH236 was one of a late pair of Vulcans built with a slightly longer wheel base. Although the body differs in much detail from Ponggol SH182, the factory supplied front is identical. When new, SH236 and its sister vehicle operated in a special livery in connection with an economic conference of nations involved in the Colombo Plan and it is seen here in October 1955 with lettering Colombo Plan Conference instead of the usual fleetname.

Fleet Lists
of the Singapore Bus Operators from 1926 to 1971

Section One:
The trolleybuses and buses of the Singapore Traction Company

Section Two:
The buses of the 'Chinese' bus operators.

Changi Bus Company Limited
Easy Bus Company
Green Bus Company
Hock Lee Amalgamated Bus Company
Kampong Bahru Bus Service

Katong Bedok Bus Service
Keppel Bus Company
Paya Lebar Bus Service
Ponggol Bus Service
Tay Koh Yat Bus Company

Express service operators:

Singapore–Johore Express
Kuala Lumpur–Singapore Express
Sing Lian Express

Singapore Traction Company
Fleet list of trolleybuses and buses

Readers should be aware that registration numbers were reused after vehicles were withdrawn and some buses were re-registered in order to allow new vehicles to take an unbroken series of numbers where some older ones remained in use.

STC was permitted to allocate registration numbers itself within the range STC 1 to 999 although by no menas all were ever used. Trolleybuses carried only un-prefixed fleet numbers.

AEC MODEL 603 TROLLEYBUSES

BODY PARTS BY SHANGHAI ELECTRIC CONST. CO.

Fleet number	Date new	Withdrawn	Disposal / notes
1	1926	?	
2	1926	?	
3	1926	?	
4	1926	?	
5	1926	?	
6	1926	?	
7	1926	?	
8	1926	?	
9	1926	?	
10	1926	?	
11	1926	?	
12	1926	?	
13	1926	?	
14	1926	?	
15	1926	?	
16	1926	?	
17	1926	?	
18	1926	?	
19	1926	?	
20	1926	?	
21	1926	?	
22	1926	?	
23	1926	?	
24	1926	?	
25	1926	?	
26	1926	?	
27	1926	?	
28	1926	?	
29	1926	?	
30	1926	?	
31	1926	?	
32	1926	?	
33	1926	?	
34	1926	?	
35	1926	?	
36	1926	?	
37	1926	?	
38	1926	?	
39	1926	?	
40	1926	?	
41	1927	?	
42	1927	?	
43	1927	?	
44	1927	?	
45	1927	?	
46	1927	?	
47	1927	?	
48	1927	?	
49	1927	?	
50	1927	?	
51	1927	?	
52	1927	?	
53	1927	?	
54	1927	?	
55	1927	?	
56	1927	?	
57	1927	?	
58	1927	?	
59	1927	?	
60	1927	?	
61	1927	?	
62	1927	?	
63	1927	?	
64	1927	?	
65	1927	?	
66	1927	?	
67	1927	?	
68	1927	?	
69	1927	?	
70	1927	?	
71	1927	?	
72	1927	?	
73	1927	?	
74	1927	?	
75	1927	?	
76	1927	?	
77	1927	?	
78	1927	?	
79	1927	?	
80	1927	?	
81	1927	?	
82	1927	?	
83	1927	?	
84	1927	?	
85	1927	?	
86	1927	?	
87	1927	?	
88	1927	?	
89	1927	?	

WITHDRAWAL DATES

All 108 AEC trolleybuses were in regular use at the outset of the Pacific War. As a result of heroic efforts by the operating staff, working under extreme hardship, a number of AECs remained in service in September 1945 when the management was released from internment. The maximum number available postwar was 51 for a very short period. Actual dates of withdrawal cannot be given but the last AEC ran in late 1948, upon the arrival of the last new replacement Ransomes, while others will have fallen victim to bombs and shellfire as early as February 1942.

AEC MODEL 603 TROLLEYBUSES (continued)

BODY PARTS BY SHANGHAI ELECTRIC CONST. CO.

Fleet number	Date new	Withdrawn	Disposal / notes
90	1927	?	
91	1928	?	
92	1928	?	
93	1928	?	
94	1928	?	
95	1928	?	
96	1928	?	
97	1928	?	
98	1928	?	
99	1928	?	
100	1928	?	
101	1928	?	
102	1928	?	
103	1928	?	
104	1928	?	
105	1928	?	
106	1929	?	
107	1929	?	
108	1929	?	

DENNIS G-TYPE

BODY PARTS BY SHANGHAI ELECTRIC CONST. CO.

Registration number	Date new	Withdrawn	Disposal / Notes
STC 1	1929	1938	?
STC 2	1929	1938	?
STC 3	1929	1938	?
STC 4	1929	1938	?
STC 5	1929	1938	?
STC 6	1929	1938	?
STC 7	1929	1938	?
STC 8	1930	1938	?
STC 9	1930	1938	?
STC 10	1930	1938	?
STC 11	1930	1938	?
STC 12	1930	1938	?
STC 13	1930	1938	?
STC 14	1930	1938	?
STC 15	1930	1938	?
STC 16	1930	1938	?
STC 17	1930	1938	?

FORD (UK) MODEL AA

BODY PARTS BY SHANGHAI ELECTRIC CONST. CO.

Registration number	Date new	Withdrawn	Disposal / Notes
STC 18	1933	1939	
STC 19	1933	1939	
STC 20	1933	1939	
STC 21	1933	1939	
STC 22	1933	1939	
STC 23	1933	1939	
STC 24	1933	1939	
STC 25	1933	1939	
STC 26	1933	1939	
STC 27	1933	1939	
STC 28	1934	1939	
STC 29	1934	1939	
STC 30	1934	1939	
STC 31	1934	1939	
STC 32	1934	1939	
STC 33	1934	1939	
STC 34	1934	1939	
STC 35	1934	1939	
STC 36	1934	1939	
STC 37	1934	1939	
STC 38	01.01.35	1942	See notes
STC 39	01.01.35	1942	See notes
STC 40	01.01.35	1942	See notes
STC 41	01.01.35	1942	See notes
STC 42	01.01.35	1942	See notes
STC 43	01.01.35	1942	See notes
STC 44	01.01.35	1942	See notes
STC 45	01.01.35	1942	See notes
STC 46	01.01.35	1942	See notes
STC 47	01.01.35	1942	See notes
STC 48	01.01.35	1942	See notes
STC 49	01.01.35	1942	See notes
STC 50	01.01.35	1942	See notes
STC 51	01.01.35	1942	See notes
STC 52	01.01.35	1942	See notes
STC 53	01.01.35	1942	See notes
STC 54	01.01.35	1942	See notes
STC 55	01.01.35	1942	See notes
STC 56	01.01.35	1942	See notes
STC 57	01.01.35	1942	See notes
STC 58	01.01.35	1942	See notes
STC 59	01.01.35	1942	See notes
STC 60	01.01.35	1942	See notes

FORD (UK) MODEL AA *(continued)*

Registration number	Date new	Withdrawn	Disposal / Notes
			BODY PARTS BY SHANGHAI ELECTRIC CONST. CO.
STC 61	01.01.35	1942	See notes
STC 62	01.01.35	1942	See notes
STC 63	01.01.35	1942	See notes
STC 64	01.01.35	1942	See notes
STC 65	01.01.35	1942	See notes
STC 66	01.01.35	1942	See notes
STC 67	01.01.35	1942	See notes
STC 68	01.01.35	1942	See notes
STC 69	01.01.35	1942	See notes
STC 70	01.01.35	1942	See notes
STC 71	01.01.35	1942	See notes
STC 72	01.01.35	1942	See notes
STC 73	01.01.35	1942	See notes
STC 74	01.01.35	1942	See notes
STC 75	01.01.35	1942	See notes
STC 76	01.01.35	1942	See notes
STC 77	01.01.35	1942	See notes
STC 78	01.01.35	1942	See notes
STC 79	01.01.35	1942	See notes
STC 80	01.01.35	1942	See notes
STC 81	01.01.35	1942	See notes
STC 82	01.01.35	1942	See notes
STC 83	01.01.35	1942	See notes
STC 84	01.01.35	1942	See notes
STC 85	01.01.35	1942	See notes
STC 86	01.01.35	1942	See notes
STC 87	01.01.35	1942	See notes
STC 88	01.01.35	1942	See notes
STC 89	01.01.35	1942	See notes
STC 90	01.01.35	1942	See notes
STC 91	01.01.35	1942	See notes
STC 92	01.01.35	1942	See notes
STC 93	01.01.35	1942	See notes
STC 94	1935	1942	See notes
STC 95	1935	1942	See notes
STC 96	1935	1942	See notes
STC 97	1935	1942	See notes
STC 98	1935	1942	See notes
STC 99	1935	1942	See notes
STC 100	1935	1942	See notes
STC 101	1935	1942	See notes
STC 102	1935	1942	See notes

Note 1.38-93 were introduced on 1st January 1935 en masse to counter the withdrawal of mosquito buses from the Geylang service

Note 2:The 1935 deliveries of Fords should have been withdrawn as more diesel powered chassis were taken into stock, as from 19

Note 4: total of 110 motor buses were requisitioned

LEYLAND CUB

Registration number	Date new	Withdrawn	Disposal / Notes
			BODY BY SINGAPORE TRACTION CO.
STC 103	1937	?	Note
STC 104	1937	?	Note
STC 105	1937	?	Note
STC 106	1937	?	Note
STC 107	1937	?	Note
STC 108	1937	?	Note
STC 109	1937	?	Note
STC 110	1937	?	Note
STC 111	1937	?	Note
STC 112	1937	?	Note

NOTE: All 10 Cubs were in stock at the commencement of the occupation but none are recordes as having survived until 1945. Withdrawal dates cannot therefore be specified

ALBION Victor PK115

Registration number	Date new	Withdrawn	Disposal / Notes
			BODY BY SINGAPORE TRACTION CO.
STC 113	1938	Note 1	
STC 114	1938		
STC 115	1938		
STC 116	1938		
STC 117	1938		
STC 118	1938		
STC 119	1938		
STC 120	1938		
STC 121	1938		
STC 122	1938		Chassis nos in text
STC 123	1938		
STC 124	1938		
STC 125	1939		
STC 126	1939		
STC 127	1939		
STC 128	1939		
STC 129	1939		
STC 130	1939		
STC 131	1939		
STC 132	1939		
STC 133	1939		
STC 134	1939		
STC 135	1939		
STC 136	1939		
STC 137	1939		
STC 138	1939		
STC 139	1939		
STC 140	1939		
STC 141	1939		
STC 142	1939		

ALBION Victor PK115 *(continued)*

Registration number	Date new	Withdrawn	Disposal / Notes
			BODY BY SINGAPORE TRACTION CO.
STC 143	1939		
STC 144	1939		
STC 145	1939		
STC 146	1939		
STC 147	1939		
STC 148	1939		
STC 149	1939		

STC 150 to STC 179

ALBIONS which were ordered during August 1940 but delivery was impossible due to wartime conditions

STC 180 to STC 191

FORD (US) 118.WF (180-188); WF 114 (189) or WF116 (190 & 191) Body probably STC

BUSES REINSTATED 1945 and replacement buses and lorry buses

The prewar series interrupted at STC 199 was believed to have been continued for a short period under the post-occupation British Military Administration, probably commencing at STC 200 as there is photographic evidence of Dodge military trucks registered as follows:

STC 231 Dodge truck
STC 244 Dodge truck
STC 251 Dodge truck

Records for this period are unavailable and thus we offer only these few tantalising snippets. Reference to the text will reveal illustrations of post-occupation lorry-buses.

An interesting note is that, with the surrender of the Japanese military, there were numerous of their vehicles in Singapore and, presumably, these would have been pressed into service, although spare parts would have quickly become a problem. At least one Hino is recorded with Tay Koh Yat.

ALBION VICTOR PK115

Regn. number	Date new	Withdrawn	Disposal / Notes
			BODY BY STC extensively rebuilt
STC 1	1938/39	by 1948	Scrapped
STC 2	1938/39	by 1948	Scrapped
STC 3	1938/39	by 1948	Scrapped
STC 4	1938/39	by 1948	Scrapped
STC 5	1938/39	*circa*1952	Scrapped—Note 1.
STC 6	1938/39	by 1948	Scrapped
STC 7	1938/39	by 1948	Scrapped
STC 8	1938/39	*circa*1955	Re-registered STC 288 —Note 2.
STC 9	1938/39	by 1948	Scrapped
STC 10	1938/39	by 1948	Scrapped
STC 11	1938/39	by 1948	Scrapped
STC 12	1938/39	by 1948	Scrapped
STC 13	1938/39	by 1948	Scrapped
STC 14	1938/39	by 1948	Scrapped
STC 15	1938/39	by 1948	Scrapped

Note 1: STC 5 was largely complete in a scrapyard in 1952.
Note 2: STC 8 was rebodied with centre doorway by Lee Kiat Seng, re-registered STC 288 and retained in service as a staff bus until circa 1955

STC 16 et seq. The recovered buses were re-registered in a new series commencing STC 1. STC 1 to 15 being allocated to those Albions considered to have a medium term future, whilst STC 16 et seq were those vehicles—many, but not exclusively, Albions—that had only a short-term future, having been so dilapidated that they would have become more of a public danger than an asset in the attempt to restore bus services.

DENNIS FALCON

BODY BY LEE KIAT SENG

Regn. number	Chassis number	Date new	Withdrawn	Disposal / Notes
STC 16	101P2	1946	1956	
STC 17	102P2	1946	1956	
STC 18	103P2	1946	1956	
STC 19	104P2	1946	1956	
STC 20	105P2	1946	1956	
STC 21	106P2	1946	1957	
STC 22	107P2	1946	1963	
STC 23	108P2	1946	1957	No destination box when new
STC 24	109P2	1946	1963	Renumbered STC103 1955
STC 25	110P2	1946	1957	
STC 26	111P2	1946	1957	
STC 27	112P2	1946	1957	
STC 28	113P2	1946	1957	
STC 29	114P2	1946	1957	
STC 30	115P2	1946	1957	
STC 31	116P2	1946	1957	
STC 32	117P2	1946	1957	
STC 33	118P2	1946	1963	Renumbered STC104 1955
STC 31	119P2	1946	1951	Burned out May1951
STC 31	120P2	1946	1957	
STC 31	121P2	1946	1963	Renumbered STC105 1955
STC 31	122P2	1946	1957	
STC 38	123P2	1946	1957	
STC 39	124P2	1946	1957	
STC 40	125P2	1946	1957	
STC 41	126P2	1947	1957	
STC 42	127P2	1947	1957	
STC 43	128P2	1947	1957	
STC 44	129P2	1947	1958	
STC 45	130P2	1947	1958	
STC 46	131P2	1947	1958	
STC 47	1P232	1947	1958	
STC 48	133P2	1947	1958	
STC 49	134P2	1947	1958	
STC 50	135P2	1947	1958	
STC 51	136P2	1947	1958	
STC 52	137P2	1947	1963	Renumbered STC106 1955
STC 53	138P2	1947	1958	
STC 54	138P2	1947	1958	
STC 55	140P2	1947	1958	
STC 56	141P2	1947	1958	
STC 57	142P2	1947	1958	
STC 58	143P2	1947	1958	
STC 59	144P2	1947	1963	Renumbered STC107 1955
STC 60	145P2	1947	1958	
STC 61	146P2	1947	1958	
STC 62	147P2	1947	1958	
STC 63	148P2	1947	1958	
STC 64	149P2	1947	1958	
STC 65	150P2	1947	1958	
STC 66	151P2	1947	1958	
STC 67	152P2	1947	1958	
STC 68	153P2	1947	1958	
STC 69	154P2	1947	1958	
STC 70	155P2	1947	1958	
STC 71	156P2	1947	1958	
STC 72	157P2	1947	1958	
STC 73	158P2	1947	1958	
STC 74	159P2	1947	1958	
STC 75	160P2	1947	1958	
STC 76	161P2	1947	1958	
STC 77	162P2	1947	1958	
STC 78	163P2	1947	1958	
STC 79	164P2	1947	1958	
STC 80	165P2	1947	1958	
STC 81	166P2	1947	1958	
STC 82	167P2	1947	1958	
STC 83	168P2	1947	1958	
STC 84	169P2	1947	1951	Burned Delta Rd Terminus May 1951
STC 85	170P2	1947	1958	
STC 86	171P2	1947	1958	
STC 87	172P2	1947	1958	
STC 88	173P2	1947	1958	
STC 89	174P2	1947	1958	
STC 90	175P2	1947	1958	
STC 91	176P2	1948	1963	
STC 92	177P2	1948	1963	
STC 93	178P2	1948	1963	
STC 94	179P2	1948	1963	
STC 95	180P2	1948	1963	
STC 96	181P2	1948	1963	
STC 97	182P2	1948	1963	
STC 98	183P2	1948	1963	
STC 99	184P2	1948	1963	
STC 100	185P2	1948	1963	
STC 101	186P2	1948	1954	
STC 102	187P2	1948	1954	Number taken by STC22 1955
STC 103	188P2	1948	1954	Number taken by STC24 1955
STC 104	189P2	1948	1954	Number taken by STC33 1955
STC 105	190P2	1948	1954	Number taken by STC36 1955
STC 106	191P2	1948	1954	Number taken by STC52 1955
STC 107	192P2	1948	1954	Number taken by STC59 1955
STC 108	193P2	1948	1963	
STC 109	194P2	1948	1963	
STC 110	195P2	1948	1963	
STC 111	196P2	1948	1963	
STC 112	197P2	1948	1963	
STC 113	198P2	1948	1963	
STC 114	199P2	1948	1963	
STC 115	200P2	1948	1963	

RANSOMES SIMS & JEFFERIES TROLLEYBUSES

BODY BY LEE KIAT SENG

Fleet number	Chassis number	Date new	Withdrawn
1	4457	1948	1964
2	4453	1948	1964
3	4486	1948	1964
4	4465	1948	1964
5	4451	1948	1964
6	4463	1948	1964
7	4479	1948	1964
8	4448	1948	1964
9	4469	1948	1964
10	4450	1948	1964
11	4446	1948	1964
12	4488	1948	1964
13	4481	1948	1964
14	4490	1948	1964
15	4482	1948	1964
16	4487	1948	1964
17	4492	1948	1964
18	4475	1948	1964
19	4467	1948	1964
20	4474	1948	1964
21	4472	1948	1964
22	4449	1948	1964
23	4483	1948	1964
24	4476	1948	1964
25	4458	1948	1964
26	4491	1948	1964
27	4494	1948	1964
28	4456	1948	1964
29	4454	1948	1964
30	4489	1948	1964
31	4493	1948	1964
32	4471	1948	1964
33	4459	1948	1964
34	4480	1948	1964
35	4477	1948	1964
36	4495	1948	1964
37	4468	1948	1964
38	4460	1948	1964
39	4485	1948	1964
40	4484	1948	1964
41	4461	1948	1964
42	4462	1948	1964
43	4473	1948	1964
45	4455	1948	1964
44	4447	1948	1964
46	4478	1948	1964
47	4466	1948	1964
48	4470	1948	1964
49	4464	1948	1964
50	4452	1948	1964

ALBION FT39N

BODY BY LEE KIAT SENG

Regn. number	Date new	Withdrawn	Disposal / Notes
STC 116	1949	?	
STC 117	1949	?	
STC 118	1949	?	
STC 119	1949	?	Renumbered STC 519 in 1964
STC 120	1949	?	
STC 121	1949	?	
STC 122	1949	?	
STC 123	1949	?	
STC 124	1949	?	
STC 125	1949	?	
STC 126	1949	?	
STC 127	1949	?	
STC 128	1949	?	Renumbered STC 528 in 1964
STC 129	1949	?	
STC 130	1949	?	
STC 131	1949	?	
STC 132	1949	?	
STC 133	1949	?	
STC 134	1949	?	
STC 135	1949	?	
STC 136	1949	?	
STC 137	1949	?	
STC 138	1949	?	
STC 139	1949	1951	Arson victim
STC 140	1949	?	
STC 141	1949	?	
STC 142	1949	?	
STC 143	1949	?	
STC 144	1949	?	
STC 145	1949	?	
STC 146	1949	?	
STC 147	1949	?	
STC 148	1949	?	Renumbered STC 548 in 1964
STC 149	1949	?	
STC 150	1949	?	Renumbered STC 550 in 1964
STC 151	1949	?	
STC 152	1949	?	
STC 153	1949	?	Renumbered STC 553 in 1964
STC 154	1949	?	
STC 155	1949	?	
STC 156	1949	?	

BEDFORD OB   *BODY BY HOCK HIN THYE*

Regn. number	Date new	Withdrawn	Disposal
STC 157	1946	1957	Rebuilt and renumbered 201 in 1956
STC 158	1946	1952	
STC 159	1946	1955	
STC 160	1946	1955	
STC 161	1946	1955	
STC 162	1946	1955	
STC 163	1946	1955	
STC 164	1946	1955	
STC 165	1946	1955	
STC 166	1946	1955	
STC 167	1946	1955	
STC 168	1946	1955	
STC 169	1946	1955	
STC 170	1946	1955	
STC 171	1946	1955	
STC 172	1946	1955	
STC 173	1946	1955	
STC 174	1946	1955	
STC 175	1946	1955	
STC 176	1946	1955	
STC 177	1946	1955	
STC 178	1946	1955	
STC 179	1946	1955	
STC 180	1946	1955	
STC 181	1946	1955	
STC 182	1946	1955	
STC 183	1946	1955	
STC 184	1946	1955	
STC 185	1946	1955	
STC 186	1946	1955	
STC 187	1946	1955	
STC 188	1946	1955	
STC 189	1946	1956	
STC 190	1946	1956	Chassis used as a 'Coronation Coach' June 1953
STC 191	1946	1956	
STC 192	1946	1956	
STC 193	1946	1956	
STC 194	1946	1956	
STC 195	1946	1956	
STC 196	1946	1956	
STC 197	1946	1956	
STC 198	1946	1956	
STC 199	1946	1956	
STC 200	1946	1956	
STC 201	1946	1956	As STC 201
STC 202	1946	1953	
STC 203	1946	1956	
STC 204	1946	1956	
STC 205	1946	1956	
STC 206	1946	1956	
STC 207	1946	1956	
STC 208	1946	1956	
STC 209	1946	1956	
STC 210	1946	1956	
STC 211	1946	1956	
STC 212	1946	1956	
STC 213	1946	1956	
STC 214	1946	1956	
STC 215	1946	1956	
STC 216	1946	1956	
STC 217	1946	1956	
STC 218	1946	1956	
STC 219	1946	1956	
STC 220	1946	1956	
STC 221	1946	1953	
STC 222	1946	1953	
STC 223	1946	1953	
STC 224	1946	1953	
STC 225	1946	1953	
STC 226	1946	1953	
STC 227	1947	1953	
STC 228	1947	1953	
STC 229	1947	1953	
STC 230	1947	1953	
STC 231	1947	1953	
STC 232	1947	1954	
STC 233	1947	1954	
STC 234	1947	1954	
STC 235	1947	1954	
STC 236	1947	1954	
STC 237	1947	1954	
STC 238	1947	1954	
STC 239	1947	1954	
STC 240	1947	1954	
STC 241	1947	1954	
STC 242	1947	1954	
STC 243	1947	1954	
STC 244	1947	1954	
STC 245	1947	1953	
STC 246	1947	1954	
STC 247	1947	1954	
STC 248	1947	1954	
STC 249	1947	1953	
STC 250	1947	1954	

FORD (USA) 'School Bus' chassis Model 1946
BODY BY HOCK HIN THYE

Regn. number	Date new	Withdrawn	Disposal
STC 251	1946	by 1953	
STC 252	1946	by 1953	
STC 253	1946	by 1953	
STC 254	1946	by 1953	
STC 255	1946	by 1953	
STC 256	1946	by 1953	
STC 257	1946	by 1953	
STC 258	1946	by 1953	
STC 259	1946	by 1953	
STC 260	1946	by 1953	
STC 261	1946	by 1953	
STC 262	1946	by 1953	

ALBION VICTOR FT39N   *BODY BY LEE KIAT SENG*

Regn. number	Date new	Withdrawn	Disposal
STC 263	1950	?	
STC 264	1950	?	
STC 265	1950	?	
STC 266	1950	?	
STC 267	1950	?	
STC 268	1950	?	
STC 269	1950	?	
STC 270	1950	?	
STC 271	1950	?	
STC 272	1950	?	
STC 273	1950	?	
STC 274	1950	?	
STC 275	1950	?	
STC 276	1950	?	
STC 277	1950	?	
STC 278	1950	?	
STC 279	1950	?	
STC 280	1950	?	
STC 281	1950	?	
STC 282	1950	?	
STC 283	1950	?	
STC 284	1950	?	
STC 285	1950	?	
STC 286	1950	?	
STC 287	1950	?	

Re-registration of pre-1942 bus
ALBION PK 115   *REBODIED BY LEE KIAT SENG*

Regn. number	Previous number	Date new	Withdrawn	Disposal
STC 288	STC 8	1938	1955	Scrapped by STC

STC 289 to 299 not issued

ALBION VICTOR FT39L   *BODY BY LEE KIAT SENG*

Regn. number	Date new	Withdrawn	Disposal
STC 300	1951	?	Exact details of disposals not known but many were sold for use as school buses and took SCB series registration numbers
STC 301	1951	?	
STC 302	1951	?	
STC 303	1951	?	
STC 304	1951	?	
STC 305	1951	?	
STC 306	1951	?	
STC 307	1951	?	
STC 308	1951	?	
STC 309	1951	?	
STC 310	1951	?	
STC 311	1952	?	
STC 312	1952	?	
STC 313	1952	?	
STC 314	1952	?	
STC 315	1952	?	
STC 316	1952	?	
STC 317	1952	?	
STC 318	1952	?	
STC 319	1952	?	
STC 320	1952	?	
STC 321	1952	?	
STC 322	1952	?	
STC 323	1952	?	
STC 324	1952	?	
STC 325	1952	?	
STC 326	1952	?	
STC 327	1952	?	
STC 328	1952	?	
STC 329	1952	?	
STC 330	1952	?	

CHASSIS NUMBERS:
No chassis numbers can be matched with individual vehicles by registration number.

STC 300-349: No chassis numbers identified.

ALBION VICTOR FT39AN   *BODY BY LEE KIAT SENG*

Regn. number	Re-registered 1962 as	Date new	Withdrawn	Disposal
STC 1	STC 251	1952	?	
STC 2	STC 252	1952	?	
STC 3	STC 253	1952	?	
STC 4	STC 254	1952	?	
STC 5	STC 255	1952	?	

CHASSIS NUMBERS:
73712C/D/E/F/K

ALBION VICTOR FT39AL
BODY BY LEE KIAT SENG

Regn. number	Date new	Withdrawn	Disposal
STC 331	1952	?	
STC 332	1952	?	
STC 333	1952	?	
STC 334	1952	?	
STC 335	1952	?	
STC 336	1952	?	
STC 337	1952	?	
STC 338	1952	?	
STC 339	1952	?	
STC 340	1952	?	
STC 341	1952	?	
STC 342	1952	?	
STC 343	1952	?	
STC 344	1952	?	
STC 345	1952	?	
STC 346	1952	?	
STC 347	1952	?	
STC 348	1952	?	
STC 349	1952	?	
STC 350	1953	?	
STC 351	1953	?	
STC 352	1953	?	
STC 353	1953	?	
STC 354	1953	?	
STC 355	1953	?	
STC 356	1953	?	
STC 357	1953	?	
STC 358	1953	?	
STC 359	1953	?	
STC 360	1953	?	
STC 361	1953	?	
STC 362	1953	?	
STC 363	1953	?	
STC 364	1953	?	
STC 365	1953	?	
STC 366	1953	?	
STC 367	1953	?	
STC 368	1953	?	
STC 369	1953	?	
STC 370	1953	?	
STC 371	1953	?	
STC 372	1953	?	
STC 373	1953	?	
STC 374	1953	?	
STC 375	1953	?	
STC 376	1953	?	
STC 377	1954	?	
STC 378	1954	?	
STC 379	1954	?	
STC 380	1954	?	
STC 381	1954	?	
STC 382	1954	?	
STC 383	1954	?	
STC 384	1954	?	
STC 385	1954	?	
STC 386	1954	?	
STC 387	1954	?	
STC 388	1954	?	
STC 389	1954	?	
STC 390	1954	?	
STC 391	1954	?	
STC 392	1954	?	
STC 393	1954	?	
STC 394	1954	?	
STC 395	1954	?	
STC 396	1954	?	
STC 397	1954	?	
STC 398	1954	?	
STC 399	1954	?	
STC 400	1954	?	
STC 401	1954	?	
STC 402	1954	?	
STC 403	1954	?	
STC 404	1954	?	
STC 405	1954	?	
STC 406	1954	?	
STC 407	1954	?	
STC 408	1954	?	
STC 409	1954	?	
STC 410	1954	?	
STC 411	1954	?	
STC 412	1954	?	
STC 413	1954	?	

CHASSIS NUMBERS:
No chassis numbers can be matched with individual vehicles by registration number but some batches are known as follows:

STC 350-413—two batches, 27 and 38 but chassis in batches of 28 and 37:

NOTE: Albion used suffix letters as an integral part of the chassis number—ten letters A to L—omitting G and I.

STC 350–376 plus one: 73704E/F
73709A/B/C/D/J/K/L
73710A/B/C/D/E
73717H/J/K/L
73718A/B/C/D
73721B/C/D/E/F/K

STC 377–413 less one: 73733J/K
73735B/C
73735B/C/D/E/F/H/K
73739E/F/H/J/K/L
73740/A/B
73741A/B/C/D/E/F/H/J
73744A/B/C/D/E/F/H/J/K/L

ALBION VICTOR FT39ALX
BODY BY LEE KIAT SENG

Regn. number	Date new	Withdrawn	Disposal
STC 222	1954	?	
STC 223	1954	?	
STC 224	1954	?	
STC 225	1954	?	
STC 226	1954	?	
STC 227	1954	?	
STC 228	1954	?	
STC 229	1954	?	
STC 230	1954	?	
STC 231	1954	?	
STC 232	1955	?	
STC 233	1955	?	
STC 234	1955	?	
STC 235	1955	?	

CHASSIS NUMBERS:
These, while known, cannot be matched to individual vehicles but were:
STC 222–231: 73757K/L
(metal bodies) 73758A/B/C/D/E/F
73763B/C

STC 232–241: 73777H/J/K/L
73778A/B/C/D/E/F

ALBION VICTOR FT39ALX *(continued)*

Regn. number	Date new	Withdrawn	Disposal
STC 236	1955	?	
STC 237	1955	?	
STC 238	1955	?	
STC 239	1955	?	
STC 240	1955	?	
STC 241	1955	?	

ALBION VICTOR FT39AL
METAL BODY BY LEE KIAT SENG

Regn. number	Re-registered 1962 as	Date new	Withdrawn	Disposal
STC 6	STC 256	1954	?	
STC 7	STC 257	1954	?	
STC 8	STC 258	1954	?	
STC 9	STC 259	1954	?	
STC 10	STC 260	1954	?	

CHASSIS NUMBERS:
None traced

GUY ARAB MK IV5LWV
BODY BY LEE KIAT SENG

Regn. number	Date new	Withdrawn	Passed to	SH-series registration
STC 157	1956	Passed to >	Scrapped	
STC 158	1956	Passed to >	Scrapped	
STC 159	1956	Passed to >	Associated	SH 9306
STC 160	1956	Passed to >	Scrapped	
STC 161	1956	Passed to >	Associated	SH 9307
STC 162	1956	Passed to >	Associated	SH 9319
STC 163	1956	Passed to >	Scrapped	
STC 164	1956	Passed to >	Associated	SH 9296
STC 165	1956	Passed to >	Scrapped	
STC 166	1956	Passed to >	Associated	SH 9308
STC 167	1956	Passed to >	Scrapped	
STC 168	1956	Passed to >	Associated	SH 9320
STC 169	1956	Passed to >	Associated	SH 9309
STC 170	1956	Passed to >	Associated	SH 9292
STC 171	1956	Passed to >	Scrapped	
STC 172	1956	Passed to >	Associated	SH 9310
STC 173	1956	Passed to >	Associated	SH 9297
STC 174	1956	Passed to >	Associated	SH 9311
STC 175	1956	Passed to >	Scrapped	
STC 176	1956	Passed to >	Associated	SH 9312
STC 177	1956	Passed to >	Associated	SH 9321
STC 178	1956	Passed to >	Associated	SH 9313
STC 179	1956	Passed to >	Associated	SH 9322
STC 180	1956	Passed to >	Associated	SH 9298
STC 181	1956	Passed to >	Associated	SH 9293
STC 182	1956	Passed to >	Associated	SH 9314
STC 183	1956	Passed to >	Scrapped	
STC 184	1956	Passed to >	Associated	SH 9299
STC 185	1956	Passed to >	Scrapped	
STC 186	1956	Passed to >	Associated	SH 9314
STC 187	1957	Passed to >	Associated	SH 9316
STC 188	1957	Passed to >	Associated	SH 9317
STC 189	1957	Passed to >	Associated	SH 9294
STC 190	1957	Passed to >	Associated	SH 9295
STC 191	1957	Passed to >	Associated	SH 9323
STC 192	1957	Passed to >	Associated	SH 9324
STC 193	1957	Passed to >	Associated	SH 9325
STC 194	1957	Passed to >	Associated	SH 9318
STC 195	1957	Passed to >	United	SH 9189
STC 196	1957	Passed to >	United	SH 9190
STC 197	1957	Passed to >	United	SH 9191
STC 198	1957	Passed to >	United	SH 9192
STC 199	1957	Passed to >	United	SH 9193
STC 200	1957	Passed to >	United	SH 9194
STC 201	1957	Passed to >	Amalgamated	SH 8896
STC 202	1957	Passed to >	United	SH 9195
STC 203	1957	Passed to >	United	SH 9196
STC 204	1957	Passed to >	United	SH 9197
STC 205	1957	Passed to >	United	SH 9198
STC 206	1957	Passed to >	United	SH 9199
STC 207	1957	Passed to >	Associated	SH 8993
STC 208	1957	Passed to >	Associated	SH 8994
STC 209	1957	Passed to >	Associated	SH 8995
STC 210	1957	Passed to >	Associated	SH 8996
STC 211	1957	Passed to >	Associated	SH 8997
STC 212	1957	Passed to >	Associated	SH 8998
STC 213	1957	Passed to >	Associated	SH 8999
STC 214	1957	Passed to >	Associated	SH 9000
STC 215	1957	Passed to >	Associated	SH 9001
STC 216	1957	Passed to >	Associated	SH 9002
STC 217	1957	Passed to >	Associated	SH 9003
STC 218	1957	Passed to >	Associated	SH 9004
STC 219	1957	Passed to >	Associated	SH 9005
STC 220	1957	Passed to >	Associated	SH 9006
STC 221	1957	Passed to >	Associated	SH 9007
STC 414	1957	Passed to >	United	SH 9200
STC 415	1957	Passed to >	United	SH 9201
STC 416	1957	Passed to >	United	SH 9202
STC 417	1957	Passed to >	United	SH 9203
STC 418	1957	Passed to >	Amalgamated	SH 8897
STC 419	1957	Passed to >	Amalgamated	SH 8898
STC 420	1957	Passed to >	Amalgamated	SH 8899
STC 421	1957	Passed to >	Amalgamated	SH 8900
STC 422	1957	Passed to >	Amalgamated	SH 8901
STC 423	1957	Passed to >	Amalgamated	SH 8902
STC 424	1957	Passed to >	Amalgamated	SH 8903
STC 425	1957	Passed to >	United	SH 9204
STC 426	1957	Passed to >	United	SH 9205

CHASSIS NUMBERS:
These are recorded in the text on page 212

GUY ARAB MK IV *(continued)*

Regn. number	Date new	Withdrawn	Passed to	SH-series registration
STC 427	1957	Passed to >	Associated	SH 9008
STC 428	1957	Passed to >	Associated	SH 9009
STC 429	1957	Passed to >	Associated	SH 9010
STC 430	1957	Passed to >	Associated	SH 9011
STC 431	1958	Passed to >	United	SH 9206
STC 432	1958	Passed to >	United	SH 9207
STC 433	1958	Passed to >	United	SH 9208
STC 434	1958	Passed to >	United	SH 9209
STC 435	1958	Passed to >	United	SH 9210
STC 436	1958	Passed to >	United	SH 9211
STC 437	1958	Passed to >	Associated	SH 9012
STC 438	1958	Passed to >	Associated	SH 9013
STC 439	1958	Passed to >	Associated	SH 9014
STC 440	1958	Passed to >	Associated	SH 9015
STC 441	1958	Passed to >	Associated	SH 9016
STC 442	1958	Passed to >	Associated	SH 9017
STC 443	1958	Passed to >	United	SH9212
STC 444	1958	Passed to >	United	SH9213
STC 445	1958	Passed to >	United	SH9214
STC 446	1958	Passed to >	Associated	SH 9018
STC 447	1958	Passed to >	Associated	SH 9019
STC 448	1958	Passed to >	Associated	SH 9020
STC 449	1958	Passed to >	Associated	SH 9021
STC 450	1958	Passed to >	Associated	SH 9022
STC 451	1958	Passed to >	Associated	SH 9023
STC 452	1958	Passed to >	Associated	SH 9024
STC 453	1958	Passed to >	Associated	SH 9025
STC 454	1958	Passed to >	Associated	SH 9026
STC 455	1958	Passed to >	Associated	SH 9027
STC 456	1958	Passed to >	Associated	SH 9028
STC 457	1958	Passed to >	Associated	SH 9029
STC 458	1958	Passed to >	Associated	SH 9030
STC 459	1958	Passed to >	United	SH 9215
STC 460	1958	Passed to >	United	SH 9216
STC 461	1958	Passed to >	Associated	SH 9031
STC 462	1958	Passed to >	Associated	SH 9032
STC 463	1958	Passed to >	Associated	SH 9033
STC 464	1958	Passed to >	Associated	SH 9034
STC 465	1958	Passed to >	Associated	SH 9035
STC 466	1958	Passed to >	Associated	SH 9036
STC 467	1958	Passed to >	Associated	SH 9037
STC 468	1958	Passed to >	Associated	SH 9038
STC 469	1958	Passed to >	United	SH 9217
STC 470	1958	Passed to >	United	SH 9218
STC 471	1958	Passed to >	United	SH 9219
STC 472	1958	Passed to >	United	SH 9220
STC 473	1958	Passed to >	United	SH 9221
STC 474	1958	Passed to >	United	SH 9222
STC 475	1959	Passed to >	Associated	SH 9039
STC 476	1959	Passed to >	Associated	SH 9040
STC 477	1959	Passed to >	Associated	SH 9041
STC 478	1959	Passed to >	Associated	SH 9042
STC 479	1959	Passed to >	Associated	SH 9043
STC 480	1959	Passed to >	United	SH 9223
STC 481	1959	Passed to >	United	SH 9224

ISUZU BR351P   *ISUZU BODIES*
Air-conditioned buses

Regn. number	Date new	Withdrawn registration	Passed to	SH-series
STC 1	1962	Passed to>	Associated	SH 8919
STC 2	1962	Passed to>	Associated	SH 8920

ISUZU BR351P   *ISUZU BODIES*

Regn. number	Date new	Withdrawn registration	Passed to	SH-series
STC 3	1962	Passed to>	United	SH 9137
STC 4	1962	Passed to>	United	SH 9138
STC 5	1962	Passed to>	United	SH 9139
STC 6	1962	Passed to>	Associated	SH 8921
STC 7	1962	Passed to>	Associated	SH 8922
STC 8	1962	Passed to>	Associated	SH 8923
STC 9	1962	Passed to>	Associated	SH 8924
STC 10	1962	Passed to>	Scrapped	Destroyed prior to 1970
STC 11	1962	Passed to>	Associated	SH 8925
STC 12	1962	Passed to>	Associated	SH 8926
STC 13	1962	Passed to>	Associated	SH 8927
STC 14	1962	Passed to>	Associated	SH8928
STC 15	1962	Passed to>	Associated	SH8929
STC 16	1962	Passed to>	Associated	SH8930
STC 17	1962	Passed to>	Associated	SH8931
STC 18	1962	Passed to>	Associated	SH8932
STC 19	1962	Passed to>	Associated	SH8933
STC 20	1962	Passed to>	Associated	SH8934
STC 21	1962	Passed to>	Associated	SH8935
STC 22	1962	Passed to>	United	SH 9140
STC 23	1962	Passed to>	United	SH 9141
STC 24	1962	Passed to>	United	SH 9142
STC 25	1962	Passed to>	United	SH 9143
STC 26	1962	Passed to>	United	SH 9144
STC 27	1962	Passed to>	United	SH 9145
STC 28	1962	Passed to>	United	SH 9146
STC 29	1962	Passed to>	United	SH 9147
STC 30	1962	Passed to>	United	SH 9148
STC 31	1962	Passed to>	United	SH 9149
STC 32	1962	Passed to>	United	SH 9150
STC 33	1962	Passed to>	United	SH 9151

ISUZU BR351P *(continued)*

Regn. number	Date new	Withdrawn	Passed to	SH-series registration
STC 34	1962	Passed to>	United	SH 9152
STC 35	1962	Passed to>	United	SH 9153
STC 36	1962	Passed to>	United	SH 9154
STC 37	1962	Passed to>	United	SH 9155

ISUZU 20PA   *ISUZU BODIES*

Regn. number	Date new	Withdrawn	Passed to	SH-series registration
STC 38	1963	Passed to>	United	SH 9156
STC 39	1963	Passed to>	United	SH 9157
STC 40	1963	Passed to>	United	SH 9158
STC 41	1963	Passed to>	Amalgamated	SH 9159
STC 42	1963	Passed to>	Associated	SH 8936
STC 43	1963	Passed to>	Associated	SH 8937
STC 44	1963	Passed to>	Associated	SH 8938
STC 45	1963	Passed to>	Associated	SH 8939
STC 46	1963	Passed to>	Associated	SH 8940
STC 47	1963	Passed to>	Associated	SH 8941
STC 48	1963	Passed to>	Associated	SH 8942
STC 49	1963	Passed to>	Associated	SH 8943
STC 50	1963	Passed to>	Associated	SH 8944
STC 51	1963	Passed to>	Associated	SH 8945
STC 52	1963	Passed to>	Associated	SH 8946
STC 53	1963	Passed to>	Associated	SH 8947
STC 54	1963	Passed to>	Associated	SH 8948
STC 55	1963	Passed to>	United	SH 9160
STC 56	1963	Passed to>	Associated	SH 8949
STC 57	1963	Passed to>	Associated	SH 8950
STC 58	1963	Passed to>	Associated	SH 8951
STC 59	1963	Passed to>	Associated	SH 8952
STC 60	1963	Passed to>	Associated	SH 8953
STC 61	1963	Passed to>	Associated	SH 8954
STC 62	1963	Passed to>	Associated	SH 8955
STC 63	1963	Passed to>	United	SH 9161
STC 64	1963	Passed to>	United	SH 9162
STC 65	1963	Passed to>	United	SH 9163
STC 66	1963	Passed to>	United	SH 9164
STC 67	1963	Passed to>	United	SH 9165
STC 68	1963	Passed to>	Associated	SH 8956
STC 69	1963	Passed to>	Associated	SH 8957
STC 70	1963	Passed to>	Associated	SH 8958
STC 71	1963	Passed to>	Associated	SH 8959
STC 72	1963	Passed to>	Associated	SH 8960
STC 73	1963	Passed to>	Associated	SH 8961
STC 74	1963	Passed to>	Associated	SH 8962
STC 75	1963	Passed to>	Associated	SH 8963
STC 76	1963	Passed to>	Associated	SH 8964
STC 77	1963	Passed to>	Associated	SH 8965
STC 78	1963	Passed to>	Associated	SH 8966
STC 79	1963	Passed to>	Associated	SH 8967
STC 80	1963	Passed to>	Associated	SH 8968
STC 81	1963	Passed to>	Associated	SH 8969
STC 82	1963	Passed to>	Associated	SH 8970
STC 83	1963	Passed to>	Associated	SH 8971
STC 84	1963	Passed to>	Associated	SH 8972
STC 85	1963	Passed to>	Associated	SH 8973
STC 86	1963	Passed to>	Associated	SH 8974
STC 87	1963	Passed to>	Associated	SH 8975

ISUZU 20PA2   *ISUZU BODIES*

Regn. number	Date new	Withdrawn registration	Passed to	SH-series
STC 88	1964	Passed to>	United	SH 9166
STC 89	1964	Passed to>	United	SH 9167
STC 90	1964	Passed to>	United	SH 9168
STC 91	1964	Passed to>	Associated	SH 8976
STC 92	1964	Passed to>	Associated	SH 8977
STC 93	1964	Passed to>	Associated	SH 8978
STC 94	1964	Passed to>	United	SH 9169
STC 95	1964	Passed to>	Associated	SH 9291
STC 96	1964	Passed to>	United	SH 9170
STC 97	1964	Passed to>	United	SH 9171
STC 98	1964	Passed to>	United	SH 9172
STC 99	1964	Passed to>	United	SH 9173
STC 100	1964	Passed to>	Associated	SH 8979
STC 101	1964	Passed to>	Associated	SH 8980
STC 102	1964	Passed to>	Amalgamated	SH 8885
STC 103	1964	Passed to>	United	SH 9174
STC 104	1964	Passed to>	United	SH 9175
STC 105	1964	Passed to>	United	SH 9176
STC 106	1964	Passed to>	United	SH 9177
STC 107	1964	Passed to>	United	SH 9178
STC 108	1964	Passed to>	Associated	SH 8979
STC 109	1964	Passed to>	Amalgamated	SH 8886
STC 110	1964	Passed to>	United	SH 9179
STC 111	1964	Passed to>	United	SH 9180
STC 112	1964	Passed to>	Associated	SH 8982
STC 113	1964	Passed to>	Associated	SH 8983
STC 114	1964	Passed to>	Associated	SH 8984
STC 115	1964	Passed to>	Associated	SH 8985
STC 116	1964	Passed to>	Associated	SH 8986
STC 117	1964	Passed to>	Associated	SH 8987
STC 118	1964	Passed to>	Associated	SH 8988
STC 119	1964	Passed to>	Amalgamated	SH 8887
STC 120	1964	Passed to>	Amalgamated	SH 8888
STC 121	1964	Passed to>	Amalgamated	SH 8889
STC 122	1964	Passed to>	Associated	SH 8989
STC 123	1964	Passed to>	United	SH 9181

ISUZU 20PA2 *(continued)*

Regn. number	Date new	Withdrawn	Passed to	SH-series registration
STC 124	1964	Passed to>	United	SH 9182
STC 125	1964	Passed to>	United	SH 9183
STC 126	1964	Passed to>	United	SH 9184
STC 127	1964	Passed to>	United	SH 9185
STC 128	1964	Passed to>	United	SH 9186
STC 129	1964	Passed to>	Amalgamated	SH 8890
STC 130	1964	Passed to>	Amalgamated	SH 8891
STC 131	1964	Passed to>	Amalgamated	SH 8892
STC 132	1964	Passed to>	Amalgamated	SH 8893
STC 133	1964	Passed to>	Amalgamated	SH 8894
STC 134	1964	Passed to>	United	SH 9187
STC 135	1964	Passed to>	Associated	SH 8990
STC 136	1964	Passed to>	Amalgamated	SH8895
STC 137	1964	Passed to>	United	SH 9188

MITSUBISHI   *MITSUBISHI BODIES*

Regn. number	Date new	Withdrawn	Passed to	SH-series registration
STC 138	1964	Passed to>	Associated	SH 8991
STC 138	1964	Passed to>	Associated	SH 8991

NISSAN RX102K3   *BODIES BY FUJI HEAVY INDUSTRIES*

Regn. number	Date new	Withdrawn	Passed to	SH-series registration
STC 601	1967	Passed to>	United	SH 9225
STC 602	1967	Passed to>	Associated	SH 9044
STC 603	1967	Passed to>	Associated	SH 9045
STC 604	1967	Passed to>	Associated	SH 9046
STC 605	1967	Passed to>	United	SH 9226
STC 606	1967	Passed to>	United	SH 9227
STC 607	1967	Passed to>	United	SH 9228
STC 608	1967	Passed to>	United	SH 9229
STC 609	1967	Passed to>	United	SH 9230
STC 610	1967	Passed to>	United	SH 9231
STC 611	1967	Passed to>	United	SH 9232
STC 612	1967	Passed to>	United	SH 9233
STC 613	1967	Passed to>	United	SH 9234
STC 614	1967	Passed to>	United	SH 9235
STC 615	1967	Passed to>	United	SH 9236
STC 616	1967	Passed to>	Associated	SH 9047
STC 617	1967	Passed to>	Associated	SH 9043
STC 618	1967	Passed to>	United	SH 9237
STC 619	1967	Passed to>	United	SH 9238
STC 620	1967	Passed to>	United	SH 9239
STC 621	1967	Passed to>	United	SH 9240
STC 622	1967	Passed to>	United	SH 9241
STC 623	1967	Passed to>	United	SH 9242
STC 624	1967	Passed to>	United	SH 9243
STC 625	1967	Passed to>	United	SH 9244
STC 626	1967	Passed to>	United	SH 9245
STC 627	1967	Passed to>	United	SH 9246
STC 628	1967	Passed to>	United	SH 9247
STC 629	1967	Passed to>	United	SH 9248
STC 630	1967	Passed to>	Associated	SH 9049
STC 631	1967	Passed to>	Associated	SH 9050
STC 632	1967	Passed to>	Associated	SH 9051
STC 633	1967	Passed to>	Associated	SH 9052
STC 634	1967	Passed to>	Associated	SH 9053
STC 635	1967	Passed to>	Associated	SH 9054
STC 636	1967	Passed to>	Associated	SH 9055
STC 637	1967	Passed to>	Associated	SH 9056
STC 638	1967	Passed to>	Associated	SH 9057
STC 639	1967	Passed to>	Associated	SH 9058
STC 640	1967	Passed to>	Associated	SH 9059
STC 641	1967	Passed to>	United	SH 9249
STC 642	1967	Passed to>	United	SH 9250
STC 643	1967	Passed to>	United	SH 9251
STC 644	1967	Passed to>	Amalgamated	SH 8904
STC 645	1967	Passed to>	Amalgamated	SH 8905
STC 646	1967	Passed to>	Amalgamated	SH 8906
STC 647	1967	Passed to>	Amalgamated	SH 8907
STC 648	1967	Passed to>	Amalgamated	SH 8908
STC 649	1967	Passed to>	United	SH 9252
STC 650	1967	Passed to>	Amalgamated	SH 8909
STC 651	1969	Passed to>	Associated	SH 9060
STC 652	1969	Passed to>	Associated	SH 9061
STC 653	1969	Passed to>	Associated	SH 9062
STC 654	1969	Passed to>	Associated	SH 9063
STC 655	1969	Passed to>	Associated	SH 9064
STC 656	1969	Passed to>	Associated	SH 9065
STC 657	1969	Passed to>	Associated	SH 9066
STC 658	1969	Passed to>	Associated	SH 9067
STC 659	1969	Passed to>	Associated	SH 9068
STC 660	1969	Passed to>	Associated	SH 9069
STC 661	1969	Passed to>	Associated	SH 9070
STC 662	1969	Passed to>	Amalgamated	SH 8910
STC 663	1969	Passed to>	Amalgamated	SH 8911
STC 664	1969	Passed to>	Associated	SH 9071
STC 665	1969	Passed to>	Associated	SH 9072
STC 666	1969	Passed to>	Associated	SH 9073
STC 667	1969	Passed to>	Associated	SH 9074
STC 668	1969	Passed to>	Associated	SH 9075
STC 669	1969	Passed to>	Associated	SH 9076
STC 670	1969	Passed to>	Associated	SH 9077
STC 671	1969	Passed to>	Associated	SH 9078
STC 672	1969	Passed to>	Associated	SH 9079
STC 673	1969	Passed to>	Associated	SH 9080
STC 674	1969	Passed to>	Associated	SH 9081
STC 675	1969	Passed to>	Associated	SH 9082
STC 676	1969	Passed to>	Associated	SH 9083
STC 677	1969	Passed to>	Associated	SH 9084
STC 678	1969	Passed to>	Associated	SH 9085
STC 679	1969	Passed to>	Amalgamated	SH 8912

NISSAN RX102K3   *(continued)*

Regn. number	Date new	Withdrawn	Passed to	SH-series registration
STC 680	1969	Passed to>	United	SH 9253
STC 681	1969	Passed to>	United	SH 9254
STC 682	1969	Passed to>	United	SH 9255
STC 683	1969	Passed to>	United	SH 9256
STC 684	1969	Passed to>	Associated	SH 9086
STC 685	1969	Passed to>	Associated	SH 9087
STC 686	1969	Passed to>	Associated	SH 9088
STC 687	1969	Passed to>	Associated	SH 9089
STC 688	1969	Passed to>	Associated	SH 9090
STC 689	1969	Passed to>	United	SH 9257
STC 690	1969	Passed to>	United	SH 9258
STC 691	1969	Passed to>	United	SH 9259
STC 692	1969	Passed to>	United	SH 9260
STC 693	1969	Passed to>	Associated	SH 9091
STC 694	1969	Passed to>	Associated	SH 9092
STC 695	1969	Passed to>	Associated	SH 9093
STC 696	1969	Passed to>	Associated	SH 9094
STC 697	1969	Passed to>	Associated	SH 9095
STC 698	1969	Passed to>	Associated	SH 9096
STC 699	1969	Passed to>	Associated	SH 9097

NISSAN MODEL 4R94   *BODIES BY FUJI HEAVY INDUSTRIES*

Regn. number	Date new	Withdrawn	Passed to	SH-series registration
STC 700	1969	Passed to>	Amalgamated	SH 8913
STC 701	1969	Passed to>	Amalgamated	SH 8914
STC 702	1969	Passed to>	Associated	SH 9098
STC 703	1969	Passed to>	Associated	SH 9099
STC 704	1969	Passed to>	Associated	SH 9100
STC 705	1969	Passed to>	Associated	SH 9101
STC 706	1969	Passed to>	Associated	SH 9102
STC 707	1969	Passed to>	United	SH 9261
STC 708	1969	Passed to>	Associated	SH 9103
STC 709	1969	Passed to>	Associated	SH 9104
STC 710	1969	Passed to>	Associated	SH 9105
STC 711	1969	Passed to>	Associated	SH 9106
STC 712	1969	Passed to>	United	SH 9262
STC 713	1969	Passed to>	United	SH 9263
STC 714	1969	Passed to>	United	SH 9264
STC 715	1969	Passed to>	United	SH 9265
STC 716	1969	Passed to>	United	SH 9266
STC 717	1969	Passed to>	United	SH 9267
STC 718	1969	Passed to>	United	SH 9268
STC 719	1969	Passed to>	Associated	SH 9107
STC 720	1969	Passed to>	Associated	SH 9108
STC 721	1969	Passed to>	United	SH 9269
STC 722	1969	Passed to>	United	SH 9270
STC 723	1969	Passed to>	United	SH 9271
STC 724	1969	Passed to>	United	SH 9272
STC 725	1969	Passed to>	United	SH 9273
STC 726	1969	Passed to>	United	SH 9274
STC 727	1969	Passed to>	Associated	SH 9109
STC 728	1969	Passed to>	Associated	SH 9110
STC 729	1969	Passed to>	Associated	SH 9111
STC 730	1969	Passed to>	United	SH 9275
STC 731	1969	Passed to>	United	SH 9276
STC 732	1969	Passed to>	Associated	SH 9112
STC 733	1969	Passed to>	Associated	SH 9113
STC 734	1969	Passed to>	Associated	SH 9114
STC 735	1969	Passed to>	Associated	SH 9115
STC 736	1969	Passed to>	Associated	SH 9116
STC 737	1969	Passed to>	Associated	SH 9117
STC 738	1969	Passed to>	Associated	SH 9118
STC 739	1969	Passed to>	Associated	SH 9119
STC 740	1969	Passed to>	Associated	SH 9120
STC 741	1969	Passed to>	Associated	SH 9121
STC 742	1969	Passed to>	United	SH 9277
STC 743	1969	Passed to>	United	SH 9278
STC 744	1969	Passed to>	United	SH 9279
STC 745	1969	Passed to>	United	SH 9280
STC 746	1969	Passed to>	Associated	SH 9122
STC 747	1969	Passed to>	United	SH 9281
STC 748	1969	Passed to>	United	SH 9282
STC 749	1969	Passed to>	Associated	SH 9122

SINGAPORE NISSAN BODIES

STC 750	1970	Passed to>	Amalgamated	SH 8915
STC 751	1970	Passed to>	Amalgamated	SH 8916
STC 752	1970	Passed to>	Amalgamated	SH 8917
STC 753	1970	Passed to>	Amalgamated	SH 8918
STC 754	1970	Passed to>	United	SH 9283
STC 755	1970	Passed to>	Associated	SH 9124
STC 756	1970	Passed to>	Associated	SH 9125
STC 757	1970	Passed to>	Associated	SH 9126
STC 758	1970	Passed to>	United	SH 9284
STC 759	1970	Passed to>	United	SH 9286
STC 760	1970	Passed to>	Associated	SH 9127
STC 761	1970	Passed to>	Associated	SH 9128
STC 762	1970	Passed to>	Associated	SH 9129
STC 763	1970	Passed to>	Associated	SH 9130
STC 764	1970	Passed to>	Associated	SH 9131
STC 765	1970	Passed to>	Associated	SH 9132
STC 766	1970	Passed to>	Associated	SH 9133
STC 767	1970	Passed to>	Associated	SH 9134
STC 768	1970	Passed to>	Associated	SH 9135
STC 769	1970	Passed to>	Associated	SH 9136
STC 770	1970	Passed to>	Associated	SH 9286
STC 771	1970	Passed to>	Associated	SH 9287
STC 772	1970	Passed to>	Associated	SH 9288
STC 773	1970	Passed to>	Associated	SH 9289
STC 774	1970	Passed to>	Associated	SH 9290

Easy Bus Company

30 Jurong Road, Singapore, 21.
Eventually became part of United Bus Company. Vehicles were built to narrow width, with 2+1 cross seating.

Known Fleet Details

Regn number	Chassis make	Body/ seating	
S 8368	Chevrolet n/c	B RP	
SC 3483	Ford n/c	B21C	
SH 163	Ford n/c	B21C	
SH 245	Austin CXD	B C	
SH 261	Austin CXD	B C	
SH 298	Austin CXD	B C	
SH 305	Austin CXD	B C	
SH 405	Austin CXD	B C	new 1955
SH 456	Austin CXD	B C	new 1955
SH 558	Austin CXD	B C	
SH 770	Austin CXD	B C	
SH 805	Austin FFK	B32C	

Changi Bus Company Limited

200 Changi Road, Singapore
Eventually became part of Associated Bus Services. A curiosity is the avoidance of the digit '5' in registration numbers.

Known Fleet Details

Regn number	Chassis make	Body/ seating	
S 347	Ford n/c	B RP	scrapped 1942
S 1139	Bedford n/c	B RP	ex military chassis?
S 2499	Ford n/c	B23RP	
S 2766	Austin n/c	B RP	ex military chassis
S 2777	Ford n/c	B RP scrapped	
S 3238	Bedford OWB	B RP	
S 3809	?? n/c	B ?	
S 3810	Fargo n/c (USA)	B C	
S 3811	Fargo n/c (USA)	B C	
S 3812	Fargo n/c (USA)	B C	
S 4320	Ford n/c	B RP	
S 4863	Ford n/c	B ?	scrapped 1942
S 6349	Dodge n/c	B RP	
S 8201	Chevrolet n/c	B C	
S 8202	Chevrolet n/c	B C	
S 8207	Ford n/c	B C	
S 8224	Ford n/c	B ?	
S 8883	Ford n/c	B ?	scrapped
S 9020	Ford n/c	B ?	
S 9786	Chevrolet n/c	B ?	
S 9787	Ford n/c	B C	scrapped
S 9788	Chevrolet n/c	B C	
SC 1911	Chev Maple Leaf	B C	
SC 1912	Chev Maple Leaf	B C	
SC 1913	Chevrolet n/c	B C	
SC 1914	Chevrolet n/c	B C	
SC 1917	Chevrolet n/c	B F	scrapped 1/56
SC 1920	Chevrolet n/c	B C	
SC 1921	Chevrolet n/c	B C	
SC 1923	Chevrolet n/c	B ?	
SC 1926	Chevrolet n/c	B C	scrapped 1/56
SC 1928	Chevrolet n/c	B F	
SC 6349	Dodge n/c	B ?	
SC 9211	Vulcan 6PF	B C	(rebodied 1956)
SC 9212	Vulcan 6PF	B C	
SC 9213	Vulcan 6PF	B C	
SC 9214	Vulcan 6PF	B C	
SH 141	Vulcan 6PF	B C	(rebodied 1956)
SH 142	Vulcan 6PF	B C	
SH 143	Vulcan 6PF	B C	
SH 144	Vulcan 6PF	B C	
SH 193	Austin CXD	B C	new 1952
SH 194	Austin CXD	B C	new 1952
SH 196	Austin CXD	B C	new 1952
SH 197	Austin CXD	B C	new 1952
SH 198	Austin CXD	B C	new 1952
SH 199	Austin CXD	B C	new 1952
SH 213	Seddon Mk4	B C	new 1953
SH 214	TSM L6PA7	B C	new 1953
SH 216	TSM L6PA7	B C	new 1953
SH 217	TSM L6PA7	B C	new 1953
SH 243	TSM L6PA7	B C	
SH 244	TSM L6PA7	B C	
SH 246	TSM L6PA7	B C	
SH 247	TSM L6PA7	B C	new 1952
SH 266	TSM L6PA7	B C	new 1952
SH 267	TSM L6PA7	B C	new 1952
SH 301	Seddon Mk11	B C	new 1954

Changi Bus Co Ltd (continued)

Regn number	Chassis make	Body/ seating	
SH 302	Seddon Mk11	B C	new 1954
SH 326	Austin CXD	B C	new 1954
SH 327	Austin CXD	B C	new 1954
SH 328	Austin CXD	B C	new 1954
SH 329	Austin CXD	B C	new 1954
SH 330	Austin CXD	B C	new 1954
SH 331	Austin CXD	B C	new 1954
SH 336	Fargo f/c	B C	new 1954
SH 337	Fargo f/c	B C	new 1954
SH 338	Fargo f/c	B C	new 1954
SH 339	Fargo f/c	B C	new 1955
SH 340	Fargo f/c	B C	new 1955
SH 346	Seddon Mk6	B C	new 1955
SH 347	Seddon Mk6	B C	new 1955
SH 348	Fargo f/c	B C	new 1955
SH 367	Fargo f/c	B C	new 1955
SH 460	Fargo f/c	B C	new 1955
SH 461	Fargo f/c	B C	new 1955
SH 462	Fargo f/c	B C	new 1955
SH 463	Fargo f/c	B C	new 1955
SH 464	Fargo f/c	B C	new 1955
SH 466	Fargo f/c	B C	new 1955
SH 467	Fargo f/c	B C	new 1956
SH 468	Fargo f/c	B C	new 1956
SH 469	Fargo f/c	B C	new 1956
SH 470	Fargo f/c	B C	new 1956
SH 471	Fargo f/c	B C	new 1956
SH 472	Fargo f/c	B C	new 1956
SH 473	Fargo f/c	B C	new 1956
SH 474	Fargo f/c	B C	new 1956
SH 476	Fargo f/c	B C	new 1956
SH 477	Fargo f/c	B C	new 1956
SH 478	Fargo f/c	B C	new 1956
SH 479	Fargo f/c	B C	new 1956
SH 601	Seddon	B C	
SH 602	Seddon	B C	
SH 603	?	B C	
SH 604	Fargo	B C	
SH 606	Fargo	B C	
SH 607	Fargo	B C	
SH 608	Fargo	B C	
SH 609	Fargo	B C	
SH 772	Albion VT17AL	B C	
SH 776	Albion VT17AL	B C	
SH 792	Fargo	B C	
SH 801	Fargo	B C	
SH 802	Fargo	B C	
SH 803	Fargo	B C	
SH 804	Fargo	B C	
SH 806	Fargo	B C	
SH 807	Fargo	B C	
SH 879	Fargo	B C	
SH 880	Fargo	B C	
SH 881	Fargo	B C	
SH 986	Fargo	B C	
SH 987	Fargo	B C	
SH 988	Fargo	B C	
SH 989	Fargo	B C	
SH 990	Fargo	B C	
SH 991	Fargo	B C	
SH 992	Fargo	B C	
SH 993	Fargo	B C	
SH 994	Fargo	B C	

Green Bus Company Limited

Originally of 2 Angullia Road, Singapore
Later of 35 King Albert Park, Singapore.
Ticket System: Bell Punch (London)
Eventually became part of United Bus Service

Known Fleet Details

Regn number	Chassis make	Body/ seating	
S 1137	Ford n/c	B RP	
S 1457	Ford n/c	B	
S 1484	-??- n/c	B	
S 1968	Chevrolet n/c	B	
S 2115	Ford n/c	B	
S 2451	Chevrolet n/c	B RP	to store shed
S 2452	Ford n/c	B	sold to Paya-Lebar
S 3239	Ford n/c	B	scrapped
S 7555	Ford n/c	B	ex Kampong Bahru
S 8087	Ford n/c	B RP	
S 8088	Ford n/c	B RP	
S 9233	Chevrolet n/c	B	

Green Bus Co (continued)

Regn number	Chassis make	Body/ seating		
SC 1986	Chev Maple Leaf	B27C		
SC 6780	Vulcan 6PF	B	F	
SC 7141	Vulcan 6PF	B		
SC 8212	Vulcan 6PF	B		
SC 8213	Vulcan 6PF	B		
SC 8881	Vulcan 6PF	B	C	
SC 8886	Morris OP/R	B	C	
SC 8887	Morris OP/R	B	C	
SC 9332	Morris OP/R	B	C	
SH 101	Morris OP/R	B	C	New 1951
SH 102	Morris OP/R	B	C	New 1951
SH 104	Morris OP/R	B	C	to Tye Lye, Malcca
SH 136	Fargo n/c	B	C	see note 1
SH 147	Fargo n/c	B	C	see note 1
SH 148	Fargo n/c	B	C	see note 1
SH 149	TSM L6PA7	B	C	
SH 155	TSM L6PA7	B	C	
SH 156	TSM L6PA7	B	C	
SH 157	TSM L6PA7	B	C	
SH 158	Fargo n/c	B	C	see note 1
SH 159	Fargo n/c	B	C	see note 1
SH 160	Fargo n/c	B	C	see note 1
SH 175	Fargo n/c	B	C	see note 1
SH 178	TSM L6PA7	B	C	
SH 180	TSM L6PA7	B	C	
SH 201	TSM L6PA7	B	C	new 1952
SH 208	TSM L6PA7	B	C	new 1952
SH 209	TSM L6PA7	B	C	new 1952
SH 210	TSM L6PA7	B	C	new 1952
SH 219	TSM L6PA7	B	C	new 1952
SH 221	TSM L6PA7	B	C	new 1952
SH 231	TSM L6PA7	B	C	
SH 237	TSM L6PA7	B	C	
SH 238	TSM L6PA7	B	C	
SH 239	TSM L6PA7	B	C	
SH 241	Seddon Mark 7	B	C	
SH 285	TSM L6PA7	B	C	
SH 286	Fargo	B	C	
SH 287	Fargo	B	C	
SH 289	Seddon Mark 7	B	C	new 1954
SH 290	Seddon Mark 7	B	C	new 1954
SH 291	Seddon Mark 11	B	C	new 1954
SH 311	Seddon Mark 7	B	C	
SH 355	Seddon Mark 7	B	C	new 1955
SH 366	Seddon Mark 11	B	C	
SH 411	Seddon Mark 7	B	C	
SH 446	Seddon Mark 11	B42C		1955, later SCB19
SH 447	Seddon Mark 11	B42C		1955, later SCB20
SH 449	Seddon Mark 7	B	C	new 1955
SH 450	Seddon Mark 7	B	C	
SH 544*	Fargo KS60	B	C	
SH 546	Fargo KS60	B	C	
SH 548*	Fargo KS60	B	C	
SH 566	Fargo KS60	B	C	
SH 567	Fargo KS60	B	C	
SH 575	Fargo KS60	B	C	Seddon style front
SH 576	Fargo KS60	B	C	Seddon style front
SH 597	Seddon Mark 17	B	C	

BELOW: Green Bus SC 6780, a Vulcan 6PF with centre sliding door.

Hock Lee Amalgamated Bus Company Ltd

295 Alexandra Road, Singapore, 3.
Eventually became part of the Amalgamated Bus Company, in which it was the major influence.

Known Fleet Details

Regn number	Chassis make	Body/ seating		
S 1101	Chevrolet n/c	B	?	
S 1751	Bedford OWB	B	RP	
S 2407	Ford n/c	B	?	scrapped
S 4001	Ford n/c	B	F	
S 5888	Ford n/c	B	RP	
S 7004	Ford n/c	B	?	scrapped
S 8063	Albion f/c	B	?	
S 8098	Ford n/c	B	?	
S 8142	Ford n/c	B	RP	
S 8143	Ford n/c	B	RP	
S9326	Chevrolet n/c	B	RP	
SC 872	Chev Maple Leaf	B	C	
SC 3077	Fargo n/c (USA)	B	C	
SC 3078	Fargo n/c (USA)	B	C	
SC 7198	Vulcan 6PF	B	C	
SC 7199	Vulcan 6PF	B	F	note **front** entrance
SC 7220	Morris OP/R	B	C	note 1
SC 7990	Vulcan 6PF	B	C	note 1
SC 7991	Vulcan 6PF	B	C	note 1
SC 8220	Vulcan 6PF	B	C	
SC 8437	Morris OP/R	B	C	note 1
SC 8982	Albion FT39N	B	?	
SC 8983*	Albion FT39N	B	?	
SC 9695	Vulcan 6PF	B	C	note 1
SH 123	Vulcan 6PF	B	C	note 1
SH 137	Vulcan 6PF	B	F	note 1
SH 139	Albion FT39N	B	F	
SH 140	Albion FT39N	B	F	
SH 153	Albion FT39N	B	C	note 1
SH 166	Vulcan 6PF	B	C	note 1
SH 167*	Vulcan 6PF	B	C	note 1
SH 168	Vulcan 6PF	B	C	note 1
SH 169	Vulcan 6PF	B	C	note 1
SH 170	Albion FT39N	B	?	
SH 171	Seddon Mk4	B	C	
SH 173	Vulcan 6PF	B	?	
SH 181	Albion FT39N	B	?	
SH 185	Vulcan 6PF	B	C	note 1
SH 186	Vulcan 6PF	B	C	note 1
SH 187	Albion FT39N	B	C	note 1
SH 189	Vulcan 6PF	B32C		note 1
SH 203	Albion FT39L	B	C	
SH 204	Albion FT39L	B	?	
SH 205	TSM L6PA7	B	C	
SH 206	Albion FT39L	B	C	
SH 284	Albion FT39L	B	C	
SH 384	Albion FT39AL	B	C	
SH 385	Albion FT39AL	B	C	
SH 386	Albion FT39AL	B	C	
SH 387	Albion FT39AL	B	C	
SH 388	Seddon Mk6	B	C	
SH 389	Seddon Mk6	B	C	
SH 390	Seddon Mk10	B23C		
SH 391	Seddon Mk10	B23C		
SH 392	Seddon Mk10	B23C		
SH 393*	Seddon Mk6	B	C	
SH 394*	Seddon Mk6	B	C	
SH 395	Seddon Mk10	B23C		
SH 396	Seddon Mk10	B23C		
SH 397	Seddon Mk6	B	C	
SH 398	Seddon Mk6	B	C	
SH 399	Dennis Teal	B46C		
SH 400	Dennis Teal	B	C	
SH 401	Dennis Teal	B	C	
SH 402	Dennis Teal	B	C	
SH 403	Dennis Teal	B	C	
SH 404	Dennis Teal	B	C	
SH 480	Albion FT39ALX	B44C		new 1955
SH 481	Albion FT39ALX	B44C		new 1955
SH 482	Albion FT39ALX	B44C		new 1955
SH 483	Albion FT39ALX	B44C		new 1955
SH 484	Albion FT39ALX	B44C		new 1955
SH 485	Albion FT39ALX	B44C		new 1955
SH 486	Albion FT39ALX	B44C		new 1955
SH 487	Albion FT39ALX	B44C		new 1955
SH 488	Albion FT39ALX	B44C		new 1955
SH 489	Albion FT39ALX	B44C		new 1955
SH 490	Albion FT39ALX	B44C		new 1955
SH 491	Albion FT39ALX	B44C		new 1955
SH 494	Dennis Teal	B	C	new 1956
SH 495	Dennis Teal	B	C	new 1956
SH 496	Albion FT39ALX	B	C	
SH 497	Albion FT39ALX	B	C	
SH 757	Dennis Falcon	B33C		note 2 (ex STC)
SH 809	Albion VT17BL	B44C		note 3
SH 810	Albion VT17BL	B44C		
SH 811	Albion VT17BL	B44C		
SH 812	Albion VT17BL	B44C		
SH 814	Albion VT17BL	B44C		
SH 815	Albion VT17BL	B44C		

Hock Lee Amalgamated (continued)

Regn number	Chassis make	Body/ seating		
SH 816	Albion VT17BL	B44C		
SH 818	Albion VT17BL	B44C		
SH 820	Albion VT17BL	B44C		
SH 821	Albion VT17BL	B44C		
SH 822	Albion VT17BL	B44C		
SH 823	Albion VT17BL	B44C		
SH 824	Albion VT17BL	B44C		
SH 825	Albion VT17BL	B44C		
SH 826	Albion VT17BL	B44C		
SH 827	Albion VT17BL	B44C		
SH 828	Albion VT17BL	B44C		
SH 829	Albion VT17BL	B44C		
SH 830	Albion VT17BL	B44C		
SH 831*	Albion VT17BL	B44C		
SH 925	Albion FT39AL	B C	note 4	
SH 926	Albion FT39AL	B C	note 4	

Notes:
1. These vehicles had a doorway position forward of centre.
2. This is the only recorded example of an ex STC vehicle in the service of a Chinese Bus Company.
3. The batch of 20 VT17BLs were all equipped with factory built Leyland Comet type fronts. SH 831 is not confirmed as an Albion but is thought to have been the 20th vehicle.
4. The origin of these 2 vehicles is not known: perhaps they were imported from Malaya. They carried bodies equipped with old-fashioned slatted windows.

Kampong Bahru Bus Service

81-3 Bukit Timah Road, Singapore, 9.

Eventually became part of Amalgamated Bus Company.

Known Fleet Details

Regn number	Chassis make	Body/ seating		
S 7555	Ford n/c	B		Sold to Green Bus
SC 6110	Ford n/c	B		Sold to Ponggol
SH 121	TSM L6PA7	B C		
SH 161	Vulcan 6PF	B C		
SH 162	Vulcan 6PF	B C		
SH 211	TSM L6PA7	B C		
SH 252	TSM L6PA7	B C		
SH 265	TSM L6PA7	B C		
SH 277	TSM L6PA7	B C		
SH 279	TSM L6PA7	B C		
SH 288	TSM L6PA7	B C		
SH 299	TSM L6PA7	B C		
SH 377	TSM L6PA7	B C		
SH 448	Fargo f/c	B C	new 1955	

Katong Bedok Bus Service

638 Bedok Road, Singapore, 16.

Eventually became part of Associated Bus Service

Known Fleet Details

Regn number	Chassis make	Body/ seating		
S 1377	Ford n/c	B RP		
S 1401	Commer n/c	B RP	scrapped	
S 2414	Ford n/c	B ?		
S 5560	Ford n/c	B RP		
S 6890	Ford n/c	B ?		
S 8101	Chevrolet n/c	B ?		
S 8102	Chevrolet n/c	B ?		
S 9054	Dodge (USA)	B RP		
SC 1440	Chev Maple Leaf	B C		
SC 3466	Chev Maple Leaf	B ?		
SC 7338	Bedford (OB)	B C		
SC 9534	Vulcan 6PF	B C		
SC 9598	Vulcan 6PF	B C		
SC 9599	Vulcan 6PF	B C		
SH 131	Vulcan 6PF	B C		
SH 132	Vulcan 6PF	B C		
SH 133	Vulcan 6PF	B C	to store shed	
SH 134	Vulcan 6PF	B C		
SH 224	TSM L6PA7	B C	later Mercedes engine	
SH 225	Albion FT39N	B31C	see note 1	
SH 226	TSM LP6A7	B C		
SH 227	TSM LP6A7	B C		
SH 228	TSM LP6A7	B C		
SH 293	TSM LP6A7	B C		
SH 294	TSM LP6A7	B C		
SH 295	TSM LP6A7	B C		
SH 296	Albion FT39N	B31C	new 1954 see note 2	
SH 297	TSM LP6A7	B C	new 1954	
SH 422	Fargo	B C	new 1955	
SH 423	Fargo	B C	new 1955	
SH 424	Dennis Teal	B C	new 1955	
SH 425	Fargo	B C	new 1955	
SH 426	Fargo	B C	new 1955	
SH 427	Fargo	B C	new 1955	
SH 428	Fargo	B C	new 1955	

Katong Bedok (continued)

Regn number	Chassis make	Body/ seating		
SH 429	Fargo	B C	new 1955	
SH 430	Dennis Teal	B C	new 1955	
SH 431	Dennis Teal	B C	new 1955	
SH 432	Dennis Teal	B C	new 1956	
SH 433	Dennis Teal	B C	new 1956	
SH 434	Dennis Teal	B C	new 1956	
SH 623	Mercedes-Benz	B C		
SH 627	Mercedes-Benz	B C		
SH 700	Mercedes-Benz	B C		
SH 775	Mercedes-Benz	B 40C		
SH 777	Mercedes-Benz	B 40C		
SH 782	Mercedes-Benz	B 40C		
SH 798	Mercedes-Benz	B 40C		
SH 799	Mercedes-Benz	B 40C		

Notes:
Note 1: SH 225/96 had bodies which appeared to be built from kits imported from Great Britain.
Note 2: The two Albion FT39Ns were fitted with bodies that may have been supplied ckd from Great Britain. (see illustration)

BELOW: SH 297 was a Katong Bedok Tilling Stevens LP6A7 new in 1954.

Keppel Bus Company

259 Tanjong Pagar Road, Singapore, 2.

Eventually became part of Amalgamated Bus Company.

Known Fleet Details

Regn number	Chassis make	Body/ seating		
S 905	Ford n/c	B RP		
S 1192	Bedford (OB)	B RP		
S 1192	Bedford (OB)	B C		
S 2480	Bedford (OB)	B C		
S 2725	Bedford (OB)	B ?		
S 3012	Bedford OB (P4)	B C		
S 5134	Ford n/c	B ?	to Tay Koh Yat	
S 7618	Bedford OB (P4)	B C		
S 7666	Ford n/c	B ?		
SC 3223	Bedford OB (P4)	B C		
SC 4334	Chev Maple Leaf	B C		
SC 7068	Vulcan 6PF	B C		
SC 7969	Vulcan 6PF	B C		
SC 7970	Vulcan 6PF	B C		
SC 8971	Vulcan 6PF	B C		
SH 122	TSM L6PA7	B C		
SH 124	Vulcan 6PF	B C		
SH 125	Vulcan 6PF	B C		
SH 126	Vulcan 6PF	B C		
SH 127	Vulcan 6PF	B C		
SH 128	Vulcan 6PF	B C		
SH 129	TSM L6PA7	B C		
SH 215*	TSM L6PA7	B C		
SH 255*	TSM L6PA7	B C		
SH 256	TSM L6PA7	B C		
SH 257	TSM L6PA7	B C		
SH 258	Albion FT39N	B C		
SH 259	Albion Ft39N	B C		
SH 260	Albion FT39N	B C		
SH 274	Albion FT39N	B C		
SH 276	Albion FT39N	B C		
SH 419	Albion FT39AL	B C	new 1955	
SH 420	Albion FT39AL	B C	new 1955	
SH 421	Albion FT39AL	B C	new 1955	
SH 455	Albion FT39AL	B C	new 1955	
SH 875	Mercedes-Benz	B C		
SH 910	Mercedes-Benz	B C		
SH 911	Mercedes-Benz	B C		

Breakdown Wagon

SG 4646	Ford n/c			

Paya Lebar Bus Service

408F/G Yio Chu Road, Singapore, 19.
Eventually became part of Associated Bus Services.

Known Fleet Details

Regn number	Chassis make	Body/ seating		
S 1151	Chevrolet n/c	B	?	new 1946
S 2452	Ford n/c	B	?	ex Green Bus
S 2466	Ford n/c	B	?	new 1946
S 1680	Chevrolet n/c	B	C	
S 1980	Chevrolet n/c	B	?	
S 2189	Chevrolet n/c	B	?	
S 2412	Chevrolet n/c	B	?	
S 2415	Chevrolet n/c	B	C	
S 4358	Chevrolet n/c	B	C	
S 4384	Chevrolet n/c	B	C	
S 4969	Chevrolet n/c	B	RP	
S 5525	Chevrolet n/c	B21C		new 1946
S 8097	Chevrolet n/c	B	RP	
S 8515	Chevrolet n/c	B	RP	
S 8810	Chevrolet n/c	B	RP	
S 8815	Chevrolet n/c	B	?	
SB 3775	Seddon Mk10	B23C		Private Bus
SC 1922	Chevrolet n/c	B	C	new 1947
SC 1931	Chevrolet n/c	B	C	
SC 3375	Chevrolet n/c	B	?	
SC 3722	Chevrolet n/c	B	?	
SC 4356	Chevrolet n/c	B	?	
SC 4358	Chevrolet n/c	B	C	
SC 4384	Chevrolet n/c	B	?	
SC 8691	Vulcan 6PF	B	C	
SC 9015	Vulcan 6PF	B	C	
SH 103	Vulcan 6PF	B	C	note 1
SH 130	Vulcan 6PF	B	C	note 1
SH 152	Vulcan 6PF	B	C	
SH 165	Vulcan 6PF	B	C	
SH 192	Vulcan 6PF	B	C	
SH 223	TSM L6PA7	B	C	
SH 249	TSM L6PA7	B	C	
SH 251	TSM L6PA7	B	C	
SH 263	Fargo f/c	B	C	new 1954
SH 268	Fargo f/c	B	C	new 1954
SH 269	Fargo f/c	B	C	new 1954
SH 273	TSM L6PA7	B	C	
SH 275	TSM L6PA7	B	C	
SH 278	TSM L6PA7	B	C	
SH 280	Fargo f/c	B	C	new 1954
SH 281	Fargo f/c	B	C	new 1954
SH 283	Fargo f/c	B	C	new 1954
SH 304	Fargo f/c	B	C	new 1954
SH 306	TSM L6PA7	B	C	
SH 307	TSM L6PA7	B	C	
SH 308	TSM L6PA7	B	C	
SH 309*	TSM L6PA7	B	C	
SH 314	Fargo f/c	B	C	new 1955
SH 315	Fargo f/c	B	C	new 1955
SH 316	Fargo f/c	B	C	new 1955
SH 317	Fargo f/c	B	C	new 1955
SH 318	Fargo f/c	B	C	new 1955
SH 356	Fargo f/c	B	C	new 1956
SH 357	Fargo f/c	B	C	new 1956
SH 358	Fargo f/c	B	C	new 1956
SH 359	Fargo f/c	B	C	new 1956
SH 539	Fargo f/c	B	C	new 1956
SH 540	Fargo f/c	B	C	new 1956

Paya Lebar (continued)

SH 541	Fargo f/c	B	C	new 1956
SH 542	Fargo f/c	B	C	new 1956
SH 618	Fargo f/c	B	C	
SH 841	Fargo f/c	B	C	
SH 842	Fargo f/c	B	C	
SH 856	Fargo f/c	B	C	
SH 857	Fargo f/c	B	C	
SH 858	Fargo f/c	B	C	
SH 859	Fargo f/c	B	C	
SH 860	Fargo f/c	B	C	
SH 861	Fargo f/c	B	C	
SH 872	Fargo f/c	B	C	
SH 873	Fargo f/c	B	C	
SH 937	Fargo f/c	B	C	
SH 938	Fargo f/c	B	C	
SH 939	Fargo f/c	B	C	
SH 940	Fargo f/c	B	C	

Notes: 1. Replaced by Fargos, thus:

SH 103	Fargo f/c	B	C
SH 130	Fargo f/c	B	C

Ponggol Bus Service Company

5 Hillside Drive, Singapore, 19.
Eventually became part of Associated Bus Services

Known Fleet Details

Regn number	Chassis make	Body/ seating		
S 1681	Chevrolet n/c	B	C	
S 4783	Cevrolet n/c	B	RP	
SC 3368	Chev Maple Leaf	B	C	
SC 5525	Chev Maple Leaf	B	?	
SC 6110	Ford n/c	B	C	ex Kampong Bahru
SC 6442	Ford n/c	B	C	
SC 6443	Ford n/c	B	C	
SC 8045	Vulcan 6PF	B	C	
SC 8896	Vulcan 6PF	B	C	
SH 138	Vulcan 6PF	B	C	
SH 182	Vu;lcan 6PF	B	C	
SH 248	TSM L6PA7	B39C		
SH 264	TSM L6PA7	B	C	
SH 312	Fargo f/c	B36C		new 1954
SH 319	Fargo f/c	B	C	new 1955
SH 598	Fargo f/c	B	C	
SH 599	Fargo f/c	B	C	
SH 600	Fargo f/c	B	C	
SH 647	Fargo f/c	B	C	
SH 648	Fargo f/c	B	C	
SH 649	Fargo f/c	B	C	
SH 965	Fargo f/c	B	C	

LEFT: Keppel Bus Company SH 455, an Albion FT 39AL passes an advertisement for a well known cocoa of the time.

Tay Koh Yat Bus Company Limited

57 Beach Road, Singapore, 7.
Eventually became part of United Bus Company, in which it was
the major influence.

Known Fleet Details

Regn number	Chassis make	Body/ seating	
S 995	Ford n/c	B21C	
S 1002	Ford n/c	B21C	
S 1004	Ford n/c	B C	
S 1331	Ford n/c	B20C	
S 1708	Ford n/c	B C	
S 1710	Ford n/c	B ?	
S 2056	Ford n/c	B C	
S 2128	Ford n/c	B C	
S 2180	Ford n/c	B C	
S 2182	Commer n/c	B21C	
S 2185	Ford n/c	B14F	burnt out 5/56
S 2218	Ford n/c	B ?	
S 2461	Ford n/c	B ?	
S 2462	Ford n/c	B ?	
S 2728	Chevrolet n/c	B C	
S 2729	Chevrolet n/c	B C	
S 2730	Chevrolet n/c	B C	
S 2731	Hino n/c	B ?	ex Japan
S 3222	Chevrolet n/c	B F	
S 3223	Ford n/c	B C	see note 1
S 3991	Chevrolet n/c	B C	
S 3992	Ford n/c	B C	
S 5134	Ford n/c	B C	ex Keppel
S 6550	Ford n/c	B ?	
S 7514	Ford n/c	B F	
S 7516	Ford n/c	B C	
S 7517	Dodge n/c	B F	
S 8003	Ford n/c	B ?	
S 8004	Ford n/c	B C	
S 8333	Ford n/c	B C	
S 8340	Ford n/c	B C	
S 8982	Ford n/c	B ?	
S 9026	Ford n/c	B C	
SC 581	Chev Maple Leaf	B C	
SC 2095	Chev Maple Leaf	B27C	
SC 2096	Chevrolet n/c	B C	
SC 2097	Chevrolet n/c	B C	
SC 2098	Ford n/c	B C	
SC 2099	Ford n/c	B C	
SC 2101	Ford n/c	B C	
SC 2517	Ford n/c	B C	
SC 2519	Ford n/c	B C	
SC 3377	Austin CXB	B ?	
SC 3992	?	B ?	
SC 4636	Austin CXB	B C	
SC 5335	Albion FT39N	B C	
SC 7095	Morris OP/R	B F	see note 2
SC 7113	Morris OP/R	B F	see note 2
SC 7391	Morris OP/R	B F	see note 2
SC 7700	Morris OP/R	B30F	see note 2 new 1950
SC 7878	Albion FT39N	B C	
SC 8004	?	B ?	
SH 135	Bedford OWB	B F	Duple body?
SH 145	Leyland OPS	B35F	see note 3
SH 151	Bedford OWB	B F	Duple body?
SH 190	Sentinel SLC6	B37F	see note 4
SH 191	Sentinel SLC6	B37F	see note 4
SH 200	Albion FT39N	B C	
SH 202	Albion FT39N	B C	
SH 212	TSM L6PA7	B40C	
SH 220	Albion FT39N	B F	see note 5
SH 222	Albion FT39N	B F	see note 5
SH 232	Albion FT39N	B F	see note 5
SH 234	Albion FT39N	B F	see note 5
SH 240	Commer f/c	B31F	see notes 5/6
SH 262	TSM L6PA7	B C	
SH 270	TSM L6PA7	B 40C	
SH 272	Albion FT39N	B ?	
SH 282	Commer f/c	B F	see notes 5/6
SH 292	TSM L6PA7	B C	
SH 300	TSM L6PA7	B C	
SH 303	TSM L6PA7	B C	
SH 313	Albion FT39N	B C	
SH 320	Commer Avr III	B41F	new 1954
SH 321	Commer Avr III	B41F	new 1954
SH 322	Commer Avr III	B41F	new 1954
SH 324	Fargo f/c	B F	new 1954
SH 325	Commer Avr III	B41F	new 1954
SH 333	Commer f/c	B C	notes 5/6
SH 342	Albion FT39N	B C	new 1954
SH 343	Commer Avr III	B41F	new 1954
SH 345	TSM L6PA7	B C	new 1954
SH 350	Fargo f/c	B C	new 1954
SH 353	Albion FT39N	B C	new 1954
SH 354	Fargo f/c	B C	new 1954
SH 363	Albion FT39	B C	new 1954
SH 368	Commer Avr III	B41F	new 1954
SH 369	Albion FT39	B40C	new 1954
SH 370	Commer Avr III	B41F	new 1954
SH 373	Fargo f/c	B C	new 1954
SH 380	TSM L6PA7	B C	
SH 383	Fargo f/c	B C	new 1954

Tay Koh Yat (continued)

Regn number	Chassis make	Body/ seating	
SH 410	Fargo f/c	B C	new 1954
SH 412	Albion FT39AL	B C	new 1954
SH 413	Albion FT39AL	B C	new 1954
SH 414	Albion FT39AL	B C	new 1954
SH 515	Albion FT39AL	B C	new 1956
SH 516	Albion FT39AL	B C	new 1956
SH 517	Albion FT39AL	B C	new 1956
SH 518	Albion FT39AL	B C	new 1956
SH 519	Albion FT39AL	B C	new 1956
SH 520	Fargo f/c	B C	new 1956
SH 521	Albion FT39AL	B C	new 1956
SH 522	Albion FT39AL	B C	new 1956
SH 523	Albion FT39AL	B C	new 1956
SH 524	Albion FT39AL	B C	new 1956
SH 614	Albion FT39ALX	B C	
SH 615	Albion FT39ALX	B C	
SH 616	Albion FT39ALX	B C	
SH 632	Albion FT39ALX	B C	
SH 633	Albion FT39ALX	B C	
SH 634	Albion FT39ALX	B C	
SH 635	Albion FT39ALX	B C	
SH 636	Fargo	B C	
SH 843	Ford Thames	B C	
SH 844	Ford Thames	B C	
SH 845	Ford Thames	B C	
SH 846	Ford Thames	B C	
SH 847	Ford Thames	B C	
SH 865	Fargo	B C	
SH 868	Fargo	B C	
SH 878	Ford Thames	B C	
SH 888	Ford Thames	B C	
SH 889	Albion VK41L	B C	
SH 890	Albion VK41L	B C	
SH 902	Albion VK41L	B C	
SH 903	Albion VK41L	B C	
SH 904	Albion VK41L	B C	
SH 905	Albion VK41L	B C	
SH 906	Albion VK41L	B C	
SH 907	Albion VK41L	B C	
SH 908	Albion VK41L	B C	
SH 909	Albion VK41L	B C	
SH 912	Albion VK41L	B C	
SH 913	Albion VK41L	B C	
SH 914	Albion VK41L	B C	
SH 915	Albion VK41L	B C	
SH 917	Fargo	B C	
SH 918	Fargo	B C	
SH 928	Fargo	B44C	
SH 929	Fargo	B44C	
SH 935	AEC Ranger	B C	Note 7
SH 941	Ford R226	B D	Note 8
SH 942	Ford R226	B D	Note 8
SH 953	M-Benz	B C	
SH 954	M-Benz	B C	
SH 971	M-BenzLP1113	B 43C	
SH 972	Ford R226	B C	
SH 973	Ford R226	B C	
SH 974	Ford R226	B C	
SH 975	Ford R226	B C	
SH 976	Ford R226	B C	
SH 977	Ford R226	B C	
SH 978	Albion VK41L	B 41C	
SH 979	Albion VK41L	B 41C	
SH 980	Albion VK41L	B 41C	
SH 981	Albion VK41L		

Express service operators:

Singapore - Johore Express

132 Rochore Road, Singapore, 7.
Operates between Singapore and Johore Bahru, across the Causeway.
Known Fleet Details

Regn number	Chassis make	Body/ seating	
S 623	Bedford OB	C21F	note 1
S 624	Bedford OB	C21F	
S 625	Bedford OB	C21F	
S 626	Bedford OB	C21F	
S 627	Bedford OB	C21F	
S 628	Bedford OB	C21F	
S 629	Bedford OB	C21F	
S 630	Bedford OB	C21F	
SC 2116	Bedford OB	C21F	
SC 2811	Bedford OB	C21F	
SH 106	Vulcan 6PF	C C	note 2
SH 107	Vulcan 6PF	C C	
SH 108	Vulcan 6PF	C C	
SH 109	Vulcan 6PF	C C	
SH 110	Vulcan 6PF	C C	
SH 111	Vulcan 6PF	C C	
SH 112	Vulcan 6PF	C C	
SH 113	Vulcan 6PF	C C	
SH 114	Vulcan 6PF	C C	
SH 115	TSM L6PA7	C C	
SH 116	TSM L6PA7	C C	
SH 117	TSM L6PA7	C C	
SH 118	TSM L6PA7	C C	
SH 119	TSM L6PA7	C C	
SH 120	TSM L6PA7	C C	
SH 235	Vulcan 6PF	C C	See note 3.1955
SH 236	Vulcan 6PF	C C	See note 3.1955
SH 787	Seddon	C C	

Notes:
1 The Bedfords were later sold for further service in Malaya
2 The Vulcans were equipped with 2+1 seating.
3 When new, these carried Colombo Plan livery

Kuala Lumpur - Singapore Express

63 Klyne Street, Kuala Lumpur
Known Fleet Details

Regn number	Chassis make	Body/ seating	
SH 229	Seddon Mk4		C24F

Sing Lian Express Limited

23 Beach Road, Singapore, 7.
Operates Malacca - Singapore express service across the Causeway.
Known Fleet Details

Regn number	Chassis make	Body/ seating		
SC 7130	Morris OP/R	B	F	New 1948
SC 7131	Morris OP/R	B	F	New 1948
SC 8114	Vulcan 6PF	B	F	New 1948
SH 154	Vulcan 6PF	B	F	New 1951
SH 172	TSM L6PA7	B	F	New 1953
SH 183	Vulcan 6PF	B29F		New 1953
SH 218	TSM L6PA7	B	F	New 1954
SH 229	Seddon Mk7	B24F		

REGISTERED IN MALACCA				
M 2841	Vulcan 6PF	B	F	New 1950
M 3050	Vulcan 6PF	B	F	New 1950
M 4019	Vulcan 6PF	B	F	New 1950
M 4758	TSM L6PA7	B	F	New 1953
M 6157	Dennis Teal	B	F	New 1957
M 6241	Bedford	B	F	New 1947

BELOW: This Albion Viking VK41L, SH 979, new to Tay Koh Yat in August 1968, is seen in simplified 'silver' livery with coloured bands and is a harbinger of the future shape of the Singapore bus.